AA

KEYGUIDE

CANADA

288

CONTENTS

KEY TO SYMBOLS

⊕ Map reference
✉ Address
☎ Telephone number
🕐 Opening times
💰 Admission prices
Ⓜ Underground station
🚌 Bus number
🚆 Train station
⛴ Ferry/boat
🚗 Driving directions
ℹ Tourist office
🎫 Tours
📖 Guidebook
🍴 Restaurant
☕ Café
🍷 Bar
🏬 Shop
① Number of rooms
❄ Air conditioning
🏊 Swimming pool
🏋 Gym
❓ Other useful information
▷ Cross reference
★ Walk/drive start point

262

155

124

217

CONTENTS | CANADA

UNDERSTANDING CANADA

Understanding Canada is an introduction to the country, its geography, economy, history and its people, giving a real insight into the nation. Living Canada gets under the skin of Canada today, while The Story of Canada takes you through the country's past.

UNDERSTANDING CANADA

Canada is one of the world's most exciting and rewarding countries to visit. The variety is huge: Stupendous mountain peaks vie with wide, rolling prairies, great lakes, dense forest and wave-battered ocean shores. From the midnight sun of the north to the vineyards and fruit orchards of the south, the country unfolds as an unending mosaic. Sophisticated cities and rural communities house a close-knit population as diverse as the land. And in the north, the winter sky glows with the swirling luminescence of the northern lights.

VAST AND FROZEN GIANT

Say "Canada" and the first three adjectives that pop into most people's minds are "huge," "cold" and "empty." This "big frigid" stereotype makes some Canadians bridle, and it is a bit simplistic, but like all stereotypes it contains a germ of truth. Canada is immense. Almost unimaginably so. Bigger than any country on Earth except Russia, it sprawls more than 6,000km (3,720 miles) from the Atlantic to the Pacific and fills four and a half time zones. An office worker in St. John's, Newfoundland, gets home for supper just about the same time his colleague in Vancouver over on the west coast is getting back to his desk from lunch. From south to north, the country is almost as vast. It stretches from the vineyards of the Niagara Peninsula, where sunset is determined by hour, to the edge of the polar ice cap, where it's determined by month. Even Canada's provinces are huge. It takes 24 hours of solid driving just to get across the province of Ontario, for example, and the entire United Kingdom would fit comfortably into British Columbia three times, with plenty of room left over for Greece.

And let's be honest about this: it can be extremely cold. Stand still at the corner of Victoria and Albert streets in Regina, Saskatchewan, in mid-January for more than five minutes and your cheeks will freeze. But go to the same street corner in mid-July and you could fry eggs on the sidewalk. And what about Victoria on the west coast? Every February, when Montréalers and Calgarians are still digging themselves out of mountainous snowdrifts, the Victorians go out and count flowers. In 2005 4.8 billion daffodils, lilies, peonies, primroses, violets and snowdrops bloomed. Canada cold? For sure, but not everywhere and not all the time.

URBAN POPULATION

It is only partly true that Canada is empty, with just 32.6 million people (2006 census)—only about half as many as France. About 70 percent of Canadians live within 200km (124 miles) of the US border, and the population along some parts of that long narrow strip can be pretty dense. In fact, most Canadians are urbanites, and close to a third of them live in just three cities: Montréal, Toronto and Vancouver. Montréal and the province of Québec are almost as French as, say, Nice and Normandy. Nova Scotia and Newfoundland have strong communities descended, respectively, from Scottish and Irish immigrants; other Europeans made for Ontario and the Prairies; British Columbia's capital still has a very English feel and Chinese settlers made Vancouver their home. However, today there's a much greater spread of nationalities, with Montréal, Toronto and Vancouver each having almost 20 different language groups.

Trying to stuff all that landscape and all those cultures into a short trip is pretty well impossible. Just driving from Montréal to Toronto, for example. takes at least five hours, and Toronto to Vancouver takes three days and four nights on Via Rail's transcontinental train. But flying into the big cities will give you quick access to a wide variety of landscapes and people.

Toronto is the gateway to Niagara Falls, the Great Lakes and Canada's industrial heartland; Montréal opens up the way for a thorough exploration of French Canada, from the fishing villages of the Gaspé Peninsula to the ski resorts of the Laurentians; and Vancouver, of course, is the gateway to the Pacific coast and the British Columbia interior. The empty spaces are never far away. The Parc de Mont-Tremblant, for example, a mountainous, lake-spattered wilderness more than half the size of Luxembourg, is just a two-hour drive from the cafés and clubs of downtown Montréal.

But don't overlook the smaller cities. The old port of Halifax makes a great base for exploring the Gaelic- and French-speaking villages of the Atlantic Provinces, and Calgary and Edmonton are gateways to the Rocky Mountains and the wheat fields of the Prairies.

POLITICAL DIVISIONS

Canada is the only monarchy on the North American continent and Canada's ultimate head of state is still the British monarch—at present, Queen Elizabeth II. Her representative in Ottawa is the governor general, a job once held by British peers and minor royalty but now awarded to a prominent Canadian who is appointed to the job for five years or so. It's a purely ceremonial role. The governor general gives royal assent to every law passed by parliament.

The 10 provinces are, in theory at least, equal in autonomy, with their own legislatures, health and school systems (and their own lieutenant-governors for ceremonial occasions). But they're wildly unequal in just about everything else. Québec, for example, with more than 1.5 million sq km (half a million sq miles) of territory, is about three times the size of France. Tiny Prince Edward Island, on the other hand, is less than 6,000sq km (2,375sq miles), which is plenty, considering its population of 133,000 is smaller than that of an average Toronto borough in Canada's most populous province, Ontario. They don't even speak the same language.

Québec is French-speaking, New Brunswick is bilingual (French and English), and the rest are all English, although they accord varying degrees of services to their French-speaking citizens.

Three territories, the Yukon, the Northwest Territories and Nunavut, also have their own legislatures, but defer to the federal government on many matters. The vast majority of the people in Nunavut, the newest territory, are native Inuit and the discussions in its legislature in Iqaluit are often in Inuktitut rather than French or English.

DEMOGRAPHICS

Canada began as a clash between the French and the British, plus a dash of native North American. But it wasn't long before the Scots and the Irish showed up to add a Gaelic touch to the mix. Succeeding waves of eastern Europeans, Jews (first Sephardic and then Ashkenazi), Italians, Greeks, Germans, Lebanese, Chinese and Japanese made Canada into one of the most multicultural nations on earth. More recent arrivals include Southeast Asians from Vietnam and Cambodia, Indians and Pakistanis, Iranians and Arabs, and Latin Americans from Nicaragua, Guatemala and Mexico.

CLIMATE

According to an old joke, Canadians split their year into two parts: 10 months of winter and 2 months of bad skiing. An exaggeration, maybe (southern areas are mostly warm from May to end September), but Canadian winters are truly the stuff of legend. January temperatures in Montréal, which shares the same latitude as Venice, often drop to -20°C (-4°F). In cities like Edmonton, Winnipeg and Regina, the mercury regularly drops to -40°C (-40°F) and stays there for a week or two. On the other hand, Prairie summers can be blisteringly hot, with temperatures well over 40°C (104°F). The only relief are the fierce rain storms.

Brutal winters and scorching summers, however, are not universal. In Victoria, British Columbia, the temperature seldom drops below freezing, and flowers start blooming in early February. January in Vancouver is more likely to be damp than white and sometimes that warm, Pacific weather leaks through the valleys of the Rockies into Calgary in the form of winds called Chinooks, which can make the temperature rise by as much as 20 degrees C (36 degrees F) in a day.

Victoria and Vancouver have another distinction: They're the only parts of the country that get a real spring, a season that starts in February on the West Coast and lingers well into May. The post-winter period in the rest of Canada, on the other hand, is nasty, muddy and short, erupting into summer with a speed that's almost rude. But what the east lacks in spring it makes up for with its long, glorious fall. The hills and valleys of Ontario, Québec and the Maritimes, in particular, blaze with glowing foliage. The red maple leaf on the Canadian flag is highly appropriate.

UNDERSTANDING CANADA

CANADA'S REGIONS

NEWFOUNDLAND AND LABRADOR

One province in spite of the ungainly name. It joined the Canadian federation in 1949, making it the youngest province and a place apart, with a fierce sense of identity and its own distinctive accent. Most of its 510,000 people live on Newfoundland, many of them in tiny villages with captivating names like Heart's Delight and Heart's Content that cling tenaciously to the rocky coast.

ATLANTIC PROVINCES

Even if all three of the Atlantic Provinces—Nova Scotia, New Brunswick and Prince Edward Island—were merged into one, the result would still be by far the smallest province. But what the Maritimes lack in size, they make up for in history. They are among the most settled regions in Canada and the coastline is dotted with historic villages, where French, English and even Gaelic are spoken. The lush farmland of the St. John River Valley, the tides of the Bay of Fundy, the warm-water beaches of Prince Edward Island, and the mountains of Cape Breton are among the region's most famous attractions.

QUÉBEC

The heartland of French Canada. More than 80 percent of its 7.6 million residents are French-speaking, which sets it apart from all of North America. Most of its cities, towns and villages are strung along the shores of the St. Lawrence River, but its northernmost point is on the same latitude as Greenland. Its capital, Québec City, is one of the oldest settlements in North America and the continent's only walled city north of Mexico. And while Québec is not a Maritime province or even considered an Atlantic province, it has one of the longest, most varied and most beautiful coastlines in the east.

ONTARIO

Canada's richest and most populous province. Its wealth is centered on the industrial cities of the Great Lakes—Toronto, Windsor, Hamilton, Oshawa and Thunder Bay—and in northern mining towns like Timmins and Sudbury. But it's not all industry and commerce. Toronto is the cultural heart of English Canada and one of the most important theater cities in the world. The Niagara Peninsula is on the same latitude as northern California, and has some of Canada's best farmlands and vineyards. To the north, the wilderness stretches all the way to the shores of James Bay.

THE PRAIRIES

Manitoba, Saskatchewan and Alberta are collectively referred to as the Prairies, and indeed, much of the landscape is flat and filled with wheat farms and cattle ranches, but the landscape is more varied than many people think. Woodlands account for more than half the entire region and Manitoba's Lake Winnipeg is large enough to qualify as an inland sea. The Badlands in the southern parts of Alberta are rich in dinosaur fossils and stories of fugitive outlaws. Western Alberta has some of the highest peaks in the Rocky Mountains and two of Canada's most famous national parks—Banff and Jasper.

BRITISH COLUMBIA

Canada's opening on the Pacific has a coastline of deep fiords and and rain forests. The Coast Mountains stretch along the Pacific shores from North Vancouver's city limits to Alaska while the Purcell, Kootenay, Selkirk,

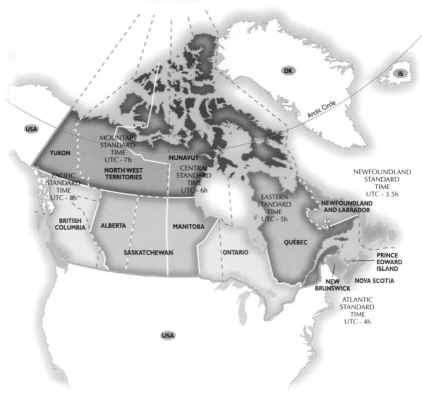

DK

IS

Arctic Circle

USA

YUKON

MOUNTAIN
STANDARD
TIME
UTC - 7h

NUNAVUT

NORTH WEST
TERRITORIES

CENTRAL
STANDARD
TIME
UTC - 6h

NEWFOUNDLAND
STANDARD
TIME
UTC - 3.5h

PACIFIC
STANDARD
TIME
UTC - 8h

EASTERN
STANDARD
TIME
UTC - 5h

NEWFOUNDLAND
AND LABRADOR

BRITISH
COLUMBIA

ALBERTA

MANITOBA

SASKATCHEWAN

ONTARIO

QUÉBEC

PRINCE
EDWARD
ISLAND

NEW
BRUNSWICK

NOVA SCOTIA

ATLANTIC
STANDARD
TIME
UTC - 4h

USA

CANADIAN POPULATION BY MOTHER TONGUE	
English	18 million
French	6.8 million
Chinese	1 million
Italian, German (each)	500,000
Arabic, Punjabi, and Spanish	350,000
Portuguese, Polish, Tagalog	250,000
Dutch, Udu, Ukrainian, Vietnamese	150,000
Other	2 million
Cree	79,000
Inuktitut	32,000
Other First Nations	100,000

the Yukon, the Northwest Territories and Nunavut, are quite different. Deciduous forests and high mountains make some of the Yukon look more like an extension of British Columbia than part of the Arctic. The Kluane National Park, in fact, has Canada's highest mountains and some of its fiercest rivers. Visitors to the Northwest Territories can sail on Great Slave Lake or travel west from Yellowknife to see Virginia Falls in Nahanni National Park. Nunavut is Canada's newest jurisdiction and is administered by the Inuit. It is home to three of the most remote national parks in the world: Auyuittuq, Sirmilik and Quittinirpaaq.

Monashee, Cariboo and Columbia mountain ranges ripple across the southern interior like rocky waves. Between them lie deep valleys and long narrow lake systems. Most of the province's 4.3 million people live in the Lower Mainland area around Vancouver, where the Fraser River empties into the Strait of Georgia. Victoria, the provincial capital, has the mildest climate in the country; it attracts so many retirees that the locals refer to it as God's waiting room.

THE FAR NORTH

That vast stretch of land and ice north of the 60th parallel is really Canada's last frontier. Its three jurisdictions,

Above *A grizzly bear playing with a log*
Far left *Point Amour Lighthouse, Newfoundland & Labrador*
Left *Western Brook Pond at Gros Morne National Park*

THE BEST OF CANADA

MONTRÉAL

Basilique Notre-Dame de Montréal (▷ 64) Historic buildings line delightful old street and house restaurants, galleries and shops.

Mont-Royal (▷ 69) In the center of the city, this area offers sights, walks and tours.

Réseau Pietonnier Souterrain (▷ 72) The miles of passages that make up the Underground City.

Vieux Montréal (▷ 84) Historic buildings line delightful old street and house restaurants, galleries and shops.

QUÉBEC

Citadelle (▷ 98) Started in 1820 by the French and added to by the English, this is still a working garrison.

Auberge St-Antoine (▷ 110) Hotel of great character in historic Lower Town.

Montmorency Falls (▷ 97) Unexpectedly impressive so close to Québec City.

Terrasse Dufferin (▷ 102) Summer street performers entertain and in winter a tobaggan run down the stairs.

QUÉBEC PROVINCE

Canadian Museum of Civilization, Gatineau (▷ 116) Architecturally unique, with displays as diverse as Canada itself.

Murray Premises Hotel, St. John's (▷ 173) Luxury hotel located in former warehouse on the harbor.

Whale-watching in Tadoussac (▷ 118) A great flotilla of whales summer in the plankton-rich waters of the St. Lawrence.

ATLANTIC PROVINCES

Bay of Fundy tides (▷ 146) One of the world's marine wonders, Fundy tides rise and fall 16m (52ft).

Cape Breton Highlands National Park (▷ 144) Breathtaking scenery along a wild rocky coastline.

Gros Morne National Park (▷ 145) Spectacularly beautiful, with geology of international importance.

Kings Landing, New Brunswick (▷ 145) Splendidly re-created 19th-century Loyalist settlement.

Louisbourg, Nova Scotia (▷ 150) The great fortress of New France guarding the entrance to the St. Lawrence.

Lunenburg, Nova Scotia (▷ 151) A World Heritage Site and one of Nova Scotia's most historic and attractive towns.

Ryan Duffy's, Halifax (▷ 171) Famous for its steak and seafood.

St. Andrews-by-the-Sea, New Brunswick (▷ 155) Picturesque town with elegant houses and tree-lined streets.

TORONTO

CN Tower (▷ 182) Erected in 1976, this 553.33 (1,815ft 5in) tower is still an icon for the city.
Harbourfront Centre (▷ 186) The dockland area is a new area of commercial and leisure activity.
Royal Ontario Museum (▷ 190) Bewildering array of choices with something to interest everyone.
Truffles (▷ 205) Classy restaurant with arguably the best food in town (some say in Canada).

ONTARIO

Kakabeka Falls, Ontario (▷ 226) Dramatic falls sometimes called the Niagara of the North.
Niagara Falls, Ontario (▷ 214) Probably the most famous waterfall in the world.
Niagara-on-the-Lake, Ontario (▷ 219) One of the most delightful and historic townships in Ontario.
Pillar and Post Inn, Niagara-on-the-Lake (▷ 247) Lovely country inn in friendly community.
Science North, Sudbury (▷ 226) Award-winning science center in two snowflake-shaped buildings.
Upper Canada Village, Ontario (▷ 227) Imaginative re-creation of early Ontario life.

THE PRAIRIES

Badlands of Alberta (▷ 252) Dramatic with their stark beauty, ocher-colored soil and arid landscapes.
Heritage Park, Alberta (▷ 259) Historic village transporting you back to early 20th-century Calgary.
Manitoba Museum, Winnipeg (▷ 265) Spectacular museum with excellent dioramas and historical displays.
Polar bears in Churchill (▷ 251) A veritable wildlife paradise on the shores of Hudson Bay.
Riding Mountain National Park (▷ 261) Rising like an island in the farmland, with three distinct landscapes.
Tavern in the Park, Winnipeg (▷ 281) Glass-roofed atrium, outdoor terrace and some of the best food in the West.

Clockwise from left to right The Zion's Lutheran Church, in Lunenburg; ever popular whale-watching boat tour, Whitless Bay, Newfoundland & Labrador; the sun going down over Riding Mountain National Park

BRITISH COLUMBIA AND THE ROCKIES

Athabasca Falls, Alberta (▷ 295) Very photogenic as the Athabasca River tumbles over rocky ledges.
Banff and Banff National Park (▷ 288) Make the town your base for visiting the sights of the national park with its spectacular lakes, hot springs and mountains.
Fort Langley, British Columbia (▷ 292) Carefully re-constructed Hudson Bay Company trading post.
Jasper National Park (▷ 296) Incredibly blue lakes, steaming hot springs and dramatic peaks.
Museum of Anthropology, Vancouver (▷ 306) Fine museum of the art and lifestyle of the First Nations.
Pacific Rim National Park (▷ 302) Virgin forests, fantastic beaches and remote offshore islands.
Rolling breakers on Vancouver Island (▷ 312) The rolling swells of the Pacific break directly on Long Beach.
Takakkaw Falls, British Columbia (▷ 317) Spectacular falls in splendid setting.

THE NORTH

Dawson City, Yukon (▷ 348) Living history and one of Canada's most unusual communities.
Kluane National Park (▷ 349) Majestic mountainscapes in Canada's highest mountains.
Northern lights in Yellowknife (▷ 353) Wildlife and northern lights reflected in the Great Slave Lake.
Virginia Falls, Northwest Territories (▷ 349) Remote, dramatic and twice the height of Niagara.

TOP EXPERIENCES

Hike out to Newfoundland's Signal Hill National Historic Site for a grand view of St. John's and its snug harbor.

Ride the passenger ferry across Halifax harbor for a view of one of the most fascinating ports in North America.

Go to a church-hall lobster supper in any of a dozen or so Prince Edward Island villages.

Rent a kayak in Tadoussac and paddle up the Saguenay River to look for beluga whales.

Walk the ramparts of Québec City, the only walled city in North America north of Mexico.

Take a romantic evening stroll to the lookout on Mont Royal for a bird's-eye view of Montréal, North America's only French-speaking metropolis.

Go to solemn Mass in Montréal's magnificently ornate Basilique Notre-Dame on Sunday morning.

Pick a bar, any bar, on Montréal's rue St-Denis and sit outside sipping a beer, a glass of wine or a cognac and watch some of the country's most stylish men and women stroll by.

Go to a National Hockey League game in Montréal, Ottawa, Toronto or Vancouver. Failing that, go to any neighborhood rink and watch a Pee Wee tournament.

Skate on the Rideau Canal through the heart of Canada's capital city, Ottawa.

Paddle a canoe through the waterways of Ontario's Algonquin Park, one of the more accessible wilderness areas in Canada.

Go Saturday shopping in Toronto's Kensington Market, where there is a chaotic fusion of cultures, smells, food, secondhand goods and street performers.

Ride the Algoma Central Railway train through the blazing fall shades of the Agawa Canyon north of Sault-Ste-Marie, Ontario.

Take the train (or fly, if you're short of time) from Winnipeg to Churchill on the shores of Hudson Bay to see the polar bears.

Spend a night in a tepee at Wanuskewin Heritage Park near Saskatoon. Canadian aboriginals started camping here more than 1,500 years ago.

Cheer the chuck wagon races at the Calgary Stampede. For sheer excitement it's hard to beat.

Rent a horse and a guide, or join a group, in either Jasper or Banff and go horseback riding in the Rockies.

Hike right past the well-walked Lake Louise in Banff National Park and climb to Lake Agnes, surrounded by snowcapped peaks.

Rent a bicycle and ride around Vancouver's Stanley Park. If you're really energetic, jog or walk.

Pick a clear day or evening and take a 1.6km (1-mile) ride to the top of Grouse Mountain on the Skyride for a glorious view of Vancouver and the Pacific.

Take a floatplane trip from Vancouver for a remote fishing trip, or just flightseeing.

Watch the Northern Lights from an out-of-town viewpoint, or go up on MIdnight Dome, near Dawson City, on June 21 to see the sun at midnight.

Below *Looking out over Signal Hill, St. John's, Newfoundland*

LIVING CANADA

CANADIAN SOCIETY

Toronto writer Peter Newman once complained that Canadians are the only people on Earth who aspire to be Clark Kent rather than Superman—an ironic jibe given that one of the two men who created the Man of Steel was Canadian-born Joe Shuster. While the stereotype is probably overstated, Canadians are, by and large, a diffident group of people (except at hockey games, of course). They tend to end every sentence with an interrogative "eh," for example, as if not quite sure of where they stand. They also tend to identify themselves by what they're not—English-speaking Canadians are "not American," for example, and, sadly, a significant number of French-speakers identify themselves as "not-Canadians." Part of the blame probably rests with the country's fractured origins. The founding nationalities—French and English—weren't exactly close to start with and spent the first century or so pretty much keeping out of each other's way. That meant that the succeeding waves of immigrants—Celts, Jews, Ukrainians, Italians, Greeks, Asians and Latin Americans—did much the same and formed what Canadians prefer to call a cultural mosaic. The end result isn't neat or tidy or homogenous, but it is interesting.

PARADES TELL THE STORY
In the past, nothing reflected Canada's cultural clashes and compromises better than the parades of Montréal. On June 24—Québec's Fête Nationale—thousands of separatists and nationalists took to the streets for a huge parade. This parade has latterly become increasingly representative of Québec's diversity, with ethnic dancers and Scottish pipe bands. A week later, on Canada Day, the Federalists staged a more modest march, and this is now a huge multinational party ending with a big fireworks display. On March 17, Montréalers of every political, linguistc and ethnic stripe turn out to celebrate St. Patrick's Day, which marks the end of winter. They hold fast to the notion that "Everyone is Irish on St. Patrick's Day."

Clockwise from top *Vibrant celebrations at Montréal International Jazz Festival; lagoon and stores in West Edmonton Mall; Canadian author Neil Bissoondath*

NO HYPHENS HERE

Novelist Neil Bissoondath would appear to be a poster boy for Canada's "cultural mosaic." Of East Indian descent, he was born in Trinidad and came to Canada in the 1960s—the perfect multicultural Canadian. But he has stubbornly refused the hyphenation process that gave us "Greek-Canadians" and "Italian-Canadians," partly because he didn't want to have to describe himself as an East-Indian-Trinidadian-Canadian, but mostly because he thought it was just plain wrong. In his 1994 book, *Selling Illusions*, Bissoondath argued that multiculturalism, with its festivals and celebrations, was paternalistic and con-descending, and created a kind of "gentle and insidious cultural apartheid." "Multiculturalism," he wrote, "has done little more than lead an already divided country down the path to further social divisiveness."

NATIONAL SYMBOLS

Canadian comedians have been known to poke fun at the fact that their national symbols are a leaf and a beaver, but the nation obviously thought long and hard before reaching these decisions. Canada, as a country, came into being in 1867, but it was nearly 100 years before it got its official maple-leaf flag. It took even longer to get a national anthem: "O Canada", already a century-old patriotic song, wasn't formally adopted until 1980.

The beaver, of course, represents the source of prosperity for the original colony, when fur trading created fortunes which in turn established cities and ultimately helped to create a nation. Hunted nearly to extinction by the middle of the 19th century, this endearing and industrious creature is now protected and is once again thriving in the wild.

WEATHER REPORT

Common phrases you'll hear in Canada: "Cold enough for ya?" (winter), and "Hot enough for ya?" (summer). The weather is something of an obsession, which is hardly surprising—if it's going to be 40 below with snow up to your armpits, you really do need to know about it. And in summer you have to know which factor sun-screen to wear. There are also add-ons to the basic forecasts that make them even more fascinating: There's the wind-chill factor (feels colder) and humidity levels (feels hotter), plus visibility, pressure, urban smog alerts, and trends and comparisons for real enthusiasts. Canada ranks high among the "greenest" countries, but stands to be one of the most affected as the global situation worsens, so climate change is a major concern here.

THE GREAT INDOORS

Canada is a paradise for outdoor types, but in winter many Canadians tend to prefer the Great Indoors. Albertans, for example, have the West Edmonton Mall (▷ 275) featuring more than 800 stores, 100 places to eat, 20 movie theaters and the world's largest indoor amusement park. Mont-réalers can live a full life without ever going outdoors, thanks to their Underground City (▷ 72, 73), which has access to 2,000 stores, restaurants and services, 7 hotels, 40 entertainment venues, 10 métro and 2 train stations, 2 bus depots, and countless offices and apartment buildings. Similarly, Toronto has the PATH system, a 27km (17-mile) system linking 1,200 stores, services, entertainments and transportation access.

In recent years Canada has shown a remarkable ability to crank out pop divas. So much so, you could be forgiven for thinking there are no male singers in the country. Sure, homegrown fans swoon over rock bands like the Tragically Hip, and chanteur Roch Boivin sets francophone female hearts aflutter everywhere. But none of these male stars can match the sheer world-busting fame of Céline Dion, Alanis Morissette, Avril Lavigne and Shania Twain. Go beyond the boundaries of pop songs, and that list of female superstars could be expanded to include jazz-singer Diana Krall and Cape Breton fiddler Natalie MacMaster. When it comes to the performing arts, Canadian women are top of the bill.

But beyond the musical stage, the genders even out. Filmmakers Denys Arcand and Atom Egoyan, and playwrights Michel Tremblay and Luc Plamondon, for example, have lit world stages and screens with their works. Canadian writers both male and female have made winning the Booker Prize look almost routine. Michael Ondaatje won it in 1992 for *The English Patient*, for example, and Margaret Atwood won it in 2000 for *The Blind Assassin*. When Yann Martel won the Booker for *The Life of Pi* in 2002, contenders included fellow Canadians Rohinton Mistry and Carol Shields.

REINVENTING AN OLD ART

In 1984, Guy Laliberté, a fire-eater and musician, brought together street-performers from around the world to create Cirque du Soleil. They proceeded to revolutionize the ancient art of the circus. Instead of grumpy tigers and a random sequence of separate acts, Cirque du Soleil combined theater, music, lights, dance, acrobatics and dazzling costumes into a seamless spectacle that has become a worldwide success.

The troupe currently has 18 different shows, including international touring shows, arena shows, and resident shows in Las Vegas (six), Walt Disney World, China and Japan. In 2007 they attracted 10 million fans.

The Cirque's huge International Headquarters is still in Montréal, located alongside the TOHU Circus Arts Complex, with its Circus Arts School and performance space.

Clockwise from top The distinctive yellow and blue big tops of Montréal's Cirque Du Soleil; Canadian singer Avril Lavigne; the entrance to Toronto's CBC Building, with a shining steel pillar supporting the semi-circular mirrored glass frontage

REACHING EVERYONE

Drawing together an officially bilingual, culturally diverse population scattered thinly over a vast landscape has been the daunting mandate of the CBC since the state-owned broadcasting corporation was set up in 1936. Its two national television networks (one French and one English) and four national radio networks (two French and two English) reach every nook and cranny of the country, from downtown Toronto to Inuvik, way up north in the Arctic.

The proliferation of private networks and cable channels has diminished the role of the CBC, but it still provides an important platform for Canadian entertainers and journalists. English-language programming has focused primarily on variety and information, while the French television network has produced such classic melodramas as *La Famille Plouffe* and *Il Lance, Il Compte*.

MIRVISH FAMILY IN TORONTO

The son of Russian Jewish immigrants, Ed Mirvish has become a household name in the city he adopted in the 1920s. With his wife Anne, he opened Honest Ed's (▷ 197), a discount store with bargain prices and free turkey handouts. Turning to the theater business, he saved the Royal Alexandra Theatre from demolition and, with his son David, built the state-of-the-art Princess of Wales Theatre. Today, with a third theater on the books and more than 500 theatrical productions to their credit, the Mirvishes are front and center in Toronto's entertainment business. In October 2008, the North American premiere of Andrew Lloyd Webber's *The Sound of Music* came to the Princess of Wales Theatre. As in the UK, the role of Maria went to the winner of a prime-time TV talent contest.

BUILDING AN EMPIRE

In the 1920s, Roy Thomson was trudging around the mining towns of northern Ontario trying to sell De Forest Crosley radios, but not having a whole lot of luck. He figured he'd sell more if reception was better and decided that the only way to achieve that would be to open a radio station. So he did—in North Bay.

This was the start of what was to become one of the biggest media empires in the world. By 1964, the Thomson family controlled hundreds of newspapers and radio and television stations in Canada, the United States and Britain (including the venerable *Times* of London). Roy, a working-class lad who'd grown up in his mother's Toronto boarding house, became Lord Thomson of Fleet.

REGULATED CULTURE

Defining what is and what is not a "Canadian song" is a serious business for Canadian bureaucrats—and for Canadian singers, musicians and radio stations. Canada has devised a set of radio and television rules to protect its "cultural industries" from the American giant next door. Radio stations, for example, must air a certain percentage of Canadian songs, as defined by bureaucratic guidelines. The results can sometimes be silly: One year, for example, the albums of pop-star Bryan Adams were shut out because he'd co-written the music with an American. But supporters say the rules have helped to create the conditions that produced such homegrown stars as Avril Lavigne and Shania Twain.

TOP SPORTS

The three most important words in Canadian sport are hockey, hockey and hockey, and that means ice hockey, not the version played on grass. The Iroquois game of lacrosse might be Canadians' official national sport, but hockey is their passion. "You don't like hockey," according to writer Stuart McLean, "you believe in it." Which helps explain why there are about as many indoor ice rinks in the country as there are churches. In even the tiniest towns kids can get quality ice time to learn the basic skills of skating and stick handling. Canada's other icy obsession, curling, is even more eccentric. This Scots-bred sport, which involves sliding 18kg (40lb) lumps of granite down long ice sheets, has more than a million aficionados in more than 1,200 clubs across the country. The national television network clears the airwaves to broadcast the national "brier," or championship. Not surprisingly, other winter sports such as skiing and snowshoeing are also popular, and while soccer's generally a dud as a spectator sport, thousands of kids play it every summer. There are even cricket teams—one of which stunned the world as well as the Canadians by winning a game against Bangladesh in the 2003 world Cup in South Africa.

Clockwise from top *Don Walchuk competes in the men's curling gold medal match played during the Salt Lake City Winter Olympic Games; event at the Calgary Stampede; Saskatoon ice hockey team in action*

CURLING

Who but Canadians would try to make a hit movie about curling? The result—*Men With Brooms*—wasn't quite the box-office smash its producers hoped for, in spite of the presence of homegrown stars Paul Gross and Leslie Nielsen. Still, the 2002 movie has its hilarious moments as its four unlikely heroes from a northern mining town try to earn the respect of their neighbors by winning the coveted Golden Broom. The final scenes even manage to make so-called "ice-bowling" look exciting. But best of all, the movie is an affectionate portrayal of the important place that curling holds in the hearts of small-town Canadians all across the country.

POLITE RULE-FOLLOWERS

For a magic moment during the 1988 Olympics, Canada thought it had the fastest sprinter on Earth when Jamaican immigrant Ben Johnson of Toronto won gold by running the 100m (109 yards) in 9.79 seconds. But Johnson tested positive for illegal steroids and was stripped of his medal—a severe blow to the country's self-image as a diffident nation of polite rule-followers.

Canada regained some measure of its lost honor, however, in 1996, when another Jamaican immigrant, Donovan Bailey, won the gold medal in the 100m with an impressive time of 9.84 seconds.

WOMEN IN HOCKEY

When the women's hockey team won gold for Canada at the 2002 Winter Olympics in Salt Lake City and the 2006 games in Torino, Italy, it was a dream come true for millions of fans. It was also eloquent proof that hockey, one of the toughest games in the world, was no longer an exclusive male preserve. Female players aren't allowed to slam each other into the boards the way the men do, but their no-hitting game is fast and exciting. So far, the elite National Hockey League hasn't signed any women, but a couple of minor-league teams have used female goalies, and one of the Olympic team, Hayley Wickenheiser, played forward with a professional men's team in Finland in 2004.

BOMBARDIER'S MARVEL

In 1958, Québecer Joseph-Armand Bombardier invented an odd contraption that looked a little like a motorcycle but with a tread and skis instead of wheels. This new winter vehicle was an instant success. Inuit hunters, for example, now zip around the Arctic on snowmobiles rather than on dogsleds. Farther south, a couple of million Canadians ride off into the wilderness on marked trails, with everything from fuel and repair stations to lodgings and restaurants. There's even a snowmobile Grand Prix at Valcourt in Québec, Bombardier's birthplace and manufacturing plant. The Grand Prix Ski-doo de Valcourt, the most important event in Canada and one of the most significant in North America, brings together elite racers to compete in an oval track and in snow-cross events.

A POPULAR SOLUTION

One of the world's most popular sports owes its birth to the ingenuity of a young Canadian teacher who was looking for a way to keep his charges interested in their gym class. It was back in 1891, and James Naismith, an Ontario native and fresh graduate of Montréal's McGill University and Presbyterian Theological College, was trying to teach physical education at the International Young Men's Christian Training College in Springfield, Massachusetts. It was winter, so they couldn't exercise outdoors. Naismith's solution? He nailed a couple of peach baskets to the walls of the gym, and—presto—the game of basketball was born. He even talked the janitor into climbing a ladder to retrieve the ball each time a point was scored—the hole in the bottom was one innovation he didn't think of

THE FRENCH EFFECT

Depending on how you look at it, Canada has either been blessed with two founding cultures or has been cursed with two warring partners. But even for the pessimists, there is no doubt that *le fait français* (the French fact) lends flash and flair to what could have been a monochromatic culture. There are French-speaking (or francophone) communities across the country, especially in northeastern Ontario and along the Acadian shores of New Brunswick, Nova Scotia and Prince Edward Island, but the province of Québec is French Canada's heartland. More than 80 percent of Québec's 7.6 million citizens count themselves francophones, and in some parts of the province resident anglophones are as rare as Sherpas. That kind of heft has allowed Québec to develop a rich and unique culture with its own pop stars, soap operas, writers, painters and musicians. Schools like the Université de Montréal, Université du Québec à Montréal and Québec City's Université Laval are among the world's finest French-language institutions. And there's simply no denying that French Canada, with its sense of fashion and style and its delight in fine dining and nightlife, has enriched the country.

PARLEZ-VOUS ANGLAIS?
Montréal is North America's only French-speaking metropolis and the second largest French-speaking city in the world. It also has a large English-speaking population, however, and while anglophones sometimes grumble about language restrictions imposed by the provincial government in Québec City, they also revel in living in one of the continent's most distinctive and cosmopolitan cities. Their language is peppered with French expressions (such as *dépanneur* for convenience store), and conversations in the trendy bars and restaurants of St.-Denis and Crescent streets often flit almost effortlessly back and forth between the two languages. Succeeding waves of Italians, Greeks, Portuguese, South and East Asians, Haitians and Latin Americans have added even more spice to the city's rich cultural stew.

From left to right *Rue St.-Louis in Québec; an old-fashioned gas station; bilingual sign warning of wildlife on the road in Manitoba*

INTO THE MAINSTREAM

Until a disgruntled René Lévesque broke with the Québec Liberal Party in the early 1960s, the separatist movement in Québec was pretty much a fringe affair with little mainstream support. Lévesque, however, had a common touch that endeared him to all Québecers. He was also a former television journalist who could explain his ideas in beguilingly reasonable terms. He eschewed the word "separatist" and called himself a sovereignist instead. But just what he meant by sovereignty was a little unclear. He always linked it to a special association with the rest of Canada, an ambivalence that has bedeviled the movement ever since, with the *purs-et-durs* demanding full independence and the softer nationalists hoping for some less final solution.

LOSS OF FAITH

One of the most startling phenomena of the last half-century has been the collapse of Roman Catholic authority in Québec. As recently as the early 1960s, the Church ran the province's schools, hospitals and social services. Large families and almost universal Mass attendance at church were the norm. Just about every village and city neighborhood had a cathedral-size stone church. But today those churches are virtually empty. Québec has one of the lowest church-attendance rates in Canada and one of the lowest birth rates in the world. The turnabout seems a little ungrateful: Québec's bishops might sometimes have been a little authoritarian, but no institution did more than the Church to preserve the French fact in Canada.

QUÉBEC ON FILM

Moviemaker Denys Arcand's critically acclaimed *Decline of the American Empire* (1986) offers an incisive if not particularly attractive portrait of Québec's modern and very secular bourgeoisie. Its main characters, four university professors and their various partners, gather for a dinner party and discuss the problems of sexuality, success, fidelity, intimacy, and ageing. The movie won an Academy Award nomination and four Canadian Junos. A more recent Arcand movie, *Jésus de Montréal*, takes a gentler look at post-Catholic Québec and its loss of faith. It follows the adventures of a group of young actors who make pornographic films by day, and every evening re-enact Christ's crucifixion for pilgrims to a Montréal shrine.

IRISH CONNECTION

Many French-speaking Quebecers have names that are more Gaelic than Gallic. Ryans and O'Neills are particularly common. Most of these French-speaking Gaels can trace their lineage back to the immigrants who arrived in Canada in the 19th century to escape the potato famine in Ireland. Most of them journeyed in deplorable conditions aboard overcrowded ships. Hundreds of new arrivals died of cholera in the fever sheds of the quarantine centers. Encouraged by their bishops and parish priests to help their suffering fellow Catholics, many French Canadian families adopted the orphaned children, but out of respect for their parents and their heritage, allowed them to keep their Irish names.

Canada's 10 autonomous provinces have exclusive jurisdiction over their own education, culture, health care and social policy. So provincial politics is as important to most Canadians as national politics. In French-speaking Québec and industry-rich Ontario, who runs the provincial government is often more important than who's in charge in Ottawa. The Liberals have run the federal government for all but 15 of the last 70 or so years. In spite of the fact that Québec's campaign for more autonomy and even independence has dominated the national agenda since the 1960s, the prime minister's job has gone to Québecers for 33 of the last 35 years—a statistic that rankles westerners in Alberta and British Columbia. In fact, western discontent led to the creation of the Canadian Alliance, which merged with the Progressive Conservatives in 2003 to form the Conservative Party, which in turn won the 2006 general election.

Above *Ministers gather in the Senate Chamber, Ottawa*

CANADA'S PARLIAMENT

The Canadian Parliament mimics its British counterpart with a 301-seat House of Commons holding the real power, and a 105-seat Senate filling in for the House of Lords as a "chamber of sober second thought." Canada's senators are appointed for life. Because senate seats come with a handsome salary and plenty of perks, and because they're often handed out to the party faithful, Canada's Upper House is sometimes referred to as the Grateful Dead (the name of a popular rock group in the 1970s). "How does a senator wink?" the old joke goes. "He opens one eye." The jokes are not entirely fair, since the Senate committees do some of the most effective work on Parliament Hill.

CHRISTIAN POLITICIANS

Christianity has played a sometimes contradictory role in Canadian politics—especially on the Prairies. Bible Bill Eberhart, for example, founder of his own Protestant sect, turned to the scriptures and the funny-money theories of Major C. H. Douglas to create the populist, right-wing Social Credit Party that held power in Alberta between 1935 and 1971.

Baptist preacher Tommy Douglas, on the other hand, was inspired by the social Gospel and dreams of the New Jerusalem to found the Co-operative Commonwealth Federation, forerunner of the socialist New Democratic Party. In 1961, while he was premier of Saskatchewan, Douglas introduced Canada's first universal Medicare plan, overruling the angry protests of the province's doctors. The rest of the country followed suit some five years later.

STORY OF CANADA

THE BEGINNINGS OF CANADA

The Hurons who greeted French explorer Jacques Cartier when he arrived in Canada in 1534 were the descendants of the Asiatic peoples who had started arriving in the Americas 13,000 years earlier. Most of them probably trekked from Siberia to Alaska over a now-vanished land bridge and spread out across the continent, creating a rich tapestry of cultures and languages. Pre-Columbian Canada was, in fact, at least as diverse as Europe. The salmon-rich rivers and seas of the West Coast, for example, allowed the seafaring Haida people, of the Queen Charlotte Islands, to develop a complex culture rich in art and sculpture. In the Arctic, the Inuit not only survived by hunting seals and whales in one of the world's most hostile climates, they flourished, developing beautiful decorative arts. The seminomadic nations of the Iroquois Confederacy developed a sophisticated political system in the eastern woodlands, with a constitution that laid out rights and obligations and enfranchised women. Contrary to popular myth, however, North America was not an entirely peaceable land. The Huron and the Iroquois, for example, had clearly never heard of Jean-Jacques Rousseau's "noble savage," and fought over territory and resources with the same vigor as, say, the British and the French.

CANOE

It's no wonder the semi-nomadic hunters and farmers of what's now eastern Canada never developed the wheel; in a land of trees and hills, it would not have been much use. Instead, some unknown wilderness genius invented the birch-bark canoe, a fast, maneuverable craft superbly adapted to a land of lakes and rivers. It was strong and flexible, yet light enough to be carried around rapids. If a rock did puncture its tough skin, the canoe could be quickly patched with a piece of bark and some tar (pitch). A scarcity of craftsmen and suitable trees has made bark canoes rare, but the design lives on, using a variety of modern materials.

TOTEM POLE

Most West Coast totem poles are made of cedar, which carves easily and has a natural resistance to rot. But there the similarities end. Each nation or tribe has an individual style. The Haida, for example, barely sculpt their poles, carving instead low-relief figures that look as if they have simply been wrapped around one half of the trunk. Their Tsimshian neighbors on the mainland carve away much more vigorously, creating birds with projecting beaks and men with projecting arms. For both Haida and Tsimshian totem poles are not simply a random assortment of carved figures, but a banner to proclaim their identity. The animal and human figures on each pole represent a collage of personified family, tribal myths and history.

IGLOO

Life in an igloo is not as chilly or precarious as it might appear. To begin with, two blubber lamps and body heat will keep the temperature hovering around 14°C (57°F), not exactly toasty, but not like living in a refrigerator, either. A few furs and it's not not only warm, it's also comfortable. It's sturdy, too, even when made from blocks of snow carved from fresh drifts. Dome-shaped buildings stand up well, anyway, as Inuit hunters discovered long ago, but the harsh arctic climate gives the igloo added strength. Fresh snow melts when it lands on an igloo then refreezes, a constant process that hardens the igloo into a solid lump that could support considerable snow drifts and even a full-size polar bear, should one happen along.

FIRST ENCOUNTER

Some time in the summer of 1007, a Norse woman named Gudrid, wife of Thorfinn, gave birth to a son named Snorri—an event that would hardly be worth a mention if it weren't for the fact that it happened at l'Anse aux Meadows in what is now Newfoundland. That made Snorri the first European child born in North America. His parents soon abandoned their settlement on the rugged coast after one too many run-ins with the local natives, but this was 500 years before Christopher Columbus set sail for the West Indies. Norse explorations of Canada's east coast began in 1001, but attempts at settlement were short-lived. Stories of their adventures, however, became part of European lore.

MAPLE SYRUP

Legend has it that an Iroquois chief and his wife were responsible for the discovery of one of Canada's sweetest treats. In a fit of pique, apparently, the chief hurled his axe at a tree. His intrigued and perhaps fearful wife collected the faintly sweet sap that dripped from the resulting hole in the bark, and boiled the next day's hunt in it—thereby inventing both maple syrup and sugar-cured venison. Canadian maple farmers still boil sap to produce 80 percent of the world's supply of maple syrup, although these days they use plastic tubes to collect the stuff and industrial-size boilers to reduce it—a process that requires 20L (5 gallons) of sap to produce just 1L (2 pints) of syrup. The end result is delicious.

Opposite clockwise Huron Ouendat Indian Village, Georgian Bay; three carved totem poles in Vancouver's Stanley Park; the painting Mah-Min (1848) by Paul Kane, in Montréal's Musée des Beaux-Arts

NOUVELLE FRANCE

French navigator Jacques Cartier was looking for gold, diamonds and a route to China when he explored the St. Lawrence River in the mid-1500s. He failed on all three counts, but his voyages brought him as far inland as what is now Montréal, opening the way for later adventurers to prosper on more prosaic products. Salt cod, for example, a Lenten staple in Catholic France, brought in enough money to build the magnificent walled city of Louisbourg on Cape Breton Island, while merchants in Québec City grew rich buying beaver pelts from native tribes with axes, guns and, less creditably, booze. Catholic missionaries followed traders into the wilderness, braving hardship and martyrdom to convert the Huron and Iroquois tribes. All this commerce and conversion, along with a few well-armed troops, made the colony's fertile lowlands safe enough for farmers and tradespeople. Slowly, Nouvelle France evolved into a mirror of the mother country, with walled cities full of stone homes and grand churches, and a countryside peopled with tenant farmers and aristocratic seigneurs. But the colony was never well defended, and the Seven Years War effectively ended the French Regime, with British troops capturing Québec City in 1759 and Montréal a year later.

CANADA'S FIRST SOCIAL CLUB
Samuel de Champlain, explorer of note, was also Canada's first bon vivant. During the grim winter of 1606, he founded the *Ordre du bon temps* (Order of Good Cheer), to buck up the spirits at the tiny French outpost of Port-Royal in what is now Nova Scotia. Colonial officers prepared feasts for themselves and local native leaders, using the region's ample fish and game, and organized music, jokes and skits to keep everyone merry. These soirées began with a ceremonial procession led by the host for the evening, proudly wearing the order's chain around his neck.

FASHION STATEMENT

It was male vanity that made many of Canada's early merchants wealthy. What they had that European haberdashers needed were beaver pelts—not for fur coats, but to make the tall, stylish felt hats that were all the rage among European men from about 1550 to 1850. At first, traders preferred old pelts that native trappers had used as coats for a couple of years. That sort of wear and tear got rid of the coarse guard hairs and made it easier for hatmakers to get at the dense underfur they used to make sturdy, water-resistant felt. However, Russian techniques for removing guard hairs cheaply eventually made new furs more desirable than "coat grade" pelts.

ORIENTAL OBSESSIONS

Robert Cavalier Sieur de La Salle was so obsessed with finding a route through North America to China that many of his contemporaries doubted his sanity. And the man certainly did travel a lot—to Lake Michigan in 1679 and to the mouth of the Mississippi in 1682, for example. He never made it to China but was murdered in Texas by mutineers while trying to invade Spanish territory in 1687. Back home on the island of Montréal, where he held land near the rapids that blocked the way west, his neighbors were generally unimpressed. They derisively referred to his estate as *la Chine* (China), a name that even today is attached to the city borough of Lachine and the nearby rapids.

FEMALE POWER

Montréal owes much of its early success to the religious fervor of two formidable French women. The first was Jeanne Mance, who abandoned the comforts of her well-to-do home in France in 1635 to help Paul Chomedy de Maisonneuve establish what they hoped would be a model Christian community in the middle of the wilderness. She was Canada's first lay nurse and built Canada's first hospital. The second was Marguerite Bourgeoys, who was the city's first schoolteacher and founder of a religious order that still runs schools in Canada. Marguerite Bourgeoys's nuns also taught homemaking skills to the "Filles du Roy," young, orphan girls who came to Canada at royal expense to find husbands among the largely male settlers; an important part of establishing the colony.

THE SCOTS CONNECTION

Scotsman James Johnstone seems to have had a habit of picking losing causes. First, he joined Bonnie Prince Charlie's failed Highland rebellion in 1745 and only barely survived the disastrous Battle of Culloden. Fourteen years later, he was in a French uniform fighting yet another losing battle against the British, this time to defend Québec City against the army of General James Wolfe, who'd served as a major on the winning side at Culloden. When the brief battle ended, both Wolfe and French General Louis-Joseph de Montcalm were dead, leaving Johnstone, Montcalm's aide-de-camp, to parlay a battlefield ceasefire with fellow Highlander General James Murray, Wolfe's second in command. Legend has it the language of negotiation was their mutual Gaelic.

Opposite clockwise *Oil painting in Ottawa's National Gallery; Fortress Louisbourg; fur trappers display, Glenbow Museum, Calgary*

WESTWARD HO!

Canada owes its early expansion to a combination of redcoats, railroadmen and daring. The redcoats were the North West Mounted Police, a tiny force of 300 lightly armed men who rode west to patrol a wilderness the size of European Russia. They used courage, discipline and not a little bluff to drive American whiskey traders from the Prairies, to pacify the native tribes and to make the land safe for settlement. This also made way for an audacious gamble—building the Canadian Pacific Railway across 4,000km (2,500 miles) of muskeg and mountains to link Montréal to the British colonies on the West Coast. The project nearly bankrupted the tiny dominion, but its completion in 1885 assured Canada's nationhood. British Columbia entered the Confederation and new settlers poured into the west, transforming the Prairies into a breadbasket, and tapping into the mineral and lumber wealth of the Rockies and the West Coast. But opening the west didn't happen without bloodshed; two uprisings led by the mixed-race, French-speaking Métis of Manitoba and Saskatchewan gave Canada its first and last taste of warfare with native tribes and created a bitterness that endured for decades.

FREEDOM FIGHTER OR TRAITOR?

The strongest resistance to western expansion came from the Métis, a mixed-race nation of devoutly Catholic, French-speaking buffalo hunters and farmers who feared that new settlers would drive them from their lands and destroy their way of life. Largely because the government did little to reassure them, they rebelled twice. In 1870, their magnetic leader Louis Riel declared a provisional government and executed a white settler who defied his authority. Canadian troops crushed the second rebellion of 1885 and Riel surrendered. His subsequent trial and execution split Canada along linguistic lines: The French hailed him as a visionary freedom fighter; the British condemned him as a half-mad traitor and murderer. The tragic truth was probably somewhere in the middle.

Above clockwise *Donald Smith, (1820–1914) marking the completion of the Canadian Pacific Railroad joining the Eastern seaboard to Vancouver; recruitment poster for the Royal Canadian Mounted Police; Québec's Terrasse Dufferin, with Château Frontenac behind*

RED RIVER CARTS

While American settlers moved their goods west in huge covered wagons, early Canadian homesteaders favored the much humbler Red River cart, a two-wheeled vehicle designed by the Métis to haul their goods around on hunting trips. The carts were hardly pretty, but they were easy to build, easier to repair, and were superbly adapted for wilderness travel. Their outward-angled wheels allowed them to carry loads of more than 360kg (800lb) without sinking into the soft prairie dirt, and their watertight construction meant the boxes could double as rafts once the wheels were removed. The carts did have one irritating characteristic, however—their greaseless axles emitted a high-pitched squeal that could be heard for miles.

MOUNTED POLICE AND SITTING BULL

When Superintendent James Morrow Walsh of the North West Mounted Police heard that Sitting Bull and 5,000 followers had crossed the border from the US into Canada in 1877, he figured he had better go and lay down the law for the Sioux leader, whose tribesmen had just wiped out the US Seventh Cavalry.

To accomplish this daunting task, he took with him exactly three men. But happily all went well. Morrow, a bit of a dandy in his buckskin coat, got along famously with Sitting Bull. The pair spent the best part of a day together, and Sitting Bull agreed to respect the laws of the Great White Mother (Queen Victoria)—which is just as well, since Walsh had only 90 men under his command to enforce those laws.

GASSY JACK

When John (Gassy Jack) Deighton arrived by rowboat on the south shore of Burrard Inlet in 1867, he had "little more than $6 in his pocket, a few sticks of furniture, a yellow dog, and a bottle of whiskey." But within 24 hours he'd opened the first bar in what would one day become Vancouver. The Globe Saloon was not much more than a shack, but it served as a blessed oasis for the workers from a nearby sawmill, who had nowhere else to go.

Life wasn't easy, though. "Surrounded by Indians, I dare not look outdoors after dark," Jack wrote his brother Tom back home in Yorkshire. "There was a friend of mine, about a mile distant, found with his head cut in two." Gassy Jack kept his head and continued to provide a haven for the sawyers.

TACITURN WISDOM

The North West Mounted Police owed much of their early success in the west to the skills of a short, bowlegged, hard-drinking man named Jerry Potts. The son of a Scottish trader and a Blackfoot woman, Potts seldom spoke more than two words at a time. "What's over that hill, Jerry?" the disoriented Mounties would often ask. "Nother hill," was Potts's invariable reply. But the stubbly little Potts was a superb guide, tracker and hunter. His 22-year career with the police began in Fort Benton in 1874, when he led Commissioner George French's lost column to water and pasture, and found suitable campgrounds for them. He also taught the Mounties how to do business with the First Nations peoples according to their own traditions.

The two world wars of the 20th century had oddly contradictory effects on Canada. On the one hand, they helped the country mature and take its place on the world stage. On the other, they threatened to tear it apart. The valor of Canada's troops at the Battle of Vimy Ridge during World War I was unexcelled, and the country's contribution to World War II, especially the war at sea, was prodigious for a nation of fewer than 15 million people.

But at home the bitter conscription battles of both wars split the country along linguistic lines, leading to riots, internment and tottering governments. French Canadians argued fiercely against being forced to fight wars they viewed as both foreign and imperial. Yet, despite their opposition to the draft, French Canadians volunteered for service in numbers roughly proportionate to their share of the population.

Meanwhile, the population was changing. Canadians were abandoning the land and moving into the towns and cities, and by the midpoint of the century, Canada had become an urban country. It was also more multicultural than before, in spite of its often unwelcoming immigration policies.

Above left to right *British ex-servicemen and their families arriving to start a new life in Canada, 1927; memorial to the Canadian soldiers who died at Vimy Ridge in France; Cunard shipping line poster*

NATION OF IMMIGRANTS?

Modern Canada prides itself on being a nation of immigrants, but for the first half of the 20th century, at least, it had pretty strong opinions about who it wanted. British and American farmers topped the list, followed by immigrants from Europe. Less welcome were people with a different culture, religion or skin color. Canada showed just how callous it could be in May 1914, when the *Komagata Maru* arrived in Vancouver with 376 immigrants from India, all British subjects. After two months of stalling and political maneuvering, the Canadian navy escorted the vessel and its passengers out of the harbor while cheering Vancouverites looked on.

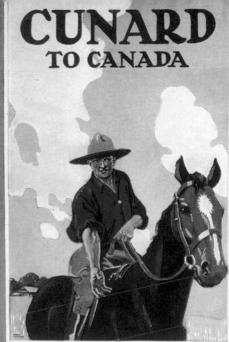

NOBEL PRIZE

After reading an article about the pancreas in the fall of 1920, Dr. Frederick Banting jotted down an idea that led, after two years of twists and turns, to the discovery of insulin as a treatment for diabetes. It also led, unfortunately, to an unseemly battle over who should get the credit. Banting claimed that he and graduate student Charles Best had done all the important work and deserved all the glory. He deliberately set out to discredit his overseer at the University of Toronto, J. R. R. Macleod, and his protegé, James Collip. When the Nobel Committee shared the 1923 prize for medicine between Banting and Macleod, an angry Banting split his share with Best and Macleod also shared his prize with Collip.

GANGSTERS IN MOOSE JAW

Moose Jaw, Saskatchewan, was a pretty lively place during the 1920s, thanks to Prohibition in the United States. Some of the continent's biggest gangsters used it as a hideout and a depot for smuggling booze into the States. River Street (aka Little Chicago) became the hub for gambling, prostitution and bootlegging. Particularly appealing to mobsters was a network of tunnels under the town that had been built to hide illegal Chinese immigrants. One frequent visitor was Al Capone, who used to stay in a River Street hotel whenever Chicago got too hot for him. Legend has it that an ill Capone had a doctor brought to his room to remove an infected tonsil—without anesthetic.

CANADA'S MOST INTERESTING MAN

When King George VI paid a visit to Montréal in 1939, his host was Camillien Houde, the city's irrepressible mayor. As the two drove past cheering crowds, the enormously popular Houde told the King with a grin, "Some of this is for you, your majesty."

Later at dinner, Houde made the King hoot with laughter when he breezily showed him a list of topics his worried advisors had forbidden him to raise. One of them, no doubt, was the impending war with Germany. While it was raging, Houde was interned for opposing the draft.

In spite of Houde's politics, however, the Queen reportedly told friends in England that the mayor was the most interesting man she'd met in Canada.

VICTORY AT SEA

Angus Walters doesn't look like the finest seaman that Canada ever produced. Pictures show a small, almost wizened, man wearing a cloth cap and an enigmatic smile. But Walters was the skipper of the legendary *Bluenose*, a sleek Nova Scotia schooner that fished the Grand Banks of Newfoundland in the 1920s and 1930s. In 1921, Walters and the *Bluenose* wrested the Fishermen's Cup from the Americans and held it for the next 17 years, in spite of the best efforts of leading boat designers in American ports such as Gloucester, Massachusetts, and Portsmouth, Maine, to come up with something fast enough to beat them. "The wood of the vessel that will beat the *Bluenose*," Walters once boasted, "is still growing."

LOSS OF INNOCENCE

Canada celebrated its 100th birthday in 1967 with a giddy year of parties, fireworks and royal visits. There was a centennial song, a centennial flag and hundreds of centennial projects, including a World's Fair in Montréal and a UFO landing pad in St. Paul, Alberta. But just three years after all this merriment, armed soldiers were patrolling the streets of Montréal in the wake of a series of terrorist kidnappings, and just six years after that, French-speaking Québec elected its first separatist government.

The roots of the unrest could be traced to the 1950s, when French Canada began to lose its Catholic fervor and assert itself as a political power to be reckoned with. At the time, the huge baby-boom generation, galvanized by the civil-rights struggle and antiwar movement in the United States, started to look around for causes of its own.

But it wasn't all power and protest. The same forces also generated a torrent of literature, music and art. Somewhat later, in 1982, Canada also got a new constitution of its own, along with a Charter of Rights and Freedoms. Canada began carving out a role for itself on the world stage as a peacekeeper and a mediator between the rich and the poor.

STRAINED RELATIONS

Canadian prime ministers have often had a strained relationship with American presidents. Prime Minister John Diefenbaker, for example, claimed that President Jack Kennedy had referred to him as an s.o.b. in a briefing paper. Kennedy denied the charge, saying "I couldn't have called him an s.o.b., I didn't know he was one—at that time." Diefenbaker's successor, Lester Pearson, had an even more abrupt encounter with President Lyndon Johnson in 1964. In a speech at Temple University in Philadelphia, Pearson criticized American policy in Vietnam and called for a pause in the bombing of Hanoi. Later, at a presidential meeting in Washington, President Johnson thumped Pearson on the chest and responded with an angry, "You don't come down here and piss on my rug."

Above clockwise *President John F. Kennedy (center) with John Diefenbaker (right); Toronto's eminent CN Tower; Canadian Prime Minister Pierre Trudeau (right), with industry minister Herb Gray*

YVETTE AUX BARRICADES!

A character in a children's textbook helped save Canada from disintegration in 1980. As Québec prepared for its first referendum on independence, separatist forces under the charismatic René Lévesque were well supported by men but not so much by women. Lise Payette, a TV talk-show host turned separatist politician, suggested it was meekness not conviction that kept women in the pro-Canada camp. She compared them to the fictional Yvette, the mild-mannered mother of a traditional family in a textbook that had been used to teach Québec children to read. Outraged pro-Canada women made their vote and helped turn the tide and win the day for national unity.

TRUDEAUMANIA

Driving his convertible Mercedes or striding around in a flowing cape with a female celebrity in tow, Pierre Elliott Trudeau often seemed more like a movie star than a politician. Prime Minister of Canada for 16 years (1968–1984), he was a respected diplomat whose extraordinary popular appeal in Canada was dubbed Trudeaumania.

Behind his undoubted charm was a formidable intelligence. His aim was to create a "just society" where all Canadians would feel at home and be treated equally.

In 2000, the news of Trudeau's death sparked a huge public outpouring of grief. To many Canadians, he remains the very embodiment of their nation.

RELIEF ON ICE

It was supposed to be a cakewalk. There was no way, Canadians firmly believed, that Soviet amateurs could beat Canada's seasoned professionals at hockey. To predict anything but a rout was heresy. "We'll need calculators to keep score," confident pundits predicted. Instead, the eight-game series in 1972 opened with a seven-to-three Soviet victory that rocked the country. From then on it was a heart-stopping roller-coaster ride that had thousands of Canadians ducking work and skipping school to watch the games. Only when Paul Henderson scored the winning goal in the dying seconds of the last game to give Canada a razor-thin victory with four wins and a tie, did the nation heave a sigh of relief and get back to work.

RUNNING FOR HOPE

After jogging 5,390km (3,369 miles) from St. John's, Newfoundland, to the western shore of Lake Superior, Terry Fox stopped outside the city of Thunder Bay. He was tired and his chest ached. A medical examination confirmed his worst fears: The cancer that had taken his right leg three years earlier had spread to his lungs. His dream of running right across Canada was over.

Less than a year later, on June 28, 1981, Fox died at his home in British Columbia. But the image of Terry Fox, his curly head bobbing as he half-jogged, half-hopped the very long and lonely miles, captured Canada's imagination. Now, every year, thousands of runners keep his Marathon of Hope alive with sponsored jogging to raise money for cancer research.

JITTERY INDECISION

It couldn't have been much closer. On October 30, 1995, Québecers voted to stay in Canada—just barely. The difference wouldn't have filled a good-size bar. The final score: 49.4 percent for independence, 50.6 against. The cliffhanger ended a decade of constitutional to-ing and fro-ing that obsessed Canada's political and chattering classes. Meanwhile, for millions of others the whole French-English argument seemed sterile and irrelevant. As accords and crises followed each other with dizzying frequency, Canadians with names like Nguyen, Guiterrez and Singh increasingly tuned out. Even some Québec heroes were losing interest. When Formula 1 driver Jacques Villeneuve opened a restaurant on Montréal's trendy Crescent Street, he called it Newtown—the English translation of his family name. And there seemed to be so many more important issues. Canada sent soldiers and sailors to the first Gulf War, and more soldiers to keep the peace amid the ruins of what had been Yugoslavia. Meanwhile, writers such as Michael Ondaatje *(The English Patient)* and Margaret Atwood *(Cat's Eye)*, pop stars like Céline Dion, Alanis Morissette and Bryan Adams, extravaganzas like Montréal's Cirque du Soleil and world-beater companies such as Bombardier were giving Canada a new presence on the world stage.

BOUCHARD

When Lucien Bouchard stepped forward to lead Québec's independence forces in 1995, nationalists were delirious. A wily politician given to changing parties, Bouchard began with the populist Creditistes, moved to the separatist Parti Québécois, switched to the Conservatives and then founded the Bloc Québécois. He also served in the cabinet and as ambassador to France.

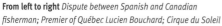

From left to right *Dispute between Spanish and Canadian fisherman; Premier of Québec Lucien Bouchard; Cirque du Soleil*

THE GREAT TURBOT WAR

The Great Turbot War of 1995 pitted Canada's tiny navy— seven ships and a submarine—against a fleet of Spanish trawlers fishing off the Grand Banks of Newfoundland. Given that the trawlers were armed with nothing more deadly than nets and hooks, the match was hardly fair, but the conflict made Canada's diminutive fisheries minister, Brian Tobin, something of a hero. Even British fishermen—no fans of Spanish fishing practices— hoisted Canadian flags in his honor. Canadians accused the Spanish of overfishing, cut their nets and confiscated one of the trawlers, escorting it into St. John's Harbour in triumph. The Spanish protested and declared that all this happened in international waters and the Canadians were little better than pirates.

INDESTRUCTIBLE TILLEYS

Alex Tilley claims he makes the best darned yachting hat in the world, an uncharacteristically forceful claim for a Canadian entrepreneur. But the stylishly brimmed canvas hat is good enough to have impressed Canada's armed forces, which ordered 6,000 of the things to protect its sailors from the broiling heat during the first Gulf War in 1991. "Tilleys" quickly became a hot barter item among the forces of other nations as well. But the military endorsement wasn't Tilley's best marketing coup. About 10 years earlier, an Ontario zookeeper had reported his Tilley had made a trip through an elephant's digestive system and emerged at the other end somewhat soiled but unscathed. The story, Tilley says, "turned out to be a fantastic selling point."

CANADIAN PEACEKEEPERS

Canadians have become so used to thinking of their soldiers as peacekeepers, they actually seem embarrassed when they show they can fight, too. This might explain why the government kept so quiet about the 1991 Battle of the Medak Pocket. Nearly 900 members of Princess Patricia's Canadian Light Infantry took part in that desperate two-day firefight to prevent Croatian regulars from murdering Serb villagers. The Canadians, about half of them weekend reservists, drove a wedge between the two sides and successfully stopped the killing. But they didn't come home to the hero's welcome they might have expected, in fact, they had to wait nine years before their government finally honored them with a military unit commendation.

MOHAWKS DON'T PLAY A ROUND

A dispute over a golf course led to the most serious First Nation uprising in modern Canada. In 1990, the town of Oka, Québec, near Montréal, tried to level a small pine forest to add a few holes to its municipal course. Mohawks from the nearby community of Kanehsatake, however, considered the threatened forest sacred ground and took up arms to defend it. The town sent in the Québec police, the Mohawks opened fire, and a policeman was killed. What followed was a tense 78-day stand-off between the army and armed Mohawks, who occupied a local social club and blockaded one of the four major bridges leading to Montréal Island. The Mohawks finally surrendered, but ultimately they achieved their aim and the golf course extension was never built.

A NEW ERA

The first years of the third millennium have seen much political upheaval in Canada. In 2004, the so-called "sponsorship scandal" broke, revealing the misuse of public funds by Liberal governments since 1993, under prime ministers Jean Chretien and Paul Martin. Feelings of alienation in western Canada together with outrage in Québec led to the defeat of the Liberals in a confidence vote in Parliament in 2005 and, subsequently, in the general election of January 2006. A new Conservative government was installed headed by Albertan Stephen Harper with, rather surprisingly, strong representation from the province of Québec. Most Canadians hope this will usher in a period of relative calm.

ARCTIC ICE

Since 2003, when the Diavik Diamond Mine opened, the capital of the Northwest Territories, Yellowknife, has become the diamond capital of North America, and other mines are under development. The diamonds mined are extremely pure and are highly prized by specialists. The region now rates as the world's third-largest diamond producer.

A VICIOUS CIRCLE

With climate change already impacting on the Arctic ice-cap, a spotlight has been thrown on this region that has little to do with ecological matters and everything to do with the oil that lies beneath it and potential oil exploration. Canada, the US (Alaska), Russia, Denmark (which owns Greenland) and Norway form a ring around the Arctic Circle and sovereignty issues have become a hot topic. Whatever the eventual resolution, there is much irony in the fact that they will be taking advantage of global warming to utilize even more of the fossil-fuels that are held to be its cause. An added headache for Canada will be the need to patrol a vast northern frontier if and when the Northwest Passage opens and becomes a reality.

NORTHERN DREAM

A long-held dream came true in 1999 for the Inuit people of the north when the Canadian government sliced off the eastern half of the Northwest Territories to create Nunavut, a vast piece of land four times the size of Spain.

The Inuit constitute about 85 percent of the region's 29,000 people, and Inuktitut is the official language of the courts and legislature. Nunavut doesn't have the same autonomy as the other Canadian provinces, but its existence gives the Inuit people an unprecedented level of self-government. Its 19-member legislature tries to blend British parliamentary rules with Inuit traditions of consensus government. There are no political parties, for example, and the legislature selects the premier from among its members.

Above *Swearing-in ceremony for the Members of the Legislative Assembly of Nunavut in Iqaluit, April 1, 1999*

ON THE MOVE

On the Move gives you detailed advice and information about the various options for traveling to Canada before explaining the best ways to get around the country once you are there. Handy tips help you with everything from buying tickets to renting a car.

ARRIVING

ARRIVING BY AIR

The major international airports in Canada are in Toronto, Montréal and Vancouver. International flights are also handled at the Ottawa and Québec City airports, and in other major cities such as Halifax, Edmonton, Calgary and Winnipeg, which are all connected to each other as well as to nearby cities in the US. All have efficient websites (▷ panel opposite) with information that includes airport and/or terminal plans, details of terminal facilities, transportation options and flight schedules.

MAJOR 'GATEWAY CITY' INTERNATIONAL AIRPORTS
Vancouver International Airport (YVR)

Located 15km (9 miles) south of downtown, Vancouver International Airport (tel 604/207-7077) has the

TRANSFERS TO MAJOR CITY DOWNTOWNS

AIRPORT	DISTANCE TO CITY	TAXI	CAR	TRAIN/SUBWAY
Vancouver International	15km (9 miles)	**Price:** Allow about $30. **Journey time:** About 30 min	South of city via Highway 99, the Arthur Laing Bridge and Grant McConachie Way	In 2009 the Canada Line rapid transit line, linking the airport with downtown, is due to open.
Toronto Pearson International Airport	27km (17 miles)	**Price:** In region of $45–$50 **Journey time:** 45 min (longer during rush hour)	Northwest of downtown by the Queensway and Highway 427 north	n/a (but see bus/long-distance bus details)
Montréal-Trudeau International Airport	15km (9 miles)	**Fixed-rate fare:** $35 (drivers accept credit cards). **Journey time:** 30 min (depends on traffic)	West of city via Autoroute Ville-Marie (Highway 720) and Autoroute 20 west.	Plans for a rail link are under discussion, but it's not imminent
Ottawa International Airport	11km (7 miles)	**Price:** About $25 **Journey time:** Around 20 min	South of downtown via Bronson Avenue south and Airport Parkway	n/a
Jean Lesage International Airport, Québec City	20km (12 miles)	**Fixed-rate fare:** $30 **Journey time:** Allow 20 min	West of downtown via Blvd. Charest, Highway 40 north, Blvd. Wilfrid-Hamel and Route de l'Aéroport	n/a

full range of passenger facilities, including duty-free stores, cafeterias, restaurants, money exchange services, tourist information and car rental desks.

An Airport Improvement Fee is imposed on all departing passengers, who have to pay $5 for flights within British Columbia or the Yukon and $15 for travel to other parts of the world. However, this is not applied to passengers in transit. This fee is now included in your fare.

Toronto Pearson International Airport

Lester B. Pearson Airport (Terminal 1, tel 416/247-7678; Terminal 3, tel 416/776-5100; Toll-free 1-866/207-1690) is 27km (17 miles) northwest of downtown. A $4.5 billion improvement and expansion project has resulted in two superb terminals (curiously numbered 1 and 3) linked by a free monorail shuttle. Pleasant and efficient, the terminals are dotted with original artworks and museum displays, and the

comprehensive range of services includes restaurants, duty-free stores and currency exchange.

All departing passengers have to pay the $20 Airport Improvement Fee; people in transit have to pay $8.

Montréal-Trudeau International Airport

Montréal's international airport (pictured left; tel 514/394-7377 or 1-800/465-1213) is 15km (9 miles) west of downtown. It has many food outlets and stores. All major car rental services have desks on the main floor and there's also a tourist information booth.

Departing passengers (but not those in transit) have to pay the Airport Improvement Fee of $15; credit cards are accepted.

Ottawa Airport

About 11km (7 miles) south of downtown, Ottawa Airport (tel 613/248-2125 or 2141) is small compared with the three airports above, but nevertheless has all the regular

facilities you would expect. It also levies an Airport Improvement Fee of $15 on all departing passengers.

Jean Lesage International Airport

Québec City's international airport (tel 418/640-2700) is located 20km (12 miles) west of downtown. It has food facilities, duty-free and gift shops, currency exchange, ATMs and car-rental desks.

An Airport Improvement Fee ($15) is included in the price of outbound tickets.

BUS/LONG-DISTANCE BUS

Airporter bus (tel 604/946-8866 or 1-800/668-3141; www.yvrairporter.com) a shuttle service to the downtown hotels and transport terminals
Frequency: Every 20 mins, 9am–9.30pm in summer, a little less frequently the rest of the year
Airport Express bus to and from downtown hotels and the bus station (tel 905/564-3232 or 1-800/387-6787; www.torontoairportexpress.com)
Frequency: Runs on a 20- to 30-minute schedule
Price: $17 one way (single), $30 round trip (return)
Ticketing: Reservations can be made online
Journey time: About 45 min depending on traffic
Regular transit bus is the cheapest option (tel 416/393-4636; www.ttc.ca), providing a number of options, all of which pick up at Terminals 1 and 3

L'Aérobus shuttle service (tel 514/842-2281) runs between airport and downtown Central bus station located at the corner of de Maisonneuve and Berri streets (metro Berri-UQAM)

Shuttle bus service to major hotels downtown (tel 613/260-2359; www.yowshuttle.com)
Frequency: Regular service every half-hour all day
n/a (no shuttle bus service downtown)

Price: $14 one way (single), $21 round trip (return)
Ticketing: May be purchased at the Airporter counter, from hotel concierges or on the bus
Journey time: 45 min
»» 192 "Airport Rocket" all-day service to the Kipling subway station at the west end of the Bloor-Danforth line (journey time: 20 min)
»» 58A Malton all-day service to Lawrence West (journey time: 1 hour)
»» 300A 24-hour route along the Bloor-Danforth corridor (journey time: 45 min)
»» 307 Eglinton West 24-hour service to Eglinton West station (journey time: 45 min)
Price: Regular transit fare of $3 for all options, includes subway transfer

Frequency: Buses depart every 5 min during the day
Price: $14 one way (single), $24 round trip (return). From the central bus station there's a free shuttle service to more than 40 hotels in downtown Montréal
Ticketing: Tickets can only be purchased on the spot
Price: $14 one way (single), $24 round trip (return).
»» OC Transpo Route also serves the airport journey
Frequency: Every 15 min **Price:** $3, or two advance tickets 95¢ each way

GETTING AROUND

AIR TRANSPORTATION

Since Canada is such a huge country, the second biggest in the world, air travel is generally the fastest and most practical means of getting from region to region. In some instances in the north, it is the only way of getting to particular communities.

AIRLINES
Air Canada
Air Canada (tel 1-88/247-2262) is the country's largest carrier and, in many instances, it has a monopoly. It serves more than 60 countries worldwide, including 10 airports in the UK and more than 90 in the US. In addition to its regularly scheduled services, its subsidiary, Air Canada Jazz (tel 888/247-2262), offers budget flights. Their low fares are available only by advance reservation

and payment, and changes to reservations are either not allowed or incur substantial charges.

Other Canadian Airlines
» WestJet, founded in 1996 to provide a budget air service in western Canada, now serves 27 destinations right across Canada, 12 US airports and 7 in Mexico and the Caribbean. For reservations, phone 1-888/937-8538.

» Based In Montréal, Air Transat is best known for its charter flights to Europe during the summer, and services to vacation destinations in Florida and the Caribbean in the winter months. For general information and reservations, tel 1-877/872-6728.

» Northern Canada (Yukon, the Northwest Territories and Nunavut) is served by Air Canada. Other carriers include Canadian North (tel 1-800/661-1505), First Air (tel 1-800/267-1247 and Air Inuit (tel 1-800/361-2965). Be warned that flights are very expensive. In addition, there are many charter companies providing air services to remote areas; the tourist offices are the best places to obtain further information about these (▷ 378).

US Airlines
The major US airlines offer regular flights between the US and Canada. American Airlines (tel 1-800/433-7300), Delta (tel 1-800/221-1212), Northwest (tel 1-800/225-2525), United (tel 1-800/241-6522), and US Airways (tel 1-800/428-4322; in the UK tel 0845 600 3300) all service Canada's major airports. Visitors from outside North America may find it worthwhile investigating prices for international connections on the busy US–Canada routes. There are many special offers, but these generally require you to fly at specified times or dates.

Other International Airlines
International airlines with nonstop services between Europe and one of Canada's major cities (Toronto, Montréal and Vancouver) include Air France (tel 1-800/375-8723; in the UK tel 0870/142-4343); British Airways (tel 1-800/AIRWAYS; in the UK tel 0871/850-9850); KLM, operated by Northwest (tel 1-800/225-2525), and Lufthansa (tel 1-800/399-5838, in the UK tel 0871/945-9747). Qantas offers flights from Australia (1-800/227-4500; in Australia 13 13 13).

AIRLINE WEBSITES		
CANADIAN AIRLINES	**US AIRLINES**	**OTHER INTERNATIONAL AIRLINES**
Air Canada www.aircanada.ca	American Airlines www.aa.com	Air France www.airfrance.com
Air Canada Jazz www.flyjazz.ca	Delta www.delta.com	British Airways www.ba.com
WestJet www.westjet.com	Northwest www.nwa.com	KLM www.klm.com
Air Transat www.airtransat.com	United www.united.com	Lufthansa www.lufthansa.com
Canadian North www.cdn-north.com	US Airways www.usairways.com	Qantas www.qantas.com
First Air www.firstair.ca		
Air Inuit www.airinuit.com		

MAJOR AIRPORTS OF EACH PROVINCE AND TERRITORY
St. John's, Newfoundland
Charlottetown, Prince Edward Island
Halifax, Nova Scotia
Saint John, New Brunswick
Québec City and Montréal, Québec
Ottawa and Toronto, Ontario
Winnipeg, Manitoba
Regina and Saskatoon, Saskatchewan
Calgary and Edmonton, Alberta
Victoria and Vancouver, British Columbia
Yellowknife, Northwest Territories
Whitehorse, Yukon
Iqaluit, Nunavut

SECURITY CONCERNS

You must carry government-issued photo identification if you take a flight within Canada and produce this when you check in. For foreign visitors, a passport is proof of identity. Canadians can use a driver's license or medical card, provided it contains a recent photograph.

Before boarding, all passengers and their carry-on baggage must pass through x-ray machines and be prepared to open all bags and have personal effects checked before boarding the plane.

CHECK-IN TIME

As a rule of thumb, passengers on international flights to the US or other overseas destinations should check in at least three hours before take-off. For flights within Canada, this time can be cut slightly depending on the airport. For example, at St. John's, Newfoundland, you can check in an hour before departure because it is a small airport. At Lester B. Pearson in Toronto, Canada's biggest and busiest facility, it is advisable to check in at least two hours before take-off because there can be a lot of security to pass through; you could miss your flight if you arrive later. All that being said, it is always important to contact your airline just prior to flying and ask what time they recommend you check in.

DOMESTIC AIRPORTS

» Winnipeg International Airport (tel 204/987-9400; www.waa.ca) is about a 20-minute drive northwest of the city (allow longer in heavy traffic). A cab will set you back $15 or more, but a city bus costs just $2.25 (tel 204/986-5700; www.winnipegtransit.com).

» Calgary International Airport (tel 403/735-1200; www.calgaryairport.com) is 16km (10 miles) north of the city. The trip downtown will take you about 30 minutes and a cab will set you back about $30. Calgary Airport is serviced by several of the major US carriers.

» Edmonton International Airport (tel 1-800/268-7134, 780/890-8382 or 1-800/268-7134; www.edmontonairports.com) is nearly 30km (19 miles) south of the city. A cab will set you back at least $35 and take a good half-hour; the sky shuttle bus costs $15 one way, $25 round trip and takes more or less the same time.

» Saskatchewan's capital, Regina, has a small airport (tel 306/761-7555; www.yqr.ca) that is only a 15-minute drive west of the city. It will take five minutes to check in and another five minutes for security, so arriving an hour in advance of your take-off time would be more than adequate.

» Halifax International Airport (tel 902/873-4422; www.halifaxairport.com) is 35km (22 miles) north of downtown—an attempt (not always successful) to avoid the fogs that affect the coastal area. It's always worth checking for flight delays before setting out. Extensive construction work in front of the terminal building has reduced parking and made the rental car area rather less accessible. Allow extra time for drop-off before your flight. Taxis to Halifax city center cost $53. There is a shuttle service to downtown hotels (tel 902/873-2091), which costs $18 one way (single) and $24 for a round trip (return); allow at least 45 minutes for the journey.

» The capital of Newfoundland, **St. John's** has a small airport (tel 709/758-8500 or 1-800/758-8500 www.stjohnsairport.nf.ca), 4.5km (3 miles) from downtown. A taxi will cost about $20 and take 15 minutes. There is no shuttle bus.

Details of other airports in Canada can be obtained from the appropriate provincial or territorial tourist office.

CITY TRANSPORTATION: TORONTO

In general, Canada's cities have invested in extensive public transportation systems, which makes travel around them relatively easy for visitors. The major cities, Toronto, Montréal and Vancouver, have excellent and reliable public transportation. Both Toronto and Montréal operate subway systems as well as buses and streetcars. In Vancouver, the transit system consists of buses, trolleys, the SeaBus catamaran ferries and the above-ground Skytrain rail service, providing a number of ways of getting around.

PUBLIC TRANSPORTATION

Toronto Transit Commission (TTC) The TTC (tel 416/393-4636; www.toronto.ca/ttc) operates buses, streetcars, the subway, and a light rapid transit system (RT).

One-way (single) fares, which can include transfers from one mode to another, are $2.75 for adults, $1.85 for students and seniors, and 70¢ for children under 12. Tickets (small metal tokens) can be purchased at all subway stations and at other authorized places displaying the TTC sign.

TTC Tips

» You need a ticket or exact change on buses and streetcars; drivers do not give change but they do give out free transfers if you intend continuing your journey on the subway.
» In subway stations, look for the push-button transfer machine found beyond the turnstile.
» Visitors can purchase a day pass for $9, good for unlimited travel on any day of the week (start of service until 5.30am next day), including public holidays.

TORONTO SUBWAY

The Toronto Subway has three lines: the Bloor-Danforth line, which crosses the metropolitan area from east to west; the Yonge-University-Spadina line, which forms a great north–south loop and Sheppard, from Sheppard-Yonge to Don Mills There are 65 stations, with buses and streetcars to the rest of the city. The popular harborfront area is accessible via the streetcar system from Union Station all along the waterfront to Exhibition station.

Subway Tips

» The Toronto subway opens at 6am every day except Sunday, when it opens at 9am; the system operates until 1.30am daily.
» "Ride Guides" with maps of the subway system are available at all subway stations, tourist offices and other public places.

TAXIS

The most expensive mode of transportation is the taxi—fares soon mount, especially at rush hour. Taxi stands can be found outside the major hotels. Cabs can also be hailed on the street, or contacted by telephone. You should tip the driver 10–15 percent of the fare.

Above *Passengers prepare to board a street car tram in Toronto*
 Left *Yellow taxi cab in Vancouver*

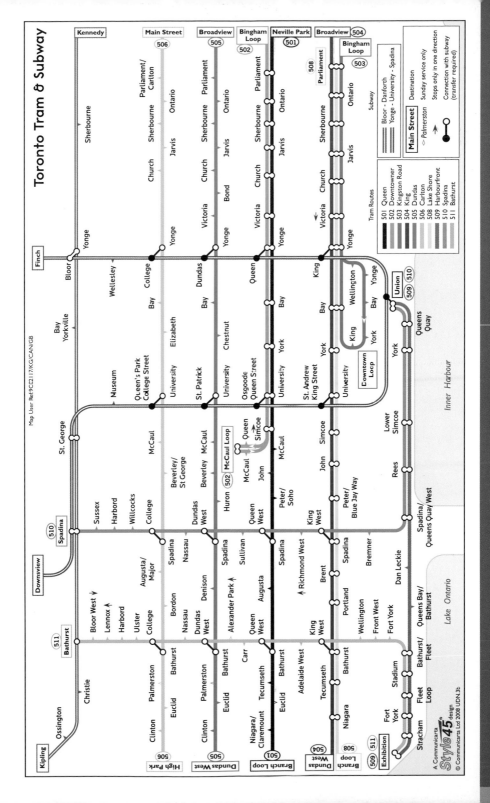

Toronto Tram & Subway

Map User Ref:9CC2117/KG/CAN/GB

A Communicarta **Style45** design
© Communicarta Ltd 2008 UDN.3b

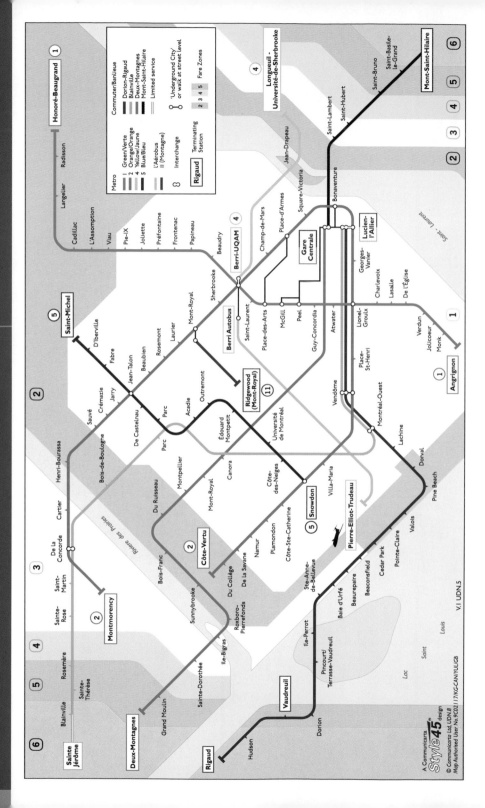

CITY TRANSPORTATION: MONTRÉAL

PUBLIC TRANSPORTATION

The Société de Transport de Montréal (STM), tel 514/786-4636; press 8 for English; www.stcum.qc.ca) runs all city buses plus the subway system (métro), which has four color-coded lines and 68 stations. The métro's green and orange lines cross downtown, the yellow goes to the islands and south shore, and the blue serves the university. There are four suburban commuter lines managed by the Agence Métropolitaine de Transport (AMT; www.amt.qc.ca).

A ticket for a one-way (single) ride on the bus or métro costs $2.75 for adults and $1.75 for seniors, students and children. A strip of six tickets costs $12.25 for adults and $6.50 for seniors, students and children. Suburban trains have fare zones as indicated on the map, the fare increasing the farther you travel.

Color-coded Lines

There are four color-coded métro lines—green, orange, yellow, and blue—and also four above-ground suburban commuter train lines. Métro lines are referred to by their color, suburban trains by their suburban destination (or start point).

Terminating Stations

When journeying by métro, look for the name of the station at the terminus of the line to ascertain the direction of travel. For example, the terminating stations on the orange line are Côte Vertu and Montmorency.

Navigation

Follow the color-coded sign with the name of the terminus in the direction you wish to travel. For example, if you are at Berri-UQAM and you wish to go to Atwater, you would take the green line in the direction of the Angrignon terminus.

Interchanging Lines

Some métro stations are served by more than one line. These are indicated by white circles on the map. It is easy to change from line to line—all you have to do is follow the color-coded sign in the direction of the terminus you want.

Interconnections with Suburban Trains

From several métro stations, covered walkways (indicated by dots on the map) link to the two downtown suburban train stations — Central and Windsor. The suburban train to Blainville links to Vendôme métro station. Connections between métro and suburban trains are indicated by a double white circle.

Montréal Métro Tips

» One-day passes allowing unlimited travel cost $9; three-day passes are $17. In summer, these passes are on sale at all the downtown métro stations; off season you must go to the central Berri-UQAM station.

» In every métro station, a transfer can be obtained from the push-button machine signed "Correspondance," enabling you to transfer to any bus.

» Free maps of the métro system are available in all stations and include a map of Montréal's extensive Underground City (▷ 72–73), together with a list of what is available at each station.

» The métro is open daily 5.30am–1am.

» If you start your journey on a bus, you will need a ticket or exact change.

TAXIS

Taxis are the most expensive means of transportation, but are convenient and plentiful in Montréal. Taxi stands are at many hotels and stategic points downtown and taxis can be hailed on the street or contacted by telephone. You should tip the driver 10–15 percent of the fare.

UNDERSTANDING THE MONTRÉAL MÉTRO

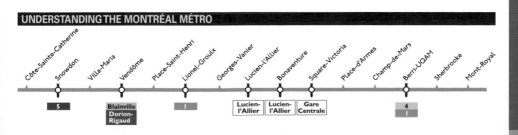

CITY TRANSPORTATION: VANCOUVER

TRANSLINK

The Vancouver transit system, Translink (tel 604/953-3333; www.translink.bc.ca), includes buses, trolleys, SeaBus ferries and the above-ground Skytrain. Services run from 6.30am until about 1am (earlier on Sundays). The fare system is rather complex, with three zones operating during weekday business hours. The fare is the same for all: $2.50 one way (single) for adults, $1.75 for seniors and children. If you cross a zone, you pay more during weekday business hours. Transfers are available between modes, and day passes cost $9 for adults and $7 for seniors and children. FareSaver 10-ticket deal is $19 for adults and $16 for seniors and children.

Skytrain has 33 stations along a 49.5km (31-mile) track that runs between downtown Vancouver, Burnaby, New Westminster and Surrey.

The **SeaBus** catamarans cross Burrard Inlet to the north shore

from the Waterfront station. The 15-minute trip is popular with visitors.

Translink Tips

» Be sure to have a ticket or the exact change for rides on the buses and trolleys; drivers do not give change, but they do give out transfers.
» Tickets can be purchased at a number of convenience stores and drugstores; look for the "FareDealer" sign.

» The trip-planning facility on the website gives the bus numbers and other details for getting to and from the city's top tourist attractions and other amenities such as parks.

TAXIS

Taxi stands are located in front of all the major hotels. Taxis can also be contacted by telephone. Hailing cabs on the street is less common than in other major cities. Tip the driver 10–15 percent of the fare.

Above left A cab awaits the next fare **Above** *BC Ferries leaving Schwartz Bay, Vancouver Island* **Below left** *The Skytrain prepares to depart Vancouver*

TRANSPORTATION OUTSIDE CITIES

FERRY SERVICES

On both the east and west coasts of Canada, ferries form an important part of the highway system as well as offering major means of access from the US.

Nova Scotia

» Bay Ferries (tel 1-888/249-7245; www.nfl-bay.com) operates a fast service by catamaran between Portland and Bar Harbor, in Maine and Yarmouth. The trip takes only three hours and reservations for all vehicles are essential in the summer.

Bay Ferries also operates a ferry between Digby, Nova Scotia, and Saint John, New Brunswick. This three-hour crossing of the Bay of Fundy is spectacular and therefore popular, so reserve well in advance.

Prince Edward Island (PEI)

The province of Prince Edward Island is accessible by the Confederation Bridge (▷ 152), but there is still one ferry in operation.
» Northumberland Ferries (tel 1-888/249-7245; www.peiferry-bay. com) runs a service from May to mid-December between Caribou, Nova Scotia and Wood Islands, PEI; the trip takes 75 minutes. Like the bridge tolls, fares are paid only on leaving the island. The service runs back and forth constantly in the

high season; no reservations are accepted, so this may be slow at peak periods.

Newfoundland

» Two different ferries operated by Marine Atlantic make the crossing to Newfoundland from Nova Scotia (tel 1-800/341-7981; www.marine-atlantic.ca). North Sydney, Nova Scotia, to Port-aux-Basques, Newfoundland runs year round and takes about five to seven hours. The other runs between North Sydney and Argentia, Newfoundland (Jun–early Sep, Mon, Wed and Thu, then Mon only to end Sep) a 14-hour trip. Many visitors cross by one and return by the other; reservation is essential in summer.

Victoria, British Columbia

Three different ferries operate between the US state of Washington and Victoria, the capital of British Columbia.
» Black Ball Transport (tel 250/386-2202; www.cohoferry.com) runs a 90-min service between Port Angeles and Victoria, and carries both cars and passengers.
» Clipper Navigation (tel 1-800/888-2535 or 250/382-8100; www.victoriaclipper.com) runs a two- to three-hour catamaran service for passengers only between Seattle and Victoria. They also run from Seattle to the San Juan Islands.
» From June to October, San Juan Cruises (tel 1-800/443-4552; www.whales.com) operates a three-hour service between Bellingham and Victoria, and includes a free salmon dinner on the return run.

British Columbia Coast

» BC Ferries (tel 1-888/223-3779 or 250/396-3431; www.bcferries.com) operates a number of routes with more than 40 ports of call. Their key services operate between the British Columbia mainland and Vancouver Island, notably the one-hour crossing from Horseshoe Bay (in North Vancouver) to Nanaimo, and the two-hour service between Tsawwassen (19km/12 miles south

MAJOR FERRY SERVICES		
	from	**to**
East Coast	Portland, Maine	Yarmouth, Nova Scotia
	Bar Harbor, Maine	Yarmouth, Nova Scotia
	Digby, Nova Scotia	Saint John, New Brunswick
	Pictou, Nova Scotia	Wood Islands, Prince Edward Island
	North Sydney, Nova Scotia	Port-aux-Basques, Newfoundland
	North Sydney, Nova Scotia	Argentia, Newfoundland
	St. Barbe, Newfoundland	Blanc Sablon, Québec
West Coast	Port Angeles, Washington	Victoria, British Columbia
	Seattle, Washington	Victoria, British Columbia
	Bellingham, Washington	Victoria, British Columbia
	Horseshoe Bay (Vancouver)	Nanaimo, British Columbia
	Tsawwassen (Vancouver)	Swartz Bay, British Columbia
	Port Hardy (Vancouver Island)	Prince Rupert, British Columbia
	Prince Rupert, British Columbia	the Queen Charlotte Islands

of Vancouver) and Swartz Bay, just north of Victoria.

BC Ferries' famous Inside Passage service, which runs between Port Hardy on Vancouver Island and Prince Rupert, takes 15 hours (reservations are mandatory). An assured service between Prince Rupert and the Queen Charlotte Islands is also available.

LONG-DISTANCE BUSES

Travel by long-distance bus is relatively cheap and it gives access to most of the country. The major company is Greyhound Canada (tel 1-800/661-8747; www. greyhound.ca), but there is a host of smaller ones. Greyhound covers most of western Canada, the Yukon and Ontario, with frequent cross-border links to US cities; it also owns the Québec-based Voyageur company, which operates routes between Montréal and Ottawa.

Discovery Pass

» Greyhound offer a variable-length Discovery Pass, which offers unlimited travel on Greyhound lines and those of selected partners (see website). It covers most of the country except Newfoundland.

» Prices start at $329 for a seven-day pass (passes are also available for 15, 30 and 60 days).

» Certain restrictions apply, so it is best to contact them before planning your trip in detail. If you buy online, passes must be purchased at least three weeks in advance (two weeks for Canadian residents).

WINTER TRAVEL

Canada functions relatively normally throughout its long cold winter. Severe storms will disrupt travel while they are in progress, but everything is geared up to get things back to normal as quickly as possible. If you are nervous about driving in snow, take the train or long-distance bus. Both services run year round and there are surprisingly few delays due to bad weather. The same is true for flights. Canadian airports are well equipped to de-ice aircraft and clear runways of snow.

You should be equipped with warm mittens, a hat, scarf, a warm coat and boots; long underwear is also advisable.

Driver Precautions in Winter

Make sure your car is fitted with snow tires or chains.

On long trips make certain you carry the following in case you break down or get stuck in a snow drift:
» spare food
» flashlight (torch)
» blanket
» candle (this keeps the temperature in the car above freezing, but you must keep a window open a crack for ventilation)
» cell phone with fully charged battery.
For more on preparing for a breakdown or accident, ▷ 52.

TRAINS

Canadian trains are clean, fast and efficient, and are a pleasant way of seeing this scenic country. Most of the passenger service is provided by VIA Rail (tel 1-888/842-7245; www.viarail.ca). In Europe, you can contact 1st Rail in the UK (tel 0845 644 3545; www.1strail.com); in Australia, contact Asia Pacific (tel 02 9319 6624; www.aptms.com.au).

VIA RAIL SERVICES
The Canadian

Canada's most famous train crosses the country between Toronto and Vancouver three times a week in each direction, and the schedule allows passengers to see the Rockies in daylight. The trip takes three days and three nights. Various classes of travel are available, from Comfort Class seats to Sleeper Class berths and bedrooms (Silver and Blue); sleeper class fares include all meals, priority boarding, and use of the Silver and Blue lounge at Toronto Union Station. All travelers have access to the Skyline car, with its observation dome, and the dining car.

The Hudson Bay

Leaving Winnipeg, this train travels 1,700km (1,054 miles) through the untamed beauty of northern Canada to Churchill on the shores of Hudson Bay. It runs three times a week in each direction and takes one and a half days (two nights). Two classes are offered: Sleeper and Comfort (economy).

The Corridor

VIA Rail offers a regular service in what it calls "The Corridor," crossing between Windsor and Québec City. VIA's Renaissance cars between Montréal and Toronto and between Montréal and Québec City run a particularly good and efficient service.

VIA RAIL CONTACTS IN CANADA	
From all over Canada and the USA	
tel 1-888/842 7245; www.viarail.ca	
From Montréal	
tel 514/989-2626	
From Toronto	
tel 1-888/842 7245	
From Moncton	
tel 506/857-9830	

Left *Traveling the Icefields Parkway, Lake Louise, on board a snocoach, built to drive safely on snow*
Bottom left *Taking a break at Bow Lake in the Icefields Parkway*

ON THE MOVE | GETTING AROUND

Other VIA Rail Trains

The Malahat runs between Victoria and Courtenay on Vancouver Island; the Skeena runs from Prince Rupert through the mountains to Jasper, with an overnight stop at Prince George. The Chaleur is a splendid trip from Montréal to Gaspé along the shores of the Baie des Chaleurs; and the Ocean links Montréal to Halifax on the Atlantic coast.

AMTRAK

From the US, Amtrak (tel 1-800/872-7245; www.amtrak.com) has a regular train service to Montréal from New York and Washington; to Toronto from Chicago and New York; and to Vancouver from Seattle.

OTHER TRAIN SERVICES—TOURS AND DAY TRIPS
Rocky Mountaineer Railtours

Rocky Mountaineer runs a two-day trip between Vancouver and either Banff or Jasper through the Rockies. Both routes overnight in Kamloops, so the whole trip is in daylight, a spectacular experience. For information, contact Rocky Mountaineer Railtours in Vancouver (tel 604/606-7245 or 1-877/460-3200; www.rockymountaineer.com).

Day Trips

» From Skagway, Alaska, the White Pass and Yukon Narrow-Gauge Railway (▷ 351) runs trips to the top of the White Pass and back daily from early May to late September (tel 1-800/343-7373; www. whitepassrailroad.com). Passports are required to cross the US/Canadian border.

Above *Canadian VIA Rail train*
Right *Driving on the highway leading to Montréal's airport*
Bottom right *Road signs*

VIA RAIL FARE CONCESSIONS

CANRAILPASS
» Offers 12 days of travel in Comfort class over a 30-day period
» High-season (June to mid-October) rates are $837 for adults, $538 for seniors, students and children
» Low-season rates are $523 for adults, $471 for seniors, students and children
» Seats are limited, so reserve as early as possible

CORRIDORPASS
» Offers 10 days of unlimited travel in the Windsor–Québec City corridor
» VIA 1 adults $714; seniors, children, students $643; Comfort: adults $299, seniors, children, students $269
» The price is the same year round, and the pass must be purchased at least five days before the first date of travel

NORTH AMERICA RAIL PASS
» With Amtrak, VIA Rail offers a North America Rail Pass valid for 30 days in Economy class and giving access to over 900 cities.
» High-season rates (late-May to mid-October) are $1,149 for adults, $1,034 for seniors, students and children
» Low-season rates are $675 for adults, $608 for seniors, students and children
» Seats are limited, so reserve as early as possible

DRIVING

Canadian highways are generally well maintained and present few problems in the inhabited south and between main towns and cities. However, once you venture off the beaten path, you may encounter unsurfaced sections that can make for difficult driving in wet weather. The harsh winters also have an effect—edges often crumble and potholes appear.

DRIVING YOUR OWN CAR

From the US, crossing the Canadian border presents few problems. You must have proof of identity and citizenship, vehicle registration papers and proof of insurance coverage with you, and be prepared for the vehicle to be searched for illegal substances.

REGULATIONS

» In Canada, you drive on the right and pass on the left.
» Right turns are allowed at red lights, after coming to a full stop, unless otherwise indicated—but not in Montréal, where it's illegal.
» All persons in a vehicle must wear seat belts.
» Speed limits are given in

kilometers per hour (▷ 373 for conversion chart) and vary slightly between provinces. Generally, expect speed limits of 100kph (62mph) on expressways, between 70 and 90kph (43 and 56mph) on other major roads, and 50kph (31mph) or less in urban areas.

GAS (PETROL) STATIONS

These are found along major routes and on the approaches to cities. In the north, you should fill your tank regularly as gas stations are sometimes far apart. The distance to the next station is usually signed. Fuel is sold by the liter. Like everywhere else in the world, the price is rising rapidly and additionally varies from province to province. UK visitors will find the cost very low but for visitors from the US the price per gallon may be as much as 25 percent more expensive.

RENTING A CAR

To rent a car, you must be over 21, and have ID and a valid driver's license, which you need to have held for at least a year. Drivers over 80 may need to provide a medical certificate as a guarantee of competence. Reservations can

usually only be made using a credit card as a guarantee, and at the moment of rental, the company will take an imprint of your card for the full expected amount. Some rental companies may accept a debit card, but check in advance. Also check any restrictions on taking the vehicle out of the province in which you organize the rental.

It is easy to rent a car in Canada, but rental vehicles are at a premium in the tourist season (mid-May to mid-October), so make an early reservation.

Rates and Companies

Car rental rates vary widely across Canada, depending on location,

RENTAL TIPS

» Don't forget that Canadian taxes (GST plus provincial tax—▷ 372) will be added to quoted rental rates.

» If you want to drop off the car in a different place from where it was rented, there's likely to be a huge surcharge to cover the cost of getting it back.

» Unless you have collision insurance (Loss Damage Waiver) provided by your credit card, you will have to pay extra for insurance against accident or damage. This can add several dollars to the daily rate.

» Be careful to check whether your daily rental charge covers unlimited mileage, or whether an additional charge cuts in after a set daily limit.

availability and how long you want a vehicle for. Starting rates can be as low as $25 a day for a compact model. It's worth checking on fly-drive deals.

RECREATIONAL VEHICLES

Trailers (caravans) and other types of recreational vehicle are subject to the same entry requirements and driving regulations as cars. RVs (motor caravans) can be rented from specialist companies in most provinces, but the supply of vehicles is often limited so reservations should be made well in advance, especially for the summer. Specialist companies may be found online, for example, Owasco Recreational Vehicles (2000 Champlain Avenue, Whitby, Ontario, tel 1-866/755-9482; www.owasco.com), have a wide range of recreational vehicles for long- and short-term rentals.

Many campgrounds handle RVs, since a lot of Canadians have them. Each provincial government tourist office can supply a list of campgrounds detailing their facilities and costs (▷ 378).

DRIVING IN REMOTE AREAS OR IN WINTER

For more on driving in extreme conditions see Winter Travel ▷ 48.

BREAKDOWN OR ACCIDENT

If you are going to drive long distances in Canada, especially in remote areas, it might be a good idea to take out membership of the Canadian Automobile Association (tel 613/247-0117; www.caa.ca). They or their local affiliate can help you in case of breakdown.

Members of the American Automobile Association are entitled to full service with the CAA, but must have their membership card with them.

In case of an emergency or accident, call 911 (▷ 375) where possible, and be sure to report any accident to the police. This is usually a condition of your insurance coverage.

Top *Long journey ahead for a lone truck*
Below *Typical street signs on Castlefield Avenue, Toronto*
Bottom right *A car is dwarfed by the vastness of the Canadian Rockies*

MAJOR CAR RENTAL COMPANIES			
NAME	TELEPHONE		WEBSITE
	CANADA	USA	
Avis	800/272-5871	800/331-1212	www.avis.com
Budget	800/472-3325	800/527-0700	www.budget.com
Dollar	800/800-3665	800/800-3665	www.dollar.com
Hertz	800/263-0600	800/654-3131	www.hertz.com
National	800/CAR-RENT	800/CAR-RENT	www.nationalcar.com
Thrifty	800/THRIFTY	800/THRIFTY	www.thrifty.com

Distance and duration chart — major points on Canada's road network. Cities (along the diagonal): Calgary, Charlottetown, Dawson, Edmonton, Fredericton, Halifax, Montréal, Ottawa, Prince George, Québec, Regina, Saskatoon, Thompson, Thunder Bay, Toronto, Vancouver, Victoria, Whitehorse, Winnipeg, Yellowknife.

```
         8132 6232  335 7453 8222 *6150 5903 1442 6515 1142 1302 3301 3320 *5648 1407 1741 5053 2111 4045
             14347 8311  700  415 1950 2221 9545 1630 7004 7427 7914 4811 2719 9631 9829 13157 6033 11934
                   6049 13708 14437 12405 12123 4803 12731 7304 6929 8928 9536 11904 6342 6540 1218 8327 5757
                        7632 8402 *6330 6048 1248 *6655 1228  853 2852 3500 *5828 1631 2005 4859 2251 3637
4675                           750 1311 1542 8906  951 6325 6748 7235 4132 2040 8952 9150 12518 5354 11255
2795 7104                          2040 2311 9635 1720 7054 7517 8005 4901 2809 9721 9919 13247 6123 12024
 294 4645 2468                          203 7604  242 5022 5445 5933 2830  539 *7650 *7848 11215 4051 9952
4315  375 6743 4285                         7322  431 4740 5203 5651 2548  437 *7408 5018 10933 3809 9711
4744  231 7173 4715  444                         7929 2502 2127 4126 4734 7102 1552 1750 3624 3525 3832
*3530 1155 5958 *3500  795 1224                        5348 5811 6258 3155  806 *8015 *8213 11541 4417 10318
*3360 1328 5788 *3330  967 1397  199                         344 2245 2153 4521 2641 2839 6114  944 4851
 756 5381 2049  745 5021 5451 4236 4066                          2024 2616 4944 2716 2914 5738 1407 4516
*3767  924 6196 *3737  564  993  252  445 4473                        3103 5431 4715 4914 7738 1854 6515
 751 3940 3235  776 3580 4010 2795 2625 1512 3032                         2328 4820 5018 8345 1221 7123
 816 4125 2984  526 3765 4194 2980 2810 1262 3217  256                        *7148 *7346 10714 3550 9451
1588 4125 3759 1298 3765 4195 2980 2810 2034 3217  937  821                         344 5203 3611 5013
1987 2688 4416 1957 2327 2757 1543 1373 2693 1780 1252 1437 1438                        5401 3809 5211
*3277 1673 5705 *3247 1313 1743  542  450 3983  795 2542 2727 2727 1290                        7137 4714
 972 5575 2777 1160 5215 5645 *4430 *4260  737 *4667 1651 1636 2408 2887 *4177                        5914
1054 5660 2862 1242 5299 5729 *4515 *4345  822 *4752 1736 1721 2493 2972 *4262  109
2327 6953  495 2318 6590 7022 5807 5637 1580 6044 3084 2833 3606 4265 5554 2308 2393
1315 3348 3744 1285 2988 3417 2203 2033 2022 2440  580  765  766  660 1950 2216 2300 3593
1783 6129 2332 1494 5769 6199 4984 4814 1550 5221 2260 2010 2782 3442 4731 2324 2408 1901 2770
```

The above chart lists major points on Canada's road network. Use the chart to gauge the distance in kilometres (green) and duration in hours and minutes (blue) of a car journey. An * indicates a quicker route via the US.

VISITORS WITH A DISABILITY

The travel industry in Canada has become increasingly aware of the needs of visitors with disabilities. Unfortunately, the process is a slow one and there is still much room for improvement. There is all too often a difference between what ought to be there and what is actually in place. This makes getting around with a disability frustrating at times, although there has definitely been progress toward making amenities and tourist sites accessible to all.

GENERAL ADVICE
» If you have a disability, plan your trip carefully and check facilities in advance.
» Where possible, travel with able-bodied friends or consider touring with a travel agent who specializes in travel for people with disabilities and makes arrangements easier.
» Contact both your departure and arrival airports in advance to let them know what assistance you will require. Airports and airlines are exemplary in helping travelers with disabilities—as long as they have advance warning.
» Make hotel reservations well in advance and again be specific about your requirements.
» Before any trip, do some research and find out what your rights actually are. Never hesitate to let it be known if you encounter unhelpful or obstructive behavior. There is often a legal requirement for your needs to be met.

WHAT TO EXPECT ONCE YOU ARE IN THE COUNTRY
» By law, all public buildings must have wheelchair access and provide special toilets.
» By municipal ordinance, curbs in the major urban centers are dropped at cross streets to meet the needs of wheelchair users. This is not, however, always the case outside the major cities.

Public Transportation
» Buses in the major cities are increasingly being adapted to accommodate wheelchairs. This is less frequently the case in rural areas. Once again, careful checking in advance will make you aware of major problems.
» All VIA Rail trains can accommodate wheelchairs as long as 48 hours' notice is given.

Hotels
» Some of the major hotels provide wheelchair access and some offer special suites for guests with disabilities. Careful checking in advance will avoid problems.
» Be aware that strict codes are in effect for new properties but older accommodations and restaurants may still have barriers.
» Details of hotels accessible to visitors with disabilities can usually be obtained from local tourist offices (▷ 378–379).

OFFICIAL POLICY
The Canada Transportation Act lays out the government of Canada's commitment to equitable access to transportation services for all. Under the Act, the Canadian Transportation Agency (an arm of the federal government) has the power to remove "undue obstacles" from Canada's transportation network, and this applies to planes and airports, trains and stations, and ferry services and their terminals.

For more information, contact the Accessible Transportation Directorate, Canadian Transportation Agency, Ottawa, Ontario, K1A 0N9, tel 819/997-6828 or 800/883-1813; www.cta-otc.gc.ca/index_e.html.

You should indicate your language preference (English or French) and the alternative format you require. This agency produces a number of publications, including:
» *The Accessibility Complaint Guide*, which summarizes the provisions of the Canada Transportation Act and gives advice about how to deal with any problems that might occur.
» *A Guide for Persons with Disabilities—Taking Charge of the Air Travel Experience*, a booklet addressing issues such as seat selection, getting to the terminal, checking in, boarding and leaving the aircraft.

USEFUL ORGANIZATIONS
» The Canadian Association of the Deaf (www.cad.ca) protects and promotes the rights, needs and concerns of deaf Canadians.
» The Canadian National Institute for the Blind (www.cnib.ca) provides services to individuals with loss of vision.
» The Canadian Paraplegic Association (www.canparaplegic. org) assists those with spinal cord injuries and other disabilities.
» The National Federation of the Blind (www.nfb.ca), increases awareness of rights and responsibilities for blind, deaf-blind and partially sighted individuals; also produces the Blind Monitor magazine available in Braille, large print, diskette, audiocassette and email formats.

OTHER SOURCES OF TRAVEL INFORMATION
Society for Accessible Travel and Hospitality www.sath.org
Touring Friends Assisted Travel Association www.mgl.ca/~touring/
Disability Travel and Recreation Resources (International) www.makoa.org/travel.htm
Accessible Travel Source www.access-able.com
Scoot Around America (delivers scooters and wheelchairs to hotels in major cities throughout North America, including Montréal, Toronto, Vancouver and Victoria) www.scootaround.com

REGIONS

This chapter is divided into the nine regions of Canada (▷ 8–9). Places of interest are listed alphabetically in each region.

Canada's Regions

MONTRÉAL

The vibrant and beautiful city of Montréal encompasses the joie de vivre of the Old Country and the entrepreneurial optimism of the New World. It's the biggest French-speaking city outside of Paris, but enjoys a better—and well deserved—reputation for the warmth of its welcome to visitors. Time your visit to coincide with one of the city's many festivals, or simply join the Thursday "cinq-à-sept" (a sort of 5–7pm happy hour) crowd on a downtown patio for one of the great Montréal experiences.

Though suburbs extend onto the mainland, Montréal mainly occupies an island in the mighty St. Lawrence River, and rising at the heart of the city is glorious Mont Royal, a vast park with panoramic views. Both of these not only add to the visual appeal of the city, they make it eminently breathable and cater to leisure pursuits, from a gentle stroll to an exhilarating ride over the rapids in a jet-boat.

The downtown hub has everything you would expect: soaring skyscrapers; vast shopping malls; broad boulevards and leafy squares; world-class cultural venues, galleries and museums; beautiful churches; and some of the finest restaurants and hotels on the continent. And when the winter chill sets in you can dive underground and enjoy the same amenities via the Reseau Pietonnier Souterrain ("the Reso"). In addition, there are little pockets of history close at hand, such as delightful Vieux Montréal, home to the first settlers, and the "Golden Square Mile," preserving the mansions of the 19th-century rich.

Take time to explore neighborhoods like the Latin Quarter, The Village, Mile End and The Plateau, with streets of traditional Montréal residential architecture (rowhouses with outside staircases and balconies), trendy one-off boutiques and lively restaurants. Discover here the long-established Jewish, Greek and Italian communities who contribute so much to the cosmopolitan feel of this fascinating city. It's Canadian, it's French, and it's much, much more besides.

MONTRÉAL

REGIONS | MONTRÉAL • CITY MAPS

↑ Biodôme de Montréal,
Parc olympique,
Jardin botanique
de Montréal

0 ——————— 200 m
0 ——————— 200 yds

I

Rue Kimberley

BOULEVARD ST-
LAURENT

RUE ST-URBAIN

Rue

Rue du Berger

St-Dominique

R Charlotte

Rue de Montigny Ouest

Clark

Rue Balmoral

Pl du
Marché

← Parc du
Mont-Royal

AVENUE DU PARC

Rue Hutchison

Rue Durocher

Rue Aylmer

SHERBROOKE OUEST

Rue de Bleury

Rue Burke

Rue de la Concorde

Place-
des-Arts

RUE STE-CATHERINE OUEST

Musée d'art
contemporain,
Places-des-Arts

CHINATOWN

2

Rue

138

Avenue

Avenue

Union

Rue

du

Rue

Président-Kennedy

BOULEVARD DE MAISONNEUVE

Rue City Councillors

Rue Mayor

Rue St-

Rue

Rue St-Edouard

Rue St-Alexandre

Jeanne

Mance

✝

Aylmer

Musée McCord
d'histoire canadienne

McGill

Square Phillips

Place

Rue Dowd

Rue

Rue de Bleury

Rue Hermine

Rue St-Alexandre

Rue Anderson

Rue de Bleury

MARIE

3

Rue Victoria

Musée des
beaux arts
de Montréal

Centre
Eaton

Cathédrale anglicane
de Christ-Church

Phillips

R Hôt

**Les Aîles
de la Mode**

Avenue

Avenue

Côte

du

Beaver

OUEST

VILLE

Rue

Mansfield

OUEST

McGill

Rle Palace

Cathcart

Rue

RUE

Réseau
Piétonnier Souterrain
(Underground City)

Place
Ville-Marie

LÉVESQUE

Union

Hall

VIGER

Square-
Victoria

AVENUE

AUTOROUTE

720

Rue Bisso

4

College

RENE

UNIVERSITY

Pl Mount Royal

Rue

STE-CATHERINE

Rue

BOULEVARD

Rue

Belmont

Rue de la Gauchetière Ouest

GARE
CENTRALE

Metcalfe

Square
Dorchester

Cathédrale
Marie-Reine-du-Monde

Mansfield

5

RUE PEEL

Rue Cypress

112

Rue de la Cathédrale

Rue

RUE ST-ANTOINE OUEST

Rue

Stanley

Place
du
Canada

1000 de la
Gauchetière

Bonaventure

Rue Drummond

A

B

C

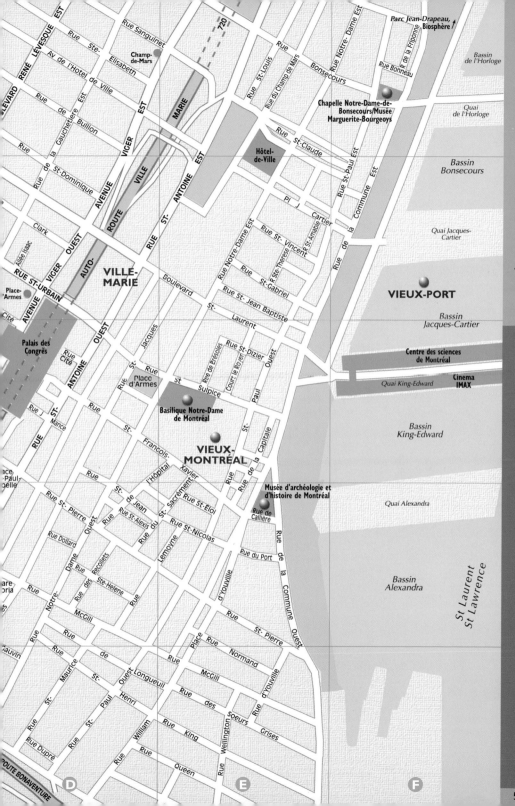

Rue Sanguinet

Rue Ste.-Elisabeth

Av de l'Hotel de Ville

Rue de la Gauchetière Est

Rue Bullion

Rue de St-Dominique

Clark

Allée Isaac

Place-d'Armes

RENÉ LÉVESQUE EST

Rue Ste.-

MARIE

ROUTE

VILLE

AVENUE

VIGER

RUE ST-URBAIN

AVENUE VIGER OUEST

Cité

Champ-de-Mars

Rue St-Louis

Rue du Champ de Mars

VILLE-MARIE

Boulevard

Jacques

Rue Notre-Dame Est

Rue St-Vincent

Rue Ste-Thérèse

Rue St-Gabriel

Rue St-Jean Baptiste

St-

Laurent

Rue St-Claude

Hôtel-de-Ville

Pl J

Rue St-Paul Est

Cartier

Rue St-Amable

Rue de

la Commune Est

Rue Bonsecours

Rue Notre-Dame Est

Rue Bonneau

Rue de la Friponne

Parc Jean-Drapeau, Biosphère /

Chapelle Notre-Dame-de-Bonsecours/Musée Marguerite-Bourgeoys

720

Bassin de l'Horloge

Quai de l'Horloge

Bassin Bonsecours

Quai Jacques-Cartier

VIEUX-PORT

Bassin Jacques-Cartier

720

Palais des Congrès

Rue Cité

Rue St-

Rue

Place d'Armes

St-

Paul

St-

Rue de la Capitale

Rue de Brésoles

Cour le Royer

Rue St-Dizier

Sulpice

Basílique Notre-Dame de Montréal

VIEUX-MONTRÉAL

Centre des sciences de Montréal

Quai King-Edward

Cinema IMAX

Bassin King-Edward

ace Paul-elle

Rue François-

Xavier

l'Hôpital

St-

Rue

de Jean

Rue St-Pierre Ouest

Rue St-Alexis

Rue St-Sacrément

du St-

Rue St-Eloi

Rue St-Elol

Rue St-Nicolas

Lemoyne

Rue de Callière

Musée d'archéologie et d'histoire de Montréal

Rue du Port

Rue de la Commune Ouest

Quai Alexandra

Rue Dollard

Rue des Récollets

Ste-Helene

Dame

Notre-

MCGILL

de

Rue d'Youville

Rue

St-Pierre

Rue d'Youville

Rue d'Youville

Bassin Alexandra

St Laurent
St Lawrence

are oria

Maurice

St-

Ouest

St-

Paul

Henri

Longueuil

MCGill

Rue des

Rue

Place

Rue

Normand

William

Rue King

Rue Wellington

Rue des Soeurs Grises

St-Pierre

Rue Dupre

Rue

Queen

ROUTE BONAVENTURE

D   **E**   **F**

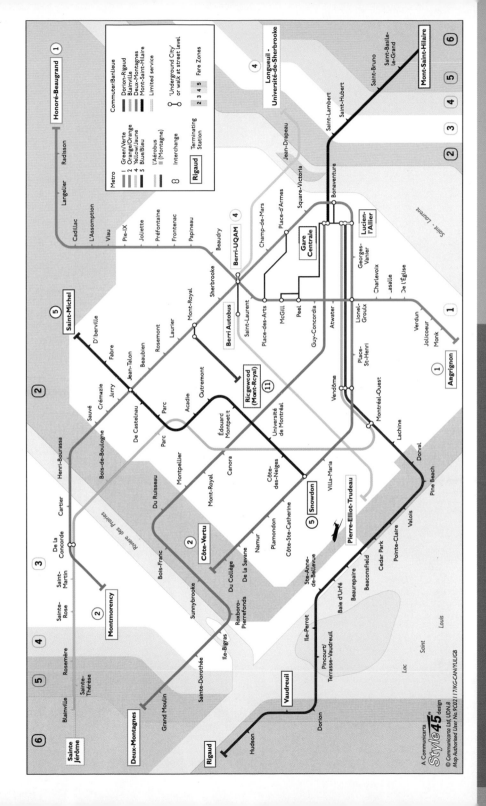

REGIONS MONTRÉAL • CITY MAPS

BASILIQUE NOTRE-DAME DE MONTRÉAL

▷ 64–65.

BIODÔME DE MONTRÉAL

www.biodome.qc.ca

In 1992, the Olympic velodrome underwent a spectacular refit and reopened as an indoor ecological park. Under the 190m (625ft) span of its vast scalloped roof, four ecosystems representing the Americas have been re-created.

The Tropical Forest—a lush and humid South American rain forest—is home to animals such as capybaras, golden lion tamarin monkeys, anacondas, parrots, piranhas and poison arrow frogs. Hardwoods and conifers flourish in the Laurentian Forest, where beavers, porcupines, otters and lynx prowl around.

In the replica St. Lawrence ecosystem, cold salty waters are home to hundreds of fish and seabirds. Polar World includes a rocky stretch of Labrador coastline populated by Atlantic puffins, common murres, black guillemots and an Antarctic setting for the stars of the Biodôme, the penguins.
✚ Off map, 58 B1 ✉ 4777 avenue Pierre-de-Coubertin, Montréal, Québec, H1V 1B3 ☎ 514/868-3000 🕐 Late Jun–early Sep daily 9–6; rest of year Tue–Sun 9–5 ✋ Adult $16, child (5–17) $8 🚇 Viau 🍴 La Brise, Le Nordet Bistro 🏧

BIOSPHÈRE

www.biosphere.ec.gc.ca

The Biosphère can be found in the geodesic dome created by visionary American architect Richard Buckminster Fuller (1895–1983) as the US Pavilion for the 1967 World's Fair.

Principally dedicated to the St. Lawrence River and the Great Lakes, the Biosphère is North America's only museum devoted to water, and each of its exhibition halls showcases a specific aspect, with interactive displays and multimedia presentations. From the fourth-floor terrace there is a good view of the whole complex.
✚ Off map, 59 F1 ✉ 160 chemin Tour-de-l'Isle, Île-Ste-Hélène, Montréal, Québec,

Left *Statue of Mother and Child at the Chapelle de Notre-Dame-de-Bonsecours*
Above *Intricate structure of the Biosphère, set on Île Ste.-Hélène near the Old Port*

H3C 4G8 ☎ 514/283-5000 🕐 Jun to end Oct daily 10–6; rest of year Tue–Sun 10–6 ✋ Adult $9.50, child (17 and under) free 🚇 Jean Drapeau 🚌 167 Casino, 169 Île Ronde (in season) 🏧

CATHÉDRALE ANGLICANE DE CHRIST-CHURCH (CHRIST CHURCH CATHEDRAL)

www.montreal.anglican.org/cathedral

The Anglican cathedral is a fine example of neo-Gothic architecture, with its flamboyant triple portico. Built in 1856–59, Christ Church had problems with the strength of its foundations right from the start, and by 1927 the stone spire was leaning precariously and had to be removed; the aluminum substitute was added in 1940. In the 1980s, developers built the huge postmodern tower behind the church and the shopping mall below it, and as a result the cathedral finally stood on firm foundations—both financially and architecturally.

The nave, with its Gothic arches, leads to the chancel, with carved stone screens and a copy by Poade Drake of Leonardo da Vinci's *Last Supper*. Be sure to visit the Lady Chapel where the icon of the Holy Trinity, by Montréal artist Viorel Badoiu, is displayed, as it's a superb work of art.
✚ 58 B3 ✉ 635 rue Ste-Catherine Ouest, Montréal, Québec ☎ 514/843-6577 (text 3 for recorded information) 🕐 Daily (tel

for info on services and noontime concerts) ✋ Free 🚇 McGill

CATHÉDRALE MARIE-REINE-DU-MONDE (MARY, QUEEN OF THE WORLD CATHEDRAL)

www.cathedralecatholiquedemontreal.org

A reproduction—on a smaller scale—of St. Peter's in Rome, Montréal's Catholic cathedral was built between 1870 and 1894 in the heart of what was then the city's Anglo-Protestant business sector, a strong statement of Montréal's Catholic heritage and the city's position as the "Rome of the North American continent." The plans for the cathedral were drawn up by architect Victor Bourgeau, and its fine-cut stone facade is topped by the patron saints of Montréal's parishes of 1890.

Inside, the nave is dominated by a fine replica of Gian Lorenzo Bernini's baroque baldachin, the canopy over the altar. It was handmade in Rome in 1900 by Victor Vincent. Crafted in red copper, it is decorated with gold leaf. Large dramatic paintings by Georges Delfosse represent episodes in the history of the Canadian Church.
✚ 58 B5 ✉ 1085 rue de la Cathédrale, Montréal, Québec, H2B 2V4 (main entrance boulevard René Lévesque) ☎ 514/866-1661 🕐 Daily; guided tours in summer (tel for info, and for times of Masses) ✋ Free 🚇 Bonaventure

BASILIQUE NOTRE-DAME DE MONTRÉAL

INFORMATION

www.basiliquenddm.org

➕ 59 E3 ✉ 110 rue Notre-Dame Ouest, Montréal, Québec, H2Y 2V5 ☎ 514/842-2925, 866/842-2925 🕐 Daily, except during Mass (tel for times); sound and light shows: Tue–Sat eve at varying times in year (tel for exact times) ✋ Adult $4, child (1–17) $2. Sound and light shows: adult $10, child (1–17) $5 🚌 20-min guided tours in French (free with admission) 🚇 Place d'Armes 🎁 Religious gifts

INTRODUCTION

Luciano Pavarotti sang here, Céline Dion was married here and absolutely everyone who visits Montréal comes here—tour buses line up around the block. The twin towers of Montréal's most famous church rise over 69m (226ft) on the south side of place d'Armes in the heart of Old Montréal. Once they dominated the whole city, but now they are dwarfed by high-rise office blocks.

The church, built on classical principles but with striking neo-Gothic ornamentation, was designed by James O'Donnell, an Irish architect living in New York, who supervised its construction from 1824 to his death in 1829. John Ostell completed the towers according to the original design in 1843, and Victor Bourgeau was responsible for the interior, finished about 1880. On the facade, note the statues of the Virgin Mary (Notre Dame), St. Joseph and John the Baptist. The east tower contains the 11.8-ton "Gros Bourdon" which is rung only on special occasions. The west tower contains a 10-bell carillon. When consecrated in 1829, Notre Dame was the biggest church in North America.

WHAT TO SEE

THE INTERIOR

The magnificent interior of the basilica never ceases to amaze, with its hand-carved wood—mainly red pine—painted and decorated with 22-carat gold. It's an experience just to walk down the nave—68m (223ft) long, 21m (69ft) wide and 25m (82ft) high—toward the altar and be bathed in the light of the three rose windows. The stained-glass windows, depicting scenes from Montréal's history, were designed by J.-B. Lagacé and produced in Limoges in 1930–31.

The altar and impressive reredos were designed by Victor Bourgeau and carved by Henri Bouriché, with central statues of white pine representing scenes of sacrifice from the Bible. To the left is the huge pulpit, also designed by Bourgeau and carved by Louis-Philippe Hébert; note the statues of Ezekiel and Jeremiah at its base.

Notre Dame's massive organ, one of the biggest in Canada, was made by Casavant and has nearly 7,000 pipes, 97 stops, four manual keyboards and a pedal-board. Because of its excellent acoustics, the basilica is frequently used for concerts. There is also a sound and light show, celebrating the founding of the city and the basilica.

CHAPELLE DU SACRE COEUR

The original Sacred Heart Chapel was added to the church in 1888–91 for intimate services, principally weddings. In 1978, it was completely destroyed in an arson attack but, rebuilt and reconsecrated in 1982, it is now a masterpiece in its own right, combining the architecture of the former chapel with contemporary elements. The galleries and side altars were reconstructed as before; the vault, however, is of steel covered with linden wood, with skylights bringing in daylight.

Dominating the chapel is an impressive bronze reredos, the work of Charles Daudelin. Cast in 32 panels by the Morris Singer Foundry in Basingstoke, England, it is 17m (56ft) high and represents humanity making its way along the difficult paths of life toward heaven. On sunny afternoons, the head of Christ at the top is bathed in sunlight entering through the skylights, a spectacular and inspiring effect.

TIPS

» Try to visit the basilica at lunchtime, when there are fewer tour groups.

» Alternatively, attend Mass, which is the only time you can see the interior with all the lights on.

» You are not allowed to walk around the basilica during Mass.

REGIONS **MONTRÉAL • SIGHTS**

Above left *The interior of the Basilique Notre-Dame, with a lit backdrop highlighting the ornate altar*
Left *A distinctive landmark, day or night*

CHAPELLE NOTRE-DAME-DE-BONSECOURS AND MUSÉE MARGUERITE-BOURGEOYS

www.marguerite-bourgeoys.com

With its copper steeple and large statue of the Virgin with arms outstretched toward the river, this little chapel has long been a city landmark. Before the expansion of the port, the statue was visible from way downstream.

Marguerite Bourgeoys arrived in Montréal in 1653, founded the city's first school and an order of teaching nuns, and built the original chapel on this site in 1678. Canonized in 1982, her tomb is in the chapel. The museum displays objects related to the chapel and its foundress.

🚩 59 F1 ✉ 400 rue St-Paul Est, Montréal, Québec, H2Y 1H4 ☎ 514/282-8670 🕐 May–end Oct Tue–Sun 10–5; Nov to mid-Jan and Mar–end Apr 11–3.30 (tel for hours of summer presentations about Marguerite Bourgeoys, and for Masses) 🎫 Museum: adult $6, child (6–12) $4, family $12 🚇 Champ de Mars

JARDIN BOTANIQUE DE MONTRÉAL (BOTANICAL GARDENS)

www2.ville.montreal.qc.ca/jardin

These glorious gardens extend to more than 73ha (180 acres), and display more than 22,000 species of plants, including 3,000 trees and 1,500 types of orchid. Created in 1931 by Brother Marie-Victorin, the gardens have 10 exhibition greenhouses and some 30 thematic gardens.

The Japanese Garden aims to create a feeling of serenity by balancing the elements, while the tranquil Chinese Dream Lake Garden was inspired by gardens from the Ming Dynasty (1368–1644). These two gardens are beautiful in spring, summer and fall. The First Nations Garden represents the natural environment, and is at its best in midsummer, as are the Annuals and Perennials gardens.

Two conservatories cover the tropical regions, while another is devoted to ferns. Flowering orchids are displayed in a conservatory resembling an ancient ruined fortress. In the Garden of Woodlessness are penjings—miniature trees that embody the Chinese art of living sculpture. The Roseraie, with more than 10,000 rose bushes, is at its best in August.

The Insectarium, in the shape of a giant bug, is great fun, and though many of the specimens on display are dead they offer plenty of surprises to visitors who might have expected nothing more than "creepy-crawlies." There are gleaming, jewel-like beetles, gloriously colored butterflies and strange-looking creatures like the Fulgoridae from Costa Rica. Other sections have fascinating displays relating to the social habits of insects such as ants and bees, and more than 75 vivariums contain live exhibits.

🚩 Off map, 58 B1 ✉ 4101 rue Sherbrooke Est, Montréal, Québec, H1X 2B2 ☎ 514/872-1400 🕐 Mid-May to end Oct daily; rest of year Tue–Sun 🎫 Mid-May to end Oct: adult $16, child (5–17) $8. Rest of year: adult $13.50, child (5–17) $7 (entrance includes conservatories and Insectarium) 🚇 Pie 1X or Viau ⬜ 🏛

MONT-ROYAL
▷ 69–70.

MUSÉE D'ARCHÉOLOGIE ET D'HISTOIRE DE MONTRÉAL
▷ 71.

MUSÉE D'ART CONTEMPORAIN (MUSEUM OF CONTEMPORARY ART)

www.macm.org

The contemporary art museum, with its distinctive modern architecture, is part of Montréal's great cultural complex, place des Arts. It moved to this spot in 1992.

The permanent collection comprises some 7,000 works, produced by 1,500 artists, of whom 1,200 (80 percent) are living. It includes the largest collection of art by Paul-Émile Borduas in existence. The works are shown in ever-changing thematic exhibitions, and the museum is constantly making acquisitions that it considers significant of the latest trends, in traditional media as well as the most innovative means of expression. Keep an eye out for Geneviève Cadieux's giant lips, La Voie Lactée, that crown the building.

🚩 58 B2 ✉ 185 rue Ste-Catherine Ouest, Montréal, Québec, H2X 3X5 ☎ 514/847-6226 🕐 Tue–Sun 11–6 (also Wed 6–9pm) 🎫 Adult $8, child (over 12; ID required) $4, family $16 🚇 Place des Arts 🍴 🏛

MUSÉE DES BEAUX-ARTS DE MONTRÉAL (MONTRÉAL MUSEUM OF FINE ARTS)

www.mmfa.qc.ca

The venerable Museum of Fine Arts, founded in 1860, is one of Canada's oldest museums. Located in buildings on both sides of Sherbrooke Street, you can get from one side to the other via an underground link. The permanent collection represents art from antiquity to contemporary times, and the museum is also well known for its temporary exhibitions.

On the north side of Sherbrooke Street is Edward and William Maxwell's imposing 1912 neo-classical building. It houses the Canadian Collection of sculpture portraying the traditional lifestyles and legends of the people of the Far North, and the Decorative Arts Galleries. On the south side, the main building, designed by Moshe Safdie and opened in 1991, houses the galleries of European and Contemporary Arts.

Under Sherbrooke Street, large galleries display African, Oceanic, Oriental, Middle Eastern, pre-Columbian, Roman, Greek and Egyptian art. The Inuit Galleries display sculpture portraying the traditional lifestyles and legends of the people of the Far North. Tapestries, furniture, porcelain and silver are highlights of the Decorative Arts Galleries.

🚩 Off map, 58 A3 ✉ 1379 and 1380 rue Sherbrooke Ouest, Montréal, Québec, H3G 2T9 ☎ 514/285-2000, 800/899-6873 🕐 Tue 11–5, Wed–Fri 11–9, Sat–Sun 10–5 🎫 Free for permanent collection, donation appreciated; temporary exhibitions Adult $15, child (over 12) $7.50 (adults half-price Wed 5–8.30) 🚇 Guy-Concordia 🍴 ⬜ 🏛

MUSÉE MCCORD D'HISTOIRE CANADIENNE (MCCORD MUSEUM OF CANADIAN HISTORY)

www.mccord-museum.qc.ca

In 1965, the McGill Union Building was converted into a museum to house the vast collections of David Ross McCord (1844–1930), whose abiding ambition was to shed light on the history and cultures of Canada. This ambition has well and truly been achieved, and today, the museum is considered one of North America's most significant historical institutions.

The collection numbers more than a 1.3 million objects, including beaded Indian headdresses, hand-forged tools, fine porcelain, glass negatives, and historical letters and documents. The renowned costume and textile collection has a plethora of women's dresses and accessories, all made and worn in Canada. An impressive collection of paintings evokes visual memories of the 18th and 19th centuries. There's even a huge totem pole in the stairwell, with the stairs built around it.

However, the McCord is probably most famous for the Notman Archives. Montréal photographer William Notman (1826–91) recorded people, places and events in the city and Canada over his long career, leaving nearly half a million photographs of 19th- and early 20th-century life.

➕ 58 A3 ✉ 690 rue Sherbrooke Ouest, Montréal, Québec, H3A 1E9 ☎ 514/398-7100 🕐 Tue–Fri 10–6, Sat–Sun 10–5; also in summer Mon holiday weekends 10–5 ♿ Adult $12, child (6–12) $4, student (ID required) $6, family $22 🚇 McGill 🔲 🏛

PARC JEAN DRAPEAU

Parc Jean Drapeau, made up of two islands in the St. Lawrence River, is one of Montréal's most precious resources. Île Ste.-Hélène was named in 1611 by Samuel de Champlain after his wife, Hélène Boulé. In 1760 the Chevalier de Lévis burned his regimental colors here before surrendering to the British army. After the conquest, the island

was fortified by the British and then handed over to Canadian troops after confederation in 1867. It became a city park early in the 20th century. Linked to Montréal by the Jacques Cartier Bridge since 1930, it was dramatically increased in size in the 1960s to host the World's Fair, Expo '67.

Today Île Ste.-Hélène is best known for its huge amusement park, La Ronde, but is also home to the Biosphère (▷ 63) and the Stewart Museum (mid-May to early-Oct daily 10–5; rest of year closed Tue), housed in the Old Fort and devoted to European settlement in Québec. The Stewart Museum has a fascinating model of Montréal as it would have been in 1760.

Île Notre Dame, a totally artificial construction, is home to the Montréal Casino, the Gilles Villeneuve motor racing circuit, and a lovely floral park.

➕ Off map, 59 F1 🚇 Jean-Drapeau (Île-Ste.-Hélène) 🚢 From Vieux-Port in summer months

PARC OLYMPIQUE (OLYMPIC PARK)

www.rio.gouv.qc.ca

In 1976, the XXI Olympiad was celebrated in Montréal, leaving the city a legacy of debt and a very fine collection of sports facilities.

Above *The iconic Montréal Tower in the Olympic Park*

Resembling a giant mollusk because of its elliptical shape, the Olympic Stadium is dominated by its tower, which rises 175m (574ft) at a 45-degree angle, and by its strange roof, which looks like a plate of meringues. Originally the brainchild of French architect Roger Taillebert, the stadium was completed with the expertise of local engineers. The "Big O," as it is called by Montréalers, has no interior columns to block the view. Controversial, hugely expensive and for many years incomplete, the stadium is nevertheless a very striking architectural achievement.

The spine of the tower can be mounted by a funicular elevator. Three huge skylight windows give spectacular views. In the tripod base of the tower, several of the Olympic swimming pools are open to the public. The former velodrome has been transformed into the Biodôme (▷ 63).

➕ Off map, 58 A1 ✉ 4141 avenue Pierre-de-Coubertin, Montréal, Québec, H1V 3N7 ☎ 514/252-4141 🕐 Observation Tower: daily, mid-Jun to early Sep 9–7; rest of year 9–5. Closed early Jan to mid-Feb; Stadium and Sports Centre: daily, by guided tour only, mid-Jun to early Sep regular departures from 10am; rest of year 11, noon, 1.30, 2.30, 3.30 ♿ Ascent of tower: adult $14, child (5–17) $7. Guided tours: Adult $8, child (5–17) $6.25 🚇 Pie IX or Viau

MONT-ROYAL

INTRODUCTION

In Montréal, "la Montagne" (the Mountain) is not only at the heart of the city, but also part of its soul. The bulky lump of Mont-Royal rises 228m (748ft), graced on its main summit by a lovely 200ha (494-acre) park that's perennially popular with residents and is precious to them.

Mont-Royal is one of a series of eight peaks in the St. Lawrence Valley that were created during tectonic activity some 60 million years ago. Rising dramatically from the otherwise flat landscape, these are the Collines Montérégiennes (Monteregian Hills), from the Latin name for Mont-Royal—*mons regius*. According to most historians, Mont-Royal gave the city its name when, in 1535, Jacques Cartier scrambled to the top and exclaimed "It's a royal mountain!" when he saw the view. There are other versions of how Montréal was named, but this is the one that's most popularly accepted. The park was created in 1876 by the great landscape architect Frederick Law Olmstead, of Central Park, New York, fame.

For the visitor, the wonderful park at the summit provides some spectacular views of the entire island and the St. Lawrence River. The artificially created Lac aux Castors (Beaver Lake) has year-round appeal—in the winter months, the snow is cleared from the surface and it makes a splendid skating rink; in summer, paddle boats can be rented. To climb the mountain on foot from downtown, walk to the top of rue Peel and follow the path with short staircases to a steep flight of 200 steps (allow 20 minutes).

WHAT TO SEE

MONT-ROYAL'S VIEWPOINTS

A five-minute walk from the parking area is the Chalet and Kondiaronk Viewpoint. From the large stone "chalet," built in 1931–32, the view is spectacular: The silver ribbon of the St. Lawrence winds its way around the city. Farther afield, several of the Monteregian Hills can be identified, notably the imposing lump of Mont St.-Hilaire. At night, the view of the illuminated city is equally wonderful. While taking in the view, spare a moment to look for the carved squirrels on the chalet's roof. From the Camilien Houde Viewpoint, the northern and eastern parts of the city are visible, dominated by the huge form of the Olympic Stadium. The St. Lawrence can be seen flowing toward Québec City. To the south, some of the Monteregians are visible, while to the north are the Laurentian Mountains (▷ 125).

THE SMITH HOUSE

By Beaver Lake, alongside the main parking lot, is the restored Smith House, built as a farmhouse in 1858. It now serves as an information center and is the hub of park activities, but most interesting is the permanent exhibition that delves into the history of the site, from the First Nations presence to the current concerns and actions relating to the conservation of the natural environment. There is also a section about the works of art that are dotted around the park, making this a perfect first stop on any visit to Mont-Royal. The pleasant café, serving organic and Fairtrade food and drink, also makes a good last stop.
🕐 Mon–Fri 9–5, Sat–Sun 10–6

PARK ACTIVITIES

Mont-Royal has a natural environment of indigenous plants and animals, and guided tours help visitors to appreciate the landscape. The deciduous woodland makes for some excellent birding, particularly during migration seasons, and the fall colors are glorious too. Up here among the trees, you can enjoy hiking

INFORMATION
www.lemontroyal.qc.ca
✚ Off map, 58 A1 ☎ Les amis de la Montagne: 514/843-8240 🚇 Mont-Royal, then bus 11

Left View of the Montréal skyline from Mont-Royal

TIP

» Montréalers do not appreciate remarks
about the height of their mountain—if
you're used to higher peaks, try not to
say so.

trails that are all but oblivious of the surrounding city, and in winter there's
cross-country skiing and a short downhill ski slope. It is also possible to join the
volunteer workforce that helps to conserve the environment, maintaining trails
and weeding out invasive plants.

L'ORATOIRE ST.-JOSEPH (ST. JOSEPH'S ORATORY)

www.saint-joseph.org

Set on the north slope of Mont-Royal, this famous Roman Catholic shrine is
visited by millions of pilgrims every year. Its huge dome, one of the biggest in
the world, is visible from all over the northern part of the city. Founded in 1904
by Brother André, the basilica was inaugurated in 1955. The interior has an
austerity that is in itself impressive. That's not to say it is without decoration,
and there are some fine artworks inside, notably the mural (1954), by Canon
Pruvost on the wall alongside the escalator; *The Nativity* (1872), by Napoléon
Bourassa, at the back of the nave; the *Way of the Cross* series, designed by
Roger de Villiers, arranged around the nave; and the decor of the Chapel of the
Blessed Sacrament, glowing with Vermont marble and gold leaf. The stained
glass windows are also interesting. One series (1958–1961) depicts ways in
which St. Joseph, the patron saint of Canada, is said to have had a hand in
specific events in Canadian history. Other features to seek out include the
crypt church, beneath the main basilica, and the tomb of Brother André.

A renovation project, due to complete in 2009, includes the restoration
of existing buildings, construction of new visitor facilities, improved access
(including elevators and escalators) and environmental protection.

✉ B3800 chemin Queen-Mary, Montréal, Québec, H3L 2M1 ☎ 514/733-8211 ⊗ Daily (tel
for hours of Masses) ⊚ Côte-des-Neiges ▭

MORE TO SEE

Mont-Royal has three cemeteries on its northern slopes, along with the
Université de Montréal, the city's largest institution of higher learning, its
campus dominated by a distinctive art deco tower. The city's most prestigious
residential areas, Westmount and Outremont, are also located on its slopes.
The 83m (272ft) metal cross (La Croix) on the summit commemorates the
placing of a wooden cross on the mountain in January 1643 by the city's
founder, Maisonneuve, after the new settlement was saved from a flood. A
hundred lightbulbs illuminate the cross at night, so that it can be seen from all
over the city. More visible by day is the enormous transmission tower.

Above right *Mont-Royal's park*
Below *It's a challenging climb up to
the Oratoire St.-Joseph*

MUSÉE D'ARCHÉOLOGIE ET D'HISTOIRE DE MONTRÉAL (POINTE-À-CALLIÈRE MUSEUM OF ARCHEOLOGY AND HISTORY)

On the spot where Montréal began in 1642, this fascinating and innovative museum is devoted to what can be the dry topic of archeology. Opened in 1992, on the 350th anniversary of the foundation of Montréal, the museum occupies a striking modern building designed by Dan Hanganu. The structure is dominated by a tower, which is strange since most of what you see inside is underground. The "point" of Pointe-à-Callière no longer exists. Originally it lay between the St. Pierre River, which used to run along place d'Youville to join the St. Lawrence at this point, but the St. Pierre was covered over in the 19th century. The name Callière refers to the second governor of Montréal, Hector de Callière, who built his house near here.

INSIDE THE MUSEUM

It's a good idea to start your visit with the multimedia presentation, which lasts about 15 minutes. This is a very high-tech but clear introduction to the city. Afterward, you can descend into the basement to see the remains of buildings that have stood on this spot since the 17th century. Next, walk through the huge brick conduit into which the St. Pierre River was channeled in 1832 to find yourself in a large archeological crypt, with remains of the foundations of the city walls, old streets and buildings.

You even meet a few of the former residents en route, by means of laser holograms. They answer your questions in both French and English, and really bring the place to life. From the crypt, take the elevator up into the old Customs House, built in 1836–38, where there are more displays on the history of this location. To put it all in perspective take an elevator ride to an outdoor observatory at the top of the tower for an excellent view of the port, river and part of Old Montréal; and there are more great views and good food at the museum's restaurant, L'Arrivage.

The museum also has temporary and traveling exhibitions, recent examples of which have included an exploration of 200 years of migration from France, and a showing of First Nations artifacts from the French Royal collections. Both of these exhibitions were produced in collaboration with museums in France.

INFORMATION

www.pacmuseum.qc.ca

🔁 59 E4 ✉ 350 place Royale, Montréal, Québec, H2Y 3Y5 ☎ 514/872-9150 🕐 Late Jun–end Aug Mon–Fri 10–6, Sat–Sun 11–6; Sep–late Jun Tue–Fri 10–5, Sat–Sun 11–5 💰 Adult $13, child (6–12) $5 or (over 12) $7 🚇 Place d'Armes 🍴 L'Arrivage—fresh, creative menu, plus city's best view of Vieux-Port 📷

Below *An informative walk through the history of Montréal in the Musée d'Archéologie et d'Histoire*

INFORMATION

www.tourism-montreal.org

🛈 Centre Infotouriste, 1001 Carré
Dorchester, Montréal, Québec

☎ 514/873-2015 Ⓜ Peel

INTRODUCTION

Beat the weather and explore Montréal via more than 33km (20 miles) of subterranean passageways in the Underground City. Temperatures in Montréal change dramatically from season to season. Nearly 3m (10ft) of snow falls every winter and temperatures can dip to -35°C (-31°F). In July, the mercury soars to a hot and sticky 35°C (95°F). Living with such a climate has many problems, some of which have been solved by the development of a weatherproof, covered-in system in the downtown business district, which gives priority to pedestrians. The connections are not always underground—there are also light, airy atriums full of stores and restaurants. The walkways connect more than 60 buildings, 8 hotels, about 1,700 stores, 200 or so restaurants and bars, 1,600 apartments, about 40 entertainment venues, 2 train stations, 2 bus termini, 10 métro stations, some 10,000 indoor parking places, about 45 bank branches, 2 universities, the place des Arts cultural center, the Palais des Congrès, and nearly 2.3 million sq m (25 million sq ft) of office space.

To appreciate the extent of the Underground City, just head off for a walk through some of it. The following highlights have linking instructions and details of how to reach each one separately. The idea of an underground city dates back to Leonardo da Vinci, but Montréal's began in the 1960s with the construction of the place Ville-Marie complex over the railroad tracks. At the same time, the métro was built, with stations connected by a network of covered passageways to many downtown facilities. Today, the entire business district is interconnected by a vast web of underground passageways.

WHAT TO SEE

PLACE VILLE-MARIE TO PROMENADE CATHÉDRALE

This was where the Underground City began. A huge cruciform tower and three smaller buildings, developed in 1959–62, sit on a shopping plaza and parking garage, covering the railroad tracks as they enter Central Station. Conceived by I. M. Pei, place Ville-Marie was the largest mixed office and commercial complex in the world when it opened. The cruciform shape reflects the city's origin as a Catholic mission, and its title comes from the city's first name, Ville-Marie (City of Mary). Stand in the outdoor plaza here and look north—there is a superb view up McGill College Avenue of McGill University and Mont-Royal. From place Ville-Marie, take the underground passageway to the Centre Eaton and then continue into Les Ailes de la Mode (nearest métro is McGill). When Eaton's department store closed, the massive building was redeveloped to house a number of clothing stores with a spectacular skylight. Attached to Les Ailes to the east is the Promenade Cathédrale. The construction of this architecturally impressive complex successfully underpinned the rapidly sinking Cathédrale Anglicane de Christ-Church (▷ 63).

🚇 Bonaventure or McGill

LES COURS MONT-ROYAL TO 1000 DE LA GAUCHETIÉRE

www.le1000.com

This elegant complex, with its enclosed interior courtyards, originally housed the Mount Royal Hotel; it was redeveloped in 1988. Note the huge bird figures hanging from the roof. The work of Inuit sculptor David Piqtoukun, they represent Tingmiluks, shamans who are able to transform themselves into birds. Return to place Ville-Marie, and walk in the other direction through Central Station to 1000 de la Gauchetière, at 205m (672ft) the tallest building in the city, with a huge and spectacular indoor skating rink on the main floor. Follow the walkway to place Bonaventure and then follow signs to place de la Cité Internationale; after that, continue toward Square Victoria métro station, turning right just before the station and following signs along a long passageway to the Montréal World Trade Centre (see below).

✉ 1000 de la Gauchetière ☎ 514/395-0555 💷 Adult $5.75, child (12 and under) $3.75, family $16; skate rental: $5 🚇 Peel or Bonaventure

CENTRE DE COMMERCE MONDIAL DE MONTRÉAL

Quite the most spectacular part of the Underground City, the Montréal World Trade Centre comprises an entire city block enclosed as an atrium. High, light and luminous, the complex surrounds a fascinating fountain and a piece of the Berlin Wall given to Montréal on the city's 350th anniversary in 1992 as a monument to peace.

🚇 Square Victoria

TIPS

» Signing in the Underground City is not as good as it could be. Arm yourself with a map and ask for directions from locals.

» Montréalers proudly call their métro system (▷ 45) "the largest underground art gallery in the world." Many stations, designed by different architects to link into the area in which they are located, have relevant artworks.

» Within the Réso and Montréal's métro stations escalators are few and far between, and those that exist are often not working. Be prepared for some stair-climbing.

Far left *Ice-skating at 1000 de la Gauchetière* **Bottom left** *The Montréal World Trade Centre* **Below** *Entrance to the Underground City and the shopping arcade, now 33km (20 miles) of passages*

VIEUX MONTRÉAL (OLD MONTRÉAL)

INFORMATION

www.vieux.montreal.qc.ca

✚ 59 E3 ℹ 174 rue Notre-Dame Est, on corner of place Jacques Cartier, Montréal, Québec ☎ 514/873-2015 Ⓜ Champ-de-Mars, place d'Armes, or Square Victoria

INTRODUCTION

In the old part of the city, narrow cobblestone streets are lined with beautifully restored historic stone buildings now housing design boutiques, art galleries and restaurants. There are two ways of exploring this fascinating area, and ideally you should try to do both. You can get an excellent overview by taking a ride in a horse-drawn *calèche*, a pleasant and informative tour with commentary by the driver. They are stationed on place d'Armes and you can choose how long you'd like the tour to be. After you've rumbled over the cobbles, just set out on foot and wander. Try to make time for a return trip after dark, when the bars and restaurants are at their best and certain buildings are imaginatively illuminated to emphasize the splendid architecture.

The site of the first settlement of Montréal, established by the French in 1642, retains much of its original layout, though only one of the early buildings remains—the Sulpician Seminary, dating from 1685. The picturesque stone houses and converted warehouses you see today reflect the heyday of the city as a major port throughout the 1800s and into the first half of the 20th century. The port was eventually replaced by a modern facility upstream and this area fell into decline, which turned out to be no bad thing. When its historic importance was recognized in the 1960s its fine old structures stood ready for restoration and an excellent job was made of it, combining heritage preservation with the creation of a vibrant living neighborhood.

WHAT TO SEE

RUE ST.-PAUL

The main thoroughfare is rue St.-Paul, Canada's oldest commercial street, and though it inevitably gets crowded with visitors at peak times it has managed to avoid becoming nothing but a tourist trap. People live and work (and play)

Above Outdoor skating at Marché Bonsecours, a romantic setting at night

here, too, and this mix give it an appealing character. Of course there are places to buy postcards and souvenirs, but there is also a concentration of very good commercial art and craft galleries and design boutiques. Crafts of the highest quality are also showcased in the imposing Marché Bon-secours (350 rue St.-Paul Est, tel 514/872-7730), including the boutique and gallery of the Québec arts council. The massive dome on the market building shares the skyline with the landmark tower of the Chapel of Notre-Dame-de-Bon-Secours (▷ 66).

THE SQUARES

There are delightful squares within Vieux Montréal, each with a different character. Champ-de-Mars, linking the old and new parts of the city, is wide open, with neat lawns and the scant remains of the old city walls. Place Jacques Cartier is spacious, too—paved, but with a double row of trees and colorfully planted tubs. Overlooked by a statue of Admiral Lord Nelson atop a tall column, it's a summer hotspot of sidewalk cafés and street performers. Place Royale, once a fur-trading marketplace, is now an elegant space with the stately Customs House along one side and the "sharp end" of Point-à-Callière (▷ 71) on the opposite side. At the center of the square a platform commemorates the 1701 Peace Treaty of Montréal. Place d'Youville has interesting, modern landscaping as well as traces of the past.

ON THE SIDESTREETS

Offshoots of the main street and the squares also contain plenty of hidden wonders, and it's worth diving down any side street that seems appealing. You will discover such places as tiny rue St.-Amable, almost invisable on the west side of place Jacques Cartier, where local artists display their canvasses for sale. The Château Ramezay, on rue Notre-Dame Est, is worth seeking out too. Built in 1705 for the Governer of Montréal, it is now a museum (Jun–end Sep daily; rest of year Tue–Sun), with a unique take on Montréal history. Works of art range from First Nations artifacts to the works of the foremost Montréal artists, including landscapes, portraits, drawings and etchings. Most fascinating of all is the Québec Ethnological Collection, reflecting the daily lives of local people from the 18th and 19th centuries, and the Photographic Collection which, again, shows the lives of real Montréalers. There's a lively program of temporary exhibitions and events, and once you've soaked up all the heritage inside the building, you can have a stroll around the lovely 18th-century garden, which combines formal layouts, English-style gardens, a kitchen garden, herb garden and small orchard.

TIPS

» Don't forego a ride in a horse-drawn carriage (calèche) if you are here in cooler weather—cozy rugs are tucked around your knees to keep you warm.
» The roof-top bar of the Hotel Nelligan is a great place to hang out on summer evenings.
» See also Vieux-Port (▷ 76), which borders the Vieux Montréal area.

Bottom left and below *Views of the imposing Marché Bonsecours*

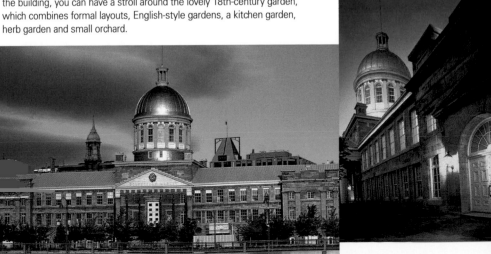

SQUARE DORCHESTER (DORCHESTER SQUARE)

Dorchester Square and its southern continuation, place du Canada, is an area of interesting buildings centered on a pleasant green space.

The Centre Infotouriste is in the Dominion Square Building, an attractive 1927 Florentine stone structure. Counterclockwise is Le Windsor, a former hotel and slim 45-story tower housing the Canadian Imperial Bank of Commerce, built in 1962. The Laurentienne Building is set at an angle to the street, and behind it looms the 50-floor IBM Marathon Building. St. George's Anglican Church, hidden away in the corner, was built in 1870 in Gothic Revival style, and the former Windsor train station, with its towers and turrets, dates from the 1880s. On the south side, Hôtel Marriott Château Champlain, with distinctive half-moon windows, is known as the "cheese-grater". The tallest building in the city is 1000 de la Gauchetière, its copper rotundas reflecting the domes of Cathédrale Marie-Reine-du-Monde across the street (▷ 63). The silver-granite Sun Life Building occupies the whole east side of the square.

✚ 58 A5

Above *The community turns out for Winter Follies at the Quays in the Old Port*
Right *The illuminated quays of Vieux-Port provide a dazzling snapshot*

VIEUX-PORT (OLD PORT)

www.oldportofmontreal.com

Reborn in the 1990s as a waterfront recreational space, Montréal's old port has a history stretching back to the arrival of the first settlers in 1642. Through the years of fur trading, river-based trade and international ocean-going steamships the port developed alongside Montréal's role as transportation hub for the whole of Canada.

By the 1980s the port was in decline, but the adjacent Vieux-Montréal (▷ 76) area had been declared a historic district and a decision was made to turn the derelict port into a linear park, stretching for 2.5km (1.5 miles) along the St. Lawrence River. Rusty rail tracks and crumbling buildings were removed, a waterfront promenade

laid out, and new facilities added. In its new incarnation the Vieux Port opened in 1992 to mark the 350th anniversary of the founding of the city. Three years later, the restored Lachine Canal, a national historic site, was reopened for pleasure boating, with a canalside path for and an interpretive center.

Some original port buildings survive, most visibly the Clock Tower, now restored as an interpretive center and viewpoint, reached by a climb of 192 open metalwork steps. Shed 16, a former warehouse, largely retains its original appearance, but now houses the Labyrinthe, a children's indoor maze. One of the new building in the Vieux-Port, on King Edward Pier, is the

Montréal Science Centre (▷ 85), an exciting place designed to stimulate interest in and knowledge of many aspects of science and technology. It also contains an IMAX theater. Behind the Quays Promenade, rue de la Commune is an attractive row of old stone buildings dotted with bars and restaurants.

The port is a hive of recreational activity year-round, with a winter skating rink, summer cruises, plenty of scope for cycling and rollerblading, festivals, fireworks, concerts and exhibitions.

✚ 59 F2 🛈 Old Port of Montréal Inc, 333 rue de la Commune Ouest, Montréal, Québec, H2Y 2E2 ☎ 514/496-PORT, 800/971-PORT 🚇 Champ de Mars, place d'Armes or Square Victoria

WALK

MONTRÉAL'S OLD CITY AND PORT

Walking around the old quarter of Montréal evokes the days when the tiny French mission struggled for survival, but also provides evidence of the city's phenomenal growth in the 19th century. Highlights include the magnificent Basilique Notre-Dame, the 19th-century buildings of rue Ste.-Hélène, and some wonderful viewpoints of the city old and new.

THE WALK

Lenght: 3.5km (2 miles)
Allow: 2.5 hours (not including visits)
Start and end at: place d'Armes
How to get there: Take the métro to place d'Armes station, which is two blocks north of the starting point on place d'Armes

★ Start the tour at the place d'Armes, visiting the Sulpician Seminary on the south side of the square, along with the Basilique Notre-Dame.

❶ When built in 1829, the Basilique Notre-Dame was the largest church on the North American continent. The interior is gorgeous (▷ 64–65). To the left is the Sulpician Seminary. The rustic building behind the wall is the oldest in the city, built in 1685 by the Sulpician priests, and is a fine example of fieldstone construction, notable for its dormer windows and clock dating from 1701.

Walk across place d'Armes to the Bank of Montréal at 119 St.-Jacques.

❷ The bank's head office occupies an imposing neoclassical structure built in 1848 by John Wells, inspired by the Pantheon in Rome. Take a look at its grandiose interior.

Leave the bank and turn right. Cross St.-Jacques to see the Old Royal Bank at 360 St.-Jacques.

❸ This massive Florentine palace, built in 1928 by York and Sawyer, was the first building in Montréal to rise higher than the towers of Notre-Dame. Go up the stairs into the huge banking hall to see the splendid coffered ceiling. Side rooms have vaulted ceilings decorated with gold leaf.

Turn left after leaving the bank and go left on rue Dollard. Cross

Notre-Dame, turn right, then turn left along picturesque rue Ste.-Hélène, with its gas lamps and fine stone buildings. Turn left on Lemoyne, then right on St.-Pierre, and walk into place d'Youville to visit the Centre d'Histoire de Montréal at No. 335 St.-Pierre and the Youville Stables at No. 298 place d'Youville.

❹ Built in 1903, the red-brick building housing the Centre d'Histoire de Montréal was once the Central Fire Station. Now it charts the history of the city with a series of interesting displays (summer Tue–Sun; winter Wed–Sun). The squat but substantial 1828 Youville Stables were constructed as potash warehouses. Walk through the porte cochère (old carriage entrance) into the lovely central courtyard.

Continue along place d'Youville to Pointe-à-Callière.

Left The busy harbour at the Old Port, filled with pleasure craft

5 On May 17, 1642, Montréal was established here, where once the St. Pierre River joined the St. Lawrence River. Construction of the port facilities has pushed the St. Lawrence some distance away and the St. Pierre River has been underneath place d'Youville since the 19th century. Today, Pointe-à-Callière is dominated by the huge concrete building housing the Musée d'Archéologie et d'Histoire de Montréal (▷ 71).

Cross rue de la Commune. Turn right and walk to the entrance to the Vieux-Port (where you can cross the railroad). Turn left, and then left again at the Promenade du Vieux-Port to come to the Esplanade du Vieux-Port.

6 This pleasant park offers a wide variety of attractions, as well as fine views of the city and the river. On the King Edward Pier is the Montréal Science Centre (▷ 85).

Continue to quai Jacques Cartier for more views. Turn left, leave the Vieux-Port, and cross rue de la Commune into place Jacques Cartier.

7 Lined with outdoor cafés and full of street performers, flower vendors and artists, this street is lively all summer, especially in the evenings.

Walk along rue St.-Paul to your right to visit Marché Bonsecours and then the Chapelle Notre-Dame-de-Bonsecours.

8 The impressive stone façade and Renaissance-style dome of the former Bonsecours Market building, built in 1845 by William Footner, today houses an interesting collection of boutiques, craft stores and restaurants (▷ 83). The "sailors' church" of Notre-Dame-de-Bonsecours (▷ 66) has

long had a special place in the hearts of Montréalers. Before the expansion of the port necessitated the reclaiming of land behind the church, the statue of the Virgin was a landmark from far downstream. It is worth taking a look inside and visiting the church's museum.

Cross St-Paul and walk up rue Bonsecours on your left. Turn left on rue Notre-Dame, and on your left, at No. 280, is Château Ramezay, built 1705 (▷ 75).

9 Today, Château Ramezay houses a fascinating museum devoted to the city's history. At the rear of the building, the Jardin du Gouverneurs is cultivated with the types of flowers, fruit and vegetables that would have been grown here during the French regime. Across the street from the garden is the monumental Second Empire Hôtel-de-Ville, Montréal's City Hall. Originally built in 1878, it was rebuilt after a fire in 1922. Above the main entrance is the balcony from which French

President Charles de Gaulle made his famous "Vive le Québec libre" speech in 1967.

Walk back to place d'Armes along rue St-Paul—the oldest street in Montréal, which dates to 1672—and through Cours Le Royer, where old stone warehouses, constructed in 1861–74 are now condominium apartments. This completes the tour.

WHEN TO GO
This is a year-round walk, but it's especially splendid early on a summer evening or on a crisp day in the fall.

WHERE TO EAT
BORIS BISTRO
✉ Rue McGill ☎ 514/848-9575
A trendy place offering Mediterranean cuisine with Asian influences; under 18s are only allowed on the terrace.

BONAPARTE
✉ Rue François-Xavier ☎ 514/844-4368
A charming restaurant in a historic stone building with good-value fixed-price meals.

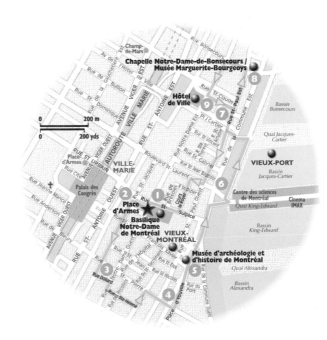

INTERNATIONAL MONTRÉAL

This walk explores the city's newest quartier—the Quartier International—which is an interesting mix of modern architecture, art installations and revitalized city squares. From here, explore the city's Chinatown, skirt modern shopping malls and the city's premier center for the arts, then head out to the Latin Quarter for superb French-style architecture, trendy shopping and vibrant nightlife.

THE WALK

Length: 4km (2.5 miles)
Allow: 3 hours (not including visits)
Start: Place du Canada/Square Dorchester
How to get there: Take the métro to Bonaventure and exit through the lobby of the Marriott Chateau Champlain Hotel. Place du Canada is directly in front.

★ Place du Canada and Square Dorchester are adjoining green spaces in the heart of the city, dotted with trees and monuments and surrounded by a pleasant blend of modern and historic buildings. Busy Boulevard René-Lévesque Ouest cuts between the two areas, but traffic lights will make the crossing easier for you.

From Place du Canada, with the Marriott hotel behind you and Square Dorchester ahead, go right along rue René-Lévesque.

❶ On the right you will see the Cathédrale Marie-Reine du Monde (▷ 63), and after crossing rue Mansfield, you will pass between place Ville-Marie and the Fairmont le Reine Elizabeth Hotel. Place Ville-Marie is a distinctive cruciform tower, with a shopping plaza at the base that marks the hub of the Underground City (▷ 72–73). The Fairmont le Reine Elizabeth is one of Montréal's grandest hotels, but is perhaps most famous as the place where John and Yoko held a seven-day "bed-in" and recorded "Give Peace a Chance" in 1969.

At rue University turn right.

❷ This broad thoroughfare has been transformed into a grand approach to the Quartier International, with modernist, back-lit columns on either side. These have been designed to represent international flags.

At rue St.-Antoine Ouest turn left and continue to Square Victoria.

❸ You are now in the new Quartier International, a revitalized area where nondescript commercial development has been transformed with stunning modern architecture, elegant squares and lots of public art inside and outside the buildings. As part of the plan square Victoria was remodeled and landscaped, and it is now a lovely grassy space with lawns and trees, a water feature with 29 fountains, and a statue of Queen Victoria atop a massive plinth. There's also an authentic Parisian art deco métro entrance, a gift to Montréal from the people of the French capital and Montréal's only métro entrance that's outdoors. The square is surrounded by striking modern office buildings, including the World Trade Centre (▷ 73).

Continue along rue St.-Antoine and turn left onto place Jean-Paul-Riopelle (pictured left).

4 Place Jean-Paul Riopelle was created out of a former parking lot as a focal point for the Quartier International. Named after the renowned Québec artist, its main feature is his sculpture fountain, moved here from the Parc Olympique and encircled by a ring of fire. After dark (from about 6.30pm to 11pm) underground lighting and mist blowers create a stunning effect. The trees on the square are varieties indigenous to the area and provide shade in summer.

At northern edge of place Jean-Paul-Riopelle, go left on avenue Viger Ouest and right on rue St.-Alexandre; you could detour ahead a short way to visit the Basilique St.-Patrick. Turn right (or left, if returning from the Basilique St.-Patrick) on rue de la Gauchetiere into Montréal's Chinatown, marked by a traditional-style gateway.

5 Smaller than it used to be, Chinatown is still a colorful area of food stores, restaurants and herbalists. Rue de la Gauchetière is pedestrian-only here and is often the scene of outdoor events. After several blocks, on the corner of rue Clark is a small park named after Dr. Sun Yat-Sen, the "father of modern China." The Chinese Catholic church is at 205 de la Gauchetière. On rue Viger, one block to the south, the Holiday Inn Select hotel was built according to the principles of feng shui and its rooftop air-conditioning plant is hidden inside bright Chinese-style pagodas.

Continue along rue de la Gauchetière to boulevard St.-Laurent to exit Chinatown through another traditional gateway. Turn left on boulevard St.-Laurent, cross boulevard René-Lévesque, then go left on rue Ste.-Catherine and continue between Complexe Desjardins and the Place des Arts.

6 Complexe Desjardins incorporates a mall with 110 stores, restaurants and services around the central Grande-Place, with a fountain and a program of events and activities. Three towering office blocks rise above it. Across the road, the place des Arts is a showpiece of Montréal's cultural life that incorporates five performance halls and the Musée d'Art Contemporain (▷ 66), which was the only museum in Canada dedicated to contemporary art until Toronto opened one in 2006. The complex also includes a café-bistro, gift shops and information center, all linked below ground but also with a splendid above-ground area that hosts festivals and open-air shows.

To get back to place du Canada, you can take the métro a couple of stops from place des Arts (direction Angrignon) to Peel, then walk three blocks south on rue Peel. If you don't want any more walking at all, continue on the métro to Lionel-Groulx and change to the orange line (direction Montmorency) to Bonaventure. If you still have energy to spare, walk west from place des Arts on boulevard de Maisonneuve to rue Metcalfe, then turn left and continue to place du Canada.

WHEN TO GO

Winters can be bitter in Montréal and the height of summer can sometimes be rather hot for pounding city streets. Otherwise any dry day is a good day to enjoy this walk. Weekdays see the most life in the Quartier International and offer the best ambience on the squares. The walk experience will be enhanced if it coincides with one of the many summer events that enliven Chinatown, rue Prince-Arthur or the Place des Arts concourse.

WHERE TO EAT
CHEZ CHINE
☎ 514/878-9888, 888/878-9888
In the uniquely Chinese-style Holiday Inn, serves authentic Chinese food including good dim sum lunches.
LA ROTONDE
☎ 514/847-6900
The restaurant at the Musée d'Art Contemporain is a stylish place to enjoy excellent Provence cuisine.

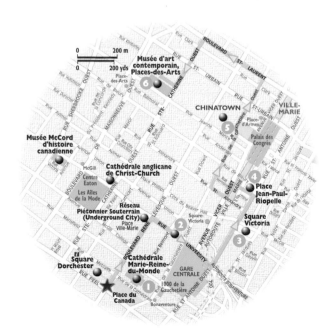

SHOPPING

ATWATER MARKET
www.marchespublics-mtl.com
Saved from demolition in the late 1960s, this distinctive building with a tall clock tower carries on a long tradition of supplying fresh produce from the countryside. It includes a gourmet food shop and a bakery.
✉ 138 avenue Atwater, Montréal, Québec ☎ 514/937-7754 ⏱ Mon–Wed 8–6, Thu–Fri 8am–9pm (till 7 Thu Jan–end Apr), Sat–Sun 8–5 Ⓜ Lionel-Groulx 🚌 78, 195

BELLINI SHOES
If you get excited by shopping for shoes, try Bellini. It has a huge range of footwear, for men and women, that bridges all tastes and budgets, and all the shoes are imported from Italy.
✉ 1119 rue Ste.-Catherine Ouest, Montréal, Québec, H3B 1H8 ☎ 514/843-7860 ⏱ Mon–Wed 9.30–6, Thu–Fri 9–9, Sat 9–5, Sun 12–5 Ⓜ Peel 🚌 15

BIDZ
There's an enormous selection of beads from all over the world to be found here, and you can have some

fun stringing them into necklaces, bracelets and earrings. There are also some funky pieces made by artists-in-residence.
✉ 3945A rue St.-Denis, Montréal, Québec, H2W 2M4 ☎ 514/286-2421, 1-877/324-5537 ⏱ Mon–Wed and Sat 11–6, Thu–Fri 11–7, Sun 12–5 🚌 Mont-Royal 🚌 30

BOUTIQUE POM' CANELLE
An exclusive boutique selling designer fashions for children aged 3 to 16. If your young teen is brave enough to be individual, or your toddler won't drool all over the Lily Gaufrette or Pinco-Palleno creations, you can dress them up beautifully.
✉ 4860 rue Sherbrooke Ouest, Montréal, Québec, H3Z 1H1 ☎ 514/483-1787 ⏱ Mon–Fri 10–6, Sat 10–5 Ⓜ Vendôme or Villa-Maria, then bus 24

COMPLEXE DESJARDINS
www.complexedesjardins.com
Linked to the Underground City, this office and shopping complex is the largest building downtown. The shopping area is around La Grande-Place, and has more than 100 units

including fashion, gifts, services and eateries. Events include exhibitions, charity events, cultural festivals and even blood-donor sessions.
✉ 150 rue Ste.-Catherine Ouest/175 boulevard René-Lévesque Ouest, Montréal, Québec, H5B 1E9 ☎ 514/281-1870 ⏱ Mon–Wed 9–6, Thu–Fri 9.30–9, Sat 9.30–5, Sun, 12–5 Ⓜ Place-des-Arts 🚌 15, 150 🍴 A good selection of cafés, bistros, fast food, and quality restaurants

HENRI HENRI
www.henrihenri.ca
This hat shop may not have coined the phrase "hat trick," but they certainly did their bit when, in the 1940s and 1950s, they gave a hat to each Canadiens hockey player who scored three goals in a game. Classic headgear for men, such as Stetson, Biltmore and Borsalino, plus Donegal tweed caps.
✉ 189 rue Ste.-Catherine Est, Montréal, Québec, H2X 1K8 ☎ 514/288-0109, 1-888/388-0109 ⏱ Mon–Thu 10–6, Fri 10–9, Sat–Sun 9–5 Ⓜ St-Laurent or Berri-UQAM 🚌 15

Above Jet-boating on the Lachine Rapids

JEAN-TALON

www.marchespublics-mtl.com
In the heart of Little Italy, this bustling market has been a popular shopping destination for many years, and the range of goods reflects its cultural diversity.

✉ 7075 avenue Casgrain, Montréal, Québec ☎ 514/277-1588 🕐 Mon–Wed and Sat 8–6, Thu–Fri 8am–9pm, Sun 8–5 🚇 Jean-Talon 🚌 Little Italy, south of Jean-Talon, east of St.-Laurent

MAISONNEUVE MARKET

www.marchespublics-mtl.com
As well as hosting vendors selling local produce, this lively market is a cultural center for festivals, music, dance, theater and other activities.

✉ 4445 rue Ontario Est, Montréal, Québec ☎ 514/937-7754 🕐 Mon–Wed 7–6, Thu–Fri 7am–8pm, Sat 7–6, Sun 7–5 🚇 Pie IX 🚌 125 🚇 Hochelaga Maisonneuve

MAISON SIMONS

This is a great store, with fashions for women and men, and a homewares department. Customers travel substantial distances to stock up on outfits here. It's strong on stylishly tailored outfits, but there are clothes for all occasions.

✉ 977 rue Ste.-Catherine Ouest, Montréal, Québec, H3B 4W3 ☎ 514/282-1840 🕐 Mon–Wed 10–6, Thu–Fri 10–9, Sat 9.30–5, Sun 12–5 🚇 Peel or McGill 🚌 15

MARCHÉ BONSECOURS

www.marchebonsecours.qc.ca
One subway stop from the ultramodern Underground City is this magnificent old building, a former public market and city hall. Headquartering the Institute of Design and the Conseil des Métiers d'Art du Québec (both of which have galleries), it houses 15 boutiques selling top-quality crafts, fashions, jewelry, furniture and gift items, and exhibitions of arts and crafts.

✉ 350 rue St.-Paul Est, Old Montréal, Québec, H2Y 1H2 ☎ 514/872-7730 🕐 Late Jun–early Sep daily 10–9, rest of year daily 10–6 (open until 9pm Thu–Fri Apr–late Jun and early Sep–end Dec) 🚇 Champ-de-Mars 🍴 Two restaurants and a historical banquet

MONTRÉAL EATON CENTRE

http://centreeaton.shopping.ca
Linked to the Underground City and McGill subway station, this mall has stores of every kind, banks and other services, and eating places. There's also a movie multiplex. Spacious and chic, it's the biggest shopping destination in the city, and includes currency exchange..

✉ 705 rue Ste.-Catherine Ouest, Montréal, Québec, H3B 4G5 ☎ 514/288-3708 🕐 Mon–Fri 10–9, Sat 10–5, Sun 11–5 🚇 McGill 🚌 15 🍴 A vast selection of international fast foods, coffee houses and the Restofiore restaurant.

OGILVY

www.ogilvycanada.com
This fine old store has a classy atmosphere and a reputation for high-quality goods. Established in 1866, and in this location since 1912, it is home to about 50 smart franchises, including Hugo Boss, Aquascutum and Anne Klein. If you are there at noon you'll hear the lone bagpiper play—a store tradition that dates back to 1927.

✉ 1307 rue Ste.-Catherine Ouest, Montréal, Québec, H3G 1P7 ☎ 514/842-7711 🕐 Mon–Wed 10–6, Thu–Fri 10–9, Sat 9–5, Sun 12–5 🚇 Peel 🚌 15

OLIVIERI

Warm, welcoming and very user-friendly, this bookstore and bistro is run with great enthusiasm by people with a passion for literature. It has a vast section devoted to Québecois, French and foreign novels, but you can also pick up a good, lightweight novel for vacation reading, and there's a kids' corner.

✉ 5219 Chemin de la Côte des Neiges, Montréal, Québec, H3T 1Y1 ☎ 514/739-3639 🕐 Mon–Sat 10–10, Sun 11–7 🚇 Côte des Neiges 🚌 165, 535 🍴 Bistro offers a selection of homemade dishes

PLACE MONTRÉAL TRUST

http://placemontrealtrust.shopping.ca
Linked to the Underground City, midway between the two busiest subway stations, this bright and lofty mall has about 170 stores, including boutiques and specialty stores.

✉ 1500 avenue McGill College, Montréal, Québec, H3A 3J5 ☎ 514/843-8000 🕐 Mon–Tue 10–6, Wed–Fri 10–9, Sat 10–5, Sun 11–5 🚇 McGill or Peel 🚌 15 🍴 Food court, including vegetarian and Oriental cuisine, plus three coffee shops

ENTERTAINMENT AND NIGHTLIFE

AMC FORUM 22

www.amctheatres.com
No less than 22 of the highest-tech movie theaters. All the latest releases, plus some foreign-language and arthouse offerings.

✉ Pepsi Forum, 2313 rue Ste.-Catherine Ouest, Montréal, Québec, H3H 1N2 ☎ 514/904-1250 🕐 Daily 💰 Adult $13 ($10 before 6pm), child (under 12) $8 🚇 Atwater 🚌 15, 57

BOURBON COMPLEX

Montréal is a particularly gay-friendly city, with more than 100 gay establishments. This one, covering a city block, is reputedly the biggest in the world. It includes a retro disco, hotel, sauna and bathhouse.

✉ 1474 rue Ste.-Catherine Est, Montréal, Québec, H2L 2H9 ☎ 514/529-6969, 1-514/866-8668 🕐 Daily, till 3am 💰 No cover charge 🍴 Bars and restaurants

CASINO DE MONTRÉAL

www.casino-de-montreal.com
This spectacular waterfront building on an island in the St. Lawrence River offers five floors of gaming, entertainment and dining. There are more than 115 tables and 3,200 slots, a keno lounge and electronic horse racing. The cabaret features world-renowned performers and dancers. Patrons must be over 18, and a dress code applies.

✉ 1 avenue du Casino, Montréal, Québec, H3C 4W7 ☎ 514/392-2746, 800/665-2274 🕐 Sun–Thu 9am–3am, Fri–Sat 24 hours 💰 Free admission; charge for cabaret 🚇 Jean-Drapeau, then 🚌 167 🍴 Bars and restaurants

COMEDYWORKS

www.comedyworksmontreal.com
In this venue, upstairs from Jimbo's pub, there's comedy every night, with a definite emphasis on

Above *Montréal's modern glass and steel Casino, beside the St. Lawrence River*

audience participation—whether it's taking to the stage on open-mic nights or just heckling the paid acts. There's regular improvised comedy and headline acts on weekends.
✉ 1238 Bishop Street, Montréal, Québec, H3G 2E3 ☎ 514/398-9661 ⊙ Nightly 8.30pm, plus late show 11pm Fri and Sat ⛄ Varies $5–$12 ⓜ Lucien L'Allier or Guy-Concordia ⓐ 15, 150

CENTRE PIERRE PELADEAU
www.centrepierrepeladeau.com
Superb acoustics and intimate size make for enjoyable concerts, which feature music and performers from all over the world, plus dance and drama.
✉ 300 boulevard Maisonneuve Est, Montréal, Québec, H2X 3X6 ☎ 514/987-6919 ⊙ Year round ⛄ Varies ⓜ Berri-UQAM ⓐ 15

ERNIE BUTLER'S COMEDY NEST
www.comedynest.com
There's an international line-up of top comedians on the bill here. Wednesday is open-mic night for budding comedians and on the first Friday of the month there's an improv show. Dinner and show packages are also available.
✉ Pepsi Forum, 3rd floor, 2313 rue Ste.-Catherine Ouest, Montréal, Québec, H3H 1N2 ☎ 514/932-6378 ⊙ Wed–Sat 8.30,

plus late show 10.30 Fri and Sat ⛄ Wed $5 otherwise $12. Dinner and show: $25 ⓜ Atwater

LE FESTIN DU GOUVERNEUR
www.festin.com
Staff in period costume serve your dinner and drinks, while musicians, singers and comedians entertain in the historic surroundings of the fort on St. Helen's Island. It's a fun bilingual evening, as long as you enter into the spirit.
✉ Fort de l'Île Ste.-Hélène, Parc Jean Drapeau, Montréal, Québec H3C 4G8 ☎ 514/879-1141, 800/713-0111 ⊙ Apr–Oct nightly 6pm (also 8.30pm if sufficient demand); Nov and Jan–Mar nightly 6pm; Dec Sun–Thu 7pm, Fri–Sat 6pm and 8.30pm ⛄ Adult $46–$48, child (under 12) $22.50–$24.50 ⛴ From Old Port (summer only) ⓜ Jean-Drapeau

HOUSE OF JAZZ
This is still one of the city's premier jazz clubs. Live music nightly from top names, local acts and jam sessions.
✉ 2060 Aylmer Street, Montréal, Québec, H3A 2E3 ☎ 514/842-8656 ⊙ Mon–Fri 11.30am–1am , Sat–Sun 5.30pm–3am; live music starts after 6.30 ⛄ $5 cover charge for evening shows; mandatory coat check $2; drink minimum Fri–Sat ⓜ McGill ⓐ 15, 125 🍴 American-style restaurant serves ribs, chicken, potato skins

PLACE DES ARTS
www.pda.qc.ca
World-class venue, central to Montréal's cultural life, with five halls totaling 6,000 seats. Full schedule of classical music, ballet and opera.
✉ 175 rue Ste.-Catherine Ouest, Montréal, Québec, H2X 1Z8 ☎ 514/842-2112 ⊙ Box office: Mon–Sat 12–8.30 ⛄ Varies ⓜ Place des Arts ⓐ 15, 80, 129 🍴 Bistro restaurant

SEGEL CENTRE FOR THE PERFORMING ARTS
www.saidyebronfman.org
The center incorporates the main theater, the 177-seat Studio, a state-of-the-art 77-seat movie theater, the ArtLounge exhibition space, a performing arts academy and is

the home of the renowned Yiddish Theatre. The productions are varied, high quality, and mostly in English.
✉ 5170 Chemin de la Côte Ste.-Catherine, Montréal, Québec, H3W 1M7 ☎ 514/739-2301, 1-866/842-2112 ⊙ Year-round ⛄ From $30 ⓜ Côte-Ste.-Catherine or Snowdon ⓐ 17, 129 west

TOHU
www.tohu.ca
In the same complex as the Cirque du Soleil's headquarters and the National Circus School, this is an intimate venue for original shows featuring innovative performances. Recent productions have mixed circus arts with martial arts and modern dance, or with whimsical fantasy. It also hosts the annual show by the National Circus School.
✉ 2345 rue Jarry Est, Montréal, Québec H1Z 4P3 Tel 514/376-8648, 1-888/376-8648 ⊙ Year-round ⛄ Varies, from $20 ⓜ Jarry, then bus 193 east or D'Iberville, then bus 94 north

SPORTS AND ACTIVITES
LACHINE RAPIDS TOUR
www.jetboatingmontreal.com
The mighty St. Lawrence River flows over the Lachine Rapids just upstream from Montréal, and you can take an exhilarating ride over them on a one-hour jet-boat ride. You can also jet-boat up to the rapids and raft down them, or take a speedboat trip with high-speed twists and turns.
✉ Clock Tower Pier, Old Port, Montréal, Québec ☎ 514/284-9607 ⊙ May to Oct 10-6, every two hours ⛄ Adult $60, child (6-12) $40, youth (13–18) $50 ⓐ 14 ⓜ Champ de Mars

MONTRÉAL ALOUETTES
www.montrealalouettes.com
McGill University stadium has been developed and expanded to a capacity of 20,000. It has hosted the Alouettes Canadian football team's home games since 1998, and the team—five-time winners of the Grey Cup—are always worth seeing.
✉ Percival Molson Memorial Stadium, 475 avenue des Pins Ouest, Montréal, Québec, H2W 1S4 ☎ 514/871-2255 ⊙ Late

Jun–early Nov 🚶 $16–$50 🚇 McGill
🚌 Free shuttle every 5 min from McGill and Square Victoria

MONTRÉAL CANADIENS
http://canadiens.nhl.com
Superb venue, and top-quality hockey from the 24-time Stanley Cup champions, the Canadiens attracts tumultuous support. Attending a game is quite an experience, and when it comes to choosing who to cheer for, take your cue from those around you.
✉ Bell Centre, 1260 rue de la Gauchetière Ouest, Montréal, Québec, H3B 5E8 ☎ 514/790-1245, 800/361-4595 🕐 Sep–end Mar 🚶 From about $25 🚇 Bonaventure or Lucien-L'Allier 🚌 61, 36, 107, 74, 75

FOR CHILDREN
BIOSPHÈRE
www.biosphere.ec.gc.ca
Built as the US Pavilion for Expo '67 and an icon of contemporary architecture, this huge geodesic sphere is now an environmental museum, with displays on the ecosystem of the St. Lawrence River, sustainability and the Biosphère's green technology (▷ 63).
✉ 160 chemin Tour de l'Îsle, Île-Ste.-Hélène, Montréal, Québec, H3C 4G8 ☎ 514/283-5000 🕐 Jun–Oct daily 10–6; rest of the year Tue–Sun 10–6 🚶 Adult $9.50, child (17 and under) free 🚇 Jean-Drapeau

BIODÔME DE MONTRÉAL
▷ 63

LABYRINTHE DU HANGAR 16
www.labyrintheduhangar16.com
A 2,430sq m (27,000sq ft) warehouse converted into a great maze game, where you have to discover and solve clues that lead you through the corridors, while tackling obstacles and various surprises along the way.
✉ Clock Tower Pier, Vieux-Port, Montréal, Québec, H2L 4K3 ☎ 514/499-0099 🕐 Mid-May to mid-Jun and Sep Sat–Sun 11.30–5.30; mid-Jun to late Aug daily 11–9 🚶 Adult $13, child (4–12) $9.75 or (13–17) $12 🚇 Champ-de-Mars 🚌 14

FESTIVALS & EVENTS

MARCH
ST. PATRICK'S DAY
Parade with marching bands and floats, and lots of traditional Irish music and dancing.
✉ Montréal, Québec ☎ 514/932-0512

APRIL
BLUE METROPOLIS INTERNATIONAL LITERARY FESTIVAL
http://blue-met-bleu.com
More than 120 authors take part in on-stage interviews, an award presentation, readings, comedy and music events.
✉ Montréal, Québec ☎ 514/937-BLEU

JUNE/JULY
CANADIAN GRAND PRIX
www.grandprix.ca
The Formula 1 race is held at the Circuit Gilles Villeneuve on Île Notre-Dame over the second weekend of June.
✉ Montréal, Québec

MEGADÔME DE MONTRÈAL
www.megadome.ca
High-tech video games and laser-tag, things to climb on, ball games, and arts and crafts activities—if you have very active kids then they will have hours of fun at this giant complex.
✉ 6900 boulevard Décarie, Montréal, Québec ☎ 514/344-3663 🚇 Namur 🚌 17, 92, 160

MONTRÉAL SCIENCE CENTRE
www.montrealsciencecentre.com
After a complete makeover in 2007, the center is more exciting than ever, opening up a world of fun and understanding that only the latest interactive exhibits can bring. Young visitors can take part in a TV newsroom broadcast, walk right into a brain, and explore all kinds of virtual experiences. There's also an IMAX theater.
✉ King Edward Pier, Vieux-Port, Montréal, Québec H2Y 2E2 ☎ 514/496-4724,

JULY–END AUGUST
JUST FOR LAUGHS COMEDY FESTIVAL
www.hahaha.com
For these 10 days Montréal is the happiest city in the world, as top comedians from all over come to do their stuff. Stage shows are broadcast worldwide.
✉ Montréal, Québec ☎ 888/244-3155, 514/845-2322

SEPTEMBER
HOT-AIR BALLOON FESTIVAL
www.balloongatineau.com
Around 150 hot-air balloons take to the sky, and on the ground there are fairground rides, shows and fireworks.
✉ Gatineau, Québec ☎ 819/243-2330

877/496-4724 🕐 Mon–Fri from 8.30am, Sat–Sun from 9.30am; closing time varies seasonally 🚶 Adult $12, child (4–12) $9 (13–17) $11, family $38. Various combined tickets with IMAX also available 🚇 Place d'Armes or Champ-de-Mars 🍴 Café Arsenik serves light meals, snacks, ice creams

PEPSI FORUM
Older kids who are not easily overwhelmed might meet their match in this huge complex, with more than 200 of the latest interactive games and simulators, a 30m (100ft) climbing wall, movie theaters, pool tables, bowling and Montréal Hall of Fame.
✉ 2313 rue Ste.-Catherine Ouest, Montréal, Québec, H3H 1N2 ☎ 514/933-6786, 888/613-6786 🕐 Daily 🚶 Activities priced separately (arcade games are expensive) 🚇 Atwater 🚌 15, 57

EATING

PRICES AND SYMBOLS

The restaurants are listed alphabetically. The prices are for a two-course lunch (L) and a three-course à la carte dinner (D). Prices in pubs are for a two-course lunchtime bar meal and a two-course dinner in the restaurant, unless specified otherwise. The wine price is for the least expensive bottle.

For a key to the symbols, ▷ 2.

ALPENHAUS

www.restaurantalpenhaus.com
You could believe yourself to be in an alpine chalet in this great little fondue restaurant, with its rustic decor of rough-hewn lumber supporting a log ceiling. In addition to the cheese or meat fondues, the menu offers European dishes such as schnitzels, sausages and pastas, plus steaks, rack of lamb and smoked salmon.
✉ 1279 rue St.-Marc, Montréal, Québec, H3H 2E8 ☎ 514/935-2285; 866/935-2285 🕐 Mon–Wed noon–3, 5.30–10, Thu–Fri 10am–10.30pm, Sat 4.30–10.30, Sun 5.30–10 🍴 $30, D $45, Wine $18 🛈 Guy-Concordia

AUBERGE LE ST-GABRIEL

www.auberge1754.com
Part of the Marriott Springhill Suites Hotel, this restaurant claims to be the oldest in North America, with a historic dining room and a lovely terrace. Food is an inventive mixture of traditional French and Québec. The wine list has a good international selection. Sunday brunch (which includes a clown for the kids) is popular.
✉ 426 rue St.-Gabriel, Montréal, Québec, H2Y 2Z9 ☎ 514/878-3561 🕐 Tue–Fri 6–10.30; Apr–end Nov also open for lunch weekdays 12–2.30 🍴 L $20, D $30, Wine $25 🚌 14, 55

BEAVER HALL

www.beaverhall.ca
This smart lunch-only restaurant was an instant hit with Montréal's business community for its interesting menu of classic bistro food, made from the freshest produce and beautifully presented. There's a great, buzzing atmosphere and a lot of animated chatter from happy patrons.

✉ 1073 côte du Beaverhall, Montréal, Québec H2Z 1S5 ☎ 514/866-1331 🕐 Mon–Fri 11–3 🍴 L $25, Wine $32.50 🚇 Square Victoria

BEN'S MONTREAL-DELI

Locked into the 1950s, with its formica and chrome interior, soda-fountain counter and diner-style seating, this deli goes back even further—to 1908, when the Kravitz family started the business. It's big on smoked-meat sandwiches and platters, but also has other basics like burgers and pasta.
✉ 990 boulevard de Maisonneuve Ouest, Montréal, Québec, H3A 1M5 ☎ 514/844-1000 🕐 Sun–Wed 7.30am–2am, Thu 7.30am–3am, Fri–Sat 7.30am–4am 🍴 L $8–$15, D $10–$15 🚇 Peel or McGill 🚌 15, 420 🚇 Downtown, corner of Metcalfe

BONAPART

www.bonaparte.com
This Old Montréal restaurant is great for a romantic, special-occasion dinner, but don't miss coming here if there's no occasion

to celebrate. The food is fabulous, and the surroundings are elegant, yet welcoming and comfortable. The French menu features the best of Québec's regional produce in main courses such as lobster flavored with vanilla and served with a spinach fondue, wild boar marinated with red wine, or leg of duck confit with fricassée of mushrooms and sweet garlic. There's also a six-course tasting menu and an outstanding wine list of more than 500 labels.

✉ 447 rue St.-François-Xavier, Montréal, Québec, H2Y 2T1 ☎ 514/844-4368 ⏰ (theater menu 5.30–6.30pm) ✋ L $25, D $50, Wine $35 🚇 Place d'Armes 🚌 Vieux Montréal, between rue Notre-Dame and rue St-Paul Ouest

BORIS BISTRO
www.borisbistro.com
Delightful bistro with a stunning summer terrace located at the edge of Old Montréal. The menu features items such as minted duck salad, smoked fish, salmon tartare, grilled trout, locally made sausages, and passion-fruit mousse dessert.

✉ 465 rue McGill, Montréal, Québec, H2Y 2H1 ☎ 514/848-9575 ⏰ Daily in summer months 11.30–11; call for off-season hours ✋ $15–$25 🚇 Square Victoria 🚌 57

BOULANGERIE OLIVE ET GOURMANDO
www.oliveetgourmando.com
Small café and bakery with delicious coffee, croissants and pastries, and out-of-the-ordinary gourmet sandwiches and salads. Everything is made on the premises and is very fresh. Credit cards are not accepted.

✉ 351 rue St.-Paul Ouest, Montréal, Québec, H2Y ☎ 514/350-1083 ⏰ Tue–Sat 8–6 (Thu to 11); closed Sun and Mon ✋ D $10–$15 🚇 Square Victoria

BRUTOPIA
www.brutopia.net
This is a lively place with three bars on three floors, three terraces and nightly entertainment. The pub food is influenced by many cuisines of the world, from Chinese dumplings to Mediterranean squid to classic

Canadian burgers. Mexican favorites have a strong presence and there are vegetarian choices too. Beer is brewed on the premises, including German-style pale ale, British-style IPA and Nut Brown Ale, beers with honey and fruit overtones, and seasonal varieties.

✉ 1219 rue Crescent, Montréal, Québec H3G 2B1 ☎ 514/393-9277 ⏰ Sat–Mon 3pm–3am, Fri noon–3am (food served until 11pm) ✋ $15, D $20 🚇 Lucien-L'Allier, Guy-Concordia

CAFÉ DES BEAUX-ARTS
www.mmfa.qc.ca
This is an elegant bistro with dark wood, honey-toned walls, white table linen, and a chic bar area. The menu has such offerings as duck confit and deer steak with mushrooms, walnuts, cranberries and red wine sauce. Save some room for the heavenly crème brûlée.

✉ Musée des Beaux-Arts, 1384 rue Sherbrooke Ouest, Montréal, Québec, H3G 1J5 ☎ 514/843-3233 ⏰ Thu–Tue 11–5, Wed 11–8; lunch served 11.30–2.30 ✋ L $20, D $25, Wine $29 🚇 Guy-Concordia 🚌 24 🚇 Downtown, at Sherbrooke and Bishop

CAFÉ VASCO DA GAMA
www.vascodagama.ca
Not surprisingly, this café is based on Portuguese cuisine, but, like the great explorer himself, dishes venture a bit farther afield. Breakfast choices include various omelettes, bagels, muffins and a healthy helping of goat milk yogurt with honey and fruit. The rest of the day the menu includes sandwiches and salads, with tapas served after 4pm and a selection of traditional desserts such as apple crumble and crème brulée. If it's picnic weather, you could opt for a lunch box to go.

✉ 1472 rue Peel, Montréal, Québec, H3A 1S8 ☎ 514/286-2688 ⏰ Mon–Wed 7–7, Thu–Fri 7am–9pm, Sat–Sun 9–6 ✋ L $12, D $20, Wine $32 🚇 Peel

CASA GALICIA
www.casagaliciamontreal.com
Traditional Spanish food, accompanied by flamenco shows

on weekends, is the attraction here, with deliciously authentic paella and tapas joined on the menu by Portuguese specialties such as grilled sardines.

✉ 2087 rue St.-Denis, Montréal, Québec, H2X 3K8 ☎ 514/843-6698 ⏰ Tue–Fri 11.30am–2pm, 5–11pm, Sat 5pm–midnight, Sun–Mon 5–11pm ✋ L $30, D $50, Wine $29 🚇 Sherbrooke

CHEZ CHINE
Don't be put off by the Holiday Inn location—after all, this Holiday Inn Select was totally created using the principles of feng shui, and there's a "pagoda" on the roof (actually hiding the air-conditioning plant). Chez Chine offers upscale gourmet Cantonese cuisine in fabulous surroundings, either indoors or in a pagoda-shaded garden with a fish pond. Dim sum is a popular lunch option, and the seafood dishes are outstanding. The menu also includes European and North American dishes, and breakfast.

✉ 99 avenue Viger Ouest, Montréal, Québec, H2Z 1E9 ☎ 514/878-9888, 888/878-9888 ⏰ Mon–Fri 6.30–10am, 11.30am–2pm, 5.30–10pm, Sat–Sun 7–11am, 11.30am–2pm, 5.30–10pm ✋ L $15, D $30, Wine $26 🚇 Place d'Armes

CLUB CHASSE ET PECHE
www.leclubchasseetpeche.com
This place is so hard to spot it's almost as if they are trying to keep their wonderful food a secret. Look for the sign with the coat of arms logo—there's no restaurant name—then take your seat in the stone-walled dining room ready to enjoy such offerings as chilled lobster soup with bell pepper or foie gras poêlé with fig and Serrano ham to start, followed by veal short rib and sweetbread with bacon and artichoke, or rabbit with langoustine and parsley root.

✉ 423 rue St.-Claude, Montréal, Québec, H2Y 3B6 ☎ 514/861-1112 ⏰ Tue–Fri 11–2, 6.30–10, Sat 6.30–10 ✋ L $30, D $55, Wine $33 🚇 Champ-de-Mars, Place d'Armes

LE COMMENSAL

One of a popular chain of vegetarian restaurants offering a vast buffet that includes some clearly indicated vegan options. You help yourself and then pay by the weight of the food on your plate, so it's difficult to anticipate the cost, particularly when everything looks so tempting. There are about a dozen desserts, too, again with vegan possibilities.

✉ 1204 avenue McGill College, Montréal, Québec, H3B 4J8 ☎ 514/871-1480 ⏰ Daily 11.30–10 ✋ $10–$15, D $15–$20 🚇 McGill 🚌 15

DELMO

www.delmo.ca

In this beautifully renovated old building in Vieux-Montréal seafood and meat dishes share equal billing on the interesting menu. You could start with a classic soup, Village Bay oysters or a plate of charcuterie, then choose a main course such as salmon pot-au-feu, moules marinière, bison, or *confit de canard à l'orange*. Top of the dessert list is the delicious pecan and maple pie. The long wine list includes a few half-bottles and several available by the glass.

✉ 211 rue Notre-Dame Ouest, Montréal, Québec, H2Y 1T4 ☎ 514/336-1869 or 514/448-1869 ⏰ Mon–Tue 11.30am–11pm, Wed–Fri 11.30am–midnight, Sat 5pm–midnight, Sun 5pm–11pm ✋ L $30, D $45, Wine $30 🚇 Place d'Armes

L'EXPRESS

In a long, narrow room, with a checkerboard floor, zinc bar and pub-style furniture, classic, unpretentious bistro fare includes pâté, caviar, *bouillabaisse*, steak tartare, fresh seafood, and *steak-frîtes*. The wine list is exclusively French, and cocktails are also available. Reservations are essential; when you call, ask for directions—it's not easy to spot from the outside.

✉ 3927 rue St.-Denis, Montréal, Québec, H2W 2M4 ☎ 514/845-5333 ⏰ Mon–Fri 8am–2am, Sat–Sun 10am–2am ✋ L $13–$20, D $20–$30, Wine $19 🚇 Sherbrooke 🚌 30, 144

GIBBY'S

www.gibbys.ca

If you like oysters, this is the place to go. It's equally renowned for succulent steaks and seafood, plus home-made bread, pastries and chocolates. A fine old archway leads into the courtyard where Gibby's occupies a converted 19th-century stable.

✉ 298 Place d'Youville, Montréal, Québec, H2Y 2B6 ☎ 514/282-1837 ⏰ Daily 5–11 or 11.30pm (opens 4.30pm Sat) ✋ D $65, Wine $28 🚇 Square Victoria 🚌 61, 75

LE JOLI MOULIN

www.lejolimoulin.com

The place that tempted its proprietors out of retirement has quickly become renowned for its friendly ambience and efficient service as well as the quality of the food. Specializing in aged AAA Alberta steaks, roast prime rib of beef and seafood, it also offers good-value table d'hôte menus and an excellent range of French, Italian and New World wines.

✉ 1201 avenue Van Horne, Montréal, Québec H2V 1K4 ☎ 514/276-5654 ⏰ Tue–Thu 11.30am–3pm, 5–11pm, Fri 11.30am–3, 5pm–midnight, Sat 5pm–midnight, Sun 5–11pm ✋ L $30, D $50, Wine $27 🚇 Outremont

MAIKO SUSHI

www.maiko-sushi.com

Sit at the sushi bar and watch the preparation then choose from the artistic offerings there or take a table and select from an interesting menu that includes teriyaki, seafood, grilled rack of lamb and filet mignon.

✉ 3877 rue Bernard Ouest, Montréal, Québec H2V 1T6 ☎ 514/490-1225 ⏰ Mon–Fri 11.30am–2.30pm, 5pm–10pm, Sat–Sun 5pm–10pm ✋ L $15, D $30, W $22 🚇 Outremont

MANGO BAY

www.mangobay.ca

A genuine tropical experience is guaranteed at this downtown restaurant, with its glowing dusky orange decor set off by lush exotic foliage and even a waterfall. The owner/chefs hail from the Caribbean, so the food is entirely authentic—succulent goat curry, jerk chicken, oxtail and ackee with salt fish are among the specialties. There's a good selection of rum-based drinks too, and live entertainment is a regular feature.

✉ 1202 rue Bishop, Montréal, Québec, H3G 2E3 ☎ 514/875-7082 ⓦ Mon–Thu 11.30am–10pm, Fri 11.30am–midnight, Sat 3pm–midnight, Sun 3–10pm 🍴 L $15, D $26, Wine $30 Ⓜ Guy-Concordia

NUANCES
www.casino-de-montreal.com
Nuances is one of the most highly rated restaurants in North America, presenting gourmet French cuisine in formal surroundings. The combinations of tastes and textures is nothing short of artistic: asparagus and lobster chartreuse appetizer, loin of lamb cooked in clay with gnocchi, parmesan-breaded eggplant (aubergine) and bell-pepper ratatouille. Dress code calls for business-style attire. No diners under 18.
✉ Casino du Montréal, 1 avenue du Casino, Montréal, Québec, H3C 4W7 ☎ 514/392-2708, 800/665-2274 ⓦ Sun–Thu 5.30–11, Fri–Sat 5.30–11.30 🍴 D $100, Wine $54 Ⓜ Jean-Drapeau then free shuttle bus 🚌 Casino bus 167

PHILINOS
www.philinos.com
Tastes of the Mediterranean as only the Greeks know how are on offer at this restaurant near Parc Mont Royal. The simplicity of the décor is reflected in the unfussy treatment of traditional Greek classics such as stuffed vine leaves, moussaka, *souvlaki* and *kotopoulo*, with specialties including platters for two featuring seafood, a selection of meats or vegetarian dishes. The wine list is international, including plenty of Greek labels.
✉ 4806 avenue du Parc, Montréal, Québec, H2V 4E6 ☎ 514/271-9099 ⓦ Sun–Thu noon–11pm, Fri–Sat noon–midnight 🍴 L $16, D $30, Wine $27 🚌 80

LE PIMENT ROUGE
Widely regarded as serving the best Szechuan cuisine in the city, this is a chic restaurant in a historic building. The carefully prepared and presented dishes include Szechuan shrimp and beef with mango strips and Kahlua sauce. Dressy casual attire is the norm.

✉ 1170 rue Peel, Montréal, Québec, H3B 4P2 ☎ 514/866-7816 ⓦ Mon–Thu, Sun 11.30–11, Fri–Sat 11.30am–midnight; closed major holidays 🍴 L $23, D $45, Wine $38 Ⓜ Peel, Bonaventure 🚌 15, 107, 150

LES REMPARTS
www.restaurantlesremparts.com
Set in the stone cellars of the Auberge du Vieux-Port (▷ 91–92), this is an elegant and romantic restaurant. The emphasis is on fresh market produce from Québec. Savory dishes are served in a grand manner with a passion for detail.
✉ 97 rue de la Commune Est, Montréal, Québec, H2Y 1J1 ☎ 514/876-0081 ⓦ Mon–Fri 5–10; Sat–Sun 5–10.30 🍴 More than $25 Ⓜ Champ-de-Mars or Place d'Armes 🚌 55

REUBEN'S
www.reubensdeli.com
Trying the smoked meat is one of Montréal's famous "experiences" and Reuben's is one of the best places, with succulent and tasty lean beef served on good rye bread. The 10oz smoked meat sandwich is the menu highlight, but you can also get steaks and charbroiled chicken, pasta and pizza, burgers, gourmet sandwiches and salads. The surroundings are pleasant and cozy, with nice booths and great jazz murals on the walls.
✉ 1116 rue St.-Catherine Ouest, Montréal, Québec, H3B 1H4 ☎ 514/866-1029 ⓦ Mon–Wed 6.30am–midnight, Thu–Fri 6.30am–1am, Sat 8am–1am, Sun 8am–midnight 🍴 L $12, D $20, Wine $28 Ⓜ Peel

RESTAURANT LE CAVEAU
Something of a Montréal institution, this restaurant offers traditional French cuisine notably duck, rack of lamb and seafood dishes.
✉ 2063 rue Victoria, Montréal, Québec, H3A 2A3 ☎ 514/844-1624 ⓦ Daily 5–10 🍴 $15–$20 Ⓜ McGill 🚌 24

LES 3 BRASSEURS
www.les3brasseurs.ca
Occupying a beautifully restored former bank building in the heart of Vieux Montréal, this microbrewery

Above *Weinstein and Gavino's Pasta Bar*

restaurant has a great atmosphere. Gleaming vats, visible from the street and the interior, are the first clue that a great beer experience awaits, and you can order a taster consisting of several small glasses. The food specialty is a selection of flamms (similar to a pizza "but better"), and the long menu of other choices includes mussels Provencale, beef carbonnade, sauerkraut with German sausage, grills and burgers, sandwiches and salads. Beer is an ingredient in many of the dishes. There are four other locations in Montréal.
✉ 105 rue St.-Paul Est, Montréal, Québec ☎ 514/788-6100 ⓦ Daily from 11.30am 🍴 L $17, D $30, Wine $29.95 Ⓜ Place d'Armes

WEINSTEIN AND GAVINO'S PASTA BAR
There's always a buzzing atmosphere in this trendy Italian place. There's an open gallery upstairs, plus a terrace for warm weather. Long list of fresh, home-made antipasti, soups, salads, pastas and pizzas, along with main courses.
✉ 1434 rue Crescent, Montréal, Québec, H3G 2B6 ☎ 514/288-2231 ⓦ Sun–Wed 11–11, Thu–Sat 11– midnight 🍴 L $15, D $25, Wine $33 Ⓜ Guy-Concordia 🚌 15

STAYING

PRICES AND SYMBOLS

Prices are the starting price for a double room for one night, unless otherwise stated. Breakfast is included unless noted otherwise. All the hotels listed accept credit cards unless otherwise stated. Note that rates vary widely throughout the year.

For a key to the symbols, ▷ 2.

ANNE MA SOEUR ANNE

www.annemasoeuranne.com
In a beautiful late 19th-century heritage building in the upscale Plateau district, this is a chic boutique hotel right in the heart of the best Latin-Quarter shopping and eating out area. The decor is modern and stylish, with much use of wood and granite, and the excellent in-room facilities include high-speed wireless internet, voice mail, microwave, toaster-oven and coffee-maker. There's a pleasant small garden, and some of those balconies for which Montréal is famous.
✉ 4119 rue St.-Denis, Montréal, Québec, H2W 2M7 ☎ 514/281-3187, 877/281-

3187 🖑 $80–$265, including Continental breakfast (delivered to the room) ⓘ 17
🚇 🚉 Mont-Royal, Sherbrooke

AU GÎTE OLYMPIQUE

www.gomontrealgo.com
A warm welcome is assured at this B&B, not just from the owner, but from pet shnauzer Sasha. In addition to the ground-level lounge, there's a snug basement sitting room with rattan furniture and a second TV. Breakfast is taken at one large table in the dining room or, in summer, on garden terraces.
✉ 2752 boulevard Pie IX, Montréal, Québec, H1V 2E9 ☎ 514/254-5423, 888/254-5423 🖑 $105–$125, breakfast included ⓘ 5 (all non-smoking), 1 apartment 🚇 🚉 Pie I

AUBERGE DE LA FONTAINE

www.aubergedelafontaine.com
B&B (pictured above) in a peaceful location on Mont Royal, overlooking pretty Parc Lafontaine. Beautiful rooms and suites; some rooms have whirlpool tub, balcony or view over the park. Continental breakfast

buffet includes bread, pastries, cheese and cold meats, yogurt and fresh fruit. Guests have free access to kitchen noon to midnight for beverages and snacks, or to use the stove or microwave.
✉ 1301 rue Rachel Est, Montréal, Québec, H2J 2K1 ☎ 514/597-0166, 800/597-0597 🖑 $120–$289, breakfast included ⓘ 21
🚇 🚉 Mont Royal 🚌 14

AUBERGE DU VIEUX-PORT

www.aubergeduvieuxport.com
An 1882 building houses this fine hotel, with stone walls, wooden beams and gleaming hardwood floors. Bedrooms have huge brass or wooden beds, private bathroom, cable TV, stereo system and voice mail—there's even an umbrella. The roof terrace has wonderful views, and gourmet dinners are served here when the city puts on fireworks displays.
✉ 97 rue de la Commune Est, Montréal, Québec, H2Y 1J1 ☎ 514/876-0081, 888/660-7678 🖑 $175–$360 ⓘ 38 (all non-smoking) 🚇 🚉 Champ-de-Mars 🚌 55

CHÂTEAU VERSAILLES

www.versailleshotels.com

Renovation has added imaginative touches to the historic architectural features in this luxury hotel, with bold shades offset by ornate white plaster moldings and huge old fireplaces. The walls are hung with Matisse reproductions and the wooden furniture has been custom made. Bathrobes and Fruits et Passion bathroom packs are provided, and rooms all have cable TV, Nintendo, minibar, hairdryer, coffee-maker and modem point.

✉ 1659 rue Sherbrooke Ouest, Montréal, Québec, H3H 1E3 ☎ 514/933-8111, 888/933-8111 ♨ $165–$290 🛈 65 🌀 🅿 Guy-Concordia 🚍 15, 57, 165

FAIRMONT QUEEN ELIZABETH

www.fairmont.com

The choice of royalty and celebrities ever since it opened in 1958. John Lennon's famous bed-in, during which he wrote and recorded "Give Peace a Chance," was held here in Suite 1742 in 1969. Rooms have cable TV, Play Station and a video check-out facility. Premier rooms and suites have the best views. The Beaver Club restaurant is renowned for gastronomic dining, and there's a modern health club. Immediate access to the Underground City.

✉ 900 boulevard René Lévesque Ouest, Montréal, Québec, H3B 4A5 ☎ 514/861-3511, 800/257-7544 ♨ $189–$599 🛈 1,039 🌀 🔽 🛄 Indoor 🅿 Bonaventure 🚍 150, 410, 420, 535, 935

LE GERMAINE

www.hotelboutique.com

The theme at Le Germaine is stylish loft living, with natural lighting enhancing the earth tones, leather chairs, dark wood, glass and mirrors. Furniture is sleek and modern, beds have down comforters (duvets) and high-quality linen; other little luxuries include fresh fruit, bottled water, bathrobe, large-screen TV (with cable and VCR), minibar and CD-clock-radio.

✉ 2050 rue Mansfield, Montréal, Québec, H3A 1Y9 ☎ 514/849-2050, 877/333-2050

♨ $210–$275, breakfast included 🛈 101 (all non-smoking) 🌀 🔽 🅿 Peel 🚍 15

HOTEL LE SAINT-MALO

www.hotel-saint-malo.com

Convenient for the Musée des Beaux-Arts and the upscale shopping of the Faubourg Ste.-Catherine, this is a smart European-style hotel with well-lit rooms in restful shades that are accented by fine modern art prints and coordinating fabrics. All rooms have individual temperature controls, high-speed internet, cable TV, minibar and private bathroom.

✉ 1455 rue du Fort, Montréal, Québec, H3H 2C2 ☎ 514/931-7366 ♨ $105–$111 🌀 🅿 Guy-Concordia

MANOIR HARVARD

www.manoirharvard.com

Proudly displaying its Grand Prix du Tourisme awards, this picturesque B&B in a Victorian mansion offers five large rooms that are stylishly designed with plain, pale walls, dark antique furniture and hardwood floors. All have a private bathroom, and some overlook the beautiful garden, which guests are welcome to enjoy. Breakfasts are a real feast.

✉ 4805 avenue Harvard, Notre-Dame de Grâce, Montréal, Québec, H3X 3P1 ☎ 514/488-3570, 888/373-3570 ♨ $125–$175, breakfast included 🛈 5 (all non-smoking) 🌀 🅿 Villa Maria

PIERRE DU CALVET

www.pierreducalvet.ca

You won't find a more historic place to stay in Montréal. Built in 1725, the hotel is named after an influential free-thinker (they'll tell you his story if you ask). Built in typical French colonial style, it contains a pleasing array of antiques, family heirlooms and portraits. Bedrooms have some huge old beds, including four-posters, and such modern conveniences as modem points. Breakfast is served in the Greenhouse, a Victorian conservatory with plants, a fountain and exotic birds.

✉ 405 rue Bonsecours, Montréal, Québec, H2Y 3C3 ☎ 514/282-1725 ♨ $265–$325 🛈 9 🌀 🅿 Champ-de-Mars

RÉSIDENCES UNIVERSITAIRES DE L'UQAM

www.residences-uqam.qc.ca

Budget accommodations on campus, close to the lively Latin Quarter. The studio rooms, with one double bed, private bathroom and kitchen/dining area, are most compact; there are also two-bedroom units (one double, one single) with full kitchen and bathroom, and some with eight bedrooms that are good for groups. Bed linen and towels are provided, and there's a café and laundry room on the premises. Guests have the use of the university sports facility.

✉ 303 boulevard René Lévesque Est, Montréal, Québec, H2X 3Y3 ☎ 514/987-6669 🕐 Mid-May to mid-Aug ♨ $50–$60 🛈 432 🅿 Berri-UQAM 🚍 14, 15, 150

RUBY FOO'S

www.hotelrubyfoos.com

If you don't want to drive into the city, this motel is perfect, just off the Trans-Canada Highway. Rooms and two-bedroom suites are modern, with light-wood furniture, and some have kitchenettes. All rooms have cable TV, coffeemaker and high-speed internet access.

✉ 7655 boulevard Decarie, Montréal, Québec, H4P 2H2 ☎ 514/731-7701, 800/361-5419 ♨ $160–$255 🛈 198 🌀 🔽 🛄 Outdoor, heated

SQUARE PHILLIPS

www.squarephillips.com

This 10-story historic building was given a complete transformation and is now a superb apartment hotel, offering a range of modern studios and suites each with one or two separate bedrooms, space to work, free high-speed Internet, and a fully equipped kitchen, with stove, refrigerator, microwave, dishwasher and all the necessary pots and pans. You can be quite self-contained here, but the hotel also has a breakfast lounge, 24-hour valet and concierge servce and many other services.

✉ 1193 Place Phillips, Montréal, Québec H3B 3C9 ☎ 514/393-1193; 866/393-1193 ♨ $145–$323, including breakfast 🛈 160 🌀 🔽 🛄 Indoor 🅿 McGill

QUÉBEC CITY

Celebrating its 400th birthday in 2008 and the 250th anniversary of the Battle of the Plains of Abraham in 2009, Québec City is Canada's oldest city and was designated a UNESCO World Heritage Site in 1985. It is the capital of the province of Québec, and though it is smaller than Montréal, has a stately grandeur and an appealing array of French-style architecture and fine museums, galleries and heritage sites.

The city, on the north bank of the St. Lawrence River, is cut in two by a sheer cliff. On its top, the Upper Town has outgrown its still-complete 4.6km (3 miles) of city walls, but the area that lies within is a delightful historic ensemble in gray stone. The most prominent building here is the Château Frontenac hotel, in the style of a grand French château, on the place d'Armes. Spreading out from this focal point are narrow streets of elegant granite buildings and the wide boardwalk of the Terrasse Dufferin and Promenade des Gouverneurs, which skirt the clifftop and give magnificent river views. Here, too, is the Citadel, reflecting the city's strategic location, and the Plains of Abraham battle site.

Descend the 170 steps of the steep Escalier Casse-Cou (Breakneck Steps) or take the funicular down to the Lower Town, an atmospheric cluster of narrow cobblestone lanes lined by historic stone buildings, many of which house interesting little shops or restaurants. Centered on the place Royale, it's a pleasant place to wander and leads to riverside walkways. Also down here, the historic port area has had a facelift to provide recreational and cultural amenities.

Québec City is more than of historic interest, though. The cultural scene is vibrant and wide-ranging, there is a full calendar of festivals, such as the Snow Goose Festival and the Summer Festival, and plenty of land- and water-based activities.

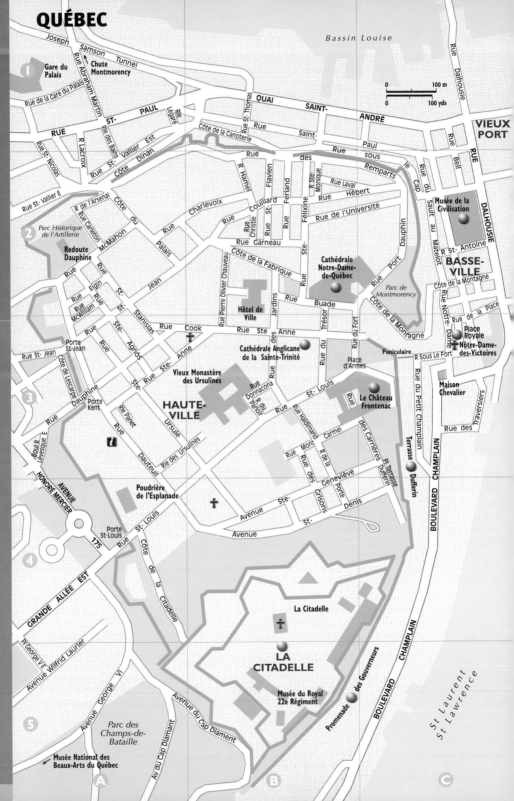

QUÉBEC

Bassin Louise

VIEUX PORT

Joseph
Samson
Tunnel

Gare du Palais
Chute Montmorency

Rue de la Gare du Palais
Rue Abraham Martin

RUE ST- PAUL

QUAI SAINT- ANDRÉ

R Lacroix
Rue des Bains
Rue St-Nicolas
Vallier Est
Côte Dinan
Côte de la Canoterie

Rue St. Thomas
Rue St- Thomas
Rue saint

Rue Paul sous les Remparts
le Cap
Rue du Sault au Matelot

Rue St- Vallier E
R de l'Arsenal
Rue Carleton
Côte du Palais
McMahon
Charlevoix
Rue Hamel
Flavien
Ferland
R Ste- Monique
Rue Laval
Rue Hébert

Musée de la Civilisation

Parc Historique de l'Artillerie

Redoute Dauphine
Rue
Rue Elgin
Rue McWilliam
St-
Stanislas
Ste- Agnès
Rue
Jean
Rue Christle
Couillard
Rue de l'Université
Félixine
R St-Antoine

BASSE-VILLE

Côte de la Montagne
Côte Notre-Dame

Rue Garneau
Côte de la Fabrique
Cathédrale Notre-Dame-de-Québec
Rue Port
Dauphin
Parc de Montmorency

Porte St-Jean
Côte de Lescarpe
Dauphine
Porte Kent
Cook
Rue Ste- Anne
Rue Pierre Olivier Chauveau
Jardins
Rue des
Hôtel de Ville
Buade
Trésor
Côte de la Montagne
Rue de la Place
Place Royale
Notre-Dame-des-Victoires

Rue St- Jean
Rue Ste- Anne
Cathédrale Anglicane de la Sainte-Trinité
Place d'Armes
Funiculaire
R Sous Le Fort

HAUTE-VILLE
Vieux Monastère des Ursulines
Rue Donnacona
R du Parloir
St- Louis
Rue du Fort
Le Château Frontenac
Maison Chevalier

Rie Panet
Rue
Ursule
Rie des Ursulines
Dauteuil
St- Louis
Rue Haldimand
Carmel
des Carrières
Rue des

Poudrière de l'Esplanade
Rue Mont-
R de la
Ste-
Pl. Terrasse Dufferin
Terrasse Dufferin

AVENUE HONORÉ MERCIER
Boul R Lévesque E
Avenue
Avenue Ste-
Genevieve
porte
Denis
Grisons
St-
BOULEVARD CHAMPLAIN
Rue du Petit Champlain

Porte St-Louis
Côte de la Citadelle
Rue St- Louis
175

GRANDE ALLÉE EST
Pl. George V E
Avenue Wilfrid Laurier
Avenue George VI
Av du Cap Diamant
Avenue du Cap Diamant

La Citadelle
LA CITADELLE
Musée du Royal 22e Régiment
Promenade des Gouverneurs
BOULEVARD CHAMPLAIN

St Laurent
St Lawrence

Parc des Champs-de-Bataille
Musée National des Beaux-Arts du Québec

0 — 100 m
0 — 100 yds

A   B   C

QUÉBEC CITY STREET INDEX

Left *The Montmorency Falls cascade down from the Laurentians into the St. Lawrence River*
Above *The archaic interior of Holy Trinity Anglican Cathedral*

CATHÉDRALE ANGLICANE DE LA SAINTE-TRINITÉ (HOLY TRINITY ANGLICAN CATHEDRAL)

www.ogs.net/cathedral

Standing behind a screen of trees, this wood-frame church, with its 47m-high (154ft) spire, was the first Anglican cathedral to be built outside the British Isles. Consecrated in 1804, it was modeled after the famous church of St. Martin-in-the-Fields in London's Trafalgar Square.

Holy Trinity is utterly Georgian in both feeling and atmosphere, hardly surprising since it was paid for by King George III. The interior is unexpectedly spacious. Its furnishings include the royal pew—decorated in royal blue and reserved for British sovereigns or their representatives. This, the bishop's chair and the box pews, were made of oak from Windsor royal forest.

✠ 94 B3 ✉ 31 rue des Jardins, Québec City, Québec, G1R 4L6 ☎ 418/692-2193 🕐 Daily ♿ Free 🎫 Guided tours May–end Oct

CATHÉDRALE NOTRE-DAME-DE-QUÉBEC (NOTRE-DAME CATHEDRAL)

www.patrimoine-religieux.com

Québec's Roman Catholic cathedral stands in the heart of the Upper Town, facing the Hôtel de Ville. Distinguished by its neoclassical facade and two dissimilar towers, the cathedral has an opulent interior. On entering, your eyes are imme-

diately drawn toward the sweeping wooden canopy high over the altar. Made by André Vermare and finished in gold, it glows in splendor.

During the 1759 siege, the cathedral was destroyed by British bombardments. Rebuilt soon afterward, it was destroyed again by fire in 1922, but was again rebuilt, to the original plans.

In 1993, a funeral chapel was dedicated to the first bishop of Québec, Monsignor de Laval. At its heart is a bronze statue of the bishop in a prone position, eyes toward the heavens. A map of his immense diocese is etched in the black granite floor.

✠ 94 B2 ✉ 16 rue de Buade, Québec City, Québec, G1R 4A1 (main entrance on rue Ste.-Famille) ☎ 418/694-0665 🕐 Daily, Mon–Sat from 7.30am, Sun from 8.30am. Closes at 4, 5 or 6pm, depending on season ♿ Adult $2, child (under 17) free; crypt: Adult $2, child (under 17) $1 🎫 Guided tours (call for hours)

CHÂTEAU FRONTENAC

www.fairmont.com/frontenac

This massive structure of green-roofed turrets and towers is Québec City's most stylish hotel (▷ 110–111), and is inextricably linked with the city's image. Named for one of the greatest and most flamboyant French governors, Louis de Buade, Comte de Frontenac, the original hotel was built by Bruce Price in 1893 for the Canadian Pacific

Railway, in the style of a Loire Valley château. The distinctive central tower was added in 1920–24.

Famous guests have included King George VI and Queen Elizabeth, Princess Grace of Monaco, Chiang Kai-shek, Charles de Gaulle, Ronald Reagan, François Mitterrand, Prince Andrew and Alfred Hitchcock. Château Frontenac hosted the Québec Conferences of World War II, when US President Franklin D. Roosevelt and British Prime Minister Winston Churchill planned the Normandy landings.

✠ 94 C3 ✉ 1 rue de Carrières, Québec City, Québec, G1R 4P5 ☎ 418/692-3861 🕐 Tours: daily ♿ $8.50

CHUTE MONTMORENCY (MONTMORENCY FALLS)

www.sepaq.com

No visit to Québec City would be complete without taking a trip to see this waterfall, just 15 minutes' drive from downtown. The Montmorency River cascades 83m (272ft) from the clifftop to a deep, bowl-shaped basin at an average rate of 35,000L (9,247 US gallons) per second—more during the spring melt. A 400th-anniversary initiative has introduced floodlighting of the falls after dark that makes a pretty scene. The visit begins with a ride up from the parking lot in an enclosed cable car, with spectacular views of the falls, the St. Lawrence River and the Île d'Orléans.

At the top there's a theater and the imposing Manoir Montmorency, with an interpretation centre and a good restaurant, then from here you walk on a level pathway along the clifftop to the Bridge over the Falls. This suspension bridge, 100m (328ft) above the top of the falls, provides an exciting view of the plummeting waters. The surrounding parkland offers excellent walks.

✠ Off map, 94 A1 ✉ Parc de la Chute Montmorency, 2490 avenue Royal, Beauport, Québec, G1C 1S1 ☎ 418/663-3330 🕐 Daily; Lower Park and cable car closed off season ♿ Cable car: adult $8.25, child (6–16) $4, family $26.50 round trip 🚗 10km (6 miles) east off Highway 440

INFORMATION

www.lacitadelle.qc.ca

✚ 94 B5 ✉ Citadelle mailing address: C.P. 6020, Succursale Haute-Ville, Québec City, Québec, G1R 4V7; access is via Côte de la Citadelle ☎ 418/694-2815 ♿ Admission by guided tour only (lasts 1 hour), Apr–end Oct several times daily (call for hours); Nov–end Mar daily 1.30pm 🕐 Adult $10, child (8–17) $5.50, family $22

INTRODUCTION

This vast defensive earthwork, covering 15ha (37 acres) is still an active military garrison, and if you wish to see the inside you must join one of the guided tours (led by soldiers) and stay with the group—whatever you do, don't wander off on your own. Once you have penetrated the vast array of moats and bastions and joined a tour, you will be taken onto a huge parade ground surrounded by buildings bearing the names of the various campaigns of the regiment, including Vimy, the Somme, Normandy and Korea. It's well worth walking around the *enceinte* (ramparts), either completely or in part.

The Citadelle was designed according to a defense system developed by the famous French military engineer Vauban, and is a four-pointed polygon, each point forming a bastion. Started in 1820, it took 30 years to complete and encloses two buildings constructed by the French, plus later additions. It is still a military base, home of the elite Royal 22e Régiment—the "Van Doos" (from Vingt Deux)—the Canadian army's only completely French regiment. It's also the summer home of the Governor General.

WHAT TO SEE

MUSÉE DU ROYAL 22E RÉGIMENT

www.r22er.com

This small museum, which you will visit on the tour, is located in a 1750 French powder magazine and an 1842 British military prison. It preserves historical documents, a collection of guns and small arms, insignias, medals, uniforms and other exhibits covering the history of the Royal 22nd. Don't miss the diorama illustrating the principal battles fought around Québec under the French regime. In summer, traditional military ceremonies such as the Changing of the Guard take place (Jun 24–early Sep daily 10am), and it's something to see. Soldiers in scarlet jackets and bearskin hats are accompanied by the regimental band and by Batisse, the regimental goat.

FORTIFICATIONS AND GATES
www.pc.gc.ca
An entire network of walls and gates, erected under both the French and English regimes, encircles the old part of the city of Québec, stretching over a total 4.6km (2.9 miles), making this the only historic district in North America to have preserved its ramparts.

Québec City was a site of great strategic and tactical importance to both the French and the British—the key to communication with the mother country, and the place where fresh supplies were stored and relief was housed. Its defense system therefore reflects the evolution of European fortification techniques from the 17th to 19th centuries, when more advance weaponry brought the era of fortified cities to an end. After the British garrison departed in 1871, there were plans to demolish what remained, but in 1874 Lord Dufferin (Governor General of Canada 1872–78) began a movement to preserve them. As a result, the Terrasse Dufferin was built over the cliffs (▷ 102–103), and the original narrow gates were replaced to provide easier movement between the old and new parts of town. The current St.-Louis and Kent gates were built between 1878 and 1881, and the St.-Jean Gate between 1938 and 1939. In 1983, Parks Canada rebuilt the Prescott Gate over Côte de la Montagne in order to complete the walkway.

Near the St.-Louis Gate is the Fortifications of Québec Initiation Centre and Esplanade Powder Magazine (May to mid-Oct 10–5), beneath the city's ramparts. Exhibitions concentrate on the history of Québec's defensive system. There's an interesting model illustrating the various fortification projects drawn up for the city. The powder magazine, built in 1815, is the only one to have been restored out of many gunpowder stores located here.
✉ Mailing address: 100 rue St.-Louis, PO Box 10, Station B Postal Terminal, Québec City, Québec, G1K 7A1 ☎ 418/648-7016 ⏰ Interpretation Centre, Esplanade Powder Magazine: early May to mid-Oct daily 10–5; rest of year by reservation ✋ Adult $3.90, child (6–16) $1.90 👆 Guided walks Jun to mid-Sep (extra charge)

ARTILLERY PARK NATIONAL HISTORIC SITE
www.pc.gc.ca
Artillery Park, in the heart of Old Québec, has a remarkable history. First used by French soldiers, it was occupied by the British garrison from 1763 to 1871, and its name comes from the Royal Artillery Regiment quartered here for most of that time. It later became an industrial complex comprising a munitions factory, workshops and foundries—the Québec Arsenal, the first of its kind in Canada. When it finally closed in 1964, the site was taken over by Parks Canada.

The Arsenal Foundry now serves as an interpretation and reception center, and contains a wonderful scale model of Québec City, made in 1808 in the tradition of military engineers. The Dauphine Redoubt, a remarkable fortified building, was originally equipped with a battery of cannon. Built by the French in 1712, it served as barracks before becoming home to the Arsenal superintendents. Inside, you can visit the 19th-century kitchen, the luxurious English officers' mess and the Arsenal superintendents' lounge. The officers' quarters have been restored with period furnishings.
✉ Mailing address: 2 rue d'Auteuil, PO Box 10, Station B, Québec City, Québec, G1K 7A1 ☎ 418/648-4205 ⏰ Artillery Grounds: all year; Arsenal Foundry, Dauphine Redoubt, Apr to mid-Oct daily 10–5, rest of year by reservation; Officers Quarters: early Jul–late Aug daily 10–5 ✋ Artillery Grounds: free. Arsenal Foundry, Dauphine Redoubt, Officers' Quarters: adult $4, child (6–16) $2

TIPS
» Don't arrive late for the Changing of the Guard—not even a minute—they won't let you in.
» Ceremonies can be cancelled because of bad weather or operational considerations.
» Try not to laugh when Batisse, the regimental goat, puts in an appearance.

Above left *This cannon atop the Citadelle gives a good idea of what potential attackers would have faced*
Below *Colorful military pomp is still a feature of this active garrison*

MUSÉE DE LA CIVILISATION (MUSEUM OF CIVILIZATION)

www.mcq.org

Located in the Lower Town close to the river, this museum, designed by architect Moshe Safdie, occupies a modern building that is beautifully integrated into the architecture of the old city. Its copper roof is pierced by stylized dormer windows, and it has a glass campanile and monumental staircase. The Maison Estèbe, a four-story French Regime stone house of 1751, is incorporated into the museum. Excavations carried out during construction unearthed many treasures.

Exhibitions are thematic devoted to civilization in the broadest sense. There's a wonderful collection of Québécois furniture, sculpture and crafts, as well as important Amerindian objects. The museum's lively integrated approach to history and culture adds a great deal of fun to the experience of discovery and works for all ages.

✠ 94 C2 ✉ 85 rue Dalhousie, C.P. 155, Succursale B, Québec City, Québec, G1K 7A6 ☎ 418/643-2158, 1-866/710-8031 ◷ Late Jun–early Sep daily 9.30–6.30; rest of year Tue–Sun 10–5 ✋ Adult $10, child (12–16) $4; free Tue Nov–May and Sat 10–12 Jan–Feb ▢ ▣

MUSÉE NATIONAL DES BEAUX-ARTS DU QUÉBEC (QUÉBEC ART GALLERY)

www.mnba.qc.ca

Québec's art gallery occupies two buildings on the Plains of Abraham. The original, constructed in 1933, was joined to a former prison in 1991 by a modern wing. The prison building, which retains the original cells, is more interesting architecturally than the rest. The Wolfe monument outside the museum marks the spot where British General James Wolfe died in the famous battle of 1759.

The permanent collection of more than 27,000 works is primarily devoted to Québec art. The early works are dominated by religious subjects and sculptures made for churches, and reflect the importance the Roman Catholic Church held in Québec society. Among the non-religious works are paintings by Jean-Paul Lemieux and Horatio Walker. The Brousseau Collection of Inuit Art, more than 2,500 works in various media, has been a highlight of the gallery since its acquisition in 2005.

✠ Off map, 94 A5 ✉ Parc des Champs-de-Bataille, Québec City, Québec, G1R 5H3 ☎ 418/643-2150, 1-866/220-2150 ◷ Jun–Sep 1 daily 10–6 (also Wed 6–9pm); rest of year Tue–Sun 10–5 (also Wed 5–9pm) ✋ Free; temporary exhibitions: adult $15, child (12–17) $4, family $30 H11 🍴 ▣

PLACE ROYALE

Place Royale is a delightful cobblestone square in the heart of the Lower Town. It is lined with tall stone houses in the French Regime style, rebuilt to give the square its original appearance (before it was blasted to bits by the British). At its heart is a bust of Louis XIV, a copy of the 1686 original that gave the square its name.

The Church of Notre-Dame-des-Victoires commemorates two victories over the British in the 17th and early 18th centuries.

The attractive adjoining streets reward exploration. Maison Chevalier, on rue de Marché Champlain, offers a free exhibition (Jul, Aug daily; Sep–end Jun weekends), featuring 18th- and 19th-century interior designs.

✠ 94 C3 🚋 Lower Town Funicular between Terrasse Dufferin and Lower Town, $1.75 one way (7.30am–11.30pm or midnight)

Right *Looking down on place Royale*
Below *Mural in place Royale*

INFORMATION

✚ 94 C3 ✉ Dufferin Terrace: adjoining place d'Armes in front of the Château Frontenac hotel
✚ 94 B5 ✉ Governors' Walk: access from the west end of the Dufferin Terrace or from avenue du Cap-Diamant in National Battlefields Park ☻ Promenade des Gouverneurs closed in snow and ice of winter, Nov–end Apr 👆 Free

INTRODUCTION

Stretching along the clifftop, these two connected boardwalks have stunning views across the river and the Lower Town. They start right in the heart of the Upper Town, outside the Château Frontenac Hotel, and from there it's a glorious—if in places vertiginous—route along the high cliffs to the Plains of Abraham. If you are daunted by the 310 steps up to the Plains of Abraham at the end, you can either just turn round and head back, or start out from the Plains of Abraham and go down the steps instead. The walk takes about 20 minutes each way (not counting climbing the steps). Since the river narrows at Québec City, there can be a wind-tunnel effect on more blustery days. In winter the snow is not cleared and the Promenade des Gouverneurs section may be closed. Other than that, it's good at any time of year and there are places along the way to get a drink or an ice cream.

WHAT TO SEE

TERRASSE DUFFERIN

There's something of the look of an English Edwardian seaside promenade to this wide, level boardwalk, with a grand hotel across the lawns to the rear and six wrought-iron gazebos—named Frontenac, Princess Louise, Lord Lorne, Victoria, Dufferin and Plessis—offering shelter from the summer sun. And yet this staid image is completely misleading. This is far more lively, with nice weather bringing out plenty of walkers, joggers and street entertainers, and the snow heralding the opening of the exciting toboggan run down the staircase. There are plenty of binocular stations along the way too, in case something catches your eye in the distance. Near the Château Frontenac, the Frontenac Kiosk houses the top of the funicular, which runs down to the Lower Town (▷ 100).

Above *The Terrasse Dufferin has superb views over the river*

The history of the Terrasse Dufferin is almost as interesting as the view. In 1630, Samuel de Champlain (whose statue stands here) moved up from the bottom of the cliff and built the first Château St. Louis here as a defense against the Iroquois and the English. This château served as the residence of the French and British governers until it was destroyed by fire in 1834. Lord Durham, the British governor at the time, built a platform over the ruins that was accessible to the public. It became such a popular visit that it was increased in size in 1854. In 1878–79, Governor General Lord Dufferin worked with architect Charles Baillairgé to extend the boardwalk once more as part of his vast beautification project for Québec ($\triangleright$ 99). It was opened on June 9, 1879 and has remained a cherished part of the city ever since. In 2005, reconstruction work began, and archeologists took the opportunity to investigate the site, revealing the remains of four forts and two châteaus on the site. Many artifacts and much knowledge about the city's early years were discovered.

PROMENADE DES GOUVERNEURS

Leading off from the end of the Terrace Dufferin, this boardwalk hugs the cliff-face about 90m (300ft) above the river, circling around beneath the outer wall of the Citadelle ($\triangleright$ 98–99) and Cap Dimant. The views are magnificent, encompassing the Lower Town, the St. Lawrence, the Île d'Orleans, and the town of Lévis on the opposite bank. On a clear day, you might even see Mont-Ste.-Anne. The Promenade, opened in 1960, culminates in the 310 steps up to the Plains of Abraham, site of the decisive battle in the Seven Years' War in which the British General James Wolfe defeated the Marqis de Montcalm's French troops.

TIP

» The town of Lévis, seen across the river, is pronounced "lay-vee". There's no more obvious way of declaring yourself a tourist than to pronounce it like the jeans..

Left *A cruise ship gleams at night while moored in the Old Port*

QUÉBEC CITY RAMPARTS

Not only is Québec the oldest city in Canada, it is also North America's only walled city, complete with a massive citadel, gates, and cannon. Strolling around these impressive fortifications is a unique way to appreciate its splendid site, captivating architecture and natural beauty. Historic Québec was added to UNESCO's World Heritage List in 1985.

THE WALK

Length: 5km (3 miles)

Allow: about 2 hours

Start and end at: Place d'Armes in front of the tourist office (Infotouriste) on rue Ste.-Anne

How to get there: Place d'Armes is in the heart of Québec City near the Château Frontenac hotel

★ From the place d'Armes, walk to your left toward the UNESCO monument. Behind it, there is a monument commemorating Samuel de Champlain, founder of Québec in 1608. You are now on the Terrasse Dufferin (▷ 102–103).

Walk along it to your right past the top of the cable car (funicular) to the Lower Town, and the covered pavilions. To your left, beyond the

Château Frontenac, is the Jardin du Gouverneurs, with its monument to both Wolfe and Montcalm. Cross the end of the toboggan slide to rue des Carrières and take the Escalier de la Terrasse up 65 steps to rue St.-Denis (there's a big sign for Parc des Champs de Bataille) and the Citadelle.

❶ Climb about another 50 steps for a really splendid view. High above the river and town, this is a great place to sit and picnic. You can look down into the outer moat of this formidable defense fortress whose construction began in 1820 on the orders of the Duke of Wellington.

Follow the star-shape of the Citadelle, to your right, to the main entrance, which you will see below

you. Cross the entrance road—Côte de la Citadelle. Bear right to follow the city walls. You might prefer to walk just inside the walls rather than on top of them. There are views ahead (outside the walls) of the Québec Parliament building and the Cross of Sacrifice, a memorial to Canadians who lost their lives in World War I.

❷ You then come to Porte St.-Louis (St.-Louis Gate), which is one of the three picturesque gates that were built into the walls between 1878 and 1881.

You can cross rue St.-Louis on top of the wall or you can descend to the street to visit the Fortifications of Québec Initiation Centre (summer months only). Return to the walls

Left *The striking Château Frontenac is named for a French governor, the Comte de Frontenac*
Above *The Château Frontenac overlooks the Terrasse Dufferin, a wide wooden boardwalk*

and continue along the top. To your left is the Québec Parliament and the site where the Ice Palace is constructed every February for the Québec winter Carnaval.

❸ Next you come to Porte Kent (Kent Gate) named after the Duke of Kent, father of Queen Victoria and Governor General of Canada 1792–94. Cross here to rue Dauphine.

The wall and path descend to Porte St.-Jean (St. Jean Gate), crossing rue St.-Jean and becoming place d'Youville, to your left. After crossing the Porte St/-Jean, you can descend into Parc de l'Artillerie (Artillery Park).

❹ Just inside the walls of this section of the Upper Town are several buildings, originally built for military purposes and later used to manufacture armaments. Until World War II, this was the Canadian Arsenal in Québec. To your right, a former armaments building is now an interpretive center (open summer months). Cross rue Richelieu. Parc de l'Artillerie continues with the Dauphine Redoubt (summer months), to your right. Built in 1712–48, it was part of the defense system that Governor Frontenac

put in place to defend the western side of the city. It was later used by British troops and then became a munitions factory in 1882.

Follow the walls and descend the steps. Cross Côte-du-Palais. The buildings of the Hôtel-Dieu loom ahead to the right. Continue to follow the walls—you are now on rue des Remparts, towards the northeast corner of the walls, with fine views over the city below. To your right is the Augustinian monastery. The Augustinian nuns founded the Hôtel-Dieu in 1637, making it the oldest hospital in North America. It's been on this site since 1644. Rue des Remparts swings to the right beyond rue Hébert, and there are views of the Château Frontenac ahead. Walk into Parc de Montmorency (Montmorency Park) from rue des Remparts.

❺ Montmorency Park was the site of the Canadian Parliament in 1850–66. Parliament met in the old Bishop's Palace. The palace burned

down, and by the time it was rebuilt Parliament had moved to Ottawa.

From the park, take the pedestrian bridge across Côte de la Montagne and climb the 83 steps back to place d'Armes.

WHEN TO GO
The walk is possible year-round, except in heavy snow; it's superb on a mild summer evening.

WHERE TO EAT
✉ Restaurant Gambrinus, 15 rue du Fort, ☎ 418/692-5144.

WHERE TO STAY
✉ Le Château de Pierre, 17 avenue Ste.-Geneviève, ☎ 418/694-0429.

SHOPPING

5 NATIONS INDIAN ART GALLERY

Originally founded as an outlet for Iroquois craft, this store now represents artists from First Nations throughout North America. There's another outlet on rue du Petit Champlain, and at Kahnawake (▷ 132).
✉ 20 rue Cul-de-Sac, Québec City, Québec, G1K 8L4 ☎ 418/692-1009 🕐 Daily 9–9 (shorter hours in winter) 🚌 1

ARTISANS DU BAS-CANADA

www.artisanscanada.com
For more than 50 years this family-run store has been providing a showcase for the work of around 500 Canadian artists and artisans. Everything here is guaranteed to be authentic.
✉ 30 Côte de la Fabrique, Québec City, Québec, G1R 3V7 ☎ 418/692-2109, 888-339-2109 🕐 Daily 10–6

BOUTIQUE CANADEAU

www.canadeau.com
On one of the main shopping streets of Old Québec City, this friendly store has a great range of Canadian-made products. In addition to Inuit soapstone sculptures from Nunavut, there are collector's knives, fur and leather items, exquisite gold jewelry and patterned tundra sweaters.

✉ 1124 rue St.-Jean, Québec City, Québec, G1R 1S4 ☎ 418/692-4850 🕐 Daily 10–6 🚌 800

LE CAPITAINE D'A BORD/ PLEIN AIR D'A BORD

www.capitainedabord.com
These twin stores—one with a nautical flavor, the other with landlubbers in mind—are close neighbors on the oldest street in North America. Under the same management, they stock a large range of sweaters, pants (trousers), footwear, waterproof jackets and shirts with labels like Lacoste, Paul and Shark and Michel Beaudouin.
✉ 59 and 63 rue du Petit-Champlain, Québec City, Québec, G1K 4H5 ☎ 418/694-0624 🕐 Mid-May to mid-Oct daily 9am–11pm; rest of year Thu–Fri 9–9, Sat–Wed 9–6

CHOCO-MUSÉE ÉRICO

www.chocomusee.com
The museum exploring the history of chocolate is interesting, of course, but it's the home-made chocolates that are the real attraction here. The finest French and Belgian chocolate covers delectable fillings with no artificial flavors or preservatives.
✉ 634 rue St.-Jean, Faubourg St.-Jean Baptiste, Québec City, Québec, G1R 1P8

☎ 418/524-2122 🕐 Daily 10–5.30 (to 9pm Thu–Fri), Sun 11–5.30 (May–late Sep may close later) 🚌 800, 801

CUIR LA POMME

www.lapomme.qc.ca
This is the outlet for the leather creations of more than a dozen Québec fashion designers. Exclusive garments are offered at extremely reasonable prices, and a multilingual staff is welcoming and helpful. If you don't see what you want, it can be tailored for you.
✉ 47 rue Sous-le-Fort, Québec City, Québec, G1K 4G9 ☎ 418/692-2875 🕐 Jun–end Oct daily 9am–10pm; rest of year daily 9.30–5.30 🚌 1 🚋 Petit Champlain, near bottom of cable car

GALERIES D'ART INUIT BROUSSEAU ET BROUSSEAU

www.artinuit.ca/sculptures
This gallery, next to Le Château Frontenac, is dedicated to promoting the work of the finest Inuit artists from Arctic Canada, and has a superb display of museum-quality pieces with a guarantee of authenticity. The staff are very knowledgeable, and purchases can be shipped abroad for you.
✉ 35 rue St.-Louis, Québec City, Québec, G1R 3Z2. Also at Pierres Vives, 23½ rue du

Petit-Champlain and 428-A rue Victoria, St. Lambert, Québec, G1K 4H5 ☎ 418/694-1828 ⏰ Daily 9.30–5.30

GALERIES DE LA CAPITALE
www.galeriesdelacapitale.com
This mega-mall (pictured opposite) has 280 stores, 30 food options and 20 visitor attractions, including a large indoor amusement park and an IMAX movie theater.
✉ 5401 boulevard des Galeries, Québec City, Québec, G2K 1N4 ☎ 418/627-5800 ⏰ Mon–Wed 9.30–5.30, Thu–Fri 9.30–9, Sat 9–5, Sun 10–5 (individual store hours may vary)

LIBRAIRIE DU NOUVEAU MONDE
Behind the Musée de la Civilisation, this store has books in English and French covering diverse subjects, with a good selection of Québec special interest titles.
✉ 103 rue St.-Pierre, Québec City, Québec, G1K 7A1 ☎ 418/694-9475 ⏰ Daily 9–6

LOUIS PERRIER JOAILLIER
www.louisperrier.com
In the heart of the Old City, Louis Perrier's store showcases stunning, elegant pieces of gold jewelry set with richly colored stones. Carrying on a 50-year family tradition, Louis' daughter, Brigitte, now heads a team of young designers. Pieces are not cheap, but they are hard to resist.
✉ 48 rue du Petit-Champlain, Québec, City, Québec, G1K 4H4 ☎ 418/692-4633 ⏰ Sat–Wed 10–5, Thu–Fri 10–9 🚌 1

PEAU SUR PEAU
www.peausurpeau.qc.ca
You can dress yourself up from head to toe in leather here, and then get a leather suitcase to pack it all in. Even if you don't want to buy, it's worth coming into the store just for the smell of leather. Everything comes from Québec or from international designers who use the best-quality skins for their original styles. They also have a shoe shop at 85 rue du Petit-Champlain.
✉ 70 boulevard Champlain, Québec City, Québec, G1K 4H7 ☎ 418/692-5132 ⏰ Sat–Wed 9–6, Thu–Fri 9–9

PLACE LAURIER
www.placelaurier.com
Eastern Canada's largest shopping mall, with 350 stores, anchored by Zellers, Sears and The Bay. Extended nine times since it was first built, it's a light, airy space with seemingly limitless choices for clothing, leisure, sports goods and homewares. Free mall services include coat-check and loan of strollers and wheelchairs.
✉ 2700 boulevard Laurier, Ste.-Foy, Québec, City, Québec, G1V 4J9 ☎ 418/651-5000, 800/322-1828 ⏰ Mon–Wed 10–5.30, Thu–Fri 10–9, Sat 9–5, Sun 12–5 (individual store hours may vary) 🚗 5km (3 miles) west near bridges on boulevard Laurier 🍴 Restaurants and fast food

LES PROMENADES DU VIEUX-QUÉBEC
More of an exclusive retail enclave than a mall in the usual sense, with just a dozen or so classy boutiques. The surroundings are equally chic, blending modern style with old wood and brass. Designer fashions for men, women and children, arts and crafts, jewelry, cosmetics, candies and Christmas items (year-round).
✉ Rue Buade or rue du Trésor, Québec City, Québec, G1R 4A2 ☎ 418/692-6000 ⏰ Daily 10–5

QUÉBEC PUBLIC MARKET
Markets are always entertaining, but add the French element—particularly the wonderful selections of cheeses—and you have something really special. This is a good place to buy maple syrup products, and the locally grown fruits and vegetables are excellent.
✉ 160 Quai St.-André, Québec City, Québec, G1K 7C3 ☎ 418/692-2517 ⏰ Apr–end Dec daily 10–6; Jan–end Mar Thu–Sun 🚌 Vieux Port area

ENTERTAINMENT AND NIGHTLIFE
CINEPLEX ODEON PLACE CHAREST
www.cineplex.com
Eight-screen movie theater showing the latest Hollywood releases in French and English.

✉ 500 rue du Pont, Québec City, Québec, G1K 6N4 ☎ 418/529-7771 ⏰ Programing starts around 2pm 🖐 Adult $8.50, child (under 14) $5.95; Tue $4.95 for all ages

GRAND THÉÂTRE DE QUÉBEC
www.grandtheatre.qc.ca
This is the premier theater in the province, home to Opera de Québec and the Québec Symphony Orchestra. Two concert halls provide a full schedule of dance, drama and music.
✉ 269 boulevard René-Lévesque Est, Québec City, Québec, G1R 2B3 ☎ 418/643-8131, 877/643-8131 ⏰ Year-round 🖐 $36–$150 🚌 800, 801

THÉÂTRE PETIT CHAMPLAIN
Atmospheric little galleried theater, with old stone walls. Regular performances by Francophone musicians of all kinds.
✉ 68 rue du Petit-Champlain, Québec, City, Québec, G1K 4H4 ☎ 418/692-2631 ⏰ Thu–Sat night 🖐 Varies

CAFÉ DES ARTS
This is an unusual place offering unusual entertainment of a more cerebral variety—mime, poetry, jazz and *chansons*.
✉ 1000 rue St.-Jean, Québec City, Québec, G1R 1R6 ☎ 418/694-1499 ⏰ Shows start around 8.30 🖐 Small cover charge; depends on show

FOR CHILDREN
PARC AQUARIUM DU QUÉBEC
www.sepaq.com
To build-up anticipation to the main attraction—an acrylic walk-through tunnel in a 350,000L (91,000 gal) tank with more than 650 marine animals—there are outdoor habitats for polar bears and seals, and a pavilion housing 3,500 fish. Dress for the cold.
✉ 1675 avenue des Hotels, Ste.-Foy, Québec City, Québec, G1W 4S3 ☎ 418/659-5264, 1-866/659-5264 ⏰ May–early Oct daily 10–5, rest of year daily 10–4 🖐 Adult $15.50, child (3–5) $5.50, child (6–12) $10.50, (13–17) $12.75, family $49 or $54.50

PRICES AND SYMBOLS

The restaurants are listed alphabetically. The prices are for a two-course lunch (L) and a three-course à la carte dinner (D). Prices in pubs are for a two-course lunchtime bar meal and a two-course dinner in the restaurant, unless specified otherwise. The wine price is for the least expensive bottle. For a key to the symbols, ▷ 2.

AU PETIT COIN BRETON

One of three locations in the city (also on boulevard Laurier and Grande Allée) serving around 80 varieties of crêpes. These range from the gourmet brunch variety (weekends only) to delicious desserts, with a huge variety of main-course fillings. There is also a large range of salads. Staff in costume evoke an atmosphere of old Brittany.

✉ 1029 rue St.-Jean, Québec City, Québec, G1R 1R9 ☎ 418/694-0758 ⏱ Mon–Wed 11–2, 5–9, Thu–Fri 11–10, Sat 9am–10pm ✋ L $10–$20, D $10–$20

AUX ANCIENS CANADIENS

www.auxancienscanadiens.qc.ca
Come here for Canadian cuisine at its finest, served in the oldest building in Québec City (1675). The menu features such local dishes as boar and pig's knuckles ragout with meatballs, meat pie with pheasant, buffalo casserole and caribou cooked with creamy blueberry wine sauce. Maple syrup features strongly in the desserts, and other sweet temptations include apple cheesecake with creamy caramel sauce.

✉ 34 rue St.-Louis, CP 175, Succursale Haute-Ville, Québec City, Québec, 1R 4P3 ☎ 418/692-1627 ⏱ Daily 12–9 ✋ L $22, D $35, Wine $39 🚌 7, 11

L'ASTRAL

www.loewshotels.com
You don't just come to this revolving restaurant for the stunning view; the French cuisine, utilizing fresh local ingredients, is accomplished and very tasty. You might start with a parfait of duck foie gras, cranberry and raisin bread and baby watercress salad with kiwi-champagne vinaigrette, followed by grilled salmon with sweetcorn foam, blackened butter, caramelized Anjou pears and sweet pea coulis. The evening sophisticated atmosphere is enhanced by the resident pianist.

✉ Loews Le Concorde Hotel, 1225 cours du Général-de-Montcalm, Québec City, Québec, G1R 4W6 ☎ 418/647-2222, 800/463-5256 ⏱ Mon–Fri 6.30am–11am, 11.45–3, 6–11pm; Sat 11.45–3, 5.45–11pm, Sun 10–3, 6–11pm ✋ L $35, D $45, Wine $30

CAFE DU MONDE

www.lecafedumonde.com
A huge map of the world adorns one wall, but this waterfront eatery is unmistakeably Parisian, from the stylish interior design to the five-spit French rotisserie to the classic bistro menu. *Steak-frites*, Toulouse sausage Dijonnaise, moules marinière, *bouillabaisse*,

beef tartare and black pudding with apples, onions and Calvados are all there, alongside a few pasta dishes and superior open sandwiches, and the brunch menu is definitely worth getting up for. Located at the Cruise Ship Terminal, the café has wonderful views over the river, and the open kitchen is fun to watch too.

✉ 84 rue Dalhousie, Québec City, Québec, G1K 4B2 ☎ 418/692-4455 ⊙ Mon–Fri 11.30am–11pm, Sat–Sun 9.30am–11pm ✋ L $25, D $40, Wine $26

LE COCHON DINGUE

www.cochondingue.com

For many years this restaurant has been a landmark in the city's eating out scene. Located in a century-old house, with a beautiful garden terrace, it offers great bistro favorites such as steak and fries, Burgundy pork stew, mussels, and Tartiflette, plus European-style sandwiches, home-made soups, salads, delicious desserts and breakfasts too. Fixed-price menus are good value.

✉ 46 boulevard René-Lévesque Ouest, Québec City, Québec G1R 2A4 ☎ 418/523-2013 ⊙ Mon–Wed 9.30–5.30, Thu–Fri 9.30–9, Sat–Sun 9.30–5 ✋ L $15, D $35, Wine $26

COMMENSAL

Québec City has a plethora of French restaurants, which are not noted for being particularly vegetarian-friendly, so this is a great find for those who don't eat meat. Healthy and ethical food is prepared using interesting recipes and you serve yourself from the hot and cold buffet, then pay by the weight on your plate. Bring your own wine.

✉ 80 rue St.-Jean, Québec City, Québec ☎ 418/647-3733 ⊙ Daily 11am–10pm ✋ L $15, D $20

LA CREMAILLIERE

This special occasion restaurant in an elegant historic building in the heart of the Upper Town is long-established and highly regarded for its fine French and Italian cuisine. Table d'hôte menus offer four or five courses, and main courses have included Québec red deer with grand

veneur sauce, Atlantic salmon with spinach leaves and a dash of curry and saffron sauce, rib of veal with herbs and white wine, and red tuna with tomatoes, olive oil and basil.

✉ 73 rue Ste.-Anne, Québec City, Québec, G1R 3X4 ☎ 418/692-2216 ⊙ Daily 11am–2.30, 5.30–11pm ✋ L $47, D $47, Wine $39

LAURIE RAPHAEL

www.laurieraphael.com

Here you will dine on the creations of one of Québec's foremost chefs, Daniel Vézina, whose innovative approach has earned many awards and accolades. Amid stunning decor you can sample such taste combinations as Nova Scotia scallops with coconut milk, black tea and exotic fruits. Equally excellent ideas are brought to dishes featuring Boileau deer, St.-Apolinaire duck and Gaspor Farm piglet, while desserts include classics with a modern twist. The fixed price "Chef! Chef!" menu is an exciting, good-value option. It also runs cookery classes, demonstrations, plus a boutique selling Québec artisan foods and products.

✉ 117 rue Dalhousie, Old Port, Québec City, Québec G1K 9C8 ☎ 418/692-4555 ⊙ Tue–Fri 11.30–2, 5.30–10, Sat 5.30–10 ✋ L $23, D $75, Wine $30

D'ORSAY

Exposed stone walls, gleaming dark wood and crisp white linen set the scene for the international cuisine. You might start with wood-smoked, rum-flavored salmon or snails with tomato and garlic sauce, followed by one of the sizzling fajita dishes, a classic pasta, mussels cooked in one of several sauces, or perhaps bison and beer osso bucco. There are plenty of choices, but save room for one of the delectable desserts.

✉ 65 rue de Buade, Québec City, Québec, G1R 4A2 ☎ 418/694-1582 ⊙ Daily 11.30am–3am ✋ L $35, D $45, Wine $24

PANACHE

www.saint-antoine.com

The massive wooden beams and rough stone walls of a former 19th-century warehouse have been

given a touch of modern chic, just as the traditional French Canadian cuisine on the menu has been given its own modern slant. The ingredients are sourced locally, so that you could choose Arctic char from Gaspesie, Cap St.-Ignace Guinea hen with lovage-scented jus, or St.-Appolinaire duck glazed with maple syrup. If you are up to it, there's a seven-course Signature Menu including wine selections for $169. There's an interesting breakfast menu, too.

✉ Auberge St.-Antoine, 8 rue St.-Antoine, Québec City, Québec, G1K 4C9 ☎ 418/692-2211, 888/692-2211 ⊙ Mon–Fri 6.30–10.30am, noon–2pm, 6–10pm, Sat–Sun 7–11am, 6–10pm ✋ L $35, D $75, Wine $35

RISTORANTE IL TEATRO

www.lecapitole.com

In the former Cinéma de Paris, so it's a perfect setting for a meal before or after a show. Fine Italian cuisine is accompanied by a good list of Italian wines, and the atmosphere is cozy and relaxed. There's a great terrace for summer dining, with a view of the fortifications and place d'Youville.

✉ Le Théâtre Capitole, 972 rue St.-Jean, Québec City, Québec, G1R 1R5 ☎ 418/694-9996, 800/238-3730 ⊙ Daily 7am until late evening ✋ L $30, D $50, Wine $30

VERSA

www.versarestaurant.com

With cool lighting and a simple, but stylish elegance, this is a magnet for the local trendy set. The menu is designed to amuse, with interesting combinations such as tempura breaded chicken with sweet-sour sauce and Jack Daniels, salmon tartar with wazabi mayonnaise, Rice Krispies and shallots, or shredded duck with deep-fried potatoes, raw milk cheese and a duck stock glaze. There's also an oyster bar and a canapé menu offered at the cocktail hour (5–7pm).

✉ 432 rue du Parvis, Nouvo St.-Roch, Québec City, Québec, G1K 6H8 ☎ 418/523-9995 ⊙ Mon–Fri 11.30am–11pm, Sat–Sun 5–10pm; bar open daily until 3am ✋ L $15, D $30, Wine $32

PRICES AND SYMBOLS

Prices are the starting price for a double room for one night, unless otherwise stated. Breakfast is included unless noted otherwise. All the hotels listed accept credit cards unless otherwise stated. Note that rates vary widely throughout the year.

For a key to the symbols, ▷ 2.

APPARTEMENTS-HOTEL BONSEJOURS

www.bonsejours.com

If you're staying for any length of time, this city-center apartment hotel offers the space to spread out and make a home away from home. The suites include a fully equipped kitchen or kitchenette and bathroom, and the larger ones have one or two bedrooms separate from the living area, accommodating up to six people. Just because you have a kitchen, you don't have to cook—there's a café on site and room service is available. You also get cable TV and free local telephone calls.
✉ 237 rue St.-Joseph Est, Québec, Québec, G1K 3A9 ☎ 418/681-4375, 866/892-8080 🖐 $85 ➊ 14 (all non-smoking) 🌀

AUBERGE INTERNATIONALE DE QUEBEC

www.cisq.org

Just because this is a hostel doesn't mean it's inconvenient. Located inside the old city walls, it's 15 minutes' walk from the train and bus stations and close to all the principal heritage sites. A member of the Hostelling International Network, the Auberge offers private and family rooms, with or without private shower room, in addition to shared dorms for between four and 12 guests (single-sex or co-ed).
✉ 19 rue Ste.-Ursule, Québec City, Québec, G1R 4E1 ☎ 418/694-0755, 866/694-0950 🖐 Private double room: $74; dorms $28 per person (higher rate includes breakfast) ➊ 62 (all non-smoking)

AUBERGE ST.-ANTOINE

www.saint-antoine.com

A massive restoration of a derelict warehouse has created a hotel of enormous character. Whether it's brick walls, huge beams and traditional-style furnishings, or clean lines, plain pastel walls and ultra-modern pieces; all have plenty of flair and just a touch of whimsy.

The 007 Suite has both in spades. Some rooms have a rooftop terrace or balcony.
✉ 8 rue St.-Antoine, Québec City, Québec, G1K 4C9 ☎ 418/692-2211 🖐 $249 ➊ 95 (89 non-smoking) 🌀

AUBERGE DU TRESOR INN

Claims to fame abound here, including the fact that it is the oldest inn in North America. There has indeed been an inn on this site since 1640, and none could deny its romantic ambience even were it not for the availability of "Romantic Packages" and "Romantic Dinners." The location simply cannot be faulted, facing the Château Frontenac across leafy place d'Armes in the heart of the Upper Town.
✉ 20 rue Ste.-Anne, Québec City, Québec, G1R 3X2 ☎ 418/694-1876, 800/566-1876 🖐 $80 ➊ 24 (all non-smoking) 🌀

LE CHÂTEAU FRONTENAC

www.fairmont.com

This landmark hotel is the city's most prestigious place to stay, with a commanding presence above it. The rooms are restful, in warm autumnal shades, with classic dark wood furniture, and have individual climate control. There's a superb leisure suite with large pool, kid's wading pool, whirlpool, steam rooms, exercise room and spa. The variety of eating options ranges from formal restaurant to bistro and afternoon teas.

✉ 1 rue des Carrières, Québec City, Québec, G1R 4P5 ☎ 418/692-3861, 800/257-7544, 800/441-1414 ✋ $179 🚻 618 🚭 📺 🏊 Indoor

GITE COTE DE LA MONTAGNE

www.gitedelamontagne.com

This historic building nestles beneath the imposing Château Frontenac. It has three spacious rooms, characterized by gleaming wooden floors and exposed stone walls, with private or shared bathroom and cable TV. There's a terrace with a lovely view of the river and the price includes a good breakfast.

✉ 54 côte de la Montagne, Québec City, Québec, G1K 3W3 ☎ 418/694-4414, 888-794-4414 ✋ $250 🚻 3 all non-smoking

GITE LA BOHEME

www.gites-classifies.qc.ca/boheme.htm

The cozy, color-coordinated bedrooms here have individual furnishings set against gleaming hardwood floors, and guests also have the use of a pleasant sitting room and pretty garden terrace. Breakfasts are particularly good, including lots of fresh fruit along with hot and cold dishes.

✉ 650 rue de la Reine, Québec City, Québec, G1K 2S1 ☎ 418/525-7832, 866/525-7832 ✋ $65 🚻 5 (all non-smoking) 🚭

HAYDEN'S WEXFORD HOUSE

www.haydenwexfordhouse.com

Dating from 1832, this splendid old stone house, bedecked with shutters and window boxes, was originally built for James Hayden from Wexford, Ireland—hence the name, which is emblazoned on the facade in its original form. The rooms, with sloping ceilings and dormer windows, are prettily

decorated and have queen-size beds; they share two luxurious modern bathrooms.

✉ 450 rue Champlain, Québec City, Québec, G1K 4J3 ☎ 418/687-5460 ✋ $110 🚻 3 (all non-smoking)

HOTEL MANOIR DE L'ESPLANADE

www.manoiresplanade.ca

Beautifully renovated, this 1845 building offers roomy accommodations that are full of character, including some exposed brick and stone walls, old fireplaces and high ceilings. The fourth-floor attic rooms are particularly pretty and have good views, but bear in mind that there's no elevator. Modern amenities include private bathroom, cable TV and free wireless Internet access in the rooms. At certain times a minimum stay of two nights is required.

✉ 83 rue d'Auteuil, Québec City, Québec, G1R 4C3 ☎ 418/694-0834 ✋ $95 🚻 36 (all non-smoking) 🚭

HOTEL-MUSEE PREMIERES NATIONS

www.maisonpremieresnations.com

It is worth venturing the 15–20 minute drive out of the city to stay at this unique luxury hotel in the heart of the Huron-Wendat lands. One building looks like a partly built wooden teepee and it has spacious modern interiors. Works by First Nations artisans adorn the walls and the gourmet restaurant offers a taste of traditional cuisine. All of the rooms and suites overlook the Akiawenrahk River and have every modern convenience. The area offers further tribal experiences along with walks through beautiful scenery.

✉ 5 place de la Rencontre "Ekionkiestha," Wendlake, Québec, G0A 4V0 ☎ 418/847-2222, 866/551-9222 ✋ $135 🚻 55 (all non-smoking) 🚗 North of city via Autoroute 73 (Highway 175) then east on Highway 369 (exit 150) or rue de la Faune (exit 154)

HOTEL PUR

www.hotelpur.com

Here you'll find another facet to a city that's noted primarily for its history. This is an ultra-modern, 18-story designer hotel located

on a chic downtown street full of fashion boutiques, hip restaurants and vibrant nightlife. In addition to the sleek and classy decor, luxurious bedlinen, pillow-top beds and down comforters (duvets), the rooms here have iPod compatible alarm clocks and big flat-screen TVs with on-demand movies. The hotel also has the city's largest indoor swimming pool and a fitness center.

✉ 395 rue de la Couronne, Québec City, Québec, G1K 7X4 ☎ 418/647-2611, 800/267-2002 ✋ $116 🚻 239 (215 non-smoking) 🚭 📺 🏊 Indoor

HÔTEL TERRASSE-DUFFERIN

www.terrasse-dufferin.com

With its quiet but spectacular location overlooking the St. Lawrence River close to the Chateau Frontenac, this small hotel has simple rooms and more elaborate suites with kitchen facilities and splendid views. It combines the Chateau's location with extremely reasonable prices.

✉ 6 place de la Terrasse-Dufferin, Québec City, Québec, G1R 4N5 ☎ 418/694-9472, 800/694-9472 ✋ $79 🚻 22 (all non-smoking) 🚭 Most units

L'HÔTEL DU VIEUX QUÉBEC

www.hvq.com

This is a privately owned hotel standing in a prime location within the walls of North America's only fortified city. There's a very friendly atmosphere throughout, and the owners offer free guided walks in July and August. A rather eccentric arrangement of staircases leads to an array of no-frills rooms that reflect the age of the building, some with exposed stone walls and sloping ceilings, and all with private bathroom, cable TV and mini-refrigerator. Local calls are free. A lively bistro-restaurant spills onto the sidewalk in summer.

✉ 1190 rue St.-Jean, Québec City, Québec, G1R 1S6 ☎ 418/692-1850, 800/361-7787 ✋ $109–$239; high-season rate includes continental breakfast 🚻 41 (23 non-smoking) 🚭

QUÉBEC PROVINCE

Québec is Canada's largest province and, as the heartland of its French population, the only province where French is the official language (though there are few here who don't understand English). The province covers more than 1.6 million sq km and stretches nearly 2,000km (1,240 miles) from the US border to the Arctic Ocean. The variety in the landscapes is truly remarkable—gentle pastures, vast forests, mountains more than 1,600m (5,250ft) high, craggy coastlines, more than a million lakes and rivers, and inhospitable tundra populated only by the hardiest wildlife.

Most of the population inhabits the southern quarter, and most sizeable towns and cities, including Québec City and Montréal, cluster along the St. Lawrence River, a historic lifeline and still a busy waterway for freight, cruise ships and leisure craft. South of the river are the fertile lands of the Cantons de l'Est and, farther east, the Gaspésie peninsula, which juts out into the Gulf of St. Lawrence and contains one of the province's highest peaks, Mont Jacques-Cartier. North of the river there's the glorious Saguenay Fjord, with the whale-watching center of Tadoussac at its mouth and lovely Lac St.-Jean to the north. Conveniently close to Montréal is the winter sports resort of Mont-Tremblant, while over in the west the Gatineau Valley is renowned for brilliant fall colors to rival Vermont.

Though the climate can be brutal in winter, Québec summers are beautiful, and it is renowned for food production—wonderful cheeses, maple syrup, organic fruit and vegetables, all kinds of meat and poultry, and even vineyards. Wild game is plentiful, the lakes and rivers are full of freshwater fish, and the Gulf of St. Lawrence gives up a succulent bounty. Pair this with Québec's French culinary heritage and you can expect some of the finest food in North America in the company of friendly locals who take pride and pleasure in sharing it with you.

Left *United Church reflected in the lake at Knowlton* **Above** *Lake Maphrémagog, Magog*

CANADIAN MUSEUM OF CIVILIZATION
▷ 116–117.

CANTONS-DE-L'EST (EASTERN TOWNSHIPS)
www.easterntownships.org
Land of mountains, lakes and delightful villages, the Eastern Townships are a unique mixture of Anglo-Saxon charm and Québécois joie de vivre. Despite their name, they are actually in the southwest of the province, just east of Montréal. After the American Revolution, the land along the border east of that city was surveyed and granted to Loyalists, mainly from New England, who preferred to live on British soil rather than in the new United States. The towns and villages reflect their heritage. From 1850 on, however, more and more French-speaking people moved into the region, and today the population is more than 50 percent Francophone.

The mountains here are part of the Appalachian Chain. Nearly 1,000m (3,280ft) high, they are rolling and tree-covered, with lakes filling the valleys. Montréalers escape to the ski slopes in winter and the lakes in summer. For visitors, there are delightful villages and a stunningly located abbey.

Knowlton is an attractive Victorian village with a variety of craft stores, art galleries, restaurants, and boutiques on England Hill, which descends to the mill stream. It is now part of the municipality of Lac-Brome, and the buildings are an eclectic mix of styles—including some costly homes on the shores of the lake. Ducks reared here are a delicacy in many of the local restaurants.

Magog has a wonderful site on the north end of beautiful Lake Memphrémagog. Summer boat trips (mid-May to end Sep daily) give constantly changing views of islands and the surrounding Appalachian peaks, notably Mt. Orford. A monastery, on the shores of the lake, has a fairy-tale quality, with striking white-granite and multicolored-brick buildings. The splendid modern church is open to the public. The monks are famous for Gregorian chant (Eucharist 11am, Vespers 5pm). They also raise Charolais cows and produce cheese, notably L'Ermite and St. Benoit.

The forested Mt. Orford National Park covers 57sq km (22sq miles) of the Appalachians and is dominated by its namesake mountain, which rises 876m (2,873ft). It's a popular ski resort, and in summer it is sometimes possible to take the chairlift up Mt. Orford for a magnificent view of Lake Memphrémagog and the surrounding mountains.

Granby Zoo, with 1,000 animals, is a great attraction for children (▷ 132).

✚ 406 U17 ℹ Tourisme Cantons-de-l'Est, 20 rue Don-Bosco Sud, Sherbrooke, Québec, J1L 1W4 ☎ 819/820-2020, 800/355-5755

CHARLEVOIX COAST
▷ 118–119.

GASPÉSIE
▷ 120–122.

ÎLE D'ANTICOSTI
www.sepaq.com
Nature lovers in search of tranquillity will adore Anticosti. Just over 300 people live on this huge island (covering nearly 8,000sq km/ 3,120sq miles), which resembles a giant cork in the mouth of the St. Lawrence estuary. It is a paradise for birders (up to 220 species, including bald eagles, have been spotted here). Impressive rock formations, caverns and waterfalls have been carved out of its fossil-rich limestone, and about 200 shipwrecks lie off the island's rocky shores.

If you can, plan at least a two-day visit; the Anticosti Reserve, run by Sépaq (a government agency), offers summer (Jun–end Aug) and winter (mid-Jan to mid-Apr) vacation packages of differing lengths that include air transfer, accommodations in inns or cabins; meals and rental of a four-wheel-drive vehicle, essential for getting around. Be sure to include a trip to the spectacular Vauréal Falls. The limestone cliffs rise dramatically from Baie de la Tour, 24km (15 miles) east of Vauréal Falls and the falls plunge 76m (249ft) into a steep-walled canyon.

Anticosti was once part of the seigniory of Louis Jolliet, who explored the Mississippi. In 1895, it was purchased for $125,000 by wealthy French chocolate-maker Henri Menier as a private hunting and fishing reserve. Menier introduced, among other things, 220 white-tailed deer; today, the herd numbers, conservatively, 120,000, the greatest concentration of these deer in North America. Menier is commemorated in the name of the island's only community, Port-Menier.

✚ 407 W14 ℹ Sépaq, Box 179, Port-Menier, Québec, G0G 2Y0 ☎ 418/535-0156, 800/665-6527)

CANADIAN MUSEUM OF CIVILIZATION

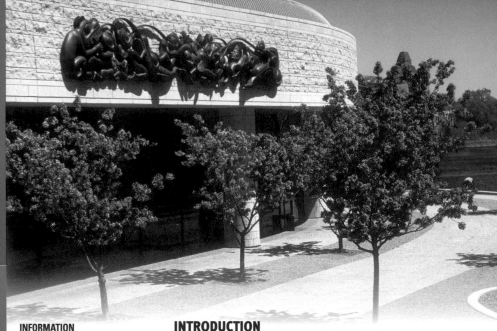

INFORMATION

www.civilization.ca

✚ 221 A2 ✉ 100 Laurier Street, Gatineau, Québec, K1A 0M8 ☎ 819/776-7000, 800/555-5621 🕙 May–Jun, Sep to mid-Oct daily 9–6 (also Thu 6–9); Jul–end Aug daily 9–6 (also Thu–Fri 6–9); mid-Oct to end Apr Tue–Sun 9–5 (also Thu 5–9 and Mon during March break) 💺 Adult $10, child (3–12) $6 or (over 12) $8, family $25; free Thu 4–9. Combined tickets available with IMAX Theatre, Canadian War Museum and special exhibitions 🎧 45-min tours of permanent galleries and selected temporary exhibitions (register at information desk, where schedules are available); $3 🍴 Café du Musée: elegant restaurant, outdoor terrace in summer 🍽 Voyageurs Cafeteria; Café Express; Café du Musée 🎁 Canadian crafts and souvenirs

Above *This wonderful museum presents Canada's history in a lively and entertaining way*

INTRODUCTION

This is one of Canada's finest museums, with fabulous displays on the culture and traditions of First Nations and settlers, all housed in a spectacular building.

Established in 1856, it is one of the oldest museums in North America. It started out in Montréal as the collection of the Geological Survey of Canada, then was moved to Ottawa, where it soon outgrew its Metcalf Street home. In 1982 the federal government launched a plan to rehouse the museum in a purpose-designed building across the river and seven years (and £340 million) later it opened in its current location. Douglas Cardinal, of Edmonton, Alberta, was the architect and his flowing building—there are no straight lines—has become not only a much-loved addition to the Ottawa riverscape but also an icon of Canadian architecture.

The museum has four levels of galleries, plus gardens outside and on the roof, so even if you have all day to spend here, there could well be just too much to fit in. The first thing to do is pick up a museum map in the lobby and prioritize your options. You might also want to find out about the times of the 45-minute guided tours of certain galleries (and register for any that you want to take), and get show times for the IMAX theater.

WHAT TO SEE

THE GRAND HALL AND FIRST PEOPLES

From the outside, the museum's curved lines and stylistic features give some hint of the rich First Nations culture to be found inside, but little can prepare you for the breathtaking Grand Hall, stretching the full four-story height of the museum, with floor-to-ceiling windows all along one wall. Here, displays focus on the supremely artistic West Coast tribes, with six replica houses on a simulated shoreline and forest background, dotted with the biggest and best collection of totems in the world. The array of incredible carvings include works by the renowned artist, Bill Reid (1920–1998), whose mother was of the Haida nation.

LEVEL TWO

Level two has several areas where temporary exhibitions are staged. Here too is the Canadian Postal Museum, showing the development of communications in this vast country, right up to the latest technological systems, and the Canadian Children's Museum. This interactive area leads young visitors through an International Village where they can learn through play and interaction with museum staff. The entrance to the IMAX theater is on this level.

CANADA, PLACES AND PEOPLE

On level three, the Canada Hall is a fascinating portrayal of various environments spanning the entire country and 1,000 years of history, from the early Viking visitors through the 1890s. Here you can explore around 20 re-created historic streets and individual buildings, with related artifacts, with highlights including a New France town square, a sumptuous merchant's townhouse and an Ontario shopping street. As you tour this part of the museum, be prepared for some of the exhibits engaging you in conversation. The resident theater company, Dramamuse, bring many of the scenes quite literally to life. They interpret the displays in an entertaining way, using a blend of scripted scenes and interactive improvisation, so they will answer questions from visitors about the lives of their characters, who include a fur trader, innkeeper, Victorian lady, and others.

LEVEL FOUR

Up on level four, the museum's newest exhibit, "Face to Face," is about people rather than places. You can discover first hand, through recordings and memoirs, the stories of people who have helped in one way or another to shape the country, together with related photographs and artifacts.

TIPS

» The Grand Hall has storytelling, native performance and craft demonstrations.
» The museum gardens are delightful— a Japanese Garden up on the roof, and Canada Garden at ground level, with native plants. There's also a kids' play area.

Left *History comes to life at the Canadian Museum of Civilization*

CHARLEVOIX COAST

INFORMATION

www.tourisme-charlevoix.com

✚ 406 U16 ℹ Association Touristique Régionale de Charlevoix, 495 boulevard de Comporté, La Malbaie, Québec, G5A 3G3 ☎ 418/665-4454, 800/667-2276

INTRODUCTION

The Charlevoix Coast, on the north shore of the St. Lawrence River, is a UNESCO World Biosphere Reserve, with captivating mountain, river and village scenes. Officially it starts in Beaupré, northeast of Québec City, and finishes at Tadoussac on the Saguenay River. It is one of Québec's most varied and beautiful regions, a combination of mountains sweeping down to the water's edge, attractive villages nestling in the valleys, and the mighty St. Lawrence. It is rural and wild, with ever-changing views of the river and the opposite shore, and on a bright summer day it is stunning. Whale-watching tours leave from Tadoussac, and Baie-Ste.-Catherine has a viewpoint high above the river on Pointe-Noire on Highway 138, just before the descent to the Saguenay—as well as the views, there are displays and films on the marine mammals.

The name Charlevoix comes from the Jesuit father François-Xavier de Charlevoix (1682–1761), the first historian of New France. As early as the 1760s, people visited the Charlevoix for its beauty. Later, lavish summer homes were built in places like La Malbaie, and cruise ships brought wealthy tourists to its shores. In 1899, Canada Steamship Lines built the enormous Manoir Richelieu as a luxury hotel.

WHAT TO SEE

WHALES

Every June, whales swim from the Atlantic up the St. Lawrence to the deep waters off Tadoussac at the mouth of the Saguenay River, waters that are rich in all kinds of flora and fauna. The tidal St. Lawrence sweeps into its tributary every day and in turn is invaded by the freshwaters of the Saguenay, creating a habitat where plankton flourish. This attracts small fish and shellfish on which the whales feed. It is a wonderful experience to see these huge creatures. The most common species are fin and minke, and there is a resident population of white whales (belugas). Occasionally, humpback whales are seen, and if you are very lucky you may glimpse the great blue whale, the biggest mammal on earth, which can be as long as 30m (98ft).

All through the summer there are whale-watching cruises from the wharf at Tadoussac. The St. Lawrence River is more than 10km (6 miles) wide at this point, and it is in the middle that the whales rise to the surface. Great jets of water issue from their blowholes just before they surface, so it isn't too difficult to locate them. There are wonderful views of Tadoussac, the mouth of the Saguenay and the 15m-high (50ft) lighthouse that marks the junction of the two rivers.

CHARLEVOIX COMMUNITIES

A row of attractive communities lies strung out along the Charlevoix Coast. Baie-St.-Paul has a beautiful site among rolling hills on the bay formed by the Gouffre River as it joins the St. Lawrence. It has inspired many artists and today there are a dozen or more art galleries in the town, giving Baie-St.-Paul an enviable reputation as a cultural center. High in the hills on the west side, the Maison de Tourisme de Baie-St.-Paul has displays on the Charlevoix crater and fine views.

Les Éboulements sits more than 300m (1,000ft) above the river, with splendid views. In 1710, Pierre Tremblay settled here and had a large family. He is the ancestor of all the Tremblays living in Québec today—the Montréal telephone directory lists nearly 6,000.

St.-Joseph-de-la-Rive, an old ship-building community squeezed between the St. Lawrence and the mountains, has lovely views of Les Éboulements, the river and the enchanting Isle-aux-Coudres, which can be reached by ferry from St.-Joseph. This island, 11km (7 miles) long and up to 5km (3 miles) wide, is a haven of rural peace and charm. In 1535, Jacques Cartier named it for the hazelnut trees (*coudriers*) that once grew here in abundance. From Pointe-de-l'Islet at the southern end there are exceptional views of Baie-St.-Paul, while from Pointe-du-Bout-d'en-Bas at the northern end, Les Éboulements can be seen high on its cliff. Ste-Irénée is best known for the prestigious international music festival held between late June and August at the Domaine Forget Music and Dance Academy.

Three communities hug the shores of La Malbaie—Pointe-au-Pic, Cap-à-Aigle and La Malbaie itself. Legend has it that the bay was given its name, *malle baye* (bad bay), in 1608 by Samuel de Champlain, founder of Québec City, who anchored his ships offshore only to find that by the next tide they had run aground. Since the 19th century La Malbaie has been a popular resort, its most famous hotel being the Manoir Richelieu in Pointe-au-Pic, a vast château and casino overlooking the St. Lawrence. Pointe-au-Pic has recently been designated a Canadian National Historic Site, generally percieved to be a precursor to UNESCO World Heritage listing, for its importance as a historic resort.

The pretty cove of Port-au-Persil on the St. Lawrence has long been a favorite with artists, and has a tiny church and a small waterfall.

Left *Low tide in the harbor of Baie-St.-Paul*
Below left *Detail of the interior of the cathedral of Ste.-Anne-de-Beaupré*
Below right *Baie-St.-Paul has many delightful art and craft galleries*

GASPÉSIE

INTRODUCTION

Also known as the Gaspé Peninsula, this rugged, remote area of eastern Québec juts into the Gulf of St. Lawrence between Chaleur Bay and the mouth of the river. It is about 240km (150 miles) long and 115–135km (70–85 miles) wide, with a mountainous, forested interior divided by rivers and lakes and a glorious scenic coast with fossil beds of worldwide renown. Its highest peak is Mont-Jacques Cartier (1,268m/4,160ft) in the Chic-Choc Mountains (▷ 128–129 drive and ▷ 130–131 walk).

It was in 1534 that French explorer Jacques Cartier planted a cross at Gaspé, claiming the land in the name of the king of France. There's a running dispute about where exactly he put this cross—a stone cross in front of the cathedral commemorates the event, and there's a bronze monument on the cliff top in front of the Musée de la Gaspésie. Both spots have their champions. From the Mi'kmaq to the arrival of Jacques Cartier, the Acadians, the Loyalists, and the settlers from the British Isles, people came here to exploit the rich fisheries.

WHAT TO SEE

FORILLON NATIONAL PARK

This wonderful park is like a massive tilted block arising from the sea. Shaped by erosion, it has a rugged coastline of sheer limestone cliffs, notably Cap Bon Ami and Cap Gaspé on the north side. The interpretive center in Cap-des-Rosiers has large aquariums, displays and films. Plaques along a short discovery trail explain the geographical features of the park and describe its wildlife. Cruises (late Jun–early Sep) leave the nearby wharf to view the cliffs up close.
✚ 407 W14 ℹ 122 boulevard de Gaspé, Gaspé, Québec, G4X 1A9 ☎ 418/368-5505; 1-888/773-8888; daily 🅿 Adult $7.80, child (6–16) $3.90, family $19.60

GASPÉ

The administrative and commercial center of the peninsula, Gaspé has a fine hillside site, dominated by a former religious building on the hilltop, which

INFORMATION

www.tourisme-gaspesie.com
✚ 407 V15 ℹ Association Touristique Régionale de la Gaspésie, 357 Route de la Mer, Ste-Flavie, Québec, G0J 2L0 ☎ 418/755-2223, 1-800/463-0323

Above *A traditional clapboard house overlooking the sea*
Left *The Ste. Anne River in Gaspésie Provincial Park*

Above *Aerial view of the coastal village of Percé, with the Rocher Percé beyond*
Opposite *Pilgrims flock to Cap-de-la-Madeleine Shrine, Trois-Rivières*

today houses the hospital. The Cathédrale de Christ-Roi is an all-wood structure built in 1969, its somewhat strange exterior contrasting with the spacious and impressively simple interior. The back wall is dominated by a luminous abstract glass window by Claude Théberge and Pierre Osterrath. Gaspé is where Jacques Cartier claimed New France for France in 1534, and the Musée de la Gaspésie includes an excellent exhibit on him (late Jun–late Oct daily 9–5 or 6, rest of year Mon–Fri 9–12, 1–4.30, Sun 1–4.30).

✚ 407 W14 ℹ 27 boulevard York East, Gaspé, Québec, G4X 2K9 ☎ 418/368-8525

PARC NATIONAL DE LA GASPÉSIE

Encompassing the highest peaks of the Chic-Choc Mountains, including Mont-Jacques Cartier, Mont-Albert, whose unique ecosystem fosters the survival of rare plants, Mont-Richardson, and Mont Ste.-Anne (▷ 130–131), the park covers 802sq km (310sq miles). The park has an important conservation role to play, protecting a representative sample of Québec Appalachians wildlife, such as caribou, moose and deer. It offers 140km (87 miles) of hiking trails in its deep valleys and forested slopes, including the Ernest-Laforce trail which is easily accessible by car; information is available at the interpretive center.

✚ 406 V15 ℹ 900 route du Parc, Ste-Anne-des-Monts, Québec, G4V 2E3 ☎ 418/763-3181
⏱ Daily 🎟 Adult $3.50, child (6–17) $1.50, family $7

PERCÉ

Percé is the scenic culmination of the Gaspé Peninsula. Here, the rock has been squeezed, folded and pushed into an incredible variety of cliffs, bays and hills. Most famous of all is the great pierced rock, Rocher Percé, a limestone block 438m (1,437ft) long and 88m (289ft) high, formed by layers of sediment deposited on the seabed about 375 million years ago. It had two arches until 1848, when one collapsed, leaving just one hole and a separate block known as the Obelisk. A boat trip to Bonaventure Island (mid-May to mid-Oct daily) passes close to the rock and then makes a circular tour of the island, which is famous for its seabirds, especially the huge gannet colony (an estimated 110,000 birds) on the cliffs on the far side.

✚ 407 W15 ℹ 142 route 132, Percé, Québec, G0C 2L0 ☎ 418/782-5448

BATTLE OF THE RESTIGOUCHE NATIONAL HISTORIC SITE

The final naval battle between France and Britain for possession of North America took place at the mouth of the Restigouche River. The French were defeated on July 8, 1760, sealing the fate of New France. On display are remains of the French frigate *Machault*, part of a relief expedition dispatched to retake Québec, which had fallen to the British the previous fall. A dramatic interpretation re-creates the battle.

✚ 406 V15 ✉ Highway 132, Pointe-à-la-Croix, Québec, G0C 1L0 ☎ 418/788-5676,
1-888/773-8888 ⏱ Jun to mid-Oct daily 9–5 🎟 Adult $3.90, child (6–16) $1.90, family $9.80

PARC NATIONAL DE MIGUASHA

The remarkably rich fossil beds exposed in a cliff on the shores of Chaleur Bay are protected in the Parc du Miguasha and are included on the UNESCO World Heritage List. A walk along the "Evolution of Life" trail will take you back in time, with information boards along the way documenting the evolution of living creatures from prehistory to the present day. The museum holds a diverse collection of more than 10,000 fossils—among them some truly impressive specimens—going back 380 million years, including some that help us to understand how fish evolved into land animals.

✚ 406 V15 ✉ 231 Route Miguasha Ovest, Nouvelle, Québec, G0C 2E0 ☎ 418/794-2475
⏱ Jun–end Aug daily 9–6; Sep to mid-Oct daily 9–5; mid-Oct to end May Mon–Fri 8.30–12, 1–4.30; closed over Christmas break 🎟 Park: adult $3.50, child (6–17) $1.50, family $7.
Museum: adult $12, child (6–17) $5.50, family $27.50

ÎLE D'ORLÉANS
www.iledorleans.com

Beautiful and fertile, the almond-shaped Île d'Orléans is about 40km (25 miles) long and sits wedged in the St. Lawrence River as it widens after passing Québec City. Settled by the French in the early 17th century, it has Norman-style stone farmhouses, ancestral country homes and several fine old churches. Église St-Pierre (May–end Oct daily), built in 1717–19 and now classified as an historic monument, is Québec's oldest country church.

The island is noted for its fresh produce, and in summer it becomes a vast open-air market, with vegetables and fruit—especially strawberries—on sale at roadside stands. You can visit a cheese dairy, sugar-shacks, vineyards, cidermakers, and pick-your-own fruit farms, and there's also a *chocolaterie* in Ste-Pétronille (year round), at the western end of the island.

The jewel of the island is the meticulously restored Manoir Mauvide-Genest (late Jun to mid-Oct daily) in St-Jean, a French manor house built in 1734. Costumed guides re-create the life of a wealthy seigneur during the French regime.

✚ 406 U16 ℹ Chambre de Commerce de l'Île d'Orléans, 490 Côte du Pont, St-Pierre, Québec, G0A 4E0 ☎ 418/828-9411, 866/941-9411

LAC ST-JEAN
www.tourismesaguenaylacsaintjean. qc.ca

Named for Father Jean Dequen, who visited its shores in 1647,
Lac St-Jean was originally called Piékouagami (Flat Lake) by the Montagnais. Large (1,350sq km/ 526sq miles) and saucer-shaped, it is the source of the mighty Saguenay River and supports a highly prized species of trout known as *ouananiche*.

In 1912, French author Louis Hémon stayed in the village of Péribonka and was inspired to write his beautiful love story *Maria Chapdelaine*, which is celebrated at the Louis Hémon Museum (Jun-Sep daily; Oct-May Mon–Fri). The author's life is traced from his birth in Brittany to his tragic death, at the age of 33, under a train in Chapleau, Ontario.

On a magnificent site beside falls on the Ouiatchouan River is the fascinating deserted village of Val-Jalbert (May–end Oct daily), once a flourishing mill town. After the mill closed in 1927, the population drifted away and the village fell into ruins, but it has since been re-created as a tourist attraction. The 400-step climb (or cable-car ride) to the top of the 72m (236ft) falls is rewarded with lovely views.

✚ 406 U16 ℹ Fédération Touristique Régionale du Saguenay-Lac-St-Jean, 412 boulevard Saguenay Est, Bureau 100, Chicoutimi, Québec, G7H 7Y8 ☎ 418/543-9778, 877/253-8387

LES LAURENTIDES
▷ 124–125.

SAGUENAY FJORD
▷ 126–127.

TROIS-RIVIÈRES
www.tourismetroisrivieres.com

An important industrial hub especially noted for its pulp and paper mills, Trois-Rivières stands at the confluence of the St. Lawrence and Maurice Rivers. At its mouth, this mighty tributary branches around two islands—hence the name Trois-Rivières (Three Rivers). In 1634, Samuel de Champlain sent the Sieur de Laviolette to establish a fur trading post here, making Trois-Rivières the second-oldest settlement in New France.

Some of the oldest buildings stand on rue des Ursulines. The most striking is the Ursuline Convent, with its silver dome and large wall sundial, built soon after the Ursulines arrived in 1697. A museum (mid-Mar to late Apr Wed–Sun 1–5; late Apr–early Nov Tue–Sun 10–5; rest of year by appointment) tells the story. Other attractions include the Québec Museum of Folk Culture (Jun–early Sep Mon–Fri 10–6, rest of year Tue–Sun 10–5) and the Pulp and Paper Exhibition Centre (Jun–Oct daily 10–6).

In Cap-de-la-Madeleine, a twin community, the river mysteriously froze over in the mild winter of 1878–79 just long enough for the inhabitants to cross it carrying stone to build a new church. In gratitude, the parish priest created a shrine devoted to the Virgin in the old chapel and, ever since, pilgrims have flocked to the site. In 1964, the gorgeous octagonal Rosary Basilica (daily) was built to accommodate them. It is huge and has a magnificent interior with seating for 6,000 and no columns to block the view.

Les Forges du St-Maurice (mid-May to mid-Oct daily), the old ironworks on the banks of the St. Maurice River, was Canada's first industrial community, and iron was smelted here between 1730 and 1883. The blast furnace and forges are open to visitors.

✚ 406 U17 ℹ 1457 rue Notre-Dame Centre, Trois-Rivières, Québec, G9A 4X4 ☎ 819/375-1122, 800/313-1173

LES LAURENTIDES

INTRODUCTION

The Québec Laurentians stretch right across the province north of the St. Lawrence River. The mountains were formed in Precambrian times, more than 500 million years ago, and are part of the Canadian or Laurentian Shield, a vast horseshoe of land that nearly encircles Hudson Bay.

Few people lived here before the arrival in the mid-19th century of a Roman Catholic priest, Antoine Labelle, who devoted his life to persuading his fellow French Canadians to settle in the Laurentians rather than seeking work in the "Protestant" United States. Labelle founded more than 20 parishes north of Montréal; today, most of these are still named after their parish saint, such as St.-Jérôme, St.-Sauveur, Ste.-Adèle, Ste.-Agathe and Ste.-Marguerite.

LAURENTIAN RESORTS

The 1930s saw the beginning of the ski industry, and the parishes turned into retreats for wealthy Montréalers. Boating, swimming, fishing, hiking, horseback riding and golf are popular pastimes in the summer, while in the fall the tree-clad mountains become a riot of color and attract many visitors. St.-Sauveur-des-Monts, the oldest resort, is surrounded by mountains. Often called "La Petite Suisse des Laurentides," the village abounds in restaurants. The main street, rue Principale, has little boutiques and handicraft stores, while the nearby parish church sports a distinctive silver roof and steeple.

The lively resort of Ste.-Agathe is located around the lovely Lac-des-Sables (Sandy Lake). A boat cruise on the lake (early Jun to mid-Oct daily) enables you to see the palatial residences where many famous visitors have stayed, including Jacqueline Kennedy, Queen Elizabeth II and Baron Von Ribbentrop.

The resort of Tremblant, surrounded by wilderness, is an amazing place. The striking buildings here house every type of restaurant, bar, boutique and accommodations imaginable. The resort takes its name from the Laurentians' highest peak, Mont-Tremblant (960m/3,150ft), which dominates the site—the streams tumbling off this great ridge create the sensation of trembling.

INFORMATION

www.laurentides.com
www.tremblant.ca
✚ 412 U17 ℹ️ Association Touristique des Laurentides, Porte du Nord (exit 51, Autoroute 15) ☎ 450/224-7007, 800/561-6673; mailing address: Tourisme Laurentides, 14 142 rue de la Chapelle, Mirabel, Québec, J7J 2C8

Tremblant

✚ 412 T17 ℹ️ 48 chemin de Brébeuf, Mont-Tremblant, Québec J8E 3B1
☎ 819/425-9930 ℹ️ 5080 montée Ryan, Mont-Tremblant, Québec, J8E 1S4
☎ 819/425-2434

Above *The Village Pietonnier is at the heart of the Tremblant resort*
Opposite *The church in Ste.-Adele*

SAGUENAY FJORD

INFORMATION
www.tourismesaguenaylacsaintjean.
qc.ca

✚ 406 U16 ℹ️ Fédération Touristique
Régionale du Saguenay-Lac-St.-Jean,
412 boulevard Saguenay Est, Bureau
100, Chicoutimi, Québec, G7H 7Y8
☎ 418/543-9778, 877/253-8387

INTRODUCTION

The Saguenay is not a long river by any means, but it is incredibly dramatic. It flows out of Lac-St-Jean (▷ 123), drops about 90m (300ft) through a wild and rocky upper section, then, for its final 60km (37 miles), it is transformed into a deep and majestic fjord—the most southerly fjord in the northern hemisphere, in fact. In places it can be as wide as 1,500m (5,000ft), and it has an average depth of 240m (787ft). Few highways touch its edges, and by far the best way to appreciate its stark and dramatic natural beauty is from the water. Cruises on the fjord are among the most impressive and popular activities in Québec, and are available from both Tadoussac and Chicoutimi.

The deep channel through which the Saguenay flows beyond Chicoutimi was gouged by glaciers 60 million years ago. When the ice receded, the sea invaded, and today tidewaters still reach Chicoutimi. The upper section of the river has been extensively harnessed for industry—La Baie, on a magnificent site on an inlet of the fjord, is dominated by port installations and aluminum plants, but the town also has the award-winning Musée du Fjord (late Jun–early Sep daily; rest of year Tue–Fri all day, Sat–Sun afternoons), which explores the ecology and geology of the area. The bay is actually called Baie des Ha! Ha!— according to local legend, early explorers, who mistook it for the main stream, gave it this name, "ha ha" meaning dead end. In contrast, human influence is unknown in the lower section of the river and the scenery is gloriously unspoilt.

The Saguenay region was struck by a great flash flood in mid-July 1996, which caused extensive damage in La Baie and Chicoutimi, leveling an entire neighborhood and forcing the evacuation of 16,000 people. Canada's first billion-dollar natural disaster, it had the unexpected benefit of covering the highly toxic sediments at the bottom of the Saguenay and Ha! Ha! rivers with a thick layer of new sediment, thus neutralizing the threat to the ecosytem.

Above *Saguenay Fjord, as seen from above Ste.-Rose-du-Nord*

WHAT TO SEE

CAP TRINITÉ

The highlight of any cruise on the fjord is the arrival at dramatic Cap Trinité, which rises 500m (1,600ft) out of the dark waters. The name comes from the three ledges that punctuate the face of the cape; on the first of these, about 180m (600ft) above the water, there is a statue of the Virgin, carved in 1881 by Louis Jobin. He undertook the work at the request of Charles-Napoléon Robitaille, whose life was saved twice after an appeal to the Virgin. The statue, which stands 9m (30ft) high, had to be transported here by boat, then painstakingly raised into position in three separate sections. Energetic visitors can walk the steep path in the Parc du Saguenay (▷ below) to the top of Cap Trinité and then descend to the statue, from where there is a superb view.

VIEWPOINTS

It is quite possible to enjoy the fjord from the land—viewpoints are accessible from Highway 172 on the north side, and also from Highway 170 on the south side. The pretty village of Ste.-Rose-du-Nord has an exceptional site with excellent vistas, especially from the wharf. From St-Fulgence there are views of the final stretches of the fjord. In the city of Chicoutimi there's a marvelous panorama from Croix de Ste.-Anne (St. Anne's Cross) on the north side of the Saguenay. Late-afternoon light is best for photography here. From the wharf in the community of L'Anse-St.-Jean on the St. Jean River, there are more great views and a covered bridge, built over the river in 1929.

PARC DU SAGUENAY (SAGUENAY PARK)

This park was created in 1983 to protect the edges of the fjord, and covers about 284sq km (110sq miles) between La Baie and Tadoussac. The most popular and accessible section is on the edge of Baie-Éternité, where the Éternité River joins the main stream. This is one of the most attractive coves on the Saguenay, dominated by twin capes, Trinité and Éternité. An interpretive center has displays on the origins of the fjord.

✚ 406 U16 ✉ Saguenay-St. Lawrence Marine Park Headquarters 91 Notre-Dame, Rivière-Éternité, Québec, G0V 1P0 ☎ 418/272-1556 ⏲ Baie-Éternité: daily; trails closed mid-Nov to mid-Dec and Apr. Baie-Ste.-Marguerite and Baie-du-Moulin-à-Baude areas: mid-May to end Oct ✋ Adult $3.50, child (6–17) $1.50, family $7

TIP

» The trail in the Parc du Saguenay that leads to the statue of the Virgin is plagued by mosquitoes in midsummer, so apply plenty of repellent.

Above *Whale-watching trips are well organized and very popular*
Left *One of the whales that frequent Saguenay Fjord*

THE RESPLENDENT GASPÉ PENINSULA

This drive offers some of the most dramatic landscapes in all of Québec, including the extraordinary cliffs of Forillon National Park, and culminates in the scenic wonder of Percé. The native peoples, the Mi'kmaq, called it *gespeq,* meaning "end of land."

THE DRIVE

Distance: 237km (147 miles)
Allow: 2 days if possible
Start: Just before Grande-Vallée on the north shore
End: Grande-Rivière on the south shore on Highway 132
How to get there: The start point is on Highway 132

★ Just before Highway 132 descends into Grande-Vallée, there is a turnout (pull-off, or lay-by) with a fine view of the town nestled around its bay. Highway 132 winds up and down, between water level, sometimes high above it. Drive 64km (40 miles) to Rivière-au-Renard.

❶ Rivière-au-Renard is the most important fishing community of Gaspésie. There are commercial wharves, fish-processing plants and an impressive fishing fleet. Today, shellfish dominates the market.

Continue 6km (4 miles). You will pass an information office for Forillon National Park on the right. To spend time in the park you must purchase a daily permit (Jun–end Oct). About 10km (6 miles) from Rivière-au-Renard is L'Anse-au-Griffon.

❷ This small fishing community's name may come from a ship, the *Griffon,* or it may refer to the gray color of the seabed—*gris fonds.* As you drive through, notice the large yellow clapboard house on the right. The Manoir LeBouthillier was built in the 1850s by John LeBouthillier, a wealthy cod merchant and exporter from Jersey, in the Channel Islands. This was a second home, for business trips, and is open to the public (Jun to mid-Oct daily).

Some 11km (7 miles) farther on is Cap-des-Rosiers.

❸ Stop at the lighthouse, Canada's tallest, for views of Cap Bon Ami and Cap Gaspé. It stands in a park with picnic tables and amenities.

After leaving Cap-des-Rosiers, you enter Forillon National Park.

❹ This wonderful park is like a huge tilted block rising from the sea. Shaped by erosion, it has a rugged coastline of sheer limestone. It is worth detouring to the Interpretive Centre, 2km (1.2 miles) along the Cap Bon Ami road (mid-Jun to mid-Sep).

Continue on Highway 132 across the peninsula. The mountains are part of the Appalachian chain, which starts far to the south in Alabama, USA. The final 50km (31 miles) of the International Appalachian Trail cross the park to end at Cap Gaspé.

⑤ About 8km (5 miles) farther, you will get a sudden view of the Baie de Gaspé and beyond, toward Percé. If it is clear, you may be able to distinguish the famous rock.

Continue 11km (7 miles) to Penouille Peninsula and Information Centre.

⑥ This sandy protrusion into the bay boasts the best beach in the area. You can walk or bicycle (no cars allowed) along the 4km (2-mile) trail or take the small train (mid-Jun to end Aug, modest fee).

Highway 132 leaves Forillon National Park and detours around the Baie de Gaspé crossing the Dartmouth River at its mouth by a long bridge. After driving 20km (12 miles) from Penouille (or 42km/26 miles from Cap-des-Rosiers) you reach Gaspé.

⑦ Gaspé is the administrative and commercial hub of the peninsula. Dominated by a former religious building, which today houses the hospital, the town has a fine site on a hillside sloping down to the York

Opposite *Jagged rock formations on the coastline of Forillon National Park*
Below *A waterfall cascades down a mossy rock face in the park*

River where it joins the Dartmouth River as it widens out to become the Baie de Gaspé.

Leave Gaspé by the bridge over the York River and turn left, keeping on Highway 132. (Avoid Highway 198.) After 48km (30 miles), at Pointe-St.-Pierre, take rue du Quai, on the left, for a short distance to the water's edge and a view of the famous rock at Percé. Rocher Percé disappears from view as you begin your entry to Percé by a steep, winding, undulating route over about 6km (4 miles).

⑧ Renowned for its beauty, Percé is the scenic culmination of the Gaspé Peninsula. Most famous of all is the great pierced rock that gave the town its name. Rocher Percé is a huge limestone block 438m (1,437ft) long and 88m (289ft) high. Until 1848, it had two arches. Then one of them collapsed, leaving just one hole and a separate block known as the Obelisk. You can park in the town and walk out (at low tide) to the rock. You can hike to the top of Mont-Ste.-Anne (▷ 130–131), take the boat tour to Bonaventure Island (▷ 122), or admire the fine views from all of Percé's headlands.

Drive 9km (5.5 miles) from Percé to L'Anse-à-Beaufils.

⑨ This small community has a general store, built in 1928, which still has its original wainscoting (paneling) and a collection of period tools (Jun to mid-Sep).

Continue 7km (4 miles) to reach Cap d'Espoir, the last place with a view of Percé. The coast now begins to swing west for 16km (10 miles) to Grande-Rivière, where the drive ends.

WHEN TO GO
Boats cross to Bonaventure Island only from June to mid-October; Percé is splendid year round, but can get overcrowded in season.

WHERE TO EAT
✉ Restaurant de la Vallée, 44 St.-François-Xavier O, Grande-Vallée ☎ 418/393-2880
✉ Restaurant Adams, 20 rue Adams, Gaspé ☎ 418/368-4949

WHERE TO STAY
✉ Motel Atlantique, 1334 Highway 132, Cap-des-Rosiers, Gaspé ☎ 418/892-5533
✉ Motel Adams, 20 rue Adams, Gaspé ☎ 418/368-2244

PANORAMA FROM MONT-STE.-ANNE

The summit of Québec's Mont-Ste.-Anne, visible from afar in the Gulf of St. Lawrence, offers magnificent panoramas of the town of Percé, the surrounding area (including Bonaventure Island), and, if conditions are clear, the coast of New Brunswick and Île d'Anticosti. The reddish conglomerate rock dramatically distinguishes it from the limestone of Rocher Percé.

THE WALK

Distance: 5km (3 miles)
Allow: at least 2.5 hours
Start/end: Church of St.-Michel-de-Percé, on rue de l'Église
Ascent: 320m (1,100ft)
How to get there: Take Highway 132 along the north coast of Gaspésie, then follow directions to Percé as detailed in the drive, ▷ 128–129

★ There's some parking next to the church; otherwise town parking areas are not far away. Walk behind the church and follow the rough

gravel road signed "Chemin du Mont-Ste.-Anne." Walk about 500m (540 yards) until you reach a trail intersection; take the left fork. The trail continues to climb steeply. In another 500m (540 yards), you come to the Belvédère One viewpoint.

❶ From here there's a splendid view over the town, its famous rock and the stone church from where you set off.

Instead of continuing on the main trail, take the Sentier des Belvédères

by the viewpoint on your right. This woodland trail is more pleasant than the main trail, and takes in two more viewpoints.

❷ From Belvédère Two, you can see Bonaventure Island, the famous bird sanctuary (▷ 122). From Belvédère Three, the view is much the same as from Belvédère One except that you are higher. The town of Percé below was an important fishing center for many years. The Mi'kmaq came here for the cod, and a French fishing station was established in 1673.

Above *The statue of St. Anne*
Left *The famous limestone Rocher Percé*
Below *Mont-Ste-Anne's Belvedere One has spectacular views*

It was, however, after the British conquest that development really began. In 1781, Charles Robin came from Jersey and established the Robins Company to market cod. By 1850, the company owned about 30 buildings, many of which still stand, and by the end of the century, Percé was Canada's cod capital. In 1912 the railroad arrived, followed by the road in 1920. These brought tourists, today the lifeblood of Percé since there are practically no cod left.

The Sentier des Belvédères rejoins the main trail, which climbs very steeply. You will get a view of the mountain peak ahead. The trail climbs the north side of the peak; the south side falls away very abruptly. At this point, you seem to be almost directly on top of the *rocher*. Another 1km (0.6 miles) along, you'll see the intersection of the Sentier de la Falaise trail, but continue up the main trail—you can descend by this alternate trail from the summit. The main trail is very obvious, because it is used by ATVs (All Terrain Vehicles) and thus wider and rutted. Some 500m (540 yards) along, having climbed 320m (1,050ft), you reach the summit.

❸ The statue of St. Anne here is the focus of pilgrimages in summer, especially on July 26, St. Anne's day. The mountain was a holy place for the native peoples, who talked of "the god on the mountain." The French dedicated the summit to St. Anne, the patron saint of fishermen, because its height made it a landmark for shipping in the gulf. The view embraces the whole bay, Bonaventure Island and, to your right, the coast of New Brunswick. The land that you can see in front and to the left is the Île d'Anticosti (▷ 115).

Take the Sentier de la Falaise trail for the first part of the descent. It is only very slightly longer, and less steep than the road. About 500m (540 yards) down, you come to lookouts Belvédères Four and Five, which offer the best views of Percé. You can avoid Belvédère Four and return directly to the main trail if you wish to save a few minutes.

❹ The peninsulas visible below are, right to left: Cap Blanc, Cap Canon, Mont Joli (with a cross), Cap Barré, Les Trois Soeurs (Three Sisters), and the Pic de l'Aurore.

Rejoin the main trail and be prepared for a steep descent. Don't try to do it too quickly and don't look directly down if you suffer from vertigo! On your right, you will pass the beginning and end points of the Sentier des Belvédères and other trails. On the main trail, signs indicate that the descent will be 10 percent over the next section. On reaching the intersection with the Chemin de la Grotto, turn right to return to the church.

WHEN TO GO
Unless you want to join them, avoid the summer pilgrimage days, notably July 26, when the route is crowded with followers.

PUBLIC RESTROOMS
There are wilderness latrines at the summit.

WHERE TO EAT
✉ Café le Croque-Lune, 162 Highway 132 Ouest, Percé ☎ 418/782-2911
You can purchase food for a picnic at the Boulangerie Le Fournand on Percé's main street (194 Highway 132 Ouest ☎ 418/782-2211).

WHERE TO STAY
✉ Hotel-Motel Manoir de Percé, 212 Highway 132 Ouest, Percé ☎ 418/782-2022

CHICOUTIMI

ECCE MUNDO

www.eccemundo.com

Spectacular and sophisticated show featuring dance through the ages—classical to jazz and rock 'n' roll—plus acrobatics, and song (in six languages).

✉ C.P. 1252, Chicoutimi, Québec, G7H 5G7 ☎ 418/549-4101, 800/563-4101 ⏰ Jul, Aug Tue–Sun 💰 Adult $45, child (under 12) $20

GATINEAU

CASINO DU LAC-LEAMY

www.casino-du-lac-leamy.com

Gaming, entertainment and conference complex with more than 60 tables, 1,800 slots, ritzy shows in the performance hall and interior gardens. Patrons must be over 18, and there's a dress code.

✉ 1 Boulevard du Casino, Gatineau, Québec, J8Y 6W3 ☎ 819/772-2100, 800/665-2274 ⏰ Daily 9am–4am 💰 Casino free; performances from $15 🚌 Outaouais bus: 21 🚗 East of downtown Ottawa across Ottawa River 🍴 Bars and restaurants

IMAX

www.civilization.ca/imax.html

In the Canadian Museum of Civilization (▷ 116–117), this big-screen theater shows large-format movies with surround sound.

✉ 100 Laurier Street, Gatineau, Québec, J8X 4H2 ☎ 819/776-7000 ⏰ Daily 10–10 (call for info about English screenings) 💰 Adult $9.50, child (under 13) $7 or (14–17) $8. Combined ticket with museum: adult $17, child $10 🚗 8 from Ottawa

GRANBY

LA FLAMME

www.la-flamme.com

Check out this family business that specializes in warm fabric, leather and fur coats by Québec designers—Simon Chang, Marisa Minicucci, Hilary Radley, Jane Adams—and top international names.

✉ 328 rue Principale, Granby, Québec, J2G 2W4 ☎ 450/378-8484 ⏰ Mon–Sat 9–5.30 (till 9 Thu–Fri)

GRANBY ZOO AND AMAZOO

www.zoodegranby.com

There are more than 800 animals here, including the big ones children love—elephants, giraffes, bears, gorillas, alligators, camels—in addition to smaller ones such as meerkats, monkeys and tiny Przewalski's horses. Also animal rides and a waterpark.

✉ 525 rue St.-Hubert, Granby, Québec, J2G 5P3 ☎ 450/372-9113, 877/472-6299 ⏰ May–late Aug daily 10–7; late Aug to mid-Oct Sat–Sun 10–5 💰 Adult $23.99, child (2–4) $10.99, (5–12) $17.99 🚗 At intersection of routes 112 and 139 🍴 Various restaurants

PALACE DE GRANBY

www.ovation.qc.ca

Features touring theater companies, music of all kinds—rock, singer-songwriters, classical, opera and other events.

✉ 135 Principale, Bureau 20, Granby, Québec, J2G 2V1 ☎ 450/375-2262, 800/387-2262 ⏰ Year-round 💰 From $25

KAHNAWAKE

5 NATIONS INDIAN ART GALLERY

Within the Mohawk Territory of Kahnawake, this is the largest gallery of Iroquois art in Canada, housed in a beautiful wood building. Inside is a wonderful array of arts and crafts, all fashioned from natural resources. It's part of a heritage village where you can visit longhouses, watch traditional dancing, and see buffalo, deer and horses.

✉ Route 138 Est, P.O. Box 1679, Kahnawake, Québec, J0L 1B0 ☎ 450/632-1059 ⏰ Daily 9–5 🚇 Angrignon, then bus 🚌 CITSO Kahnawake bus 🚗 10 minutes from Montréal, between Mercier Bridge and highways 20, 15 and 10

KNOWLTON
THEATRE LAC BROOME
www.theatrelacbroome.ca
Professional summer theatre is hosted here, with an eclectic mix of classical and innovative drama and musicals. Shows are in English.

✉ 9 Mont-Echo, Knowlton, Québec, J0E 1V0 ☎ 450/242-2270 (box office) ⏰ Jun–end Aug Tue–Sat 8pm (also 2pm Thu) 💲 $10–$35 🚗 Downtown, south of intersection of Knowlton and Lakeside roads

MONTEBELLO
PARC OMEGA
www.parc-omega.com
Here you drive through the 600ha (1,500-acre) enclosure and see wild animals, including bison, bear, boar, moose and wolves, in their natural habitats. Station FM88.1 on the car radio gives information about the animals. Out of the car, there's a deer enclosure to wander through, an otter pool and birds of prey.

✉ Route 323 North, Montebello, Québec, J0V 1L0 ☎ 819/423-5487 ⏰ Summer daily 9.30–6; winter 10–4 💲 Adult $13, child (6–15) $9, child (2–5) $5 🚗 2km (1.2 miles) north of Montebello on Highway 323 🍴 Log-built cafeteria, with terrace overlooking the lake, serves light meals

MONT TREMBLANT
GRAY ROCKS RESORT
GOLF COURSE
www.grayrocks.com
Two beautiful courses both with 18 holes and well in excess of 5,500m (6,000 yards). Voted the best family golf resort in Québec in one golf magazine, they also offer a good challenge for experienced golfers.

✉ 2322 rue Labelle, Mont Tremblant, Québec, J8E 1T8 ☎ 819/425-2771,

800/567-6767 ⏰ Spring–end Oct depending on weather 💲 $30–$115 🚗 5km (3 miles) north of St.-Jovite on Highway 327

HELLY HANSEN
www.hellyhanson.com
If you wind up in Mont Tremblant in winter without the right outdoors gear, this place can fix you up for all kinds of demanding conditions. It stocks Lifa and Helly Hansen clothing, accessories and equipment, along with Merrell footwear, and helpful staff can advise about the technicalities of layering fabrics.

✉ 116 Chemin Kandahar, Mont Tremblant, Québec, J8E 1B1 ☎ 819/681-4990 ⏰ Daily 8.30am–10pm

PERCÉ
BOUTIQUE AU BON SECOURS
This artisan-owned craft shop was once a pharmacy, and is now Percé's oldest store. It carries a great selection of original craft work by the owner and others; one reason to come is for the superb sandstone bird sculptures by Québec artist, Suzanne Tétreault-Massé.

✉ 150 Ouest Route 132, Percé, Québec, G0C 2L0 ☎ 418/782-2011 (off-season 514/245-0173) ⏰ May–end Oct daily 9–9

PIEDMONT
ANTIQUITÉS HIER POUR DEMAIN
An attractive white clapboard house is the home of this antiques shop, which specializes in Québec pine furniture from the 18th and 19th centuries. There's a good selection of small items, including some beautiful pieces of folk art, woodcarving and old toys.

✉ 914 boulevard des Laurentides, Piedmont, Québec, J0R 1K0 ☎ 450/227-4231 ⏰ Fri–Sun 11–5 🚗 On Highway 117

PIERREVILLE
AU VIEUX THÉÂTRE DE PIERREVILLE
www.vieuxtheatre.com
This former movie theater has lots of character, and cabaret-style seating. It hosts concerts and comedy.

✉ 33 rue Maurault, Pierreville, Québec, J0G 1J0 ☎ 450/568-0909, 877/568-0909

⏰ Shows some Saturday nights, plus summer season 🚗 On route 132, 30km (19 miles) east of Sorel

POINTE-CLAIRE
Y BOURBON STREET WEST
Street scene mural, brick walls, and polished wood, coupled with a friendly mood on the dance floor, attracts all ages. Live bands—blues (Tuesdays), R&B, soul, and rock—and comedy (Wednesdays). Drive home service available.

✉ 1866 boulevard des Sources, Pointe-Claire, Québec, H9R 5B1 ☎ 514/695-6545 ⏰ Music starts Tue and Sun 9.30, Wed 9, Thu 10, Fri–Sat 10.30

STE.-ANNE-DE-BEAUPRÉ
PROMENADE STE.-ANNE
www.miromar.com
For a change from the big malls and chic boutiques, you can indulge in pure bargain-hunting at this discount strip mall. Substantial savings on designer clothes for the whole family, accessories and homeware, including Levi's, Fila, Niko Leather, Benetton and Liz Claiborne.

✉ 10909 boulevard Ste.-Anne, Ste.-Anne-de-Beaupré, Québec, G0A 3C0 ☎ 418/827-3555 ⏰ Mon–Wed 9.30–5.30, Thu–Fri 9.30–9, Sat–Sun 9.30–5 🚗 20 min east of Québec City, 2km (1 mile) beyond Ste.-Anne-de Beaupré Basilica on Route 138

ST.-BERNARD-DE-LACOLLE
IGL
www.igldutyfree.com
A big white building by the main highway to the US border, where you can pick up duty-free items before you leave Canada. All the usual liquor, wine, perfumes, watches, jewelry and gift items, as well as clothing and souvenirs.

✉ Intersection of Route 15 and Route 87, St.-Bernard de Lacolle, Québec, J01 1V0 ☎ 450/246-2000, 1-888/-445-2222 ⏰ Daily 24 hours 🚗 South of Montréal at intersection of Route 15 and US Highway 87

ST.-FULGENCE
PARC AVENTURES CAP JASEUX
www.capjaseux.com
This adventure tourism enterprise on the Saguenay Fjord offers a variety

of things to do, including clambering through the trees on aerial rope courses, sailing, sea kayaking and climbing (made safe and easy) on the rock face.

✉ Chemin de la Pointe-aux-Pins, St.-Fulgence, Québec, G0V 1S0 ☎ 418/674-9114; 888/674-9114 (toll-free) 🕙 Daily ✋ Adult $4.39, child (5–17) $3.51. Activities: adult from $30, child from $15 🚍 Off Highway 172 between St.-Fulgence and Ste.-Rose-du-Nord

ST.-JOACHIM
CAP-TOURMENTE
www.qc.ec.gc.ca/faune/faune/html
World-famous location for viewing tens of thousands of migrating snow geese in spring and fall, with 2,400ha (5,928 acres) of tidal bulrush marshland. Many other species, observation points, information center and guide services.

✉ Canadian Wildlife Service, 570 chemin du Cap-Tourmente, St.-Joachim, Québec, G0A 3X0 ☎ 418/827-4591 🕙 Early Jan–end Oct daily 8.30–5 ✋ $6. Personal guide services: $60 per hour 🚍 Highway 360 near Beaupré

ST.-MARC-SUR-RICHELIEU
SPA GIVENCHY
www.spagivenchy.com
This spa has a fabulous location. Saltwater pumped from far below ground feeds the swimming pool and therapeutic baths. Treatments focus on shaping, revitalizing, hydrating and enhancing face and body.

✉ Hostellerie Les Trois Tilleuls, 290 rue Richelieu, St.-Marc-sur-Richelieu, Québec, J0L 2E0 ☎ 514/856-7787 🕙 Daily ✋ Treatments priced separately; massage from $115, body treatments from $65, facials from $100 🚍 On Highway 223; to the east of Montréal (south of the river), via Highway 20

SHAWINIGAN
LA CITÉ DE L'ENERGIE
www.citedelenergie.com
An old industrial area has been revitalized to form this unique and imaginative theme park beside the St. Maurice River. There is a wide variety of activities, including a science with interactive exhibits,

a multimedia show, pontoon boat trips on the river, visits to a power station and a former aluminum smelter, extensive gardens and ascent by elevator of a massive 115m-high (377ft) hydro pylon for splendid views of the area.

✉ 1000 avenue Melville, C.P. 156, Shawinigan, Québec, G9N 6T9 ☎ 819/536-8516, 866/900-248, 1-800/263-2230 🕙 Mid-Jun to early Sep daily 10–6 (last admission 3pm); rest of year Tue–Sun 10–5 (last admission 2pm). Some attractions are seasonal ✋ Adult $16, child (6–12) $9, family $36 or $38. Eclyps show $49.50 (under 13 years $20); Shawinigan Space art exhibition: adult $15, child (6–12) $8, (13 and over) $13, family $30 🚍 Highway 55 exit 211, just south of Shawinigan

SHERBROOKE
CARREFOUR DE L'ESTRIE
This is the megamall for the Eastern Townships region, with about 200 stores and 19 restaurants. It's anchored by the usual clutch of department stores—Sears, The Bay, Zellers, Maison Simons—all in bright, modern surroundings.

✉ 3050 boulevard de Portland, Sherbrooke, Québec, J1L 1K1 ☎ 819/563-1907 🕙 Mon–Wed 9.30–5.30, Thu–Fri 9.30–9, Sat 9–5, Sun 10–5 🚍 1, 3, 4, 6, 11 🚍 Portland Commercial District, off Highway 10 or 55

CENTRE CULTUREL DE L'UNIVERSITÉ DE SHERBROOKE
www.centrecultureludes.ca
Modern campus theater with an eclectic schedule, including dance, drama, classical concerts and comedy.

✉ 2500 boulevard de l'Université, Sherbrooke, Québec, J1K 2R1 ☎ 819/820-1000 🕙 Year-round ✋ Varies

GRANADA
www.theatregranada.com
Historic 1,200-seat theater that hosts touring theater companies, musicals, comedy, and classical and pop concerts.

✉ 53 rue Wellington Nord, Sherbrooke, Québec, J1H 4P9 ☎ 819/565-5656 🕙 Year-round ✋ Varies $17.50–$60; dinner and show packages available

Above *A flock of snow geese*

LE VIEUX CLOCHER DE SHERBROOKE
www.vieuxclocher.com
Venue for touring performers, including rock bands, solo artists, comedians and family entertainers.

✉ 1590 rue Galt Ouest, Sherbrooke, Québec, J1H 2B5 ☎ 819/822-2102 🕙 Year-round ✋ Varies; from $17.50 🚍 3, 4, 5, 7, 8, 9

TERREBONNE
THÉÂTRE DU VIEUX-TERREBONNE
www.theatreduvieuxterrebonne.com
This theater hosts drama, dance, song, classical music, jazz and comedy. Most are in French, but some productions in English.

✉ 866 rue St.-Pierre, Terrebonne, Québec, J6W 1E5 ☎ 450/492-4777, 866/404-4777 🕙 Year-round ✋ Varies; $20–$60 🚍 North of Montréal, on north bank of the Thousand Islands River

TROIS-RIVIÈRES
D'ARTAGNAN'S
www.ledartagnans.com
Brick walls and a cavernous interior set the scene for this long-established night spot, with dancing to DJs on Friday and Saturday and a lively bar atmosphere the rest of the week. The heated terrace is as crowded as the inside.

✉ 282 Des Forges, Trois-Rivières, Québec, G9A 2G8 ☎ 819/694-4457 🕙 Daily 12pm–3am ✋ Cover charge Fri–Sat 🚍 Downtown, between rue Notre-Dame and rue Royale

FESTIVALS AND EVENTS

FEBRUARY
GRAND PRIX SKI-DOO
www.grandprixvalcourt.com
In the town where the Bombardier snowmobile was invented, this three day competition includes speed and extreme events.
✉ Valcourt, Québec ☎ 450/532-3443, 866/532-7543

MAY
INTERNATIONAL NEW MUSIC FESTIVAL
www.fimav.qc.ca
Celebrating its 25th anniversary in 2008, this festival stages 26 concerts of progressive rock, jazz, electroacoustic and contemporary music; the largest of its kind in North America.
✉ Victoriaville, Québec ☎ 819/752-7912

JUNE
FESTIVAL INTERNATIONAL DANSE ENCORE
http://festival-encore.com
Since 1995 this dance festival has been going from strength to strength, producing a varied program of the highest quality, including contemporary ballet in theaters, all kinds of other dance—including salsa and hip hop—on open-air stages, masterclasses and competitions.
✉ Trois-Rivières, Québec ☎ 819/376-2769, 877/533-2673

INTERNATIONAL GARDEN FESTIVAL
www.jardinsmetis.com
More than 40 garden designers and landscape architects from around the world create fabulous and innovative gardens for this festival, which continues until early October.
✉ Grand-Métis, Québec ☎ 418/775-2222

L'OUTAOUAIS EN FÊTE
www.imperatif-francias.org
To welcome in the summer, Gatineau celebrates for five days, with a grand parade, open-air activities, concerts, craft shows, fireworks and of course, eating and drinking. There's also a midway (funfair) and children's entertainment.
✉ Gatineau, Québec ☎ 819/684-8460

JULY
FETE DU LAC DES NATIONS
www.fetedulacdesnations.com
Massive fireworks competition, with more than 30 shows in the space of six days. There's also a craft village and other attractions.
✉ Parc Jacques Cartier, Sherbrooke, Québec ☎ 819/569-5888

LAC ST.-JEAN INTERNATIONAL SWIMMING MARATHON
www.traversee.qc.ca
Since 1955 Lac St.-Jean has been the venue for this exciting open-water swimming event, with long-distance races accompanied by small craft and cruise boats full of spectators. Ancillary events include a street banquet for 10,000 people (all seated!), shows and fireworks.
✉ Lac St.-Jean, Québec ☎ 418/275-2851

MOUNTAIN BIKE FESTIVAL
www.velirium.com
Mont-Ste.-Anne hosts a full schedule of downhill and cross-country events on two wheels, including World Cup and National Championship races. Also extreme sports demonstrations and children's races. Held over three weekends.
✉ Mont-Ste.-Anne, Québec ☎ 418/827-1122

AUGUST
BIG BROME FAIR
www.bromefair.com
This agricultural show in late August/September is more than 150 years old and as well as the prize cattle and other farming events, there's lots of entertainment, a midway (fairground rides) and shopping opportunities.
✉ 345 Stagecoach Road, Brome, Québec ☎ 450/242-3976

TROIS-RIVIÈRES GRAND PRIX
www.velirium.com
It's not Formula 1, but the town's streets become a race-track for Formula Ford, Formula 1600, Grand Am, CASCAR and others, accompanied by entertainment and fireworks.
✉ Trois-Rivières, Québec ☎ 819/370-4787

SEPTEMBER
SYMPHONY OF COLOURS
www.tremblant.com
The fabulous fall colors of the Laurentians are celebrated with concerts and the Grand Prix of Colours climb, or you can take the gondola to the summit of Mont Tremblant for a panoramic view over the spectacular sea of red, orange and yellow leaves. The festival wraps up at Halloween with a costume ball.
✉ Mont-Tremblant, Québec ☎ 819/681-3000

WINE HARVEST FESTIVAL
www.fetedesvendanges.com
More than 150 Québec wine and artisan food producers present this celebration of the wine harvest on the shores of Lake Memphrémagog.
✉ Magog-Orford, Québec ☎ 819/847-2022

WESTERN FESTIVAL
www.festivalwestern.com
Rodeos, country music, a parade and other attractions bring the cowboys to town for Eastern Canada's biggest Western event.
✉ St.-Tite, Québec ☎ 418/365-7524

OCTOBER
INTERNATIONAL FESTIVAL OF POETRY
www.fiptr.com
Ten days of events and activities involving many of the town's cafés, restaurants and art galleries as well as theaters to showcase poets from around 30 countries.
✉ Trois-Rivières, Québec ☎ 819/379-9813

EATING

REGIONS | QUÉBEC PROVINCE • EATING

PRICES AND SYMBOLS

The restaurants are listed alphabetically within each town. The prices are for a two-course lunch (L) and a three-course à la carte dinner (D). Prices in pubs are for a two-course lunchtime bar meal and a two-course dinner in the restaurant, unless specified otherwise. The wine price is for the least expensive bottle.

For a key to the symbols, ▷ 2.

AYER'S CLIFF
AUBERGE RIPPLECOVE INN

www.ripplecove.com

Refined French and international cuisine is served here, in an elegant lakeside Victorian dining room. The lunch menu might include snow-crab cake, Wiener schnitzel and stir-fried Szechuan shrimp, while at dinner there's a four-course table d'hôte menu, a Canadian menu and a Québec menu—and a pianist accompanying your meal with classical music.

✉ 700 Ripplecove Road, Ayer's Cliff, Québec, J0B 1C0 ☎ 819/838-4296, 800/668-4296 ◷ Year-round for lunch and dinner ✋ L $22, D $55 (4 courses), Wine $20 ⛟ On Highway 141, 8km (5 miles) south of Highway 55, intersection 21

LA BAIE
L'AUBERGE DES 21

www.aubergedes21.com

Right on the shore of the Saguenay Fjord, this is a delightful inn serving exceptional regional cuisine, with some dishes inspired by traditional First Nations recipes. Menus change with the seasons, but have included caribou with wild juniper berries and gin sauce, and Native-style smoked salmon, served hot with maple vinegar and white butter sauce. Menus are table d'hôte, with five courses at dinner.

✉ 621 rue Mars, Ville de la Baie, Québec, G7B 4N1 ☎ 418/697-2121, 800/363-7298 ◷ Daily 7–10, 12–2, 6–9 ✋ L $15, D $46, Wine $40 ⛟ Off Highway 372 in La Baie, via rue Bagot

BEAUPORT
MANOIR MONTMORENCY

www.sepaq.com/chutemontmorency

The dining room offers spectacular views of the Montmorency Falls. Excellent Québec cuisine, blending traditional French recipes with local ingredients. The park fee will be refunded if you show your restaurant receipt.

✉ 2490 avenue Royale, Parc de la Chute-Montmorency, Beauport, Québec, G1C 1S1 ☎ 418/663-3330 ◷ Daily 10–10 ✋ L $13, D $30, Wine $29.95 ⛟ Metrobus 800, then bus 50

CHICOUTIMI
LE PRIVILÈGE

www.leprivilege.ca

Chicoutimi's finest restaurant is run by Diane Tremblay, one of Canada's most accomplished chefs. Her skill and excellent local produce make for a memorable meal, which might start with gnocchi of smoked salmon with parmesan and sauce *à la brunoise,* with vegetables and shrimp. Recent main courses have included Saguenay venison on a bed of lentils, and fjord duck marinated in herbs, with a sauce of Séchouan pepper and vanilla. There is also an eight-course Menu Dégustation.

✉ 1623 boulevard St.-Jean-Baptiste, Chicoutimi, Québec, G7H 7T9 ☎ 418/698-6262 ◷ Mon–Fri 10–7 ✋ D $55, Wine $20

GASPÉ
CAFÉ DES ARTISTES
Just over 1km (half a mile) from the Musée de la Gaspésie, this charming café doubles as a gallery for the work of local artists, notably the owners. The simple table d'hôte menu includes home-made ice creams and home-roasted coffee.
✉ 249 boulevard de Gaspé, Gaspé, Québec, G4X 1A5 ☎ 418/368-2255 🕐 Jun to mid-Sep daily 11–10 🍴 L $10, D $16–$20

MAGOG
A LA PAIMPOLAISE
www.paimpolaisedemagog.com
This is a lovely old Breton-style crêperie, with various fillings that you can build in the same way you'd choose pizza toppings. There's more than crêpes on the menu though, with specialties drawing from local produce to produce traditional cuisine such as rabbit chasseur, Madeira kidneys, fresh salmon with ginger butter and cheese or meat fondue. The table d'hôte menu is especially good value, starting at around $20.
✉ 2760 Route 112, Magog, Québec, J1X 5R9 ☎ 819/843-1502 🕐 May to mid-Oct daily from 5pm, plus Sun brunch 10am; Winter: closed Mon–Tue 🍴 Sun Brunch $22.50, D $40, Wine Bring your own

MONT TREMBLANT
LA TABLE ENCHANTÉE
www.mt-tremblant.com/table
Attractive gardens and natural wood inside give a nice country feel to this little restaurant in the heart of the Laurentians, which specializes in game and traditional cuisine. There's a moderate, well-chosen wine list.

✉ 1842 Highway 117 North, Mont Tremblant, Québec, J8E 2Y2 ☎ 819/425-7113 🕐 Tue–Sun 5–10 🍴 D $25, Wine $22.50 🚌 On Highway 117, 1km (0.6 mile) north of intersection wth Montée Ryan

PERCÉ
LA NORMANDIE DINING ROOM
www.normandieperce.com
White walls and bright red roof stand out on the seashore, and the hotel restaurant looks out over Percé Rock and Bonaventure Island. It is known for some of the best food in the area, and there is an extensive four-course table d'hôte menu.
✉ Hotel La Normandie, 221 Highway 132 Ouest, Percé, Québec, G0C 2L0 ☎ 418/782-2112 🕐 Jun–end Sep daily 7.30–10am, 6–9pm 🍴 D $25–$40, Wine $20 🚌 Orléans Express, Gaspé route 🚌 Downtown, on waterfront

ST.-FAUSTIN-LAC-CARRÉ
LA CABANE À SUCRE MILLETTE INC.
www.tremblant-sugar-shack.com
Sugar shacks are great to visit when the sap is flowing (Mar–end Apr), but here you can tour the boiling room and maple grove year-round. More to the point, you can sample real down-home Canadian cooking in a traditional log building: Laurentian pea soup, smoked maple syrup ham, baked beans and sausages in maple syrup. Desserts include scrumptious sugar pie, pancakes with maple syrup, and maple taffy on snow. Reservation essential.
✉ 1357 rue St.-Faustin, St.-Faustin-Lac-Carré, Québec, J0T 1J3 ☎ 819/688-2101, 877/688-2101 🕐 Mar–end Apr Tue–Sat 11.30–8, Sun 11.30–7pm; rest of year meals only when open for a group reservation 🍴 $10–$17 (all courses, maple taffy and tea or coffee included) 🚌 15 minutes' drive south of Tremblant on Highway 117

ST.-LAURENT
LE CANARD HUPPÉ
www.canard-huppe.com
This delightful island inn is run by chef Philip Rae, so it is not surprising that eating in the dining room here is a particular treat. The aim of the kitchen is to present a flavor of the island using local produce wherever possible. So you might start your meal with a terrine of local game with multicolored jellies and hams, or marinated trout and house-smoked salmon with apple and cheddar in a basil emulsion. Equally delectable main courses might include rack of Island lamb in a maple mustard crust or beef *filet mignon* with roasted red peppers, glazed shallots and black pepper sauce. Reservations are essential.
✉ 2198 chemin Royal, St.-Laurent, Île d'Orléans, Québec, G0A 3Z0 ☎ 418/828-2292, 800/838-2292 🕐 Daily 6pm–8pm 🍴 D $38, Wine $33 🚌 Near southern end of island, 6km (4 miles) from the bridge

TADOUSSAC
RESTAURANT LE BÂTEAU
www.lebateau.com
A big model sailboat on the signboard heralds your arrival at this informal restaurant, which has a wonderful view over the water. Lunch and dinner are both served buffet style, with tasty Québecois dishes that include delicious home-made soups, beef and vegetables, seafood, rounded off with traditional pies for dessert.
✉ 246 rue des Forgerons, CP 127, Tadoussac, Québec, G0T 2A0 ☎ 418/235-4427 🕐 May–end Oct daily 11–2.30, 5–9.30; also sandwiches 11–5 🍴 L $11, D $17, Wine $18 🚌 In middle of village

TROIS-RIVIÈRES
LE SACRISTAN
This is a handy place to stop for a quick snack, serving an interesting selection of soups, salads, hot and cold sandwiches and desserts. You can turn it into a meal with the "Bistrot Formule" of soup, salad, grilled sandwich, dessert and glass of wine for an all-in price, or choose the daily-changing special, which might be carbonnade of beef, couscous with chicken, sausages with lentils, or chili con carne.
✉ 300 rue Bonaventure, Trois-Rivières, Québec, G9A 2B1 ☎ 819/694-1344 🕐 Mon–Fri 8am–6pm 🍴 L $16.50 🚌 Downtown, between rue Notre-Dame Centre and rue Royale

PRICES AND SYMBOLS

Prices are the starting price for a double room for one night, unless otherwise stated. Breakfast is included unless noted otherwise. All the hotels listed accept credit cards unless otherwise stated. Note that rates vary widely throughout the year.

For a key to the symbols, ▷ 2.

BAIE-ST.-PAUL
AUBERGE LA MAISON OTIS

www.maisonotis.com

A traditional Québec-style hotel, extended to provide a beauty suite, swimming pool, restaurant and café. The attractive bedrooms come in various sizes and have beautiful furniture. Outside, there are lovely gardens and a stylish terrace.

✉ 23 rue St. Jean Baptiste, Baie-St.-Paul, Québec, G0A 1B0 ☎ 418/435-2255, 800/267-2254 🖐 $208, with dinner ⓘ 30 🔄 🏊 Indoor

GASPÉ
L'HOTEL DES COMMANDANTS

www.hoteldescommandants.com

Mellow earth tones add a richly warming effect to this stylish hotel,

though the stunning view over the bay is likely to be something of a distraction. In addition to the range of modern rooms, the hotel has a health center offering various treatments and therapies, a cinema, cabaret shows, a bar-restaurant and the Terra Nova restaurant.

✉ 178 rue de la Reine, Gaspé, Québec, G4X 1T6 ☎ 418/368-3355, 800/462-3355 🖐 $115 ⓘ 70 (all non-smoking) 🔄 🚗 Downtown, one block back from coast road (Highway 198)

LAC BROME
AUBERGE LAKEVIEW

www.aubergelakeviewinn.com

This is a listed historic building from 1874, in a convenient location for Lac Brome and many other Eastern Township attractions. Rooms come in several styles, but all have elegant decor and handcrafted furniture. The spacious studios come with whirlpool baths and a balcony. The plush dining room offers formal service and five-course gourmet dinners; there's also an English-style pub serving regional specialties and local and imported beers.

✉ 50 rue Victoria, Lac-Brome City, Knowlton, Québec, J0E 1V0 ☎ 450/243-6183, 800/661-6183 🖐 $136, with dinner ⓘ 28 🔄 🚗 Outdoor heated 🚗 Off Lakeside Road (Highway 243), near south end of lake

AUBERGE QUILLIAMS

www.aubergequilliams.com

The address says it all—this lovely hotel has a splendid location right on Lac Brome, and it's backed by the Quilliams wildlife reserve, a marshland rich in birdlife, where you can canoe from the hotel's dock. There are various types of room, from the standards with queen-size bed to large suites with separate living area, kitchenette and a couple of double sofa beds. All rooms have a balcony, wireless internet access, coffee-maker and terrycloth robes. The restaurant offers French cuisine and an award-winning wine list.

✉ 572 chemin Lakeside, Lac Brome, Québec, J0E 1R0 ☎ 450/243-0404, 888/922-0404 🖐 $149 ⓘ 38 (30 non-smoking) 🔄 🏊 Indoor 🚗 5km (3 miles) south of Highway 10 (exit 90, Knowlton/Lac Brome), on route 243

MAGOG

CHATEAU DU LAC
www.lechateaudulac.com
Very French-looking, this elegant auberge is just a short walk from Lake Memphremagog and the town center. It was built as a private mansion in 1867 and has been very tastefully renovated to provide a high standard of accommodations. Its enduring popularity means that an expansion is on the cards. The rooms are individually styled and have private bathrooms, some with whirlpool tubs, cable TV, internet access and clock radios.
✉ 85 rue Merry Sud, Magog, Québec, J1X 3L2 ☎ 819/868-1666, 888/948-1666 ⍟ $129 ➀ 8 (all non-smoking) ⬤ 🅿 Near northeastern tip of lake, near junction of highways 112 and 141

MONT TREMBLANT

FAIRMONT TREMBLANT
www.fairmont.com
Superb year-round resort set beneath the highest peaks in the Laurentians. Popular with winter sports enthusiasts, but there's lots to do all year, much of it right in the hotel, including swimming pools, a health and fitness suite, and a kids' club. Regular rooms and suites have fairly standard hotel furnishings, cable TV, coffeemaker, hairdryer and minibar. Fairmont Gold guests get special treatment, with their own lounge, concierge and check-in. Many rooms have wonderful mountain views and windows open to let in the clean air.
✉ 3045 chemin Principale, Mont Tremblant, Québec, J8E 1B1 ☎ 819/681-7000 ⍟ $539 ➀ 314 ⬤ 🔻 ⬛ Indoor and outdoor, heated 🅿 In resort village

PERCÉ

LE MIRAGE
www.hotellemirage.com
Every single room in this friendly, family-run hotel has a spectacular view of the famous Percé Rock and Bonaventure Island, and they have nice big windows to make the most of it. Some rooms have glossy hardwood floors, while others are carpeted, and all have quality fabrics

that coordinate with the stylish design; extended cable TV and hair-dryers are provided. The extensive grounds include a tennis court and pool. Boat trips and whale-watching can be arranged.
✉ 288 Highway 132 Ouest, Percé, Québec, G0C 2L0 ☎ 418/782-5151, 800/463-9011 ⬤ Mid-May to mid-Oct ⍟ $98 ➀ 67 (50 non-smoking) ⬤ ⬛ Outdoor, heated 🚌 60 🅿 West of Percé on Highway 132

ST.-LAURENT

LE CANARD HUPPÉ
www.canard-huppe.com
Peacefully located in a rural area, this pretty little auberge is noted for its restaurant (▷ 137) as well as its comfortable accommodations. Two lodges contain the rooms, which are all different but they all have splendid old-style furniture and restful decor. One is a suite with a fireplace and whirlpool tub.
✉ 2198 chemin Royal, St.-Laurent, Île d'Orléans, Québec, G0A 3Z0 ☎ 418/828-2292, 800/838-2292 ⍟ $128 🅿 Near southern end of island, 6km (4 miles) from the bridge

TROIS-RIVIÈRES

GOUVERNEURE
www.gouverneur.com
The featureless modern architecture might not be all that appealing and the rooms are much like any other business hotel, but standards are high and this is a good choice for its downtown location and facilities. The rooftop swimming pool, for instance, has great views, and comprehensive dining options include a great seafood buffet on Friday and Saturday nights. Rooms include coffee-makers, wireless high-speed internet and voice mail, and business class rooms also have a minibar, work table and free breakfast. Packages and promotions offer good value.
✉ 975 rue Hart, Trois-Rivières, Québec, G9A 4S3 ☎ 888/910-1111 ⍟ $92 ➀ 127 (114 non-smoking) ⬛ Outdoor 🔻 🅿 Downtown, corner of rue Laviolette

Above *Wakefield Mill, in Wakefield*

MANOIR DE BLOIS
www.manoirdeblois.com
Built in the early 19th century, this former family home retains its fine architectural features and is appropriately furnished with antiques. Each room is individually decorated in warm colors and has a private bathroom, and high ceilings add to the already spacious feel.
✉ 197 rue Bonaventure, Trois-Rivières, Québec, G9A 2A9 ☎ 819/373-1090, 800/397-5184 ⍟ $99.95 ➀ 5 (all non-smoking) 🅿 Downtown, off rue Royale

WAKEFIELD

WAKEFIELD MILL
www.wakefieldmill.com
This lovely inn is in the heart of the hills and forests of Gatineau Park. Exposed brick walls, hardwood floors and mellow tones are set off by soft calico sofas and historical pictures. Some rooms include a Jacuzzi and a fireplace, and many have wonderful views of the falls; all have old-Canadian furnishings and satellite TV. There are also some luxury suites.
✉ 60 Mill Road, Wakefield, Québec, J0X 3G0 ☎ 819/459-1838, 888/567-1838 ⍟ $102 ➀ 26 ⬤ ⬤ 🅿 Half-hour drive north of Ottawa off Highway 5, and along Highway 105

ATLANTIC PROVINCES

Add all four of the Atlantic Provinces together—New Brunswick, Nova Scotia, Prince Edward Island, and Newfoundland and Labrador—and you still wouldn't match the area of any other single Canadian province. Nevertheless, they have historical, geographical and cultural riches that far outmatch their size.

As the part of Canada that's closest to Europe, this is where the early explorers and settlers first landed—Vikings 1,000 years ago, John Cabot in 1497, the first French settlers in 1605, quickly followed by the British. Later, steamships brought millions of immigrants across the Atlantic, and their first landfall was Halifax, capital of Nova Scotia. Many liked what they saw and stayed on the east coast, and the influences are still apparent: a distinctive Scottishness persists in Nova Scotia (New Scotland); there's still a hint of Irish brogue in the accent of the Newfoundlanders; and 50 percent of the population of New Brunswick, the only officially bilingual province in Canada, have French as their first language. History was made again on Prince Edward Island in 1867, when Canada was declared a nation in Charlottetown.

There is stunning scenery everywhere, with great mountain ranges, vast forests, the world's highest tides in the Bay of Fundy, unspoiled sandy beaches with the warmest water north of the Carolinas, and the tundra of Labrador with its large herds of caribou. Prince Edward Island is more gentle, a rural gem with blood-red soil that's most famous for potatoes and Lucy Maud Montgomery's *Anne of Green Gables* stories.

Halifax is the biggest and liveliest city, while the other provincial capitals—Fredericton, Charlottetown and St. John's—retain a charming small-town feel. All around the coast are achingly picturesque fishing villages, rocky coves and harbors. Come for the scenery, the Celtic music, the historic sites, the hiking or the whale-watching, and don't leave without eating some of the local lobster.

ANNAPOLIS ROYAL

www.annapolisroyal.com

On the wide basin of the Annapolis River, where it meets the Bay of Fundy, tiny Annapolis Royal is a place of immense historic charm, and its main street is lined by elegant homes, craft shops, art galleries and restaurants. Twice a day, the huge Fundy tides (▷ 146–147) rush in, reversing the flow of the river with a mighty thrust that generates the town's electricity.

Annapolis Royal was the first French colony in North America, settled 15 years before the Pilgrim Fathers landed in the US. It was also the most fought over place in Canada during the hostilities between the English and French. Port Royal National Historic Site (mid-May to mid-Oct daily), about 10.5km (6.5 miles) west of town across the causeway, recalls those days. It was built in 1605 and survived only until 1613, but the compound, reminiscent of an old Normandy farm, has been meticulously reconstructed.

Canada's oldest national historic park, Fort Anne (mid-May to mid-Oct daily), off Upper St. George Street, was built by the French in 1702–08, with later additions by the British. It houses historical displays, plus the huge Heritage Tapestry that illustrates four centuries of Annapolis Royal history.

✚ 407 W16

L'ANSE AUX MEADOWS

Head north from Gros Morne to the northern tip of Newfoundland and you'll find a place of enormous historic significance to the whole of North America. L'Anse aux Meadows (Jun to mid-Oct daily) is an excavation and partial reconstruction of the only Viking settlement found on the Continent. It provides a fascinating insight into the lives of those early explorers who based themselves here for seasonal forays from Scandinavia in search of fish and berries. They also made trips from their settlement here to the mainland of North America.

✚ 407 X12

AVALON PENINSULA

Sometimes called "Canada's Far East," this is the most easterly part of the entire North American continent, suspended from the rest of Newfoundland by a narrow isthmus. It's wild and beautiful, with the vital city of St. John's (▷ 154) on its eastern coast, a distinctive lifestyle and sense of history. European settlement started early here, and British fishermen first visited around the 1520s.

The rugged beauty of the coastline is matched by the wonders of nature: whales at St. Vincent's and at the ecological reserve of Witless Bay (where thousands of humpbacks and minkes come to feed); and seabird colonies on the islands of Witless Bay and at Cape St. Mary's in the southwest, home to northern gannets, razorbills and murres. And most years there is the spectacle of 10,000-year-old icebergs drifting past.

The most easterly point is Cape Spear. From this headland there are wonderful views and it's a prime whale-watching spot. Now a national historic park, the cape has a visitor center (mid-May to mid-Oct daily) and two lighthouses. It's supremely peaceful, but nature has its hazards too, so heed the safety notices.

Northwest of St. John's, at Harbour Grace, the Conception Bay Museum (July–early Sep) recalls the town's role in transatlantic aviation—a number of pioneering flights set out from here. Farther north still, Trinity Bay has a trio of communities with names that beckon: Heart's Delight, Heart's Desire and Heart's Content. At the last, in 1866, the transatlantic communications cable ended. The old cable station is now a dedicated museum (mid-May to late Sep daily).

On the west coast lies Placentia, its name derived from the French *plaisance*, given to it in 1662 when it became capital of the French colony. Located on a narrow strip of land, the town is overlooked by the remains of the 17th-century French fortress atop Castle Hill (visitor

Above *Preserved Douglas DC3 "Spirit of Harbour Grace", Conception Bay Museum*
Opposite *Church at Harbour Grace*

center: mid-May to mid-Oct daily; grounds: year round).

✚ 407 Z13 ⓘ 1st floor, Gentara Building, 348 Water Street, St. John's, Newfoundland and Labrador, A5C 5M2 ☎ 709/576-8106

BADDECK

www.visitbaddeck.com

Baddeck lies at the heart of Cape Breton island on the shore of St. Patrick's Channel, part of the enormous Bras d'Or Lake, and because of this scenic location the 1,000-strong community swells in summer with visitors. The town has a long history of attracting emigrating Scots, one of whom was Alexander Graham Bell (1847–1922), inventor, researcher and all-round genius, who in 1885 built a summer home here.

Bell's many achievements are recalled at the Alexander Graham Bell National Historic Site (May–Oct daily; Nov–Apr by arrangement; www.pc.gc.ca) at the east end of the village on Chebucto Street (Highway 205). It was, of course, the telephone that made the inventor rich and famous, but his experiments delved into many other areas. In 1907, Bell's Silver Dart flew across Baddeck Bay in the first manned flight in Canada. Later, one of his hydrofoils, the HD-4, set a world record with a speed of 114kph (almost 71mph) on Bras d'Or Lake.

✚ 407 X15

Above *View of the coast along the Cabot Trail* **Right** *The Acadian flag flies at the City Hall, Fredericton* **Opposite** *Lifeguard lookout post at Neil's Harbour on the Cabot Trail*

BONAVISTA PENINSULA
www.bonavista.net

It is thought that John Cabot's first North American landfall in 1497 might have been on this scenic spot on Newfoundland's east coast. "O buona vista," the Italian-born explorer is said to have declared, and few would hesitate to echo his sentiment. Today, a statue of the explorer stands above Cape Bonavista and its pounding waves. The red and white lighthouse here (mid-May to late Sep daily) dates from 1843, and costumed guides re-create life in the 1870s.

About 5km (3 miles) from the cape is the tranquil community of Bonavista, a thriving center for international trade only a generation ago, when its little harbor was filled with schooners and its docksides were alive with scurrying workers. The Ryan Premises (mid-May to late Oct daily; www.pc.gc.ca) on the waterfront, are the former headquarters of James Ryan Ltd., which created an economic empire here based on the Labrador and Newfoundland inshore fisheries. The company closed in 1978, but the buildings have been restored to tell the story. Also on the harborfront is a locally built replica of John Cabot's ship, the *Matthew* (mid-May to end Sep daily; www.matthewlegacy.com), in which he crossed the Atlantic from Bristol in England.

Another explorer, Portuguese Gaspar Corte Real, arrived on Trinity Sunday 1501, and thus the tiny coastal village of Trinity was named. Trinity's main claim to fame today is the New Founde Land pageant (Jul–Labor Day weekend Wed, Sat and Sun 2pm), a musical parade through the town with vignettes of characters from Trinity's history. Hiscock House (mid-May to late Sep daily) is a typical early 20th-century merchant's home, where guides in period costume show you around.
➕ 407 Y12

CAMPOBELLO ISLAND
www.campobello.com

At the point where the Atlantic Ocean roars up into the Bay of Fundy lies Campobello, one of the Fundy Islands (▷ 146–147) and long famous for its invigorating climate. In the late 19th century the island attracted wealthy US industrialists keen to escape the city. Among those who had vacation houses here were James and Sara Delano Roosevelt, whose son Franklin later became US president (1933–45). Young Franklin spent his summers on Campobello, which he called his "beloved island," and later he and his wife Eleanor bought their own summer home here. In 1921, FDR contracted polio. He did not return to Campobello for 12 years, by which time he was president. The 34-room Dutch-gabled Roosevelt Cottage (late May to Oct daily) is now the focal point of the 1,133ha (2,800-acre) Roosevelt-Campobello International Park (daily; www.fdr.net), impeccably maintained by the governments of both Canada and the United States as an international peace park. Simply furnished, the house is a poignant return in time, full of reminders of its former owners. The neighboring visitor center (late May to Oct daily) offers excellent interpretive displays on Roosevelt's life.

Walk down to the wharf for the splendid view of the coast and Eastport, Maine—if the famous fog hasn't set in—or explore the hiking trails and drives that wind through the forest to headlands and rocky shores.
➕ 407 W16 🚢 From L'Etete (near St. George), New Brunswick, or from Eastport, Maine (US); both services via Deer Island

CAPE BRETON HIGHLANDS NATIONAL PARK
www.pc.gc.ca

Cape Breton is one of the most beautiful places in eastern Canada, and its scenery is nowhere more breathtaking than in the northern part of the island, where the Cabot Trail (▷ 160–161 drive and ▷ 162–163 walk) winds through dense forests and skirts sections of wild, rocky coastline. Much of this road falls within the Cape Breton Highlands National Park, which was created in 1936 and encompasses 950sq km (366sq miles). You need a permit to enter the park, even if you are just driving through, and you can pick this up, along with a free map, from the information centers (see below), the Whale Centre in Pleasant Bay or the Celtic Bakery in Dingwall. The national park has 265 hiking and walking trails, ranging from short family walks to challenging overnight adventures. Some lead to view-points offering panoramas of the spectacular coastline; others explore forests and secluded lakes. Here, moose, black bear, bobcats and coy-otes roam, while bald eagles circle overhead. Off the coast, whales and dolphins break the surface, watched by a multitude of seabirds—there is no shortage of whale-watching trips between June and September, no-tably from Chéticamp and Pleasant Bay (▷ 160–161), but you can often see the marine mammals from the coastal viewpoints.

✚ 407 X15 🚹 Ingonish and Chéticamp information centers; early May–late Oct daily ✋ Permit: adult $7, child $3.50, children under 6 free

FREDERICTON

www.tourism.fredericton.ca
On a wide bend of the Saint John River, New Brunswick's capital is an attractive city of elm-lined streets and elegant houses, and you can easily explore it on foot. Its cultural heart is the restored Historic Garrison District, with museums, galleries, craft shops, guards' drill re-enactments and free entertainment every evening in July and August. The city stages lots of festivals too, including the June river festival, Highland Games in July and, the biggest of them all, the Harvest Jazz and Blues Festival in September. Opposite the Legislative Building is the modern Beaverbrook Art Gallery (daily; www.beaverbrookartgallery.org), the finest art gallery in Atlantic Canada. Pride of place goes to Salvador Dalí's huge *Santiago el Grande*, high above the entrance lobby. There are also good collections of Canadian and British paintings. From Fredericton, drive east for 34km (21 miles) on the

Trans-Canada Highway 2 to reach King's Landing Historical Settlement (Jun to mid-Oct daily; www.kingslanding.nb.ca), a splendidly re-created 19th-century Loyalist settlement amid woodland, pasture and riverbank. Staffed by costumed interpreters, it's one of the largest cultural sites of its kind in Canada and includes homes, farms and workshops, plus a fascinating water-driven sawmill.

✚ 407 W16 🚹 11 Carleton Street, Fredericton, New Brunswick, E3B 4Y7 ☎ 506/460-2041, 1-888/888-4768

FUNDY NATIONAL PARK AND ISLANDS

▷ 146–147.

GROS MORNE NATIONAL PARK

www.pc.gc.ca
This wild area of fiords, sea coast, forest and mountains on Newfoundland's west coast was designated a World Heritage Site by UNESCO in 1987, not only for its spectacular scenic beauty but also for the global importance of its geology. The flat-topped and almost barren ocher-hued Tablelands (4km/2.5 miles from the Discovery Centre on highway 431) are peridotite from the Earth's mantle which moved hundreds of kilometers to their present position some 450 million years ago.

The formation at Green Point, 12km (7.5 miles) north of Rocky Harbour, a tilted, slanted chunk of rock that rises abruptly from the ocean, is considered one of the best examples of exposed sedimentary rock in the world; there are guided walks with naturalists in summer.

The best introduction to Gros Morne is at the Discovery Centre (May to end Oct daily) in Woody Point on Highway 431. It has a wonderful location, and its displays explain the geological phenomena that attract international interest. The Park Visitor Centre (year-round daily, but winter opening uncertain; check before visiting), on Highway 430 near Rocky Harbour, also has back-ground information (▷ 156–157).

About 27km (17 miles) north of Rocky Harbour is Western Brook Pond; this is something of an understatement, it's 16km (10 miles) long, bordered by cliffs up to 700m (2,300ft) high, and is 160m (525ft) deep and up to 3km (2 miles) wide. It's an oligotrophic lake, containing almost no nutrients and supporting little plant life—this water is some of the purest in the world.

There is a dramatic view of the remarkable Western Brook Pond from highway 430, but the only way to appreciate this scenic fiord-lake fully is to walk to its edge (6km/4 miles return) and take the boat trip (Jun to end Sep daily). Face to face with nature at its wildest, it's truly awe-inspiring.

About 6km (4 miles) south of the pond is Broom Point (mid-May to mid-Oct daily; reservations tel 709/458-2730), which offers an insight into the lives of a mid-20th-century fishing family.

✚ 407 X13 ✉ Gros Morne National Park Headquarters, Rocky Harbour, Newfoundland and Labrador, A0K 4N0 ☎ 709/458-2417 🕐 Daily ✋ Adult $9, child (6–16) $4.50, family $18 (includes Discovery Centre) ✈ Deer Lake Airport (32km/20 miles from park entrance) 🚌 Connections to Rocky Harbour from airport and ferries

FUNDY NATIONAL PARK AND ISLANDS

INFORMATION

www.pc.gc.ca

➕ 407 W16 ℹ️ Visitor Centre, Highway 114, Alma, New Brunswick, E4H 1B4
☎ 506/887-6000 🕐 Mid-May to mid-Oct daily; mid-Oct to mid-May Mon–Fri
🖐 Adult $7, child (6–16) $3.50, family $17.50

INTRODUCTION

Situated on the Bay of Fundy and southern New Brunswick's last true wilderness, this 206sq km (80sq mile) park is a wonderful combination of coastal highlands and shoreline. The bay, with its vast tidal range and cold waters, influences the entire park. You can experience the tidal fluctuation strolling on the beach and watching fishing boats come and go. There are also more than 100km (60 miles) of inland trails to explore, as well as the bay's islands.

One of the world's marine wonders, the Bay of Fundy experiences the highest tides anywhere on the planet. At the head of the bay, the gravitational pull of the sun and moon causes tides that rise and fall up to an incredible 16m (52ft) twice a day—every day! This huge rise is caused by a combination of factors—like water in a bathtub, the water in the bay has a natural rocking motion, called a *seiche*, that takes about 12 hours to rock from the mouth of the bay to its head and back again. This coincides with the frequency of the pulse from the Atlantic tides that flood into the bay. Accentuating the rise even further is the shape of the bay; because it becomes narrower and shallower towards its head, the water is forced higher up the shores.

Other places in the world have large tides, but their tidal ranges measure only about 10m (30ft) and they don't move as much water; in the Bay of Fundy, the tidal contribution is equal to the total daily discharge of all the world's rivers.

WHAT TO SEE

NATIONAL PARK COASTLINE

At the park's eastern entrance is Alma Beach, where many visitors time their arrival with low tide so that they can walk across the kilometer-wide (0.6-mile) tidal flats. A pole in the sand indicates how deep the water is at high tide. Be sure to walk back well before high tide, in less than an hour it is waist-deep.

In the 19th-century, a thriving sawmill stood at the mouth of the Point Wolfe River, 10km (6 miles) southwest of Alma. By the 1920s, however, all the accessible trees had been cut and the mill closed. You can follow a path overlooking a small gorge and dam and view the cove that once filled with schooners to transport the wood; explanatory panels tell the story. Look here for the old wooden covered bridge. At low tide you can walk down the long beach with its wide gravel bar, though be sure to check the tide tables before wandering too far (it is easy to become stranded as the tide rises).

At Herring Cove, 4km (2.5 miles) southwest of Alma, you can explore the tidal pools, seaweed-draped rocks and mud flats at low tide, and then return at high tide to find them all gone.

A good way to see the Fundy coastline is by joining one of the popular guided sea-kayaking trips that go out of Alma (▷ 164), with trips to suit novices and families as well as experienced paddlers. Another fun pastime at low tide is beachcombing, with plenty of shells and sealife washed up on the shore.

CALEDONIA HIGHLANDS
Stretching back from the coast are forested highlands, a wilderness area with dense forest, rivers with waterfalls, and plentiful wildlife. Fundy is on the Atlantic bird migration route, and more than 260 species have been identified within the park; 95 of these have nested in the park and the peregrine falcon has been reintroduced. The park has excellent visitor facilities, including campgrounds and a nine-hole golf course (mid-May to early Oct). The sharp rise in altitude within the Highlands makes for an interesting mix of trees, which in turn results in wonderful fall colors. These forests are home to 38 species of mammal, ranging from chipmunks and red squirrel to massive moose.

CAMPOBELLO ISLAND
▷ 144.

DEER ISLAND
Deer and the other two islands—Campobello and Grand Manan—lie in the mouth of Passamaquoddy Bay. They are evergreen-cloaked, often windswept and fog-bound, but are popular because they are so peaceful and have abundant wildlife—particularly birds and whales. Island life is dominated by the sea, and the high tides, whirlpools and swirling currents of the bay act as giant pumps, bringing up the nutrients that feed tiny marine organisms. These, in turn, are food for all kinds of sea creatures, and the 900 people who reside on Deer Island, which lies on the 45th Parallel midway between the Equator and the North Pole, live largely by harvesting lobsters and clams and by salmon farming. Off Deer's southern tip is the Old Sow Whirlpool, the largest tidal whirlpool in the western hemisphere. It is best viewed from Deer Island Point, three hours before high tide at new and full moon. There's a campground, picnic tables and a pebble beach, but swimming is not recommended!
🞣 407 W16 🛈 Lord's Cove, Deer Island, New Brunswick, E5V 1W2 🚢 Free ferry from L'Etete, near St. George, New Brunswick

GRAND MANAN ISLAND
Grand Manan is the largest of the Fundy Islands, and has towering cliffs, rugged scenery and a population of about 1,000. This is the North American capital for dulse, an edible seaweed used as a seasoning or eaten raw as a snack (an acquired taste). The island is also a bird sanctuary, where a total of 230 species have been sighted, and Machias Seal Island offshore has a puffin colony. Interestingly, Machias Seal is the subject of a boundary dispute between Canada and the US, an unresolved leftover from the War of 1812.
🞣 407 W16 🛈 1141 Route 776, Grand Manan, New Brunswick, E5G 4K9 ☎ 506/662-3442, 1-888/525-1655 🚢 From Blacks Harbour, New Brunswick

TIPS
» If you walk out on beaches at low tide, be aware of the times when the tide changes. The water rushes in—from nothing to waist-deep in less than an hour—and it's not always easy to scramble up the cliffs.
» Moose sometimes gather at the roadside in the evening and may wander onto the road, so drivers need to be aware of the hazard. Aside from not wanting to hurt the moose, their bulk and weight makes it like driving into a brick wall, and human fatalities are not uncommon.

Opposite *Point Wolfe is a great place for birding and beachcombing*
Below *Point Wolfe River Gorge, once busy with loggers and ships*

HALIFAX

INFORMATION

www.halifaxinfo.com

⊞ 407 X16 ℹ Scotia Square Visitors Centre, 5251 Duke Street, Halifax, Nova Scotia ☎ 902/490-4000 ℹ Waterfront Visitor Info Centre, Sackville Landing, Halifax, Nova Scotia ☎ 902/424-4248

INTRODUCTION

Halifax is the international gateway to the Atlanic Provinces, with the second-largest natural harbor in the world. Unsurprisingly, it can be wet and foggy, and it can be very windy, but on a fine summer's day or during its comparatively mild winter it is an exciting and interesting place to visit. Many attractions are along the waterfront, but the best place to start is up on Citadel Hill—for its fortress and panoramic overview of the city. Ferries cross the harbor to the twin city of Dartmouth.

Halifax was founded in July 1749 on land the native peoples called Chebucto (Big Harbor), and from the start it was a military stronghold. The city's history was frequently eventful, but one episode left a terrible mark. In December 1917, during World War I, the *Mont Blanc*, a French munitions ship carrying picric acid, guncotton, TNT and benzol, had a fatal collision with the *Imo*, a Belgian relief ship, in The Narrows of the harbor. There followed the greatest man-made explosion the world saw prior to the bombing of Hiroshima in 1945. A huge area of the city was completely flattened, more than 2,000 people died and 9,000 were injured, many blinded for life.

WHAT TO SEE

CITADEL NATIONAL HISTORIC SITE

Halifax is crowned by Citadel Hill, where the massive star-shaped fortress still dominates the city despite modern high-rise construction. There are views in every direction: of the city (including the famous Town Clock), the harbor, Dartmouth, across The Narrows, and the bridges that connect it to Halifax. Fortified since 1749, the present Citadel was completed in 1865. Inside, you are back

Above *Halifax's huge natural harbor has hosted the Tall Ships Race*

in the year 1869 when the 78th Highland Regiment was stationed here, now represented by costumed guides dressed in MacKenzie tartan kilts, feathered bonnets and bright red doublets. You can visit the Army Museum, barracks, guardroom, garrison cell, and powder magazine, and see the "Tides of History," a spectacular audiovisual presentation.

✉ Halifax, Nova Scotia, B3K 5M7 ☎ 902/426-5080 ⏰ Daily (animation Jun–Sep 15) ✋ Jun to mid-Sep adult $10.80, child (6–16) $5.40, family $26.90; May, mid-Sep to end Oct adult $7.05, child $3.40, family $17.60 ▢ ▦

THE WATERFRONT

Halifax's magnificent natural harbor extends nearly 16km (10 miles) inland—only Sydney Harbour in Australia is larger. It remains ice-free all winter and is almost divided into two by a stretch called The Narrows, which separates the outer harbor from the Bedford Basin. The city's lively waterfront area is colorful and fun, with a walkway stretching for 4km (2.5 miles), waterfront restaurants, fine museums, and the ever-present salty smell of the ocean. Besides all the activity on the water, there's much to see and do on land.

A group of old warehouses on Upper Water Street were innovatively renovated in the 1970s and are now collectively known as the Historic Properties. An early but still very successful urban regeneration scheme, they house restaurants, craft stores and offices. There's a particularly good food market area offering fresh fish and seafood to eat in or take out, breads, coffee and more. From here, you can walk along to the casino in one direction and to Pier 21 (▷ below) in the other. Along the way you'll pass the Maritime Museum (▷ below), *Bluenose II* if it's visiting (▷ 151, Lunenburg), tugboats, the Dartmouth ferry and the Court House. HMCS *Sackville* (May–end Dec daily can be visited at HMC Dockyard, Jan–end Apr on reservation, tel 902/427-2837), a World War II corvette floating at Sackville Landing. The sole survivor of more than 100 corvettes built to escort convoys, restored as a museum commemorating all who served in the Canadian Navy.

MARITIME MUSEUM OF THE ATLANTIC

The city's distinguished seafaring history is reflected in this excellent museum on the waterfront, partly located in a 1879 ship's chandlery. It houses a collection of full-size and model ships, some of them floating, tells the stories of the *Titanic* (150 of the drowned were buried in Halifax, many unidentified) and the Cunard Steamship Line (Samuel Cunard was from Halifax), and has an excellent film about the Halifax Explosion (▷ Introduction). Other displays include shipwrecks, hidden treasures and a reconstruction of the ship's chandlery of 100 years ago.

✉ 1675 Lower Water Street, Halifax, Nova Scotia, B3J 1S3 ☎ 902/424-7490 ⏰ May–end Oct daily; rest of year Tue–Sun ✋ May–Oct adult $8.50, child (6–17) $4.50, family $22; Nov–Apr adult $4.50, child $2.50, family $10.75 ▦

PIER 21

www.pier21.ca

Pier 21, at the end of the waterfront walkway, was Canada's "front door" from 1928 to 1971. More than a million immigrants entered the country here (not to mention wartime evacuees, refugees and war brides). Today, it's an interactive visitor center where Canadians can record their memories. The dramatic multimedia presentation is a fascinating and emotional experience for immigrants and their descendants. It also includes the World War II balcony overlooking the harbor where half a million troops boarded ships to serve in Europe. In October 2007, the Harbourside Gallery was opened, a vast space for temporary exhibitions on themes of immigration and nation-building.

✉ 1055 Marginal Road, Halifax, Nova Scotia, B3H 4P6 ☎ 902/425-7770 ⏰ May–end Nov daily; rest of year Tue–Sat ✋ Adult $8.50, child (6–16) $5, family $21 ▢ ▦

Above *The Citadel Signal Mast*
Below *The Town Clock is one of the city's most recognized landmarks*

HOPEWELL ROCKS

www.thehopewellrocks.ca

It is a strange experience to be walking on the seabed, knowing that within a few hours the water will be 10m (30ft) deep on that very spot. To get the best of this unique place on Shepody Bay, visit first at high tide, when the bay is dotted with tiny tree-covered islands, then return at low tide to walk among them. The "islands" are actually narrow red sandstone columns up to 15m (50ft) high and wider at the top.

Hopewell Rocks are 47km (25 miles) south of Moncton on Highway 114, going toward Fundy National Park. At the top of the cliff is an interpretive center with displays explaining the Fundy phenomenon. Make sure you consult the tide tables to time your visit so that you don't get cut off by waters that rise at up to 2.4m (8ft) per hour. At low tide you can get to the rocky beach via a steep staircase.

407 W16 131 Discovery Road, Hopewell Cape, New Brunswick, E4H 4Z5 506/734-3534, 1-877/734-3429 (toll-free within Canada) Mid-May to mid-Oct daily Adult $8, child (5–18) $5.75, family $20

LABRADOR

www.gov.nf.ca/tourism

This is one of the last great wilderness areas on the face of the Earth, where glacial action, erosion and internal upheaval have carved a land of unsurpassed beauty.

There are towering mountains, massive rock faces, huge lakes and fast-flowing rivers. The air is clean, the water is pure and there is an amazing diversity of wildlife.

Labrador stretches 1,000km (600 miles) south to north, from the Strait of Belle Isle to the shores of Ungava Bay, and covers a staggering 1,560,000sq km (600,000sq miles). Much of Labrador is inaccessible, but there's the scenic coast route from Blanc Sablon, Québec in the south to Cartwright, and the Trans-Labrador Highway, which comes in from Baie Comeau, Québec, in the west and runs through Labrador City to Goose Bay. In 2009 a new section will link Cartwright and Goose Bay. Some parts have gravel surfaces and there may be winter closures (tel: 709/896-7840 to check on road conditions). Communities farther north can be reached only by coastal ferries. Much of Labrador is easier to reach in winter, with a snowmobile or dogsled! The people have to be self-reliant to survive in this some-times hostile land.

In the 16th century, the old Basque community of Red Bay, 78km (48 miles) from Blanc Sablon, now a National Historic Site, was the whaling capital of the world; the interpretation center here (early-Jun to early-Oct daily) has items retrieved from shipwrecks.

The paved section of Highway 510 ends at Red Bay, but a gravel road continues another 65km (40 miles) north to Mary's Harbour, from where you can cross (mid-Jun to mid-Sep two ferries daily, tel 709/921-6216) to Battle Harbour. Here, mercantile saltfish premises established in the 1770s developed into a thriving community recognized as the "Capital of Labrador" for 200 years or so. Since the decline of the cod fishery, Battle Harbour has been deserted, but is now a National Historic Site, with restored historic structures, walkways and work areas, and a collection of fishery-related items.

409 V12 Newfoundland and Labrador Tourism 709/896-3489; 1-866/41-1044

LOUISBOURG FORTRESS

www.pc.gc.ca

The fortress of Louisbourg glowers into the mists, fogs and storms of the North Atlantic, a mighty symbol of the fierce struggle between France and Britain. This was the great fortress of New France guarding the entrance to the St. Lawrence River and the approach to Québec. Not only did it have the largest garrison in North America, it was also a commercial hub with a harbor, governor's palace, hospital, homes, arsenals and warehouses.

Construction of the star-shaped fortified town began in 1719. The Canadian government has now faithfully re-created about a quarter of the original site to reflect a town of the 1740s covering 4.8ha (12 acres), with more than 50 buildings and extensive stone fortifications. From the visitor center, you can walk or take a shuttle bus to the fortress. In summer costumed interpreters re-enact every level of society.

407 Y15 259 Park Service Road, Louisbourg, Nova Scotia, B1C 2L2 902/733-2280 Mid-May to end Oct daily 9.30–5; full animation and services Jun–end Sep, limited May and Oct Adult $16.50, child (6–16) $8.50, family $40.50 Bakery and restaurant

Left *Hopewell Rocks, supporting tiny islets, are exposed at low tide*

LUNENBURG

One of Nova Scotia's most historic and beautiful towns, Lunenburg has narrow streets lined with colorful buildings that reflect its seafaring heritage and now also provide shopping for some very original products. The buildings in Lincoln and Pelham streets have antiques and craft shops that are great for browsing. In 1995, UNESCO, when adding Lunenburg to its list of World Heritage Sites, declared it to be an "outstanding example" of British colonial settlement in North America. Set on a neck of land 92km (57 miles) east of Halifax, the town maintains its original rectangular grid pattern and the wonderful variety of brightly painted wood-framed buildings that the early settlers constructed here.

ON THE WATERFRONT

The attractive waterfront remains active with the fishing and shipbuilding activities that have been the backbone of the town's prosperity for 250 years. Here, the Fisheries Museum of the Atlantic (May–end Oct daily; rest of year Mon–Fri), in a group of red-painted buildings, includes floating vessels at the wharfside, and you can board the banks schooner *Theresa E. Connor*, the *Cape Sable*, an early steel-hulled side trawler and the Cape North trawler.

The museum also has an exhibit dedicated to the famous *Bluenose*, which was built in Lunenburg. It was the undefeated champion of the North Atlantic fishing fleet from 1921 to 1942. In 1963, an exact replica 43.6m (143ft) long, was constructed, and the *Bluenose II* offers summer tours and cruises up and down the coast between Halifax and Lunenburg. A schedule of her visits is available from the tourist information center or at www.bluenose2.ns.ca.

MARITIME HERITAGE

Established in 1753, Lunenburg was the next British colonial settlement in Nova Scotia after Halifax and soon became the focus of a bustling economy based on fishing, shipbuilding and maritime commerce. By the 19th century, the town was thriving, its harbor filled with masts and sails. Today it's also home to one of the largest fish and seafood processing plants in the world. The most important catch of Lunenburg's vessels, the scallop, is now king.

INFORMATION

www.explorelunenburg.ca

➕ 407 X16 ℹ Blockhouse Hill Road, Lunenburg, Nova Scotia ☎ 902/634 8100 🕒 May–end Oct daily; closed rest of year

Above *Few commercial docks are as picturesque as those at Lunenburg*

PRINCE EDWARD ISLAND

INFORMATION
www.peiplay.com
✚ 407 X15 ℹ 6 Prince Street (Box
2000) Charlottetown, Prince Edward
Island, C1A 7N8 ☎ 902/368-4444,
1-8000/463-4PEI; www.gov.pe.ca/
visitorsguides

INTRODUCTION

This tranquil island, and Canada's smallest province at 230km (140 miles) from tip to tip, is affectionately known as "Spud Island" for the principal crop that comes out of its bright red soil (look for the brick-red souvenir "PEI Dirt Shirt," dyed with earth!). The island is an extremely popular holiday destination for residents of the other Atlantic provinces, and is fast gaining ground with people from farther afield, who enjoy its peaceful, gently rolling countryside, its fine beaches and its unhurried pace of life. There's a tradition of fiddle music here to rival that of Cape Breton, plus an island-wide culinary love affair with seafood—in addition to the excellent restaurants, you'll see signs inviting you to "Lobster Suppers" in the most unlikely places.

The island is also the home of the much-loved fictional character in *Anne of Green Gables*. In 2008 the island celebrated the centenary of the publication of Lucy Maud Montgomery's engaging story, adding to the already ubiquitous presence of her young heroine in souvenir shops, hotel theme packages and island attractions.

Getting to the island has been easy since the Confederation Bridge—at 13km (8 miles) the longest bridge in the world over ice-covered waters—opened in 1997. You cross for free, but pay a toll ($39.50 for cars) on the way back. The island is also connected by ferry to Pictou, Nova Scotia. There's a good network of mostly quiet roads. By far the greatest charm of PEI lies in its lovely landscapes and sea views, and the provincial government have devised and signposted three day-long routes for making the most of them—the North Cape Coastal Drive covers the west of the island, the Blue Heron the center, and the Kings Byway the east. The island is basically crescent-shaped, its much-indented coastline dotted with lighthouses, and there is no shortage of superb sandy beaches (some are tinged red by the same oxide that colors the soil). Inland, which is never farther than 16km (10 miles) from the coast, the altitude rarely exceeds 90m (300ft).

Above *Cyclists touring the perimeter of Prince Edward Island*

HIGHLIGHTS

CHARLOTTETOWN

For a provincial capital, Charlottetown is laid-back and modest in size, but in Canadian history it has an important place. It was here in 1864 that representatives of the island, New Brunswick, Nova Scotia, Québec and Ontario met to discuss the creation of a new nation, and this led to the Confederation of Canada in 1867. The meeting took place in Province House, the grand provincial legislature building and also a national historic site (Jun–late Oct daily; late Oct–end May Mon–Fri), part of which has been restored to its 1864 appearance. On the waterfront, where the delegates landed in 1864, Founders Hall (mid-May to early Oct daily; early Oct to mid-May Tue–Sat) relates Canadian history through multimedia displays and theater, and there's a waterfront boardwalk with interpretive panels. History aside, this is a pleasant little city by the sea, with decent shopping and a lively festival each summer.

🚩 407 X15 ✉ Prince Street, Charlottetown, Prince Edward Island, C1A 7N8 ☎ 902/368-4444, 1-800/464-4PEI

PRINCE EDWARD ISLAND NATIONAL PARK

The national park stretches for 40km (25 miles) along the shores of the Gulf of St. Lawrence from Cavendish to Dalvay, and encompasses some large and highly mobile sand dunes that are a rare phenomenon in North America. Walking trails thread through a varied landscape of dunes, red sandstone cliffs and some of the finest saltwater beaches in Canada, and the Interpretation Centre (mid-May to early Oct daily) at Greenwich has displays on the ecology of the area, plus a 3-D model of the entire Greenwich Peninsula.

🚩 407 W15 ℹ️ 2 Palmers Lane, Charlottetown, Prince Edward Island, C1A 5V6 ☎ 902/672-6350 🕐 Daily (animation late Jun–late Aug) 🎟 Adult $7, child (6–16) $3.50; mid-Sep to end May free 💻 🏛

CAVENDISH

Up on the north coast, Cavendish has become a major tourist center for one reason only—it was the home of author Lucy Maud Montgomery, who has made PEI famous worldwide. At least eight houses on the island claim some connection with the author, but here you'll find the original Green Gables House, where young Maud, as she was known to her family, often came to visit her relatives. It's now a national historic site where you can tour the house and farmyard, and there are regular summer events. The author's grave can be seen in the Cavendish Community Cemetery. To cater to the huge numbers of visitors who come for the "Anne" sites, a number of other attractions have sprung up, not all of them quite in keeping with the rural idyll portrayed in the books. The re-creation of Avonlea Village (▷ 165) has a degree of charm—and children love it—but you might want to bypass the cluster of family fun parks, waxworks displays, and weird-and-wonderful themed exhibits that cluster around Highway 6. Beyond you will find a superb beach with miles of unspoiled sands and warm, shallow water and scenic routes to places like lovely Rustico Bay, just to the east.

🚩 407 W15 ✉ Intersection of Routes 13 and 6 for entrance to national park ☎ 902/063-7830

BASIN HEAD FISHERIES MUSEUM

PEI maintains a strong fishing heritage ($65-million-worth of lobsters were landed in 1995), and over in the east off Route 16 near the little town of Souris (French for mouse; the town was named after a one-time infestation), this museum gives a feel for the life of the inshore fishermen. Displays include fishing shacks and a cannery to visit.

🚩 407 X15 ✉ Basin Head, near Souris, Prince Edward Island ☎ 902/357-7233 🕐 Jun–end Sep daily 🎟 Adult $4 💻 🏛

TIPS

» Stop at the visitor center on the New Brunswick side of Confederation Bridge for splendid views of the graceful structure.

» The PEI Heritage Passport will save 35 percent on admission to any three of the seven attractions in the scheme (tel: 902/368-6600 for details).

Below *Green Gables House, in the PEI National Park, near Cavendish*

INFORMATION

www.stjohns.ca

✚ 407 Z13 ℹ 1st Floor, Gentara Building, 348 Water Street, St. John's, Newfoundland and Labrador, A1C 5M2

☎ 709/576-8106

TIPS

» Take a boat tour from St. John's to view whales among 10,000-year-old icebergs.

» When the sun goes down and the attractions close, seek out a pub with live traditional Newfoundland music.

» If you are around in July and August, a military tattoo takes place on Signal Hill, performed by students in the 19th century uniform of the Royal Newfoundland Companies.

ST. JOHN'S

The capital of Newfoundland faces the Atlantic Ocean on the Avalon Peninsula, and its location is nothing short of spectacular, on hills that rise behind a superb natural harbor whose narrow entrance is appropriately called The Narrows. The city's major attractions are clustered on, and below, the great rock of Signal Hill; be warned, the hilltop is prone to very strong winds—which is why there are no trees. There are wonderful trails starting from Cabot Tower: to the Queen's Battery, with its views of the city, and the Ladies Lookout, the highest point on Signal Hill at 160m (525ft); you can even descend the North Head to The Narrows by a really steep path on the ocean side (not advisable if it is windy!).

Some skeptics dispute St. John's two major claims to fame: that John Cabot entered the harbor in 1497 to "discover" the New World; and that on August 5, 1583, Sir Humphrey Gilbert chose this spot to proclaim Queen Elizabeth I's sovereignty over Newfoundland, the first act in the creation of the vast British Empire. But it doesn't matter. There is no doubt in anyone's mind that this is a city with a very long history. A community first sprang up here because of the rich fishery, the city grew commercially in the 19th century, and the harbor was an important gathering place for convoys during World War II. St. John's has a character all of its own, and its citizens adore their rocky, wind-blown city.

WHAT TO SEE

SIGNAL HILL NATIONAL HISTORIC PARK

Today, it would be unthinkable to visit St. John's without driving up here for the panoramic view across the city, harbor and coastline—Cape Spear, North America's most easterly point, is visible to the southeast. The hill, now a national historic site, is topped by the squat stone Cabot Tower, the city's best-known landmark, built in 1897 to commemorate the 400th anniversary of John Cabot's arrival. Today, it houses displays on communications. As early as 1704, signal flags were flown from the summit to announce the arrival of vessels, but in 1901 communications history was made here when Guglielmo Marconi received the first transatlantic wireless signal—the letter "s" in Morse code, from Poldhu in Cornwall, England, more than 2,700km (1,700 miles) away.

✉ Signal Hill Road, St. John's, Newfoundland and Labrador, A1C 5M9 ☎ 709/ 772-5367

🕐 Daily. Visitor center: mid-May to mid-Oct daily; mid-Oct to mid-May Mon–Fri 🅿 Adult $4, (6–16) $2 🏛

Above *Fine old clapboard houses, painted in pastel hues, line Gower Street*

ST. ANDREWS-BY-THE-SEA

www.standrewsnb.ca

St. Andrews sits at the end of a peninsula jutting into Passamaquoddy Bay, part of the Bay of Fundy, and is a captivating, neat and orderly community, with elegant houses along wide, tree-lined streets. Kept free of fast-food outlets and chain stores, the main street is an attractive mix of restaurants and small stores selling crafts, antiques and general supplies.

The first people to settle St. Andrews were Loyalists from the United States, who moved here after the American Revolution. More recently, the town has attracted many artists and craftspeople, who have found an outlet in the not-for-profit Sunbury Shores Arts and Nature Centre (Jul–end Aug daily; Sep–end Jun Mon–Fri) on Water Street. It houses a gallery, craft workshops and artists' studios, and hosts regular exhibitions and organizes courses. You can also join a guided nature walk from here (Jul–end Aug, Tue–Sat). Some houses are open to the public, as is the lovely 11ha (27-acre) Kingsbrae Garden (mid-May to mid-Oct daily).

There's also a harbor, with boats offering fishing or whale-watching trips.

✚ 407 W16 ⓘ Chamber of Commerce, 46 Reed Avenue, St. Andrews, New Brunswick, E5B 1A1 ☎ 506/529-3555

SAINT JOHN

www.tourismsaintjohn.com

Saint John is the largest city in New Brunswick and commonly called "Fog City" because of the dense mists that roll in off the water. A trip to see Reversing Falls Rapids is almost obligatory. At low tide, the Saint John River empties into the Bay of Fundy through a narrow rocky gorge where there is a series of rapids and whirlpools. At high tide, the force of the Fundy tides (▷ 146–147) carries water upstream, rising as much as 4.4m (14.5ft) in the gorge. This reversal of the water flow and rising of the level means that, for a very short time, boats can actually

navigate over the rapids. To view the phenomenon, go to Fallsview Park (west side of Highway 100 as it crosses the Saint John River). The Falls Restaurant in the park offers a film presentation of the phenomenon in the rooftop theater ($2.50). You really need to visit the spot twice—near low tide and near high tide—but the smell of the pulp mill can be rather strong!

Apart from the falls, don't miss the old City Market, downtown on Charlotte Street (year-round Mon–Sat), which sells lobsters, cheese, the edible seaweed dulse, and other fresh produce.

✚ 407 W16 ⓘ P.O. Box 1971, Saint John, New Brunswick, E2L 4L1 ☎ 506/658-2855, 1-866/463-8639

ST. JOHN'S (NEWFOUNDLAND)
▷ 154.

TERRA NOVA NATIONAL PARK

www.pc.gc.ca

On Newfoundland's east coast, the Terra Nova National Park protects 400sq km (154sq miles) of boreal forest and coastline. It's easy to get here by road via the Trans-Canada Highway which bisects the park.

Most of the facilities are on Newman Sound, including the Visitor Information Centre (mid-May to mid-Oct daily) at Saltons, which includes a marine exhibition area with aquariums, displays and film from an underwater camera. From here, you can take boat tours (mid-May to end Oct) to view the wildlife.

✚ 407 Y13 ☎ 709/533-2801 ⊙ Daily 🖐 Boat tours mid-May to mid-Oct; adult $5.50, child (6–16) $2.75, family $13.50

VILLAGE HISTORIQUE ACADIEN

www.villagehistoriqueacadien.com

In northern New Brunswick, on the Acadian Peninsula, this provides a remarkably authentic representation of the life of the Acadians—settlers of French descent—between about 1770 and 1939. Acadian pride shines through at the village, 50km (30 miles) east of Bathurst. More than 40 buildings are staffed by interpreters in period costume. Visitors can sample Acadian cuisine at La Table des Ancêtres and stay overnight at the Château Albert.

✚ 407 W15 ✉ 14311 Road 11 (P.O. Box 5620), Caraquet, New Brunswick, E1W 1B7 ☎ 506/726-2600, 877/721-2200 ⊙ Early Jun–late Sep daily 🖐 Adult $15, child (6–17) $10, family $36 (lower prices off season) 🍽 🏛

Below *Ferris wheel at St. John's fun fair*

BONNE BAY

Stretching deep inland from the Gulf of St. Lawrence, Bonne Bay is surrounded by the Long Range Mountains and Tablelands of Gros Morne National Park. The bay penetrates inland and divides into two sections; choose between driving the north side or the south, or do both.

THE DRIVES
Length: North side 39km (24 miles); south side 52km (32 miles)
Allow: A half-day for each drive
Start: Wiltondale
End: North side drive at Lobster Cove Head Lighthouse, Rocky Harbour; south side drive at Trout River Pond
How to get there: Turn off the Trans-Canada Highway onto Highway 422 at Deer Lake, for west coast of Newfoundland

NORTH SIDE DRIVE

★ From Wiltondale, take Highway 430 north in the direction of Gros Morne National Park. The highway climbs steeply and, after 13km (8 miles), there is a view of Bonne Bay below.

❶ The mountains drop straight into this fiord, which is over 200m (700ft)

deep. It has two main arms—the east, which is beside you, and the south—connected by a narrow strait of water known as a "tickle".

Drive 14km (9 miles) to an excellent place on the left to admire the bay.

❷ On a clear day, Gros Morne Mountain is visible to your right.

Continue for 5km (3 miles) and you will see a parking area for hikers wishing to scale Gros Morne, a tough eight hour climb. After another 2km (1.2 miles) you will reach the visitor center.

❸ In addition to background information, the center has several interesting videos explaining the park's outstanding geology.

From here, there's a detour to Norris Point (8km/5 miles), with a spectacular viewpoint on the right 2km (1.2 miles) after taking the turn. You can see the Tablelands across the water. After crossing a narrow isthmus, you will arrive at the water's edge.

❹ The Bonne Bay Marine Station here offers displays and interpretive programs in the summer months. There are also boat tours and a water taxi service to Woody Point.

Return to Highway 430. Drive 4km (2.5 miles) from the visitor center to Rocky Harbour. Take a left turn off Highway 430 and drive 1km (0.6 miles) to Salmon Point (you may see whales, if you're lucky). A further 1km (0.6 miles) takes you

to Lobster Cove Head Lighthouse.
Park and walk (five minutes) to the
lighthouse.

5 The lighthouse has been a
beacon to shipping since 1897. The
old lightkeeper's house (mid-May to
mid-Oct) has displays on the lives of
the people who have lived on this
coast for the last 4,000 years.

SOUTH SIDE DRIVE

★ From Wiltondale, take Highway
431 and follow signs for Woody
Point and Trout River. After 10km (6
miles) cross the Lomond River and
enter the Gros Morne National Park.
After 3km (2 miles), turn right, continue for 4km (2.5 miles) to Lomond.

1 This former logging community is
a great place to stop for a picnic, or
even a quick dip (although the water
is too cold to stay in for long).

Return to Highway 431. You will
climb steeply up the "Struggle" for
7km (4 miles) to the top.

2 From this viewpoint there is an
impressive view of the Tablelands
over the top of the Peak of Teneriffe.
Their orange-rust color contrasts
with the deep green elsewhere.

Continue on Highway 431 for 5km
(3 miles), enjoying views of
Glenburnie and the other small
communities. Beyond Glenburnie,
the road follows the eastern shore,
with views of the surrounding hills
and Woody Point up front.

3 In early summer, whales are
sometimes seen here chasing
schools of capelin, herring and
mackerel.

Drive 9km (5 miles) beyond
Glenburnie, taking the detour off
Highway 431 into Woody Point.

4 The community of Woody Point
was once the hub of the fishing and

lumbering industries around Bonne
Bay; its fine old homes recall the
wealth of those days.

Return to Highway 431, drive 1km
(0.6 miles) from Woody Point to the
Discovery Centre.

5 Displays at the Discovery Centre
(May–end Oct daily; Mon–Thu
rest of year) explain the geological
phenomena of the Gros Morne
National Park, which was declared a
World Heritage Site in 1987.

Continue for another 6km (4 miles)
beyond the Discovery Centre and
you come to the Tablelands Walk
(▷ 158–159).

6 On the drive here from the
Discovery Centre, notice the difference between the ocher-colored
Tablelands and Winterhouse Brook
Canyon to your left, and the green
valley ahead and to your right. The
road marks the division between
these two geological formations.

As you continue, there are views
ahead of the Gulf of St. Lawrence
as the road descends to Trout River,

which lies 12km (7 miles) from the
Tablelands walk.

7 Trout River has an active fishing
industry. Notice the black volcanic
rock all around.

Some 2km (1.2 miles) along on the
road to the campground, is a viewpoint of Trout River Pond.

8 Here you get a magnificent
view of this long narrow fiord set
between the Tablelands and the
Gregory Plateau Hills. Again, the
contrast in color between the orange
rock and the green hills is incredibly
striking. There are boat tours on
Trout River Pond (Jun to Sep).

WHEN TO GO

The north side drive is best on
sunny days that highlight the colors
(the Discovery Centre is closed
November through April). For the
south side drive, late summer is
best for weather, but there's more
chance of spotting whales earlier
in the year. December brings the
caribou down from the Tablelands,
and they are often seen, along with
moose, on the roadsides.

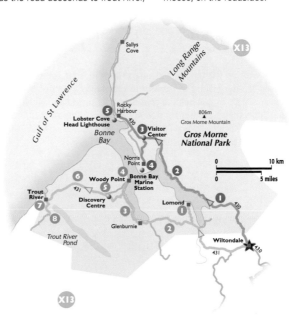

WALK

WALKING ON THE EARTH'S MANTLE

This unique walk on flat-topped and almost barren ocher-colored rock, never usually seen at the Earth's surface, is in Newfoundland's Gros Morne Tablelands. Composed of peridotite from the Earth's mantle, the Tablelands record a time when the continents of Eurasia and North America collided. Formed far below the ocean floor, they were transported hundreds of kilometers to their present position some 450 million years ago. Gros Morne National Park (▷ 145) was placed on UNESCO's World Heritage List because of the importance of its geological features.

THE WALK

Length: 4km (2.5 miles)
Allow: 1–2 hours
Start/end: In the parking area on Highway 431, 5km (3 miles) from the Discovery Centre in Woody Point (direction Trout River)
Ascent: About 60m (200ft)
How to get there: Gros Morne is in the west of Newfoundland. Turn off the Trans-Canada Highway onto Highway 422 at Deer Lake, then Highway 431 from Wiltondale

After reading explanatory panels about the geology of the area, begin your walk. You will soon pass a second trail, part of a 500m (540-yard) loop, which can be made by those not wishing to walk the whole trail (take this loop on your return). Much of the trail, except the last section, follows an old gravel roadbed, so it's reasonably flat and easy.

The path is marked by stones, and you should not wander off it—with

little vegetation, it is hard to judge distances (and heights) in the Tablelands. What looks like a short, flat and easy hike can actually be a long, hard struggle over jumbled boulders.

The ocher-colored rock here is virtually devoid of vegetation—almost desert-like. Peridotite weathers from a dark green to the rusty brown you see around you as oxygen reacts with the iron in the rock. The twisted and gnarled larch trees and alders growing here are small but they are hundreds of years old.

Continue about 1km (0.6 miles).

To your right and high above you, a deep, steep-walled basin can be made out in the mountainside. Known as a cirque, it's a remnant of retreating glaciers and is best viewed from the largish bridge over the stream flowing from it. Along the trail you will cross many streams by boardwalk bridges. At dusk or in foggy weather, take particular care—it's easy to miss your footing.

Soon afterward, to the left, there's a splendid view of the verdant South Arm of Bonne Bay below. After about 1.5km (1 mile), the path leaves the old roadway and bears right, marked by man-made stone ridges. After 2km (1.2 miles), you will reach the bottom of Winterhouse Canyon, from which the Winterhouse Brook issues.

This is a lovely place to sit on the rocks and have a picnic. Note the rocks in the stream bed, with surfaces resembling snake skin. This is peridotite which has reacted to the passage of water by breaking up into a series of tiny cracks. You can walk farther into the canyon but there is no trail and the going is rough.

Return by the same route. Just before reaching the parking area, which you can see ahead, you can follow the alternative loop trail mentioned at the start of this walk. This loop enables you to appreciate some of the plants that have managed to adapt and grow in this very harsh environment.

The pitcher plant consumes insects to make up for the nutrient-poor soil; the yellow lady's slipper grows beside streams where it can benefit from the calcium leaching out of the rock. You will also see Arctic plants,

which are at the southern limit of their growing range here.

WHEN TO GO
During the national park's Summer Interpretation Program (late Jun–Sep), when wardens lead guided tours.

WHERE TO EAT
✉ Old Loft Restaurant, Water Street, Woody Point ☎ 709/453-2294

WHERE TO STAY
✉ Victorian Manor Heritage Properties, Main Road, Woody Point ☎ 709/453-2485, 866/453-2485

Opposite *A mountain stream in the heart of the Tablelands*
Below *The tableland rocks have great geological importance*

DRIVE

DRIVE THE CABOT TRAIL

The Cabot Trail, in the northern part of Cape Breton Island in Nova Scotia, is named after the Italian explorer who is said to have landed at its northern tip in 1497. Hugging the coast, the road winds up and down, with fine views of ocean, craggy mountains, rocky inlets and dense forests. Along the way, look for moose, bald eagles, whales and a multitude of seabirds.

THE DRIVE
Length: 292km (181 miles)
Allow: 2 days
Start/end: Baddeck
How to get there: From the Canso Causeway, take Trans-Canada 105 east to Baddeck
Warning: Cape Breton, especially the Atlantic coast, is well known for its fogs. Switchbacks and almost dizzying changes of altitude can make the drive hazardous.

★ Drive west from Baddeck on Trans-Canada Highway 105 toward Canso Causeway, along the Bras d'Or Lake shore. After 8km (5 miles), at Buckwheat Corner, turn right on the Cabot Trail. Drive 52km (32 miles) and the Margaree River and harbor come into view.

❶ You follow the Margaree River through mostly agricultural country, and you'll cross the river, driving north on the undulating Gulf Coast.

After crossing the river, the village names are French and you'll see the tricolor Acadian flag along the way.

After driving another 24km (15 miles), you'll come to Chéticamp.

❷ Chéticamp is a sprawling fishing village. At 15067 Main Street, close to the Roman Catholic church of St.-Pierre, is the Coopérative Artisanale Acadienne (May–end Oct daily, then Tue and Fri 1–3pm). The community is famous for its handmade hooked rugs, and the co-op offers a good selection. There's a restaurant and a small museum (May–end Oct daily).

Drive on 8km (5 miles) to enter Cape Breton Highlands National Park. This is one of the most spectacular parts of the drive, but the road is very steep and winding in some places, with frequent switchbacks.

❸ If you drive the trail between May and October, stop at the Information Centre at the park entrance to buy a permit (adult $7, child $3.50, family $17.25. Take time here to view the interesting exhibitions and videos, and browse around the excellent bookstore (mid-May to mid-Oct daily).

At regular intervals on the route you'll find turnouts (pull-offs, or lay-bys) where you can stop and admire the views of the Gulf of St. Lawrence or take one of the walks that leads off the highway. The drive climbs 455m (1,493ft) up French Mountain, followed by 355m (1,165ft) up Mackenzie Mountain—the switchback descent from here is particularly dramatic, with views along the coast to Pleasant Bay. Drive 14km (9 miles) beyond Pleasant Bay to the Lone Shieling (parking on right).

Left *The glorious coastline is among the most scenic in eastern Canada*
Below *A whale breaking the waters around Cape Breton*

❹ The short but rewarding 15- to 20-minute walk to the Lone Shieling, a stone cottage, is through maple forest beside a stream. The tiny cottage is a replica of a Scottish sheep crofter's hut common to the Highlands and islands of Scotland. It is a tribute to the many Scots who settled in this area after the Highland Clearances in Scotland in the 18th and 19th centuries.

There are fine views as you enter the valley of the North Aspy River and as you descend to the village of Cape North on Aspy Bay. The next section of the Cabot Trail is far less scenic, being inland, but there is a very good chance that you'll see moose, especially in early morning or evening. After 34km (21 miles), there's a detour to Neil's Harbour.

❺ The 2km (1.2-mile) detour into Neil's Harbour takes you to this attractive fishing village and its sandy bay. Park by the lighthouse.

Return to the Cabot Trail and drive 6km (4 miles) to Black Brook Cove (park and walk to the beach).

❻ Scenic Black Brook Cove has pink granite rocks stretching into the sea, contrasting with the lush green forest of the hillsides inland. If you have time, walk along the coast. Strung along the next 20km

(12 miles) or so of the Cabot Trail around North Bay and Ingonish Harbour is a series of communities that together form a resort area popular for fishing, swimming, boating, whale-watching and golf.

Continue your drive beyond Middle Head for 7km (4 miles) to Cape Smokey, which rises 366m (1,200ft).

❼ The trail climbs steeply up Cape Smokey. From the lookout at the summit, the view is one of the most dramatic along the whole of the drive. The descent, a series of vertiginous switchbacks, returns to sea-level and continues south along

the Gaelic Coast. Offshore are the Bird Islands, where vast numbers of seabirds nest in summer.

Remain on the Cabot Trail and follow the winding shoreline of St. Ann's Bay to South Gut St. Ann's, or take the scenic alternative on Highway 312 along a narrow spit of land, then cross St. Ann's Bay by a two-minute ferry ride (cars $5) across the narrow outlet to join Trans-Canada Highway 105 and the Cabot Trail. After joining Trans-Canada Highway 105, turn right and continue for 19km (12 miles) for the return to Baddeck.

WHEN TO GO
It's good in all seasons if you avoid the foggy days, but summer is best for whale-spotting.

WHERE TO EAT
✉ Rusty Anchor, Pleasant Bay, Cape Breton
☎ 902/224-1313

WHERE TO STAY
✉ Inverary Resort, 368 Shore Road, Baddeck ☎ 902/295-3500, 800/565-5660
✉ Cheticamp Outfitters Inn, Cheticamp
☎ 902/224-2776

MIDDLE HEAD ON THE CABOT TRAIL

Middle Head, in Cape Breton, Nova Scotia, is a long, narrow protrusion into the Atlantic Ocean. It separates North Bay from Ingonish Harbour and has fabulous views of the rocky coast and mountains. In 1890, Henry Corson, a friend of inventor Alexander Graham Bell, built a house here after discovering this area while staying with Bell in Baddeck (▷ 143). His home became part of the national park in 1938 and, in 1951, it was replaced by Keltic Lodge, a fine hotel that's run by the provincial government of Nova Scotia.

THE WALK

Distance: 4km (2.5 miles)

Allow: about 2 hours

Start/end: Parking area signed "Trail No. 25 Middle Head" just beyond Keltic Lodge

How to get there: From the Canso Causeway, take Trans-Canada 105 through Baddeck, then turn left onto the Cabot Trail at South Gut St. Ann's or reach it via the Englishtown ferry. Drive north toward Ingonish Beach (88km/55 miles from Baddeck). Follow signs for Keltic Lodge, pass the lodge and park in the designated area

Warning: The cliffs at the tip are extremely steep and mists can descend quickly. Take care with children

At the beginning of the trail, note the old gate posts—this was once a carriage road linking a country estate with summer fishing shacks, and the gates kept the cows from wandering along the trail. The path goes up and down, with viewpoints of Cape Smokey across Ingonish Harbour on the right. After 1km (0.6 miles) you come to Trail Junction, an alternative route that you can take on your return. After a steep descent with views ahead of the peninsula, you will reach the narrow section of the headland. There are superb views in both directions—to Ingonish Island in North Bay, and across Ingonish Harbour.

Until fairly recently, there were fishermen's shacks here, along with nets, traps and drying racks. These have all been gone since the 1980s, as have the cod that were fished.

The path continues up and down, with several lookouts and benches where you can pause to rest and enjoy the surroundings. The forest of mainly beech trees gives way to dense fir on the approach to the tip of the peninsula.

In addition to the trees, other plants here include creeping juniper, black crowberry and stunted white spruce. In the winter, the wild

Atlantic winds batter this peninsula, and the salt-laden fog and rain flow over the cliffs, permeating the thin soil. Plants really need to cling on to survive.

After about 1.5km (1 mile) you come to Trail Junction No. 2, which you can follow on the return. Several paths lead from here to the cliffs at the end of Middle Head, which drop abruptly to the sea.

A plaque marks the official end of the trail. The cliffs are very impressive, with great Atlantic breakers crashing in far below. This is a very wild place and can be dangerous, as mists can descend very fast.

Return to the trail you passed earlier. A very short walk leads to a lookout at the tip of the peninsula, this time on the North Bay side.

This is where seabirds nest in spring. You will see great cormorants, black guillemots, common terns and great black backed gulls. Explanatory panels are positioned to help you identify each species. Occasionally, pods of whales and seals can be seen breaking the waves offshore. In addition, the national park is home to moose, black bear, coyote, fox and bald eagles.

Retrace your steps to the narrow section and climb the steep slope to the trail junction. About 500m (540 yards) along, is an alternative route, which is slightly longer.

This route offers great views of North Bay and barren Ingonish Island, which is topped by a lighthouse. The island is another nesting area for birds, and in 1976 it was the site of an important archeological find. Basalt chippings were found, which were the residue of centuries of spear- and arrow-point production by the Mi'kmaq. These finds have been dated as early as 9000BC, and were used to spear fish and shellfish.

Return to the parking area.

WHEN TO GO
The trail is closed in springtime, when seabirds are nesting on the cliffs. At other times, try to choose a day when the notorious Atlantic fog is unlikely to roll in off the ocean. In the fall, the foliage colors are beautiful, and this, combined with the Celtic Colours Festival, makes October a good time to be here. The information center at Ingonish is open only mid-May to mid-October.

WHERE TO EAT
✉ Atlantic Restaurant or Purple Thistle Room, Keltic Lodge, Middle Head Peninsula, Ingonish Beach ☎ 902/285-2880

WHERE TO STAY
✉ Keltic Lodge, Middle Head Peninsula, Ingonish Beach ☎ 902/285-2880

✉ Castle Rock Country Inn, 39339 Cabot Trail, Ingonish beach ☎ 902/285-2700

SOME PARK REGULATIONS
Consult onsite publications and important safety messages, and, in order to protect the environment and ensure your own safety, keep the following national park rules in mind:

» It is illegal to disturb or collect any natural, cultural or historic objects, including rocks, driftwood, plants or animals.
» Feeding, touching, enticing or hunting any wildlife is unlawful, and these activities place not only the animals at risk, but you as well.
» Store all food in the trunk of your car (where it won't attract the attention of animals) and do not drop litter—it harms wildlife, spoils the view and is subject to a $2,000 fine.
» Gathering twigs, branches, bark and dead wood for firewood is prohibited.
» Stay on established trails to avoid trampling vegetation.
» Pets are welcome (except on swimming beaches), but must be kept on a leash at all times and droppings must be picked up, even in remote areas.

Opposite *Keltic Lodge has a wonderful view over the Ingonish Coast*
Below left *The rocky coast of Cape Breton provides magnificent vistas along the walk*
Below *Cormorants are among the many seabirds found on this coast*

ALMA
FRESH AIR ADVENTURE
www.freshairadventure.com
Guided kayaking, from two-hour to multiday trips, along scenic coastline to caves and beaches. The full days trips give a real Bay of Fundy experience, on the highest tides in the world.
✉ 16 Fundy View Drive, Alma, New Brunswick, E4H 1H6 ☎ 506/887-2249, 800/545-0020 ⏰ Mid-May to mid-Sep daily ⛹ From $40 for 2 hours

ANNAPOLIS ROYAL
KING'S
www.kingstheatre.ca
This historic building hosts 50 to 70 live shows (both drama and concerts), including a summer festival and movies.
✉ 209 St. George Street, Annapolis Royal, Nova Scotia, B0S 1A0 ☎ 902/532-7704, 902/532-5466 ⏰ Year-round

ANTIGONISH
BAUER
www.stfx.ca/theatre-antigonish
Nova Scotia's longest-running professional repertory theater, home to the university community theater, Theatre Antigonish and the summer Festival Antigonish season.

✉ St. Francis Xavier University, Antigonish, Nova Scotia, B2G 2W5 ☎ 902/867-3333 ⏰ Year-round ⛹ from $11.50

BOUCTOUCHE
LE PAYS DE LA SAGOUINE
www.sagouine.com
In a re-created Acadian village, professional actors bring to life La Sagouine, an old woman with lots of tales to tell. It is mostly in French, but there are daily English-language tours, and the colorful musical shows and special events are always entertaining for younger children.
✉ 57 Acadie Street, Bouctouche, New Brunswick, E4S 2T7 ☎ 506/743-1400 ⏰ Mid-Jun to mid-Sep daily 9.30–5.30 ⛹ Adult $14 ($11 in fall), child (5–16) $8 ($5 in fall), family $34 ($25 in fall) 🚌 Off Highway 11 at exit 32 El'Ordre du Bon Temps restaurant serves traditional Acadian dishes and seafood (closed after end Aug)

BURLINGTON
BURLINGTON AMUSEMENT PARK
www.burlingtonamusementpark.com
As well as the longest karting track east of Montréal, with some two-seater carts for an adult with child, this park has minigolf, bumper cars and boats, baseball batting cages, trampolines, and a roller-coaster.

✉ Route 234, Burlington, Prince Edward Island, C0B 1M0 ☎ 902/836-3098, 866/644-3098 ⏰ Mid-Jun to mid-Sep daily 10–6; May to mid-Jun, late Sep weekends ⛹ Free admission, charges for rides 🍴

CAPE BRETON
CABOT TRAIL WHALE WATCHING
www.cabottrail.com/whalewatching
Sightings of whales—pilot, humpback, minke, or, more rarely, right whales, orcas, belugas and sperm whales—are pretty much guaranteed. Trips are in a traditional lobster boat or Zodiac inflatable, and the captain is knowledgeable.
✉ 23349 Cabot Trail, Pleasant Bay, Cape Breton, Nova Scotia, B0E 2P0 ☎ 902/224-1976 ⏰ Mid-May to mid-Oct daily 9–6 ⛹ Adult $44, child (8–12) $22 🚌 Northwest coast of Cape Breton, 35-min drive north of Chéticamp

CAPE BRETON HIGHLANDS NATIONAL PARK
www.pc.gc.ca
This is one of the most beautiful places in Atlantic Canada, with a stunning coastline and thickly forested mountains. There are 27 hiking trails of various lengths and you can pick up maps at the information points.

✉ Chéticamp Information Centre, Cape Breton, Nova Scotia, B0C 1L0 ☎ 902/224-2306 ⊕ Year-round; reduced service Oct–end May 🖐 Park entry permit $6 mid-May to mid-Oct

SAVOY
www.savoytheatre.com
This grand 1920s theater was converted into a movie house, converted back again in the 1970s, and restored in the 1990s after a fire. It is now one of the finest theaters in the whole of Atlantic Canada.
✉ 116 Commercial Street, Glace Bay, Cape Breton, Nova Scotia, B1A 3C1 ☎ 902/564-6668, 902/842-1577 ⊕ Year-round 🖐 $20–$40

CAVENDISH
AVONLEA
www.avonlea.ca
Anne of Green Gables was set on Prince Edward Island, and your kids can live the story and meet "Anne" at the fictional village of Avonlea, re-created in the PEI countryside. Costumed actor-guides inhabit the farm, houses and stores, and kids can attend Miss Montgomery's schoolroom. It's not just for girls—all children will enjoy the lively music shows, the games, the farm animals, and taking a wagon ride.
✉ Route 6, Cavendish, Prince Edward Island, C1E 2B7 ☎ 902/963-3050 ⊕ Mid-Jun to end Aug, daily 9–5; Sep 10–4 🖐 Adult $16.95, child $9.95 🍴 The White Sands tearoom

CHARLOTTETOWN
CONFEDERATION CENTRE OF THE ARTS
www.confederationcentre.com
Officially opened in 1964, this downtown arts center combines three theaters offering a variety of concerts and plays with an art gallery, workshops, Canadian gift store and bistro. Every summer, Confederation Centre hosts the Charlottetown Festival with nightly performances of the popular musical *Anne of Green Gables*, which has been running for more than 40 years!

✉ 145 Richmond Street, Charlottetown, Prince Edward Island, C1A 1J1 ☎ 902/628-1864 Box office: 800/565-0278, 902/566-1267 ⊕ Year-round daily

EMPIRE STUDIO 8
www.empiretheatres.com
A modern multiscreen theater showing the latest mainstream releases. It can be found at Charlottetown Mall.
✉ University Avenue, West Royalty, Charlottetown, Prince Edward Island, C1E 1Z6 ☎ 902/368-1922 ⊕ Daily 🖐 Adult $10, child (under 13) $5.50, (14–17) $8.25

OLDE DUBLIN PUB
www.oldedublinpub.com
You will find this Irish theme pub upstairs from Claddagh Room restaurant with traditional music.
✉ 131 Sydney Street, Charlottetown, Prince Edward Island, C1A 1G5 ☎ 902/892-6992 ⊕ Live entertainment: May–end Sep daily 🖐 Prices vary (but free before 8.30pm)

DARTMOUTH
ALDERNEY LANDING
www.alderneylanding.com
Performing arts center with a 285-seat theater, outdoor event plaza and art gallery. Home of the Eastern Front Theatre Company, plus professional touring drama and dance companies.
✉ 2 Ochterloney Street, Dartmouth Waterfront Park, Dartmouth, Nova Scotia, B2Y 3Z3 ☎ 902/461-4698 ⊕ Year-round 🖐 From $25

FREDERICTON
BOTINICALS GIFT SHOP AND STUDIO
www.botinicalsgiftshop.com
This attractive clapboard house, found next door to Bliss Carman House, is decked with windowboxes full of trailing plants, and fronted by garden foliage. It sells unique craftwork by a number of the top artisans in the Maritimes, including superb metal floral arrangements by John L. Welling.
✉ 65 Shore Street, Fredericton, New Brunswick, E3B 1R3 ☎ 506/454-7361, 877/454-7361 ⊕ Tue–Fri 10–6, Sat 12–6

BOYCE FARMERS' MARKET
www.boycefarmersmarket.com
This Fredericton institution was founded in the early 19th century by local benefactor William Boyce, and moved to its present home in 1951. Over 200 vendors offer local produce and specialty foods, crafts and gifts.
✉ 665 George Street, Fredericton, New Brunswick, E3A 1A3 ☎ 506/451-1815 ⊕ Sat 6am–1pm

DOLAN'S
An Irish-style pub, with a Maritime Kitchen Party Thursday, Friday and Saturday nights, featuring best East Coast Celtic talent. Classic rock other nights. Full dinner menu.
✉ Piper's Lane, 349 King Street, Fredericton, New Brunswick ☎ 506/454-7474 ⊕ Daily 🖐 $5 after 8pm Fri and Sat, otherwise free

EMPIRE THEATRES
www.empiretheatres.com
This 10-theater movieplex is an integral part of the Regent Mall. It screens the latest Hollywood releases.
✉ 1381 Regent Street, Regent Mall, Fredericton, New Brunswick, E3C 1A2 ☎ 506/458-9704 ⊕ Daily 🖐 Adult $10, child $5.50 🚌 116

KINGSWOOD ENTERTAINMENT CENTRE
www.kingswoodpark.com
A 72,000sq m (80,000sq ft) family attraction, with indoor playground, a big playclimber with slides and ball-pool, laser-tag and soft-play for toddlers. For adults there's bowling, golf and a gymnasium.
✉ 31 Kingswood Park, Fredericton, New Brunswick, E3C 2L4 ☎ 506/444-9500 ⊕ Sun–Thu 8–6, Fri–Sat 8am–10pm; hours vary seasonally 🖐 Games priced individually or in combos ranging from $6.95 to $18.95; under-6 inflatables $2.95; playclimber (3–11 years only) $4.65 🚌 15N 🚗 South of city, off Hanwell Road (Highway 640)

OFFICERS' SQUARE

Free concerts are put on in the historic Garrison District, including jazz, blues, folk, country and marching bands. There are also theater performances by the Calithumpians.

✉ Queen Street, Fredericton, New Brunswick, E3B 4Y7 ☎ 506/452-9616 🕐 Theater: Jul, Aug daily; Concerts: Jul, Aug Tue, Thu 👜 Free

REGENT MALL

www.regentmall.ca
Fredericton's biggest and newest mall is bright and attractive, and home to 115 stores and services. It's anchored by Sears, Wal-Mart, Toys'R'Us, Chapters and Sport Check, along with a good range of fashion boutiques and some interesting specialty stores.

✉ 1381 Regent Street, Fredericton, New Brunswick, E3C 1A2 ☎ 506/452-1005 🕐 Mon–Sat 10–9, Sun 12–5 🚌 116 🚗 Southern edge of town just beyond the Trans-Canada Highway/101 intersection

RIVER VALLEY CRAFTS AND ARTISAN GIFT SHOPS

Six stores and artisans' studios are grouped together on the first floor of the former Soldiers' Barracks. In these historic surroundings you can buy First Nations crafts, paintings, jewelry, pottery, soaps, Celtic art, and much more.

✉ Soldiers' Barracks, Carleton Street, Fredericton, New Brunswick ☎ 506/460-2837 🕐 Jun–end Sep daily

SCIENCE EAST HANDS-ON SCIENCE CENTRE

www.scienceeast.nb.ca
With 100 hands-on exhibits, kids can learn about the basics of science in an exciting and fun way. They can step inside a giant kaleidoscope, leave their shadow on a wall and take part in the ever popular static-electricity display that literally makes their hair stand on end.

✉ 668 Brunswick Street, Fredericton, New Brunswick, E3B 1H6 ☎ 506/457-2340 🕐 Jun–end Aug Mon–Sat 10–5, Sun 1–4; Sep–end Dec, Feb–end May Tue–Fri 12–5, Sat 10–5 👜 Adult $5, child $3, family $7

HALIFAX

CASINO NOVA SCOTIA

www.casinonovascotia.com
Waterfront casino with table games, including baccarat, blackjack, craps, roulette, more than 1,000 slot machines and a poker room. Live entertainment in concert hall.

✉ 1983 Upper Water Street, Halifax, Nova Scotia, B3J 3Y5 ☎ 902/425-7777, 888-6GAMES6 🕐 Daily 24 hours; closed holidays 👜 Free 🚌 2, 4, 6, 12, 82

DALHOUSIE ARTS CENTRE

www.artscentre.dal.ca
The Rebecca Cohn Auditorium here hosts jazz, opera, Celtic, rock and country music concerts; it's also home to Symphony Nova Scotia.

✉ 6101 University Avenue, Halifax, Nova Scotia, B3H 3J5 ☎ 902/494-3820, 800/874-1669 🕐 Year-round 🚌 1, 3, 58

EMPIRE 17 CINEMAS AND IMAX

www.empireimax.com
Halifax's principal movie destination, with a multiscreen theater showing latest first-run releases; plus Atlantic Canada's only IMAX theater, which has 2-D and 3-D movies.

✉ 190 Chain Lake Drive, Bayers Lake, Halifax, Nova Scotia, B3S 1C5 ☎ 902/876-4800 🕐 Daily 👜 Adult $10.75, child $6.50 🚌 12, 21 🚗 West of downtown via Quinpool and St. Margaret's Bay roads

GRAFTON STREET DINNER THEATRE

www.graftonstdinnertheatre.com
Lighthearted musical comedies with some audience interaction. Specially written shows focus on a particular era of the 20th century, with wait staff also in character. Three-course dinner offers limited choices.

✉ 1741 Grafton Street, Halifax, Nova Scotia, B3J 2W1 ☎ 902/425-1961 🕐 Shows 6.45–10pm 👜 Adult $35.60, child (under 12) $17.39 except Sat

HALIFAX MOOSEHEADS

www.halifaxmooseheads.ca
The Mooseheads hockey team plays in the Québec League. It may not be NHL (National Hockey League), but games are enthusiastically contested and well supported.

✉ Halifax Metro Centre, 5284 Duke Street, Halifax, Nova Scotia, B3J 3L2 ☎ 902/451-1221 🕐 Sep–end Mar 👜 Adult $13.50–$20, child (under 12) $8 🚌 1, 3, 6, 10

HALIFAX SHOPPING CENTRE

www.halifaxshoppingcentre.com
The biggest shopping mall in Halifax, anchored by Sears, Sears Outlet and Wal-Mart, with over 150 stores, including the largest Gap and Gap for Kids in the Atlantic Provinces. In bright surroundings, there's fashion, sporting goods, drugstores, homeware and bookstores, plus banks, hair salons and fast-food outlets.

✉ 7001 Mumford Road, Halifax, Nova Scotia, B3L 4N7 ☎ 902/454-8666 🕐 Mon–Sat 9.30–9.30 🚌 1–6, 9, 10, 14, 15, 18, 20, 52, 58 🚗 Ten minutes from downtown via Quinpool and Connaught

JOHN W. DOULL

www.doullbooks.com
The statues and sculptures among the floor-to-ceiling book shelves make for a highly entertaining visit to this downtown store (corner of Prince and Barrington). There's a huge stock of old books, focusing on nautical themes and books about the Atlantic Provinces. You'll also find modern first editions, academic, history and art books.

✉ 1684 Barrington Street, Halifax, Nova Scotia, B3J 2A2 ☎ 902/429-1652, 800/317-8613 🕐 Mon–Tue 9.30–6, Wed–Fri 9.30–9, Sat 10–9 🚌 6

MUSEUM OF NATURAL HISTORY

www.museum.gov.ns.ca/mnh
In addition to such exhibits as a pilot whale skeleton, stuffed moose and dinosaur fossils, there are always live displays that might include snakes, amphibians, bats, spiders and mice, plus Gus, an 80-year-old tortoise, and a living beehive.

✉ 1747 Summer Street, Halifax, Nova Scotia, B3H 3A6 ☎ 902/424-7353. Recorded information: 902/424-6099 🕐 Jun–end Oct Mon–Tue, Thu–Sat 9.30–5.30, Wed 9.30–8, Sun 1–5.30; mid-Oct to end May Tue and Thu–Fri 9.30–5, Wed 9.30–8, Sun 1–5 👜 Adult $5, child (6–17) $3, family $10–$15 🚌 8, 14, 20, 53, 59, 61, 68, 84, 86

NEPTUNE
www.neptunetheatre.com
Dating from 1915, the theater was renovated in 1997 and is home to one of the oldest professional companies in Canada. Two auditoriums feature world-class drama, music and comedy.

✉ 1593 Argyle Street, Halifax, Nova Scotia, B3J 2B2 ☎ 902/429-7070, 800/565-7345 🕐 Year-round 🚌 1, 3, 10, 14

SHAKESPEARE BY THE SEA
www.shakespearebythesea.ca
A summer season of open-air theater featuring Shakespeare favorites, an annual event since 1994 and performed in beautiful Point Pleasant Park.

✉ Point Pleasant Drive, Halifax, Nova Scotia ☎ 902/422 0295 🕐 Jul, Aug ✋ Donation ($10 suggested) 🚌 9 🚭

REFLECTIONS CABARET
www.reflectionscabaret.com
The best gay dance club in town, featuring drag shows with pop-star impersonators, karaoke every Tuesday, talent nights, movies and music videos, and live bands.

✉ 5184 Sackville Street, Halifax, Nova Scotia ☎ 902/422-2957, 877/422-2957 🕐 Mon–Sat 1pm–4am, Sun 4pm–4am

SPIRIT
www.spiritspa.ca
In a restored historic downtown building (above the Up Country furniture store), spa staff will soothe away the cares of the day and give you a fresh-air glow with their range of natural products. Services include Vichy Shower, sea scrub, hair and makeup, and sports massage.

✉ 1566 Barrington Street, Level 3, Halifax, Nova Scotia, B3J 1Z6 ☎ 902/431-8100 🕐 Daily ✋ Day rate $330 (the works); massage from $45 🚌 1, 3, 6, 10

MARYSTOWN
GOLDEN SANDS
On Burin Peninsula of Southern Newfoundland, there's miles of fine golden sand with attractions that include freshwater swimming, a huge waterslide, boat rentals, minigolf and trackless train rides.

✉ Marystown, Newfoundland and Labrador, A0E 2M0 ☎ 709/891-2400 🕐 mid-Jun to mid-Sep daily 10am–dusk (weather permitting) ✋ $4 🚌 On highway 222, 20km (12 miles) from Marystown

MONCTON
CHAMPLAIN PLACE
www.champlainplace.ca
The biggest shopping mall in the Atlantic Provinces. It's a bright, modern place, anchored by Sears, Sobeys and Wal-Mart, with a good range of specialty stores, fashions, sporting goods, electronics and homeware. There's a multiplex movie theater and an indoor-outdoor amusement park.

✉ 477 Paul Street, Dieppe, Moncton, New Brunswick, E1A 4X5 ☎ 506/857-0040 🕐 Mon–Sat 10–9, Sun 12–5; closed holidays 🍴 Usual food court outlets, plus Don Cherry's Grapevine and McGinnis Landing

CAPITOL
www.capitol.nb.ca
This fine theater has been magnificently restored to its 1920s splendor, including the original stenciling and gilded boxes; it stages drama, dance, comedy and concerts featuring all kinds of music.

✉ 811 Main Street, Moncton, New Brunswick, E1C 1G1 ☎ 506/856-4377 🕐 Year-round 🚌 1, 2, 3

CRYSTAL PALACE
www.crystalpalace.ca
Next to the Champlain Place shopping mall, this indoor and outdoor amusement park is a great reward for the kids for being good while you shopped. It includes a roller-coaster,

Jumpin' Star ride, laser-tag, Ferris wheel, bumper boats, carousel and carting.

✉ 499 Champlain Street, Dieppe, Moncton, New Brunswick, E1A 6S5 ☎ 506/859-4386 🕐 Mon–Thu 12–8, Fri 12–9, Sat 10–9, Sun 10–8 (summer daily 10–10) ✋ All-day bracelet $19.95, junior $16.95, family $62 🚌 7, 8, 9, 10, 20, 21 🍴 McGinnis Landing

EMPIRE 8
www.empiretheatres.com
Eight curved wall-to-wall screens and stadium seating, with state-of-the-art projection and sound.

✉ 125 Trinity Drive, Moncton, New Brunswick, E1G 2J7 ☎ 506/857-8903 🕐 Daily ✋ Adult $10.25, child (under 13) $5.50 🚌 Codiac bus from downtown

MAGIC MOUNTAIN
www.magicmountain.ca
Magic Mountain is Atlantic Canada's largest waterpark. When you've experienced the weird sensation of freewheeling "uphill" in your car on Magnetic Hill, you can explore the rest of the complex.

✉ TCH 2, exit 450, Moncton, New Brunswick, E1G 4R3 ☎ 506/857-9283, 800/331-9283 🕐 Mid-Jun to early Sep daily 10–6 (till 8 in high season) ✋ $21.50 (under 1.2m/48ins tall $16) 🚌 Magic Mountain route

MONCTON WILDCATS
www.moncton-wildcats.com
The Wildcats play hockey against visiting teams from the Maritimes and Québec.

✉ Moncton Coliseum, 377 Killam Drive, Moncton, New Brunswick, E1C 3T1 ☎ 506/389-5989 🕐 Sep–end Mar ✋ Adult $12, child (under 12) $9

NEW GLASGOW

GLASGOW SQUARE
www.newglasgowriverfront.ca/Glasgow/theatre2.html
A distinctive modern building, with a full schedule of drama and music, including some on the outdoor stage.
✉ 15 Riverside Parkway, New Glasgow, Nova Scotia, B2H 5E7 ☎ 902/752-4800, 888/873-0777 🕐 Year-round 🖐 Some shows are free

MAGIC VALLEY FUN PARK
www.magicvalley.ca
Nova Scotia's original theme park, with huge waterslides, pedal boats, train ride, carting, soft-play area, and live animals. Storybook Village takes younger children into the world of nursery rhymes.
✉ Highway 104, New Glasgow, Nova Scotia, B0K 2A0 ☎ 902/396-4467 🕐 Summer daily 11–6 🖐 $13.95 including all rides and attractions, $7 general admission. Individual ride prices also available 🚌 10km (6 miles) west of New Glasgow off Trans-Canada Highway at exit 20

PARRSBORO

SHIP'S COMPANY THEATRE
www.shipscompany.com
This is a unique entertainment experience: The theater is the historic vessel, MV *Kipawo*. The season includes a kids' stage.
✉ 18 Lower Main Street, Parrsboro, Nova Scotia, B0M 1S0 ☎ 902/254-3000, 800/565-SHOW 🕐 Jul to mid-Sep Tue–Sat 🖐 $20–$24

PICTOU

DECOSTE ENTERTAINMENT CENTRE
www.decostecentre.ca
This is a showcase for Nova Scotia culture with informal ceilidhs, concerts, pipebands, highland dancing and pioneer re-enactments.
✉ Water Street, Pictou, Nova Scotia, B0K 1H0 ☎ 902/485-8848, 800/353-5338 🕐 Apr–end Dec 🖐 $15–$40

SAINT JOHN

JET BOAT TOURS
www.jetboatrides.com
Tremendous jet-boat thrill ride, on the Saint John River and right into the famous Reversing Falls. The one-hour trip includes 20 minutes hanging on tight as the boat leaps through the rapids.
✉ Box 7094, Brunswick Square, Saint John, New Brunswick, E2L 4S5 ☎ 506/634-8987, 888/634-8987 🕐 Jun–end Sep daily 1pm, 3pm, 5pm (also Jul, Aug 11am, 7pm) 🖐 Adult $36.50, child (2–12) $28.95 🚌 Douglas Avenue route from City Hall, then 2-min walk 🚌 Fallsview Park, off Douglas Avenue

THE SCHOLAR'S DEN
www.abebooks.com/home/sden
Housed in a former drugstore, with the original 100-year-old storefront, apothecary's marble-top counter, oak shelving and drawers. Sells not only scholarly works, but also contemporary hardcover titles, paperbacks and vinyl records.
✉ 105 Prince Edward Street, Saint John, New Brunswick, E2L 3S1 ☎ 506/657-2665 🕐 Mon–Sat 11–5, Sun 11–5

ST. JOHN'S

AVALON MALL
www.shopavalonmall.com
Attractive mall on two levels with a large Empire Theatres multiplex. As you'd expect, there are lots of clothing outlets, plus books, music, gifts, jewelry and gadgets.
✉ 48 Kenmouth Road, St. John's, Newfoundland and Labrador, A1B 1W3 ☎ 709/753-7144 🕐 Mon–Sat 10–10, Sun 12–5 🚌 3, 4, 7, 14, 15

THE FLUVARIUM
www.fluvarium.ca
A unique insight into the life of a river, with windows below the water level of a real stream showing the day-to-day activities of trout, frogs and tadpoles. Feeding time is usually at 4pm. The second floor has interactive exhibits, videos and displays.

Right *Children enjoy the rides at the Magic Valley Fun Park*

✉ Nagles Place, Pippy Park, St. John's, Newfoundland and Labrador, A1B 2Z2 ☎ 709/754-3474 🕐 Mon–Fri 9–5, Sat–Sun 12–5, hours change seasonally, telephone for details if visiting off-season 🖐 Adult $5.50, child (under 14) $3.50

JOHNSON GEO CENTRE
This is a sensational showcase explaining why the province is so spectacular in geological terms. You start with a thrilling introductory audiovisual presentation and experience earthquakes and volcanoes, by the time you leave, geology will be so fascinating you'll be analyzing every rock you see.
✉ 175 Signal Hill Road, St. John's, Newfoundland and Labrador, A1A 1B2 ☎ 709/737-7880 🕐 Mid-May to mid-Oct daily; mid-Oct to mid-May Tue–Sun 🖐 Adult $10.25, child (5–17) $4.60 📷

NEWFOUNDLAND SCIENCE CENTRE
www.NLsciencecentre.nf.com
Up-to-the-minute science museum in one of the oldest buildings in St. John's. Kids can transform into a human gyroscope, look into the world of backyard bugs, walk like a dinosaur, or enjoy the puppet theater.
✉ 5 Beck's Cove, The Murray Premises, St. John's, Newfoundland and Labrador, A1C 5N5 ☎ 709/754-0823 🕐 Mon–Fri 10–5, Sat 10–6, Sun 12–6 🖐 Adult $6, child $4.25

THE ROOMS
www.therooms.ca
This immense structure was designed to represent the fishing rooms where families got together in times past to process their catch. Home to the Provincial Museum, Art Gallery and Archives, you should

visit for the view even if you have time for nothing else.

✉ 9 Bonaventure Avenue, P.O. Box 1800, Station C, St. John's, Newfoundland and Labrador, A1C 5P9 ☎ 709/757-8000
🕐 Jun to mid-Oct daily 10–5 (until 9 Thu and Fri), Sun 12–5; closed mid-Oct to end May Mon 🖐 Adult $5, child (6–16) $3

SHEDIAC
SANDSPIT

Along the best beach in the province, Sandspit has children's rides, carting, bumper boats, soft-play, carousel, and super-slide.

✉ Parlee Beach, 85 Ohio Road, Shediac, New Brunswick, E4P 2JB ☎ 506/532-8111
🕐 Mid-Jun to early Sep daily 8am–10pm
🖐 Free, charge for rides 🚌 Pointe-du-Chêne, off Highway 15, exit 37

UPPER CLEMENTS
UPPER CLEMENTS PARK

www.upperclementspark.com

This amusement park includes a roller-coaster, log flume, fairground rides, rope swings, paddle boats and 12ha (30-acre) wildlife park.

✉ 2931 Highway 1, Upper Clements, Nova Scotia, B0S 1A0 ☎ 902/532-7557; for Wildlife park call 902/532-5924 🕐 Mid-Jun to early Sep daily 10–6. Wildlife park: mid-May to mid-Oct 🖐 $8 plus rides: premium bracelet (covers all rides) $22.50
🚌 West end of Annapolis Valley, 8km (5 miles) west of Annapolis Royal

WOLFVILLE
ATLANTIC THEATRE FESTIVAL

www.atf.ns.ca

World-class performers present the classics; accommodations packages and backstage tours available.

✉ 504 Main Street, Wolfville, Nova Scotia, B4P 2S2 ☎ 902/542-4242, 800/337-6661
🕐 Late Jun–end Aug 🚌 Across from Acadia University

YARMOUTH
TH'YARC

www.yarcplayhouse.com

Holds live theater, music concerts and other performances, and has a gallery of local art.

✉ 76 Parade Street, Yarmouth, Nova Scotia, B5A 3B4 ☎ 902/742/8150
🕐 Mid-Mar to mid-Dec

FESTIVALS AND EVENTS

MARCH
SNO-BREAK WINTER FESTIVAL

www.tourismlabrador.com

A week of snowmobile races, Nordic skiing, adventure tours, parties and family fun.

✉ Goose Bay, Newfoundland and Labrador ☎ 709/896-3489

JUNE/JULY
CANADA'S IRISH FESTIVAL

www.canadasirishfest.com

Lively festival, with a pipe and drum parade, and music from top Canadian and Irish performers.

✉ Miramichi, New Brunswick
☎ 506/778-8810

FESTIVAL 500, SHARING THE VOICES

www.festival500.com

International festival of choral singing, with choirs from all over the world.

✉ St. John's, Newfoundland and Labrador ☎ 709/738-6013

NOVA SCOTIA INTERNATIONAL TATTOO

www.nstattoo.ca

Nightly for 10 days the Metro Centre hosts military bands, pipe bands, dancers and military displays, featuring the cream of the world's military and civilian performers.

✉ Halifax, Nova Scotia ☎ 902/420-1114

ROLLO BAY FIDDLE FESTIVAL

Permanent festival grounds host the cream of Maritimes fiddle talent, with two concerts a day and an old-time dance each night. A friendly event.

✉ Rollo Bay, Prince Edward Island
☎ 902/687-2584

JUNE–END SEPTEMBER
CHARLOTTETOWN FESTIVAL

www.confederationcentre.com

A summer-long festival of music and theatre held in the Confederation Centre for the Arts in Prince

Edward Island's capital city. It includes the ever-popular musical version of *Anne of Green Gables* which has been a keystone of the festival for more than 40 years.

✉ Charlottetown, Prince Edward Island
☎ 800/565-0278, 902/628-1864

AUGUST
ATLANTIC SEAFOOD FESTIVAL

www.atlanticseafoodfestival.com

Some of the best seafood in the world comes out of the waters off New Brunswick, and top international chefs come to work their magic on it.

✉ Moncton, New Brunswick
☎ 506/384-8585

HALIFAX INTERNATIONAL BUSKER FESTIVAL

www.buskers.ns.sympatico.ca

Street performers, including musicians, magicians, comedians, artists, jugglers, dancers and mime artists, do their stuff along the 1km (0.6-miles) waterfront site.

✉ Halifax, Nova Scotia ☎ 902/429-3910, 866/773-0655

SEPTEMBER
HARVEST JAZZ AND BLUES FESTIVAL

www.harvestjazzblues.nb.ca

Venues and streets throughout the city are buzzing with live music, and a large marquee downtown hosts big-name jazz and blues bands.

✉ Fredericton, New Brunswick
☎ 506/454-2583, 888/622-5837

OCTOBER
CELTIC COLOURS FESTIVAL

www.celtic-colours.com

One of the best Celtic music festivals in the world, with about 300 musicians from all the Celtic nations performing in a week of concerts and ceilidhs, at more than 30 venues.

✉ Sydney, Cape Breton, Nova Scotia
☎ 902/562-6700, 877/285-2321

EATING

PRICES AND SYMBOLS

The restaurants are listed alphabetically within each town. The prices are for a two-course lunch (L) and a three-course à la carte dinner (D). Prices in pubs are for a two-course lunchtime bar meal and a two-course dinner in the restaurant, unless specified otherwise. The wine price is for the least expensive bottle.

For a key to the symbols, ▷ 2.

BIG POND

RITA'S

www.ritamacneil.com

Singer-songwriter Rita MacNeil, a Canadian legend, bought this former school-house, in the place where she grew up, as her family home. When fans dropped by they were welcomed in, and her hospitality became so popular that Rita decided to open up a tearoom. A comfortable, attractive place to enjoy a pot of tea and home-baked goodies, then a visit to the gift shop. ✉ Big Pond, Cape Breton, Nova Scotia, B1J 2E2 ☎ 902/828-2667 🕐 Mid-Jun to

mid-Oct daily 10–6 🖐 L $12 🚗 40km (25 miles) west of Sydney on Highway 4

CHARLOTTETOWN

GAHAN HOUSE

www.peimenu.com/brewing

Traditional-style brewpub with polished dark wood and brick interior, in a historic building on the city's liveliest street. Six excellent ales are brewed on the premises, and brewery tours are available for groups of four or more (phone in advance). Above-average pub food. ✉ 126 Sydney Street, Charlottetown, Prince Edward Island, C1A 1G4 ☎ 902/626-2337 🕐 Mon–Thu 11–10, Fri–Sat 11am–midnight, Sun 4–10 🖐 L $18, D $23, Wine $21

FREDERICTON

BREWBAKERS

www.brewbakers.ca

Crispy pizzas from the wood-fired oven, pasta, fresh seafood, interesting salads and entrées are on the extensive menu. The

open kitchen adds to the lively atmosphere, plus a stylish bar and patio seating on an upper deck. ✉ 546 King Street, Fredericton, New Brunswick, E3B 1E6 ☎ 506/459-0067 🕐 Mon–Thu 11.30–10, Fri 11.30–11, Sat 4–11, Sun 4–9 🖐 L $15, D $28, Wine $20

EL BURRITO LOCO

www.elburritoloco-vallarta.com

The Mexican owner ensures authentic Mexican food. Guacamole made to order, fresh salsa made to a family recipe, interesting fillings for burritos, tortillas, tacos, tamales and enchiladas. ✉ 304 King Street, Fredericton, New Brunswick, E3B 1E3 ☎ 506/459-5626 🕐 Hours vary daily 🖐 L $9, D $23, Wine $18

CORA'S BREAKFAST & LUNCH

www.chezcora.com

Don't be deterred by the fact that this is a chain restaurant. It has spread across Canada is due to the popularity of its deliciously healthy meals. Mounds of fresh fruit adorn everything, and the menu basics include Cora's secret recipe French toast, crêpes, omlets, waffles, paninis and salads. There's always a thick mixed-fruit cocktail on the drinks list too. Children just love this place too.

✉ 476 Queen Street, Fredericton, New Brunswick, E3B 1B6 ☎ 506/472-2672 🕐 Mon–Sat 6am–3pm, Sun 7am–3pm 🍴 L $10 🚌 Downtown, between Westmorland and Regent streets

HALIFAX

FID

www.fidcuisine.ca

This cool, sophisticated restaurant has been focusing on sustainable organic produce since before it was the trendy thing to do, and uses it to create interesting dishes that combine classic French cuisine with Asian influences. The restaurant's unusual name comes from a mariners' tool used for splicing—see the connection? The menu changes frequently, but recent dinnertime offerings have included an appetizer of lamb shoulder confit with charred tomato, corn and heirloom beet, while main course choices roasted Atlantic monkfish with gingered kabocha squash, steamed Shanghai bok-choy and Jerusalem artichoke. Equally creative lunches include lighter dishes. Groups of six to eight people can get Monday evening cooking classes in summer.

✉ 1569 Dresden Row, Halifax, Nova Scotia, B3N 1H6 ☎ 902/422-9162 🕐 Tue 5–10pm, Wed–Fri 11.30am–2pm, 5–10pm, Sat–Sun 5–10pm 🍴 L $14, D $55, Wine $38 🚌 1, 3, 10, 14, 20 and many others 🚌 Near the Citadel, off Sackville Street

RYAN DUFFY'S STEAK AND SEAFOOD

One of Canada's top 100 restaurants every year since 1987. Steak is a serious business here. You choose your cut of corn-fed American beef at the table, then it's taken away and cooked to your liking.

✉ 5640 Spring Garden Road, Halifax, Nova Scotia, B3J 3M7 ☎ 902/421-1116 🕐 Mon–Fri 11.30–2, 5–10, Sat–Sun 5–10 🍴 L $15, D $35, Wine $23 🚌 1, 10, 80; free bus (called Fred) in summer 🚌 Downtown, near Citadel Hill

SALTY'S ON THE WATERFRONT

www.saltys.ca

Waterfront restaurant with a nautical theme. Try to get a window table because the view across the harbor is stunning. Seafood fresh out of the water is the specialty, notably lobster, mussels, Atlantic salmon, and deep-sea scallops. Lunch and dinner are also available in the bar downstairs.

✉ 1869 Upper Water Street, Halifax, Nova Scotia, B3J 1S9 ☎ 902/423-6818 🕐 Daily 11.30–10 (varies seasonally) 🍴 L $15, D $25, Wine $25 🚌 2, 4, 6, 12, 32 🚌 End of Historic Properties pier

MOBILE

CAPTAIN'S TABLE

www.captainstable.nf.ca

This restaurant is named after Newfoundland's greatest hero, Captain William Jackman, great-grandfather of the current owner-chef. Delicious fresh seafood and other traditional Newfoundland dishes. Also excellent non-fish dishes and children's menu. For dessert, try the wonderful bumbleberry pie or apple dumpling.

✉ Box 79, Mobile, Newfoundland and Labrador, A0A 3A0 ☎ 709/334-2278 ☎ Mid-Apr to end Sep daily 11.30–9; Oct to mid-Apr Wed–Sun 12–8 🍴 L $15, D $23, Wine $15 🚌 Halleran's or Lawlor's Irish Loop service from St. John's 🚌 On south coast, a 35-minute drive from St. John's along Highway 10

MONCTON

LITTLE LOUIS'

www.littlelouis.ca

Eating out in Moncton has improved enormously over the last few years and this classy restaurant is one of the finest examples. In stylish surroundings—and with live jazz Thursday to Saturday—you can enjoy the accomplished cooking of chef Andrew Stevens. There are oysters,

either raw or baked, among the appetizers, and main courses also offer some excellent seafood choices, such as Arctic Char poached in passion-fruit butter with grapefruit, glazed green asparagus and herb pasta. Meat dishes might include roast elk with licorice purée, roast squash, wilted greens and natural jus. The short selection of desserts is both interesting and creative and the excellent wine list includes more than 30 by the glass.

✉ 245 Collishaw Street, 2nd Floor, Moncton, New Brunswick, E1C 9P9 ☎ 506/855-2022 ☎ Daily from 5pm; last seating 9.30pm 🍴 D $50, Wine $29 🚌 Off Vaughn Harvey Boulevard, two blocks south of Mountain Road

ST. JOHN'S

CABOT CLUB

A superb, upscale restaurant, its refined atmosphere enhanced by classical music, a spectacular view of Signal Hill and the harbor (and passing icebergs in winter) through picture windows. Traditional Newfoundland cuisine, expertly prepared. Dress code is casual-dressy. Reservations recommended.

✉ The Fairmont Newfoundland, Cavendish Square, St. John's, Newfoundland and Labrador, A1C 5W8 ☎ 709/726-4980 🕐 Mon–Sat 6–10pm 🍴 D $30–$35, Wine $25 🚌 3, 5, 15 🚌 Downtown

SUMMERSIDE

STARLITE DINER AND DAIRY BAR

www.starlitediner.pe.ca

A total 1950s experience, with a neon-lit frontage, jukeboxes in the booths (bring plenty of quarters), waitresses in 1950s fashions, old gas pumps and Coca-Cola memorabilia inside. Good down-home cooking features burgers, hotdogs, fried clams, barbecued chicken and "the biggest breakfast in town."

✉ 810 Water Street, Summerside, Prince Edward Island, C1N 4J8 ☎ 902/436-7752 🕐 Daily 7am–10pm 🍴 L $10, D $13 🚌 East of town at Read's Corner, intersection of Highways 1A and 11

PRICES AND SYMBOLS

Prices are the starting price for a double room for one night, unless otherwise stated. Breakfast is included unless noted otherwise. All the hotels listed accept credit cards unless otherwise stated. Note that rates vary widely throughout the year.

For a key to the symbols, ▷ 2.

ALMA

CAPTAIN'S INN

www.captainsinn.ca

The bedrooms here are in a country style. All have private bathroom and TV; some have ocean views.

✉ 8602 Main Street, Alma, New Brunswick, E4H 1N5 ☎ 506/887-2017 🖐 $90 ⓘ 9 (all non-smoking) �️ 🚗 In the village

ANNAPOLIS ROYAL

QUEEN ANNE INN

www.queenanneinn.ns.ca

No expense was spared when this Victorian home was originally built, with a grand staircase, gleaming woodwork and elegant rooms, all set in spacious grounds with mature trees. Each room has a private bathroom. Breakfast is served at one large table.

✉ 494 St. George Street, Annapolis Royal, Nova Scotia, B0S 1A0 ☎ 902/532-7850 🕐 Closed Nov to mid-Apr 🖐 $89 ⓘ 12 (all non-smoking) �️

L'ANSE AU CLAIR

NORTHERN LIGHT INN

www.northernlightinn.com

Close to the border with Québec and the ferry service to Newfoundland. It has some housekeeping cottages and RV (motor caravan) sites with power hook-ups in addition to its hotel rooms and suites, all of which have cable TV and telephones.

✉ 58 Main Street, P.O. Box 92, L'Anse au Clair, Newfoundland and Labrador, A0K 3K0 ☎ 709/931-2332 🖐 $105 ⓘ 54, 5 cottages 🚗 On Labrador Strait

CHARLOTTETOWN

INNS ON GREAT GEORGE

www.innsongreatgeorge.com

This renowned inn consists of 12 properties that have been beautifully restored to provide luxury accommodations in 19th-century style. The best rooms have an open fireplace and Jacuzzi, and all are elegantly furnished with antiques.

✉ 58 Great George Street, Charlottetown, Prince Edward Island, C1A 4K3 ☎ 902/892-0606, 800/361-1118 🖐 $125 ⓘ 48 (all non-smoking) 🚗 🚾 🚗 Downtown, in the National Historic District

DINGWALL

MARKLAND COASTAL RESORT

www.marklandresort.com

This resort consists of wooden cabins, surrounded by mountains, forests and beaches.

✉ Cabot Trail, Dingwall, Cape Breton, Nova Scotia, B0C 1G0 ☎ 902/383-2246, 800/872-6084 🖐 $99 ⓘ 25 ⓒ 🏖 Outdoor (beach) 🚌 Northern tip of Cape Breton Island on the Cabot Trail

FREDERICTON
LORD BEAVERBROOK
www.lordbeaverbrookhotel.com
An elegant and comfortable hotel and a city landmark since 1947. It couldn't have a better location, neighboring the art gallery, Playhouse and Legislature, and backing onto the wide St. John River. Rooms are spacious, with cable TV.
✉ 659 Queen Street, Fredericton, New Brunswick, E3B 5A6 ☎ 506/455-3371, 888/561-7666 🖐 $205 ⓘ 168 (150 non-smoking) ⓒ 🏊 Indoor 🚌 11 🚍 Downtown

HALIFAX
HALLIBURTON HOUSE INN
www.halliburton.ns.ca
This historic property is elegantly furnished with antiques. Rooms and suites all have private bathrooms (some with whirlpools), goose-down comforters (duvets), and cable TV.
✉ 5184 Morris Street, Halifax, Nova Scotia, B3J 1B3 ☎ 902/420-0658 🖐 $159 ⓘ 29 ⓒ 🚌 7, 9

THE PEBBLE
www.thepebble.ca
In a historic home set on 2ha (5 acres) of grounds, this is bed-and-breakfast of the highest order, with two luxurious suites and warm hospitality from proprietor Elizabeth O'Carroll, who has furnished the place with great flair and attention to detail. Both of the suites are superbly furnished and have the finest bedlinens, and their spacious private bathrooms are equally stunning (one has an oval hydrotherapy bath) with cozy robes and quality toiletries. There's a cozy lounge and breakfast room, hung with original artworks by local artists, and the house is very close to the waterfront of the North West Arm, making for glorious views from both the house and its delightful garden. Breakfast might include

bruléed Irish oatmeal with fruit, cream and maple syrup or fresh waffles with berries.
✉ 1839 Armview Terrace, Halifax, Nova Scotia, B3H 4H3 ☎ 902/423-3369, 888/303-5056 🖐 $125 ⓘ 2 (both non-smoking) 🚌 West of downtown off Quinpool Road

LUNENBURG
LINCOLN HOUSE
www.lincolnhouse.ca
With its turret, dormer windows and wrought-iron fence, this historic B&B is right at home in the Lunenburg UNESCO World Heritage Site. Inside, the decor is pure Victorian, with hardwood floors, ornate fireplaces, stained glass, antique furniture and quality linens.
✉ 130 Lincoln Street P.O. Box 322, Lunenburg, Nova Scotia, B0J 2C0 ☎ 902/634-7179, 877/634-7179 ⓒ Mid-May to mid-Oct 🖐 $85, breakfast and afternoon tea included ⓘ 4 (all non-smoking)

MONCTON
CHATEAU MONCTON
www.chateau-moncton.nb.ca
This motel is in a distinctive five-story building right beside the Petitcodiac River. The bar has a superb river view. Bedrooms and suites (some with whirlpool bathtub) have extended cable TV, high-speed internet access and free local calls.
✉ 100 Main Street, Moncton, New Brunswick, E1C 1B9 ☎ 506/870-4444, 800/576-4040 🖐 $119 ⓘ 106 (70 percent non-smoking) ⓒ 🍴 🚌 1, 2, 3, 4, 7, 8, 9, 10, 16, 23 🚍 Downtown, near train station

NORTH RUSTICO
NORTH RUSTICO MOTEL AND COTTAGES
www.nrmci.com
Overlooking lovely North Rustico Harbour, and handy for the attractions of Cavendish and the national park, this is a friendly family-run establishment. There's a range of wooden cottages with porches, and a small motel block. The snug cottages, all warm pine inside, are equipped with full-size refrigerator, microwave and a gas barbecue

outside. In the morning, guests congregate in the enclosed sundeck at the house for the breakfast buffet. There is a swimming pool, playground and laundry room on site.
✉ Highway 6, North Rustico, Prince Edward Island, C0A 1N0 ☎ 902/963-2253, 800/285-8966 ⓒ May–end Oct 🖐 $80, breakfast included only at some times of year ⓘ 23 🏖 Outdoor 🚌 Highway 6, 8km (5 miles) east of Cavendish

ST. JOHN'S
THE MURRAY PREMISES HOTEL
www.murraypremiseshotel.com
Overlooking the harbor, this former salt-cod warehouse dating from 1846 is now a luxurious boutique hotel. Up-to-the-minute facilities include whirlpool baths, cable TV, internet connections and voice mail. Dotted around are fascinating reminders of its past, and the old beams, exposed brickwork and quirkily slanting roofs all add to the atmosphere.
✉ 5 Becks Cove, St. John's, Newfoundland and Labrador, A1C 6H1 ☎ 709/738-7773, 866/738-7773 🖐 $179 ⓘ 28 (all non-smoking) ⓒ

Opposite *Boats anchored at Halifax*
Below *Lincoln House, Lunenburg*

TORONTO

The provincial capital of Ontario is Canada's New York—its financial center, culture and entertainment capital, shopping mecca, and more, and while it might not quite be "the city that never sleeps," it doesn't get a lot of rest. Downtown is a constant hive of activity, whether you are dodging the suits plowing purposefully between the skyscrapers of the Financial District or milling around with the shoppers around Yonge or Bloor streets. You might find your way barred because there's a movie or music video being filmed on the streets; you might chance upon an open-air concert on a city square. It all adds to the buzz. After dark it's full of theater-goers, nightclubbers, restaurant patrons and, in summer, locals just hanging out on patios.

Toronto's location on the shores of Lake Ontario give it a certain open-air freshness, although humidity can give rise to smogs in the sweltering summer. Nevertheless, the lakeshore and islands are a huge bonus, providing leisure pursuits, waterfront walks and even beaches within walking distance of downtown.

Though Toronto as we see it today has largely developed over the last 40 years or so, it has a history going back to the early pioneers. In and around the downtown core there are a number of historic sites and leafy streets of heritage homes, and Queen's Park offers a stately ensemble comprising the Provincial Legislature, Toronto University and the fabulous Royal Ontario Museum.

TORONTO

↑ Casa Loma

↑ Black Creek Pioneer Village

400 m
400 yds

YORKVILLE

Rosedale Val

Scollar Street
Collier

CHURCH ST

Saint Paul's

Prince Arthur Avenue
Yorkville Ave

Spadina
Madison Avenue
Road
Spadina

Saint George

Cumberland
Bellair St
Bay St

Asquith Ave
Bloor / Yonge
Roys
Sq

BLOOR STREET WEST

BLOOR STREET EAST

Ontario Science Centre, Toronto Zoo

Devonshire Pl
Royal Ontario Museum

Gardiner Museum of Ceramic Art

Sultan

Balmuto

Charles Street West
Charles Street East

Museum

Lennox Street
Herrick St

Howard
Sussex
Ave

Sussex
Glen Morris St

BP
Nichol Ln
St George
Huron
St

Saint Mary St

Isabella Street

Gloucester Street

Emsley

Nicholas St
Saint

Irwin Ave
Joseph
Phipps

Dundonald St

Wellesley

Wellesley Street East

HARBORD STREET

Markham
Croft
Lippincott
Brunswick
Major
Robert
Mews
Classic Ave
Willcocks St

HOSKIN AVE

Tower Rd

Hart House Circle

Wellesley Street West

Maitland Street

Church St

Alexander Street

Wood Street

Ulster St
Bancroft Ave
Russell St

University of Toronto

Galbraith Rd
College Rd
Kings Rd

Queen's Park

QUEENS PARK CRES W
QUEENS PARK CRES E

Ontario Legislature

Grosvenor St

Breadalbane St

Surrey
Grenville St

YONGE STREET

CARLTON STREET

College St

Granby Street
McGill Street

COLLEGE STREET

Bellevue
Augusta Street
Oxford
Nassau Street
Leonard Ave
Wales St

Glasgow St
Cecil Street
Huron
Ross St
Henry
McCaul
Orde St
Murray St

Laplante Ave
Elizabeth St

Gerrard Street West

Gerrard Street East

Walton St

Barnaby Pl

Mutual St

Kensington Market

CHINATOWN

Baldwin
Darcy Street

Kensington Ave
Larch
Grange Ave

Elm St
St Patrick St
Edward St

Gould Street

Dalhousie Street

DUNDAS STREET

Dundas
Art Gallery of Ontario

The Grange
Grange Park
Grange Rd

St George
Stephanie St
John St
Bulwer St
Soho

Saint Patrick Street
Simcoe Street
University Avenue
Centre Ave
Chestnut St
Armoury St

BAY STREET
Sheppard St

Eaton Centre
James Street

Victoria Ln
Bond St
Victoria
Shuter St

Willison Sq
Phoebe St

Toronto City Hall

Osgoode
Nathan Phillips Square

Albert St

Queen

QUEEN STREET EAST

Museum of Contemporary Canadian Art

QUEEN STREET WEST

Denison Avenue
Augusta Avenue
Cameron
Vanauley Street

RICHMOND STREET WEST

Nelson St
Duncan St
York St

Temperance St

Lombard Street

RICHMOND STREET

Portugal Sq
Maud St
Camden St
Brant
Portland St
Morrison St
Oxley St
Charlotte St

Peter St
Pearl St

St Andrew St

St James Park

ADELAIDE STREET

ADELAIDE STREET WEST

Tecumseth St
Stewart St
Brant Pl

Mercer St
John St
Clarence Sq

Millstone Lane

King

Colborne St

KING STREET EAST

KING STREET WEST

Draper St
Niagara Street

Windsor Street
Wellington Street West

Piper Street

Hockey Hall of Fame

Wellington St
Scott Ln

WELLINGTON STREET

FRONT STREET EAST

St Lawr Ma

FRONT STREET WEST

Station St
York St

UNION STATION

The Esplanade

Wilt

Fort York

Housey Street

Blue Jays Way

Rogers Centre

CN Tower
Bremner Blvd

Rees St
Lower Simcoe St

Union BAY STREET

Wiltshire

GARDINER EXPRESSWAY

LAKE SHORE BLV

Ontario Place

BATHURST BLVD W
LAKE SHORE

Queens Quay West

Stadium Road
Lower Spadina Ave

Robertson Crs

Queens Quay West

Bay St

Queens Quay East

Cooper St
Freeland St

HARBOURFRONT

Nautical Centre

York Quay Centre

Queens Quay Terminal

Harbourfront Centre

Island Ferry Docks

Toronto Harbour

↓ Toronto Islands

A | B | C

TORONTO STREET INDEX

REGIONS TORONTO • CITY MAPS

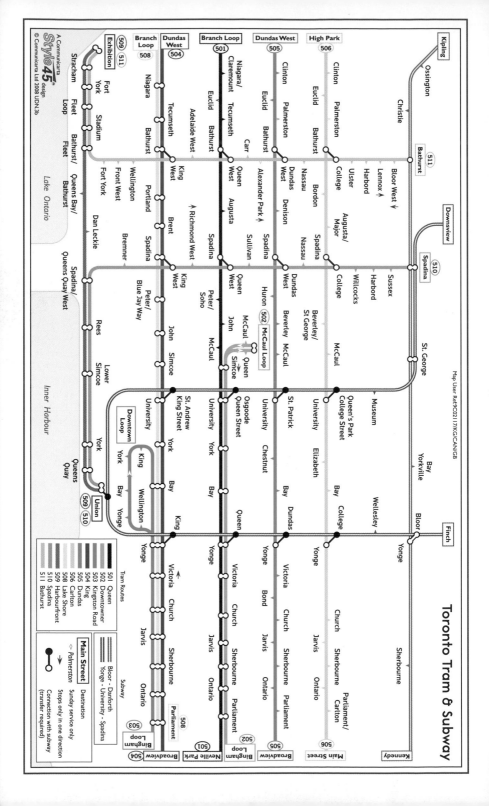

Toronto Tram & Subway

Lake Ontario

Inner Harbour

Map User Ref:9C0211/KG/CAN/GB

A Communicarta
Style45 design
© Communicarta Ltd 2008 UDN.3b

ART GALLERY OF ONTARIO

In November 2008, after a complete transformation, this already world-class art gallery reopened in a stunning new building by the internationally renowned Toronto-born architect, Frank Gehry. Massively increased in size, it features a curved glass façade that sweeps upward from Dundas Street, housing a sculpture gallery and allowing sight of many artworks by passersby, a central block and a Contemporary Art wing overlooking Grange Park at the rear. Throughout the building, the use of glass not only floods the interior with natural light but also incorporates the surrounding cityscape into the scheme.

THE THOMSON COLLECTION

The transformation of the gallery was prompted by the donation in 2002 of the collection of some 2,000 works amassed by Canadian millionaire Kenneth Thomson, who also provided some funding for the $254 million cost of the project. The collection includes works by notable Canadian artists, including Tom Thomson, the Group of Seven, and Paul Kane, and European art spanning many centuries:18th and 19th-century paintings, sculpture, medieval and religious art. One of the highlight is Rubens' *The Massacre of the Innocents*.

CANADIAN GALLERIES

With its exhibition space increased by 164 percent, the Canadian works are particularly interesting. It includes one of the biggest and best collections of Inuit art in the world, plus many important works by post-Confederation artists such as Emily Carr, Cornelius Krieghoff, Tom Thomson and the Group of Seven and leading contemporary artists.

EUROPEAN ART AND THE HENRY MOORE GALLERY

The gallery holds an important collection of European masterpieces, including works by Van Gogh, Van Dyck, Picasso, Magritte, Degas, Monet, Rodin and many others. It also has the world's largest collection (more than 900 pieces) of Henry Moore works, including bronzes and original plasterworks. Moore had a particular affection for the city of Toronto and personally donated a large number of these works to the AGO.

INFORMATION

www.ago.net

✚ 176 B3 ✉ 317 Dundas Street West, Toronto, Ontario, M5T 1G4 ☎ 416/979-6648, 1-877/225-4246 🕓 Reopening end of 2008; call for information 🖐 Call for information 🚌 505 Ⓜ St. Patrick 🍴 🏛

Opposite *The distinctive red brick Flatiron Building framed by Brookfield Place's two towers*
Below *Model of the staircase in the new and improved Art Gallery of Ontario*

CN TOWER

INFORMATION

www.cntower.ca

🕂 176 B4 ✉ 301 Front Street West, Toronto, Ontario, M5V 2T6 ☎ 416/868-6937 🕐 Daily (times vary seasonally); closed Dec 25 💵 Look Out, Glass Floor and Skypod: Adult $26.50, child (4–12) $20.50; Look Out and Glass Floor only: adult $22, child (4–12) $15. Taxes not included. Free if you have a restaurant reservation 🍴 360 The Restaurant at the CN Tower 🚇 Union Station 🚃 Streetcar 510 🚆 GO-Train to Union Station 🍽 Horizons Café and Marketplace Café

INTRODUCTION

After all these years, this building is still an icon for the city. The view from the top of the 553.33m (1,815ft 5in) CN Tower in downtown Toronto is spectacular. On a clear day you can trace Yonge Street as it disappears in a straight line over the far horizon and see small planes pass beneath you. It's great to stay up there long enough to watch the sun go down and the city light up far below. For a really special treat, you can dine in the revolving 360 Restaurant (▷ 202) while the cityscape and lake drift slowly past the window. To get up the tower, you take a stomach-churning ride in an external glass elevator at a speed of 6m (20ft) per second.

The CN Tower was not intended to be a tourist attraction, but was constructed to solve a communications problem. In the 1960s, Toronto's low-rise skyline was transformed with a cluster of downtown skyscrapers that got in the way of the airwaves, so in 1976 Canadian National Railways (CN) built the tower to hold microwave receptors and an antenna, giving Torontonians some of the clearest TV and radio reception in North America. CN had the foresight to provide viewing platforms, too, and it soon became not only a city icon, but also a place visitors just have to go. Since the railroad company sold the tower, the CN in the name has been adapted to stand for "Canada's National."

WHAT TO SEE

THE LOOK OUT AND GLASS FLOOR

The big bulge two-thirds of the way up, at a height of 346m (1,136ft), is the Look Out, reached via the glass elevator. Here, you can spend some time inside, identifying the city landmarks, before descending one floor to an observatory. If you have a good head for heights, you can even stand on a (strong) glass panel and look straight down at the ground far below.

If you don't want to ride the elevator you can't get up the tower—unless, that is, you join in one of the organized Stair Climbs in which thousands of

Above People viewing Toronto from above through the glass floor in the CN Tower

people climb the 1,776 stairs to raise money for charity. Both the United Way and the World Wildlife Fund hold annual climbs that raise more than $1.5 million in total. In 1989, Brendan Keenoy set a world record for the fastest climb, accomplishing it in just 7 minutes and 52 seconds. And in 2002, paraplegic athlete Jeff Adams went up the stairs in a wheelchair to support a campaign highlighting accessibility issues. The stairs are not otherwise accessible to the public.

SKYPOD

From the Look Out level, there's an internal elevator up to the SkyPod, another 209m (686ft) above the ground. You emerge onto the highest man-made observatory in the world, where the thick enclosing glass curves beneath you to maximize the wonderful views. Visibility can be over 160km (100 miles), and if humidity is low and clouds are few, you might just make out the spray of Niagara Falls and the city of Rochester, New York state, on the far side of the lake.

TIPS

» Arrive early in the day, as the lines to ascend the tower can be long at peak times.

» Unless you've teenagers in your party, you'll probably want to hurry past the tacky offerings—video-game arcades, motion simulators, etc.—at the bottom of the tower. However, the 15-minute "To The Top" movie about the construction of the tower is interesting.

» Check the weather before you plan your trip—it's a lot of money to pay just to have your head in the clouds.

» Be aware that on windy days you can feel the tower swaying (up to 1.8m/6ft from the vertical). Staff will tell you that it's quite normal, but it can still be very unnerving.

» The best way to get here is to take the subway to Union Station and follow the Skywalk.

» If you make a reservation to dine in the 360 Restaurant (▷ 202), you'll avoid any wait to get to the top on busy days. Afterward you can walk down to the Look Out and glass-floor level.

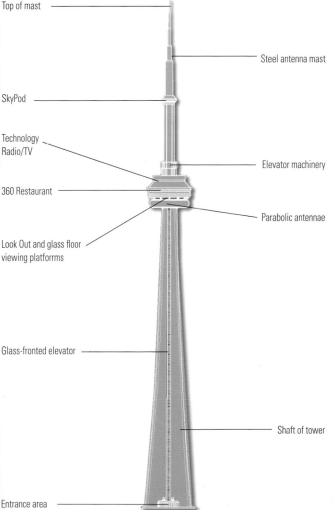

Top of mast

Steel antenna mast

SkyPod

Technology
Radio/TV

Elevator machinery

360 Restaurant

Parabolic antennae

Look Out and glass floor
viewing platforrms

Glass-fronted elevator

Shaft of tower

Entrance area

BLACK CREEK PIONEER VILLAGE
www.blackcreek.ca

A complete small rural community, of the type you would have found in southern Ontario in the early Victorian era, is a delightfully unexpected find in the northern part of the city. The 40 homes, workshops, stores and other buildings have been constructed and laid out as a town, with tree-lined dirt roads, boardwalks and split-log fencing around old-fashioned gardens. The friendly, knowledgeable staff create a welcoming down-home atmosphere, and it's on the site of a real pioneer farm.

Most of the buildings are occupied by costumed interpreters, who bring the whole experience to life. Craftspeople are actually working, farmers are tending animals, housewives are sewing or spinning in their parlors, and all are ready to chat to you about what life was like in pioneer days. This is a lovely place to spend a summer's day, and in winter roaring fires will warm you while you have a chat with the various craftspeople about their work.

✚ Off map,176 B1 ✉ 1000 Murray Ross Parkway, Toronto, Ontario, M3J 2P3 ☎ 416/736-1733 ⊙ Daily May—end Dec; closed Christmas Day 🖐 Adult $13, child (4–15) $9 🚇 Finch 🚌 60 🍴 🏛

CASA LOMA
www.casaloma.org

Casa Loma, with its turrets and towers, chimneys and machicolations, has been described as a mixture of 17th-century Scottish baronial architecture and 20th-Century Fox. It's a rich man's fantasy on a grand scale.

The rich man was stockbroker Sir Henry Pellatt, and his architect was Edward Lennox. Construction began in 1911, and they gave it 15 bathrooms, 5,000 electric lights, an elevator, a private telephone, and every other luxury money could buy. By the time the house was finished, three years later, it had swallowed up $3.5 million of Pellatt's fortune. It needed 40 servants to maintain it, and the cost of its upkeep skyrocketed just as his fortunes took a downturn. Ten years later he had to sell his dream home and auction off his belongings, and in 1939 he died almost penniless.

For years Casa Loma was neglected and sat unoccupied while the city debated tearing it down, but in 1937 the Kiwanis Club suggested making it into a tourist attraction; they still run it on behalf of the city today. Keep an eye out for the 244m (266-yard) tunnel that leads to the stables, which have mahogany stalls and Spanish tiles.

✚ Off map, 176 A1 ✉ 1 Austin Terrace, Toronto, Ontario, M5R 1X8 ☎ 416/923-1171 ⊙ Daily 9.30–5 (last admission 4; closes 1pm Dec 24); closed Dec 25, Jan 1 🖐 Adult $17, child (4–13) $9.25 🚇 Dupont 🚌 127 🏛

CN TOWER
▷ 182–183

FORT YORK
www.fortyork.ca

In 1793, Toronto, then called York, was founded at this very spot, and became the capital of Upper Canada. Today, the Gardiner Expressway and railroad tracks have replaced the fort's defenses and the waters of Lake Ontario no longer lap against its walls, but it still gives a vivid insight into Toronto's history.

It may be hard to visualize this peaceful spot as the scene of bitter military action, but an American army invaded this growing community on April 27, 1813, and attacked Fort York. Vastly outnumbered, the fort's defenders retreated, but not before they had blown up the city's gunpowder supply, destroying the

Clockwise from left *The fairytale turrets of the Casa Loma; glazed ceramic statue of the Virgin Mary and Christ Child in the Gardiner Museum; man dressed as a British soldier, Fort York*

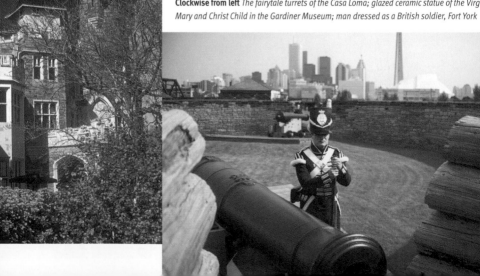

fort and killing hundreds of the attackers.

Fort York was rebuilt immediately after the War of 1812, and a number of the structures you see today date from that time. The officers' quarters and soldiers' barracks reflect life in a military base in the 1830s. Other buildings house exhibits on the history of the fort and Canadian military history since the War of 1812. There are seasonal tours given by guides in period costume, as well as summer events such as military drills and musket firing. Fife and drum music and demonstrations of military drill and drumming are staged by costumed interpreters. There's a pedestrian walkway leading up from the streetcar stop on Fleet Street, but it's very steep and not recommended for small children, the elderly or people with mobility difficulties.

✚ 176 A4 ✉ 100 Garrison Road, Toronto, Ontario, M5V 3K9 ☎ 416/392-6907 🕐 Daily 10–4 or 5; closed Dec 17–Jan 1 ✋ Adult $6, child (12 and under) $3 or (over 12) $3.25 🚇 Bathurst 🚌 Streetcar 511 💻

GARDINER MUSEUM OF CERAMIC ART
www.gardinermuseum.on.ca
This little gem occupies an engaging modern building which has been extended to allow for its expanding collection, for special exhibitions and for a gourmet restaurant with a view on the new third floor. The Gardiner is Canada's only museum entirely devoted to ceramic art, and was founded in 1984 by local philanthropists George and Helen Gardiner to house the comprehensive collection they had amassed from Europe, Asia and the Americas. The pieces are arranged chronologically, starting with a fine display of pre-Columbian objects, predominantly unglazed earthenware, figures, vessels and ritual items.

There is a splendid collection of 15th- and 16th-century Italian majolica, tin-glazed earthenware from Faenza, Florence, Urbino and Venice, and some 17th- and 18th-century

delftware from England, named because of its similarity to the products of the Dutch town of Delft. Note in particular the chargers—large plates with portraits of English monarchs. Meissen, Du Paquier, Sèvres, and the great English companies of Worcester, Chelsea and Derby represent 18th- century European porcelain. The exquisite scent bottles come from different parts of Europe, but particularly notable are the elaborate rococo models made in England. The 19th-century Minton china is excellent, and an interesting display of contemporary ceramics brings the collection up to date.

✚ 176 B1 ✉ Brookfield Place, 111 Queen's Park, Toronto, Ontario, M5S 2C7 ☎ 416/586-8080 🕐 Mon–Thu 10–6, Fri 10–9, Sat–Sun 10–5 ✋ Adult $12 child (13 and over) $6; free Fri 4–9 🚇 Museum 🍴 Jamie Kennedy at The Gardiner

HARBOURFRONT CENTRE
▷ 186–187

HOCKEY HALL OF FAME
www.hhof.com
This shrine to Canada's sporting obsession has a comprehensive collection of hockey memorabilia and features hockey greats such as Maurice "The Rocket" Richard, Bobby Orr and Wayne Gretzky. There are extensive interactive consoles where you can experience the challenges that have made these sporting heroes great, and you can see the original Stanley Cup, North America's oldest sports trophy.

✚ 176 C4 ✉ 30 Front Street, Toronto, Ontario, M5E 1X8 ☎ 416/360-7765 🕐 Late Jun–end Aug Mon–Sat 9.30–6, Sun 10–6; rest of year 🚇 Union Station ✋ Adult $13, child (4–13) $9

KENSINGTON MARKET
www.kensington-market.ca.com
Canada's 2006 census revealed that Toronto had become one of the world's most multicultural places, and one of the best areas to appreciate this diversity is at Kensington Market. Portuguese spice merchants, Chilean butchers, Laotian restaurants, Jamaican fast food—

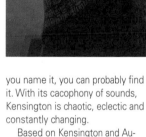

you name it, you can probably find it. With its cacophony of sounds, Kensington is chaotic, eclectic and constantly changing.

Based on Kensington and Augusta avenues and Baldwin Street, the market is an amazing potpourri of businesses and street vendors amid a warren of narrow streets. Houses have been converted into individualistic stores and informal restaurants that spill out onto the street, and people fill just about all of the available space between them.

You can buy all kinds of food here—fresh fish, vegetables, unusual cheeses, fruit, bread, nuts, exotic spices—and there are stores selling carpets and furniture. This is also a great place to seek out secondhand or vintage clothing.

If you want the full market experience, go on a Saturday, when it's at its busiest.

✚ 176 A3 🚇 St. Patrick 🚌 Dundas streetcar

HARBOURFRONT CENTRE

INFORMATION

www.harbourfront.on.ca

🔲 176 B5 ✉ 235 Queens Quay West, Toronto, Ontario, M5J 2G8 ☎ 419/973-4600 (admin), 416/973-3000 (info hotline), 416/973-4000 (box office) 🕐 General area always accessible; call for event information 🏛 Free access; charges vary for individual events 🚇 Union Station 🚋 Streetcar 509, 510 from Union Station 🛍 Large variety of stores and craft shops 🍴 Restaurants at Pier 4 and in Queen's Quay Terminal. Cafés and fast food

INTRODUCTION

This former dockland area is now a shining beacon of cultural, commercial and leisure activities. Between downtown and the lakeshore, there might seem at first glance to be little more than a tangle of railroad tracks heading for Union Station and traffic thundering by on the wide Gardiner Expressway. Look closer, however, and you will see that these are just barriers separating the bustle of the city streets from a different world of waterfront shopping and entertainment. On the section between York and Spadina is a superb 4ha (10-acre) leisure complex that has transformed the old docklands.

In 1974, the center, then known simply as Harbourfront, was set up as a nonprofit organization (so events are reasonably priced or free) to bring a wide variety of artists and art forms to the people of Toronto, to introduce ideas that would not normally be showcased at commercial venues, and to push the boundaries of creative expression. At just about any time of the year, you can drop by the Harbourfront Centre and find something going on, even if it's just Torontonians taking the air beside the water.

WHAT TO SEE

PERFORMANCES AND FESTIVALS

The Harbourfront Centre has a full and exciting schedule of music, dance, drama and other events, both inside and in the open air, by international performers. It's also the venue for various festivals, including the World Stage Festival each April, hosting theater companies from all over the world. The well-established Harbourfront Reading Series is one of the most admired public reading events in the world, and has hosted more than 2,500 distinguished authors, including a dozen Nobel laureates. The International Festival of Authors is another popular event where you can rub shoulders with literary icons. On summer Sunday afternoons, various outdoor "cushion concerts" take place, including storytelling for children and live music. World culture is a particular focus of the center, with recent events showcasing Caribbean, Iranian, Taiwanese, Latin American, Yiddish and South Asian culture.

GARDENS AND GALLERIES

The enchanting Music Garden, outside Queen's Quay Terminal (▷ below), was designed jointly by renowned cellist Yo Yo Ma and landscape artist Julie Moir Messervy to reflect Bach's First Suite for Unaccompanied Cello. The separate areas of the garden each represent a different movement within the suite. Notice, too, the maypole and the Music Pavilion, designed and created by Canadian artists. The garden makes an appropriate and scenic setting for the center's Summer Music in the Garden series of open-air concerts (Thu 7pm and Sun 4pm, weather permitting). Another horticultural attraction is the Artists' Gardens, where plants are used to create living installations.

York Quay Centre hosts exhibitions in a broad range of media, including photography and multicultural themes. Meanwhile, the Power Plant specializes in contemporary art, including paintings, sculpture and installation work, and, though it exhibits work from the rest of Canada and other countries, it maintains a strong commitment to Toronto artists. The Canada Quay Building also stages temporary exhibitions; features include computer-based displays.

SHOPPING

The York Quay Centre, at 235 Queen's Quay West, includes the Bounty Contemporary Canadian Crafts store, where you can buy quality Canadian crafts made by some of the country's brightest and most innovative artists. You can also see some of these crafts in the making, in the studios of the artists-in-residence. On summer weekends, the open-air International Market at the water's edge has vendors selling arts and crafts from across the globe, including native works, Oriental textiles and South American jewelry.

Queen's Quay Terminal, at 207 Queen's Quay West, is a glittering and imaginative conversion of a 1920s warehouse that contains more than 30 chic stores, galleries and restaurants, the former selling crafts, fine arts and designer clothing (▷ 197). Luxury condominiums and offices are on the upper floors, with some of the best lake views in the city.

ACTIVITIES

There is always plenty to see and do on the water. Nearby, ferries leave for the Toronto Islands and a variety of boat tours are available. The Nautical Centre offers all kinds of water-based activities, including sailing, kayaking, sightseeing cruises, and environmental awareness events. In winter, you can bring your ice-skates (or rent them) and skate to music at Toronto's biggest open-air ice rink, with changing facilities and hot food and drinks to warm you up. If it all sounds too energetic, the wide waterfront boardwalk is great for a leisurely stroll.

Clockwise from top left *Queen's Quay terminal; boats moored at Harbourfront; York Quay Centre; boarding a tour boat at Queen's Quay terminal*

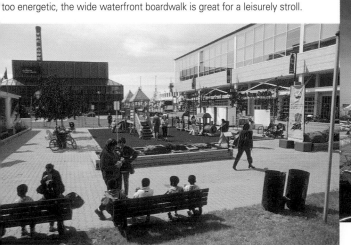

MUSEUM OF CONTEMPORARY ART

www.mocca.toronto.ca

In 2005 this exciting gallery was born out of the former Art Gallery of North York and contains a permanent collection of more than 400 works by around 150 of Canada's foremost contemporary artists. In addition to providing this showcase for the most influential home-grown talent, there is a lively program of temporary exhibitions covering all media, sometimes offering comparisons between the Canadian art scene and those of other countries. Always thought-provoking, the museum takes a bold approach to its active acquisitions program. Make a point of seeing the Book Sculptures: Brother (Bunk Beds) by Micah Lexier is an amusing work combining photographs, cardboard, wood and paper.

✚ Off map, 176 A3 ✉ 952 Queen Street West, Toronto, Ontario M6J 1G8 ☎ 416/395-0067 🕐 Tue–Sun 11–6 ✋ Free 🚋 501 Queen Street

ONTARIO PLACE

www.ontarioplace.com

In 1971, Ontario Place was constructed as a futuristic showcase for the province of Ontario, brightening up what was then an underdeveloped waterfront area and including the construction of three man-made islands and lagoons. Today, it has developed into a popular amusement park, with more than 30 exciting rides, lots of things for children to do and top-quality entertainment.

Outdoor attractions are open only in summer, including The Festival of Fire fireworks displays on four nights in June and July, but entertainments continue year round in the IMAX movie theater, the Atlantic Pavilions—with nightclub, rooftop terrace and 450-seat theater—and the 16,000-capacity Molson Amphitheatre, hosting concerts starring big-name international performers.

✚ Off map, 176 A5 ✉ 955 Lakeshore Boulevard West, Toronto, Ontario, M6K 3B9 ☎ 416/314-9900; 866/663-4386 🕐 Jun–end Aug daily from 10am; May

and Sep weekends; closing time varies ✋ "Play-all-day": adult and child over 5 $22, child (4–5) $12, under 3 free. Grounds only: adult $13, child (4–5) $7, under 3 free. Also individual attraction prices 🚋 Streetcar 509 from Union Station or 511 from Bathurst Station to Exhibition Place, then walk 🍴 Restaurant in Atlantis Pavilions; also a variety of fast-food outlets

ONTARIO SCIENCE CENTRE

www.ontariosciencecentre.ca

This is the science center to beat them all. You don't just stand and look here, but can really get involved with the exciting and entertaining exhibits. There are 13 multi-themed exhibition halls with more than 800 high-tech, interactive displays, plus live hands-on demonstrations and an OMNIMAX theater with a giant 24m-wide (80ft) domed screen.

In the Space Hall you can use a rocket chair to navigate on the Moon; in the Sports Hall you can test yourself by climbing a rock wall or racing an Olympic bobsled; in the Food Hall you can choose your favorite meal and check its nutritional value. You can find out how weather systems form in the Earth Hall and perform chemical experiments in the Matter, Energy and Change display.

Popular sections include the Science Arcade, with its demonstrations about generating your own electricity, and the Human Body exhibit, where you can learn how to catch a criminal with DNA fingerprinting. And when you have had enough with doing all that, you can sink back into a tilted seat at the OMNIMAX theater and enjoy a specially filmed large-format movie on its huge wrap-around screen, with 13,000W of digital sound.

There are daily science demonstrations, so check on arrival to see what's on.

✚ Off map, 176 C1 ✉ 770 Don Mills Road, Toronto, Ontario, M3C 1T3 ☎ 416/696-1000, 888/696-1110, 416/696-3127 (info line) 🕐 Daily 10–5; closed Dec 25 🚇 Eglinton, then take bus 🚌 34 ✋ Adult $14, child (4–12) $8, youth (13–17) $10. With IMAX: adult $20, child (4–12)

$10, youth (13–17) $14. IMAX also available separately 🍴 Galileo's Bistro 🎫 Lobby café 🎁 Mastermind toy store

ROGERS CENTRE

www.rogerscentre.com

The Rogers Centre is a superb multipurpose megastadium with a massive retractable roof that makes it a year-round, all-weather facility. The Rogers Centre is huge, covering 186,000sq m (2 million sq ft), and at 95m (310ft) high it could accommodate a 31-story building even with the roof closed. It also has a luxury hotel built into one side, with many rooms overlooking the field (▷ 198).

The Rogers Centre is first and foremost a sports venue, being home to the Toronto Blue Jays baseball team and the Toronto Argonauts (▷ 200), who play in the Canadian football league. It also hosts other sporting events, pop and rock concerts, trade shows and festivals (▷ 201). Seating capacity is around 50,000. If the roof needs to close over any of these events, it takes 20 minutes for the 11,175-tonne structure to slide across the 3.2ha (7.9-acre) opening.

You can get a behind-the-scenes tour, which includes the Blue Jays Hall of Fame, the Press Box and the museum, with event memorabilia, a model of the stadium and a multiscreen video wall.

✚ 176 B4 ✉ I Blue Jays Way, Toronto, Ontario, M5V 1J3 ☎ 416/341-1707 🕐 Guided tours daily, when there are no events scheduled ✋ Adult $13.25, child (12–17) $9.25, child (5–11) $7.75 🚇 Union Station

ROYAL ONTARIO MUSEUM

▷ 190–192.

ST. LAWRENCE MARKET

www.stlawrencemarket.com

This historic market building contains a wonderful assortment of stands on its main floor, selling a huge variety of foods. It is particularly well known for fresh fruit and vegetables (locally grown in season), but is also home to dozens of meat and deli vendors and fishmongers.

In season, you can buy fresh cut flowers, and there are carts piled high with an array of crafts and specialty items.

Cheese and dairy foods, dry goods and organic health foods are available on both levels, and there's prepared food to eat on the spot. Try the peameal bacon on a bun. Peameal bacon is salt- and sugar-cured extra-lean ham, rolled in cornmeal. It's a trademark Toronto delicacy (though it is available throughout Canada) and Torontonians eat it for breakfast.

There has been a market in this area since at least 1803, but not in the present building. This was originally built in 1844 to serve as Toronto's first city hall, and only became a market in 1899 when the city administration moved into what is now "Old" City Hall on the corner of Bay and Queen streets.

The old council chamber still exists on the second floor and now houses the Market Gallery, with photographs, paintings and documents relating to Toronto.

The market is lively and fun at any time, but more so on Saturdays, which is the busiest day. This is also the day when a smaller farmers' market is open in the north market building directly across Front Street from St. Lawrence Market's main doors.

🕂 176 C4 ✉ 92 Front Street East, Toronto, Ontario, M5E 1C4 ☎ 416/392-7120 🕔 Tue–Sat 🚇 Union Station 🍴

TORONTO ISLANDS
www.toronto.ca/parks/island
The Toronto Islands are just a short distance from the shore, but the ferry ride to get there makes it feel like a real excursion.

Centre Island is the principal destination for most visitors to the islands, and has a superb beach, Centreville amusement park (▷ 201) and an animal park. Other facilities include barbecues and picnic tables, tennis courts, bicycle rental, playgrounds, wading pools and fast-food outlets.

To the west is Hanlan's Point (where there's a clothing-optional beach), named after the Hanlan family, who were among the first year-round inhabitants of the Toronto Islands. Toronto City Centre Airport is here, from where you can go on helicopter sightseeing trips (▷ 200).

From the ferry dock, you can walk to the 1806 Gibraltar Point Lighthouse, Toronto's oldest surviving structure, which has a wonderful site on the lakeshore. It is also home to the Gibraltar Point Centre for the Arts, promoting artistic achievement and development.

Ferries go to different points on the islands, so make sure you get on the right one for the area you want to visit, though you can rent bicycles and buggies to get around once you are there.

🕂 Off map, 176 C5 ☎ 416/392-8188 (Toronto Parks and Recreation), 416/392-8193 (ferry info) ⛴ From Mainland Ferry

Docks at foot of Bay Street to Hanlan's Point, Centre Island and Ward Island, 10-min trip, daily, every 20 min, but first and last ferry times vary seasonally (no winter service to Centre Island) ✋ Ferry round trip: Adult $6, child (under 14) $2.50 🍴 Iroquois and Paradise restaurants 🛋

TORONTO ZOO
▷ 193.

YORKVILLE
This is Toronto's ritziest neighborhood, where Bugattis vie with Porsches for parking spaces, and is synonymous with haute couture boutiques, exclusive art galleries, designer stores and expensive restaurants. In addition, the annual glamfest of the Toronto International Film Festival is based here, attracting Hollywood's biggest names.

Back in the 1960s, this was an altogether different place—the hub of the city's counterculture, and proving ground for Canadian musicians such as Neil Young, Joni Mitchell and Gordon Lightfoot, who went on to find lasting international renown.

Today, the Victorian townhouses have been expensively restored. Many of them contain antiques shops, art galleries and designer boutiques. There's a pleasant village atmosphere and an almost tangible aroma of privilege and wealth.
🕂 176 B1 🚇 Bay

Top right *Toronto's modern marina and the small island of Hanlin's Point*

ROYAL ONTARIO MUSEUM

INTRODUCTION

After an ambitious expansion and renovation project, many priceless items in this world-class museum can now be seen for the first time. Because of the size of the museum and the bewildering array of choice, careful planning is necessary to get the best out of your visit. The first consideration is timing. School groups tend to come during the mornings, and mid-week afternoons seem to be the quietest times to visit. When you arrive, pick up a museum map, then head for the Samuel Hall-Currelly Gallery area, an elegant space designed specifically for orientation purposes. Here you can sit in comfort and identify your priorities from the map, and also view displays that offer an overview of the many collections. If you particularly want hands-on exhibits, head for the CIBC Discovery Gallery and the Patrick and Barbara Keenan Family Gallery of Hands-on Biodiversity on level two or the Digital Gallery on level one.

The original ROM building is nearly 100 years old, officially opened by the then Governor-General of Canada on March 19, 1914. At that time it housed the five separate museums of the University of Toronto, but these were amalgamated and brought under provincial government control as the Royal Ontario Museum in 1955. By this time a new wing had been added (in 1933) and further expansion became necessary as the world-class collections continued to grow. HM Queen Elizabeth II opened another new building in 1984.

However, it is the most recent expansion that has had the greatest impact of all. The Michael Lee-Chin Crystal, which opened in June 2007 and added a massive 7,500sq m (80,000sq ft) of exhibition space, is a stunning piece of architecture by Daniel Libeskind. Daring, controversial and inspired by the museum's mineral collection, it bursts out of the old building like a gigantic cartoon explosion, with prisms of glass and metal spiking skyward and out over the Bloor Street sidewalk. Love it or hate it, it provides imaginative exhibit spaces that are flooded with light and offers a tantalizing glimpse of some of the museum's star attractions to passersby.

WHAT TO SEE

CHINESE COLLECTIONS

Among the four galleries devoted to Chinese art and archeology, the undisputed highlight is the stunning Bishop White Gallery of Chinese Temple Art. One of the foremost collections of its kind in the world, the gallery contains three complete and remarkably well preserved temple wall paintings dating from the Yuan Dynasty (AD1271–1368), along with an array of beautiful, delicately painted statues. The largest of the murals, 11.6m (38ft) wide and 5.8m (19ft) high, depicting the Buddha of the Future, was painstakingly restored in 2005. Equally breathtaking is the Gallery of Chinese Architecture, which contains a Ming tomb and several large structures, including a reconstruction of an Imperial Palace building from the Forbidden City. The Joey and Toby Tanenbaum Gallery of China is another world-class collection of Chinese objects, including ceramics dating back to prehistoric times and more recent pieces of furniture and works of art.

DINOSAURS AND NATURAL HISTORY

Canada's Badlands (▷ 252–255) have given up some of the world's finest specimens of dinosaur bones and fossils, and the James and Louise Temerty Galleries of the Age of Dinosaurs have a stunning collection amounting to 20 complete or nearly complete skeletons, 50 dinosaur specimens and 350 fossils dating as far back as 250 million years ago. Displayed to their best possible advantage in the new Michael Lee-Chin Crystal extension, the skeletons are

INFORMATION

www.rom.on.ca

⊞ 176 B1 ✉ 100 Queen's Park, Toronto, Ontario, M5S 2C6, main entrance on Bloor Street West ☎ 416/586-8000 (recorded information) 🕐 Daily 10–5.30 (also Fri 5.30–9.30) 💵 Adult $20, child (5–14) $14; free 45 mins before closing; half price Fri 4.30–9.30 (except special ticketed exhibitions) 🚇 St George 🚌 5, 142 🎫 Free guided tours daily 🍽 C5 Restaurant, Food Studio 🛍 🏧

Opposite *The striking new crystalline extension is the centerpiece of the ROM's ambitious expansion program*
Below *Stone statue of an ancient Chinese warrior*

TIPS

» Buy tickets online to avoid having to line up, although you will be charged an extra $1. Online tickets are not dated and can be used on any day during the coming year, but only for a single visit. Make sure the barcodes have printed clearly.

» A limited number of strollers (pushchairs) and wheelchairs are available free of charge, and large-print museum information can be picked up at the admissions desk.

» You can get in for half price on Fridays after 4.30pm and for free on Wednesdays after 4.30pm.

flooded with natural light and give an excellent impression of their size and power. The Barosaurus, at 27.5m (90ft) long, is the largest dinosaur skeleton ever mounted in Canada. You can walk all the way around many of the exhibits, and touch-screen stations answer many questions and offer fun facts.

Sharing Level 2 is the Gallery of the Age of Mammals, which continues the story of mammal development following the extinction of the dinosaurs. More than 400 specimens here include large and small, familiar and highly unusual creatures, with the mastodon and other Ice-Age animals a particularly popular exhibit. A favorite exhibit with children is the Bat Cave, a re-creation of the St. Clair cave in Jamaica that you can walk right into, with sound effects, plenty of bats roosting high up in rocky crevices, and other nocturnal creatures. There are also galleries of birds and reptiles, and the fun Gallery of Hands-on Biodiversity, with exhibits you can actually handle.

WORLD CULTURE

A fabulous array of items from all over the world is on show in the World Culture Galleries, inclluding finds from ancient Cyprus, the Prince Takamado Gallery of Japan, with an outstanding collection of ceramics, sculpture, paintings, armour and tea ceremony artifacts. The Sir Christopher Ondaatje South Asian Gallery explores more than 5,000 years of history, including fine and decorative arts, weapons, religious items and textiles. There are also superb collections from Europe, Africa and the Middle East, from Egyptian mummies and funerary objects to delicate Greek figurines and medieval suits of armour.

CANADIANA

The history of Canada is represented in fascinating and lively style. The Daphne Cockwell Gallery of Canada: First Peoples contains a wonderful collection of artifacts that offer a comprehensive insight into the culture of the indigenous population before the arrival of the European settlers, laid out here in consultation with the museum's six Native advisors. There is a superb collection of First Nations art, including Canada's largest collection of works by pioneer artist Paul Kane, the "Father of Canadian Art." One of the most lively sections of the whole museum, this gallery includes a theater for live performances of tribal music and dance and the screening of films. The Sigmund Samuel Gallery of Canada portrays Canadian history after the first Europeans arrived, and has a rich collection of furniture, decorative and applied arts. A highlight here is a display of early 19th-century French carved panelling from Québec.

Above *The dinosaur skeletons are always among the museum's most popular exhibits*

TORONTO ZOO

Covering 287ha (710 acres) in the valley of the Rouge River at Scarborough 37km (23 miles) northeast of Toronto, this enormous zoo, with 10km (6 miles) of walking trails, opened in 1974. It is more a celebration of wildlife than a zoo in the traditional sense, and its concept has always been to allow visitors to see the animals in as natural a setting as possible. More than 5,000 animals, representing more than 460 species, come from all six of the world's major zoo-geographic regions.

In addition to the outdoor paddocks, there are four giant indoor pavilions and several smaller indoor viewing areas. The zoo is a nonprofit organization, and in addition to the public access, it maintains a serious commitment to scientific research and conservation. The annual running costs are around $24 million, and those who balk at paying for parking in addition to admission should know that this alone pays the animals' food bill.

THE CONTINENTAL AREAS

Not surprisingly, the spectacular wildlife in the African area is one of the most popular—elephants, giraffes, rhinos, antelopes, crocodiles—even a termite mound. And, most popular of all, a troop of western lowland gorillas.

The Australasian continent has a large number of species that are not found anywhere else in the world, such as the Komodo dragon, and there are also plenty of kangaroos and wallabies, emu, possums, wombats and the Tasmanian devil. In addition, the Edge of Night exhibit switches night and day so that the nocturnal marsupials are active when visitors are present. There's also an Indomalayan pavilion, with a tropical rainforest and waterfall, clouded leopards, exotic birds and a Sumatran orangutan family; the Eurasia area, with camels, Siberian tigers and Barbary apes; the Americas, featuring animals as diverse as polar bears and Brazilian cockroaches, and including alligators, sloths, bird-eating spiders and llamas.

The rugged Canadian Domain features elk and moose, bison and musk oxen, grizzly bears, cougars, Arctic wolves, and bald eagles, and there's a spectacular variety of waterfowl on Weston Pond. A new Tundra area, with polar bears, is due to open in 2009.

INFORMATION

www.torontozoo.com

✚ Off map, 176 C1 ✉ Meadowvale Road, Scarborough, Ontario, M1B 5K7 ☎ 416/392-5929 🕐 Early Mar to mid-May and Sep 2 to mid-Oct daily 9–6; mid-May to Sep 1 9–7.30; mid-Oct–early Mar 9.30–4.30 (last admission 1 hour before closing) 🎫 Adult $20, child (4–12) $12 🚇 Kennedy then bus 86A, or Sheppard then bus 85 🚆 GO train to Rouge Hill then bus 85 🅿

TIPS

» Arrive early and even then don't try to see everything, it's just too big. But don't miss the gorillas.
» Wear comfortable shoes. Even if you take the Zoo-mobile ($5 per day), there's plenty of walking to do.
» Pick up a schedule for the daily "Meet the Keeper" events and feeding times.
» If you're coming with kids, be aware that the Kids Zoo includes a huge water-play area so they'll want their swimsuits and towels

Below *A laid back polar bear dries off at Toronto Zoo*

THE HEART OF TORONTO

This walk in Canada's most important city includes a glimpse of the vibrant financial area, the underground system of passageways lined with stores and food outlets, a number of unusual art works, and a look at what Toronto has done with its magnificent waterfront.

THE WALK

Length: 4.8km (3 miles)
Allow: 2–2.5 hours (not including visits)
Start and end at: Nathan Phillips Square in front of Toronto City Hall ✛ 176 B3
How to get there: Nathan Phillips Square is on Queen Street West; subway: Queen or Osgoode

★ Nathan Phillips Square is an attractive focal point for the distinctive 1965 City Hall. In front of the curved, twin buildings, there's an open area and water feature used for summer sunning and winter ice skating.

From here, cross Bay Street to your left. On the corner with Queen Street you see Old City Hall.

❶ Built in 1889–99 by Edward James Lennox at a cost of $2.5 million, it served as both a courthouse and municipal offices. Today, it houses the criminal court.

Walk behind Old City Hall, cross James Street and enter the Eaton Centre.

❷ Designed by Eberhard Zeidler in 1977, the impressive atrium, with its arched glass and steel roof, is over 262m (860ft) long. It features a flock of sculpted Canada geese in full flight by Michael Snow, as well as nearly 300 stores and restaurants.

Walk through and out on the other side onto Yonge Street.

❸ "The longest street in Canada" was built by Governor Simcoe in 1795 as a military road connecting Toronto to Lake Simcoe to the north.

Continue south on Yonge Street for four blocks, then turn right on King Street.

❹ This is the financial heart of Canada. To your right is Scotia

Plaza, owned by the Bank of Nova Scotia. Across the street, step inside Commerce Court, owned by the Canadian Imperial Bank of Commerce, created in 1929–30 by architects York and Sawyer. In the 1970s, the tower was added next door, to your right.

Walk through a sort of metal kaleidoscope that joins the two together. Turn left in the newer building and walk outside into the courtyard. Turn right and out onto Bay Street. Then turn left and cross Wellington Street. Across the street, the two triangular gold-sheathed towers are the Royal Bank of Canada. At 181 Bay Street, enter Brookfield Place.

❺ This complex boasts the most elegant galleria in the city. Designed by Skidmore, Owings, and Merrill in 1993, the long, elegant atrium is five floors high and incorporates two older buildings, plus two unusually shaped office towers.

Left *The glazed roof of the Eaton Centre atrium with its sculptured flock of 60 Canada geese*

Return to Bay Street and turn left, cross Front Street and look to your right for a great view of the CN Tower. Here, Bay Street goes under the railroad tracks. Cross the street to the west sidewalk (pavement) leading through a tunnel. Just before you emerge from the tunnel, on your right is the Air Canada Centre, home to the Toronto Maple Leafs (▷ 200). Walk alongside the stadium and then under the Gardiner Expressway. This is a horrible section of the route and you may wonder where it's all leading, but the waterfront is really worth the effort. Cross Harbour Street and Queen's Quay, and then walk between the Westin Harbour Castle Hotel and Harbour Square to come to the waterfront.

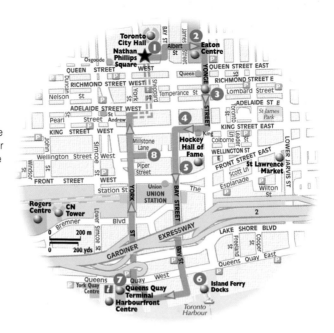

❻ Across the water, you can see the Toronto Islands. Ferries to the islands leave from the dock.

Turn right at the water's edge and follow the path in front of the condominiums and around the York Street slip. Ahead to your right is Queen's Quay Terminal.

❼ Classy stores occupy the light and airy ground level of Queen's Quay Terminal (▷ 187, 197). At the far end there are waterfront restaurants and cafés.

Cross Queen's Quay and walk away from the lake on York Street. Go under the expressway and railroad tracks again. You can take the Teamway, a covered sidewalk on the west side of York Street, leaving it to go outside at Front Street. Cross the street and walk past the Fairmont Royal York Hotel (▷ 207). Walk one more block and then turn right at Wellington Street. The black glass buildings on both sides of the street are part of the Toronto-Dominion Centre. Go into the Maritime Life Tower on your right to visit the TD Gallery of Inuit Art.

❽ The TD Gallery contains a selection of Toronto-Dominion bank's superb collection of Inuit art that should not be missed.

Walk back outside again, cross Wellington Street, and enter the middle of the buildings of the TD Centre across the street. In the courtyard, officially called The Pasture, the sculpture of seven peaceful bronze cows is the work of Saskatchewan sculptor Joe Fanfare. Cross King Street and enter First Canadian Place. Take the escalator down to experience a bit of Toronto's underground city on the PATH Walkway, a subterranean shopping complex that connects the business district. From First Canadian Place, you can follow the signs back to City Hall. You will pass below the Richmond Adelaide Centre and the Sheraton Centre. You will then find yourself in the parking area of Nathan Phillips Square. Take the steps up and you are back where you started.

WHEN TO GO
You can do this walk anytime, but spring, early summer and fall are the best. High summer gets very hot and humid, which also exacerbates the effect of traffic pollution. Winters, of course, can be very cold.

WHERE TO EAT
ACQUA
✉ Brookfield Place, 10 Front Street West, ☎ 416/368-7171

PIER 4 STOREHOUSE RESTAURANT
✉ 245 Queen's Quay West ☎ 416/203-1440

BATON ROUGE
✉ 216 Yonge Street ☎ 416/593-9667

PLACES TO VISIT
BROOKFIELD PLACE
www.brookfieldproperties.com
✉ 181 Bay Street

TD GALLERY OF INUIT ART
✉ 79 Wellington Street West ◉ Mon–Fri 8–4

SHOPPING

ALL THE BEST FINE FOODS

www.allthebestfinefoods.com

The name says it all, and the display in the century-old storefront defies you to keep on walking. The shop is well placed for exclusive Rosedale, and it has an outstanding cheese selection, freshly baked goods, gift baskets, tableware and other items for stylish entertaining.

✉ 1101 Yonge Street, Toronto, Ontario, M4W 2L7 ☎ 416/928-3330 ⏱ Mon–Wed 8.30–6.30, Thu–Fri 8.30–7, Sat 8.30–6, Sun 10–5 🚇 Summerhill 🚌 97B 🚶 North of Bloor, near Marlborough Avenue/Price Street intersection

BOUNTY

www.harbourfrontcentre.com

A range of contemporary Canadian crafts, including ceramics, blown glass, jewelry, wood and fiber crafts. Many of the items have been made by the professional artists-in-residence at the onsite craft studios (where you can watch the work in progress).

✉ Harbourfront Centre, 235 Queen's Quay West, Toronto, Ontario, M5J 2G8 ☎ 416/973-4993 ⏱ Tue and Sat–Sun 11–6, Wed–Fri 11–8 🚇 Union Station 🚋 Streetcar 509, 510

DR. FLEA'S

www.drfleas.com

An undercover market houses more than 400 independent vendors selling everything from crafts to music, baby goods and toys. The farmers' market has fresh produce and bread.

✉ 8 Westmore Drive, Toronto, Ontario, M9V 3Z7 ☎ 416/745-3532 ⏱ Sat–Sun 10–5 🚇 Royal York, then bus 73 🚌 73 🚗 Highway 27 and Albion Road, 25 min from downtown

EATON CENTRE

www.torontoeatoncentre.com

A trailblazer in the world of shopping, this is one of the most visited places in Toronto (▷ 194), but even with a million visitors a week it rarely feels crowded (except the food court on weekday lunchtimes). There are nearly 300 stores, and Sears is the main anchor store.

✉ 220 Yonge Street, Toronto, Ontario, M5B 2H1 ☎ 416/598-8700 ⏱ Mon–Fri 10–9, Sat 9.30–7, Sun 12–6 🚇 Queen or Dundas 🚌 97B 🍴

ESKIMO ART GALLERY

www.eskimoart.com

There are touches of the Arctic about this excellent gallery of Inuit sculpture, with frosted-glass shelving, pedestals that simulate icebergs and icy blue lighting. It displays Canada's largest collection of contemporary Inuit soapstone carvings, reflecting the warm emotions that exist in the cold north.

✉ 12 Queen's Quay West, Toronto, Ontario, M5J 2V3 ☎ 416/366-3000 ⏱ Mon–Fri 10–7, Sat–Sun 10–6 🚇 Union Station 🚋 Streetcar 509, 510 🚶 Harbourfront

HAZELTON LANES

www.hazletonlanes.com

Toronto's most upscale shopping mall, in ritzy Yorkville, is filled with top fashion designers, including Chanel, Stella McCartney, Prada and many more. There are also fine jewelers, lifestyle boutiques—and a Rolls Royce dealership.

✉ 58–87 Avenue Road, Toronto, Ontario ☎ 416/968-8680 ⏱ Mon–Wed, Sat 10–6, Thu–Fri 10–8, Sun 12–5 🚇 Bay, St George 🚌 142 🚶 Just north of Bloor; underground parking available

HOLT RENFREW

www.holtrenfrew.com

This long-established, exclusive store has the oldest existing contract with Christian Dior and five generations of royal warrants. In addition to prestigious designer fashions for men and women, it has accessories, cosmetics and fragrances, and a spa.

✉ 50 Bloor Street West, Toronto, Ontario, M4W 1A1 ☎ 416/922-2333 🕐 Mon–Wed and Sat 10–6, Thu–Fri 10–8, Sun 12–6 🚇 Bay 🚌 6A, 6B 📍 Downtown, just west of Yonge 🔲

HONEST ED'S

A huge signboard with 22,000 flashing lights heralds a place that's world-famous for its brash, fun approach to discount retailing (a sign inside reads "don't faint at our prices, there's no place to lie down"). In business since 1948, it has 14,400sq m (160,000sq ft) of bargains including clothing, gifts, homewares and food.

✉ 581 Bloor Street West, Toronto, Ontario, M6G 1K3 ☎ 416/537-1574 🕐 Mon–Fri 10–9, Sat 10–6, Sun 11–6 🚇 Bathurst 🚌 Streetcar 511 📍 Corner of Bloor and Bathurst; parking to rear, off Lennox Street

KALIYANA

www.kaliyana.com

This is a real find—a classy store with uncluttered racks of gorgeous clothes in sleek styles and unusual colors, all in washable natural fibers. Smart enough for the office and comfortable enough for lounging around, and best of all, you won't get turned away if you're bigger than size 10, as they go up to a size 24.

✉ 2516 Yonge Street, Toronto, Ontario, M4P 2H7 ☎ 416/480-2397 🕐 Mon–Wed and Sat 10–6, Thu–Fri 10–7, Sun 12–5 🚇 Eglinton 🚌 97+ 📍 Yonge and Eglinton

QUEEN'S QUAY TERMINAL

A very smart mall with soaring ceilings, lots of glass giving natural light (and lake views), and more than 30 outlets that have a mainly Canadian focus—Arctic Nunarut, Canadian Naturalist, Oh Yes! Toronto, Proud Canadian Design and Tilley Endurables (▷ below). There's also designer clothing, fine art and Venetian glass. The food court overlooks the lake, and serves Japanese, Italian, seafood and diner-style food.

✉ 207 Queen's Quay West, Toronto, Ontario, M5J 1A7 ☎ 416/203-0510

🕐 Daily 10–5 🚇 Union Station 🚌 Streetcar 509, 510 🍴

TILLEY ENDURABLES

www.tilley.Ú

The flagship store of a Toronto business success story sells tough, practical clothing for travelers. It started with Alex Tilley's simple need for a good sailing hat, and now the clothing is sold all over the world.

✉ 900 Don Mills Road, Toronto, Ontario, M3C 1V6 ☎ 416/441-6141 🕐 Mon–Wed 9–8, Thu–Fri 9–9, Sat 9–6, Sun 11–5 🚌 25+, 403 📍 Uptown, two traffic lights north of Eglinton

WORLD'S BIGGEST BOOKSTORE

Now part of the giant Chapters-Indigo chain, this is not the biggest any more, but the name was accurate when it opened, and who's going to quibble when they see 27km (17 miles) of shelves and 143,000 titles in 65 departments? There's a database that contains every book that is in print in the world.

✉ 20 Edward Street, Toronto, Ontario, M5G 1C9 ☎ 416/977-7009 🕐 Mon–Sat 9am–10pm, Sun 11–8 🚇 Dundas 🚌 97B 📍 Downtown, off Yonge just north of the Eaton Centre and Dundee Street West

ENTERTAINMENT AND NIGHTLIFE

AIR CANADA CENTRE

www.theaircanadacentre.com

This complex includes the huge 5,200-seat Sears Theatre, which stages ice shows and concerts by touring international stars. There are also plenty of food choices, including a pub and a bar.

✉ 40 Bay Street, Toronto, Ontario, M5J 2X2 ☎ 416/815-5500 🕐 Year-round 🚇 Union Station 🚌 Streetcar: 6A, 97B

BABAL·Ú

www.babaluu.com

Soft seating and pools of light on the hardwood dance floor create a party atmosphere at this tapas bar. The music includes salsa, mambo, Afro-Cuban and Brazilian. Free salsa lessons 9–10pm except Saturday.

✉ 136 Yorkville Avenue, Lower Level, Toronto, Ontario, M5R 1C2 ☎ 416/515-

0587 🕐 Tue–Sun 6pm–2am 🖐 Cover $8–$12 🚇 Bay 🚌 Streetcar 6, A, B 📍 Bloor-Yorkville; north of Bloor between Yonge Street and Avenue Road

CANADA SQUARE

www.cineplex.com

Eight big, curved screens and stadium seating make for enjoyable viewing of the latest releases.

✉ 2190 Yonge Street, Toronto, Ontario, M4S 2C6 ☎ 416/646-0444 🕐 Daily 🖐 Adult $10, child (under 14) $8 🚇 Eglinton 🚌 32B, 32C, 61+, 97+ 📍 Uptown, at Eglinton Avenue West

CANSTAGE

www.canstage.com

In a renovated old factory, Canada's largest contemporary theater company stages serious drama, classics, comedies and small-scale musicals. Canstage also stages productions at the St. Lawrence Centre on Front Street and outdoors in High Park in the summer.

✉ 26 Berkeley Street, Toronto, Ontario, M5A 2W3 ☎ 416/368-3110, 887/399-2651 🕐 Year-round 🖐 $20–$89 🚇 King, then eastbound streetcar to Berkeley

C'EST WHAT?

www.cestwhat.com

A young (early 20s) crowd come to this brewpub showbar to relax on the comfy couches and enjoy an eclectic mix of quality indie pop, jazz, folk and blues. Good food and 35 draft beers.

✉ 67 Front Street East, Toronto, Ontario, M5E 1B5 ☎ 416/867-9499 🕐 Daily 11.30am–2am (no music Mon) 🖐 $5–$8 🚇 King 🚌 Streetcar 504 (King) 📍 Downtown, corner of Church

ELGIN & WINTER GARDEN

www.heritagefdn.on.ca

One of Ontario's historic sites, this is the last "double-decker" Edwardian theater in the world—Elgin downstairs, Winter Garden above. The calendar includes a variety of drama, music and comedy.

✉ 189 Yonge Street, Toronto, Ontario, M5B 1M4 ☎ 416/314-2901 🕐 Year-round 🚇 Queen 🚌 Streetcar 97B 📍 Downtown, between Queen and Dundas

FAMOUS PEOPLE PLAYERS

www.fpp.org

World-renowned puppeteers create a remarkably exciting show using huge puppets and black lighting. A meal is an integral part of the show.

✉ 110 Sudbury Street, Toronto, Ontario, M6J 3S6 ☎ 416/532-1137, 1-888/453-3385 ⏰ Tue–Sat ✋ Dinner and show: adult $54.50, child $39.95 🚋 Streetcar to Dovercourt 🚇 South of Queen between Lisgar and Dovercourt

FLY

www.flynightclub.com

Currently the hottest gay club in the city, it is popular with straight clubbers too for its top-rated DJs, superior sound and light systems, and party atmosphere. Fans of the TV show *Queer as Folk* might recognize it as "Babylon."

✉ 8 Gloucester Street, Toronto, Ontario, M4Y 1L5 ☎ 416/910-5426 ⏰ Fri 10pm–3am, Sat 10pm–6am ✋ $10–$20 🚇 Wellesley 🚋 97B 🚇 Downtown at Gloucester and Yonge, two blocks north of Wellesley

FOUR SEASONS CENTRE FOR THE PERFORMING ARTS

www.coc.ca

This superb theater, opened in 2006 complete with all the latest technological and acoustic devices, was built for the Canadian Opera Company and the Canadian Ballet. Its five-level, horseshoe-shape main auditorium, the R. Fraser Elliott Hall, lends an intimacy that belies its 2,000-plus capacity.

✉ 145 Queen Street West, Toronto, Ontario ☎ 416/306-8231, 416/363-6671 ✋ $60–$275; free concerts Tue, Thu at noon, first wed of month 5.30 🎧 Guided tours Sat 11.45 and 12 🚇 Osgoode (direct access) 🚋 Streetcar 501 🚇 Downtown, at southeast corner of Queen Street West and University Avenue (on-site parking)

THE GUVERNMENT

www.theguvernment.com

Incorporating the huge and classy Kool Haus venue, this multi-faceted club complex hosts Canadian and international big-name performers and DJs in seven separate rooms. Both a dress code and age limits apply.

✉ 132 Queen's Quay East, Toronto, Ontario, M5A 3Y5 ☎ 416/869-0045 ⏰ From 7pm; DJs Fri–Sat from 10 ✋ $10–$15 🚇 Union Station 🚋 Streetcar 75 🚇 Corner of Lower Jarvis Street

HARBOURFRONT CENTRE

▷ 186–187.

HORSESHOE

www.horseshoetavern.com

With an eclectic schedule of top-quality alternative rock, pop and contemporary country music, including many rising (and risen) stars, Horseshoe is located in the back room of a traditional-style pub. It has a great sound system and room for about 350 people.

✉ 370 Queen Street West, Toronto, Ontario, M5V 2A2 ☎ 416/598-4753 ⏰ Daily 12pm–2am; live music Mon–Thu 9pm–1am, Sat–Sun 9–2.30 ✋ $5–$10 🚇 Queen then streetcar west to Spadina, or Spadina then streetcar south to Queen

LAUGH RESORT

www.laughresort.com

Top international comedians bring down the house: Chris Rock, Adam Sandler, David Spade, Ray Romano and Ellen Degeneres have all been on the bill here. Wednesday is new laughs night, for unknown comics.

✉ 370 King Street West, Toronto, Ontario, M5V 1J9 ☎ 416/364-5233 ⏰ Wed–Sat 8.30 (also 10.45 Fri–Sat) ✋ $7–$15 🚇 St. Andrew 🚋 Streetcar 504 🚇 In the Entertainment District

MASSEY HALL

www.masseyhall.com

The grande dame of the city's music halls, dating back to 1894. It hosts pop, rock and classical music.

✉ 178 Victoria Street, Toronto, Ontario, M5B 1T7 ☎ 416/593-4822 🚇 Queen or Dundas 🚋 Streetcar 97B, 501, 502 🚇 Off Yonge Street, opposite Eaton Centre, on Shuter

MOLSON AMPHITHEATRE

Open-air facility with reserved seating for 9,000 and lawn space for 7,000 more. Concerts include rock, jazz, hip-hop, blues and country.

✉ Ontario Place, 909 Lakeshore Boulevard West, Toronto, Ontario, M6K 3L3 ☎ 416/260-5600 ⏰ May–Oct 🚇 Bathurst, then streetcar 511 🚇 Exhibition, then walk south

MYSTERIOUSLY YOURS…

www.MysteriouslyYours.com

The audience participates in solving the crime in this highly entertaining interactive murder-mystery, which unfolds during dinner.

✉ 2026 Yonge Street, Toronto, Ontario, M4Z 1Z9 ☎ 416/486-7469, 800/668-3323 ⏰ Fri, Sat, some Thu and some Wed matinees ✋ $65–$70, including dinner and taxes; matinee $53, including lunch 🚇 Davisville or Eglinton 🚋 Streetcar: 97B, 97+ 🚇 Uptown, north of Bloor on west side of Yonge

POLSON PIER

www.polsonpier.com

One of Toronto's largest entertainment complexes, incorporating the Sound Academy nightclub, with DJs, live bands and special events, a drive-in movie theater, a huge lakeshore patio with a swimming pool and masses of sports amenities.

✉ Polson Street, Toronto, Ontario M5A 1A4 ☎ 416/469-5655, 416/461-3625 ⏰ Year-round, some attractions are seasonal ✋ Separate charges for each facility 🚇 Union Station then take bus 🚋 72A, 172A 🚇 Off Cherry Street in docks area

PRINCESS OF WALES

www.mirvish.com

Built in the 1990s, this 2,000-seat theater has a huge stage suitable for the most spectacular Broadway shows, including the North American premiere of Andrew Lloyd Webber's *Sound of Music* in 2008.

✉ 300 King Street West, Toronto, M5V 1H9 ☎ 416/593-4142 ⏰ Year-round 🚇 St. Andrew 🚋 Streetcar King Street

ROGERS CENTRE

www.rogerscentre.com

In addition to sporting events, Rogers Centre hosts concerts by megastars, opera, circus, ice shows, and such events as the Chinese New Year Festival and Canadian Aboriginal Festival.

1 Blue Jays Way, Toronto, Ontario, M5V 1J1 ☎ 416/341-3000 ⏰ Check local listings for schedule ⬡ ⓜ Union Station or St. Andrew 🚃 Streetcar 510 🍴

ROYAL ALEXANDRA
www.mirvish.com
This is a pretty, restored beaux-arts theater with 1,495 capacity. It's the oldest continuously operating theater in North America, staging mostly musicals.
✉ 260 King Street West, Toronto, Ontario, M5V 1H9 ☎ 416/593-4142, 800/724-6420 ⓜ St. Andrew 🚃 Streetcar King Street 🚃 Between Simcoe and Duncan

ROY THOMSON HALL
www.roythomson.com
Superb modern hall, home to Toronto's Symphony Orchestra and Mendelssohn Choir. Presents top international classical performers.
✉ 60 Simcoe Street, Toronto, Ontario, M5J 2H5 ☎ 416/872-4255 ⓜ St. Andrew 🚃 Streetcar 504

SECOND CITY
The company that inspired the US hit TV show *Saturday Night Live* presents revues, improv, character performers and short plays. Past members include Mike Myers, John Candy and Gilda Radner.

✉ 51 Mercer Street, Toronto, Ontario, M5V 9G9 ☎ 416/343-0011 ⏰ Daily ⬆ $23–$28 (improv show free after main performance) ⓜ St. Andrew 🚃 Streetcar 504 (King), 510 (Spadina) 🚃 Downtown, just south of King Street West between Peter and John streets

SONY CENTRE
www.monaco.com
Formerly the Hummingbird Centre, this is the largest venue in the city, staging opera, Broadway-style shows, ballet and concerts.
✉ 1 Front Street East, Toronto, Ontario, M5E 1B2 ☎ 416/393-7429 ⓜ Union Station or King Street 🚃 65A, 72A

TORONTO CENTRE FOR THE ARTS
www.tocentre.com
A beautiful modern building containing three halls—the mainstage theater, a studio theater and a recital hall for musicals and concerts.
✉ 5040 Yonge Street, Toronto, Ontario, M2N 6R8 ☎ 416/733-9388 ⓜ North York Centre or Sheppard 🚃 Streetcar 97B, 97C 🚃 North York, north of Sheppard

YUK YUK'S COMEDY CABARET
www.yukyuks.com
Founded here in Toronto in 1976, this comedy club chain has fostered much Canadian talent, and hosted

the likes of David Letterman, Jerry Seinfeld and Robin Williams from the US. Amateur nights are Tuesdays.
✉ 224 Richmond Street West, Toronto, Ontario, M5V 1V6 ☎ 416/967-6425 ⏰ Tue–Sun ⬆ $11–$18 (amateur nights $3) ⓜ Osgoode 🚃 Streetcar 501 🚃 Downtown, between Duncan and Simcoe

SPORTS AND ACTIVITIES
DON VALLEY GOLF COURSE
Howard Watson designed this 18-hole course, taking advantage of the rolling landscape. It's a challenging par 71, with signature par 5 at the 12th hole.
✉ 4200 Yonge Street, Toronto, Ontario, M2P 1N9 ☎ 416/392-2465 ⏰ When weather permits ⬆ $52–$59 (9 holes $28–$33) ⓜ York Mills 🚃 97 🚃 At intersection of Yonge Street and William Carson Crescent

HARBOURFRONT CANOE AND KAYAK CENTRE
www.paddletoronto.com
You can take to the water right in the city and explore the secluded beaches, bird sanctuaries and picnic areas of the Toronto Islands. You can go it alone or join in with a group.

Below *The Elgin Theatre*

283A Queen's Quay West, Toronto, Ontario, M5V 1A2 ☎ 416/203-2277, 800/960-8886 🕒 Mid-May to late Sep Mon–Fri 10–8, Sat–Sun 10–6; Jan to mid-May for indoor pool sessions and courses ✋ $25–$35 per hour; $60–$70 per day (plus damage deposit) 🚇 Union Station, then Queen's Quay West streetcar 🚊 Streetcar 509, 510

HELICOPTER COMPANY INC.
www.helitours.ca
If you think the view from the top of the CN Tower is impressive, wait till you've seen it from a helicopter! Flights of 10 to 15 minutes whisk you over the city and offer spectacular photo-opportunities.
✉ Toronto City Centre Airport, Hangar 6, Suite 212, Toronto, Ontario, M5V 1A1 ☎ 416/203-3280 🕒 Daily; reservations required ✋ From $95 per passenger 🚇 Union Station, then streetcar 🚊 509 to Bathurst, then airport ferry

TORONTO ARGONAUTS
www.argonauts.ca
Founded in 1873, this team, whose home is the Rogers Centre, holds the Canadian Football League record for the most championship victories.
✉ Rogers Centre, 1 Blue Jays Way, Toronto, Ontario, M5V 1J3 ☎ 416/341-2700 🕒 Season Jun–end Nov 🚇 Union Station 🚊 Streetcar 510

TORONTO BLUE JAYS
www.bluejays.ca
Major league baseball team, twice winners of the World Series. Great action on the field and a buzzing atmosphere.
✉ Rogers Centre, 1 Blue Jays Way, Suite 3200, Toronto, Ontario, M5V 1J1 ☎ 416/341-1000, 888/OK-GO-JAY

🕒 Apr–end Sep ✋ $9–$62 🚇 Union Station 🚊 Streetcar 510

TORONTO FC
The city's professional Major League soccer team came into being in 2006, and in 2007 got a new 20,000-seat stadium—BMO Field at Exhibition Place. It also serves as the National Soccer Stadium, and home games are played here against North America's finest teams.
✉ BMO Field, 170 Princes' Boulevard, Exhibition Place, Toronto M6K 3C3 ☎ 416/360-4625 🕒 End Mar to late Oct 🚊 29 Dufferin; streetcar 509 Lakeshore or 511 Bathurst 🚆 GO train to Exhibition 🚌 West of downtown, off Lakeshore Boulevard

TORONTO LYNX
www.lynxsoccer.com
The Lynx, an amateur soccer team, play in the North American A-League. Home games are played to enthusiastic support at the Centennial Stadium or Varsity Centre.
✉ 100 East Mall, Suite 11, Toronto, Ontario, M8Z 5X2 ☎ 416/251-4625 🕒 May–late Jul ✋ $15 🚇 Royal York, then bus 48; for Varsity Centre: St George 🚌 West of city, between Eglinton and Rathburn; Varsity Centre at Bloor West and Devonshire Place, west of Queen's Park

TORONTO MAPLE LEAFS
http://mapleleafs.nhl.com
Toronto's National Hockey League team whips up the excitement at the Air Canada Centre.
✉ Air Canada Centre, 40 Bay Street, Suite 400, Toronto, Ontario, M5J 2X2 ☎ 416/815-5500 🕒 Season: Sep–end Apr ✋ From $30 🚇 Union Station 🚊 Streetcar: 6, 6A, 97B

TORONTO RAPTORS
www.nba.com/raptors
Without a basketball team for 50 years, Toronto got the Raptors up and running in 1995, and they've made their mark in the NBA, frequently reaching the playoffs. The fan base is growing, and there's strong support at home games at the Air Canada Centre.
✉ Air Canada Centre, 40 Bay Street, Suite 400, Toronto, Ontario, M5J 2X2 ☎ 416/872-5000 🕒 Oct–end Jun 🚇 Union Station 🚊 Streetcar: 6, 6A, 97B

HEALTH AND BEAUTY
CLEAR
www.cleardayspa.com
A chic, modernist spa where highly trained professionals pamper the Toronto elite. The Waterfall Room's wet-body treatments are a highlight.
✉ 300 York Mills Road, Toronto, Ontario, M2L 2Y5 ☎ 416/386-0300 🕒 Mon 11–6, Tue 10–6, Wed 9–7, Thu–Fri 9–8, Sat 9–6; closed Sun ✋ Treatments priced individually: manicure $22, 1-hour massage $80 🚊 Northwest corner of Bayview and York Mills Road

ICI PARIS
www.iciparis.ca
An oasis of calm in dynamic Riverdale, focusing on holistic treatments and natural skin care.
✉ 370 Danforth Avenue, Toronto, Ontario M4K 1N8 ☎ 416/461-1774 🕒 Mon–Fri 9–8, Sat 9–6, Sun 10–3 ✋ Treatments priced separately; facials from $75, massage from $45 (30 min) 🚇 Chester 🚊 Streetcar: 504, 505

FOR CHILDREN
BATA SHOE MUSEUM
www.batashoemuseum.ca
Most children will love this museum with its fascinating collection of shoes through the ages. There are elongated pointed-toe boots worn by Gothic knights, silk boots worn by Victorian ladies, sandals with huge soles worn in the Sahara to protect their wearers from the hot sand, and tiny lotus shoes worn by Chinese women whose feet were bound from birth to keep them small. Shoes worn by famous people

include Elton John's silver-and-red platform boots, Robert Redford's cowboy boots and John Lennon's "Beatle Boots."

✉ 327 Bloor Street West, Toronto, Ontario, M5S 1W7 ☎ 416/979–7799 ◷ Mon–Wed, Fri–Sat 10–5, Thu 10–8, Sun 12–5 ♿ Adults $12, child (5–17) $4, family $18–30 (free Thu 5–8) 🚇 On Bloor Street West at corner of St. George Ⓜ St. George

CENTREVILLE
www.centreisland.ca

This 240ha (600-acre) park, themed around a century-old Ontario village, has more than 30 rides and attractions that include an antique carousel, Ferris wheel, log flume, boats, bumper cars, train rides and pony rides. It appeals most to children under 10.

✉ Centre Island, Toronto, Ontario, M5J 2G2 ☎ 416/203-0405 ◷ Jun–early Sep daily 10.30am–dusk; May and late Sep Sat–Sun (subject to change) ♿ Admission free. All-day pass for rides: over 1.2m (4ft) tall $29.50, under 1.2m $21, family $90 🚢 From foot of Bay Street and Queen's Quay

FORT YORK
▷ 184–185.

ONTARIO PLACE
▷ 188.

ONTARIO SCIENCE CENTRE
▷ 188.

RIVERDALE FARM
www.friendsofriverdalefarm.com

Little ones will love this turn-of-the-20th-century farmstead in the heart of the city, where they can see horses, donkeys, sheep, chickens, cows, goats and pigs. There are regular demonstrations, including cow and goat milking, buttermaking, sheep-shearing, spinning, storytelling and sing-alongs.

✉ 201 Winchester Street, Toronto, Ontario ☎ 416/392-6794 ◷ Daily 9–5 ♿ Free Ⓜ Castle Frank, then bus 65+ south 🚋 Streetcar: 506 🚇 Cabbagetown, off Parliament Street

TORONTO ZOO
▷ 193.

FESTIVALS AND EVENTS

JANUARY
WINTERCITY
www.toronto.ca/special_events/wintercity
Indoor and outdoor events bring the city to life for two weeks in the depths of winter, with music, skating shows, street theater, acrobatics and comedy.
✉ Toronto, Ontario ☎ 416/395-0490

MARCH
CANADA BLOOMS: THE TORONTO FLOWER AND GARDEN SHOW
www.canadablooms.com
Some 2.4ha (6 acres) of gardens and 150-plus stands promoting horticulture at the Metro Toronto Convention Centre. Fun events, such as a celebrity flower-arranging competition.
✉ Toronto, Ontario ☎ 416/447-8655

MAY
GREEN TORONTO FESTIVAL
www.toronto.ca/greentorontofestival
Environmentally friendly festival based on Yonge-Dundas Square, with more than 100 eco-exhibitors, live music, guest speakers, locally grown food, and a traffic-free Yonge Street on the second day.

MILK INTERNATIONAL CHILDREN'S FESTIVAL OF THE ARTS
www.harbourfront.on.ca
One of the best children's festivals in North America, with theater, music and puppet shows.
✉ Toronto, Ontario ☎ 416/973-4000

AUGUST
CANADIAN NATIONAL EXHIBITION
www.theex.com
One of the biggest exhibitions in North America, with a permanent home on the lakefront. "The Ex" has hundreds of exhibitors and attractions.
✉ Toronto, Ontario ☎ 416/393-6300

SEPTEMBER
TORONTO INTERNATIONAL FILM FESTIVAL
www.tiff09.ca (date changes each year)
The movie industry comes to Toronto to showcase hundreds of movies, and the place is heaving with celebrities.
✉ Toronto, Ontario ☎ 416/968-FILM

OCTOBER
CANADIAN INTERNATIONAL MARATHON
www.runtoronto.com
A serious event for the runners (qualifying speed; no walkers), but there's ancillary entertainment for spectators.
✉ Toronto, Ontario ☎ 416/972-1062

NOVEMBER
CANADIAN ABORIGINAL FESTIVAL
www.canab.com
This three-day event at the Rogers Centre is a celebration of First Nations culture, including a pow wow, music awards, lacrosse and the arts.
✉ Toronto, Ontario ☎ 519/751-0040

PRICES AND SYMBOLS

The restaurants are listed alphabetically within each town. The prices are for a two-course lunch (L) and a three-course à la carte dinner (D). Prices in pubs are for a two-course lunchtime bar meal and a two-course dinner in the restaurant, unless specified otherwise. The wine price is for the least expensive bottle.

For a key to the symbols, ▷ 2.

360 THE RESTAURANT AT THE CN TOWER

www.cntower.ca

The world's tallest revolving restaurant has won some of the highest awards for its food and wine (from the world's highest wine cellar). All diners enjoy the spectacular views, and the complete circuit takes 72 minutes. If you eat a main course, you are entitled to a free trip up the tower. There's also a cafe from which to enjoy the view.

✉ CN Tower, 301 Front Street West, Toronto, Ontario, M5V 2T6 ☎ 416/362-5411 ⏰ Mon–Sat 11–2, 4.30–10.30, Sun 4.30–10.15 🖐 L $45, D $54, W $40 🚇 Union Station, then via SkyWalk

BATON ROUGE

www.batonrouge-restaurant.com

This is a cool and classy bar-restaurant. There's premium-quality steak and Danish baby back ribs, tender chicken and other southern American dishes cooked over hickory and aromatic hardwoods. Although the name implies it, the restaurant has nothing to do with Louisiana. The company originated in Montréal and is French for "Red Stick."

✉ Toronto Eaton Centre, 216 Yonge Street, Toronto, Ontario, M5B 1N5 ☎ 416/593-9667 ⏰ Mon–Thu 11–11, Fri 11am–midnight, Sat 11.30am–midnight, Sun 12–10 🖐 L $18, D $35, Wine $28 🚇 Dundas or Queen 🚌 97B

BISTRO 990

A bright, striped awning, a Citroen 2CV parked outside, Picasso-style drawings, fresh flowers, French doors…it's a little corner of Paris in downtown Toronto. The menu is bursting with French bistro classics. And you are likely to be rubbing shoulders with celebs if Hollywood is in town (which it often is).

✉ 990 Bay Street, Toronto, Ontario, M5S 3A8 ☎ 416/921-9990 ⏰ Mon–Fri 12–3, 5–11, Sat 5–11, Sun 5.30–10 🖐 L $25, D $60, Wine $15 🚇 Wellesley 🚌 6A, 6B 🚇 Downtown, just north of Wellesley

BOAT HOUSE GRILL

www.boathousegrill.sites.toronto.com

In the southeast corner of the main level of this upscale mall, this restaurant is particularly popular in summer when you can dine on the lakeside patio, but in winter it's also a great spot to stoke up after skating at the fabulous Harbourfront outdoor rink nearby, with the same great view through the windows. There's a long menu to suit all tastes, including seafood such as blackened Mahi Mahi or traditional fish and chips, succulent steaks, chicken and ribs, pasta, pizzas, and burgers.

✉ Queen's Quay Terminal, 207 Queen's Quay West, Toronto, Ontario M5J 1A7 ☎ 416/203-6300 ⏰ Daily 11am–midnight 🖐 L $20, D $35, W $26 🚇 Union station, then streetcar 🚌 509, 510 🚇 Downtown, on the lake shore just west of Harbour Square

BRIGHT PEARL

www.brightpearlseafood.com

An almost luminous presence on Spadina, this bright yellow and green building is unmistakeably part of Toronto's downtown Chinatown. In an area not short of Chinese restaurants, this one is a stand-out for quality too. The freshest possible seafood comes live from the tank and dim sum—between 80 and 100 varieties—is served all day (with "happy hour" at certain times of the day).

✉ 346–8 Spadina Avenue, Toronto, Ontario M5T 2G2 ☎ 416/979-3988 🕒 Daily 9am–11pm 🖐 L $15, D $25, W $30 🚇 St. Patrick 🚌 510 Spadina, 505 Dundas 🚍 Downtown, northeast corner of Spadina and Dundas

BUNGALOW CAFE

www.bungalowcafe.ca

This is a cool venue in cool King West Village, serving dishes that have good flavor combinations without being overfussy. There are pastas, such as chicken Croole penne with mushrooms and green peppers, or linguini with smoked salmon and spinach, and entrées such as mustard- and rosemary-crusted pork chop with maple-glazed apples, or chicken breast stuffed with goat cheese and bacon with a mustard and tomato sauce. Weekly special promotions include 2-for-1 pastas (Mon) or appetizers (Wed) and $5 glasses of wine on Thursdays.

✉ 934 King Street West, Toronto, Ontario ☎ 416/214-CAFÉ 🕒 Mon–Fri from 4pm, Sat from 6pm, Sun 11am–4pm 🖐 L $27, D $40, W $36 🚌 504, 508 King Street West 🚍 Downtown, west of Bathurst near Strachan Avenue intersection

CANOE

www.oliverbonacini.com/canoemovie.html

The views are spectacular, but it would take a lot to distract you from the food. This is one of Canada's finest restaurants, serving outstanding Canadian cuisine, and the provenance of the ingredients are often right there on the menu—Cumbrae Farms Steak Tartare with truffle crème fraiche and black trumpets, or chilled Yarmouth lobster and scallop with sweet mustard, Pelee Island caviar and tarragon cream, and that's just for starters. Main courses might include Spring Bank bison striploin with northern woods mushrooms, confit Yukon and peppercorn sauce, or broiled British Columbia sablefish with foie gras, yellow foots, soybean cassoulet and black mustard dressing. The tasting menu is a tempting option. There's a business dress/smart casual dress code.

✉ 54th Floor, Toronto Dominion Bank Tower, 66 Wellington Street West, Toronto, Ontario M5K 1H6 ☎ 416/364-0054 🕒 Mon–Fri 11.45am–2.30pm, 5–10.30pm 🖐 L $50, D $80, W $40 🚇 Union or King 🚍 Downtown, between Bay and York streets, one block south of King

CAPTAIN JOHN'S HARBOUR BOAT

www.captainjohns.ca

This restaurant is on a ship, with its prow pointing straight up the longest street in the world (Yonge). The menu is mostly seafood—the Alaskan king crab feast is highly recommended—with lobster St. Tropez (marinated in cream and pernod), or shark steak. There's a bar up on deck, with lakeshore views.

✉ 1 Queen's Quay East, Toronto, Ontario, M5E 1A1 ☎ 416/363-6062 🕒 Mon–Sat 11–11, Sun 10.30am–11pm 🖐 L $20, D $30, Wine $25 🚇 Union Station 🚌 6, 97B 🚍 Downtown, on lake at foot of Yonge Street, next to Island Ferry Terminal

CHIADO

www.chiadorestaurant.ca

The cuisine is described as "progressive Portuguese" and the décor is elegant and as artistic as the food on the plates. Fresh fish is flown in daily from Portugal, then expertly turned into dishes such as the starter of grilled squid with fresh coriander, lemon and garlic with roasted sweet peppers, charred tomato and caramelized leeks and the main course pan-seared filet of grouper with marine salt, dry spices and fresh herbs. There are equally interesting organic meat dishes and some stunning desserts, plus a tapas menu.

✉ 864 College Street, Toronto, Ontario M6H 1A3 ☎ 416/538-1910 🕒 Mon–Fri 12–2.30, 5–10, Sat–Sun 5–10 🖐 L $25, D $70, W $45 🚌 506 College Street

MONTANA

www.montanaonline.ca

Huge, brash, lively restaurant, with some of the most cheerful and energetic wait staff you'll see anywhere. The food inclines in various directions, including Italian, but in its heart it is steadfastly North American. Upstairs there's a sports bar with pool table and the Mustang Room with DJ (Thu–Sat). No children are allowed.

✉ 145 John Street, Toronto, Ontario, M5V 2E4 ☎ 416/595-5949 🕒 Sun–Wed 11am–midnight, Thu 11am–1am, Fri–Sat 11am–2am 🖐 L $15, D $25, W $25 🚇 Osgoode 🚌 Streetcar 501 🚍 Entertainment district, southeast corner of John and Richmond

EMBRUJO FLAMENCO

www.embrujoflamenco.com

Here's something you might not expect to find in Greektown—a Spanish tapas restaurant—but its exciting flamenco shows, Spanish wines and regional cuisine might tempt you off the souvlaki trail. The selection of tapas includes authentic classics such as Jamon Serrano, chorizo and cheese in flaky pastry and fried squid with garlic, as well as more unusual choices: shrimps in chocolate sauce, perhaps, or grilled ostrich in a wine and balsamic reduction. There are plenty of vegetarian varieties, too, and there's paella on the menu.

✉ 97 Danforth Avenue, Toronto, Ontario ☎ 416/778-0007 🕒 Mon–Thu and Sun 5–11pm, Fri–Sat 5pm–midnight 🖐 D $35, W $29 🚇 Broadview 🚍 Greektown, near Broadview Avenue intersection

FRAN'S

www.fransrestaurant.com

There are times when all you want is a good diner, and Fran's fits the bill at any time of the day or night. It never closes, and is renowned for its gargantuan all-day breakfasts, burgers, Asian-style bowl meals, charbroiled steaks, apple pie and "adult milkshakes" (with a shot of something more interesting than chocolate sauce). There are good vegetarian choices too.

 20 College Street, Toronto, Ontario, M5G 1K2 ☎ 416/923-9867 🕐 Daily 24 hours 🖐 L $15, D $25, W $24 🚇 College 🚋 506 College 🚩 Downtown, between Yonge and Bay

KI MODERN JAPANESE
www.kijapanese.com
This is a fun place to explore a full range of traditional and innovative Japanese food. You can watch the chefs prepare their artistic bites at the sushi bar, opt for the equally animated cocktail bar, where raised dining areas are surrounded by ponds, or sit in one of the more intimate dining areas. The food choices include *kushiyaki* (skewers and dips), *tempura*, *nigiri*, *sashimi*, *makimonos* and hot and cold "signature plates" such as saikyo-marinated broiled black cod with rapini, salmon roe and orange drizzle, or wok-tossed shrimp with tomato rayu-chili sauce. Sharing dishes is encouraged.

 181 Bay Street, Bay Wellington Tower, Brookfield Place, Toronto, Ontario, M5J 2T3 ☎ 416/800-1384, 416/308-5888

(reservations) 🕐 Mon–Fri 11.30am–11pm, Sat 4–11pm (bar open until 1am) 🖐 L $30, $40, W $ 🚇 Union 🚩 Downtown, between Front and Wellington streets

LA MEXICAN
In an area noted for high-end shopping, this friendly little restaurant offers good, authentic Mexican and Tex-Mex food at really good prices. All the favorites are on the menu, from the spicy black bean soup to deep-fried ice cream, with sizzling fajitas, burritos, enchiladas and chimichangas along the way. A more sophisticated dinner might start with tiger shrimps with tequila and chipotle peppers on sliced tamales, followed, perhaps, by one of the specials—leg of lamb seasoned with mild chile and herbs, baked in corn husks and served with guacamole comes highly recommended.

 838 Yonge Street, Toronto, Ontario, M4W 2H1 ☎ 416/934-0712 🕐 Daily 11am–10pm 🖐 L $20, D $35, W $25 🚇 Bloor-Yonge 🚩 Yorkville, just north of Bloor Street

MOONBEAN COFFEE COMPANY
This coffeehouse developed from a retail store selling coffee beans and specialty teas, and is a great place to

relax amid the bustle of Kensington Market. And there's a funky patio for people-watching.

 30 St Andrew's Street, Toronto, Ontario, M5T 1K6 ☎ 416/595-0327 🕐 Daily 7am–9pm 🖐 $10 🚇 St. Patrick, then streetcar 505 🚩 Streetcar: 505 on Dundas, 510 on Spadina

NORTH 44
www.north44restaurant.com
This sophisticated spot may be one of Toronto's best celebrity-spotting venues, but the food is far more rewarding. Inspired combinations, such as pistachio and spiced chocolate with foie gras and a main-course roasted squab with spun potato omelette, ramps and stewed rhubarb sit alongside straightforward prime USDA steaks that don't need anything beyond a side dish. Superb seafood includes grilled sea trout with king mushroom pot-stickers, wilted Asian greens and lemon garlic sauce. Bear in mind there's a menu of irresistable desserts, so make sure you leave some room.

 2537 Yonge Street, Toronto, Ontario, ☎ 416/487-4897 🕐 Mon–Sat 5–11pm 🖐 D $80, W $28 🚇 Eglinton 🚩 Midtown, north of Eglinton Avenue, near Keewatin Avenue intersection

OLIVIA'S AT FIFTY THREE MICROWINERY

www.oliviasat53.com

This artsy and elegant little place is a real find, where you can mingle with artists and other creative types, often to the accompaniment of live jazz. Downstairs is Toronto's first microwinery, producing South American wines from imported grapes, while upstairs you can choose from an interesting menu of skilfully prepared dishes. Start, perhaps, with grilled black tiger shrimp on watercress with pickled Spanish onion and cherry tomato confit in a lemon-tarragon dressing, then move on to a herbed roasted capon breast with a picked rhubarb purée, pomme anna and roasted asparagus, or an imaginative vegetarian risotto.

✉ 53 Clinton Street, Toronto, Ontario, M4A 2V5 ☎ 416/533-3989 ⏰ Tue–Sun 5.30–10.30pm (11.30pm on weekends), also Sun brunch from 10.30am; closing time flexible, depending on who is there and what's on ✋ Brunch $12, D $45, W $17 🚌 506 College Street westbound 🚇 Little Italy, northeast corner of College and Clinton

RECTORY CAFE

www.rectorycafe.com

If you take a trip to the Toronto Islands, seek out this lovely place at Ward's Island. With the works of local artists hanging inside, it has tables on its shady terrace and among the trees in the garden. The menu features interesting starters such as three-bean hummus with sliced fruits, vegetables and flatbreads or warm goat cheese salad with honey brandy dressing. Main courses might include beef tenderloin with a red wine reduction or pan-seared Tilapia with coconut curry reduction and jasmine rice. You can also opt for a tasty sandwich or soup for lunch.

✉ 102 Lakeshore Avenue, Ward's Island, Toronto, Ontario, M5J 1X9 ☎ 416/203-2152 ⏰ Summer daily from 11am; lunch served until 4pm, dinner from 4.30pm; Winter Wed–Sun 11am–5pm (but subject to weather conditions) ✋ L $25, D $40, W $29 ⛴ Ward's Island ferry from the Harbourfront 🚇 Ward's Island, a five-minute walk west of ferry landing or 25 minutes from Centre Island

SENATOR

www.thesenator.com

Toronto's oldest restaurant—more than 76 years in the same location—has a huge menu, starting with an impressive range of breakfast choices, including Toronto's own specialty, peameal bacon. Lunch features homemade soups, salads, sandwiches and burgers, and both lunch and dinner offer great comfort food such as fish and chips, liver and onions, meat loaf and mashed potato, and grilled salmon with citrus butter. There's a convenient take-out service too.

✉ 249 Victoria Street, Toronto, Ontario ☎ 416/364-7517 ⏰ Mon 7.30am–3pm, Tue–Fri 7.30am–3pm, 5–10.30pm, Sat 5–10.30pm ✋ L $15, D $35, W $27 🚇 Dundas 🚇 Downtown, at Yonge and Dundas Square

SHOPSY'S DELI AND RESTAURANT

www.shopsys.ca

Shopsy's attracts an eclectic clientele. It has a vast menu, featuring large portions and fresh ingredients. Branches are also on King Street and at 1535 Yonge Street.

✉ 33 Yonge Street, Toronto, Ontario, M5E 1G4 ☎ 416/365-3333 ⏰ Mon–Fri 7am–10pm, Sat 8am–10pm, Sun 11am–9pm ✋ L $13, D $18, Wine $20 🚇 Union Station or King 🚌 97B 🚇 Downtown

TRUFFLES

www.fourseasons.com

Experts agree that Truffles serves the best food in Toronto—maybe the best in the country—and it has a long list of accolades. Contemporary French cuisine is presented in extremely classy surroundings. The signature dish features spaghettini with Perigord "black gold" truffles. Dress code is casual but dressy; jackets not required.

✉ Four Season's Hotel, 21 Avenue Road, Toronto, Ontario, M5R 2G1 ☎ 416/928-7331 ⏰ Tue–Sat 6–10; closed Sun ✋ D $75, Wine $30 🚇 Museum (then walk north) or Bay (then walk west) 🚇 Downtown, north of Bloor

VITTORIO'S

Authentic Italian food at its very best is served at this long-established restaurant, where all the pasta is homemade. Highlights include pan-seared veal with Cognac, mustard and mascarpone, and an astonishing *zuppa di pesce* that has half a lobster, half a crab, scallops, mussels, shrimp, clams and calamari floating in its tasty broth. The atmosphere is great, and the graffiti wall is full of endorsements from happy diners. There's another Vittorio's on Avenue Road.

✉ 1973 Yonge Street, Toronto, Ontario M4S 1Z6 ☎ 416/482-7441 ⏰ Tue–Thu noon–2.30pm, 5.30–11pm, Fri noon–2.30pm, 5.30pm–12.30am, Sat 5.30pm–12.30am, Sun 5.30–10pm ✋ L $25, D $45, W $27 🚇 Davisville 🚇 Midtown, between St. Clair and Eglinton, near Imperial Street intersection

WAYNE GRETZKY'S

www.gretzkys.com

If your party includes a hockey devotee, you'll be very popular if you bring them here, but the food is enough of an enticement to non-sport fans. Containing the famous player's own collection of hockey memorabilia (awards, uniforms and skates, sticks, pucks, photographs and more), it also has a sport bar screening live games. The food includes barbecue specialties and comfort food such as Grandma Gretzky's Famous Meatloaf, wood-oven pizzas and hand-made pasta dishes. In summer, the rooftop patio is a great place to hang out, with its own barbecue menu, and year-round you can get a dinner-and-show package with the famous Second City comedy club nearby.

✉ 99 Blue Jays Way, Toronto, Ontario, M5V 9G9 ☎ 416/979-PUCK ⏰ Mon–Thu 11.30am–1am, Fri–Sat 11.30am–2am, Sun 11.30am–11pm ✋ L $30, D $45, W $28 🚇 St Andrew 🚌 510 Spadina, 504 and 508 King Street 🚇 Downtown, two blocks north of Rogers Centre between Front and King streets.

STAYING

PRICES AND SYMBOLS

Prices are the starting price for a double room for one night, unless otherwise stated. Breakfast is included unless noted otherwise. All the hotels listed accept credit cards unless otherwise stated. Note that rates vary widely throughout the year. For a key to the symbols, ▷ 2.

AINSLEY HOUSE

www.ainsleyhouse.com
Gracious bed-and-breakfast in leafy Rosedale, Toronto's smartest residential area. The spacious rooms have gleaming hardwood floors with rugs and nice old furniture.
✉ 19 Elm Avenue, Toronto, Ontario, M4W 1M9 ☎ 416/972-0533; 1-888/423-3337 ♨ $80–$120; 2-night minimum stay ① 4 (all non-smoking) 🦽 ♿ Rosedale, then bus 82 to South Drive 🚌 75

AMBASSADOR INN

www.jarvishouse.com
A fine redbrick home dating to 1899, and yet just 10 minutes' walk from the Eaton Centre and two blocks from the subway. It's been lovingly restored, with original features such

as exposed brick walls and stained glass preserved. All the bedrooms have private bathrooms (some with hot tubs). There's no B&B sign outside because they prefer guests to reserve; you'll get directions when you call.
✉ 280 Jarvis Street, Toronto, Ontario, M5B 2C5 ☎ 416/260-2608 ♨ $189–$319 ① 20 (all non-smoking) 🦽 ♿ College 🚋 Streetcar 506 (Carlton) 🚌 Downtown, corner of Jarvis and Gerrard, two blocks east of Yonge

BONNEVUE MANOR

www.bonnevuemanor.com
If you prefer to stay outside the downtown area, but within easy reach of it, this beautiful brick Victorian bed-and-breakfast is an excellent choice. Within walking distance of the lakeshore and close to lovely High Park, it retains many elegant features, such as plaster mouldings and hardwood floors, and is furnished in keeping with its character. All of the rooms have private bathrooms and air-conditioning. Minimum two-night stay.

✉ 33 Beaty Avenue, Toronto, Ontario, M6K 3B3 ☎ 416/536-1455 ♿ Year-round ♨ from $99–$150 ① 3 (all non-smoking) 🚌 504, 508 King Street West

CAMBRIDGE SUITES HOTEL

www.cambridgesuiteshotel.com
This is a haven of calm in the bustling financial and entertainment district—a cool and classy modern hotel that offers two-room suites. Amenities include high-speed internet access, microwave, refrigerator and coffeemaker. Cityscape and Penthouse suites on the top floors have great views and extra luxuries.
✉ 15 Richmond Street East, Toronto, Ontario, M5C 1N2 ☎ 416/368-1990, 800/463-1990 ♨ $175–$360 ① 229 🦽 📺 Charge ♿ Queen 🚌 97B; streetcar 501 (Queen), 502 (Downtowner) 🚏 Corner of Yonge and Richmond

CARLTON—TORONTO TOWNHOUSE

www.torontotownhouse.com
This lovely 140-year-old house has delightful gardens front and rear and has won several Toronto Tourism

awards for its cozy accommodations. The rooms and suites are bright and nicely furnished, stylished without being cluttered, and some have a private deck or balcony. The hearty breakfast includes fresh fruit, homemade granola and a hot item, such as pancakes, omelets or French toast. In addition to free wireless internet access, guests can make free long-distance calls to anywhere in North America.

✉ 213 Carlton Street, Toronto, Ontario, M5A 2K9 ☎ 416/323-8898, 877/500-0466 💵 $109–$169 🛏 9 (all non-smoking) 🚇 🅿 College 🚋 Streetcar 506/306 (Carlton) 🚌 Downtown/Cabbagetown, just west of Parliament Street

FAIRMONT ROYAL YORK
www.fairmont.com/royalyork
A Toronto landmark since 1929 and long-time choice of visiting royalty and celebrities. The 28-story hotel retains its original hand-painted ceilings, travertine pillars and glittering chandeliers. Guest rooms are exceptionally elegant, but even more opulent are the suites and the exclusive Fairmont Gold section, where the level of pampering reaches monumental heights. There are five restaurants, a sky-lit swimming pool, a spa, and a fitness facility. The hotel is directly connected to underground shops and the subway.

✉ 100 Front Street West, Toronto, Ontario, M5J 1E3 ☎ 416/368-2511, 800/257-7544 💵 $189–$309 🛏 1,365 (all but 150 non-smoking) 🚇 🅿 🏊 Indoor 🚇 Union Station 🚌 Downtown, opposite Union Station

FOUR SEASONS
www.fourseasons.com
The Four Seasons, in the upscale neighborhood of Yorkdale, is a 32-storey tower of sheer luxury. It also contains what many consider to be Toronto's finest restaurant, Truffles (▷ 205), and is crammed with Hollywood glitterati when the annual film festival is on. All rooms have a sitting area and workspace with two-line telephones and internet, and some have a balcony. The Health Club offers a range of massages,

manicures and pedicures and there are good services for families, plus complimentary limousines (mornings only) to downtown destinations.

✉ 21 Avenue Road, Toronto, Ontario, M5R 2G1 ☎ 416/964-0411 💵 $390–$925 🛏 380 (350 non-smoking) 🚇 🅿 🏊 Indoor and outdoor 🚇 Bay 🚌 Yorkville, between Bloor Street and Yorkville Avenue

GLOBAL VILLAGE BACKPACKERS TORONTO
www.globalbackpackers.com
Bright and lively hostel in a central location, near CN Tower, and housed in a former Spadina Hotel that was once a celebrity haunt for the likes of Jack Nicholson and the Rolling Stones. There are spacious dormitories with linen supplied free. Self-serve kitchen, laundry, secure storage for luggage and internet access are available. Public areas with bright native-art murals include a games room with pool table, bar and outdoor deck with barbecue parties in summer.

✉ 460 King Street West, Toronto, Ontario, M5V 1L7 ☎ 416/703-8540, 888/844-7875 💵 $73 (double occupancy); $27 per person in dormitory 🛏 190 beds 🚇 🅿 St. Andrews 🚋 Streetcar 510 (Spadina), 504 (King) 🚌 Downtown, King and Spadina

NEILL-WYCIK COLLEGE HOTEL
www.neill-wycik.com
Relaxed and friendly students' residence with compact rooms, close to downtown and 10 minutes' walk from the bus station. Occupies 15 floors of a 22-story building; each floor has four apartments, consisting of four or five bedrooms, two bathrooms and a kitchen/lounge area. Linen is supplied, but no crockery or kitchen utensils. A renovated on-site café with outdoor patio is where breakfast is served 7–11am. There's a sauna, rooftop sundeck and 24-hour concierge.

✉ 96 Gerrard Street East, Toronto, Ontario, M5B 1G7 ☎ 416/977-2320, 800/268-4358 🕐 Early May–late Aug 💵 $66–$72 🛏 300 🚇 🅿 College 🚋 Streetcar 506 (Carlton) 🚌 Gerrard East and Church

RENAISSANCE TORONTO HOTEL DOWNTOWN
www.marriott.com
Next door to the CN Tower, this is the first hotel ever to be an integral part of a sports complex, curving around one side of the Rogers Centre. Inside it's sheer luxury, and 70 rooms have picture windows overlooking the stadium. However, you should be aware that TV cameras often pan across here during games—one couple famously got caught on camera engaged in an entirely different sport.

✉ 1 Blue Jays Way, Toronto, Ontario, M5V 1J4 ☎ 416/341-7100, 800/237-1512 💵 $179–$599 🛏 348 (all non-smoking) 🚇 🏊 Indoor 🚇 Union Station 🚋 Streetcar 509, 510

VICTORIA
www.hotelvictoria-toronto.com
This European-style boutique hotel is close to all the action of downtown Toronto, at the heart of the theater and financial districts. Its classy lobby leads straight onto Yonge Street. The bedrooms all have identical Regency stripe wallpaper and coordinated fabrics, with private bathroom, cable TV, internet access, and voice mail. Deluxe rooms also have mini-refrigerator and coffeemaker. Guests can use the health club at the nearby Plaza Club.

✉ 56 Yonge Street, Toronto, Ontario, M5E 1G5 ☎ 416/363-1666, 800/363-8228 💵 $115–$159 🛏 56 (all non-smoking) 🚇 🅿 King 🚌 97B

WESTIN HARBOUR CASTLE
www.starwoodhotels.com
This huge, glittering, classy hotel has a wonderful lakeshore setting. Rooms have extended cable TV, video games, dual phone lines, voice mail and honor bars. In addition to a revolving rooftop restaurant, there's the trendy Toula, offering Italian cuisine along with more great views across the harbor.

✉ 1 Harbour Square, Toronto, Ontario, M5J 1A6 ☎ 416/869-1600, 800/228-3000 🕐 Year-round 💵 $159–$389 🛏 977 🚇 🏊 Indoor 🚇 Union Station 🚌 6A, 97B; streetcar 509, 510

ONTARIO

Forty percent of Canadians live in Ontario, largely in the most southerly 20 percent of the province, making this area one of the most densely populated in the entire country. The attraction is easy to see. Not only does southern Ontario have a climate good enough to sustain a thriving wine-producing industry, but the string of towns and cities along the St Lawrence River and near the shores of the Great Lakes—including both the national and provincial capital—are attractive, lively, booming and easy to reach. This, of course, makes it great for visitors too, not to mention the presence of Canada's number one attraction, Niagara Falls.

Ontario has much to offer visitors, and locals, with a love of the great outdoors. It borders four of the five Great Lakes, and there are thousands more lakes and rivers throughout the province, making it great for water-borne activities such as kayaking, white-water rafting, sailing, swimming and fishing. There are some excellent scenic cruises too, such as around the Thousand Islands in the St Lawrence river or the equally picturesque Georgian Bay on Lake Huron. There's terrific hiking, including the Bruce Trail and in the Algonquin Provincial Park, and although there are no really high mountains, there's good downhill skiing at Collingwood and excellent cross-country (Nordic) elsewhere in the province.

History is here to discover too: First Nations heritage; living history re-creations of early pioneer settlements; military reenactments at genuine forts; sites associated with the Underground Railroad, which brought slaves from America to freedom north of the border; and excellent museums and historic buildings to visit. All of this combines to build up a picture of how Ontario—and Canada as a whole—developed over the centuries.

Away from all the obvious attractions, there are charming little townships and artsy communities that may surprise you with an excellent art gallery or perhaps an enthralling festival, bursting with the characteristic enthusiasm that abounds in this prosperous province.

ALGONQUIN PROVINCIAL PARK

www.algonquinpark.on.ca

The call of a loon echoes from a rocky lakeshore, the golden sunset silhouettes a solitary pine tree and a moose raises its massive head to stare at a beaver forging a ripple across a glassy pond; Algonquin Park is the essence of the wilderness. Established in 1893 and covering 7,630sq km (2,946sq miles) of maple-clad hills, lakes, rivers and bogs, this is Ontario's best-known provincial park. The only way to explore the interior is by canoe or on foot, but Highway 60 crosses the park for a 56km (35-mile) stretch, offering easy access to part of it. The Visitor Centre (late April–end Oct daily; rest of year Sat–Sun only), the Logging Museum and the Algonquin Gallery (both open same hours as the Visitor Centre) are on the highway.

🔲 412 S18 ✉ Box 219, Whitney, Ontario, K0J 2M0 ☎ 705/633–5572 🕐 Daily $12.85 per car per day; additional fees for facilities such as camping (▷ 395)

GEORGIAN BAY

▷ 212.

HAMILTON

www.tourismhamilton.com

At the western end of Lake Ontario, Hamilton has a natural harbor and is known for its steel industry and often written off as a non-tourist destination, but it does have much to offer. The waterfront area has walkways, lake cruises and Canada's most famous historic warship, HMCS *Haida,* to explore (daily 10–5, mid-May to end Aug; Sep to mid-May; call 905/526-0911 for details).

The Royal Botanical Gardens (daily), occupying 1,000ha (2,470 acres) on the western side of the lake, offer splendid displays in five different areas (a shuttle-bus service runs between them Wed–Sun). The Rose Garden is at its best in early summer.

Overlooking Hamilton's harbor is the neoclassical, porticoed mansion of Dundurn Castle (late May–early Sep daily; rest of year Tue–Sun). A showpiece of 19th-century privilege, it was home to Sir Allan Napier MacNab, Canada's prime minister from 1854 to 1856, and contains a fine collection of 19th-century furnishings.

Hamilton is also home to Ontario's third-largest art gallery. The Art Gallery of Hamilton (Tue–Wed, noon–7, Thu–Fri noon–9, Sat–Sun noon–5), recently enhanced by an extension and restoration work costing $18 million, has a particularly noteworthy collection of 19th-century European art. Several interesting museums in the city include the Museum of Steam and Technology National Historic Site (Jun–early Sep Tue–Sun 11–4; early Sep–end May Tue–Sun noon–4) and the Canadian Warplane Heritage Museum (daily 9–5), with around 35 historic aircraft—some in working order—and memorabilia.

✉ 410 S19 ℹ Tourism Hamilton, 34 James Street South, Hamilton, Ontario, L8P 2X8 ☎ 905/546-2666, 800/263-8590

KINGSTON AND THE THOUSAND ISLANDS

▷ 213.

MCMICHAEL CANADIAN ART COLLECTION

www.mcmichael.com

'We fell under the spell of works by a few passionate artists who had captured not only the form and colour of the wilderness that we loved, but its very soul'—the words of Robert McMichael, explaining why he and his wife decided to collect the works of Tom Thomson and the Group of Seven. They gave their splendid collection (and their home) to the province of Ontario, and the paintings are exhibited in a stunning setting within a series of sprawling log buildings.

The original Group of Seven—Franklin Carmichael, Lawren Harris, A.Y. Jackson, Frank Johnston, Arthur Lismer, J.E.H. MacDonald and Frederick Varley—sought a Canadian way of representing their country, believing that Canadian art must be inspired by Canada itself.

Also on display are contemporary First Nations art and Inuit sculpture.

🔲 410 S19 ✉ 10365 Islington Avenue, Kleinburg, Ontario, L0J 1C0 ☎ 905/893-1121, 888/213-1121 🕐 Daily 10–4 ✋ Adult $15, child (5 and over) $12, family $30 🍴 ♿

MIDLAND

www.town.midland.on.ca

Midland, on Severn Sound of Georgian Bay, has a picturesque harbor, and is a tourist base for nearby Ste-Marie-Among-the-Hurons and the Martyrs' Shrine.

Jesuit missionaries, keen to spread the faith to the Huron, or Wendat, built a mission close to present-day Midland and called it Ste-Marie-Among-the-Hurons. But when two French Jesuit missionaries were murdered by the fierce Iroquois tribes the site was abandoned. A reconstruction of the mission (mid-May to mid-Oct daily) stands as a poignant memorial, and its 22 buildings are peopled by costumed interpreters representing the Jesuit fathers and their Huron converts.

Martyrs' Shrine (mid-May to mid-Oct daily) is a twin-steepled church 3km (2 miles) east of Midland on Route 12, built in 1926 to commemorate eight Jesuit martyrs. The striking interior features wood paneling and a cottonwood roof shaped like a ship's hull.

🔲 410 S18 ℹ 575 Dominion Avenue, Midland, Ontario, L4R 1R2 ☎ 705/526-4275

Opposite page *Mist rises from a lake in Algonquin Provincial Park*
Below *The front entrance of the McMichael Canadian Art Collection*

INFORMATION

www.pc.gc.ca
www.tobermory.org

✚ 410 S18 ℹ Bruce Peninsula
National Park and Fathom Five National
Marine Park, P.O. Box 189, Tobermory,
Ontario, N0H 2R0 ☎ 519/596-2233
ℹ Tobermory Chamber of Commerce,
P.O. Box 250, Tobermory, Ontario, N0H
2R0 ☎ 519/596-2452

Above *Beautiful Georgian Bay has rocky
shores, sand beaches and islands*
Below *A fun mural gives this Midland
house a whole new perspective*

GEORGIAN BAY

The large expanse of Georgian Bay is part of Lake Huron, but because the
Bruce Peninsula and Manitoulin Island nearly cut it off, it is almost a lake in
its own right and indeed, is sometimes referred to as the "Sixth Great Lake."
The southern part of the bay has sandy beaches and resorts; the northern
and eastern shorelines are indented; and there are thousands of small granite
islands with windswept trees and ospreys winging overhead. It's a wild area
with a raw beauty.

The Bruce Peninsula, part of the Niagara Escarpment, tilts toward the west,
with a gentle side facing Lake Huron, and huge rock walls and rugged capes on
the Georgian Bay side. It was declared a World Biosphere Reserve by UNESCO
in 1990, and is also a Canadian national park.

Manitoulin Island is the largest freshwater island in the world, covering
2,590sq km (more than 1,000sq miles). Named after Manitou, the Great Spirit,
it was set aside as an Amerindian reserve in 1837.

COMMUNITIES OF THE BAY

Penetanguishene, commonly called Penetang, is set at the head of a deep
inlet. A British naval base was located here in the 19th century, and the site
is known today as Discovery Harbour (late Jun–end Aug daily 10–5; mid-May
to late Jun Mon–Fri 10–5). In the original officers' quarters of 1845 you'll see
period furniture and, if you're lucky, a "period" officer. HMS *Tecumseth* and
HMS *Bee* are full-scale and active replicas of the original Royal Navy vessels.

Tobermory, at the tip of the Bruce Peninsula, is very much a sailors' town,
with twin harbors full of yachts and pleasure craft in the summer. It is the headquarters of two national parks: Bruce Peninsula, which protects the land, and
Fathom Five National Marine Park, an underwater park preserving the many
shipwrecks in the depths—a mecca for scuba divers. Non-divers can still see
the wrecks, and the local species of fish, in glass-bottom tour boats.

The same boat trip from Tobermory will take you to Flowerpot Island (mid-
May to mid-Oct daily), one of Ontario's recognized and highly acclaimed natural
attractions after Niagara Falls. It is renowned for its amazing rock pillars. The
best way to see the natural wonders is to take a cruise around the island, with
an option to land and follow the trails leading to the two sea stacks and a good
view of the coastline.

KINGSTON AND THE THOUSAND ISLANDS

Located on Lake Ontario just before the St. Lawrence River leaves the lake, Kingston started life as a French fur-trading settlement but was subsequently settled by Loyalists, who gave it the name. In the early 19th century, the British built a naval base and dockyard here, followed by the Rideau Canal (▷ 223) and, finally, Fort Henry. By the 1840s, Kingston was so important that it was briefly the capital of the province of Canada—its grand City Hall was built as a possible Parliament building, but it lost the honor after confederation. Today, it is a gracious place to visit, with a number of museums and historic properties. A pleasant city of limestone buildings, tree-lined streets and lake views,it retains its military role as home to the Royal Military College. It is also on the doorstep of one of southern Ontario's loveliest regions, the Thousand Islands, where the sparkling waters are dotted with, more or less, 1,000 islands.

Set on Point Henry, high above the St. Lawrence River, the massive Fort Henry (mid-May to early Oct daily) was constructed between 1832 and 1836 to protect the town, the naval dockyard at Point Frederick and the entrance to the Rideau Canal. It never saw military action, and began to decay in the early 20th century. Restored to its full splendor, it provides a real insight into mid-19th century military life, with barracks, officers' quarters, kitchens, guard room and powder magazine. The costumed interpreters are very approachable and there are military performances in summer.

THE THOUSAND ISLANDS

Called the Garden of the Great Spirit by native peoples and the Mille Îles by the early French explorers, these islands lying in clear sea-blue waters became one of the most popular vacation areas of northeastern North America in the 19th century. As it leaves Lake Ontario, the St. Lawrence is littered with islands for about 120km (75 miles). They vary in size—some are large and forested, others simply boulders of granite supporting a few jagged pine trees. No one agrees about their number—estimates vary between 990 and 1,800. In places, the rock has a pinkish hue, beautifully set off by the crystal waters and the surrounding greenery. It is possible to appreciate the region's beauty from the Thousand Island Parkway, but by far the best way is to be a passenger on one of the many boat tours.

INFORMATION

www.1000islandsgananoque.com
www.kingstoncanada.com
www.cityofkingston.ca
🚏 411 T18 ℹ️ Kingston Tourist Information Office, 209 Ontario Street, Kingston, Ontario, K7L 2Z1 ☎ 613/548-4415, 888/855-4555 ℹ️ Thousand Islands Gananoque Chamber of Commerce, 10 King Street East, Gananoque, Ontario, K7G 1E6 ☎ 613/382-3250, 1-800/561-1595

BOAT TOUR COMPANIES

Gananoque Boat Line
✉️ 6 Water Street, Gananoque, Ontario, K7G 2B7 ☎ 613/382-2144 (infoline), 888/717-4837; www.ganboatline.com

Rockport Boat Line Ltd
✉️ 23 Front Street, Rockport, Ontario, K0E 1V0 ☎ 613/659-3402, 800/563-8687; www.rockportcruises.com

Kingston 1000 Island Cruises
✉️ 261–265 Ontario Street, Kingston, Ontario, K7K 2X5 ☎ 613/549-5544; www.1000islandcruises.on.ca

Below *Cottages on the lakeshore reflect the popularity of this region*

NIAGARA FALLS

INTRODUCTION

One of the most spectacular sights in the world, the Niagara Falls is a breath-taking experience that no amount of commercialization can mar. The Niagara River divides when it reaches tiny Goat Island. About 10 percent of the water heads for the American Falls (on the US side of the river), which are more than 300m (nearly 1,000ft) wide, and 54m (177ft) high. The other 90 percent of the water heads for the Canadian, or Horseshoe Falls, so named for their shape. They are nearly 800m (2,600ft) wide and about 51m (167ft) high. The Canadian side of the falls has the best views, and attractive parks with beautiful flower displays line the river.

Avoid the town—it's tacky and touristy—and its US twin, Niagara Falls, New York, an industrial city full of chemical plants and factories exploiting the power of the falls. However, a trip to the US side can lead you to Goat Island, which separates the Canadian and American falls. There are various ways to enjoy the falls, most of which involve some degree of getting wet, but waterproofs are provided on the *Maid of the Mist* boat trip and for the walk behind the falls. You can also take a walk along the paved walkway of the Niagara River Recreation Trail (▷ 230–231). If you want to stay dry, you can always take a helicopter ride. Don't ever expect solitude—around 14 million people visit every year.

FORCE AND FLOW

The falls came into existence about 12,000 years ago, when the retreating glaciers created the Niagara Escarpment (▷ 218) and diverted the waters of Lake Erie into Lake Ontario. The top layer of rock is a hard dolomite limestone, with softer layers of sandstone and shale beneath. The force of the water tumbling over the falls cuts away at this underlying layer, causing the top layer to erode and break off. This erosion used to be about 1m (3ft) every year. In fact, 12,000 years ago the falls were 11km (7 miles) downstream. Since the 1950s, water diversion to power plants has spread the flow of water more evenly and

INFORMATION

www.niagarafallstourism.com
⊞ 411 S19 🛈 Niagara Falls Tourism, 5400 Robinson Street, Niagara Falls, Ontario, L2G 2A6 (also at Rainbow Bridge and 5440 Stanley Avenue) ☎ 905/356-6061 🚌 People Mover Bus runs along the Niagara Parkway; every 20 min in summer, reduced service off season, Apr–end Oct; adult $7.50, child (6–12) $4.50

Opposite *The Maid of the Mist is dwarfed by the falls*
Bottom left *The mighty Horseshoe Falls as seen from Maid of the Mist*
Below *The Skylon Tower looms above the trees at Niagara Falls*

thus reduced the rate of erosion, now estimated to be 36cm (1ft) every 10 years. Eventually, in a few hundred thousand years, the falls will erode their way back to Lake Erie.

In 1678, a Récollet priest, Louis Hennepin, became the first European to see the cataract. In his journal, he described it as "a vast and prodigious cadence of water which falls down after a surprising and astonishing manner, insomuch that the universe does not afford its parallel." Few have disagreed with him since. He continued: "The waters which fall from this vast height do foam and boil after the most hideous manner imaginable, making an outrageous noise, more terrible than that of thunder; for when the wind blows from off the south, their dismal roaring may be heard above fifteen leagues off." Little has changed—except that you cannot hear the falls from Lake Ontario today; traffic noise and the diversion of water to power plants have seen to that.

WATERFALL FASCINATION

Since that sighting in 1678, the falls on the Niagara River have enticed people from all over the world. By the 19th century, Niagara had become a hucksters' paradise, with every conceivable device being employed to separate visitors from their money. In 1885, the Ontario government stepped in and created Queen Victoria Park to protect the natural environment around the falls from unbridled commercial development. This was the beginning of today's Niagara Parks Commission, which regulates development in a total of 1,700ha (4,200 acres) of land along the river's edge.

In the early 20th century, Niagara attracted stuntsmen of all types. Some went over the falls in a barrel, others walked over them on a tightrope. This type of stunt was banned in 1912. Nonetheless, a total of 15 daredevils have tried to go over the falls in one way or another since then. Five of them drowned, including someone on a jetski as recently as 1991.

WHAT TO SEE

TABLE ROCK AND BEHIND THE FALLS

While they have their place in the Niagara experience, the boats, helicopters and cable cars should take second place. By far the best way to appreciate the power of the falls is to stand here at the very top, at the point where a dark green mass of water, about 2m (6ft) deep at the edge, silently slithers into the abyss. It is totally mesmerizing. It is also rather wet, especially on windy days.

The recently renovated Welcome Centre provides a viewing gallery, shops, places to eat and other amenities. A new attraction here is an exciting 4D simulation of the geological turmoil that led to the creation of Niagara Falls, produced by some of the world's top special effects experts. It's called Niagara's Fury (Jun–end Aug daily 9–9; Sep–end May daily 9–7), and you

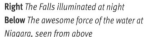

Right *The Falls illuminated at night*
Below *The awesome force of the water at Niagara, seen from above*

should visit prepared not only for being moved (literally) and startled, but also for a drop of 20°C (36°F) in temperature and a simulated snowstorm.

An appropriate follow-up is the purely natural, awe-inspiring Journey Behind the Falls (daily from 9am; closing times vary seasonally). Take the elevator 46m (150ft) down through the rock, then a short walk through tunnels leading to two portals. From here there's an incredible rear view of the falling water. Waterproof clothing is provided.

MAID OF THE MIST

A trip on one of these little boats is quite an experience. You board in calm waters (and don the waterproofs provided), then voyage right into the horse-shoe and the turmoil of water at the foot of the falls, venturing just a little bit farther than might seem sensible. Soaked by the incredible spray, you can look up at the huge wall of water plummeting down on three sides—Niagara means "thundering water."

✉ 5920 River Road ☎ 905/358-5781 🕐 30-min trips Apr–late-Oct daily ✋ Adult $14.50 child (6–12) $8.90

WHIRLPOOL AERO CAR AND WHITE WATER WALK

A little way north of the falls, the river takes a sharp turn and this creates a spectacular whirlpool midstream. It's best viewed from above, and that's where the Whirlpool Aero Car comes in. It has been gliding for about 1km (0.6 miles) across the river here since 1916 and the trip is a memorable experience. Nearby, you can take an enclosed elevator 70m (230ft) down through the rock for the White Water Walk. You emerge via a tunnel onto a boardwalk that runs alongside one of the most turbulent stretches of rapids in North America.

Whirlpool Aero Car ✉ 3850 Niagara River Parkway 🕐 Late Jun to mid-Oct from 9am; mid-Oct to late Jun daily from 10am. Closing time varies seasonally ✋ Adult $11, child (6–12) $6.50, under 5 free.

White Water Walk ✉ 4330 Niagara Parkway ☎ 905/356-2241 🕐 Late Mar–end Nov daily from 9am. Closing times vary seasonally and weather may cause closures ✋ Adult $8.50, child (6–12) $5, under 5 free

TIPS

» Arrive early or late for the popular *Maid of the Mist* boat trip on hot summer days.
» The falls are impressive in winter when partially frozen, but the spray freezes in midair and lands on you as ice pellets.
» Avoid the hucksters on Clifton Hill unless you really want your photograph taken in a barrel "going over the falls."

Above *View of the Horseshoe Falls from the Skylon Tower observation area*
Below *Aboard the* Maid of the Mist

INFORMATION

www.niagaraparks.com

411 S19 ⓘ The Niagara Parks
Commission (and Niagara Historic Sites),
7400 Portage Road South, P.O. Box 150,
Oak Hall Administrative Bldg. Niagara
Falls, Ontario, L2E 6T2 ☎ 905/356-2241

INTRODUCTION

The Niagara Parkway follows the Niagara River between lakes Erie and Ontario.
It is a wonderful drive, 53km (33 miles) long encompassing Niagara Falls
(▷ 214–217) as well as tranquil river scenes, beautiful gardens, fascinating
historic sites and the lovely community of Niagara-on-the-Lake. The Niagara
River is 56km (35 miles) long; the upper part is a wide, steadily flowing stream
with islands both large and small in its channel, and it is only after Chippawa
that it begins to pick up speed as it approaches the falls. The parkway is
slightly shorter than the river, running from Old Fort Erie to Niagara-on-the-
Lake. The best way to see it is to follow the drive in this chapter (▷ 228–229).
The Niagara Parkway was created in 1923 by the Niagara Parks Commission
(▷ 216), which still regulates development in a total of 1,700ha (4,200 acres)
of land along the river's edge.

WHAT TO SEE

NIAGARA ESCARPMENT

The Niagara Escarpment is sometimes known as Ontario's Great Wall.
Essentially, it is a massive ridge of fossil-rich sedimentary rock, which began
to form 450 million years ago. Several hundred meters (over 1,000ft) high in
places, it stretches 725km (450 miles) from Queenston on the Niagara River to
Tobermory at the tip of the Bruce Peninsula (▷ 212). In 1990, the escarpment
was declared a World Biosphere Reserve by UNESCO, and in the Niagara
peninsula, it provides good soil for the rich farmlands, orchards and vineyards.

FORT ERIE

This town stands at the point where Lake Erie empties into the Niagara River. It
is a major crossing place into the United States, with the 1927 Peace Bridge—
opened by the then Prince of Wales—connecting it to Buffalo. An interesting
place to visit is Old Fort Erie (early May–early Oct daily), a reconstruction of

a British fort built in 1747. It is the only fort in Canada to have withstood a seige—during the War of 1812—though it was destroyed by the Americans in 1814. In a scenic location the costumed guides really bring the place to life. and throughout the summer months (Jun–Aug) there are special events, themed tours and battle re-enactments.

QUEENSTON

Queenston Heights, 106m (348ft) above the river on the edge of the Niagara Escarpment, was the original location of Niagara Falls before erosion forced them upstream. This was also the site of a battle during the War of 1812, when British commander Isaac Brock was killed; a 50m (64ft) monument, currently undergoing restoration, stands here in his honor. A bridge crosses the river at this point to Lewiston, New York. At the bottom of the escarpment is Queenston, once home to the Canadian heroine Laura Secord, who, in 1813, set out on a 32km (20-mile) journey to warn the British that the Americans had crossed the river and were preparing to attack. The Laura Secord homestead (early May–early Sep daily; early Sep–early Oct Wed–Sun) is immaculately maintained. Both Brock's Monument and the Laura Secord homestead are surrounded by the formal flowerbeds and lanscaping of Queenston Heights Park. Beyond Queenston, the parkway is lined with gracious homes, orchards and vineyards in the heart of the most important fruit- and wine-producing area in Canada.

NIAGARA-ON-THE-LAKE

This community on Lake Ontario at the mouth of the Niagara River is one of the most captivating in Ontario and well known for its annual Shaw Festival (▷ 241). Settled by Loyalists after the American Revolution, it was the first capital of Upper Canada. The Americans burned it to the ground during the War of 1812, but it was rebuilt soon afterward. Since then, time seems to have stood still here, and gracious 19th-century houses stand on tree-lined streets. Nearby Fort George (Apr–end Nov daily 10–5) was built in the 1790s and is today a national historic park. It played an important role as the British headquarters during the war of 1812 and many of the key events are regularly re-enacted by costumed actors. Restored to its original condition in the 1930s, the site includes a wooden stockade, officers' quarters, guard house, powder magazine and barracks.

411 S19 Chamber of Commerce, 26 Queen Street, P.O. Box 1043, Niagara-on-the-Lake, Ontario, L0S 1J0 905/468-1950

TIPS

» A number of Niagara wineries are open to the public and offer tastings and tours.
» In summer, look for roadside stands selling juicy fresh peaches and other fruits direct from the farm.

Opposite top *The Whirlpool Aero Car poised above Niagara Parkway*
Opposite bottom *Blooms at the Niagara Botanical Gardens*
Below *Guides in period costume are on hand at Historic Fort Erie (below left)*

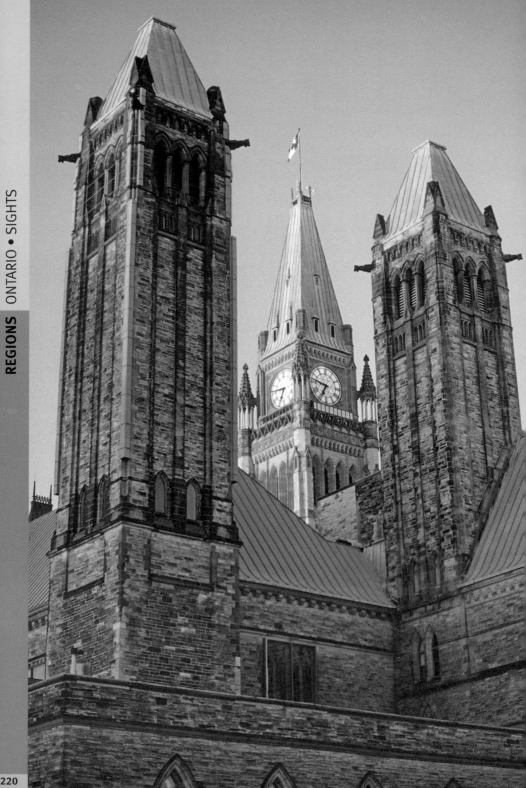

OTTAWA

INTRODUCTION

Ottawa defies the image that most people have of a national capital city. With a population of 1.2 million it is the fourth largest city in Canada and certainly it has its imposing architecture and some notably splendid museums, its bustling commercial centres of high-tech industry, and all that goes with the government offices of a capital city; but it is also very pretty and a relaxing, low-key place, full of parks and pleasant driveways, open spaces and waterways.

Located on the Ottawa River, the place which was to become the Canadian capital started life as a raucous lumber town. It was known as Bytown at the time the Rideau Canal was built (▷ 223). When Queen Victoria chose it as the new capital of her colony in 1857, the inhabitants renamed it Ottawa after the river which marks the boundary between the provinces of Ontario and Québec, and between English-speaking and French-speaking Canada.

The museums, monuments and historic sites are superb and as the city centre is quite compact it is easy to visit the main attractions at a leisurely pace. Designated a UNESCO World heritage Site in 2007, the Rideau Canal is the artery that cuts through the city and provides a playground summer and winter. A boat trip on any of the three waterways—the broad and slow moving River Ottawa, the fast-flowing Gatineau or the gentle Rideau Canal—is a great way to feel the pulse of the city and get a flavour of what it has to offer.

WHAT TO SEE

CANADA AVIATION MUSEUM
www.aviation.technomuses.ca

Housed in a huge hangar, this museum—part of the Canada Science and Technology Museum—tells the story of aeronautical history from the first attempts at flight to the jet age. It is also home to one of the most impressive collections of vintage aircraft in the world.

The emphasis here is on Canadian aircraft, but there are planes, both military and civil, from many nations, and the collection is still growing.

The Walkway of Time takes you on a journey through the eras of aviation development, while Pushing the Envelope showcases the achievements of Canada's aviation industry since 1945. Highlights include a replica of the AEA Silver Dart, built by Alexander Graham Bell's Aerial Experiment Association in 1901, plus a World War I Sopwith Snipe and a De Havilland Fox Moth.

✚ Off map, 223 B1 ✉ 11 Aviation Parkway, Ottawa, Ontario, K1K 4R3 ☎ 613/993-2010, 800/463-2038 🕐 May–end Aug daily 9–5; rest of year Wed–Sun 10–5 💷 Adult $6, student $5, child (4–15) $3, family $14 🚌 129 🛒 🏛

CANADA SCIENCE AND TECHNOLOGY MUSEUM
www.sciencetech.technomuses.ca

The Canada Science and Technology Museum is the largest of its kind in the country. Devoted to the ingenuity of Canadian inventions, every aspect of the scientific spectrum is covered, from the snowmobile to the Canadarm (part of the space shuttle). Exhibits cover transportation, astronomy, communications, space travel and computers. The Innovation Canada display is particularly fascinating, showing how this vast country's topography and climate have inspired invention. The Locomotive Hall offers an incredible display of huge and powerful locomotives, including the Canadian Pacific No. 926 steam train used across Canada right up until the early 1960s.

✚ Off map, 223 C3 ✉ 1867 St. Laurent Boulevard, Ottawa, Ontario, K1G 5A3 ☎ 613/991-3044 🕐 May–early Sep daily 9–5; rest of year Tue–Sun 9–5 💷 Adult $7.50, child (4–14) $3.50, family $18; additional $3 for the Simex Virtual Voyages™ Simulator 🚌 85, 86 🛒 🏛

INFORMATION
www.canadascapital.gc.ca
ℹ National Capital Commission Infocentre, 90 Wellington Street, opposite the Parliament Buildings ☎ 613/239-5000 (800/465-1867); year-round daily

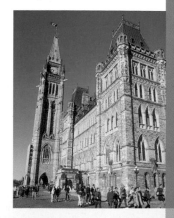

Opposite *The copper roofs, clock tower and spires, that make up the skyline of Parliament Hill*
Below *The Gothic-style Parliament Buildings*

TIPS

» Ottawa has a greater concentration of museums than anywhere else in Canada. You can see 10 of them (plus a National Arts Centre performance) for a reduced price with the 7-day Museums Passport (adult $30, family $75).

» Check out the Byward Market for fruit, bread and cheese. There are also several excellent restaurants in the neighborhood.

» If you go inside the Parliament Buildings you will have to go through security scanners, so allow extra time to stand in line for this procedure.

» The free guided tours are very popular in midsummer—arrive early and reserve your time in advance at the Info-tent.

» Pick up a self-guiding booklet to the grounds at the Info-tent.

CANADIAN WAR MUSEUM

www.civilization.ca

The Canadian War Museum, housed in a spectacular building beside the Ottawa River, is one of the world's foremost museums of military history. Designed by Raymond Moriyama, the complex geometric forms of the building resemble a fighter jet from some angles. A series of small windows high up on the walls spell out in Morse code: "Lest we forget–N'oublions jamais". The interior is equally evocative. With some 500,000 objects including artillery and military vehicles and an extensive collection of War art, the museum's permanent exhibits highlight defining moments in Canada's history. From the early days of New France through to present-day peacekeeping duties for the United Nations, Canada's military history is splendidly brought to life with full-size dioramas and displays. Highlights include memorabilia from the Battle of Vimy Ridge in 1917, the D-Day Landings of 1944, and more recently, the Iltis jeep used by Canadian peacekeepers in Bosnia.

🔲 Off map, 223 A3 ✉ 1 Vimy Place, Ottawa, Ontario, K1A 0M8 ☎ 819/776-8600, 800/555-5621 🕐 May–end Jun, Sep to mid-Oct daily 9–6 (also Thu 6–9); Jul–end Aug daily 9–6 (also Thu–Fri 6–9); rest of year Tue–Sun 9–5 (also Thu 5–9) 💰 Adult $10, child (3–12) $6, family $25. Free for veterans or members of Canada's armed forces. Combined tickets available with Canadian Museum of Civilization and its IMAX theater 🔲 🏫 🚌 8, 86, 87, 95, 96, 97

PARLIAMENT HILL

www.parliamenthill.gc.ca

Home of the Canadian government, the carved stones and copper roofs of the Canadian Parliament Buildings—commonly referred to as Parliament Hill—stand high on a bluff above the river. With their turrets and towers, these buildings are a glorious fantasy of High Victorian architecture. The best view of them is from the rear, from the Ottawa River or from Gatineau on the other (Québec) side; approaching them on Wellington Street, all you see is a large, flat, open park surrounded by three distinctive stone buildings.

The site was purchased from the British military in 1859. Three buildings were constructed in the 1860s—the one in the middle was for the Houses of Parliament and the Parliamentary Library, the east and west blocks for offices. In 1916, the Centre Block was mostly destroyed by fire. It was rebuilt in 1920 in a more sober rendering of the Gothic style. The Peace Tower, added in 1927 as a monument to Canadians killed during World War I, has a carillon of 53 bells.

Free tours of the Centre Block are offered (even when Parliament is in session). For Canadians, the tour is a something of necessary pilgrimage, but non-Canadians may prefer simply to walk around the exterior to admire the architecture and to take in the wonderful views of the city and river.

In front of the buildings is the Centennial Flame, a fountain with a natural gas flame burning at its heart. Lit in 1967 (centenary year), it symbolizes the first 100 years of Canadian Confederation and portrays the shields and emblems of all the provinces and territories, and the date each joined Canada. Head left around the Centre Block to the Summer Pavilion, for views of the Québec shore and the Canadian Museum of Civilization. At the back of the Centre Block is the extraordinary 16-sided Gothic Parliamentary Library, which survived the 1916 fire. The statues you pass are mostly of former Canadian prime ministers or the fathers of Canadian Confederation. Two commemorate British monarchs—Queen Victoria and Queen Elizabeth II.

From late June to late August, the 30-minute Changing of the Guard ceremony takes place on the main lawn (get there by 9.45am); a 30-minute bilingual sound and light show (twice a night Jul–early Sep, times vary), uses the Centre Block as a big screen.

🔲 223 B2 ✉ National Capital Commission Infocentre, 90 Wellington Street (opposite Parliament Buildings); Info-tent on Parliament Hill, mid-May–early Sep ☎ 613/239-5000, 800/465-1867 🕐 Daily

NATIONAL GALLERY OF CANADA

▷ 224–225.

RIDEAU CANAL NATIONAL HISTORIC SITE

www.pc.gc.ca

Cutting right through the heart of the capital, the Rideau Canal forms an attractive linear park. In winter, the canal becomes a 7.8km-long (4.8-mile) skating rink, known as the Rideau Canal Skateway (tel 613/239-5234 for ice conditions). In 2007 it was declared a World Heritage Site.

The canal leaves the Ottawa River by a flight of eight locks. From there it stretches some 202km (126 miles), with a total of 47 locks. It was built by the British government between 1826 and 1832 to provide a safe route between Montréal and the naval base on Lake Ontario, avoiding the stretch of the St. Lawrence River that forms the border with the US. The construction was entrusted to Colonel John By of the Royal Engineers and, although it ranks among the greatest early civil engineering works of North America, By got no credit for it—in fact, it cost so much money that he was recalled to Britain in disgrace.

✚ 223 C2 ✉ Rideau Canal Historic Site, 34 Beckwith Street South, Smiths Falls, Ontario, K7A 2A8 ☎ 613/283-5170, 1-888/773-8888

SUPREME COURT OF CANADA

www.scc-csc.gc.ca

Canada's Supreme Court Building, designed by Montréal architect Ernest Cormier, stands high above the Ottawa River, just west of Parliament Hill (▷ opposite). Set back from busy Wellington Street, the building provides a dignified setting for the country's highest tribunal.

✚ 223 B3 ✉ 301 Wellington Street, Ottawa, Ontario, K1A 0J1 ☎ 613/995-4330, 613/995-5361 (information on guided tours) 🕐 May–end Aug daily 9–5; rest of year Mon–Fri 9–5 💰 Free

Above *Locks along the Rideau Canal, a year-round focus of outdoor city life*

NATIONAL GALLERY OF CANADA

INFORMATION

http://national.gallery.ca

[+] 223 B2 [✉] 380 Sussex Drive, Box 427, Station A, Ottawa, Ontario, K1N 9N4 [☎] 613/990-1985, 800/319-2787 [🕐] May–end Sep daily 10–5 (also Thu 5–8); rest of year closed Mon [♿] Adult $9, child (12–19) $4, family $18; free Thu after 5pm. Additional charge for special exhibitions: adult $15, child (12–19) $7, family $30 [👆] Guided tours: May–end Sep daily 2pm; Oct–end Apr Wed–Sun 2pm; free [▯] [▤]

INTRODUCTION

Home to over 1,500 Canadian works of art, the result of almost 130 years of erudite collecting, the National Gallery of Canada occupies a wonderful site in the heart of the capital, with great views of Parliament Hill (▷ 222). The architecture of this building is stunning, with the glittering prisms of its tower echoing the Gothic turrets of the Parliamentary Library across the Rideau Canal. The Great Hall in particular has splendid vistas, and the elegant galleries, courtyards and skylights diffuse natural light throughout the building.

WHAT TO SEE

CANADIAN COLLECTION

Not too surprisingly, the National Gallery of Canada has the world's largest collection of Canadian art on display in the permanent collection galleries. The tone is set as soon as you enter these galleries. New France springs to life with painted and gilded altarpieces, sculptures of saints and religious paintings. Gradually, there is a transition to splendid landscapes, such as Lucius O'Brien's *Sunrise on the Saguenay*, followed by some of the famous names of Canadian art. The genre scenes of Cornelius Kreighoff and Paul Kane record the long-lost lifestyle of native Canadians. Pride of place is given to the magnificently evocative works of Tom Thomson and the Group of Seven. Thomson's *The*

Jack Pine, A. Y. Jackson's *The Red Maple* and Lawren Harris' *North Shore Lake Superior* capture the glorious wildness and stunning beauty of the country. More contemporary artists are not ignored, with fine offerings by Jean-Paul Riopelle and Paul-Émile Borduas.

MORE COLLECTIONS

The gallery owns some outstanding examples of art from other cultures. Over 400 works of art are on display in the spacious European, American and contemporary galleries, reflecting the core and substance of artistic tradition and innovation in Western culture. The collection is arranged chronologically from the Middle Ages through to today. Don't miss Lucas Cranach's *Venus* (c1518), Gian Lorenzo Bernini's marble bust of Pope Urban VIII (c1623), John Constable's *Salisbury Cathedral from the Bishop's Grounds* (1820), and the original of the much-reproduced work by Benjamin West, *The Death of General Wolfe*. In the contemporary art galleries, Barnett Newman's enormous abstract work *Voice of Fire* (1967) features three huge stripes. The American artist's work cost the Canadian taxpayer $11 million. Controversy still surrounds this purchase, so you may well find a group of out-of-towners here to see what their money was spent on. Hidden away on the lowest level, but accessible from the Great Hall, you'll find a suite of five octagonal rooms devoted to the art of the North. Full of wonderful prints and sculptures in soapstone and whalebone, they provide a great overview of Inuit art. One section is reserved for mini-exhibitions that focus on individual artists.

Important special exhibitions are presented here throughout the year, and there are also talks, art-related performances, tours and movies.

RIDEAU STREET CHAPEL

At the heart of the Canadian Galleries and adjacent to the Garden Court, you will suddenly come upon this extraordinary and dramatic presentation of the rich artistic traditions of French Canada. Previously a part of the Convent of Our Lady of the Sacred Heart in Ottawa, this splendid chapel interior was saved from threatened destruction, dismantled piece by piece and moved into the National Gallery, which was at that time under construction. The interior has been painstakingly reconstructed exactly as it was.

Designed in 1887 by the diosesan architect Canon Georges Bouillon the chapel interior is unique in the history of Canadian ecclesiastical architecture. It has a decorated neo-Gothic fan-vaulted ceiling, marbled cast-iron columns, three altars, a balcony and splendid windows. It is the only known chapel of its kind in North America.

Above *The bright fall colors of* The Pool *by Tom Thomson (1915)*
Below *The open, airy galleries display some outstanding artworks*
Opposite *The gallery building resembles a huge, glittering prism*

POINT PELEE NATIONAL PARK
www.pc.gc.ca

This tiny oasis of green, protruding into Lake Erie and the most southerly point of the Canadian mainland, was formed when tons of sand were deposited here by the retreating glaciers of the last Ice Age and a lush woodland of deciduous trees took root.

Point Pelee is on the same latitude (40°N) as Rome, and has a plant and animal life unique in Canada. For this reason, its 20sq km (8sq miles) have been preserved as a national park since 1918. It is also famous for its spring and fall bird migrations, when more than 350 species pass through. For a few days each fall, it hosts thousands of migrating monarch butterflies, on their way south to the mountains of central Mexico 3,000km (1,860 miles) away. They come to find their only food—milkweed—which grows in abundance here.

✚ 410 R20 ✉ 407 Monarch Lane, R.R.1, Leamington, Ontario, N8H 3V4 ☎ 519/322-2365, 519/322-2371 (info line) 🕐 Daily 🎟 Apr–end Oct adult $7.80, child (6–16) $3.50 family $17.10; Nov–end Mar adult $5.50, child (6–16) $2.65, family $13.50 🖥🏛

SAULT STE. MARIE
www.saulttourism.com

Sault Ste. Marie, known as "The Soo," is an industrial city on the north side of the St. Mary River. This 96km (60-mile) stretch of water connects lakes Superior and Huron and forms the international border between Ontario and the state of Michigan. In a single turbulent mile, the river drops more than 6m (20ft) in a series of rapids *(saults)*.

Mighty locks enable large ships to travel the St. Lawrence Seaway, a major shipping route between the two lakes, and the four side-by-side Sault Ste. Marie locks are the final step in the 16 locks between the Atlantic and Lake Superior. Two of these locks are 24m (80ft) wide and a massive 411m (1,350ft) long, among the longest in the world. A lock-boat cruise (mid-May to mid-Oct daily) gives you a close view of the ships on one of the world's busiest canal systems.

North of town is the wilderness of the Canadian Shield. A day trip by train (mid-Jun to mid-Oct daily 8am) runs 184km (114 miles) through this rugged landscape, with a two-hour stop at spectacular Agawa Canyon.

✚ 404 Q18 ℹ Tourism Sault Ste. Marie, 99 Foster Drive, Sault Ste. Marie, Ontario, P6A 5X6 ☎ 705/759-5432

SCIENCE NORTH AT SUDBURY
www.sciencenorth.on.ca

Sudbury sits in a huge oval-shaped crater, about 100km (62 miles) wide and 15km (9 miles) deep, in the rocky Canadian Shield in northern Ontario's vastly rich mineral belt. Nickel and copper were discovered here in 1883 during construction of the Canadian Pacific Railway, and today Sudbury is one of Canada's largest mining towns.

Science North, Sudbury's superb science museum, is housed in two glittering snowflake-shaped buildings, representing the glaciation that sculpted the landscape. They are linked by a rock tunnel, ending in a cavern where a spectacular 3-D movie is shown. From here, a ramp reveals part of the underlying bedrock. There are laser shows, an IMAX theater, tropical greenhouse, science camps and workshops.

Science North's sister attraction, Dynamic Earth (122 Big Nickel Road, Sudbury), opened in 2003 to give an in-depth (quite literally) exploration of the geology of the area. It includes a glass-elevator descent to a tour of former mine tunnels, a mining-themed kids' hands-on play area, gold panning, geology and mineral displays, an interactive nickel mining gallery, and a movie theater showing exciting geologically themed films. An ambitious expansion project will be continuing through 2009. Outside, and a landmark for visitors, is Sudbury's famous Big Nickel, a giant reproduction of the 1951 Canadian nickel coin.

✚ 405 R18 ✉ 100 Ramsey Lake Road, Sudbury, Ontario, P3E 5S9 ☎ 705/522-3701, 705/522-3700 (info line) 🕐 Daily 🎟 Adult $18, child (12 and under) $15 for each attraction or £29.95 (child $24.95) for Science North and Dynamic Earth 🍴 Lakehouse Restaurant 🏛

THUNDER BAY
www.visitthunderbay.com

Located on the northwest shore of Lake Superior, Thunder Bay is Canada's lakehead—between the Atlantic and the Great Lakes.

Old Fort William Historical Park (mid-May to mid-Oct daily), a reconstruction commemorating the fur trade, looks just as it did in 1815. The fort is huge, with a whole cast of characters. There's an Ojibwa encampment, carefree voyageurs in bright clothing, and Scottish fur traders in top hats and long coats.

The dramatic Kakabeka Falls are 32km (20 miles) west of Thunder Bay on Highway 11/17. The Kaministikwia River plunges 39m (128ft) over sheer cliffs around a pinnacle of rock, then cuts a narrow gorge where platforms and a trail offer great views. There are fossils displayed at a visitor center (mid-May to end Oct daily).

About 65km (40 miles) northeast of the city the spectacular steep-sided Ouimet Canyon, about 1.6km (1 mile) long and up to 100m (328ft) deep, is the result of a fault in the bedrock. Rare vegetation grows on the canyon floor—Arctic alpines such as fir-club moss, lichen, saxifrage and shield fern are a remnant of the last Ice Age. A trail (mid-May to mid-Oct daily) follows the top of the canyon for 1km (0.6 mile).

✚ 404 P18 ℹ Visitor Information Centre, Highway 11/17E, Thunder Bay, Ontario, P7E 5VE ☎ 807/983-2041, 800/667-8386

UPPER CANADA VILLAGE

Upper Canada Village is an imaginative re-creation of an Ontario community in the mid-19th century. Located beside the St. Lawrence River in a rural setting, it was created during the construction of the St. Lawrence Seaway in the 1950s. In order to build the new power dams and shipping channels, engineers dammed the historic Long Sault rapids to form Lake St. Lawrence, drowning 200 farms, eight villages and thousands of homes in the process. Just over 30 heritage buildings were carefully moved here to preserve them, and today the fairly tough early existence of the Loyalists who lived in this area in the 1860s is brought back to life.

VILLAGE LIFE REVISITED

The village transports you back to an era when life was simpler. The costumed staff tend livestock in barns and farmyards, spin wool and quilt, make cheese and bread, grind wheat into flour in a steam-powered mill, and travel about in every type of 19th-century conveyance imaginable—visitors can ride some of them too. Tradesmen forge iron, sharpen and solder tinware, make furniture, shoe horses, and print a newspaper. There's a flour mill, sawmill, school, church, tavern and a doctor's surgery.

The buildings show how the the early settlers progressed from pioneer shanties to substantial homes of brick and stone. The Ross farm, one of the oldest buildings, is a single-roomed log homestead of a type built by the early Loyalists. In contrast, the much larger 1860s Loucks farm has an air of substance and affluence. Crysler Hall is a magnificent and spacious mansion, once the home a prosperous landowner, and it would have been luxuriously furnished. Today, it houses the village's Orientation Centre with an audio visual show and various exhibits including an account of the "Lost Villages" submerged below Lake St. Lawrence.

INFORMATION

www.uppercanadavillage.com

 412 T18 ✉ 13740 Country Road 2, Morrisburg, Ontario, K0C 1X0

☎ 613/543-4328, 800/437-2233

🕓 Mid-May to early Oct daily 9.30–5

✋ Adult $18.95, child (5–12) $7.95, (13–25) $11.95, family 10 percent discount. Prices do not include tax

🍴 🖵 🎁

Opposite *Wooden boardwalks across the marshes in Point Pelee provide access for visitors while preserving the delicate ecology of the area*
Below *Costumed interpreters in a house in Upper Canada Village*

NIAGARA PARKWAY

This scenic drive encompasses the impressively powerful Niagara Falls, one of the world's great tourist attractions, as well as tranquil river scenes, beautiful gardens and the picturesque community of Niagara-on-the-Lake.

THE DRIVE
Length: 53km (33 miles)
Allow: A half-day
Start: Old Fort Erie
End: Niagara-on-the-Lake
How to get there: Old Fort Erie is on highway 1, 32km (20 miles) south of Niagara Falls and 2km (1.2 miles) from the Peace Bridge, a major entry point from the US (Buffalo, New York state)

The Niagara Parkway officially begins at Mather Arch on the left side of Highway 1 (going north).

❶ Surrounded by beautiful flower beds in summer, Mather Arch was constructed in 1939 as a gateway for visitors entering Canada from the US over the Peace Bridge. The bridge connects Fort Erie in Ontario with Buffalo in New York across Niagara River. It was opened in 1927 by the then Prince of Wales, and is one of four international bridges across the river.

There are many rest stops and picnic areas along the parkway. About 16km (10 miles) into the drive, you will see Navy Island.

❷ This small island was where rebel leader William Lyon Mackenzie sought refuge after the failure of his revolt in Upper Canada in 1837.

Another 2km (1.2 miles) along, in Chippawa, the parkway follows a one-way system to cross the Welland River over King's Bridge, then passes the Dufferin Islands, a series of small island parks with paths and bridges. Immediately after these islands is the International Niagara Control Works.

❸ At night, the control dam channels up to 50 percent of the water from 90m (300ft) below the city of Niagara Falls to the Sir Adam Beck Generating Stations, here and near Queenston, or to the Robert Moses Generating Station on the American side of the falls
    Immediately beyond the control works, the river is very impressive, moving at nearly 100kph (60mph) through great rapids. After 28km (17 miles) from the start of the drive, you come to Horseshoe Falls. Park across from the Table Rock complex (parking $12) and go for a stroll to view this amazing sight. Take rain gear if you have some.

❹ The Horseshoe (or Canadian) Falls (▷ 214–217) are nearly 800m (2,600ft) wide and 50m (160ft) high. From inside the Table Rock building, you can descend 38m (150ft) by elevator and walk to two observation decks behind the Falls (daily). Protective rain gear is provided. A little farther along, the American Falls can be seen on the US side of the river, and you reach the starting point for the *Maid of the Mist* boat trip (▷ 217).

Another 2km (1.2 miles) along the parkway is Rainbow Bridge.

❺ The steel-arched Rainbow (or Honeymoon) Bridge is the fifth to be built at this location. Completed in 1941, it replaced a bridge destroyed in an ice jam in 1938. On the Canadian side, there is a carillon tower with 55 bells, the largest of which weighs 10 tons.

The parkway passes underneath the Whirlpool Rapids Bridge, 2km (1.2 miles) along, then it's another 1km (0.6 miles) to the White Water Walk, and a Buddhist temple, and then another 1km (0.6 miles) to the whirlpool and Aero Car.

6 An elevator takes you down to the White Water Walk at the bottom of the gorge, a boardwalk alongside the rapids (late Mar–end Nov daily). It is almost impossible to see these rapids from above. Across the street from the White Water Walk is a large Buddhist temple, known as the Ten Thousand Buddhas Sarira Stupa—an amazing sight. The river makes an

abrupt turn northeast, and the force of the water creates a powerful whirlpool. A cable car is suspended high above it, offering impressive views (late Mar–end Nov daily). The Whirlpool can be seen from the riverbank here, but there is a better view from the other side if you continue driving another 2km (1.2 miles).

Drive almost 3km (2 miles) from here to Niagara Glen.

7 Here you can hike down the gorge, carved out by the river between 7,000 and 8,000 years ago. For the descent of over 60m (200ft), allow about 15 minutes to descend and 30 minutes to climb back up.

Continue on the parkway for 1km (0.6 miles) to reach the Botanical Gardens and Butterfly Conservatory

(daily). In another 2km (1.2 miles), you'll pass two more important power plants.

8 Below, the Sir Adam Beck Generating Station is one of Ontario Hydro's largest facilities. Across the river, the Robert Moses Generating Station serves this very industrial part of New York state.

One kilometer (0.6 miles) farther, the Queenston-Lewiston Bridge crosses the river. The parkway steeply descends the escarpment and bypasses the small village of Queenston at its foot then continues through an area of large, beautiful estates, orchards and vineyards as it approaches Niagara-on-the-Lake.

9 Niagara-on-the-Lake was settled by Loyalists after the American Revolution, and was the first capital of Upper Canada. The Americans burned it to the ground during the War of 1812, but it was rebuilt soon afterward. The town is well known for the Shaw Festival (▷ 241) and is also the jewel at the heart of the burgeoning Niagara wine industry (▷ 392–393).

WHEN TO GO
Though Niagara Falls is always busy, you don't have to drive far to get away from the crowds. Spring is lovely, fall offers local wine festivals and, in winter, the falls freeze—an incredible sight.

WHERE TO EAT
✉ Peller Estates Winery Restaurant, 290 John Street East, Niagara-on-the-Lake ☎ 905/468-4678.

WHERE TO STAY
✉ Holiday Inn, 1485 Garrison Road, Fort Erie ☎ 905/871-8333.
✉ Prince of Wales Hotel, 6 Picton Street Niagara-on-the-Lake ☎ 905/468-3246 or 888/669-5566.

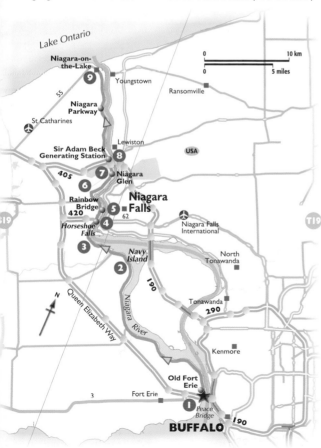

Opposite The Maid of the Mist *heads right into the spray of the falls*

NIAGARA WALK

This walk follows part of the scenic Niagara River Recreation Trail, begun in 1986. In its entirety, the paved pedestrian path stretches some 58km (35 miles) along the bank of the Niagara River from Niagara-on-the-Lake to Fort Erie.

THE WALK

Length: Just over 5km (3 miles)
Allow: 1.5 hours
Start/end: Rainbow Bridge, Niagara Falls
How to get there: From Queen Elizabeth Way, take Highway 420 into Niagara Falls and exit on River Road. From US, just cross the Rainbow Bridge.

Warning: The spray given off by the falls is likely to drench you. You may need rain gear.

From Rainbow Bridge walk toward the falls.

The steel-arched Rainbow Bridge, or Honeymoon Bridge, is the fifth to be built here, its predecessor was destroyed in an ice jam in 1938. You can walk under the bridge if you don't mind the roar of the traffic.

At the end of the bridge to the right is a carillon tower with 55 bells. Concerts are given from time to time. The cloud of spray issuing from the falls dominates the view ahead.

Cross Clifton Hill Street and follow the footpath away from the road close to the river and you come to the *Maid of the Mist.*

You can buy a ticket here and take the *Maid of the Mist* boat trip (rain gear is provided). This trip rates among the most exciting in the world (▷ 217).

About 500m (540 yards) ahead you'll see Goat Island, a tiny wooded island separating the American Falls from the Horseshoe Falls.

The American Falls, on the US side of the river, are 300m (1,000ft) wide and more than 50m (164ft) high, but count for only 10 percent of the river's flow.

Soon after this point, you will start to feel the spray from Horseshoe Falls, about 0.8km (0.5 miles) along.

At Table Rock, you can approach the very edge, where the water plunges over the cliff and is a very compelling sight. The falls are both spectacular and powerful, nearly 800m (2,600ft) wide and 50m (160ft) high, and carries 90 percent of the river's flow. The force of water continually causes large sections of rock to erode and break off, but water diversion to the power plants and generating stations has spread the flow more evenly over the falls, thus reducing the rate of erosion.

Continue walking upstream for about another 0.8km (0.5 miles).

Huge boiling rapids upstream are an impressive precursor to the falls, with water flowing at nearly 100kph (60mph). The rusty old boat caught in the midst has been there since 1918. It was a dumping scow that broke loose from its towing tug some way upstream and finally ran aground here. It took 29 hours to rescue the men on board—a breeches buoy connected to a line was shot out to them from the roof of the Electrical Development Corporation building, which you can see directly ahead.

Turn around at the Electrical Development Corporation and return to Rainbow Bridge.

WHEN TO GO

It's never quiet here, but arrive early or come in the evening, when the falls are floodlit, to avoid the crowds and longest lines for the *Maid of the Mist*.

WHERE TO EAT

✉ Edgewaters Tap and Grill, 6342 Niagara Parkway, Niagara Falls ☎ 905/356-2217.
✉ Elements on the Falls Restaurant, Table Rock, Niagara Falls ☎ 905/354-3631.

WHERE TO STAY

✉ Lion's Head Bed-and-Breakfast, 5239 River Road, Niagara Falls ☎ 905/374-1681.

Opposite *The Horseshoe Falls*
Above *The most exciting—and wettest—way to admire the majestic falls is by boat*
Below *The incredible spray is bound to make you wet at some point, but waterproofs are provided on board*

WHAT TO DO

ACTON

OLDE HIDE HOUSE

www.LeatherTown.com

An 1899 building houses Canada's largest leather store, and it's worth visiting just for the wonderful aroma inside. Stretching into the distance are coats, jackets, pants (trousers) and vests, plus purses, wallets, belt, gloves, and leather furniture.

✉ 49 Eastern Avenue, Acton, Ontario, L7J 2E6 ☎ 519/853-1031, 877/453-2843 🕓 Daily 10–6 (until 9pm on Fri) 🚌 Off Mill Street

BOWMANVILLE

MOSPORT INTERNATIONAL RACEWAY

www.mosport.com

A principal venue for Canadian motor racing, with a 4km (2.5-mile), 10-turn road course, a 0.8km (half-mile) oval, a 1km (half-mile) cart track, and Driver Development Centre. Events include CASCAR and Superbike.

✉ 3233 Concession Road #10, RR #5, Bowmanville, Ontario, L1C 3K6 ☎ 905/983-9141 🕓 Mid-May to end Sep 🖐 Usually

$15–$50; weekend rates available 🚌 100km (62 miles) east of Toronto off Highway 401 (exit 431) then east on RR #20

BRAMPTON

WILD WATER KINGDOM

www.wildwaterkingdom.com

A terrific waterpark, with a wave pool, tubes and waterslides of varying fright levels, rides and a safe play area for tinies. New in 2008 is the enormous Sports Dome, with an indoor driving range.

✉ 7855 Finch Avenue West, Brampton, Ontario, L6T 0B2 ☎ 416/369-9453, 866/794-9453 🕓 Mid-Jun to early Sep daily 10–6 (till 8 high season) 🖐 Adult $29.95, child (under 10) $21.95 (under 3) free 🚇 Yorkdale or York Mills, then GO Bus; 22 from Mississauga; 11 from Brampton 🚌 Off Highway 427

CAMBRIDGE

AFRICAN LION SAFARI

www.lionsafari.com

This huge park houses 1,000-plus exotic animals that roam freely in large game reserves. You can drive

through or take the safari bus, and there's a lake cruise and scenic railroad. Don't miss the elephant swim, and Jungle Playground.

✉ 1386 Cooper Road, Flamborough; mailing address: #RR1, Cambridge, Ontario, N1R 5S2 ☎ 519/623-2620, 800/461-WILD 🕓 May–late Jun Mon–Sat 10–4, Sat–Sun 10–5; late Jun–early Sep daily 10–5.30; early Sep to mid-Oct daily 10–4 🖐 Late Jun–early Sep adult $27.95, child (3–12) $22.95, spring and fall adult $22.95, child (3–12) $18.95. Tax not included 🚌 One hour southwest of Toronto, off Highway 401 at exit 299 (west) or exit 268A (east)

CAMPBELLVILLE

MOHAWK RACETRACK

www.woodbineentertainment.com

Beautiful woodland setting, with exciting major league harness (trotting) racing, featuring many of North America's champion horses.

✉ 9430 Guelph Line, Campbellville, Ontario, L0P 1B0 ☎ 416/675-RACE, 888/675-RACE 🕓 May to mid-Oct Thu–Sun 7.30pm, Mon 7.20pm 🖐 Free 🚌 Off Highway 401, west of Toronto

COLLINGWOOD

BLUE MOUNTAIN RESORT

www.bluemountain.ca

This is Ontario's premier winter resort, on its highest mountain, with downhill and cross-country skiing, snowboarding, tubing and tuition. Also hiking, mountain-biking, water sports in the summer months.

✉ 108 Jozo Weider Boulevard, Collingwood, Ontario, L9Y 3Z2 ☎ 705/445-0231, 1-877/445-0231 🕐 Year-round ✋ Rentals: skis $25–$46, snowboard $35–$46, Lift tickets: $40–$64 🚍 11km (7 miles) west of Collingwood off Highway 26

ELORA

KARGER GALLERY

www.kargergallery.com

The picturesque village of Elora, with its wide river rapids, is a great place to shop, with lots of friendly boutiques and interesting specialty stores. The Karger Gallery is one of the highlights, full of high-quality works from more than 100 Canadian artists–ceramics, glass, wood, metal, paintings and raku. Stunningly beautiful pieces sit alongside whimsical practical items, and the prices are very affordable.

✉ Elora Mews, 45 Mill Street West, Elora, Ontario, N0B 1S0 ☎ 519/846-2921, 877/846-1116 🕐 Daily 11–6

GANANOQUE

THOUSAND ISLANDS KAYAKING

www.1000islandskayakingco.com

Catering to beginners and more experienced kayakers, this company organizes half-day and full-day tours around the beautiful Thousand Islands, with certified guides, all equipment, and tuition provided. Full day tours include lunch, and healthy snacks are provided for 3-hour tours.

✉ 58 River Road, Lansdowne, Ontario K0E 1L0 ☎ 613/329-6265 🕐 May–Oct, by reservation ✋ Half-day $85, full day $125 🚍 Gananoque is off Highway 401, about 30km (18 miles) east of Kingston

THOUSAND ISLANDS PLAYHOUSE

www.1000islandsplayhouse.com

With one theater right on the waterfront (pictured right) and another in an old former fire station next door, this professional theater stages popular lightweight drama, music and comedy.

✉ 690 Charles Street South, Gananoque, Ontario, K7G 2T8 ☎ 613/382-7020, 866/382-7020 🕐 Mid-May to early Nov ✋ Adult $32, child $16 🚍 On bank of St. Lawrence River

GEORGETOWN

WILDWOOD MANOR RANCH

www.wildwoodranch.com

Friendly and knowlegeable guides lead rides through the 40ha (100 acres) of land owned by the ranch, including woodland and open fields, with plenty of chances of spotting local wildlife (deer, racoons, etc) along the way. Horses for all levels.

✉ RR5, Georgetown, Ontario, L7G 4S0 ☎ 905/877-6852 🕐 Trail rides by appointment only; from 1 hour to full day rides ✋ $40 per hour 🚍 One hour's drive north of Toronto (call for directions)

HAMILTON

ADVENTURE VILLAGE

www.adventurevillage.ca

This 1.2ha (3-acre) amusement park will keep the little ones happy with bumper cars, miniature golf and gemstone panning. Older children will enjoy the batting cages and climbing wall. The arcade and games room has something for all ages.

✉ 580 Van Wagners Beach Road, Hamilton, Ontario, L8E 3L8 ☎ 905/549-8727 🕐 Apr and Sep Mon–Fri 4–9, Sat–Sun 12–9 (to 10pm Fri and Sat); May Mon–Fri 12–9, Sat–Sun 10–9 (to 10pm Fri and Sat); Jun Mon–Fri 12–10, Sat–Sun 10–10 (to midnight Fri and Sat); Jul–end Aug daily 10am–midnight; Oct Sat–Sun 12–5 ✋ Activities priced separately; various packages available 🍴 🚍 East of downtown, near Stoney Creek, off Burlington Street East or QEW

CONFEDERATION PARK

www..conservationhamilton.ca

On the lakeshore, this 83ha (205-acre) park includes a terrific water park with a wave pool, scary six-story slides and fun for toddlers in a wading pool with sprays and fountains. There's also the Adventure Village with such attractions as bumper cars, climbing wall and mini golf, plus shoreline paths for skating and bicycling, and lots of lawns for running around.

✉ 585 Van Wagners Beach Road, Hamilton, Ontario, L8E 3L8 ☎ 905/457-6141 🕐 Park: daily 24 hours; Wild Waterworks: early Jun–late Jun Mon–Fri 11–4, Sat–Sun 10–6; late Jun to mid-Aug daily 10–8; last 2 weeks Aug daily 10–6

Park free; Wild Waterworks: adult $19, child (4–10) $12.30 Ollie's Landing café $ On shore of Lake Ontario, follow signs off Centennial Parkway (Highway 20) 56 (weekends and holidays)

HAMILTON PLACE THEATRE
www.hecfi.on.ca
Fine modern facility with huge stage and superior acoustics, staging drama, concerts, opera and musicals. Adjacent Studio Theatre is more intimate.
Ronald V. Joyce Centre for the Performing Arts, 1 Summers Lane, Hamilton, Ontario, L8P 4Y2 905/546-3100 Year-round

THEATRE AQUARIUS
www.theatreaquarius.org
This superb modern theater complex, with two performing spaces, features classic drama, musicals and children's shows.
190 King William Street, Hamilton, Ontario, L8R 1A8 905/522-7529, 800/465 7529 Year-round $21–$49 Downtown, between Walnut and Ferguson

KINGSTON
CATARAQUI TOWN CENTRE
www.cataraquitowncentre.ca
The largest shopping center in the area, with more than 140 stores, including Sears, The Bay, Zellers and Sport Chek;. There's also a good variety of smaller stores, places to eat and services such as free loan of strollers and wheelchairs. Events include fashion shows and family entertainment.
945 Gardiner Road, Kingston, Ontario, K7M 7H4 613/389-7900 Mon–Fri 9.30–9, Sat 9.30–6, Sun 11–5 West of the river, between Princess and Kidd, south of Highway 401 (exit 611)

FIREWORKS
www.glassrootsstudio.com
Glass artists can be seen at work in this studio and gallery in downtown Kingston, with a huge variety of their creations on sale, including wine glasses, vases, ornaments— even marbles.
56 Queen Street, Kingston, Ontario K7K

1A4 613/547-9149 Mon–Fri 9–5, Sat 10–5, Sun 11–4 Downtown, near King Street intersectiion

GRAND THEATRE
www.grandtheatre-kingston.com
Around $17 million has been spent on making the Grand Theatre "Grand Again". Behind its smart new façade, the building has two performance spaces, two licensed lounges and a patio, and an art gallery showcasing local works.
218 Princess Street, Kingston, Ontario, K7L 1B2 613/530-2050 Year-round

TIME TO LAUGH
www.timetolaugh.ca
North America's top touring comedians are on stage here. Amateur night first Wednesday of each month; improv third Wednesday.
The Hub, 394 Princess Street, Kingston, Ontario, K7L 2Z4 613/542-5233 Thu–Sat Varies, from $12.95, dinner and show packages available Downtown, eight blocks from waterfront near Barrie Street intersection

TOUCAN AND KIRKPATRICK'S
www.thetoucan.ca
The Toucan and Kirkpatrick's (upstairs) are both Irish pubs. It's the Toucan that has music—ranging from traditional folk to hot new bands, playing soul, blues, funk and Motown. There's a lively atmosphere and traditional pub fare.
76 Princess Street, Kingston, Ontario, K7L 1A5 613/544-1966 Daily Downtown, between Wellington and King Street East

LONDON
CHILDREN'S MUSEUM
www.londonchildrensmuseum.ca
Canada's first children's museum, and still one of the best. Kids can dig for dinosaur bones, hunt "underground" for cave dwellers, experience an Arctic adventure, explore life 100 years ago, and dress up like an astronaut. Outdoor playground with maze.
21 Wharncliffe Road South, London, Ontario, N6J 4G5 519/434-5726

Tue–Sun 10–5 (also Fri 5–8pm); open Mon 10–5 mid-May to early Sep $6 (under 2 free) 12 Between Queens Avenue/ Riverside Drive and Horton Street

MISSISSAUGA
LIVING ARTS CENTRE
http://livingartscentre.ca
World-class theaters with excellent acoustics, staging drama, dance, opera, comedy, and music, including classical, jazz, blues and folk.
4141 Living Arts Drive, Mississauga, Ontario, L5B 4B8 905/306-6000, 888/805-8888 Year-round Downtown transit terminal nearby Downtown across street from Square One (▷ below)

PLAYDIUM
www.playdium.com
More than 5ha (11.5 acres) of indoor and outdoor activities and conveniently close to Square One shopping. Indoor complex with 200 virtual and interactive games, plus a Ridefilm motion simulator with wrap-around screen. Outside there are baseball batting cages, a go-cart track, golf greens, volleyball and basketball courts, and a climbing tower.
99 Rathburn Road West, Mississauga, Ontario, L5B 4C1 905/273-9000 Mon–Thu 12–11, Fri 12–1am, Sat 10am–1am, Sun 10am–11pm $10–$25 Downtown transit terminal nearby Center of Mississauga, just north of Square One

SQUARE ONE
www.shopsquareone.com
It was Canada's largest shopping mall when built in 1973, and it's still Ontario's largest, with more than 360 stores and services, anchored by the big four department stores: a giant Wal-Mart, The Bay, Sears, and Zellers. There is also the Square One multi-screen cinema with 11 screens.
100 City Centre Drive, Mississauga, Ontario, L5B 2C9 905/279-7467 Mon–Fri 10–9, Sat 9.30–6, Sun 12–6 Downtown Transit Terminal nearby Downtown Mississauga, at highways 403 and 10 Around 40 outlets

NIAGARA FALLS

BRUCE TRAIL
www.brucetrail.org
Canada's oldest and longest footpath stretches 845km (525 miles) from Niagara to Tobermory in northern Ontario and there are some 430km (267 miles) of side trails branching off the main route. Much of the trail can be enjoyed on short hikes, including the highest point at Osler Bluff (8km/5 miles; approx 3 hours). There are also some short walks to specific landmarks, including the Hole in the Wall—a ladder descent through rock fissures—near Toronto.
✉ Bruce Trail Conservancy, P.O. Box 857, Hamilton, Ontario, L8N 3N9 ☎ 905/529-6821, 1-800/665-4453 ⓒ Year-round ✋ Free

CANADA ONE FACTORY OUTLETS
www.canadaoneoutlets.com
Around 40 stores selling off big-name items at up to 70 percent discount—Liz Claiborne, Ecco, Tommy Hilfiger, Reebok, and Villeroy and Boch are just some of them.
✉ 7500 Lundy's Lane, Niagara Falls, Ontario, L2H 1G8 ☎ 905/356-8989, 866/284-5781 ⓒ Mon–Sat 10–9, Sun 10–6 (closes 6pm on Mon Jan–end Apr) 🚌 Niagara People Mover (summer only) 🍴 Saint Cinnamon Bakery Café

MARINELAND
www.marinelandcanada.com
You can touch beluga whales and orcas and help feed them, then watch their show, which includes sea lions and walruses. There are also thrill rides (included in the entrance fee), many designed with children in mind. The world's largest whale habitat offers walkways and underwater viewing.
✉ 7657 Portage Road, Niagara Falls, Ontario, L2E 6X8 ☎ 905/356-9565 ⓒ Jul–end Aug 9–6; mid–May to end–Jun, Sep to mid-Oct 10–5 ✋ $36.95, child (5–9) $29.95 🚌 Niagara Parks People Mover (summer only) 🚗 1.6km (1 mile) from Horseshoe Falls 🍴 Cafeterias, snack wagons

NIAGARA FALLSVIEW CASINO RESORT
www.fallsviewcasinoresort.com
This casino occupies a massive 232,250sq m (2.5 million sq ft) complex rising 25 floors above the city. Overlooking the Falls, it has more than 3,000 slot machines and 150 gaming tables. The complex also includes a hotel, restaurants, health spa and theater providing entertainment by top international artistes. Like all gaming facilities in Ontario, the casino is managed by a branch of the government of Ontario.
✉ 6380 Fallsview Boulevard, Niagara Falls, Ontario, L2G 7X5 ☎ 888/FALLSVUE ⓒ Daily 24 hours ✋ Free; charge for theater shows. Age limit 19 🚗 Corner of Buchanan Avenue and Murray Street

OAKES GARDEN THEATRE
www.niagaraparks.com
Constructed in 1936, this amphitheater has beautiful lawns, rock gardens, lily ponds and borders overlooking the American Falls. The classical-style stage hosts a variety of plays and concerts.
✉ Niagara Parkway, Niagara Falls, Ontario, L2E 6T2 ☎ 905/356-2241, 877/642-7275 ⓒ Year-round ✋ Mostly free 🚌 5, 19, Niagara People Mover

WHIRLPOOL GOLF COURSE
www.niagaraparks.com
This has been one of Canada's top public courses since 1951, an 18-hole par 72 championship course with the backdrop of the Niagara River whirlpool and gorge. Full rental service and clubhouse.
✉ 3351 Niagara Parkway, Niagara Falls, Ontario, L2E 6T2 ☎ 905/356-1140 ⓒ Whenever weather permits ✋ Green fees: $64–$74, cart rental: $16, club rental: $30, reduced fees spring and fall 🚗 North of Rainbow Bridge on Niagara Parkway

Below *The Centrepointe Theatre, Ottawa*

NIAGARA-ON-THE-LAKE

EUROPA ANTIQUES
www.europa-antiques.com
You could spend hours browsing around this antiques shop, housed in an ivy-clad church building over 100 years old. Inside there's a range of furniture and many fascinating collectables such as bobbins, oil lamps, pewter and kitchenware.
✉ 1523 Niagara Stone Road, Virgil, Ontario, L0S 1J0 ☎ 905/468-3130
🕐 May–end Dec Mon, Wed–Fri 10–5, Sat–Sun 11–5; Jan–end Apr Sat–Sun 11–5
🚌 On Highway 55, 2km (1 mile) from Niagara-on-the-Lake

FRENCH PERFUME FACTORY
www.perfumefactory.ca
See antique stills, raw materials and the laboratory at the first perfume factory and museum in North America to open to the public. Hundreds of big-name fragrances for men and women are available at less-than-duty-free prices—along with Ombra bath products and aromatherapy oils.
✉ 393 York Road, Niagara-on-the-Lake, Ontario, L0S 1J0 ☎ 905/685-6666, 800/463-0012 🕐 Daily 10–5 🚌 Off Queen Elizabeth Way, exit 38 or via Glendale Avenue from St. Catharines

SHAW FESTIVAL THEATRE
www.shawfest.com
The only theater in the world that specializes in plays by George Bernard Shaw. It is also one of the largest repertory companies in North America.

✉ 10 Queen's Parade, Niagara-on-the-Lake, Ontario, L0S 1J0 ☎ 905/468-2172, 800/511-7429 🕐 Apr–early Nov
💵 $45–$105; lunchtime one-acts $27

WHIRLPOOL JET BOAT
www.whirlpooljet.com
This thrilling ride takes you over the Devil's Hole Rapids. For the "wet jet" you get waterproof clothing (and life jacket), but you'll probably need a change of clothes afterward. There's also the "jet dome" option, a covered vessel that keeps you dry throughout.
✉ 61 Melville Street, Niagara-on-the-Lake, Ontario, L0S 1J0 ☎ 905/468-4800, 888/438-4444 🕐 Mid-Apr to end Oct
💵 Adult $56, child (6–13) $47 🚌 Niagara Parks shuttle: Jun–end Oct daily; May Sat–Sun 🚌 Corner of Delater (off King Street) and Melville

ZOOM LEISURE
www.zoomleisure.com
If you have the time and the energy, one of the finest ways to explore historic Niagara-on-the-Lake and the surrounding winelands is on two wheels. You could just rent bicycles from this place, or take one of their guided tours, either in a group or custom-planned to your own requirements.
✉ 2017 Niagara Stone Road (Highway 55), Niagara-on-the-Lake, Ontario, L0S 1J0 ☎ 905/468-2366, 866/811-6993 🕐 Call for details 💵 Rentals from $20 (3 hours); tours from $65 🚌 Southwest of town, between Mary Street and East West Line

OAKVILLE

OAKVILLE CENTRE FOR THE PERFORMING ARTS
www.oc4pa.com
Community arts center staging theater, music, comedy, family entertainment and touring performers.
✉ 130 Navy Street, Oakville, Ontario, L6J 2Z4 ☎ 905/815-2021, 888/489-7784
🕐 Sep–end Jun 💵 Average $25–$60

OTTAWA

ABORIGINAL EXPERIENCES
www.aboriginalexperiences.com
Experiencing Canadian and American aboriginal culture is fascinating for both children and adults. Here, on an island that has been a place of celebration for 1,000 years, you can enjoy songs, drumming and dancing, and hear ancient legends. There are tepees, totem poles and canoes.
✉ Mail address: 34 Merton Street, Victoria Island, Ottawa, Ontario, K1Y 1V5
☎ 613/564-9494, 877/811-3233 🕐 Jun 21–early Sep daily 11–5 💵 Three options: "Legends" adult $7, child $4; "Discovery" adult $15, child $10; "Taste of Native Spirit" adult $20, child $14. Add-on "Creation" craft workshop $6–$14 extra 🚌 1, 2, 4, 7
🍴 Traditional aboriginal food 🎭 Authentic crafts and food

BARRYMORES MUSIC HALL
www.barrymores.on.ca
One of Ottawa's top live rock music venues since 1978, with some big names featured in its history. Sundays are Retro 1980s nights with no cover charge. Thursdays feature 1990s music, both with nightly DJs; live bands Friday and Saturday.
✉ 323 Bank Street, Ottawa, Ontario, K2P 1X9 ☎ 613/233-0307 🕐 Thu–Sun
💵 Varies 🚌 1, 2, 4, 7

BOUTIQUE LE PAPILLON
www.boutiquelepapillon.com
Elegant women in Ottawa shop at this family-run business. It's not just the fashions that set this store apart, it's the courteous, knowledgeable and honest service. Designer clothing from around the world is selected for a classic cut, wearability, modern textiles, and a contemporary sense of style.

✉ 136 Bank Street, Ottawa, Ontario, K1P 5N8 ☎ 613/237–3662 🕐 Mon–Wed and Sat 10–5.30, Thu–Fri 10–6 🚌 1, 2, 4, 7, 316

BYWARD MARKET
www.byward-market.com
Historic market in the oldest part of Ottawa, with a real buzzing atmosphere. Hundreds of vendors, under cover and lining the streets, sell fruit and vegetables, clothing, footwear, jewelry, crafts, ornaments and souvenirs. The whole area is a lively mix of restaurants, specialty stores and nightclubs.
✉ 55 Byward Market Square, Ottawa, Ontario, K1N 9C3 ☎ 613/562-3325 🕐 Daily, hours vary 🚌 1, 2, 4, 7, 14, 16, 18 (Rideau) or 3, 4 (Dalhousie)

CANADA AGRICULTURE MUSEUM
www.agriculture.technomuses.ca
This is the largest urban working farm and research station in Canada. Most children love visiting the animal barns. There is a dairy cattle barn with many different breeds, a horse and cattle barn with Clydesdales and seven breeds of beef cattle, and a small animal barn with pigs and piglets, sheep and lambs, goats, rabbits and chickens. Exhibitions include histories of tractors and hop growing. There are also live demonstrations, an arboretum and ornamental gardens.
✉ Prince of Wales Drive, P.O. Box 9724, Stn T, Ottawa, Ontario, K1G 5A3 ☎ 613/991-3044, 866/442-4416 🕐 Daily 9–5. Animal barns: open year-round. Exhibits and demonstrations: Mar–end Oct 👋 Nov–end Feb free; Mar–end Oct adult $6, child (3–14) $3, family $13 🚌 South of the traffic circle on Prince of Wales Drive 🚌 3

CANADIAN MUSEUM OF NATURE
www.nature.ca
The renovation project here is well under way, introducing new displays and multimedia and interactive technology. The Talisman Energy Fossil Gallery has 36 complete dinosaur skeletons, 3-D animations, real fossils and dramatic dioramas. The Mammal Gallery and Bird Gallery are also open, with real specimens in re-created habitats, touch-screen computer terminals and a play area. When the renovations are complete in 2010, there will also be a gallery dedicated to humans, a Water Gallery and a dynamic Discovery Centre with the latest high-tech approach to make learning fun, plus the ever popular Creepy Critters and Finders and Keepers exhibits.
✉ Victoria Memorial Building, 240 McLeod Street, Ottawa, Ontario, K1P 6P4 ☎ 613/566-4700, 800/263-4433 🕐 May–end Sep daily 9–6 (also Wed–Thu 6–8); Oct–end Apr daily 9–5 (also Wed–Thu 5–8) 👋 $5 (under 4 free), family $13 🚌 5, 6, 14 🚌 Corner of Metcalfe and McLeod; Metcalfe Street exit from Highway 417 🚫 Closed during renovation

CANADA SCIENCE AND TECHNOLOGY MUSEUM
www.sciencetech.technomuses.ca
This national museum (▷ 221) is a fantastic place for children to learn not only about science in general, but also about specific Canadian achievements. The Space exhibit has plenty of interactive displays, multimedia presentations and a simulator ride.
✉ 1867 St. Laurent Boulevard, Ottawa, Ontario, K1G 5A3 ☎ 613/991-3044, 1-866/442-4416 🕐 May–early Sep daily 9–5; rest of year Tue–Sun 9–5 👋 Adult $7.50, child (4–14) $3.50, family $18; additional $3 for the Simex Virtual voyages™ Simulator 🚌 85, 86 🚌 Southeast of downtown; exit Queensway at "St Laurent South", drive 2.6km (1.5 miles) to Lancaster Road and turn left 🚫 🚽

CENTREPOINTE THEATRE
www.centrepointetheatre.com
This modern theater hosts dance groups, theater companies, solo singers, touring bands, orchestras and comedians.
✉ Ben Franklin Place, 101 Centrepointe Drive, Nepean, Ottawa, Ontario, K2G 5K7 ☎ 613/580-2700, 866/752-5231 🕐 Year-round 👋 Usually $25–$45 🚌 95 to Baseline 🚇 O-Train to Carleton, then bus 117

COLLECTED WORKS
www.collected-works.com
This independent bookstore, in the Holland neighborhood, is owned and run by real enthusiasts—co-owner Craig Poile is a poet and playwright. You can browse at leisure, get expert advice, enjoy excellent coffee and cookies, and perhaps catch a reading or art exhibition in the back room, or a book-signing event. Well-stocked with a strong emphasis on literary fiction, poetry and children's books. Good range of titles by Canadian, American and British writers.
✉ 1242 Wellington Street West, Ottawa, Ontario, K1Y 3A4 ☎ 613/722-1265 🕐 Mon–Wed 8–6, Thu–Fri 8am–9pm, Sat 8–5.30, Sun 11–5 🚌 2 🚫

D'ARCY MCGEE'S
www.darcymcgees.ca
In its prime downtown location, this is a lovely pub with a traditional interior featuring handcarved wood, and etched and stained glass that was handcrafted in Ireland and shipped over. Traditional Celtic and East Coast music from first-rate live bands.
✉ 44 Sparks Street, Ottawa, Ontario, K1P 5A8 ☎ 613/230-4433 🕐 Sun–Tue 11am–1am, Wed–Sat 11am–2am. Live music Wed, Fri, Sat 👋 No cover charge 🚌 2, 4, 5, 6, 7

DUKE OF SOMERSET
Buzzing historic Somerset Village pub complex with a great atmosphere. It has regular live music from local rock bands, karaoke, international sport on satellite TV, and traditional pub league games.
✉ 352 Somerset Street, Ottawa, Ontario, K2P 0J9 ☎ 613/233-7762 🕐 Daily 👋 No cover charge (except charity events) 🚌 1, 2, 4, 7, 316 🚌 Corner of Bank

EIGHTEEN
www.restaurant18.com
An ultra-chic bar and restaurant, which attracts a casually sophisticated crowd. Cutting-edge cuisine, well stocked wine bar and DJ spinning acid jazz and retro soul on weekends in the bar lounge.

18 York Street, Ottawa, Ontario,
K1N 5T5 ☎ 613/244-1188 ⊙ Daily
✋ No cover charge 🚌 1, 3, 4, 306.
Transitway: 95, 97 Mackenzie King or Laurier
🚇 Byward Market

GREAT CANADIAN THEATRE COMPANY
www.gctc.ca
This is a long-established company
staging a vibrant selection of
challenging drama and comedy, and
with a commitment to produce new
Canadian work.
✉ 1227 Wellington Street West, Ottawa,
Ontario, K1Y 0G7 ☎ 613/236-5196
⊙ Sep–end Jun ✋ Previews and
matinées $29, evenings $39 🚌 2 🚇 West
of Downtown, at intersection with Holland

INUIT ARTISTS' SHOP
www.inuitart.org
Owned and operated by the artists
themselves, this is a nonprofit
(which doesn't mean items are
cheap) gallery with exquisite
examples of Inuit art, including
sculptures in caribou and whale
bone and stone, prints, wall
hangings, baskets, and dolls. The
shop also stocks books, stationery,
DVDs and CDs. Items can be
shipped worldwide.
✉ 2081 Merivale Road, Ottawa, Ontario,
K2G 1G9 ☎ 613/224-8189 ⊙ Mon–Fri
9–5, Sat 10–4 🚌 3, 4, 306 🚇 South of the
Queensway in South Ottawa

IRISH VILLAGE
www.irishvillage.ca
Four Irish pubs cluster together in
this corner of Byward Market, with
live music at Mother McGintey's and
the Heart and Crown. It's mostly
traditional Irish, but McGintey's also
has a jam session on Sundays.
✉ 67 Clarence Street, Ottawa, Ontario,
K1N 5P5 ☎ 613/562-0674 ⊙ Daily, live
music Wed–Sat 🚌 1, 3, 4, 306 🚇 Byward
Market

KANATA 24
www.amctheatres.com
AMC 24-screen megaplex with wall-
to-wall screens and stadium seating,
some with retractable armrests.
✉ 801 Kanata Avenue, Kanata, Ottawa,

Ontario, K2T 1E7 ☎ 613/599-1200 or 5500
⊙ Daily ✋ Adult $12.50, child (2–12)
$8.50 (13 and over with student ID) $10.50,
🚌 97 from Ottawa or 118, 161, 152 from
Kanata Town Centre

NATIONAL ARTS CENTRE
www.nac-cna.ca
One of the largest and most comprehensive performing arts facilities
in the world, staging theater (English
and French), dance and music.
✉ 53 Elgin Street, P.O. Box 1534 Stn B,
Ottawa, Ontario, K1P 5W1 ☎ 613/947-
7000, 866/850-ARTS ⊙ Year-round
✋ Varies 🚌 1, 2, 4, 5, 6, 7, 14

OTTAWA LITTLE THEATRE
www.o-l-t.com
One of Canada's oldest theaters
(since 1913), producing eight plays
a year. The auditorium dates from
1970 — when a fire destroyed the
original.
✉ 400 King Edward Street, Ottawa,
Ontario, K1N 7M7 ☎ 613/233-8948
⊙ Sep–end Jun Tue–Sat 8pm ✋ $24
🚌 2, 7, 14, 18 🚇 Transitway Mackenzie
King Bridge (15-min walk)

OTTAWA LYNX
http://web.minorleaguebaseball.com
Ottawa's baseball team, the Lynx,
plays visiting teams from the minor
league at the 10,000-seat open
stadium on the edge of the city.
Enthusiastic fans are as entertaining
as the game.
✉ Ottawa Lynx Stadium, JetForm Park, 300
Coventry Road, Ottawa, Ontario, K1K 4P5
☎ 613/747-5969, 800/663-0985
⊙ Apr–early Sep ✋ Adult $9–$11, child
(under 14) $7–$9 🚌 103 Lynx Shuttle, 3, 18,
🚇 South edge of city off Queensway (exit
117) at Vanier Parkway and Coventry Road

OTTAWA RENEGADES
http://slam.canoe.ca/Renegades/
A fairly new team for the city
(though it has a long history in
Canadian Football with other teams),
the Renegades came into being in
2001, and play their home games at
a 31,000-seat open-air stadium with
some canopied seating.
✉ Frank Clair Stadium (Lansdowne Park),
1015 Bank Street, Ottawa, Ontario, K1S 3W7

☎ 613/231-5608 ⊙ Season: late
Jun–end Nov ✋ $20–$70 🚌 1, 7

OTTAWA SENATORS
www.ottawasenators.com
The Senators play about 40 home
games at the Corel Centre, against
visiting National Hockey League
teams the excitement runs high.
✉ Corel Centre, 1000 Palladium Drive,
Kanata, Ontario, K2V 1A5 ☎ 613/599-0250,
800/444-SENS ⊙ Season: Sep–end Apr
(playoffs for Stanley Cup May–end Jun
if team qualifies) 🚌 401, 402, 403, 404,
405, 406 🚇 West of city off Highway 417
(Queensway) to arena-specific interchange

PLACE D'ORLÉANS
www.placedorleans.com
Wide sunlit aisles, a fountain and
children's play areas make this a
particularly pleasant mall. Anchored
by Wal-Mart and The Bay, it has
around 200 stores.
✉ 110 place d'Orleans Drive, Orleans,
Ottawa, Ontario, K1C 2L9 ☎ 613/824-9050
⊙ Mon–Sat 9.30–9, Sun 11–5 🚌 95
🚇 East of Downtown, just off RR174/
Highway 17 at place d'Orléans Drive 🍴

RCMP MUSICAL RIDE CENTRE
www.rcmp.ca/musicalride/ridecentre_e.htm
See the legendary Mounties putting
their horses through their paces
in the choreographed Music Ride
(check in summer because the team
travels a lot). You can also tour the
stables, meet the horses, visit the
riding school and farrier station, and
see the displays of gleaming tack
and ceremonial carriages.
✉ 1 Sandridge Road, Ottawa, Ontario,
K1K 0A7 ☎ 613/998-8199 ⊙ May–end
Aug daily 9–3.30; Sep Mon–Fri 9–3.30,
Oct–end Apr Tue and Thu 10–2 ✋ Free
🚌 7 🚇 Just beyond Rockcliffe Park, at
St. Laurent Boulevard

RENT-A-BIKE
www.rentabike.ca
Ottawa is great for bicycling, with
bicycle paths and weekend road
closures. This company has a large
selection of bicycles and in-line
skates for rent.
✉ East Arch, Plaza Bridge, 2 Rideau Street,
Ottawa, Ontario, K1N 8S7 ☎ 613/241-4140

◉ Mid-Apr to end Oct daily 9–5 ✋ From $9 per hour; $23 (4 hours)

RIDEAU CARLETON RACEWAY

www.rcentertainmentcentre.ca

One of Canada's fastest 1km (slightly more than a half-mile) harness racing tracks, with prime seating in the grandstands and a couple of annual races with big prize money. Also simulcast racing from tracks across North America and Australia, and 1,250 slot machines.

✉ 4837 Albion Road, Gloucester, Ottawa, Ontario, K1X 1A3 ☎ 613/822-2211 ◉ Live racing: late Mar–Dec 26 Thu, Fri and Sun 6.30pm; Jul Mon; Simulcast racing and slots: daily 9am–3am 🚌 Track's own shuttle service 🚌 Southeast of downtown beyond airport

RIDEAU CENTRE

www.rideaucentre.net

About 140 stores share this downtown mall, with Sears as the anchor. It has a classy feel to it, though after the big out-of-town malls, it seems just a little closed in. But it's definitely worth a visit for its many interesting specialty stores and individual fashion boutiques.

✉ 50 Rideau Street, Ottawa, Ontario, K1N 9J7 ☎ 613/236-6565 ◉ Mon–Fri 9.30–9, Sat 9.30–6, Sun 11–5 🚌 2, 7, 14, 18, 306, 316 🍴

R.W. KIDS

www.rwkids.com

If you want to outfit your kid like a little Canadian, this is the place to come. Family-run, it stocks a range of stylish Canadian-made clothes, including tough dungarees, denim jackets and snowsuits.

✉ 1407B Carling Avenue, Ottawa, Ontario, K1Z 7L6 ☎ 613/724-4576, 800/652-4674 ◉ Mon–Wed and Sat 9.30–5.30, Thu–Fri 9.30–8 🚌 85 Bayshore 🚌 East of Downtown, at Carling and Kirkwood–Queensway intersection 124

VALLEYVIEW LITTLE ANIMAL FARM

www.wlittleanimalfarm.com

You can't beat ordinary farm animals for amusing little kids, especially when the baby animals arrive in the spring. Rabbits, lambs, goats, cows and ducks can all be touched, fed and stroked. There's a train ride through the fields, country walks, a play area, old farm equipment, puppet shows and special events.

✉ 4750 Fallowfield Road, Nepean, Ottawa, Ontario, K2J 4S4 ☎ 613/591-1126 ◉ Mid-Apr to end Oct Tue–Sun 10–3 or 4 ✋ $6.50 🚌 West on Highway 12 🍴

VINEYARDS WINE BAR BISTRO

www.vineyards.ca

Atmospheric cellar wine bar, with snug booths and well-stocked bar of fine wines, single malts and imported beer. Live jazz Wednesday and Sunday evenings.

✉ 54 York Street, Ottawa, Ontario, K1N 5T1 ☎ 613/241-4270 ◉ Daily ✋ No cover charge 🚌 1, 3, 4, 306. Transitway: 95, 97 to Mackenzie King or Laurier 🚌 Byward Market

YUK YUK'S COMEDY CABARET

www.yukyuks.com

Comedy club's Ottawa location seats 200 for touring professional stand-up comedians. Amateur night Wednesday.

✉ Capital Hill Hotel, 88 Albert Street, Ottawa, Ontario, K1P 5E9 ☎ 613/236-5233 ◉ Wed–Thu 8.30pm, Fri 9.30pm, Sat 8pm and 10.30pm ✋ Wed $6, Thu $12, Fri–Sat $18. Dinner and show $43–$52 🚌 16, 18, 316

ZAPHOD BEEBLEBROX

Not for nothing was this place voted Ottawa's best live music and dance venue. Jewel, Alanis Morissette and Fun Loving Criminals are among countless international stars who have played to the eclectic crowd. The Rolling Stones filmed their "Streets of Love" video here in 2005. There are live bands 4 or 5 nights each week and DJs nightly.

✉ 27 York Street, Ottawa, Ontario, K1N 5S7 ☎ 613/562-1010 ◉ Daily ✋ Cover charge varies 🚌 1, 3, 4, 306. Transitway: 95, 97 to Mackenzie King or Laurier 🚌 Byward Market

RAMA

CASINO RAMA

www.casinorama.com

More than 2,400 slots and 110 gaming tables, nine restaurants, an all-suite hotel, and a 5,000-seat venue hosting an eclectic program of big-name concerts (Diana Ross, the Tchaikovsky Ballet, Santana, Gloria Estefan, Jeff Foxworthy, Ricky Skaggs) and shows. Patrons must be over 19.

✉ 5899 Rama Road; mail address: RR #6, P.O. Box 178, Rama, Ontario, L0K 1T0 ☎ 705/329-3325, 800/832-7529 ◉ Daily 24 hours 🚌 Call 705/329-5228 for special bus services 🚌 Ninety minutes north of Toronto, via Highway 400, off Highway 11 then 12

SAULT STE. MARIE

LOPLOP

www.loplops.com

This cool lounge-gallery-eatery presents live music several nights a week, with an eclectic—sometimes

eccentric—bunch of acts ranging from singer-songwriters and progressive folk to jazz, funk-groove and country-rock bands.

✉ 651 Queen Street East, Sault Ste. Marie, Ontario, P6A 2A6 ☎ 705/945-0754 🕐 Wed–Fri from 4pm, Sat from 7pm ✋ Varies by performance, from $5

STRATFORD
CHOCOLATE BARR'S
www.chocolatebarrs.com

If you feel in need of a sugar rush, Derek Barr's store is sure to satisfy. It's full of handmade chocolates and other candies, including toffee, fudge, mints and gift box selections.

✉ 136 Ontario Street, Stratford, Ontario, N5A 7Y4 ☎ 519/272-2828 🕐 Mon–Wed and Sat 9–6, Thu–Fri 9–8, Sun 11–5 (longer hours around major holidays) 🚍 Downtown, between Downie and Waterloo streets

STRATFORD FESTIVAL OF CANADA
www.stratfordfestival.ca

North America's premier classical theater company has its home at the superb 1,826-seat Festival Theatre and offers a season of Shakespeare, other classics and musicals. It has an innovative, nine-level thrust stage and no seat is farther than 20m (65ft) away. The company also stages productions at Stratford's Avon, Studio and Tom Patterson theaters.

✉ 55 Queen Street, Stratford, Ontario, N5A 4M8 ☎ 519/271-4040, 800/567-1600 🕐 Apr to mid–Nov ✋ From $29 to $109

SUDBURY
DINOSAUR VALLEY MINI GOLF
www.dinosaursudbury.com

Not one but six different mini-golf courses totaling 54 holes, with 20 huge dinosaur, dragon and insect models around the site. Dedicated to cancer families, the attraction raises money for cancer charities each year.

✉ 3316 St. Laurent Street, Sudbury, Ontario, P0M 1L0 ☎ 705/897-6302 🕐 May–early Sep daily 9–8 ✋ Adult from $7 (18 holes) to $20 (54 holes); child (under 10) $5.99–$17.99 🚍 North of Sudbury via Highway 35 (Elm Street), then Highway 18

NEW SUDBURY CENTRE
The biggest mall in northern Ontario has around 110 stores and services.

✉ 1349 Lasalie Boulevard, Sudbury, Ontario, P3A 1Z2 ☎ 705/566-9080 🕐 Mon–Fri 9.30–9, Sat 9.30–6, Sun 11–5 🚍 Northeast Sudbury at Barrydowne Road

THUNDER BAY
CANADA GAMES COMPLEX
www.gamescomplex.com

Constructed for the 1981 Canada Summer Games, this complex has a range of fitness and leisure amenities, including a 77m (253ft) pool, divided into three for lane swimming, recreational swimming and diving. There's also a diving tower and a 73m (240ft), figure-eight tube slide. Around the pool there's play equipment for children, table tennis, badminton and exercise equipment. The complex includes a jogging track, squash courts, weight rooms and other training areas. Spectator events are also held here.

✉ 420 Winnipeg Avenue, Thunder Bay, Ontario, P7B 6B7 ☎ 807/684-3311 🕐 Mon–Thu 5.45am–10pm, Fri 5.45am–9pm, Sat–Sun 8am–9pm ✋ Adult from $5.37, child (3–12) $2.80, family $16.82 (Thunderslide extra $1.87) ☕ Café 🚍 Downtown, next to Community Auditorium

COMMUNITY AUDITORIUM
www.tbca.com

Impressive 1,500-seat concert hall, home to the Thunder Bay Symphony Orchestra, with full schedule of classical concerts, musicals and rock concerts.

✉ 1 Paul Shaffer Drive, Thunder Bay, Ontario, P7B 6C7 ☎ 807/684-4444, 800/463-8817 🕐 Year-round ✋ Varies

JOYCE SEPPALA DESIGNS
www.joyceseppaladesigns.com

English-born Joyce Seppala has introduced stunning designs to cuddly fleece fabrics and linens, and the result is a range of wearable, easy-care garments that are stylish and fun. Imaginative patterns are inspired by Joyce's love of Canadian landscapes.

✉ 508 East Victoria Avenue, Thunder Bay, Ontario, P7C 1A7 ☎ 807/624-0022 🕐 Mon–Fri 9.30–5, Sat 9.30–1

MAGNUS THEATRE
www.magnus.on.ca

Northwest Ontario's professional theater company stages an interesting series of world-class drama and comedy.

✉ Dr. S. Penny Petrone Centre for the Performing Arts, 10 South Algoma Street, Thunder Bay, Ontario, P7B 3A7 ☎ 807/345-5552, 807/345-8033 🕐 Sep–end Apr (plus one summer production) ✋ $27.50–$32.50 🚍 West of downtown, off Waverley Street

SILVERCITY THUNDER BAY
www.cineplex.com

Twelve big-screen, big-sound movie theaters with stadium seating.

✉ 850 North May Street, Thunder Bay, Ontario, P7C 6A5 ☎ 807/628-8445 🕐 Daily ✋ Adult $7.50, child (13 and under) $4.20; Tue $4.20 all ages 🚍 Downtown, corner of North May and Northern

VAUGHAN
CANADA'S WONDERLAND
www.canadas-wonderland.com

Canada's premier theme park with over 200 attractions, including North America's greatest variety of roller-coasters and an 8ha (20-acre) water park that includes Canada's largest wave pool. For toddlers there's a cartoon-themed area; bigger kids and adults can scream the day away as they're hurtled around on ever more scary rides. There's a full schedule of entertainment, and live shows.

✉ 9580 Jane Street, Vaughan, Ontario, L6A 1S6 ☎ 905/832-8131 🕐 Early May–early Sep daily from 10am; Sep to mid-Oct Sat–Sun; closing time varies with season: 6, 8, 10 or 10.30pm ✋ Adult $52, child (3–6) $26, seniors $26. Grounds only: $26.49 P$8 🚍 Wonderland Express GO bus from Toronto's Yorkdale, or York Mills subway station 🚍 North of Toronto, off Highway 400, beyond the 401 🍴

FESTIVALS AND EVENTS

JANUARY
NIAGARA ICEWINE CELEBRATIONS
www.niagaraicewinefestival.com
Celebrating internationally renowned ice wine (▷ 393), with wines from more than 30 of Ontario's wineries.
✉ Niagara Falls, Ontario ☎ 905/688-0212

FEBRUARY
WINTERLUDE
www.canadascapital.gc.ca/winterlude
The capital celebrates winter with street parties, a stew cook-off, ice-carving and snow-sculpture, Inuit cultural events, the Canadian Ski Marathon, snowshoe racing and other entertainment.
✉ Ottawa, Ontario

APRIL
SHAKESPEARE FESTIVAL
www.stratfordfestival.ca
The largest classical repertory company in North America presents about 16 plays (not all Shakespeare) and fringe events until November.
✉ Stratford, Ontario ☎ 800/567-1600

SHAW FESTIVAL
www.shawfest.com
The works of George Bernard Shaw are performed during this festival, which lasts until November.
✉ Niagara-on-the-Lake, Ontario
☎ 800/511-7429, 905/468-2172

JUNE
CANADA DANCE FESTIVAL (CDF)
www.canadadance.ca
Showcases the work of contemporary Canadian choreographers.
✉ Ottawa, Ontario ☎ 613/947-7000 ext 576 ◉ Every two years

JULY
CISCO OTTAWA BLUESFEST
www.ottawabluesfest.ca
The biggest outdoor festival of its kind, over 11 days with international performers on several stages. Main stage on the grounds of City Hall. Also includes Cajun, jazz, zydeco and world music.
✉ Ottawa, Ontario ☎ 613/247-1188

KINGSTON BUSKERS RENDEZVOUS
www.kingstonbuskers.com
Four days featuring street performers from around the world, including magicians, musicians, acrobats and comedians.
✉ Kingston, Ontario

AUGUST
CANADIAN GRAND MASTERS FIDDLE CHAMPIONSHIP
http://canadiangrandmasters.ca
Some of Canada's top fiddle players compete for the national crown.
✉ Nepean, Ottawa, Ontario
☎ 613/821-3641

FERGUS SCOTTISH FESTIVAL AND HIGHLAND GAMES
www.fergusscottishfestival.com
One of North America's oldest and biggest highland games, with pipe bands, Celtic music and traditional sports.
✉ Fergus, Ontario ☎ 519/787-0099

FESTIVAL OF THE ISLANDS
www.festivaloftheislands.com www.gananoque.com/festival
Boat races, musical events, dances and barbecues culminate on the ninth day in a spectacular fireworks display over the St. Lawrence River.
✉ Gananoque, Ontario ☎ 613/382-1562

SEPTEMBER
NIAGARA WINE FESTIVAL
www.niagarawinefestival.com
Celebrating the bounty of Niagara's wineries, with tastings, tours and entertainment.
✉ St. Catharines, Ontario

OCTOBER
OKTOBERFEST
www.oktoberfest.ca
With its German heritage, this is the obvious place to enjoy traditional Oktoberfest celebrations, which continue for nine days.
✉ Kitchener, Ontario ☎ 519/570-4267

DECEMBER
CHRISTMAS LIGHTS ACROSS CANADA
www.canadascapital.gc.ca
More than 70 sites in Ottawa are illuminated, including Parliament Hill. Nearly 300,000 colorful lights are turned on, timed to coincide with similar displays across the nation.
✉ Ottawa, Ontario ☎ 800/465-1867 or 613/239-5000

EATING

PRICES AND SYMBOLS

The restaurants are listed alphabetically within each town. The prices are for a two-course lunch (L) and a three-course à la carte dinner (D). Prices in pubs are for a two-course lunchtime bar meal and a two-course dinner in the restaurant, unless specified otherwise. The wine price is for the least expensive bottle.

For a key to the symbols, ▷ 2.

GANANOQUE
GANANOQUE INN

www.gananoqueinn.com
Historic pub on the St. Lawrence River with a sophisticated formal dining room serving Continental cuisine. The informal pub, with its patio deck, has pasta, burgers and daily specials.
✉ 550 Stone Street South, Gananoque, Ontario, K7G 2A8 ☎ 613/382-2165, 800/465-3101 🕐 May–end Nov daily 7–10, 11.30–2.30, 5–9; Apr and Dec Fri–Sun 7–10, 5.30–10 🖐 L $12, D $26, Wine $27 🚇 Downtown, on waterfront

KINGSTON
CHEZ PIGGY

Hidden away in a downtown courtyard, it has been said that Chez Piggy serves the kind of food you might have in a private home and the place oozes the same kind of warmth and friendliness. The staff are bright and lively. Pick up a copy of the Chez Piggy Cookbook and re-create the experience back home.
✉ 68-R Princess Street, Kingston, Ontario, K7L 1A5 ☎ 613/549-7673 🕐 Mon–Sat 11.30am–midnight, Sun 11am–midnight 🖐 L $10, D $40, Wine $25 🚇 Downtown, at Princess and King (68-R means at the rear)

TOUCAN TANGO

In the heart of downtown, this tapas bar and restaurant has a creative menu combining traditional European and New-World flavors. Innovative touches include the Martini and Manicure packages on Wednesdays. There's a DJ on Fridays and Saturdays.
✉ 331 King Street East, Kingston, Ontario, K7L 3B5 ☎ 613/531-0800 🕐 Daily 11–10 (tapas available until midnight) 🖐 L $20, D $30, Wine $25 🍷 3 🚇 Downtown at King Street East and Brock Street, one block back from waterfront

KLEINBURG
THE DOCTOR'S HOUSE

www.thedoctorshouse.ca
Just the place for a special occasion meal, in a historic house with a superbly restored, elegant dining room, complete with beams and fireplace. In summer you can eat on the patio, overlooking glorious gardens. The menus have many interesting choices, from the starter of Prince Edward Island mussels in a Pernod cream sauce to entrées such as Muscovy duck breast with orange frangelico sauce, or honey mustard and pistachio crusted rack of lamb with roasted garlic and pepper sauce. There are good pasta dishes, and the lunch menu offers simpler entrées, including wraps. Brunch is served on Sundays.
✉ 21 Nashville Road, Kleinburg, Ontario, L0J 1C0 ☎ 905/893-1615 or 416/234-8080 🕐 Tue–Sat 11.30am–3.30pm, 5.30–11pm, Sun 10.30am–4, 5.30–11 🖐 L $30, D $55, Wine $40 🚇 At Nashville Road and Islington Avenue

MIDLAND
LIBRARY RESTAURANT

www.thelibraryrestaurant.ca
In a grand old library building, with its original woodwork and cathedral ceiling intact, this sophisticated restaurant offers beautifully presented classic dishes with modern and international influences. You could start with Indian noodle

salad and fresh vegetables, apple and creamy coconut sauce, then choose a roasted filet of Mahi Mahi with spiced Cuban citrus sauce and mango salsa. Simpler lunch choices (Friday only) might include Thai beef salad or smoked chicken pasta.

✉ 526 Hugel Avenue, Midland, Ontario, L4R 1V7 ☎ 705/528-0100 🕐 Tue–Sat 5.30–9.30 (also Fri 11.30–2) 🍴 L $15, D $35, Wine $24 🚌 Downtown, off King Street, between Dominion Avenue and Yonge Street

SCULLY'S CRAB SHACK
www.scullys.ca
With its Mardi Gras bar, French Quarter dining room and Bayou room, there's no mistaking the New Orleans influences of this fun restaurant overlooking Georgian Bay. For anyone who's left in any doubt, there are also live blues performances to set the mood. Delicious appetizers include coconut shrimp, bacon-wrapped scallops, and quesadillas, and main courses range from fajitas and jambalaya to "Nawlins Catfish" and grilled chicken or steak.

✉ 177 King Street, Town Dock, Midland, Ontario, L4R 4L3 ☎ 705/526-2125 🕐 Mon–Thu 11.30–9, Fri–Sat 11.30–10, Sun 11.30–8 (open longer hours in summer) 🍴 L $25, D $40, Wine $26

NIAGARA FALLS
BETTY'S
www.bettysrestaurant.com
Fronted by a beautiful shrub garden, this friendly restaurant has been serving home-style cooking for more than 30 years. Popular specials include roast beef or turkey, liver and onions, and seafood platters, and the menu also has a big selection of salads, burgers, hot and cold sandwiches, fish and chips and steaks. Breakfast is served (around $5–$7), and there are special deals for seniors and children.

✉ 8921 Sodom Road, Niagara Falls, Ontario, L2E 6S6 ☎ 905/295-4436 🕐 Daily 8am–9pm 🍴 L $12, D $20, Wine $20 🚌 South via Niagara Parkway, then turn right on Highway 47 and left on Highway 116

MONTICELLO GRILLE HOUSE AND WINE BAR
www.monticello.ca
A rare find in this neck of the woods—a stylish restaurant serving Louisiana cuisine. Southern favorites include Creole mussels, chicken and sausage gumbo and pecan-crusted pork loin with apple and jalapeno sauce, or a cut of corn-fed beef cooked over an open-flame grill.

✉ 5645 Victoria Avenue, Niagara Falls, Ontario, L2G 3L5 ☎ 905/357-4888, 800/843-5251 🕐 Daily noon–10 🍴 L $30, D $40, Wine $28 🚌 Just north of Victoria Park, off Clifton Hill

SKYLON
www.skylon.com
At the top of the landmark Skylon Tower, this revolving restaurant does a full circuit every hour, making for perfect views of the nearby falls over a leisurely meal. The menu features soups, salads and pasta alongside upscale classics like filet mignon Béarnaise, seafood medley or chicken breast Cordon Bleu. There are international and Ontario wine lists. The Early Dinner set menu, served at 4.30–5pm only, is good value at $36.50.

✉ 5200 Robinson Street, Niagara Falls, Ontario, L2G 2A3 ☎ 905/356-2651 🕐 Daily 11.30–3, from 4.30 for dinner 🍴 L $45, D $80, Wine $36.95 🚌 Downtown, off Stanley Avenue (Highway 102)

QUEENSTON HEIGHTS RESTAURANT
www.niagaraparks.com
Far from the bustle of the Falls, this is a relaxed and affordable restaurant overlooking the Niagara River. Try the duck confit at dinner time. In summer, there's an outdoor covered patio. Sunday brunch is popular as is the Niagara Grand Dinner Theatre (call 905/357-7818 for details).

✉ 14184 Niagara Parkway, Niagara Falls, Ontario, L0S 1L0 ☎ 905/262-4274 🕐 Late Mar–end Jan daily for lunch and dinner. Hours vary–please phone ahead. Also Sun brunch 🍴 L $25, D $30, Wine $25 🚌 18km (11 miles) north of the Falls on the Niagara Parkway near the Queenston

to Lewiston NY bridge 🚌 Niagara People Mover bus in season

NIAGARA-ON-THE-LAKE
TERROIR LA CACHETTE
www.lacachette.com
Delicious tastes of Provence are created using top-quality Niagara produce in a chic restaurant within the Strewn Winery (the wine list is exclusively Ontario). There's informal dining in the wine bar and a patio.

✉ 1339 Lakeshore Road, Niagara-on-the-Lake, Ontario, L0S 1J0 ☎ 905/468-1222 🕐 Wed–Sun 11.30–3, 5–9 🍴 L $20, D $40, Wine $28 🚌 About 6km (4 miles) west of town

OTTAWA
BLUE NILE
www.bluenileottawa.com
If you are looking for a new experience, this Ethiopian restaurant will probably fit the bill. It's especially good if you're with a group of friends because traditionally a selection of dishes are brought to the table to be shared. Vegetarian, meat and poultry dishes are mostly cooked in a rich sauce (various degrees of spiciness) and served with a unique type of flat-bread. Some involve raw meat, so check it out if this is not to your taste. The kids' menu is more Western.

✉ 577 Gladstone Avenue, Ottawa ☎ 613/321-0774 🕐 Mon 4–10pm, Tue–Sun 11–10 🍴 L $25, D $35, Wine $23 🚌 South of downtown, between Somerset Street and the Trans-Canada, at Percy Street intersection

COURTYARD RESTAURANT
www.courtyardrestaurant.com
Close to the Byward Market, this restaurant is located in an old stone building off Sussex Drive. Specializing in continental cuisine, the fish dishes are excellent. Brunch is offered on Sundays and, in the summer, you can sit outside in the attractive courtyard.

✉ 21 George Street, Ottawa, Ontario, K1N 8W5 ☎ 613/241-1516 🕐 Mon–Sat 11.30–2, 5.30–9.30; Sun brunch 11–2, dinner 5–9 🍴 L $23, D $40, Wine $30

EDOKO

www.edokosteakhouse.com

This is a stylish Japanese restaurant offering the usual entertainment from the chefs at the teppanyaki tables as well as a great sushi bar. Appetizers include various tempura dishes with dips, clear soups, sushi and sashimi selections and there are seemingly endless main courses and combinations that you can mix and match. Specialties include hot tempura seafood and teriyaki.

✉ 64 Queen Street, Ottawa, Ontario, K1P 5C6 ☎ 613/236-8885 ◷ Mon–Fri 11.30–2, 5–10, Sat 5–10 ⚑ L $20, D $40 🚇 Downtown, two blocks back from Parliament Hill, between Elgin and Metcalfe streets

MERLOT

www.merlotottawa.com

A revolving restaurant on the 29th floor of the Marriott Hotel, giving superb views of the city and the Ottawa River—a complete circuit takes about two hours, so come for a leisurely dinner. The Sunday lunch buffet is particularly popular.

✉ Marriott Hotel, 100 Kent Street, Ottawa, Ontario, K1P 5R7 ☎ 613/783-4212 ◷ Daily 6–10, also Sun 10.30–2, 5–9 ⚑ D $30–$40, Wine $33 🚍 1, 2, 4 🚇 Downtown

YANGTZE

Stands out in a long street full of restaurants, not only for the first-rate Chinese food, but also for the illuminated dome high above the entrance. Try the crispy baskets with various fillings and the excellent wonton soup.

✉ 700 Somerset Street West, Ottawa, Ontario, K1R 6P6 ☎ 613/236-0555 ◷ Mon–Thu 11am–midnight, Fri 11am–1am, Sat 10am–1am, Sun 10am–midnight ⚑ L $15, D $23, Wine $20 🚍 2, 85, 316 🚇 Near Cambridge intersection

ZAK'S DINER

www.zaksdiner.com

There's retro-fun to be enjoyed 24-hours a day in this remake of a classic 1950s diner. The breakfast menu is terrific, ranging from healthy smoothies to a massive "Lumberjack's Breakfast" (you can imagine!). Later in the day, there's a huge choice of sandwiches (including deli-style triple-deckers), soups, salads, burgers, and comfort food such as liver and onions, meatloaf with gravy, and fish and chips. Or you could just call in for a coffee with a piece of pie, fudge brownies or a banana split.

✉ 14 Byward Market Square, Ottawa, Ontario, K1N 7A1 ☎ 613/241-2401 ◷ Daily, 24 hours ⚑ L $20, D $30, Wine $18 🚇 Downtown, Byward Market

SAULT STE. MARIE

CESIRA'S

www.cesiras.com

Cesira's has been run for more than 35 years by the Aiudi family (the third generation is at the helm), and one of the reasons for its longevity is the great home-made pasta, which comes in many varieties—six types of lasagne alone. Non-pasta dishes include the classic veal parmigiana, king crab legs and filet mignon and there are vegetarian options too. Low-price meal deals and the great family-friendly atmosphere add to the appeal.

✉ 133 Spring Street, Sault Ste. Marie, Ontario, P6B 4Z9 ☎ 705/949-0600, 877/783-7362 ◷ Mon–Fri 11.30–2.30, 5–10, Sat 5–10 ⚑ L $15, D $40, Wine $27 🚇 Downtown, between Bay and Wellington streets

A THYMELY MANNER

Located in a conversion of an old home, this is widely regarded as the best restaurant in the area. Only the finest natural ingredients are used.

✉ 531 Albert Street East, Sault Ste. Marie, Ontario, P6A 2K3 ☎ 705/759-3262 ◷ Tue–Sat 5.30–11; closed public holidays ⚑ D $38, Wine $27 🚇 Between Spring and Broc

STRATFORD

CHURCH RESTAURANT AND THE BELFRY

Fine dining in the stunning surroundings of a former church, complete with vaulted ceiling and stained-glass windows, carefully lit to create a warm glow around the immaculately set tables. Chef Amédé Lamarche's menu changes every few weeks, but recent offerings have included appetizers such as licorice-crusted veal sweetbreads with honey and salsify, morels and pickled ramps with a milk and licorice reduction, and a main course of Québec rabbit: saddle with lobster and lemongrass, rack with cauliflower and peas, and leg with green curry consommé. Desserts included white chocolate and yogurt mille-feuille with roasted fig marmalade and gingerbread snap. There is a four-plate tasting menu for $90 (or $120 if you include the wine). Also on the premises, the Belfry is a cool, modern space with a simpler menu.

✉ 70 Brunswick Street, Stratford, Ontario, N5A 6V6 ☎ 519/273-3424 ◷ Church: Tue–Sat 5–8.30, Sun 11.30–1.30, 5–8; Belfry: Tue–Thu 11.30–1.30, 5–9.30, Fri–Sat 11.30–1.30, 5–midnight ⚑ Church: L $45, D $75, Wine $30; Belfry: L $25, D $40, Wine $30 🚇 Downtown, two blocks south of Ontario Street at Waterloo Street South

LET THEM EAT CAKE

www.letthemeatcake.ca

With a name like that, how could you do anything but go in? In addition to the tempting treats in the cake display case, there's a huge all-day breakfast menu, soups, salads, wraps and sandwiches, home-made pot pie, and dinner items (after 4pm only) such as roast beef, grilled Asian salmon and pesto chicken tettrazini.

✉ 82 Wellington Street, Stratford, Ontario, N5A 2L2 ☎ 519/273-4774 ◷ Daily 7am–8pm ⚑ L $15, D $27, Wine $15 (half-liter) 🚇 Downtown, south of Victoria Lake between Downie and St Patrick streets

SUDBURY

CULPEPPER'S EATERY

www.sud-biz.com/culpeppersrestaurant

A bright and cheerful atrium overlooks the dining area of this popular restaurant. It has an enormous menu of Italian, Greek and North American food. There's also a children's menu.

1835 Regent Street South, Sudbury, Ontario, P3E 3Z7 ☎ 705/522-2422 Mon–Thu 11–11, Fri–Sat 11am–midnight, Sun 10–10, holidays 4–11 L $10, D $25, Wine $25 501 South End, corner of Paris

TOMMY'S NOT HERE

http://tommysnothere.com

One of Sudbury's classiest restaurants, Tommy's Not Here offers upscale surroundings and an interesting menu with Mediterranean slant. You might start with shrimp Montebello or maple pecan brie, or one of the crisp salads. Main courses might include a classic chicken marsala or veal saltimbocca and there will be prime Canadian steaks and a selection of pasta dishes on the menu too. An interesting wine list includes European, Australian, South African and Canadian labels.

1889 Regent Street, Sudbury, Ontario, P3E 3Z7 ☎ 705/522-2822 Mon–Sat from 4pm D $50, Wine $27 South End, between downtown and the Trans-Canada, near Long Lake Road intersection

THORNHILL
THE OCTOGON

www.octagonrestaurant.com

For a formal, special occasion dinner this place is hard to beat, with its warm-hued, wood-paneled walls dotted with gilt-framed paintings and ornately carved fireplace, stained glass and objets d'art. The dinner menu has a good selection of appetizers, including clam chowder, Greek salad, escargots and oysters, while the main courses offer succulent charcoal broiled steaks, or dishes such as sole meunière, Alaska king crab legs, chicken cooked in white brandy sauce and several upscale versions of the "surf and turf" theme. Lunches are more straightforward and much less pricey.

7529 Yonge Street, Thornhill, Ontario L3T 2B4 ☎ 905/889-8989 Mon–Fri noon–2.30, 5–11, Sat 5–11, Sun 5–10 L $20, D $90, Wine $35 Northern outskirts of Greater Toronto, between Steeles Avenue and Highway 407, near Clarke Avenue intersection

THUNDER BAY
CARIBOU RESTAURANT AND WINE BAR

www.caribourestaurant.com

This is a nice-looking restaurant with a good atmosphere, and the food is both creative and unpretentious, artistically presented with no sacrifice to quantities. The wood oven is put to good use, too, not just for the interesting pizzas but also for maple-glazed salmon with fennel-orange relish, roast rack of lamb with a fresh herb crust and wild boar, simmered in a rich tomato sauce. The simpler lunch menu has pizzas, of course, and dishes like spicy pad thai, crab cakes, pasta and hot sandwiches.

727 Hewitson Street, Thunder Bay, Ontario, P7B 6B5 ☎ 807/628-8588 Mon–Wed 5–10, Thu 11.30–2, 5–11, Fri 11.30–2, 4.30–midnight, Sat 4.30–midnight, Sun 5–9 L $20, D $45, Wine $34 Downtown, just off Harbour Expressway at Balmoral Street

PORT ARTHUR BRASSERIE AND BREWPUB

www.pabrewpub.com

The Port Arthur provides a neighborhood meeting place and supplies it with great beer and food. It's a casual, family-oriented place. Popular dishes include Big G's pizza, quesadillas (tortillas stuffed with cheese and salsa), and fish and chips. There are seven beers to choose from (some seasonal), all brewed on the premises.

901 Red River Road, Thunder Bay, Ontario, P7B 1K3 ☎ 807/767-4415 Sun–Wed 11–10, Thu 11–11, Fri–Sat 11am–midnight L $15, D $28, Wine $16.50 3 Downtown, corner of Red River and Dunant

STAYING

PRICES AND SYMBOLS

Prices are the starting price for a double room for one night, unless otherwise stated. Breakfast is included unless noted otherwise. All the hotels listed accept credit cards unless otherwise stated. Note that rates vary widely throughout the year.

For a key to the symbols, ▷ 2.

GAGANOQUE

STEPHIES BED AND BREAKFAST ON THE RIVER

Overlooking the beautiful Thousand Islands, this is a comfortable and welcoming place under the same ownership as the Irish pub next door. Stylish bedrooms have king- or queen-size beds, Internet access and en-suite bathroom, and there are two suites up in the loft.
✉ 490 Stone Street South, Gananoque, Ontario, K7G 2A4 ☎ 613/382-2542 🕐 May–early Oct 👐 $130 🛈 6 (all no smoking) 💲 🚌 Downtown waterfront, at Water Street

HAMILTON

VISITORS INN

www.visitorsinn.com
Don't be deceived by the name into thinking this is just another chain motel. It is, in fact, a four-star

hotel with a stylish dining room, a swimming pool complex, and exercise room and a range of business services. The rooms have one or two queen-size beds, and there are also a number of suites which have king-size beds and Jacuzzi. There are some efficiency rooms. All have free high-speed Internet access, cordless phone, coffee makers, refrigerators, satellite/cable TV and other amenities.
✉ 649 Main Street West, Hamilton, Ontario, L8S 1A2 ☎ 905/529-6979, 800/387-4620 👐 $111 🛈 60 (47 non-smoking) 💲 🍽 🏊 Indoor 🚌 Corner of Highway 403 and Main Street West

KINGSTON

BELVEDERE

www.hotelbelvedere.com
Built in the 1880s, this mansion has been restored and converted into a pleasant hotel. The accommodation is decorated in restful tones and some of the bathrooms are fitted with a whirlpool bath.
✉ 141 King Street East, Kingston, Ontario, K7L 2Z9 ☎ 613/548-1565, 800/559-0584 👐 $119 🛈 20 (10 non-smoking) 💲 🚌 3 🚌 Downtown, on the waterfront. Near City Hall and University

NIAGARA FALLS

CAIRNGORM BED AND BREAKFAST

www.cairngorm-niagara.com
Spacious and elegant, this charming bed-and-breakfast has a lovely location overlooking the gorge. You can enjoy the view with breakfast on the balcony in summer or have breakfast in your room. The charming bedrooms have a king- or queen-size bed, wireless Internet access and a whirlpool baths in the en-suite bathroom.
✉ 5395 River Road, Niagara Falls, Ontario, L2E 3H1 ☎ 905/354-4237, 888/414-4237 👐 $100 🛈 6 (all no-smoking) 🚌 Just north of Rainbow Bridge

SHERATON FALLSVIEW

www.fallsview.com
The Sheraton Fallsview has the best location in town, directly overlooking both the Horseshoe and American falls. Modern high-rise hotel with several types of spacious rooms and suites, though not all have a view of the falls.
✉ 6755 Fallsview Boulevard, Niagara Falls, Ontario, L2G 3W7 ☎ 905/374-1077, 800/618–9059 👐 $99 🛈 402 (354 non-smoking) 💲 🍽 🏊 Indoor 🚌 6; Niagara Parks People Mover (in summer)

STONE BOUTIQUE SUITES

www.stoneboutiquesuites.com

This place is a shining beacon of modern chic. There are two suites, each self-contained, self-sufficient, and stylishly furnished and decorated. Each has a living room, kitchen and one or two bedrooms, a balcony with a view of the river and a propane barbecue. Some of the art on display is the work of the owner, an accomplished and published illustrator. There is a two-night minimum stay requirement.

✉ 5225 River Road, Niagara Falls, Ontario, L2E 3G9 ☎ 905/357-4366 ✋ $145 ① 2 suites (no smoking) 🅿 North of Rainbow Bridge between Eastwood Crescent and Otter Street

NIAGARA-ON-THE-LAKE
PILLAR AND POST INN

www.vintageinns.com

One of Canada's loveliest and highest rated country inns, dating from 1890, with a long list of guest services and amenities, including 24-hour concierge, valet, babysitting, business facilities, ticket reservations and free shuttle. Individually designed bedrooms combine floral fabrics with dark greens and reds, and each has a Victorian fireplace, large-screen TV, Play Station and Nintendo and bathrobes. The 100 Fountain Spa has undergone a huge refurbishment, and offers a wide range of treatments and pampering services.

✉ 48 John Street West, Niagara-on-the-Lake, Ontario, L0S 1J0 ☎ 905/468-2123, 888/669-5566 ✋ $200 ① 122 🅢 🛁 🏊 Indoor and outdoor 🅿 Middle of town

NOBEL
WINNETOU RESORT

http://holidayjunction.com/winnetou

Snug housekeeping cottages on the rocky shore of Georgian Bay, with a fine sandy beach on site and all kinds of boats, windsurfers and fishing. Available for single nights and weekends, as well as longer stays. In addition to wonderful views, the rustic-style timber cottages have full bathroom and kitchen, and outside barbecue and lawn furniture.

✉ 234 Dillon Road, RR#1, Nobel, Ontario, P0G 1G0 ☎ 705/342-9967, 800/567-4550 ✋ $113 ① 12 units 🏊 🚗 14km (9 miles) north of Parry Sound on Highway 69, then 10km (6 miles) west on Highway 559

OTTAWA
ALBERT HOUSE

www.albertinn.com

Second Empire-style inn, built in 1875 by Canada's chief architect, it is close to all downtown attractions. Bedrooms have old-style furniture and wallpapers, coordinated fabrics, shams and soft lighting. All have private showers or bathrooms; some with whirlpool baths. Also TV, desk, and dataport telephone.

✉ 478 Albert Street, Ottawa, Ontario, K1R 5B5 ☎ 613/236-4479, 1-800/267-1982 ✋ $118 ① 17 (all non-smoking) 🅢 🚌 16, 18, 316; Transitway 95, 97 🚌 Downtown

ARC, THE HOTEL

www.arcthehotel.com

One of Ottawa's top boutique hotels, Arc is just four blocks from the Parliament Buildings and close to shops and National Arts Centre. The bedrooms are stylishly elegant, with muted natural shades and Egyptian cotton bed linen; baths are so deep that you can wallow up to your chin.

✉ 140 Slater Street, Ottawa, Ontario, K1P 5H6 ☎ 613/238-2888, 800/699-2516 ✋ $150 ① 112 (107 non-smoking) 🅢 🛁 🚌 1, 2, 4, 7, 16, 18, 316; transitway: Mackenzie-King 🚌 Between Metcalfe and O'Connor

SAULT STE. MARIE
ALGOMA WATER TOWER INN

www.watertowerinn.com

Independent motor inn with exceptional facilities. Some rooms have a woodburning stove and some have whirlpool baths. Leisure facilities include a feature swimming pool, with kids' wading pool, whirlpool, sauna, and fitness room; the outdoor section consists of a landscaped courtyard with waterfall and rivers.

✉ 360 Great Northern Road, Sault Ste. Marie, Ontario, P6A 5N3 ☎ 705/949-8111, 800/461-0800 ✋ $145 ① 180

🅢 🏊 Indoor and outdoor 🛁 🅿 North edge of town at Great Northern Road (Highway 178) and Second Line (Highway 550) intersection

SUDBURY
PARKER HOUSE INN

www.parkerhouseinns.com

The renowned hospitality and good cooking brings visitors back to this elegant home, convenient to downtown, Science North and Dynamic Earth. All bedrooms have queen-size beds (some four-posters), private bathrooms, and facilities that include TV, VCR and modem point.

✉ 259 Elm Street, Sudbury, Ontario, P3C 1V5 ☎ 705/674-2442, 888/250-4453 ✋ $85 ① 8 (all non-smoking) 🅢 🅿 Downtown

THUNDER BAY
PRINCE ARTHUR

www.princearthur.on.ca

This hotel has the best view in the city, overlooking Lake Superior and the marina, and it's right in the heart of the action. Rooms are in plain, modern style, with light-wood furniture, big beds, satellite TV, and no distinguishing features to speak of; executive suites have more of the same in their roomy lounge area.

✉ 17 North Cumberland Street, Thunder Bay, Ontario, P7A 4K8 ☎ 807/345-5411, 1-800/267-2675 ✋ $100 ① 120 🅢 🏊 Indoor 🅿 Downtown, on the waterfront

WHITE FOX INN

www.whitefoxinn.com

Elegant mansion on a wooded estate. Rooms come in three sizes and have a combination of plain, pastel shades and interesting furniture, including hardcarved Indonesian hardwood pieces. They each have a fireplace and jet tub, and in addition to the usual TV/VCR, each room has a mini stereo and telephone with modem point.

✉ 1345 Mountain Road, Thunder Bay, Ontario, P7J 1C3 ☎ 807/577-3699, 800/603-3699 ✋ $110 ① 9 🅢 🅿 2km (1.2 miles) southeast of the city, just off Highway 61

THE PRAIRIES

The heartland of Canada is often accused of being flat and featureless—justifiably so in places. Going from east to west, the Prairies provinces are Manitoba, Saskatchewan and Alberta, with wheatfields that fill the horizons giving way to cattle ranches and oil fields. Nevertheless, if you know where to look, there are fascinating discoveries to be made here.

The northern bulk of Manitoba is uninhabited tundra, but up here is Churchill, famous for its polar bear watching tours. Look at a map and you'll be struck by how much water the province has. Lake Winnipeg is the fifth largest in the country, and running parallel to it are lakes Manitoba, Winnipegosis and Cedar, with countless satellite lakes. Winnipeg, the provincial capital, at the geographic center of North America, is a cultured place, with world-class arts facilities and a mix of modern and historic areas around the confluence of its two rivers.

Saskatchewan produces more than half of the wheat grown in Canada and averages the highest levels of sunshine in Canada. It also produces all of the RCMPs, since it is home to their training academy. Here, too, the dead-flat rumor is put to rest by the Cypress Hills in the southwest and Moose Mountain. The provincial capital, Regina, and the other big city, Saskatoon, are prosperous, vibrant places with plenty to see and do, and there are lots of historic sites throughout the province.

Alberta is to Canada what Texas is to the US—a booming province rich on oil but still hanging on to its wild-west cowboy culture in places. Pick-up trucks and stetsons aside, it's a confidently modern province with a go-ahead capital, Edmonton, and lively second city, Calgary. Add to this the famous Badlands' dinosaur heritage and the fabulous Rocky Mountains looming in the west…and you are still only scratching the surface.

BATOCHE NATIONAL HISTORIC SITE

www.pc.gc.ca

High on a bluff above the South Saskatchewan River, Batoche was the stronghold of the Métis people (a mixed French and First Nations population) and the place where they made their final stand. From here their leader, Louis Riel, declared a provisional regional government during the rebellion over land titles in 1885. Government forces were sent to quell the uprising, the insurgents were quashed and many Métis died.

A few original buildings remain on the site, which holds a special place in the history of the nation, and in 2007 an 1896 Métis home opened after restoration. Staff in period costume act out the rôle of the Métis on the site, and there's a modern interpretive center.

✚ 402 J16 ✉ P.O. Box 999, Rosthern, Saskatchewan, S0K 3R0 ☎ 306/423-6227 ◷ Early May–end Sep daily 9–5 ◔ Adult $7.05, child (6–16) $3.40, family $16.25 ▢ 🏛

CALGARY

▷ 256–259.

CARDSTON

This tiny town in southern Alberta has one major claim to fame—a monumental Mormon tabernacle (only grounds and visitor center open to non-Mormons), the largest outside the US, dedicated in 1923. A group of Mormons left Utah in 1887 and founded a settlement here. Today the town of single-story homes is overshadowed by the temple.

The Remington-Alberta Carriage Centre (daily) has one of the largest collections of horse-drawn vehicles in North America, from pioneer wagons to elegant carriages.

The town's most famous daughter was actress Fay Wray, who starred in the movie *King Kong* (1933) as the girl with the gorilla on top of the Empire State Building.

✚ 401 F17 ℹ On Highway 2, south of Fort MacLeod, Alberta, T0K 0K0 ☎ 403/653-2499

Above *A horse and carriage at the Remington-Alberta Carriage Centre*
Opposite page *A hiker walks along a trail in Cypress Hills Interprovincial Park*

CHURCHILL

www.churchill.ca

Self-styled "Polar Bear and Beluga Whale Capital of the World," Churchill sits on the shores of Hudson Bay at the mouth of the Churchill River. The town was established in 1929, though the first European, Danish explorer Jens Munck, arrived in 1619. The Hudson's Bay Company built a post here in 1717 to trade and store furs for shipment to England.

However, it's not just polar bears that are the drawcard here. Churchill is a veritable wildlife paradise, with beluga whales arriving during the summer, seals resident year-round, caribou migrating through the region twice a year, and over 250 species of birds nesting in the summer months. And in winter, the spectacular aurora borealis lights up the town's night sky.

A short boat trip across the river is Fort Prince of Wales (Jul–Aug daily), constructed by the Hudson's Bay Company (1731–71) as its trading post and defense post. The Eskimo Museum (Jun–early Nov Mon pm, Tue–Sat all day; rest of year Mon, Sat pm), in town, is devoted to Inuit history and lifestyle.

✚ 408 M13 ℹ Churchill Chamber of Commerce, 211 Kelsey Boulevard, Churchill, Manitoba, R0B 0E0 ☎ 204/675-2022 ◷ Mon, Wed, Fri 5–8pm; longer hours during whale and polar bear season

CYPRESS HILLS INTERPROVINCIAL PARK

www.cypresshills.com

Rising 600m (1,968ft) from the surrounding prairie, Cypress Hills are the highest land between the Rockies and Labrador. The 18,400ha (45,448-acre) lush forested environment is an oasis amid millions of hectares of grassland. It supports rare wildflowers (best in spring) and more than 200 species of birds, and at its heart is Fort Walsh National Historic Site (▷ 261), birthplace of the Mounties.

In Saskatchewan, the 22km (13.6-mile) unmade single-track Gap Road, leading through the heart of the park, is similar to that used by the first Mounties and before them the early settlers, while Loch Leven is home to the park administration. In the Alberta sector the major settlement is Elkwater, a pretty town on the banks of Elkwater Lake. From here it's 5km (3 miles) or so to Horseshoe Canyon for panoramic views of the prairies to the north, while Head of the Mountain offers views south over rthe border into Montana.

✚ 401 G17 ✉ 27km (17 miles) south of Maple Creek, Saskatchewan, S0N 1N0 ◔ Day pass $7 ℹ Loch Leven, ☎ 306/662-5411 ◷ Jun–early Sep Mon–Thu 8–8, Fri–Sun 8am–10pm. ℹ Elkwater ☎ 403/893-3777 ◷ Mid-May to early Sep Mon–Fri 10–6

THE BADLANDS

INFORMATION
www.traveldrumheller.com
www.dinosaurvalley.com
www.canadianbadlands.com
⊞ 401 G16 🚹 Drumheller Tourism,
P.O. Box 999, 60 – 1st Avenue West,
Drumheller, Alberta, T0J 0Y0
☎ 1-866/823-8100

INTRODUCTION
The Badlands region is full of dramatic arid landscapes and stretch roughly north to south through Alberta in the region of the Red Deer River Valley. They have a stark beauty, with ocher-hued soil that reflects the light and changes aspect constantly, glowing as the sun strikes it. The soil is dusty dry in summer and thick mud when it rains, and little grows here—hence it is bad for agriculture, it was bad for the early pioneers to travel through, and it can be bad underfoot for tourists in wet weather. Drumheller, the "dinosaur capital of the world," makes an excellent base. As well as the Dinosaur Trail (▷ 254), there's a driving loop and numerous self-guiding walks in the Dinosaur Provincial Park. Best of all, though, are the excellent ranger-led hikes and the park-bus tour, with a fascinating commentary.

NATURAL EROSION
Centuries of rain and river erosion in the Badlands have created some fascinating landscape features, including "rills"—narrow crevices incised down a hillside by rivers of rain—and the extraordinary "hoodoos," towers of soil topped by a harder stone. The latter are formed when rain washes away the surrounding softer soil but the soil beneath the harder capstone is protected. The area has a rich seam of coal, and over 120 mines were active at the peak of the industry, between the two world wars. Mining has declined in the last 30 years, resulting in the abandonment of once-thriving settlements. However, along with the discovery of the coal, another discovery was made that has kept

Above *The Dinosaur Provincial Park*

the area buzzing with visitors and scientists. In 1884, one Joseph Burr Tyrrell came to the area to map the coal deposits and happened upon the remains of a dinosaur. It was the first of many found in the area, and also a previously unknown type that is now known as Albertosaurus. The soft rocks of the Badlands were later discovered to have preserved one of the largest deposits of dinosaur bones (and some eggs) in the world, and paleontologists flocked in to dig them up. Controls had to be imposed, to prevent damage at the hands of the untrained, and to stop the finds from being shipped away to museums around the world. Today it is illegal to remove anything from the ground.

The strange landscape has also brought film crews to the area, and you may have seen it in such movies as *The Virginian, Unforgiven, Superman, Shanghai Noon, Ararat* and—appropriately—*Where the Dinosaurs Roam.*

WHAT TO SEE

THE ROYAL TYRRELL MUSEUM

www.tyrrellmuseum.com

This is one of the finest museums of its kind in the world, named after Joseph Burr Tyrrell, who made the first dinosaur fossil discoveries here in 1884. It houses a paleontology collection covering a staggering 3.9 billion years, whose most dramatic specimens date from the Mesozoic Era. There are 11 impressive exhibition areas in the museum. The Dinosaur Hall is a particular highlight, where around 40 skeletons are on display, some free standing, others tantalizingly shown on a rock surface as if they had just been found. Here you can see an Albertosaurus, the always compelling Tyrannosaurus rex and other weird and wonderful dinosaurs. Dioramas and replicas of the landscape make a fitting setting, and the night-sky effect of the lofty ceiling adds to the atmosphere.

The Age of Mammals displays skeletons from the Cenozoic era, tracing the evolution of many creatures we know today, while the Ice Ages exhibit explores the time of frozen wastes and woolly mammoths. In Cretaceous Alberta the museum has re-created the home of a pack of Albertosaurus of 70 million years ago, and another highlight is the Lords of the Land exhibit, collecting together some of the most significant finds of all. The Devonian Reef exhibit portrays the period from between 418 to 355 million years ago, when the Badlands formed part of the seabed. It is particularly fascinating because this was the era when fish first began to develop legs and emerge from the oceans, and the museum's re-creation of a reef environment, together with thousands of models, is an excellent representation of this important evolutionary progression. It is also interesting to learn that the microscopic

Above *The Royal Tyrrell Museum houses a collection of over 800 fossils and 35 dinosaur skeletons*
Bottom left *The weird and wonderful hoodoos in the Badlands*
Below *A giant Tyrannosaurus rex in downtown Drumheller*

» Don't miss the viewpoints from the top of the Horsethief and Horseshoe canyons.
» Don't try walking Badlands trails after heavy rain as they'll have a layer of slippy mud on them.

organic remains from those days laid the foundation for Alberta's current economic prosperity by transforming into oil and gas.

The Burgess Shale display continues the watery theme. It represents an area of the Canadian Rockies now protected as the Yoho National Park (▷ 317), which was also at one time beneath the ocean. Models of some of the weird and wonderful creatures that inhabited the area (at 12 times their actual size) are realistically arranged around the walk-in diorama.

New in 2008, the Great Minds Fresh Finds gallery gets right to the core of the museum's story, focusing on its scientists and their most memorable finds.

Budding paleontologists will enjoy the interactive stations in the science hall, and perhaps be inspired by watching scientists at work coaxing recent finds out of their rocky jackets. After you've seen the finds gloriously displayed, this part of the museum shows just how much painstaking work goes into revealing just one tiny bone. The museum offers a one-hour guided hike entitled Seven Wonders of the Badlands, an easy trail along a gravel path but with much to discover along the way (mid-May to late Jun, Sat and Sun 11.30 and 3.30; late Jun–end Aug daily 11.30 and 3.30; Sep daily 2.30). Several other trails begin outside the museum, including some suitable for bicycles.
✉ Highway 838, Midland Provincial Park, Drumheller, Alberta, T0J 0Y0 ☎ 403/823-7707, 888/440-4240 🕓 Mid-May to early Sep daily 9–9; early Sep to mid-Oct daily 10–5; mid-Oct to mid-May Tue–Sun and holiday Mon 10–5 💵 Adult $10, child (7–17) $6, family $30 🎧 65-min audio guides in various languages: $4 ($7 for two) 🖥 🏛

DINOSAUR PROVINCIAL PARK

Just two hours' drive from the city of Calgary, 110km (68 miles) southeast of Drumheller, the pleasant prairie grasslands suddenly give way to a startling moonscape of dry, barren land with odd pinnacles jutting skyward, some shaped like giant mushrooms, weird creatures or even humans who have been petrified without warning. Come at sunrise or sunset, when the orange glow highlights the more prominent features and it is quite magical. The landscape itself would, in fact, be enough of an attraction, but for some 65 million years it held a secret only revealed since the late 1880s—a remarkable treasure trove of dinosaur skeletons, bones and eggs. Around 300 skeletons have so far been unearthed in what is now the Dinosaur Provincial Park and a UNESCO World Heritage Site, and excavations continue.
✉ P.O. Box 60, Patricia, Alberta, T0J 2K0 ☎ 403/378-4342 🕓 Visitor center: mid-May to early Sep daily 8.30–7, early Sep–early Oct daily 10–5, early Oct to mid-Nov Wed–Fri 9–4, Sat–Sun 10–5, mid-Nov to end Mar Mon–Fri 9–4 💵 Free, but fees for bus tours and talks

Below left *A conservator at the Royal Tyrrell Museum in Drumheller*
Below right *A dinosaur guards the museum entrance*

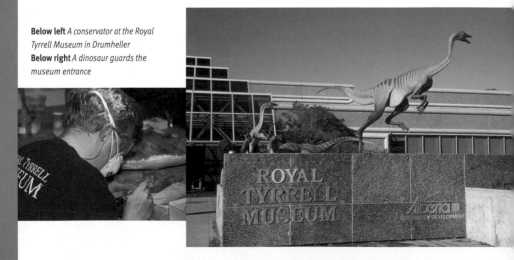

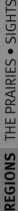

PARK VISITOR CENTRE

In 1987 the Royal Tyrrell Museum opened a field station within the park as a base for its scientists. You can learn about their work at one of the Park Visitor Centre's fossil lab talks (Jul–Aug, Tue–Sun at 2pm) and take a look at some almost complete skeletons in situ, protected under glass in four display areas. A series of guided hikes and bus tours are provided by the park to help you get the best out of your visit. Most of the hikes last for 2.5 to 3.5 hours, some more strenuous than others, and there is one full-day expedition for experienced hikers only. Don't expect to see actual excavations in progress—they are in the more remote areas—but you will see fossils and former excavation sites.

TAKE THE TOUR

The easiest way to get a good overview of the park is on the 2-hour Badlands Bus Tour. Contrary to first impressions, there is nature and wildlife in the Badlands, with cottonwood, willow and berry bushes along the riverbanks, and cacti and sage in the arid areas. Wildlife includes coyotes, antelope, rabbits and the less appealing scorpions, rattlesnakes and black widow spiders. Overhead you might spot golden eagles and prairie falcons as well as numerous smaller species. The remarkable Dinosaur Provincial Park, around 110km (68 miles) southeast of Drumheller, is a UNESCO World Heritage Site where paleontologists have unearthed in excess of 300 dinosaur skeletons. There are five interpretive hiking tours and a driving loop past some of the more interesting areas. Otherwise, take a guided hike or a bus tour (May–Oct). The Royal Tyrell Museum (▷ 253–254) has a field station where scientists are working on new discoveries. Four display areas show nearly complete skeletons in situ.

Above *Real and replica dinosaur skeletons at the Royal Tyrrell*
Below *You can climb the World's Largest Dinosaur for great views*

✚ 401 G16 ✉ P.O. Box 60, Patricia, Alberta, T0J 2K0 ☎ 403/378-4342 ⊕ Visitor Centre: mid-May to early Sep daily 8.30–7, early Sep–early Oct daily 10–5, early Oct to mid-Nov Wed–Fri 9–4, Sat–Sun 10–5, mid-Nov to end Mar Mon–Fri 9–4 ✋ Free. Fees for tours and talks

CALGARY

INFORMATION

www.tourismcalgary.com

✚ 401 F16 ℹ 200–238, 11th Avenue S.E., Calgary, Alberta, T0G 0X8

☎ 403/263-8510, 800/661-1678; also at the Calgary Tower

Above *Calgary skyline at twilight*

INTRODUCTION

Calgary is where the Prairies meet the Rockies. It sits on prairie grassland on the banks of the Bow River, and takes its influence from the cowboy culture to the east, where today thousands of miles of flat wheatland stretch away. To the west, the jagged peaks of the Rockies rise out of the horizon, their snowy caps glinting on sunny days. Calgary's compact downtown core is a concentration of high-rise towers, reflecting the city's thriving economy, with an efficient light rail transit system running through its heart. The main pedestrian focus is Stephen Street Mall, which links several modern shopping malls with older streetside emporia, cafés and restaurants. To combat the sometimes severe winter weather, shopping malls are linked to office blocks by indoor walkways, either above street level or underground; the downside of this is that the outside streets can seem a little empty and lacking in atmosphere.

Calgary was established very rapidly, initially around the site of Fort Calgary, built in 1875 just to the east of today's downtown, then later around the train station, which allowed trade to flourish and the population to grow. Beef was the major commodity, with large ranches dominating the surrounding areas; this gave way to wheat, and then to oil. Since the 1970s the city has grown, thanks to its oil and natural gas revenues, to become the major commercial hub of Alberta.

WHAT TO SEE
CALGARY TOWER
www.calgarytower.com

The tower offers one of the best panoramic views in Canada, extending from the snowcapped Rockies to the expanse of prairie. You can see the prairie while enjoying a meal in the revolving Panorama Dining Room. The tower is 190m (623ft) high and the top of the observation tower stands 1,228m (4,028ft) above sea-level. There's also a thrilling glass floor experience. The transparent area is 11m (36ft) long and more than 1.2m (4ft) wide and, with a glass wall in front, it can feel as if you are levitating high in the sky.

✉ 101 9th Avenue S.W., Calgary, Alberta, T2P 1J9 ☎ 403/266-7171 🕐 Daily hours vary seasonally; observation deck may be closed for special events 💲 Adult $12.95, child (under 17) $9.95, family $37

FORT CALGARY HISTORIC PARK
www.fortcalgary.com

The original Fort Calgary, established in 1875, served as a barracks for the North West Mounted Police, who were sent to Calgary specifically to put a stop to whiskey trading. The fort, demolished in 1914, has been reconstructed using period tools and techniques. The historic park brings history to life through interactive interpretation, exhibits, performances and activities. Visitors can even check out how they look in a Northwest Mounted Police uniform and find out how it feels to be inside one of the cells. There is an interpretive center with exhibits about Calgary from 1875 to the 1940s, plus the 1875 Fort site, the Deane House Historic Site and 16ha (40 acres) of riverside park and pathways.

✉ 750 9th Avenue S.E., Calgary, Alberta, T2G 5E1 ☎ 403/290-1875 🕐 Daily 9–5 all year 💲 Adult $10.75, child (3–6) $4.75, (7–17) $6.75

GLENBOW MUSEUM
www.glenbow.org

This is western Canada's largest museum, designed originally around the collections of local entrepreneur Eric Harvie, who bequeathed them to the city in 1966. The museum is famed for its treatment of First Nations exhibits. Go up to the third floor for the excellent Blackfoot Gallery—Niitsitapiisinni: Our Way of Life, which traces the history and culture of the people who lived in the area for centuries before the arrival of the Europeans. Members of the Blackfoot Nation have been deeply involved in the setting up and development of this gallery,

Above left *You can see the snowcapped Rockies from the Calgary Tower*
Above right *Costumed interpreters at Fort Calgary Historic Park*

and their story not only delves into their past on the northwest plains and inter-action with newcomers to their land, but also explains how their traditions still play an important part in daily life. On the same floor, Native Cultures from the Four Directions brings together art and artifacts from other original inhabitants, including Inuit and Northwest Coast nations. Before leaving the third floor, be sure to visit Mavericks: An Incorrigible History of Alberta, focusing on the sto-ries of 48 people who helped to shape Alberta. The museum's second floor has a collection of Asian sculptures, reflecting the heritage of more recent arrivals who are adding to the diverse character of the province. Up on the fourth floor there is Where Symbols Meet, relating aspects of West African achievement, and Warriors—A Global Journey Through Five Centuries, exploring various cul-tures and their approach to war. There is also a glittering mineralogy exhibition..
✉ 130 9th Avenue S.E., Calgary, Alberta, T2G 0P3 ☎ 403/268-4100 ⊗ Daily 9–5 ✋ Adult $14, child (7–17) $9, family $28

OLYMPIC STADIUM

www.canadaolympicpark.ca
In 1988, Calgary hosted the XV Winter Olympics, and this stadium was built to the west of the city. Today, it houses the Olympic Hall of Fame, with film footage and displays including a virtual reality hockey shoot-out, and serves as a winter sports center. The Olympic Park is an important training center for athletes and a recreational facility for residents and visitors, with a summer chairlift and activities including bobsleigh rides, mountain biking and mini golf.
✉ 88 Canada Olympic Road S.W., Calgary, Alberta, T3B 5R5 ☎ 403/247-5452 ⊗ May–end Sep Mon–Fri 8am–9pm, Sat–Sun 8–5.30; Nov–end Mar Mon–Fri 9–9, Sat–Sun 9–5; Apr–end May daily 8–5.30 🎧 Audio tours

CALGARY ZOO

www.calgaryzoo.org
This complex occupies 32ha (79 acres) on the banks of the Bow River east of the city and plays an important role in wildlife conservation. As well as animals from around the world, it has species found in the wilds of Canada. There is a primates exhibit; a Eurasia exhibit, including tigers and snow leopards; the Prehistoric Park, with life-size dinosaurs and a model volcano; and a tropical garden with butterflies and birds. Destination Africa includes a rainforest and Africa savannah, with appropriate wildlife. There is a full daily program of nature

Top left *Calgary Tower offers the best all-round view of the city*
Top right *The Glenbow Museum has displays relating to the early pioneers who conquered the West*

talks that focus on particular species. The zoo also runs education programs, for adults, children and families, which get you behind the scenes and closer to the animals. Register early for these because they are extremely popular.

✉ 1300 Zoo Road N.E., Calgary, Alberta, T2E 7V6 ☎ 403/232-9300 🕐 Daily 9–6 ✋ Adult $18, child (3–12) $10, (13–17) $12 HLRT: Zoo 🖥 🏛

ART GALLERY OF CALGARY
www.artgallerycalgary.org
The facades of two historic downtown buildings give way to an interior that is totally modern, with spacious galleries showcasing contemporary art. There is no permanent collection, but between 15 and 20 exhibitions a year show works of known and emerging artists, including travelling exhibitions from the major national galleries. There is also a program of music by local performers.

✉ 117 8th Avenue S.W., Calgary, Alberta T2P 1B4 ☎ 403/770-1350 🕐 Tue–Sat 10–5 (also 5–9pm first Thu of every month) ✋ Adult $5, child/student (over 6) $2.50, under 6 free; $2 noon–1pm Mon–Fri

HERITAGE PARK HISTORIC VILLAGE
www.heritagepark.ca
At nearly 27ha (67 acres), this is Canada's largest living historic village, taking you back to the Calgary of the early 20th century. The park has more than 150 buildings with a feel of the old West, and is populated by costumed "citizens." Main Street is lined with saloons, stores and tack merchants from c1910, and there's an antique midway (funfair) and a working forge. You can travel back to the halcyon days of the Canadian Pacific Railway on a locomotive, or take a carriage ride through town. And between 9am and 10am you can get a free Stampede Breakfast of cowboy-style barbecue and beans. The new Heritage Town Squarebrings the park up to the 1930s and 1940s era, complete with an old train station, transportation museum and mercantile exhibit.

✉ 1900 Heritage Drive S.W., Calgary, Alberta, T2V 2X3 ☎ 403/268-8500 🕐 Mid-May to early Sep daily 9–5; early Sep–end Oct Sat–Sun 9–5 ✋ Adult $15 ($25 including rides), child (3–17) $10 ($20 including rides), family $49 (plus $10 per person for rides) 🚆 LRT: Heritage, then shuttle bus 🍽 🏛

MORE TO SEE
PRINCE'S ISLAND PARK
Set on an artificial island in the Bow River, just off Eau Claire Market, Prince's Island is Calgary's urban park. There are formal gardens (best in the spring and summer) and lawns, hiking, bicycling and in-line skating trails, and canoe rental in the summer. Sections of deciduous woodland are home to coyotes, raccoons and other wild urban dwellers.

TIPS
» If you have children in tow, check out www.childfriendly.ca for a directory of kid-friendly businesses in Calgary, including accommodations, restaurants, attractions, entertainment, shopping, events and places that rent equipment such as strollers (pushchairs), car seats, travel cots, toys and even snowsuits.
» Calgary is a great city for cycling, with some 500km (311 miles) of cycle paths. You can pick up the Calgary Pathway and Bikeway Map from the City of Calgary Planning Information Centre on the 4th floor of the Municipal Building, 800 Macleod Trail SE, or at any Calgary Co-op store (location detailed at www.calgarycoop.com), or download it from the city website (www.calgary.ca).

Below left *Night falls on the city skyline*
Below right *The Calgary Stampede is one of Canada's most exciting annual events*

www.edmonton.com

401 F15 Edmonton Tourism, 9990 Jasper Avenue, 3rd Floor, Edmonton, Alberta, T5J 0Y9 780/424-9191, 1-800/463-4667

EDMONTON

Edmonton, the most northerly of Canada's major cities, originally grew around a Hudson's Bay Company post called Edmonton House, founded in 1795 to trade in furs with the local Cree and Blackfoot. At the end of the 19th century, the population doubled with the Klondike Gold Rush. In 1905, Alberta entered the Canadian Confederation and Edmonton was chosen as the provincial capital. In 1912 it amalgamated with the nearby town of Strathcona—today an area of early 20th-century architecture with one-of-a-kind boutiques, cafés, restaurants, antiques markets and theaters.

In downtown Edmonton, City Hall is an interesting modern glass structure built for the city's centennial in 1992. Other buildings flanking Sir Winston Churchill Square (the city's arts district) include the Art Gallery, the Citadel Theatre and the Francis Winspear Centre for Music, home to the Edmonton Symphony Orchestra. To the west is the Royal Alberta Museum (daily 9–5), which has a range of galleries explaining the natural and social history of the province, with particular emphasis on First Nations culture.

South of the river, just across from downtown on A Street, is the Muttart Conservatory (Mon–Fri 9–5.30, Sat 11–5.30), where tropical and exotic gardens are housed in a surreal collection of glass pyramids that were designed by Peter Hemingway in the early 1970s.

ALBERTA LEGISLATIVE ASSEMBLY

www.assembley.ab.ca

West of downtown is the Alberta Legislative Assembly, an imposing construction of 1913 with a dome and portico.

97 Avenue and 107 Street 780/427-2826 LRT Grandlin Daily tours from visitor center on 107th Street: May to mid-Oct hourly 9–12, half-hourly 12.30–4; rest of year Mon–Fri hourly 9–3, Sat–Sun and holidays hourly 12–4

FORT EDMONTON PARK

www.ftedmontonpark.com

Fort Edmonton was the earliest settlement here, and this re-creation takes you back to the founding of the community.

Fox Drive and Whitemud Freeway, Edmonton, Alberta 780/496-8787 Mid-May to end Jun Mon–Fri 10–4, Sat–Sun and holidays 10–6; Jul–end Aug daily 10–6, Sep Sun 10–6 Adult $13.25, child (2–12) $6.75, (13–17) $10, family $40

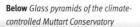
Below *Glass pyramids of the climate-controlled Muttart Conservatory*

FORT BATTLEFORD NATIONAL HISTORIC SITE

www.pc.gc.ca

Headquarters of the North West Mounted Police from 1876 until 1924, when it was abandoned, Fort Battleford has been restored to offer an insight into the role of the 19th-century Mountie in a troubled and developing land. In 1885, during the Métis uprising, when First Nations warriors converged on Battleford, the stockade provided refuge to more than 500 settlers. Standing firm against its attackers, it was in part instrumental in the uprising's failure.

Today, several of the original buildings have been restored and equipped in the style of the times. The barracks now house an interpretive center, with photographs, documents and other objects that bring the history to life, while costumed staff act as Mounties going about their daily duties. The new Visitor Centre, while blending with existing buildings, is a model of sustainable building, using solar, wind and geothermal energy.
✚ 402 H16 ✉ P.O. Box 70, Battleford, Saskatchewan, S0M 0E0 ☎ 306/937-2621 🕐 Mid-May to early Sep daily 9–5 ✋ Adult $7.50, child (6–16) $3.50, family $17.60 📷 🏛

FORT WALSH NATIONAL HISTORIC SITE

www.pc.gc.ca

Set in the lee of rolling hills and woodland on the banks of Battle Creek, Fort Walsh was an important center of law and order, and of Canadian justice. From 1878 to 1883 it was a North West Mounted Police post, and a base for their efforts to control the illicit whiskey trade from the US. When Chief Sitting Bull and a band of Sioux warriors escaped here across the US border after the Battle of Little Big Horn in 1876, the Mounties, under James Walsh (after whom the fort is named), controlled the situation. Eventually, Walsh persuaded Sitting Bull to head back over the border to life on a reservation.

Visitors can take a tour of the buildings, the townsite, two cemeteries, and the Farwell Trading Post—a reconstructed 1872 whiskey-trading post. Costumed staff re-create the pioneering atmosphere of the time.
✚ 401 G17 ✉ P.O. Box 278, Maple Creek, Saskatchewan, S0N 1N0 ☎ 306/662-3590 (May–end Oct), 306/662-2645 (off season) 🕐 Mid-May to early Sep daily 9.30–5.30 ✋ Adult $9.10, child (6–16) $4.40, family $20.10 📷

HEAD-SMASHED-IN BUFFALO JUMP

www.head-smashed-in.com

Where the foothills of the Rockies meet the Great Plains northwest of Fort Macleod (18km/11 miles, via Highway 2 and Highway 785), the bluntly named Head-Smashed-In safeguards one of the oldest, largest and best-preserved buffalo jumps in existence, listed as a UNESCO World Heritage Site in 1981. The jump can be viewed from the top and the bottom. For over 5,500 years buffalo were driven to their deaths over this precipice to provide food, clothing and bone tools for the Native Plains people. Despite the popular image of hundreds of dead buffalo, tribes are believed to have killed only as many animals as they needed for survival.

The seven-level visitor center is a remarkable work of architecture, built into the hillside with a facade that resembles eroded rock. Skylights on the hilltop bring natural light into the interior, where you begin at the top level and trace the plains ecology, the lives of the Plains nation and the way they hunted, ending at the tableau of life-size buffalo standing fearfully on a cliff-edge.

Continuing downward, further galleries deal with the arrival of Europeans and their impact, and a film about the archeological program that runs here.
✚ 401 F17 ✉ Box 1977, Fort Macleod, Alberta T0L 0Z0 ☎ 403/553-2731 🕐 Mid-May to mid-Sep daily 9–6; rest of year 10–5 ✋ Adult $9, child (7–17) $5, family $22 📷 🏛

Above *Fort Battleford National Historic Site*

REGINA
▷ 262.

RIDING MOUNTAIN NATIONAL PARK

www.pc.gc.ca

At the meeting place of three distinct landscapes—deciduous forest, boreal forest and aspen parkland—that meld over part of the Manitoba Escarpment, Riding Mountain is home to a wide variety of wildlife and plants. Wasagaming, the park's low-key main townsite, sits on the southern shore of Clear Lake, the largest stretch of water here and the focus of summer watersports and fishing. Over 400km (248 miles) of hiking trails make this one of the most accessible parks in western Canada, and back-country trails are open to mountain bikers. Anishinabe Village at Shawenequanape Kipichewin on Lake Katherine (mid-May to mid-Sep) offers the opportunity to experience First Nations culture at first hand and to sleep out in a tepee. The park is home to moose, bear, wolves, elk and plenty of birds, and there is a captive herd of bison. The famous naturalist and writer Grey Owl worked here as a keeper in the early 1930s.
✚ 403 K17 ✉ Wasagaming, Manitoba, R0J 2H0 ☎ 204/848-7275 🕐 Park: late Jun–Aug daily; spring and fall hours vary. Closed winter. Visitor Centre: Jul–late Aug daily 9.30–8; late May–end Jun and late Aug to mid-Oct daily 9.30–5.30 ✋ Day passes: adult $6.80, child (6–16) $3.40, family $16.60

INFORMATION

www.tourismregina.com

✚ 402 J17 ℹ️ Tourism Regina,
Highway 1 East, P.O. Box 3335,
Regina, Saskatchewan, S4P 3H1
☎ 306/789-5099, 800-661-5099

REGINA

The capital of Saskatchewan, Regina—named in honor of Queen Victoria—rises up out of a vast area of wheat-producing prairie as if out of nowhere. The city was founded in 1882 as the new provincial capital, replacing the original capital, Battleford, farther north. Located where the new Canadian Pacific Railway crossed the Wascana Creek, Regina was seen as a gesture of validation for the railroad and a nod toward the importance of communications, but the decision caused a great deal of controversy at the time. The new capital was incorporated as a city in 1903 and Saskatchewan became a province in 1905. In 1912 a tornado destroyed it, and what is seen today is the redevelopment that followed the disaster. Regina is the home of the Royal Canadian Mounted Police.

WASCANA CENTRE

South of the largely unremarkable downtown area is the real heart of Regina, the Wascana Centre, one of Canada's largest urban parks. It's a focus for all sorts of outdoor activities, from birding to picnics, but several museums and galleries are also here. The Royal Saskatchewan Museum (May–Labor day daily 9–5.30; rest of year 9–4.30) has three main galleries: Earth Sciences (geology), Life Sciences (ecology) and an interesting First Nations Gallery. The collection in the MacKenzie Art Gallery (Sat–Wed 10–4.30, Thu–Fri 10–9) includes regional, national and international works, including famous names such as Henry Moore and Andy Warhol, plus more than 650 contributions by Saskatchewan artists. The Saskatchewan Science Centre (Tue–Fri 9–5, Sat–Sun 12–6) is great fun for children with permanent displays and an IMAX theater.

Above *Regina's city skyline*
Below *The Legislative Building at dusk*

RCMP HERITAGE CENTRE

www.rcmpheritagecentre.com

The RCMP moved to Regina in 1882, some 10 years after the force was established at Fort Walsh (▷ 261). Although the headquarters moved to Ottawa in 1920, the Training Academy, (or Depot Division) remained here. In 2007 this new heritage centre opened to portray the history and ongoing purpose of the RCMP. Designed by internationally renowned architect Arthur Erickson, the stunning building contains artifacts and displays to tell the story in an engaging way. The imaginative March of the Mounties exhibit is a highlight. Further expansion of the center will be ongoing through 2008–9.

✚ 402 J17 ✉️ 5907 Dewdney Avenue, Regina, Saskatchewan, S4T 0P4 ☎ 306/522-7333, 1-866/567-7267 🕐 Tue–Sun 10–4.30 🏛️

SASKATOON

Saskatoon was founded on the banks of the South Saskatchewan River in 1883 by John Neilson Lake, a representative of the Temperance Colonization Society, who had secured a government grant of land. Unfortunately, Lake's efforts to establish an abstemious settlement were not altogether successful, and in the census of 1901, the population of Saskatoon was registered as a mere 113. With the opening of the Canadian Pacific Railway, however, people gradually began to look upon it as a decent place to live. Farming remains the primary industry hereabouts, and the city has become a major hub for agricultural distribution. Today, it's a friendly city with a lively arts scene.

CITY MUSEUMS

The history of Saskatoon c1910 can be relived at the Saskatchewan Western Development Museum (Jan–end Mar Tue–Sun 9–5; apr–end Dec daily 9–5), on Lorne Avenue South, which features the new Winning the Prairie Gamble exhibit. A series of dioramas and interpretive displays focuses on agricultural development in the last 150 years. The city's railroad heritage is celebrated in the Saskatchewan Railway Museum (May–end Sep daily), where visitors can take rides on working stock. The Mendel Museum (daily 9–9) on Spadina Crescent East, is the city's premier art gallery, with a revolving exhibit of contemporary and historical works by local, national and international artists.

On Highway 11, the Wanuskewin Heritage Park (daily) is Saskatoon's First Nations interpretive center, depicting the lifestyle of the Northern Plains peoples. There are tepees, dioramas explaining the techniques hunters would use to catch and kill buffalo, and a café offering a taste of First Nations cuisine. Work on a major expansion project began in October 2007. While work is in progress the Main Hall displays are housed in a temporary exhibition hall.

OTHER ATTRACTIONS

Saskatoon's most famous son was John G. Diefenbaker, who became Canada's 13th prime minister, and he is remembered at the Diefenbaker Canada Centre (daily) on Diefenbaker Place, where his office and cabinet room are displayed with a large archive relating to Canadian history and politics.

Saskatoon has five theaters and during the summer months there are various open-air concerts. You can also take a river cruise from the Mendel Gallery Wharf.

INFORMATION

www.tourismsaskatoon.com

✚ 402 H16 ℹ️ Tourism Saskatoon, 6–305 Idylwyld Drive North, Saskatoon, Saskatchewan, S7L 0Z1

☎ 306/242-1206, 800/567-2444

Below *The Delta Bessborough Hotel blends harmoniously with Saskatoon's city architecture*

WINNIPEG

INFORMATION

www.tourism.winnipeg.mb.ca

✚ 403 L17 ℹ 300–259 Portage Avenue, Winnipeg, Manitoba, R3B 2A9

☎ 204/943-1970, 1-800/665-0204

🕐 Mon–Fri 8.30–4.30

INTRODUCTION

Winnipeg is the capital of Manitoba province, the geographic heart of Canada, and marks the edge of the prairies. Downtown covers several city blocks around the Portage and Main crossroads, and is an eclectic mix of modern glass-sided skyscrapers and early 20th-century brick and stone edifices. An underground shopping mall comes into its own in the harsh Winnipeg winters. Guided tours are available, notably in the Exchange District, The Forks and St. Boniface districts, and the tourist office can provide details. For getting around, the city's free Downtown Spirit bus sytem has three routes circling the downtown area during the day in addition to its comprehensive ticketed bus network.

Winnipeg was founded as a Hudson's Bay Company outpost for trading with local First Nations tribes. The rival North West Company set up here in 1738. In 1821 the Earl of Selkirk purchased land locally, and the area was settled by Scots fleeing from the Highland Clearances. Winnipeg was declared a city in 1873 and, with the arrival of the Trans-Canada railway, became the Gateway to the West. Now the capital of Manitoba, the city's heyday was c1900–30, and the impressive Legislature Building was completed during this period.

WHAT TO SEE

THE EXCHANGE DISTRICT

The Exchange District is a National Historic Site and hailed as having the best concentration of pre-1913 architecture anywhere in North America. Its most interesting buildings include Confederation Life, a 1912 skyscraper; the 1903 British Bank of North America, the oldest bank building on "bankers' row"; the 1913 Pantages Theatre, with its lavish interior; and the 1903 Criterion Hotel. Observe trading in action from the viewing gallery of the Winnipeg Commodity Exchange (Mon–Fri), Canada's only agricultural futures and options exchange. This regenerated district also has a lively collection of arts companies, galleries, boutiques, restaurants and nightclubs. The Centennial Centre (▷ 277) is home to the Royal Winnipeg Ballet, Opera Company and Symphony Orchestra. Oseredok (Mon–Sat 10–4, also Sun 1–4 Jul–Aug), the Ukrainian cultural and

Above *The Legislative Building in Winnipeg is splendidly imposing*

educational center, commemorates the Ukrainians who settled in Manitoba through folk art and musical instruments, tools and an art gallery.

ℹ️ 133 Albert Street, 2nd Floor, Winnipeg, Manitoba, R3B 1G6 ☎ 204/942-6716

MANITOBA MUSEUM

This spectacular museum presents a history of the province, from its fossil records (dating from 80 million years ago) to its modern industries. The main theme is people and the environment, and excellent dioramas depict Manitoba's ecosystems, with beautifully preserved specimens of animals and birds.

One gallery charts the Hudson's Bay Company's development, with a replica of the two-masted ketch *Nonsuch*, which sailed from England into Hudson Bay in 1668 to found trade with Canada. The Grasslands Gallery examines European settlers and their effects on the prairie grasslands. The rise of Winnipeg city is illustrated in the Urban Gallery, with its re-created 1920s street.

✉️ 190 Rupert Avenue, Winnipeg, Manitoba, R3B 0N2 ☎ 204/956-2830 🕐 Mid-May to early Sep daily 10–5; rest of year Tue–Fri 10–4, Sat–Sun 11–5 ✋ Museum, Planetarium and Science Gallery combined tickets: adult $18, child (3–17) $12.50, family $60; individual rates also available

THE FORKS NATIONAL HISTORIC SITE

www.theforks.com; www.pc.gc.ca

On a bend in the river, this refurbished district is Winnipeg's favorite place to gather, for visitors and locals alike. The Forks combines leafy parks, river walkways, the national historic site, an excellent marketplace, eating, shopping and a host of arts organizations in regenerated Canadian Pacific Railway yard buildings. The Forks is set to become the site of a spectacular new national museum, the Canadian Museum for Human Rights, which, at the time of writing, was nearing its fundraising target of $265 million.

✉️ Main Street and Waterfront Drive, Winnipeg, Manitoba, R3C 4S8 ☎ 204/983-6757, 1-888/787-8888 🕐 Daily ✋ Free 🚌 38, free Downtown Spirit bus

ST. BONIFACE CATHEDRAL

Across the river from The Forks, and built in 1968, St. Boniface Cathedral incorporates the haunting remains of the original 1908 Gothic Revival church, which was destroyed by fire. The cathedral cemetery is the final resting place of many important French and Métis citizens, including Louis Riel (▷ 28),

Below left *Artwork on restored warehouses in the Exchange District*
Below right *The Golden Boy tops the dome of the Legislative Building*

seen by Manitobans as the founder of the province, and two of the earliest bishops—Provencher and Tache. The cathedral museum has displays relating to the rise of the Métis.

✉ 190 Avenue de la Cathédrale, St. Boniface, Manitoba, R2H 0H7 ☎ 204/233-7304 ⦿ Daily ✋ Free

DALNAVERT NATIONAL HISTORIC SITE

This is a typical well-to-do family home of the late Victorian era. Built in Queen Anne Revival style, it rejoices in luxuries of the day, including indoor plumbing, central heating and electric lighting, and is furnished and decorated in keeping with its period. The Legislative Building is in a pleasant park nearby.

✉ 61 Carlton Street, Winnipeg, Manitoba, R3C 1N7 ☎ 204/943-2835 ⦿ Mar–end Dec Wed–Fri 11–5, Sat 11–6, Sun 12–4; Jan–end Feb Sat–Sun ✋ Adult $5, child (5–17) $3, family $12

WINNIPEG ART GALLERY

www.wag.mb.ca

Just north of the Legislative Building, this lively gallery, founded in 1912, is designed by local architect Gustavo da Roza to look like a ship rising out of the water. The specialist collection comprises over 22,500 works, from a fifth-century AD Roman bust to 20th-century videos. The emphasis is on Manitoba artists, but international names are also represented. The museum has the

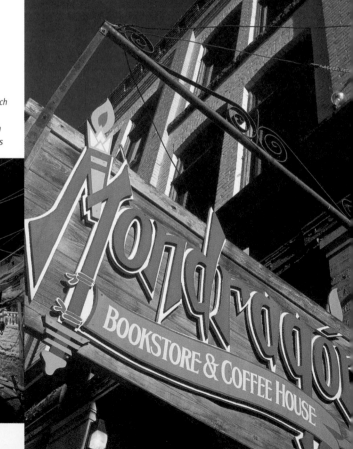

Below left *Diorama of the* Nonsuch *ketch in the Manitoba Museum*
Below right *The Exchange District is an area of restored, converted warehouses*

world's largest collection of contemporary Inuit art. Other exhibits include Gothic and Renaissance altar paintings and tapestries, mid-18th-century decorative pottery, and around 200 photographs by André Kertész, one of the founding fathers of modern photography.

✉ 300 Memorial Boulevard, Winnipeg, Manitoba, R3C 1V1 ☎ 204/786-6641 ⏲ Tue–Sun 11–5 (also Thu 5–9pm) 👋 Adult $6, child (6–12) $3, family $15

LOWER FORT GARRY

Lower Fort Garry, founded in 1881 and the oldest stone trading post still intact in western Canada, lies 32km (20 miles) north of Winnipeg and was a key component in the Hudson's Bay Company network. The bulk of trade here was in farm produce, which the company bought to feed its workers farther north on Hudson Bay itself. From the 1840s, the company expanded the fort to include a brewery, distillery, sawmill and lime kilns. In addition to its role as a fur-trading post and supply station, it later served as the first training facility for the North-West Mounted Police, forerunners of the RCMP, who arrived in 1873 to police what was then a lawless and volatile area. Today, the buildings are populated by costumed interpreters, who portray the lives of the original inhabitants.

✉ 5925 Highway 9, St. Andrews, Manitoba, R1A 4A8 ☎ 204/785-6050, 877/534-3678 ⏲ Mid-May to early Sep daily 9–5; early Sep to mid-Oct Visitor Centre 9–5 👋 Adult $7.05, child (6–16) $3.40, family $17.60 🚌 Beaver Lines bus from Winnipeg and Selkirk 🎧 Guided tours at 11am, 1pm, 3pm 🍴 🏛

MENNONITE HERITAGE VILLAGE

www.mennoniteheritagevillage.com

Set in a 16ha (40-acre) park, 61km (38 miles) south of Winnipeg, the Heritage Village re-creates the traditional lifestyle of Mennonites, a Protestant German-speaking sect, from the 17th century to the present day. There are more than 30 buildings and monuments here, including a windmill, a schoolhouse c1919, a machine shed with tools, a barn and animal pens, an 1881 church, and dwellings. Special events take place throughout the year, the biggest of which is the early August weekend of pioneer activities, including threshing with steam engines, music, food and other attractions. December sees a celebration of a traditional Christmas with sleigh rides and choirs singing carols.

✉ 231 Highway 12 N, P.O. Box 1136, Steinbach, Manitoba, R5G IT8 ☎ 204/326-9661 or 866/280-8741 ⏲ May–end Jun and Sep Mon–Sat 10–5, Sun 12–5; Jul, Aug Mon–Sat 10–6, Sun 12–6; rest of year Tue–Fri 10–4 or by appointment 👋 Adult $8, child (6–12) $2 or (13 and over) $4, family $20 💻 🏛

TIPS

» Free concerts and street entertainment are staged in summer in the Old Market Square.

» Winnipeg's West End is a renowned multicultural neighborhood and is a great place to find lots of international restaurants and food stores.

» The Promenade Taché on the St Boniface side of the river has interpretive plaques about the history of the district as well as lovely views.

» Check on the progress of the planned Canadian Museum of Human Rights, which is soon to be built at the confluence of the Red and Assiniboine Rivers. If you do nothing else, take a look at the architect's drawing of the stunning design at www.canadianmuseumforhumanrights. com.

Top left *Lower Fort Garry*
Top right *A statue of Louis Riel stands in the grounds of the Legislative Building*

PRINCE ALBERT PARK DRIVE

Prince Albert National Park, the largest protected wilderness in Saskatchewan, covers 3,875sq km (1,534sq miles) of rare environment, a mixture of boreal evergreen forest plains and fescue grassland, which at one time covered much of the Prairies but has been all but usurped by crops since the arrival of Europeans. Water makes up over 10 percent of the area with over 1,500 lakes and streams. There are few roads in the park and many of its highlights are a couple of kilometers' walk from vehicular access. However, this scenic route explores Prince Albert's forest ecosystem and the underlying effect of glaciation on the landscape.

THE DRIVE
Length: 135km (84 miles)
Allow: 3 hours
Start: Prince Albert town
End: Grey Owl parking area in Prince Albert National Park
How to get there: The starting point at Prince Albert town is located 144km (90 miles) north of Saskatoon, along Highway 11

★ Prince Albert town is one of the last major centers before you head off into the national park.

Head north out of Prince Albert on Highway 2. After 37km (23 miles), turn left on Highway 263, which is signposted "Prince Albert National Park Scenic Route."

The small settlement of Christopher Lake, just over 1km (0.6 miles) along, has a filling station and general store. Later, you'll pass the decaying wooden shacks and warehouses of a long abandoned settlement. The southern boundary of the national park (entrance fee) comes into view after 18km (11 miles).

Top *A tranquil Waskesiu Lake at sunrise*
Left *The cabin where Grey Owl lived and wrote in the 1930s*

❶ In the park, the first natural attraction is Sandy Lake on the left, where summer visitors can fish or go boating, and there is a lay-by with a great view.

The road leads on through thick, mainly evergreen, forest.

❷ It is common to see deer or elk grazing on the wide shoulder (verge) of the road.

After 10km (6 miles) you'll cross the marshy Spruce River Valley. The Spruce Highlands walk (▷ 270–271) starts just over the bridge. Continue through Prince Albert Burn, 62km (38 miles) along the route.

❸ This is an area seemingly devastated by fire, but in fact, most forest areas rely to a certain extent on fire for their continuation. Some species of plants germinate only after a fire, so in many areas controlled burning takes place.

As you come to the outskirts of Waskesiu Lake, 66km (41 miles) from Prince Albert, you'll see the banks of the lake on your left before the settlement appears.

❹ The town has a pleasant setting amid dense forest with several small beaches. Log cabins and clapboard cottages, in ample gardens, are available for rent. The oldest buildings—the Community Hall, Golf Clubhouse and Nature Centre— were built during the Depression of the 1930s by single unemployed men, who earned $5 per month plus food and housing.

When you reach Waskesiu Lake, turn left at the crossroads and drive past Kipasiwin Camping. The road leads around the lake, traveling west, and crosses the Waskesiu River. You'll also pass the marina, 6km (4 miles) farther along, before the road ends in a gravel parking area some 32km (20 miles) from Waskesiu Lake.

❺ From here you can walk or go by kayak into the heart of the park's wilderness. The best of the trails (21km/13 miles one way) is Grey Owl Trail, leading to the last resting place of writer-naturalist Grey Owl, born Archibald Stansfield Belaney in England, who lived here during the 1930s (▷ 271).

Return to your car and drive back the way you came.

WHEN TO GO
The park is always open, but activities are restricted in winter. The information center is closed early September to mid-May and hotels close October to end May.

WHERE TO EAT
✉ Mackenzie's Dining Room, Hawood Inn, 851 Lakeview Drive, Waskesiu Lake
☎ 306/663-5911.

WHERE TO STAY
✉ Elk Ridge Resort, Waskesiu Lake
☎ 306/663-4653.

Above *Windsurfers on Waskesiu Lake*

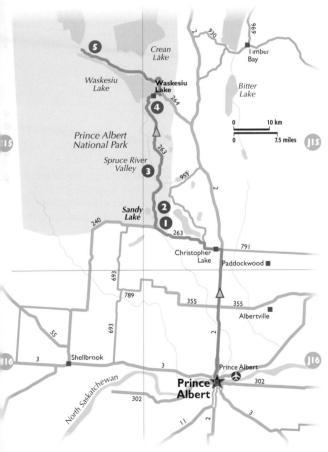

SPRUCE HIGHLANDS TRAIL
IN PRINCE ALBERT NATIONAL PARK

Prince Albert National Park is a landscape sculpted by glacial action. The Spruce Highlands are composed of glacial moraine—rocks deposited after the glaciers advanced and retreated over several stages of the last Ice Age. Several separate ridges of moraine have created an undulating landscape now overlaid with totally unspoiled forest, a mixture of evergreen and deciduous trees that is home to deer, wolves and the occasional bear.

THE WALK
Length: 8.5km (5 miles)
Allow: 5 hours
Start/end: Spruce Highlands Trail parking area on Highway 263
How to get there: From Prince Albert town (▷ 268), take Highway 2 north to the Highway 263 intersection. Turn left here for the Spruce Highlands Trail parking area
Warning: Read the advice leaflets regarding animal encounters offered by the park office before you depart. Take drinking water and snacks with you

From the parking area follow the path next to the information plaque

on the south side. Early in the walk there is a sharp rise in elevation with a seat at the top. If it's too soon to take a rest, make a right turn here.

The path levels out and leads left past a large "erratic"—a boulder left behind when the glaciers melted at the end of the last Ice Age. This area was under as much as 1,600m (5,200ft) of glacial ice, which formed some of the major lakes, carved the river valleys and shaped the drumlins, eskers, ridges and moraines that are much in evidence throughout the park.

After 700m (765 yards) you'll reach a wooden lookout tower, from where you can view much of the southern part of the park.

Notice the effect of erosion on the valley by the Spruce River. The southwestern section of the Prince Albert National Park is home to a sizable herd of plains bison.

From the tower the path leads down and up across another moraine valley to reach the start of the walk loop 300m (330 yards) away. Take the left path.

Left *Glorious sunsets bring a golden glow to Prince Albert National Park*

You'll find that the walk is easier on the return section; the steeper undulations are on the outward section.

The path leads on through thick, mainly deciduous, forest, sometimes cutting across the slope of the hills, which can be hard on the ankles. After 1km (0.6 miles) the path widens into a bright valley, then climbs to its highest point: 1,500m (4,920ft).

From here there are far-reaching views southwest.

Eventually, 3.4km (2.1 miles) from the loop start, you'll reach an intersection in the trail where it's possible to take a left to Anglin Lake. To continue on the circular Spruce River Highlands route, keep to the right. From the intersection, the route begins to swing back toward your starting point. You'll enter an area of mainly evergreen forest 1.3km (0.75 miles) beyond, where the climbs and drops are not as steep as they were on the outward path. Just before you reach the start of the loop and head back past the lookout tower for the parking area, glance over to the left.

You will see another typical geological feature of a glacial landscape. The small lake set deep in a bowl below you is known as a kettle, created when a block of ice was left behind as the main glacier retreated. The ice became covered in layers of earth but later melted, causing the earth to drop into the now empty space and fill with water.

WHEN TO GO
The park is open year-round, but the information center is closed from early September to mid-May, and hotels and restaurants are closed from October to May.

WHERE TO EAT
The nearest place for refreshments is in Waskesiu Lake, 27km (17 miles) away. ✉ Beach House, 911 Lake View Drive, Waskesiu Lake ☎ 306/663-5288 ✉ Park Centre Café, 929 Waskesiu Drive, Waskesiu Lake ☎ 306/663-5233.

WHERE TO STAY
Again, Waskesiu Lake is the nearest: ✉ Hawood Inn, Waskesiu Lake ☎ 306/663-5911 ✉ Elk Ridge Resort, Waskesiu Lake ☎ 306/663-4653.

PARK WILDLIFE
Prince Albert National Park is one of the few areas in the world where timber wolves live free and undisturbed. It is also one of the few Canadian parks with a herd of free-roaming bison. Six bison (out of 50 that were released nearby in 1969) found their way into this protected area and have now increased in number to around 220. Other wildlife includes lynx, woodland caribou, elk, moose and black bear. There are around 200 species of birds, the list including eagles, osprey, loons and hawks. The park also has Canada's largest breeding colony of white pelicans—numbering more than 15,000—on and around Lavallée Lake, but access is restricted.

GREY OWL
Credited by some with being the first ecologist, Grey Owl was born Archibald Stansfield Belaney in Hastings, England, in 1888. He emigrated to Canada in 1906, lived as a trapper and married an Ojibway woman. In 1925 he met his second wife, a Mohawk, and became a conservationist and writer, taking the name Grey Owl. He wrote three novels about life at his small cabin at Ajawan Lake at the heart of the Prince Albert National Park. Grey Owl died in 1938 and is buried near his cabin, now a popular summer hike for devotees, in spite of being a 40km (24-mile) round trip from the nearest parking area. A 1999 movie about Grey Owl was directed by Richard Attenborough and starred Pierce Brosnan in the title role.

Above *Clearly defined paths make following the Spruce Highlands Trail easy*
Below *Parks Canada has placed information boards at suitable points in the park*

WHAT TO DO

BEZANSON

ADAM RANCH
www.adamranch.net
Saddle up cowboy-style for guided rides over vast, pristine grasslands where buffalo, cattle, bear, moose and coyotes roam. Ranch activities include roping and calf-"rassling."
✉ Box 332, Bezanson, Alberta, T0H 0G0 ☎ 780/814-5618, 866/232-6283 ◷ Year-round ✋ Various packages, from around $500 for inclusive weekend; free pick-up from Grande Prairie airport ⊟ Peace Country, southeast of Grande Prairie

CALGARY

ALBERTA BOOT
www.albertaboot.com
Alberta's only western boot maker, producing over 10,000 pairs a year from cow and bull hide, as well as exotic skins. There are always 12,000 pairs in stock, and you can also get jeans, hats, shirts and belts.
✉ 614 10th Avenue SW, Calgary, Alberta, T2R 1M3 ☎ 403/263-4605 ◷ Jul–end of the Calgary Stampede Mon–Fri 9–9, Sat 9–6, Sun 11–4; rest of year Mon–Sat 9–6 FC-train: 7th Avenue ⊟ Downtown at 10th Avenue SW and 5th Street SW

BACK ALLEY NIGHTCLUB
The name might conjure up dubious

images, but don't be deterred—this is a big, fun, friendly place where you can listen to a good variety of live rock and alternative music.
✉ 4630 MacLeod Trail SW, Calgary, Alberta, T2G 5E8 ☎ 403/287-2500 ◷ Wed–Thu 8pm–2am, Fri–Sat 7pm–2am ✋ Wed, Fri, Sat $5, Thu $4 ⊟ 81 ⊞ LRT: 201

BEAT NIQ JAZZ & SOCIAL CLUB
www.beatniq.com
Beat Niq began life as a relaxed jazz café in 1997 and has expanded to become Calgary's only exclusively jazz venue. The atmosphere and music are superb, complemented by fine dining in the Piq Niq café.
✉ 811 1st Street SW, Calgary, Alberta, T2P 7N2 ☎ 403/263-1650 ◷ Thu–Sat 8pm–2.30am ✋ Usually $10; $7 for patrons of Piq Niq café ⊞ LRT: C-Train to Centre Street ⊟ Eastern downtown, between 9th Avenue and Stephen Avenue Walk

BUTTERFIELD ACRES
www.butterfieldacres.com
This is a hands-on farm, where children can get close to the animals, collect eggs, try milking, and take a hayride or a pony ride.
✉ 254077 Rocky Ridge Road, Calgary, Alberta, T3R 1A6 ☎ 403/547-3595 ◷ Jul,

Aug daily 10–4; Apr–end Jun and Sep Mon–Fri 10–2, Sat–Sun 10–4; winter special events by advance ticket purchase only
✋ Adult $12.99, child (toddlers–7) $10.99 ⊟ Northwest of Calgary, 3km (2 miles) north of the Crowchild Trail (Highway 1A) ⬚ Hot and cold drinks, snacks (Jul–Aug)

CALAWAY PARK
www.calawaypark.com
Western Canada's largest outdoor amusement park, offering 30 rides—for thrill-seekers and small children. Live entertainment, soft-play area, minigolf, and a haunted mansion.
✉ 254033 Range Road 33, Calgary, Alberta, T3Z 2E9 ☎ 403/240-3822 ◷ Late Jun–end Aug daily 10–7; mid-May to late Jun Fri 5–9, Sat–Sun 10–7; Sep to mid-Oct Sat–Sun 11–6 ✋ $29 (7–49 years), $23 (3–6 years), $21 (50 years or over), family $70. Taxes not included ⊟ 10km (6 miles) west of Calgary on Trans-Canada Highway (Highway 1) at Springbank Road ⬚Fast food and snacks

CALGARY FLAMES
http://flames.nhl.com
One of the premier franchises in the National Hockey League (NHL), the Flames attract passionate support. The splendid stadium was used in the XV Winter Olympics.

✉ Pengrowth Saddledome, 555 Saddledome Rise SE, Calgary, Alberta, T2P 3B9 ☎ 403/777-2177 🕐 Season: Oct–end Apr 👋 $30–$218 🚈 LRT: 201 Victoria Park/Stampede 🚌 Next to Stampede Ground

CALGARY STAMPEDERS
www.stampeders.com
One of the top Canadian football teams in the west, with loyal and enthusiastic fans. Games are played in the 36,000-seat stadium that hosted the opening and closing ceremonies of the XV Winter Olympics.
✉ McMahon Stadium, 1817 Crowchild Trail NW, Calgary, Alberta, T2M 4R6 ☎ 403/289-0258, 1-800/667-3267 🕐 Season: late Jun–early Nov 👋 $27–$88 🚌 University of Calgary

CALGARY ZOO
www.calgaryzoo.ab.ca
This is one of the finest zoos in North America, known for breeding endangered species. The Destination Africa exhibit includes tropical rainforest with lowland gorillas and hippo viewing pool. The Prehistoric Park re-creates the Canada of the dinosaurs, and the Botanical Garden has a butterfly garden (▷ 258).
✉ 1300 Zoo Road NE, Calgary, Alberta, T2E 7V6 ☎ 403/232-9300, 800/588-9993 🕐 Daily 9–5 👋 Adult $16, child (13–17) $10, (under 13) $8. Taxes not included 🚈 LRT: C-train Zoo 🚌 At Memorial Drive/Deerfoot Trail interchange 🍴 Five food outlets; Safari Lodge offers a hot buffet breakfast

EAU CLAIRE FESTIVAL MARKET
www.eauclairemarket.com
Established in 1993, this 21,600sq m (240,000sq ft) shopping and entertainment complex soon became central to the Calgary experience with its retailers, restaurants, nightlife and street entertainers.
✉ 200 Barclay Parade SW, Calgary, Alberta, T2P 4R5 ☎ 403/264-6450 🕐 Mon–Wed and Sat 10–6, Thu–Fri 10–8, Sun 11–5 (some retailers keep longer hours) 🚌 31, 419, 433 🚌 Prince's Island Park, at 2nd Avenue SW and 2nd Street SW 🍴 A dozen food-court eateries and 10 international restaurants

EPCOR CENTRE FOR THE PERFORMING ARTS
www.epcorcentre.org
A 2,000-seat concert hall and four theaters of various sizes are home to five arts companies, with a diverse schedule of dance, music, theater, cabaret, and comedy.
✉ 205 8th Avenue SE, Calgary, Alberta, T2G 0K9 ☎ 403/294-7455 🕐 Year-round 👋 Varies HLRT: C-Train to Centre Street, City Hall or Olympic Plaza 🚌 Downtown, overlooking Olympic Plaza ☕ Coffee bar with snacks

GALLERIA
www.calgarycraftedgifts.com
Canadian crafts are on offer here, including pottery, quilts, glass, jewelry, sculpture, fine arts, hand-crafted toys and clothing for kids, and gourmet foods. Events include art exhibitions with artists in attendance.
✉ 907 9th Avenue SE, Calgary, Alberta, T2G 0S5 ☎ 403/270-3612 🕐 Mon–Sat 10–5, Sun 12–5. Closed holidays

KART WORLD
www.kartworldcalgary.com
The whole family can have fun on this kart outlet, with two tracks. There's also mini-golf and laser tag, a games arcade and food outlets.
✉ 5202 1st Street SW, Calgary, Alberta, T2H 0C8 ☎ 403/253-8301 🕐 Daily 10–10 (weather permitting) 👋 Karting: adult $7.50–$10 per five-minute ride, child $5.50; multiple ride and multi-activity prices available; Laser Runner: $5.50 per game; mini-golf: adult $5.50, child (under 10) $4.50 🚌 Off Macleod Trail SW via 50th Avenue SE

SHIP AND ANCHOR
www.shipandanchor.com
This excellent pub and restaurant has been a fixture of Calgary nightlife for more than 15 years. Live music, sports TV and other events some nights. Open-stage jams Saturday afternoons. The pub's own record label promotes local bands.
✉ 534 17th Avenue SW, Calgary, Alberta, T2S 0B1 ☎ 403/245-3333 🕐 Daily 11am–2am 👋 Free to bar and events G7 🚌 South of downtown at 17th Avenue SW and the corner of 5th Street SW

SOUTHERN ALBERTA JUBILEE AUDITORIUM
www.jubileeauditorium.com/southern
This superb building, at South Alberta Institute of Technology, is home to the Calgary Opera and Alberta Ballet, and also hosts touring companies.
✉ 1415 14th Avenue NW, Calgary, Alberta, T2N 1M4 ☎ 403/297-8000 🕐 Year-round 🚈 C-train: SAIT/ACAD/Jubilee

STAMPEDE PARK
www.stampede-park.com
Thoroughbred and harness racing take place seven months of the year, including the Nat Christie Memorial Stake, western Canada's richest race; at other times there's simulcast betting.
✉ 2300 Stampede Trail SE, Calgary, Alberta, T2G 2W1 ☎ 403/261-0214 🕐 Thoroughbred racing: mid-Mar to end Jun, Wed and Fri 6pm, Sat, Sun and holidays 1pm. Harness racing: late Jul–late Oct. Simulcast: Wed and Fri–Sun year-round 👋 Free 🚈 LRT: 201 Victoria Park/Stampede or Erlton/Stampede

THEATRE JUNCTION/GRAND
www.theatrejunction.com
Contemporary drama is staged here, including plays and new works from the resident company.
✉ 608 1st Street SW, Calgary, Alberta, T2P 1M6 ☎ 403/205-2922 🕐 Specific dates 👋 $24–30 🍴 🚈 LRT to 1st Street station 🚌 2, 3, 17, 62, 64, 109, 116, 142, 301 🚌 Downtown cultural district, 6th Avenue SW intersection

THE UPTOWN
www.theuptown.com
This 1951 art deco movie theater now offers two venues in one. Downstairs the beautiful original main floor still shows movies (first-run, art-house, international), while the former balcony is separate, with a stage for live performances and projection facilities. There are also plans to install an art gallery.
✉ 612 8th Avenue SW, Calgary, Alberta ☎ 403/265-0120 🕐 Daily, times vary 👋 Adult $9, children (13 and under) $5, Students with ID $7; Tue and matinées $7 all ages 🚌 Downtown near 5th Street

SW intersection FC-train to 4 Street SW or 6 Street SW 🍴 Snacks include soup, samosas and smokies

COLEMAN

ALBERTA FLY FISHING ADVENTURES

www.albertaflyfishing.ab.ca

Three great trout rivers meet here, and there are 20 more less than an hour away. You can get walk-and-wade, float trips and heli-fishing with local experts, customized to anglers' abilities. Equipment and travel are included in the price.

✉ Box 1094, Coleman, Alberta, T0K 0M0 ☎ 403/563-3258, 877/363-3258 🕐 Year-round 💷 Prices depend on requirements 🚗 On Highway 3 at Crowsnest Pass in southwest Alberta

DRUMHELLER

CANADIAN BADLANDS PASSION PLAY

www.canadianpassionplay.com

In a natural rocky amphitheater, a permanent set has been built with seating for 2,500. A huge cast puts on a three-hour passion play in summer. At other times you can arrange for a guided tour and/or a visit to the Interpretive Centre. This is also the venue for the Beethoven in the Badlands concert with the Calgary Philharmonic Orchestra (June).

✉ Box 457, Drumheller, Alberta, T0J 0Y0 ☎ 403/823-2001 🕐 Mid-Jul two weekends (Fri–Sun) 3pm, 6pm 💷 Adult $30, child (12 and under) $15, family $80 🚗 Just west of Drumheller on South Dinosaur Trail, off Highway 9 🍴 Stands for light snacks and drinks

DINOSAUR TRAIL GOLF AND COUNTRY CLUB

www.dinosaurtrailgolf.com

One of the most unusual golf courses in Canada, this course offers challenges to all levels of player.

✉ Drumheller, Alberta ☎ 403/823-5634 🕐 Apr–Oct 💷 18 holes $53, 9 holes $28. Power cart rentals

THE FOSSIL SHOP

www.thefossilshop.com

The Badlands might inspire you with an interest in fossils, and here you can buy all kinds of museum-quality examples, either natural or made into jewelry. There are also books, toys and T-shirts.

✉ 61 Bridge Street, Drumheller, Alberta, T0J 0Y0 ☎ 403/823-6774 🕐 Jul–Aug daily 9–9; Sep–Jun 10–6

EDMONTON

ALBERTA CRAFT COUNCIL GALLERY AND SHOP

www.albertacraft.ab.ca

More than 200 of Alberta's finest craftspeople are represented at this enticing craft council store, where you'll find beautiful ceramics, glass art, woven fabrics, wood carvings and more, all expertly displayed in spacious and airy surroundings.

✉ 10186 106th Street, Edmonton, Alberta, T5J 1H4 ☎ 780/488-6611, 800/362-7238 (toll-free in Alberta) 🕐 Mon–Sat 10–5

CITADEL THEATRE

www.citadeltheatre.com

One of Canada's foremost arts facilities, housing five theaters and a theater school. Full calendar of performances for young people.

✉ 9828 101 A Avenue, Edmonton, Alberta, T5J 3C6 ☎ 780/425-1820, 888/425-1820 🕐 Year-round 💷 Varies 🚇 LRT: Churchill 🚌 52, 100, 112, 308 🚗 Arts District 🍴 Eastbound Bistro and Bar

EDMONTON CRACKER-CATS

www.crackercats.ca

Since the Trackers were bought, renamed and moved to Texas in 2003, the Cracker-Cats (an oil-related term) have represented Edmonton in the Golden Baseball League. They play home games at the 9,200-capacity Telus Field, one of the Minor League's best baseball parks.

✉ Telus Field, 10233 96th Avenue, Edmonton, Alberta, T5K 0A5 ☎ 780/423-2255 🕐 Season: Apr–end Sep 💷 Adult $8–$11, child (3–14) $5–$10 🚌 52 🚇 LRT: Government Centre 🚗 Rossdale

EDMONTON ESKIMOS

www.esks.com

Eskimos home games are played in the 60,000-capacity stadium built to host the 1978 Commonwealth Games. It's the only one in Canada with natural turf—one of North America's best playing surfaces.

✉ Commonwealth Stadium, 11000 Stadium Road, Edmonton, Alberta, T5J 247 ☎ 780/448-ESKS, 1-800/667-3757 🕐 Season: late Jun–early Nov 💷 Adult $29–$65, child (under 17) $14.50–$32.50 🚌 2, 120, 127 🚇 LRT: Stadium 🚗 4km (1.5 miles) northeast, near 112 Avenue and 86 Street intersection

EDMONTON OILERS

www.edmontonoilers.com

Excellent sightlines make this a good place to watch the rapid-action hockey games.

✉ Rexall Place, Northlands Park, Edmonton, Alberta, T5J 2N5 ☎ 780/414-4625, 866/414-4625 🕐 Season: Oct–end Apr 💷 $36–$1215 🚌 5, 8, 10, 127, 141, 142, 143 🚇 LRT: Coliseum 🚗 Downtown, near 74th Street and Wayne Gretzky Drive

FRANCIS WINSPEAR CENTRE FOR MUSIC

www.winspearcentre.com

World-class concert hall, home of the Edmonton Symphony, featuring classical, country, folk, jazz, dance and comedy in a dramatic setting.

✉ 4 Sir Winston Churchill Square, Edmonton, Alberta, T5J 4B2 ☎ 780/428-1414, 800/563-5081 🕐 Year-round 💷 Varies 🚌 6, 63, 64, 66 and many others 🚇 LRT: Churchill 🚗 Arts District, corner of 102nd Avenue and 99th Street

THE LAUGH SHOP

www.thelaughshop.ca

Booking professional acts, this popular stand-up comedy club is in a purpose-built, 300-seat venue. Occasional improv shows too.

✉ Londonderry Mall, 6606 137th Avenue, Edmonton, Alberta, T5C 3C8 ☎ 780/476-1010 🕐 Thu and Sat 8pm, Fri 8pm and 10.30pm; open-mic night Wed

NORTHERN ALBERTA JUBILEE AUDITORIUM

www.jubileeauditorium.com

Fan-shaped auditorium with 2,538 capacity on a 5ha (13-acre) site. Entertainments here include Broadway-style musicals, comedy and a variety of music concerts.

11455 87 Avenue, Edmonton, Alberta, T6G 2T2 ☎ 780/427-2760 🕐 Year-round 🖐 Varies 🚌 4, 6, 30, 50, 51 and many others 🚊 LRT: University 🚗 University of Alberta (new parking lot under construction; call for alternative parking details)

SAVILLE SPORTS CENTRE

www.savillesportscentre.ca
This center has eight indoor and nine outdoor tennis courts, ten curling sheets, a fitness center and a gymnasium, plus a pro shop and food lounge with pool tables and 26 TV screens.

✉ 6501 115th Street, University of Alberta, Edmonton, Alberta, T6G 2E1 ☎ 780/492-2222 🕐 Mon–Fri 6.15am–10pm, Sat–Sun 8am–10pm (open until 11pm Sep–Apr)

SCOTIABANK THEATRE/ WEST EDMONTON MALL

www.cineplex.com
There's a huge choice of movie theaters in Edmonton, and this multiplex is one of three in West Edmonton Mall. It has 13 wide, curved screens with surround-sound and stadium seating, plus an IMAX theater.

✉ #3030, 8882 170 Street, Edmonton, Alberta, T5T 4M2 ☎ 780/444-2400 🕐 Daily 🖐 Adult $12.50–$15.50, child $9–$12 🚌 1, 2, 100, 112, and many others

TELUS WORLD OF SCIENCE

www.odyssium.com
The six fascinating galleries at this major attraction include the natural world at the Green's House; the Gallery of the Gross, with everything weird about the human body; crime-solving in Mystery Avenue; and all things extraterrestrial in the Space Place. DiscoveryLand is specifically for two- to eight-year-olds, and there's also the Star Theatre, an observatory and an IMAX theater.

✉ 11211–142 Street, Edmonton, Alberta, T5M 4A1 ☎ 780/452-9100, 780/451-3344 (recorded information and advance tickets sales) 🕐 Jul–early Sep daily 10–9, rest of year daily 10–5 (also 5–9 Fri–Sat); times for some attractions may vary. IMAX daily

Right *The Epcor Centre for the Performing Arts in Calgary (see page 273)*

from 11am 🖐 Adult $13, child (4–12) $9.50, (13–17) $11, family $47.95 🚌 121, 126 🚊 LRT: Westmount 🚗 Coronation Park, at 111 Avenue and 142 Street 🍽 Light meals, snacks and beverages

WEST EDMONTON MALL

www.westedmall.com
The world's biggest shopping mall, with more than 800 stores, but it doesn't stop there. World-class leisure attractions include Deep Sea Derby (with real submarine trips), a 2ha (5-acre) indoor waterpark, a huge amusement park with thrill rides, the Sea Life Caverns, and an ice rink. Also lots of entertainment venues, sports facilities and special events.

✉ 8882 170 Street, Edmonton, Alberta, T5T 4M2 ☎ 800/661-8890, 780/444-5200 🕐 Mon–Sat 10–9, Sun 11–5, holidays 10–6 🖐 Prices vary depending on attraction, mall free 🚌 1, 2, 100, 112 and many other routes 🍽 Huge choice of fast food, snacks and restaurants

YARDBIRD SUITE

www.yardbirdsuite.com
Named after a Charlie Parker tune, this club is run by the local nonprofit Jazz Society for a discerning bunch of regulars, and delivers quality jazz from big-name performers.

✉ 11 Tommy Banks Way, Edmonton, Alberta, T6E 2M2 ☎ 780/432-0428 🕐 mid-Sep to end Jun Fri–Sat 8–1. Jam session Tue 🖐 Varies 🚌 52 🚗 Corner of 102 Street and 86 Avenue

HILL SPRING
GREAT CANADIAN BARN DANCE

www.gcbd.ca
It may not be sophisticated, but it's great fun: a roast beef dinner, a horse-drawn hayride, and an old-style barn dance with live music (and dancing tuition).

✉ Box 163, Hill Spring, Alberta, T0K 1E0 ☎ 403/626-3407, 866/626-3407 🕐 Mid-May–Jul and Oct–early Nov Fri and Sat; Aug–Sep Wed–Sat 🖐 Adult $27.50, child (under 9) $7.50 or (10–17) $20 🚗 Northeast of Hill Spring off the 505 on Wynder Road

KENOSEE LAKE
KENOSEE SUPERSLIDES

www.kenoseesuperslides.com
Waterslides range from gentle slopes to the terrifying Freefall that drops you eight stories in less than three seconds, and Bonzai Slides that bounce you to the bottom (you can rent tubes to cushion the effect). Also pools and a play area.

✉ Highway 9, Kenosee Lake, Saskatchewan ☎ 306/577-2343 🕐 Mid-Jun to end Jun Wed–Sun 10–6; Jul–Aug daily 10–6 (weather permitting) 🖐 Age 7–60 $20, child (4–6) $10; half-price last 2 hours of the day 🚗 At entrance to Moose Mountain Provincial Park and Kenosee Lake Village 🍽 Cruisers Family Restaurant

MEACHAM
HAND WAVE GALLERY

www.handwave.ca
The tiny village of Meacham is home to a large number of artists and

craftspeople, and this little gallery sells high-quality individual pieces. It showcases the work of about 75 Saskatchewan artists, specializing in such crafts as ceramics, quilting, woodcarving and metalwork.

✉ 409 3rd Avenue North, Meacham, Saskatchewan, S0K 2V0 ☎ 306/376-2221 🕐 May–end Sep Thu–Mon 11–6; Oct–end Dec 1–6; Jan–end Apr by appointment 🚌 52km (32 miles) east of Saskatoon on Highway 5, then 5km (3 miles) south on Highway 2

MISSINIPE
HORIZONS UNLIMITED
www.churchillrivercanoe.com

This company is run by experienced canoeists offering tuition, guided trips, equipment rental and shuttle service (sometimes by floatplane).

✉ Churchill River Canoe Outfitters, La Ronge, Missinipe, Saskatchewan, S0J 1L0 ☎ 877/511-2726 🕐 Mid-May to late Sep 👋 Canoe rental from $35 per day 🚌 80km (50 miles) north of La Ronge at Otter Lake

REGINA
BOOK AND BRIER PATCH
www.bookbrier.ca

Three generations of one family have run this independent store, which contains 30,000-plus titles, including mass-market paperbacks and children's books. The magazine section is huge, and there is also a wide selection of cassettes, CDs and DVDs.

✉ 4065 Albert Street, Regina, Saskatchewan, S4S 3R6 ☎ 306/586-5814 🕐 Mon–Sat 9–9, Sun 12–5 🚌 11, 13 🚌 South Regina 🍸 Cappuccino bar (Mon–Sat 8.30am–10pm)

CONEXUS ARTS CENTRE
www.conexusartscentre.ca

Home of Opera Saskatchewan, producing world-class performances in a grand theater with superb acoustics. Also hosts the Regina Symphony, touring companies and big-name touring acts.

✉ 200A Lakeshore Drive, Regina, Saskatchewan, S4S 7L3 ☎ 306/525-9999, 800/667-8497 🕐 Year-round 👋 Varies 🚌 1 (tell the driver you want the center and he/she will detour there) 🚌 Downtown

GLOBE THEATRE
www.globetheatrelive.com

A 400-seat theater-in-the-round, which each year stages six main-stage productions and four "Sandbox Series," including excellent contemporary Canadian works and international drama.

✉ 1801 Scarth Street, Regina, Saskatchewan, S4P 2G9 ☎ 306/525-6400, 866/954-5623 🕐 Year-round 👋 Main stage: from $32.50. Sandbox Series: $15 🚌 Cornwall Centre service 🚌 Downtown, in Old City Hall Mall, corner of 11th Avenue

SASKATCHEWAN ROUGHRIDERS
www.saskriders.com

Canadian Football League players, and two-time winners of the Grey Cup (but not for a while), the Riders hosted the 2003 championships.

✉ Taylor Field, 2940 10th Avenue, Regina, Saskatchewan, S4P 3B8 ☎ 306/525-2181, 888/474-3377 🕐 Season: late Jun–end Oct or early Nov 👋 $37–$70 🚌 1, 11, 13 🚌 Just west of downtown, between Saskatchewan Drive and Dewdney Avenue

SASKATCHEWAN SCIENCE CENTRE
www.sasksciencecentre.com

This science center has lots of fun learning activities, special events and visiting exhibitions. The Braintastic exhibit includes activities like constructing a model of a neuron out of candies, and having fun with optical illusions and other sensory curiosities. There's also an IMAX movie theater

✉ 2903 Powerhouse Drive, Regina, Saskatchewan, S4N 0A1 ☎ 306/791-7900, 800/667-4629 (IMAX: 306/522-4629) 🕐 Tue–Fri 9–5, Sat–Sun 12–6 (IMAX daily 12–9) 👋 Adult $8, child (3–5) $3.75, (6–13) $6. Combined tickets with IMAX: Adult $12.75, child (2 and under) $3.75, (3–5) $6, (6–13) $9.50 🚌 10, 12 (on request; tell the driver you want the Science Centre) 🚌 Wascana Park, at corner of Winnipeg Street and Wascana Drive

SOUTHLANDS SHOPPING CENTRE
http://southlandsshoppingcentre.ca

More than 85 stores and services, including Chapters and Wal-Mart.

✉ 2965 Gordon Road, Regina, Saskatchewan ☎ 306/584-7644 🕐 Mon–Tue and Sat 9.30–6, Wed–Fri 9.30–9, Sun 12–5 🚌 G7, 9, 11, 13 🚌 Corner of Albert Street South

ROSTHERN
STATION ARTS CENTRE
www.stationarts.com

A converted train station houses this arts facility, which hosts concert and theater productions.

✉ Railway Avenue, Rosthern, Saskatchewan, S0K 3R0 ☎ 306/232-5332 🕐 Year-round 👋 Varies 🚌 At entrance to Rosthern from Highway 11 🍸 Tearoom serves light meals

SASKATOON
BUD'S ON BROADWAY
www.budsonbroadway.com

Legendary venue for top-quality rock and blues, with live bands most nights and a jam session on Saturday afternoon (musicians welcome).

✉ Broadway Avenue, Saskatoon, Saskatchewan, S7N 1B5 ☎ 306/244-4155 🕐 Daily (closed Mon in winter), Jam Session Sat 3–8pm 👋 6 🚌 South of the river, just north of Main Street

PERSEPHONE THEATRE
www.persephonetheatre.org

In a beautiful new building by the river, Persephone Theatre is the city's premier theatre company. It stages six productions a year, including classics, contemporary drama, comedy and musicals.

✉ 100 Spadina Crescent E, Saskatoon, Saskatchewan ☎ 306/384-7727 🕐 Sep–end Apr Tue–Sun 👋 Varies with event, from $21 🚌 Downtown, at south end of 2nd Avenue, off 19th Street

PRAIRIE POTTERY
www.prairiepottery.com

Run by potters Ron and Rusty Kurenda, this excellent store also has a huge selection of high quality, hand-crafted ceramics from around 40 potters based in the Prairies.

✉ 150-B 2nd Avenue N, Saskatoon, Saskatchewan, S7K 2B2 ☎ 306/242-8050 🕐 Mon–Sat 10–5.30 🚌 Downtown terminal nearby 🚌 Downtown, between 22nd and 23rd streets

RODEO

www.canadiancowboys.sk.ca

A fantastic Prairies experience with events all over the province every weekend, with the Finals Rodeo in Edmonton (▷ 260) in November.

✉ Various locations; contact the Canadian Cowboys' Association, RR4, Site 412, Box 287, Saskatoon, Saskatchewan, S7K 3J7 ☎ 306/931-2700 🕐 Season: Apr–Nov

TCU PLACE

www.tcuplace.com

The city's foremost arts venue has a full program of concerts, including classical music, comedy, musicals and touring artists such as Tom Jones, George Jones and The Cult. It also operates as a convention center.

✉ 35 22nd Street E, Saskatoon, Saskatchewan, S7K 0C8 ☎ 306/975-7777, 306/975-7761 🕐 Year-round 🖐 Varies 🚌 Downtown terminal nearby on 23rd Street E 🚌 Downtown, next to Midtown Plaza, just east of Idylwyld Drive

WATROUS

DANCELAND

Traditional 1928 dance hall, famous for its dance floor, built on a cushion of horsehair. It hosts old-style dances, country rock 'n' roll, bluegrass shows, and dance competitions.

✉ RR#1, Manitou Beach, Watrous, Saskatchewan, S0K 4T0 ☎ 306/946-2743, 800/267-5037 🕐 Dances: Fri–Sat nights. Gospel shows: Sun (call for details of other events; open daily for tours) 🖐 $12.50–$20 🚌 Free shuttle service from town on dance nights 🚌 North of Watrous, off Highway 2

MANITOU SPRINGS

www.manitousprings.ca

This is one of only three places in the world where the water is so mineral-rich it keeps you afloat, and it has legendary therapeutic properties. Canada's largest indoor mineral spa has a huge pool filled with it, plus various treatments.

✉ Box 610, Manitou Beach, Watrous, Saskatchewan, S0K 4T0 ☎ 306/946-2233, 800/667-7672 🕐 Daily 9am–10pm 🖐 Day pass: adult $16.80, child (6–12) $9, (13–17) $11. Treatments priced separately 🚌 North of town on Route 365

WINNIPEG

ASSINIBOIA DOWNS

www.assiniboiadowns.com

Hosts 75 days of thoroughbred racing a year, including the Manitoba Derby. Sundays and holidays are festive, with family entertainment. Rest of the year features simulcast wagering from major tracks in Canada, the US and Australia.

✉ 3975 Portage Avenue West, Winnipeg, Manitoba, R3K 2E9 ☎ 204/885-3330 🕐 Live racing: May–end Sep. Gaming lounge: daily 9am–2am 🖐 Free, Clubhouse $2 🚌 Race Track Shuttle, "A" Trip from Main and William; "B" Trip from Portage and Ronald 🚌 Southwest of downtown, northwest of Perimeter Highway

BAYAT GALLERY

www.inuitgallery.com

This is one of the largest and finest galleries for the work of Inuit artists. Beautiful sculptures, carvings and prints are set against a stark white background. The wildlife wood sculptures by Ed Brown are a highlight.

✉ 163 Stafford Street, Winnipeg, Manitoba, R3M 2W9 ☎ 204/475-5873, 888/884-6848 🕐 Mon–Sat 10–5.30, Sun by appointment 🚌 Downtown, at Stafford and Grosvenor

BURTON CUMMINGS THEATRE

www.burtoncummingstheatre.com

A national historic theater hosting concerts, drama and musicals.

✉ 364 Smith Street, Winnipeg, Manitoba, R3B 2H2 ☎ 204/956-5656 (tickets available only from Ticketmaster ☎ 204/780-3333) 🕐 Year-round 🖐 Varies 🚌 Downtown, near Notre Dame and Ellice

CENTENNIAL CONCERT HALL

www.mbccc.ca

Home of Winnipeg's Symphony Orchestra, this is a first-class modern facility offering a full calendar of classical concerts.

✉ 555 Main Street, Winnipeg, Manitoba, R3B 1C3 ☎ 204/956-1360 🕐 Year-round 🖐 Varies 🚌 21, 22, 24, 28, 67

THE FORKS MARKET

www.theforks.com

There are around 75 stores in this complex including The Forks Market

Above *A dinosaur in Calgary Zoo's Prehistoric Park (see page 273)*

and Johnston Terminal. The market has a huge array of specialty foods, and the second floor has local arts and crafts, including aboriginal works. The Johnston Terminal has specialty boutiques, an antiques mall and the Explore Manitoba Centre with information about the province. The complex also has an IMAX theater and tourist attractions.

✉ 201 One Forks Market Road, Winnipeg, Manitoba, R3C 4L9 ☎ 888/942-6302 🕐 Jul–early Sep Mon–Sat 9.30–9, Sun 9.30–6.30; rest of year Sat–Thu 9.30–6.30, Fri 9.30–9. Johnston Terminal opens 10am 🚌 38, Downtown Spirit (free) 🚌 Downtown, east of Main Street and Union Station 🍽 Fast-food outlets and more formal restaurants

FORT WHYTE CENTRE

www.fortwhyte.org

One of Canada's foremost outdoor recreation facilities, with woods, lakes and grassland. There's a large herd of bison, a prairie dog town and an aquarium. In summer there's a tepee encampment, boating and fishing, and in winter there's a toboggan slide, skating on the lake and ice-fishing.

✉ 1961 McCreary Road, Winnipeg, Manitoba ☎ 204/989-8355 🕐 Mon–Fri 9–5, Sat–Sun 10–5 🖐 Adult $6, child (3 and over) $4 🚌 Southwest of downtown off Route 155 🍴 Light lunches, coffees

MANITOBA CHILDREN'S MUSEUM

www.childrensmuseum.com

This terrific museum is where learning flourishes. Kids can get involved in a variety of activities.

✉ Kinsmen Building, 45 Forks Market Road, Winnipeg, Manitoba, R3C 4T6 ☎ 204/924-4000 ⏰ Sun–Thu 9.30–4.30, Fri–Sat 9.30–6 👎 Adult $6.25, child (2–17) $6.75 🚌 38, Downtown Spirit (free)

MANITOBA MOOSE

www.moosehockey.com

Top National Hockey League affiliate of the Vancouver Canucks, known for high-caliber hockey and great entertainment, the Moose now play in the American Hockey League.

✉ MTS Centre, 260 Hargrave Street, Winnipeg, Manitoba, R3C 5S5 ☎ 204/987-7825, 888/626-6673 ⏰ Season: Oct–end Apr 👎 From $14 🚌 10, 11, 14–20, 33 and many more 🚗 On Portage Avenue between Hargrave Street and Donald Street

MANITOBA THEATRE CENTRE

www.mtc.mb.ca

Canada's oldest English- language theater, producing world-class plays and other shows. Venue for the Fringe Theatre Festival in July.

✉ 174 Market Avenue, Winnipeg, Manitoba, R3B 0P8 ☎ 204/942-6537, 877/446-4500 ⏰ Oct–end May 👎 $22–$80 🚌 21, 22, 24, 28, 31, 33, 67 🚗 Exchange District

MANITOBA THEATRE FOR YOUNG PEOPLE

www.mtyp.ca

This theater company specializes in performances for young people,

including traditional tales and innovative theater for teens.

✉ CanWest Global Performing Arts Centre, Forks Market Road, The Forks, Winnipeg, Manitoba, R3C 4X1 ☎ 204/942-8898, 877/871-6897 ⏰ Oct–early Apr, Jun Fri 7pm, Sat–Sun 1pm and 4pm 👎 From $12.50 🚌 38, Downtown Spirit (free)

PANTAGES PLAYHOUSE THEATRE

www.pantagesplayhouse.com

This lavish theater hosts varied entertainments, including theater and all types of music.

✉ 180 Market Avenue, Winnipeg, Manitoba, R3B 0P7 ☎ 204/989-2889 ⏰ Year-round 👎 Varies 🚌 11, 18, 29 🚗 Exchange District

RAINBOW STAGE, KILDONAN PARK

www.rainbowstage.net

A covered, comfortable outdoor amphitheater with a popular summer season of musical productions.

✉ Rainbow Stage Productions, 200-180 Market Avenue, Winnipeg, Manitoba, R3B 0P7 ☎ 204/989-5261 ⏰ Aug Sun–Fri 8pm 👎 $18–$42 🚌 18, 32 🚗 15km (9 miles) northeast of downtown's Main/ Portage intersection

SHAKESPEARE IN THE RUINS

www.shakespeareintheruins.com

After 10 years at the ruins of St. Norbert's monastery, the company has been on the move. It now stages imaginative Shakespeare productions in the beautiful conservatory in Assiniboine Park. Reservations recommended.

✉ Assiniboine Park Conservatory, Winnipeg, Manitoba ☎ 204/957-1753 ⏰ Mid-May to early Jul Tue–Sun 👎 From

$8 🚌 67, 79 🚗 South of Assiniboine River, off Croydon Avenue (Route 95)

TIMES CHANGE(D) HIGH AND LONESOME

www.highandlonesomeclub.ca

The best venue in the city for live roots, blues, bluegrass, country and soul. Jam sessions on Sunday.

✉ 234 Main Street, Winnipeg, Manitoba, R2C 0A1 ☎ 204/957-0982 ⏰ Thu–Sun 8pm–2am; also Mon–Wed 4pm–2am, but no live music 🚌 14, 38, 55 🚗 Downtown, corner of St. Mary Avenue

WEST END CULTURAL CENTRE

www.wecc.ca

After more than 10 years in its much-loved converted church (pictured below), this renowned center has been forced to give up on the shaky old building and is set to build new premises on the site. Call to check before showing up.

✉ 586 Ellice Avenue, Winnipeg, Manitoba, R3B 1Z8 ☎ 204/783-6918 ⏰ Year-round 👎 Varies 🚌 14, 31 (Ellice) and 29 (Sherbrooke) 🚗 At Sherbrooke 🍴 Snacks, plus a bar

WINNIPEG BLUE BOMBERS

www.bluebombers.com
www.canadianstadium.com

The Blue Bombers Canadian football team has enthusiastic fans, and it's fun to join them in cheering on the players at the Canad Inns Stadium, an open venue seating nearly 34,000.

✉ Canad Inns Stadium, 1465 Maroons Road, Winnipeg, Manitoba, R7B 1G7 ☎ 204/784-2583 ⏰ Season: late Jun–early Nov 👎 $15–$55 🚌 11, 12, 20, 24, 26, 66, 67, 77, 78, 79, 97 🚗 Just east of the airport, across from Winnipeg Arena

WINNIPEG JEWISH THEATRE

www.wjt.ca

Canada's only professional theater company promoting an understanding of Jewish culture through top-quality productions of established and new plays on Jewish themes.

✉ Asper Jewish Community Campus, C 148–123 Doncaster Boulevard, Winnipeg, Manitoba, R3N 2B2 ☎ 204/477-7517 ⏰ Oct to mid-May 👎 $28

FESTIVALS AND EVENTS

FEBRUARY

INTERNATIONAL NEW MUSIC FESTIVAL
www.wso.mb.ca
Beat the winter chill with this seven-day festival of music from living Canadian and foreign composers, performed by the Winnipeg Symphony Orchestra and guest soloists.
✉ Winnipeg, Manitoba ☎ 204/949-3999

MARCH

ROYAL MANITOBA WINTER FAIR
www.brandonfairs.com
Six-day agricultural show, including horse shows and commercial and rural exhibits.
✉ Brandon, Manitoba ☎ 204/726-3590, 877/729-0001

MAY

SASKATCHEWAN INTERNATIONAL TATTOO AND FESTIVAL
www.sasktattoo.com
A relatively new event (the first was in 2007), this is a stirring and entertaining celebration of the work of the Canadian armed forces, emergency services and RCMP, with an impressive pageant, plus marching bands, displays, reenactments and other entertainments.
✉ Regina, Saskatchewan
☎ 306/585-3948

INTERNATIONAL CHILDREN'S FESTIVAL
www.childfest.com
This is the time to bring your little ones to Edmonton, with five days of theater, world music and crafts, storytelling, circus artists and activities. Lots of fun and games.
✉ Edmonton, Alberta ☎ 780/459-1542

VESNA FESTIVAL
www.vesnafestival.com
A celebration of Ukrainian culture takes over TCU Place for two evenings featuring dance bands, traditional dancers, choirs and other entertainers, art and crafts and delicious Ukrainian food. Note that you'll need photo ID to get in, and there's a semi-formal dress code.
✉ Saskatoon, Saskatchewan

JUNE

NATIONAL ABORIGINAL DAY AND POWWOW
www.wanuskewin.com
Three days of traditional celebrations at the Wanuskewin Heritage Park mark National Aboriginal Day, including children's activities, dance competitions and fireworks.
✉ Saskatoon, Saskatchewan
☎ 306/931-6767, 877/547-6546

JULY

CALGARY STAMPEDE
http://calgary-stampede.com
Recalling pioneer days, this is a huge event that takes over the whole city, starting with the big parade on opening day. After that, it's 10 days of big-name concerts, a first-rate rodeo and cultural events.
✉ Calgary, Alberta ☎ 403/261-0101, 800/661-1260

WINNIPEG FRINGE THEATRE FESTIVAL
www.winnipegfringe.com
In the true tradition of the fringe philosophy, this festival stages inexpensive events and promotes interaction between audience and theater professionals. As well as shows there are open-air events, concerts, buskers and stuff for kids.
✉ Winnipeg, Manitoba

AUGUST

FOLKORAMA
www.folklorama.ca
Canada's largest and longest-running multicultural festival. Two weeks of events, showcasing more than 40 ethnic cultures.
✉ Winnipeg, Manitoba ☎ 204/982-6210, 800/665-0234

DRAGON BOAT FESTIVAL
www.dragonboat.regina.sk.ca
More than 60 teams take part in these exciting and colorful races. Alongside the water there's Asian entertainment, food and children's activities.
✉ Regina, Saskatchewan ☎ 306/525-2628 Mar–Sep only; message service only

SEPTEMBER/OCTOBER

EDMONTON INTERNATIONAL FILM FESTIVAL
www.edmontonfilmfest.com
Nine days and nights of independent cinema productions, including around 40 feature films and documentaries and some 100 short films from around the globe.
✉ Edmonton, Alberta ☎ 780/423-0844

NOVEMBER

CANADIAN FINALS RODEO AND FARMFAIR INTERNATIONAL
www.canadianfinalsrodeo.ca
The rodeo stars Canada's toughest professionals; Farmfair, at Northlands Park, is a huge agricultural show.
✉ Northlands Park, Edmonton, Alberta
☎ 780/451-8000, 888/800-7275

EATING

PRICES AND SYMBOLS

The restaurants are listed alphabetically within each town. The prices are for a two-course lunch (L) and a three-course à la carte dinner (D). Prices in pubs are for a two-course lunchtime bar meal and a two-course dinner in the restaurant, unless specified otherwise. The wine price is for the least expensive bottle.

For a key to the symbols, ▷ 2.

CALGARY

BUZZARDS COWBOY CUISINE

www.cowboycuisine.com

If you enjoy steak and ribs, this place is great. It's full of cowboy memorabilia, and the interior takes you back 100 years. It's not all steak and ribs, though; there are also chicken and fish dishes, soups and salads.

✉ 140 10th Avenue Southwest, Calgary, Alberta, T2R 0A3 ☎ 403/264-6959 🕐 Daily 11–10 🍴 L $15, D $33, Wine $28 🚊 C-train 🚌 Downtown, near 10th Avenue/1st Street intersection

LA DOLCE VITA

This Little Italy restaurant has a distinctive white exterior with wrought-iron balconies, and a chic formal interior. Traditional recipes using fresh pasta, seafood and veal combine with imaginative

presentation. There's a more casual dining room upstairs.

✉ 916 1st Avenue Northeast, Calgary, Alberta, T2E 0C5 ☎ 403/263-3445 🕐 Mon–Fri 11.30–2, 5.30–10.30, Sat 2.30–11; closed Sun 🍴 L $25, D $45, Wine $30 🚌 9 🚌 Little Italy, between 8th and 9th

EDMONTON

BACON

www.eatatbacon.com

Vegetarians, don't be deterred by the name. This friendly little place has an interesting menu of wholesome food including meat-free options such as the Vancouver Rice Bowl, with brown rice, braised greens, crispy tofu and sprouts. There is a "vegan special" on Wednesdays. Meat eaters can enjoy such dishes as braised lamb with Moroccan spices, or bison burger with molasses butter, remoulade and havarti. Friday's special is always fresh wild fish, Saturday is slow cook day and on Sunday it's just open for brunch.

✉ 6509 112th Avenue, Edmonton, Alberta, T5W 0P1 ☎ 780/477-2422 🕐 Tue–Sat 11am–3pm, 5–10pm, Sun 10am–3pm 🍴 L $20, D $35, Wine $30 🚊 Stadium, then bus 2 🚌 2 🚌 Northeast of downtown, just east of Wayne Gretzky Drive

THE CREPERIE

www.thecreperie.com

The French cuisine at this romantic spot is delectable. The house dish is, of course, stuffed crêpes, including vegetarian options.

✉ 111, 10220 103rd Street, Edmonton, Alberta, T5J 0Y8 ☎ 780/420-6656 🕐 Tue–Thu 11.30–9, Fri 1.30–10, Sat 5–10, Sun 5–9 🍴 L $15, D $28, Wine $28 🚊 LRT to Bay 🚌 1, 2, 8, 52, 112, 308 🚌 Downtown in the Boardwalk, just north of 102nd Avenue

JACK'S GRILL

www.jacksgrill.ca

The restaurant also has a beautiful courtyard with summer seating. The menu is bistro-style, with starters such as grilled romaine or an antipasto plate. Entrées might include roasted buttermilk-marinated chicken breast supreme with birch syrup glaze and 28-day aged beef rib-eye. If you plan to share a dish, be prepared for a $5 charge.

✉ 5842 111th Street, Edmonton, Alberta, T6H 3G1 ☎ 780/434-1113 🕐 Mon–Sat from 5pm 🍴 L $60, D $80, Wine $35 🚌 6, 9, 17, 51 🚌 South of the river, between 61st and 57th avenues NW, north of Southgate Centre and Whitemud Drive (Highway 2). NB If driving south, use 109th or 113rd street

LOUISIANA PURCHASE

www.louisianapurchase.ca

Owner/chef Dennis Vermette displays a deep understanding of authentic Creole and Cajun cuisines. Dishes include alligator kebab or salmon, shrimp and crawfish boudin, pecan-crusted pork tenderloin, topped with jumbo shrimp and smoked Chipotle pepper buttercream. If hot spices are not to your taste, there are plenty of tamer choices, but check before you order. Jambalaya Nights (Monday and Tuesday) are a great value.

✉ 10320 111th Street, Edmonton, Alberta, T5K 1L2 ☎ 780/420-6779 ◷ Mon–Thu 11.30–9.30, Fri 11.30–10, Sat 5–10, Sun 4.30–9 ✋ L $17, D $35, Wine $20 🚇 LRTCorona 🚌 308 or 111, 112, 309 (104 Avenue) 🚃 Downtown, between Jasper Avenue NW and 104 Avenue NW

REGINA
BUSHWAKKER BREWING CO. LTD.

www.bushwakker.com

Created from an old warehouse, this renowned brewpub retains original features, including its restored pressed-tin ceiling. You can see the brewhouse through large windows. The excellent beers are accompanied by memorable pub food.

✉ 2206 Dewdney Avenue, Regina, Saskatchewan, S4R 1H3 ☎ 306/359-7276 ◷ Mon–Thu 11am–1am, Fri–Sat 11am–2am ✋ L $8, D $16, Wine $17 🚃 Old warehouse district, at Dewdney and Cornwall

MEDITERRANEAN BISTRO

www.mbistro.ca

This smart modern bistro just off the Trans-Canada Highway is big and boisterous. It has a lengthy menu of bistro favorites, including coq au vin, linguini carbonara and shrimp seafood ravioli.

✉ 2589 Quance Street East, Regina, Saskatchewan, S4V 2Y7 ☎ 306/757-1666 ◷ Mon–Sat 11–11, Sun 5–10 ✋ L $12, D $30, W $25 🚃 East of Regina, on Trans-Canada Highway (Highway 1), just southeast of Fleet Street intersection

SASKATOON
JOHN'S PRIME RIB

www.johnssaskatoon.com

John's has been a Saskatoon institution for more than 30 years. Beef, and ribs in particular, are always good, but fresh fish, duck and game such as pheasant are also available.

✉ 401 21st Street East, Saskatoon, Saskatchewan, S7K 0C5 ☎ 306/244-6384 ◷ Mon–Fri 11am–11.30pm, Sat 4.30–11.30 ✋ L $15, D $28, Wine $25 🚃 Downtown at the corner of 21st Street and 4th Avenue

SASKATOON STATION PLACE

www.stn-biz.com/saskatoonrestaurant

This place has two Pullman railcars parked outside. You can choose between dining in these fine old relics or in the historic station building. Inside, it's decorated in Victorian style with authentic antiques and railroad memorabilia. The menu has tender ribs, succulent steaks, Greek dishes, pastas and salads.

✉ 221 Idylwyld Drive North, Saskatoon, Saskatchewan, S7L 6V6 ☎ 306/244-7777 ◷ Mon–Sat 10.30am–midnight, Sun 10am–11pm ✋ L $10, D $30, Wine $30 🚌 1, 7 🚃 At intersection with 23rd Street

WINNIPEG
AMICI

www.amiciwpg.com

Very classy upstairs Italian restaurant where the food creates the color, with Tuscan specialties on a daily-changing menu.

✉ 326 Broadway, Winnipeg, Manitoba, R3C 0S5 ☎ 204/943-4997 ◷ Mon–Fri 11.30–2, 5–11, Sat 5–11 ✋ L $25, D $45, Wine $20 🚌 29 🚃 At Hargrave Street

BLINK

www.blinkcalgary.com

Renovated in April 2008, this stylish restaurant is in a historic building. A creative approach to accompaniments enhances main courses such as rib eye of beef (with butternut squash and black truffle, crosnes, thumbelina carrots and perigueux sauce). Lunch dishes are simpler, but equally imaginative and include pastas and sandwiches.

✉ 111 8th Avenue Southwest, Calgary,

Alberta, T2P 1B4 ☎ 403/263-5330 ◷ Mon–Wed 11am–3pm, 5–10pm, Thu 11am–3pm, 5–11pm, Fri 11am–3pm, 5pm–midnight, Sat 5pm–midnight ✋ L $30, D $60, Wine $9 (all by the glass) 🚌 24, 101, 104 directions]Downtown, just off Centre Street South

RAW BAR AT THE ARTS

www.hotelarts.ca

Calgary's most stylish designer hotel contains one of the city's most outstanding restaurants. Renowned chef Duncan Ly heads a team that produces exciting Pacific-Rim influenced dishes.

✉ 119 12th Avenue SW, Calgary, Alberta, T2R 0G8 ☎ 403/266-4611, 800/661-9378 ◷ Daily 11am–2pm, 5–10pm ✋ L $40, D $60, Wine $40 🚌 17, 67, 70, 72, 73

RIVER CAFÉ

www.river-cafe.com

Nestled among the trees on this glorious island in the Bow River, the interior has natural wood and an open fireplace. All-round windows have lovely views of the park. Dedicated to supporting local farms and ethical food producers, the restaurant offers a menu of regional specialties.

✉ Princes Island Park, Calgary, Alberta; mailing address: PO Box 193, 200 Barclay Parade SW, Calgary, Alberta, T2P 4R5 ☎ 403/261-7670 ◷ Feb–Dec Mon–Fri 11am–3pm, 5pm–10pm, Sat–Sun 10am–3pm, 5–10pm (until 11pm in summer). Closed Jan ✋ L $35, D $65, Wine $28 🚃 On the island, just west of Jaipur Bridge from Eau Claire Market

TAVERN IN THE PARK

With its tall tower and mock-Tudor architecture, this is a landmark building surrounded by lovely parkland. The restaurant is in an atrium; there is also outdoor seating on the garden terrace in summer. The food is equally memorable, with gourmet European dishes bringing out the intense flavors of the fresh fish, meat and poultry.

✉ 55 Pavilion Crescent, Assiniboine Park, Winnipeg, Manitoba, R3P 2N6 ☎ 204/896-7275 ◷ Tue–Sat 11.30–2.30, 5–10, Sun 10–2, 5–9 ✋ L $15, D $50, Wine $30 🚌 67 🚃 In Assiniboine Park Pavilion

PRICES AND SYMBOLS

Prices are the starting price for a double room for one night, unless otherwise stated. Breakfast is included unless noted otherwise. All the hotels listed accept credit cards unless otherwise stated. Note that rates vary widely throughout the year.

For a key to the symbols, ▷ 2.

BATTLEFORD
GOLD EAGLE LODGE

www.goldeaglelodge.com
Set next to the casino, this modern hotel may not be very inspiring from the outside, but the rooms and suites are spacious and nicely furnished, some with Jacuzzi tubs and some with a separate kitchenette. It has a beautiful indoor saltwater swimming pool with three hot tubs, and a fitness room with exercise equipment, steam room and sauna. Breakfast is the only meal available here.
✉ 12004 Railway Avenue East, North Battleford, Saskatchewan, S9A 3W3 ☎ 306/446-8877, 866/446-8877 ✋ $97 (including Continental breakfast) ① 12 (all non-smoking) ⑤ ℙ With winter plug-ins 🏊 Indoor 🚗 On Highway 16 (Yellowhead) on southeast edge of North Battleford

CALGARY
KENSINGTON RIVERSIDE INN

www.kensingtonriversideinn.com
Rooms and public spaces in this charming hotel feature original works of art, and facilities include CD-players, high-speed internet access, and whirlpool baths in some rooms.
✉ 1126 Memorial Drive Northwest, Calgary, T2N 3E3 ☎ 403/228-4442, 877/313-3733 ✋ $284 ① 19 (all non-smoking) ⑤ 🚉 LRT C-Train to Sunnyside 🚌 4 🚗 Northwest of central downtown just west of 10th Street NW

CHURCHILL
AURORA INN

www.aurora-inn.mb.ca
In the heart of town, this hotel offers spacious living in two-story suites. The living rooms each have a comfortable sofa, dining table, cable TV with movie channel and VCR, there's a fully equipped kitchen, and the bedrooms are loft-style with private bathroom and queen-size or twin beds. The hotel also offers a complimentary laundry service, WiFi and public computer access. Book well ahead for the October and November polar bear season and be prepared to pay in full in advance.
✉ PO Box 1030, Churchill, Manitoba, R0B 0E0 ☎ 204/675-2071, 888/840-1344 ✋ $115 ① 22 [14 non-smoking]

DAUPHIN
CANWAY INN

www.canwayinnandsuites.com
This modern hotel is convenient for visiting Riding Mountain National Park. The modern bedrooms are fairly plain, but there are also deluxe rooms and suites.
✉ 1601 Main Street, Dauphin, Manitoba, R7N 2V4 ☎ 204/638-5102, 888/325-3335 ✋ $62 ① 67 (12 non-smoking) ⑤ 🏊 Indoor 🚗 2.4km (1.5 miles) south of Dauphin on highways 5A and 10A

DRUMHELLER
HEARTWOOD MANOR

www.innsatheartwood.com
This is a 1920s heritage building. There are spacious suites with whirlpool baths, rooms with sloping ceilings and dormer windows, rooms with fireplaces and two cottages. A range of professional spa treatments is also available.
✉ 320 Railway Avenue East, Drumheller, Alberta, T0J 0Y4 ☎ 403/823-6495, 888/823-6495 ✋ $110 ① 15 (all non-smoking) ⑤ 🚗 Downtown, just east of Highway 9

EDMONTON

FANTASYLAND AT WEST EDMONTON MALL

www.fantasylandhotel.com

If you want the complete West Edmonton Mall experience, reserve one of Fantasyland's 120 luxury theme rooms. Why not try sleeping in a Wild West stagecoach? There are modern regular rooms too.

✉ 17700 87th Avenue, Edmonton, Alberta, T5T 4V4 ☎ 780/444-3000, 800/737-3783 ✋ $189 ⓘ 355 (158 non-smoking) 🔆 📺 🚌 1, 2, 100, 112 (and many other routes) 🅿 Southwest corner of the mall

UNION BANK INN

www.unionbankinn.com

This fine old building is now a chic, classy boutique hotel. Rooms and suites are individually styled. Some bathrooms have jet tubs. Free cheese and wine are delivered to rooms every evening.

✉ 10053 Jasper Avenue, Edmonton, Alberta, T5J 1S5 ☎ 780/423-3600, 888/423-3601 ✋ $169 ⓘ 34 🔆 📺 🚆 LRT to Central 🚌 3, 5, 100, 120, 135 🅿 Downtown, corner of 101st Street

SASKATOON

PARK TOWN

www.parktownhotel.com

This is a distinctive and superbly renovated hotel with lovely river and parkland views. Rooms include coffeemakers, hairdryers, voice mail and TV. There's a comedy club and Irish pub on the premises.

✉ 924 Spadina Crescent East, Saskatoon, Saskatchewan, S7K 3H5 ☎ 306/244-5564, 800/667-3999 ✋ $82 ⓘ 173 🔆 📺 🚊 Indoor 🚌 6A, 7, 11, 19 🅿 Downtown, corner of 25th Street by University Bridge

WINNIPEG

5 CALGARY DOWNTOWN SUITES

www.5calgary.com

As well as being in the heart of downtown the all-suite hotel offers stylish and spacious accommodations for a reasonable price. Suites have a good-size lounge with dining area and complimentary internet access, a fully equipped kitchen and a spacious bathroom. Other than the studio suites, each has either one or two separate bedrooms. There's a good restaurant at street level, which also provides room service, a cocktail lounge, and a spa.

✉ 618 5th Avenue SW, Calgary, Alberta, T2P 0M7 ☎ 403/451-5551, 888/561-7666 ✋ $109 ⓘ 302 (280 non-smoking) 🔆 📺 🚊 Outdoor 🚆 LRT 3 St SW or 6 St SW 🚌 5, 145, 433 or BRT 301 🅿 Downtown, corner of 5th Avenue and 5th Street

BANNER

In historic Crescentwood, this is a beautiful Victorian B&B on a shady lot with mature trees and lawns. Rooms are large and snug, and the one called Secret Harbor has a private sunroom hidden away behind a corner door. Wayfarer's Rest is larger, and has its own sitting area, dressing room and private bathroom.

✉ 164 Harrow Street, Winnipeg, Manitoba, R3M 2Z2 ☎ 204/256-8721 ✋ $65 ⓘ 2 🔆 🅿 Crescentwood, to the south of the downtown area

FAIRMONT PALLISER

www.fairmont.com/palliser

Stately and luxurious, this is Calgary's finest hotel. Occupying an elegant historic building, it leaves nothing to be desired in its rooms, particularly on the Fairmont Gold floor, with its exclusive check-in/out desk and concierge services and additional amenities. There is also a range of suites, including the one where Queen Elizabeth II stayed. There are two excellent restaurants and 24-hour room service.

✉ 133 9th Avenue SW, Calgary, Alberta, T2P 2M3 ☎ 403/262-1234, 800/257-7544 ✋ $149 ⓘ 405 (360 non-smoking) 🔆 📺 🚊 Indoor 🚆 LRT Centre Street 🅿 Downtown, just west of Centre South

HOTEL ARTS

www.hotelarts.ca

If you're looking for chic, this designer boutique hotel would fit the bill. The first of its kind in the city, it has been overhauled at a cost of $10 million and is full of funky art and contemporary furniture. The rooms are luxurious and supremely stylish with their "espresso and chocolate" decor, and include flat-screen TVs, pillow-top mattresses and goose-down duvets, high-speed internet, and stunning bathrooms. There are luxury rooms and suites too. The two first-rate restaurants include the trendy Raw Bar, which offers live entertainment on weekends. .

✉ 119 12th Avenue SW, Calgary, Alberta, T2R 0G8 ☎ 403/266-4611, 800/661-9378 ✋ $349 ⓘ 185 (all non-smoking) 📺 🚊 Outdoor 🚌 403, 433 🅿 Downtown, between Centre Street South and 1st Street SW

PLACE LOUIS RIEL ALL-SUITE HOTEL

www.placelouisriel.com

This is undoubtedly the best place to stay in Winnipeg. All rooms have a fully equipped kitchen, cable TV, video games, voice mail and internet access. There's a store and an ATM in the hotel.

✉ 190 Smith Street, Winnipeg, Manitoba, R3C 1J8 ☎ 204/947-6961, 800/665-0569 ✋ $120 ⓘ 294 (non-smoking) 🔆 📺 🅿 Downtown, between York and St. Mary

WESTWAYS

www.westways.ab.ca

This is a good choice for those who prefer a more homey place. This heritage home is enhanced by paintings, antiques and ornaments. All rooms have pillow-top mattresses, bathrooms, cable TV and DVD player, and telephone with voice mail. Free use of a computer, and free beverages from the third floor pantry, which also has a microwave and refrigerator.

✉ 216 25th Avenue SW, Calgary, Alberta, T2S 0L1 ☎ 403/229-1758, 866/846-7038 ✋ $119 ⓘ 5 [non-smoking] 🚆 LRT Erlton/Stampede, then bus 🚌 403, 433 🅿 Southwest quadrant, between 1st Street SW and 2nd Street SW

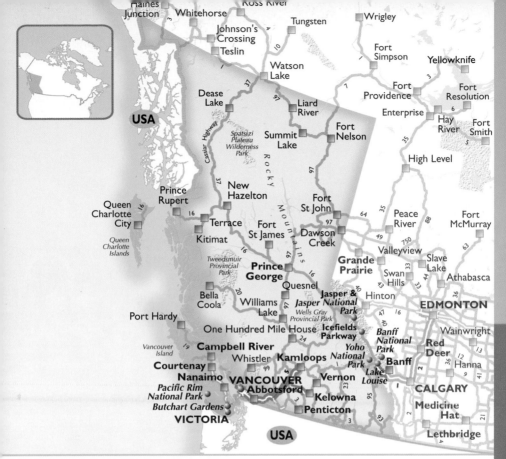

BRITISH COLUMBIA AND THE ROCKIES

This region of Canada is one of the most appealing of all, at the same time uniquely Canadian, quaintly British (even now, in places) and increasingly Pacific Rim. Its breathtaking scenery, vibrant cities, land and marine wildlife, wine-growing area, summer and winter-sports opportunities, historic sites, and wonderful First Nations art and culture combine to offer an unforgettable experience. It is also the only Canadian province that averages an above-zero winter temperature while mountain areas provide the requisite snow. Perfect.

The two main cities are the stately provincial capital, Victoria, across the Strait of Georgia on beautiful Vancouver Island, and stunning Vancouver, almost surrounded by water, with fragrant pine-clad mountains rising from its suburbs. Both routinely figure in any top ten list of best places in the world to live.

Head north from Vancouver through the Coast Mountains and in just a couple of hours you'll reach Whistler, co-host of the 2010 Winter Olympic Games and one of the finest winter sports resorts in the world. Go east from Vancouver and you will find the lush fruit-growing and wine-producing Okanagan Valley, centered on the pleasant lakeside town of Kelowna. It's a beautiful, well-watered, gently rolling landscape, but continue east and the Rocky Mountains loom large on the horizon, sheltering mirror lakes that are almost too perfect to bear.

Take the Icefields Parkway between Jasper in the north and Banff in the south for a breathtaking journey through snow-capped peaks and glacier-filled valleys, and it's quite likely that you'll also see bears, moose, elk and wild long-horn sheep along the way. Other major wildlife experiences of British Columbia and the Rockies includes huge numbers of bald eagles at Brackendale, near Squamish, the salmon run (2010 is the next good year), notably on the Adams River, and whale-watching off the west coast.

BUTCHART GARDENS

These spectacular formal gardens, planted with rare and exotic species, occupy a former limestone quarry. They celebrated their centenary in 2004, and in 2006 were designated a National Historic Site. They were created by Jenny Butchart in and around a worked-out limestone quarry of her husband Robert's Portland cement works. Her lifelong interest in plants inspired the idea, and the garden's inception coincided with a time when exotic plants were the very latest thing in garden fashion. Jenny imported hundreds of species from around the world, and over the decades, the garden has been developed and expanded to cover some 55ha (136 acres). It is still owned and run by the same family, currently by Robert and Jenny's grandson.

GARDEN TOUR

On arrival, visitors get a route map of the meandering pathways. It begins with the Sunken Gardens, 25m (82ft) down on the floor of the original quarry, with classical statuary among the plants. The Ross Fountain here was installed in 1964 to commemorate the 60th anniversary of the gardens. Next comes the Rose Garden, best in July and August, planted with hybrid tea roses around an Italian wishing well. From here you move on to the Japanese Garden, which dates to 1906 and was laid out with the help of a Japanese landscape artist—look for the rare Himalayan blue poppy. Last comes the Italian Garden, the most formal of all the garden areas, planted in 1926 on what used to be the Butcharts' tennis court.

SEASONAL ATTRACTIONS AND EVENTS

There is color and interest at any time of the year here. Even in the first quarter of the year, when everywhere else is still in the grip of winter, the indoor garden, in a stone-flagged conservatory, is an inspiration to gardeners anticipating spring, with its beds of daffodils and tulips, and flowering shrubs. Outside, stunning displays continue throughout the seasons.

Dazzling by day, the gardens sparkle when illuminated on summer evenings with thousands of lights connected to North America's largest underground wiring system. From mid-June to mid-September there's daily afternoon and evening entertainment, except on Saturdays when spectacular fireworks displays take place, followed by music from a historic pipe organ.

INFORMATION

www.butchartgardens.com

✚ 413 C17 ✉ 800 Benvenuto Avenue, Brentwood Bay, British Columbia, V8M 1J8 ☎ 250/652-4422, 866/652-4422, 250/652-5256 (recorded info) 🕐 Daily from 9am. Closing times vary seasonally, from 3.30pm in mid-winter to 9 or 10pm in summer; call for information ✋ Adult $14.50–$26.50 depending on season, child (5–12) $2–$3 or (13–17) $7.25–$13.25 🚌 75; Gray Line Tour from Victoria (Apr–end Oct); fare includes admission 🍴 Dining Room Restaurant, Blue Poppy Restaurant ☕ Coffee shop 🛍 Seeds, gardening accessories, souvenirs and First Nations crafts 📖 Flower identification guide

TIP

» If you want time to stop and smell the roses, avoid the busiest times of year, when the unbroken conga line of visitors has its own momentum.

Opposite *The gardens are a riot of color in spring and summer*
Below *There are many exotic plants in the gardens*

BANFF AND THE NATIONAL PARK

INFORMATION

www.banfflakelouise.com
www.pc.gc.ca
✚ 401 F16 ℹ️ Banff and Lake Louise Tourism Bureau, P.O. Box 1298, Banff, Alberta, T1L 1B3 ☎ 403/762-8421
ℹ️ National Park Info Centre, 224 Banff Avenue, Banff, Alberta, T1L 1K2
☎ 403/762-1550 🕐 Late Jun–end Aug daily 8–8; mid-May to late Jun and first 2 weeks in Sep daily 9–7; rest of year daily 9–5. Closed Dec 25 ✋ National Park fees: adult $8.80, child (6–16) $4.40, family $17.60

Above The rippling waters of Lake Minnewanka reflect snow-capped Mount Inglismaldie

INTRODUCTION

Surrounded by sublime mountain landscapes, Banff township sits in a natural bowl on the banks of the Bow River and makes an excellent base for touring the area. In 2008 the town of Banff replaced all its buses with a fleet of hybrid buses. Not only are they environmentally friendly, each one is totally covered with a landscape-and-wildlife painting. They operate over three routes—Banff Avenue, Tunnel Mountain and Sulphur Mountain—which cover most of the places you would want in and around town. There are also horse-drawn carriages, taxis and bicycle rentals.

You'll need a car to do proper justice to the park—start by taking the Bow Valley Parkway (▷ 291). Even if you are just driving through, you will need a national park pass (adult $9.80, child (6–16) $4,90, family $19.60), which raises funds to support visitor facilities.

EXPLORING THE NATIONAL PARK

Road conditions are good, but in winter, of course, the weather can be a factor—your hotel should be able to check for any road closures, or you can contact the national park authority. Do drive very carefully at all times and watch out for wildlife wandering onto the road ahead (and for other drivers who may brake suddenly if they see wildlife at the roadside). Summer and winter, think of any activity associated with mountains, lakes and rivers, and the great outdoors in general, and there'll be the opportunity to pursue it here. Summertime offers guided hikes, river rafting, family kayaking, horseback riding, caving, fishing, golf and helicopter sightseeing. In winter, there's downhill and Nordic skiing, ice-fishing, dogsled tours, sleigh rides, snowmobiling, tobogganning, skating and guided snowshoe walks.

The whole Rockies tourist phenomenon started when the Canadian Pacific Railway built the Banff Springs Hotel in 1888. It was modeled on a Scottish castle and named after the town of Banff in Scotland. Today, it is one of the world's great hotels, and even if you don't want to stay here, at least call in for a British-style afternoon tea or the legendary Sunday brunch, and wallow in luxury, surrounded by breathtaking mountain scenery.

The Banff National Park, Canada's first, was created in 1885 to protect the hot springs discovered during construction of the Canadian Pacific Railway. Parks Canada run a number of Interpretive Programs that offer a fascinating insight into various aspects of the national park. They also have uniformed "Roving Interpreters," who may be encountered in or out of town and are ready to answer your questions, and can recommend licensed local guides for hiking, horseback riding, fishing and climbing trips.

WHAT TO SEE

BANFF

With stupendous mountain views all around, it's hard to resist the lure of the wild, but Banff has some interesting attractions to make it worth lingering a while. It is Canada's highest town (1,383m/4,537ft) and the main tourist center for the area, with a population of around 8,000—not large by any means, but certainly geared up to cater to the 4 million or so visitors who visit the national park every year. In spite of this, it still hangs on to much of its pleasant, small town feel, particularly when a deer or wild sheep wanders in.

MUSEUMS IN BANFF

Among the town's heritage attractions, the Banff Park Museum National Historic Site (mid-May to late Sep daily 10–6; late Sep to mid-May daily 1–5) is the oldest natural history museum in Western Canada and a real relic of the past, preserved exactly as it was in 1932—which is precisely why it is listed as a National Historic Site of Canada. The exhibits are based on a collection put together for the 1893 Chicago World Exhibition to represent the wildlife of

Left *The Sulphur Mountain Gondola (cable car) on Mountain Avenue*
Below *Johnson Canyon old gas station on the Bow Valley Parkway*

this area, subsequently enlarged by the then curator, Norman Sanson, who personally collected many of the exhibits and arranged the museum displays.

The Whyte Museum of the Canadian Rockies (daily 10–5) has a more contemporary feel, with galleries of paintings and photographs showing scenes of the Rockies, and an interesting collection of artifacts related to the area, including First Nations pieces. The recreational relics are particularly fascinating, including climbing and skiing equipment from the past. The museum also has charge of seven significant historic homes in the town, from tiny log cabins to family homes.

The Buffalo Nations Luxton Museum (daily), on the Bow River, displays artifacts relating to the local First Nations tribes and hosts events, entertainments and re-enactments of their traditional lifestyles. The big stone building at 101 Mountain Avenue is Canada Place (Jun–Sep, daily), the headquarters of the national park administration. You can visit the glorious gardens, and inside there are exhibits about Canadian landscape, culture, art and inventions, with touch-screen technology and computer games to inject a bit of fun.

Banff has a summer arts festival, and year-round entertainment is provided at the Banff Centre and in the town's pubs. The town may be rather full of tourists in summer and skiers in winter, and prices may be a bit higher here, but standards are high too, with lots of expensive designer boutiques, art galleries and craft shops. It is essential to reserve accommodations well in advance for a summer stay.

HOT SPRINGS AND SULPHUR MOUNTAIN

There are eight hot springs bursting out onto Sulphur Mountain, which, not surprisingly, takes its name from the smell given off by the water as it emerges from a depth of some 3km (2 miles) below the surface. Not all of the springs are accessible, but you can take a dip in the Upper Hot Springs (daily) on Mountain Avenue, south of downtown, a particularly fun thing to do when snow is falling. The water temperature of 42°C (108°F) keeps you cozy enough.

The Cave and Basin National Historic Site (daily) is based around a spring that was discovered by railroad engineers in 1885 and actually led to the creation of the national park, Canada's first, from which the entire network of national parks has grown. Early visitors could stay in a hotel here (long gone) and bathe in the waters, but no more—the site was sacred to the local Stoney First Nations people and is now respected as such. However, visitors can tour the site, see the cave and the underground and outdoor pools and the original spring. There is also a replica of the 19th-century bathhouse, which now contains an exhibition and film about the site.

A number of trails begin here too, including a couple of short boardwalks

Below *Taking a look at Mount Rundle and Second Vermillion Lake*
Right *Banff Avenue stores at dusk*

and longer trails to view the unique environment of the nearby wetlands. An easy way up to the 2,281m (7,486ft) summit of Sulphur Mountain is on an eight-minute ride in the Banff Gondola (daily, but closed for two weeks in January for maintenance), with breathtaking views all around. At the top there's an observation deck, two restaurants and gift shop, and a number of hiking trails can be followed.

Above *The tree-fringed waters of Vermillion Lake, with spectacular mountains in the background*
Below *A view down Banff Avenue to Cascade Mountain*

BOW VALLEY PARKWAY
This is a wonderfully scenic drive, passing through some pretty aspen woodland and evergreen forest where you may see elk, moose and even an occasional bear. After 25km (16 miles), you'll come to Johnston Canyon, where you can walk along the canyon side to two pretty waterfalls (1km/0.6 miles to the first and 2.7km/1.7miles to the second) At a number of places along the Parkway, there are parking places with information panels. There is a speed limit of 60kph (37mph) on the Bow Valley Parkway, and access is restricted from 6–9pm daily from March 1 to June 25 in order to allow the wildlife free access of their natural corridor between habitats.

LAKES IN THE NATIONAL PARK
The park's lakes are justly famous. Lake Louise (▷ 298) and Moraine Lake (▷ 299) are the best known, but don't miss the lovely Lake Minnewanka. It takes its name from the Stoney nation's name, Minn-waki, or "Lake of the Spirits," which they believed inhabited its waters. The hot springs and abundant food sources made it a mecca for ancient nomadic tribes that habitually camped here. In the first half of the 20th century it was the site of a village and power plant. Thankfully, the power plant closed and the village is now hidden beneath the lake and its wild beauty restored. You can glide across its waters on a 1.5-hour narrated boat trip (mid-May to mid-Oct) to the impressive Devil's Gap, where sheer rock walls rise fjord-like from the lake. Along the way you will learn about the natural and human history of the lake.

The three Vermillion Lakes are easily reached from Banff and are very picturesque, particularly at sunset, and there are places to park at good viewing points. You can rent kayaks or canoes, or follow hiking trails.

Above *Giant Douglas firs in Cathedral Grove are hundreds of years old*
Right *One of the many outdoor murals on buildings in Chemainus*

BANFF AND THE NATIONAL PARK
▷ 288–291.

BUTCHART GARDENS
▷ 287.

CATHEDRAL GROVE
www.britishcolumbia.com/parks/?id=286
Officially MacMillan Provincial Park, after the forester who gave the land to the province, this 136ha (336-acre) park is known as Cathedral Grove. It preserves giant Douglas fir trees, some of which are up to 800 years old—the largest is 76m (250ft) high, 3m (9ft) in diameter and 9m (30ft) in circumference.

Walking between the huge trunks below the high forest canopy gives an impression of being in a vast natural cathedral. A 500m (550-yard) interpretive walk south of the highway takes you past some of the oldest trees, with explanatory panels on the temperate ecosystem along the way. A trail north of the highway leads through groves of Western Red Cedar to Lake Cameron, where you can swim or picnic.
✚ 413 C16 ✉ 114km (70 miles) north of Victoria, on Vancouver Island–take Highway 1 then go left on Highway 4 🕓 Daily, dawn–dusk 🖐 Free 🅿 $1 per hour or $3 or $5 per day

CHEMAINUS
www.chemainus.bc.ca
Street art has earned this long-established port in the southeast of Vancouver Island the title of Canada's largest outdoor art gallery. The town has risen phoenix-like from the ashes of its declining forestry industry to become a thriving artistic and commercial hub.

In 1983, following the closure of the town's large sawmill, a mainstay of the local economy for 120 years, enterprising residents set up the Festival of Murals. Building on the success of the first five murals commissioned in 1982, more than 35 now grace the walls of downtown buildings, depicting the town's history and cultural life. There are also 13 sculptures, and new artworks are added every year. A tourist train and horse-drawn tours provide an easy way to view the world's largest outdoor art gallery. Apart from the murals, the town is attractive, its painted clapboard cottages turned into boutiques selling antiques, clothing and arts and crafts. The Chemainus Theatre has a professional cast that performs throughout the year, and the town is well supplied with art galleries and eateries.
✚ 413 C17 ❗ Chemainus Visitor Information Centre, 9796 Willow Street, Chemainus, British Columbia, V0R 1K0, ☎ 250/246-3944

DUNCAN
www.duncancc.bc.ca
Duncan calls itself the "city of totems," and displays over 80 of these unique carved symbols along the Trans-Canada Highway and in the town. The Cowichan people are highly regarded for their totem-carving skills, and each totem tells a story, perhaps a legend or a real family history. Pick up a self-guiding tour map from the visitor information center, or take a free guided tour (May–end Sep) starting from the historic train station, now the Cowichan Valley Museum (Jun–Sep Mon–Sat 10–4; rest of year Wed–Fri 11–4, Sat 1–4), on Canada Avenue. At the Quw'utsun Cultural and Conference Centre (daily; www.quwutsun.ca) on Cowichan Way, you can watch totems and other items being crafted, experience a multimedia presentation on First Nations lifestyle and social history, and try your hand at native crafts or buy the real thing.
✚ 413 C17 ❗ Duncan Visitor Information Centre, 381 Trans-Canada Highway, Duncan, British Columbia, V9L 3R5, ☎ 250/746-4636, 1-888/303-3337

FORT LANGLEY
www.pc.gc.ca
This carefully reconstructed fort, 50km (30 miles) east of Vancouver, signposted off Highway 1, gives you a good idea of how the pioneers lived and traded in the early 1800s, with costumed staff setting the scene. The Hudson's Bay Company established a trading post here in 1827, at the southern narrows of the Fraser River, to trade pelts for food and other supplies with the local First Nations tribes. The trading

post was fortified in 1839 and, as the fur trade declined, Fort Langley pioneered farming and fish processing for export to San Francisco, Hawaii and Australia. During the Cariboo gold rush, when thousands made their way north from the US along the Fraser River, the governor of Vancouver Island, fearful of an American takeover, declared British Columbia a crown colony here at the fort in 1858.

Within the wooden stockade are barracks, the Big House (the chief trader's home), a forge and a storehouse, which is the only original building. Inside here you can see furs and some of the goods for which they were traded.

🚩 413 C17 ✉ PO Box 129, 23433 Mavis Avenue, Fort Langley, British Columbia V1M 2R5 ☎ 604/513-4777 🕒 Late Jun–end Aug daily 9–8, rest of year daily 10–5 💰 Adult $7.25, child (6–16) $3.50, family $18

FRASER CANYON/HELL'S GATE
www.hellsgateairtram.com
The main section of Fraser Canyon extends from Yale to Boston Bar, and Hell's Gate is its most spectacular attraction. Here, the river crashes through a narrow 35m-wide (110ft) opening between the 180m-high (600ft) canyon walls. The river is named for Simon Fraser, an American-born fur trader and explorer who navigated its length in a canoe in 1808. Today's visitors no longer need be so intrepid and can make the crossing with Airtram (mid-Apr to mid-Oct daily) on a scenic journey from the east side across the seething waters to a plateau on the west bank, a descent of 142m (500ft). Once across you'll find observation points and a display on the lifecycle of the salmon that return here to spawn each fall. There's also a restaurant, gift shop and fudge factory.

🚩 413 D16 ✉ 43111 Trans-Canada Highway, Boston Bar, British Columbia, V0X 1L0. On Highway 1, 200km (125 miles) northeast of Vancouver C604/867-9277 🕒 Mid-Apr to mid-Oct daily 10–4 💰 Adult $16, child (6–18) $10, family $42

GLACIER NATIONAL PARK
www.pc.gc.ca
The Glacier National Park is more than 12 percent solid ice; the rest is made up of the stunning mountain scenery of the Selkirk range of the Rockies. It is one of the least accessible national parks in the Rockies, with a few trails suitable only for experienced hikers/ mountaineers.

Many visitors simply sail through the park on the Trans-Canada Highway, enjoying the views from their car and halting only at the Rogers Pass Visitor Centre (daily; closed Nov Tue–Wed). Rogers Pass is a national historic site at the place where in 1882 engineer A. B. Rogers overcame huge difficulties to find a way through the mountains for the Canadian Pacific Railway's transcontinental line. The line was never stable and closed in 1916 when the Cannaught rail tunnel opened.

The park was established in 1886, shortly after the line was completed. The main attraction was, and still is, the Illecillewaet Neve Glacier, located south of the visitor center. Trails leading to stunning viewpoints were laid out by Swiss guides about a century ago, and rangers lead guided walks to see the glaciers.
🚩 400 E16 ☎ 250/837-7500 🕒 Daily 💰 Adult $7, child (6–16) $3.40, family $17.50

HOWE SOUND
www.tourismsquamish.com
The fjord-like landscape of Howe Sound is beautifully unspoiled, a stunning scene created by a mixture of receding ice flows, volcanic action and water erosion. It is an easy drive to the sound from Vancouver on the Sea to Sky Highway, or you can take a leisurely boat trip. Squamish, at the head of the sound, is known for its sporting opportunities, from gentle walks to summer and winter adrenaline sports, and is anticipating a major boost during the 2010 Winter Olympics in Vancouver/ Whistler. It's a good place to see bald eagles in winter, and also has a large artists' community, with plenty of galleries and open studios.

A big attraction in the area is the British Columbia Museum of Mining (tel 604/896-2233, www.bcmuseumofmining.org; early May to mid-Oct daily 9–4.30) at Britannia Beach, on the site of a copper mine. The mine closed in 1974, and a year later the museum opened, incorporating mine tours and mining exhibits.
🚩 413 C16 ℹ Squamish Visitor Information Centre. 102-28551 Loggers Lane, Squamish, British Columbia, V8B 0H2, ☎ 604/815-4994/5084; daily

ICEFIELDS PARKWAY
See pages 294–295.

INSIDE PASSAGE
For dramatic scenery and sightings of whales, porpoises, seals and bald eagles, the 15-hour day-trip along the Inside Passage is unbeatable. During early explorations, vessels sailing the western seaboard were at the mercy of the Pacific Ocean. The Inside Passage provided a safe route through offshore islands. Today, ferries, freight carriers and yachts ply between the islands and the forested, fjord-incised mainland. Toward the northern end of the route is the Grenville Channel, only 500m (1,600ft) wide at its narrowest point. Ferries depart from Port Hardy northbound or Prince Rupert going south (www.bcferries.com).
🚩 400 B15

Below *The Hell's Gate Airtram above the Fraser Canyon*

ICEFIELDS PARKWAY

INFORMATION

www.icefieldsparkway.ca
www.travelalberta.com

✚ 401 E15 🛈 Columbia Icefields
Centre, Icefields Parkway, Jasper,
Alberta, ☎ 877/423-7433; mid-Apr
to mid-Oct daily 9–5 or 6 🅿 Icefields
Parkway open all year, unless there's
heavy snow 🚌 Brewster Grey Line
bus from Banff to Jasper uses Icefields
Parkway 🚐 Snocoach from Columbia
Icefields Centre (May to mid-Oct daily)
🛍 Columbia Icefields Centre, North
Saskatchewan River Crossing, Sunwapta
Falls 🍴 Columbia Icefields Centre,
North Saskatchewan River Crossing,
Sunwapta Falls

Above *Bow Lake makes a perfect mirror
for the mountains above*

INTRODUCTION

This is one of the world's most spectacular drives, where majestic mountain
scenery has been sculpted by massive ice flows.

Officially Highway 93, the Icefields Parkway (▷ 318–319 drive and ▷ 320–
321 walk) reveals a never-ending series of stunning vistas as you drive the
230km (143 miles) from Lake Louise to Jasper. And, best of all, the attractions
along the route are easily accessible—at the roadside or within a short walk.
There's free parking at all the viewpoints and trailheads—but definitely no
parking along the roadside or on the verges. At km127 (mile 79) from Lake
Louise is the Columbia Icefields Centre, a comprehensive information center
with interactive displays; it also has a restaurant and Snocoach tours out onto
the ice.

The Icefields Parkway was built to provide jobs during the Depression and
was intended as a scenic route, so viewpoints and stopping places were an
integral part of the plan. It follows the route of the early fur trappers, and
several features are named after pioneers, including Hector Lake, named after
geologist James Hector, the first white man to travel the area, in 1858.

WHAT TO SEE
THE ICEFIELDS

The route is so named because it leads past the major icefields (glaciers) of the
Canadian Rockies. After 40km (25 miles) of lovely alpine meadows dotted with
lakes, you reach the first of them, the Crowfoot Glacier, whose three ice flows
resemble the claws of a bird. After Saskatchewan Crossing you enter the most
spectacular section. From the parking area for Parker Ridge, the 2.4km (1.5-
mile) trail to the ridge is a steep climb, but well worth it for the fantastic views
to the north. Farther north is the Columbia Glacier and Icefields, made up of

several glaciers (notably the Athabasca), where you can take a Snocoach ride or a guided walk out onto the ice. Do not venture out here without a guide as the hazards are many. If you get the opportunity, take a drink from the glacier meltwater. It's clean, refreshing and rich in minerals.

THE LAKES

The sapphire lakes here are a compelling attraction: tiny Herbert Lake, with a backdrop of Mt. Temple, larger Hector Lake and lovely Bow Lake, where there is a 3.4km (2-mile) lakeshore walk.

Some 40km (25 miles) into the route you'll reach the turnoff for the Peyto Lake view, which has one of the best panoramas of the entire highway, extending over pine forests to the mountain-encircled lake. The unusual blue of the lake's waters is the result of the fine rock particles that wash off the Peyto Glacier, away to the left.

VALLEYS AND WATERFALLS

Four rivers have carved their way through the mountains, sometimes tumbling as waterfalls. First is the Bow River, which flows south toward Banff, and, after crossing the North Saskatchewan River, there are terrific views of Cirrus Mountain and the Bridal Falls. Farther north are the wider, rock-strewn valleys of the Sunwapta and Athabasca rivers, with the splendid Sunwapta Falls and Athabasca Falls. The latter is the most photogenic waterfall of the route, but the Weeping Wall (105km/65 miles from Lake Louise) is perhaps the most astounding: a giant rock face with water constantly seeping down it. At km72 (mile 45) from Lake Louise, a short trail leads to Mistaya Canyon.

WILDLIFE

At various points you may catch sight of black bears and moose, and you might even see a gray wolf. More common are the shaggy, white mountain goats that frequent the area, making light work of the landscape with their suction-cupped feet. In the most northerly section, you might also encounter bighorn sheep. If you want to see the rare mountain caribou, head for the Sunwapta gravel flats/Beauty Creek area around May, when they come to feed here. Grizzlies and elk also inhabit this area. If you see a parked car, chances are there's some wildlife to see. Park safely and don't get out of your car.

Above The way to Cirrus Mountain
Left Snocoach tours of the Athabasca Glacier are popular
Below The Athabasca Falls rushing down a rocky gorge

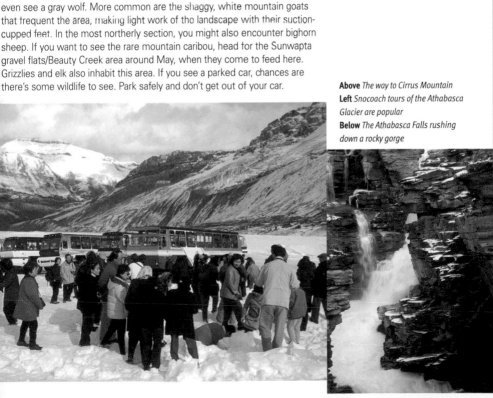

JASPER TOWN AND NATIONAL PARK

Above *The best way to explore the park is on horseback*

INFORMATION

www.jaspercanadianrockies.com
www.pc.gc.ca
www.skijaspercanada.com
www.rockymountaineer.com
✚ 400 E15 ℹ Jasper Tourism and Commerce, P.O. Box 98, Jasper, Alberta, T0E 1E0 ☎ 780/852-3858 ℹ Jasper National Park and Tourism Information Centre, 500 Connaught Drive, Jasper, Alberta, T0E 1E0, ☎ 780/852-6176; Apr to mid-Jun daily 9–5; mid-Jun to Labor Day 8–7; Labor Day–end Sep 9–6; Oct 9–5; Nov–end Mar 9–4 🚉 Rocky Mountaineer Scenic Railway, ViaRail Station, 607 Connaught Drive, Jasper, Alberta, T0E 1E0, ☎ 604/606-7245, 1-877/460-3200

INTRODUCTION

Jasper National Park is a spectacular place with towering peaks and lakes of unbelievable hues.

One hundred years old in 2007, Jasper National Park covers an area of 10,878sq km (4,200sq miles). An excellent introduction to it is a visit to the information office, almost opposite the train station in Jasper town, where you can discover why the park has a reputation for great white-water rafting in summer, and snowboarding and skiing in winter. Jasper is a stop on the Rocky Mountaineer scenic railroad that runs from Vancouver to Edmonton, and the ViaRail train Skeena, linking Edmonton with Prince Rupert on a scenic journey, also stops here. The park has more than 1,200km (660 miles) of hiking routes, mostly long range or difficult, but the main attractions and some of the best scenery are easily accessible by car or via the Jasper Tramway (▷ opposite).

Jasper was one of the first areas of the Rockies to be reached by Europeans when, in 1811, members of David Thompson's expedition to find a northern route over the mountains arrived here. One of Thompson's companions established a depot called Henry House for the North West Company (a rival of the Hudson's Bay Company, but later amalgamated with it). This was renamed Jasper House after a man called Jasper Hawse, and the name stuck when the town grew.

Activity declined through the 19th century, but the arrival of the railroad in 1908 saved the settlement. The park was created three years later.

WHAT TO SEE

JASPER TOWN

Jasper is not as pretty or as sophisticated as Banff (▷ 288–291), and those who come do so mostly for the outdoor attractions and activities of the park, giving the place the atmosphere of a real mountain town. You'll certainly want to visit the park information center (▷ Information, opposite), built in 1914 to house the park superintendent and the administrative offices, and now a national historic site in an attractive setting of flower gardens.

To learn about Jasper's history, visit the Yellowhead Museum (mid-May to mid-Oct daily; rest of year Thu–Sun), which focuses on the town's role in the fur trade and also has exhibits relating to the surrounding landscapes, plus a small art gallery.

THE WHISTLERS AND MT. EDITH CAVELL

You can ride the Jasper Tramway (mid-Apr to mid-Oct daily) to an elevaton of 2,285m (7,496ft). The Whistlers for panoramic views of the surrounding area; a steep climb, around 1.5km (just under a mile) long, takes you to the true summit.

The name of The Whistlers comes from the high-pitched whistle made by a hoary marmot when it senses danger; you may be lucky enough to see one of these engaging animals near the summit. Another panoramic viewpoint is of the serenely beautiful Mt. Edith Cavell, reached via a 4.5km (2.8-mile) twisting road.

LAKES AND HOT SPRINGS

The nearest lakes to the town (Edith and Annette) are just 5km (3 miles) to the northeast, but more dramatic are Patricia and Pyramid lakes, just over 7km (4 miles) northwest of Jasper.

All four lakes have sandy beaches, boat rental and trails to enjoy. One of the highlights of the park is Maligne Lake and the 48km (30-mile) route to reach it, passing Medicine Lake on the way. Maligne Lake Road is a good place for wildlife spotting, especially early or late in the day—look out for elk, deer, bighorn sheep, coyote and black bear. You can also hike Maligne Canyon on a 3.7km (2.3-mile) route.

Miette Hot Springs (mid-May to early Oct daily), toward the eastern border of the park and reached via a drive up the wild Fiddle Valley, has the hottest naturally occuring water in the Rockies, flowing from the mountains at a temperature of 54°C (129°F).

TIPS

» The top of The Whistlers is extremely exposed to the elements, so bring warm clothing, even in summer.

» The Columbia Icefields Centre, Athabasca Glacier, Sunwapta Falls and Athabasca Falls are also within Jasper National Park (▷ 294–295 Icefields Parkway).

Left *Malinge Lake, encircled with mountains, is the largest lake in the Rockies*
Below *Trekkers hiking up to the summit of Mount Edith Cavell*

INFORMATION

www.banfflakelouise.com

www.pc.gc.ca

➕ 401 F16 ℹ Banff and Lake Louise Tourism Bureau, P.O. Box 1298, Banff, Alberta, T1L 1B3, ☎ 403/762-8421

ℹ National Park Info Centre, 224 Banff Avenue, Banff, Alberta, T1L 1K2

☎ 403/762-1550 🕐 Late Jun–end Aug daily 8–8; mid-May to late Jun and 1st 2 weeks in Sep daily 9–7; rest of year daily 9–5. Closed Dec 25 ✋ National Park fees: adult $8.80, child (6–16) $4.40, family $17.60

ℹ Lake Louise Visitor Centre, Samson Mall 🕐 Summer months only

TIP

» The view can be spoiled by the crowds, so arrive early if you want to get the place almost to yourself.

Below Canoeing on the lake's deep, tree-fringed waters

LAKE LOUISE

Ravishing Lake Louise sits in a bowl carved by glacial ice, framed by dark green forest and with a backdrop of snowcapped mountains, and is one of the most beautiful views in the Rockies. The iridescent blue of the water is created by microscopic particles that are trapped in the spring meltwaters—these absorb the light of all the colors in the rainbow except blue and green, which are reflected back in the most astonishing way, and appear even more intense viewed from above lake level.

It was called Lake of the Little Fishes by the native Stoney Indians, but when Tom Wilson, a European outfitter working for the Canadian Pacific Railway, saw the lake in 1882, he immediately christened it Emerald Lake for its brilliant color. In 1884 it was renamed Lake Louise in honor of Queen Victoria's daughter, married to the then Governor General of Canada, Lord Lorne.

HIKING TRAILS

Though it is not possible to follow a complete circuit around the lake, there are some wonderful walks, the most popular of which are to the Plain of Six Glaciers and the climb up to Lake Agnes (▷ 320–321). A great way to enjoy the scene without the effort of hiking is from the Lake Louise Gondola (May–end Sep daily; skiers only in winter), which opens up panoramic views.

FAIRMONT CHÂTEAU LAKE LOUISE HOTEL

In 1890, the Canadian Pacific Railway built a wooden chalet for visitors, but work soon started on the Château Lake Louise Hotel (▷ 320, 321), which sits on glacial moraine left behind as the ice retreated and now dominates the lakeside. There's a viewing area in front of the hotel, with a splendid outlook toward the surrounding mountains.

KOOTENAY NATIONAL PARK

www.pc.gc.ca

Together with Banff, Jasper and Yoho, Kootenay National Park forms part of a UNESCO World Heritage Site and protects an area of 1,406sq km (550sq miles) on the western slopes of the Rocky Mountains. The least busy of the major parks in the Rockies—though it gets 3 million visitors per year—Kootenay is an easy excursion from Banff or Lake Louise. In a three-hour drive you can take in all kinds of terrain, from the glacier fields in the north, through mountains, meadows and grasslands to the arid land farther south.

Kootenay owes its existence to the road that bisects it from north to south. Construction began before World War I, but funds soon ran out, and the highway was completed with federal government funds on condition that a strip of land 8km (5 miles) each side of the road was given over to a national park.

Trails lead from the Kootenay Parkway to most of the main attractions. The best of the short trails are to Marble Canyon and Paint Pots, each about a 15-minute walk from their parking areas. At Marble Canyon the dolomite and limestone walls of the 36m-deep (120ft) gorge have been polished marble-smooth by the waters that carved it. The trail crisscrosses the rushing creek several times before reaching a waterfall. The Paint Pots are pools with a build up of minerals around their rims.

✚ 401 E16 ⓘ National Park Visitor Center, 7556 Main Street East, Radium Hot Springs, British Columbia, V0A 1M0 ☎ 250/347-9505 ⓘ Mid-May to mid-Jun and early to mid-Sep, daily 9–5; mid-Jun to early Sep daily 9–7, mid-Sep to mid-Oct daily 9–4 Park fees: adult $8.80, child (6–16) $4.40, family $17.60

MORAINE LAKE

www.banfflakelouise.com

www.pc.gc.ca

Discovered in 1899 by Walter Wilcox, who described it as a place of "inspiring solitude and rugged grandeur," Moraine Lake—the Jewel of the Rockies—sits at an elevation of 574m (1,884ft) and, like nearby Lake Louise, was created by glacial action. Though it is smaller than Lake Louise, it's no less picturesque. In fact, its location at the foot of a range of the jagged peaks of the Wenkchemna Mountains, which are much closer to the water than those surrounding Lake Louise, exaggerates the bowl-like effect and creates a much more intimate atmosphere.

A tea lodge erected in 1912 was replaced several times. The most recent (1991) lodge, designed by Arthur Erickson, is a suitably rustic place to lunch or spend the night.

Viewpoints and trails

At the outlet of the lake, a small hill, created by a landslip, makes a perfect viewing point—this is the view that appeared on old $20 bills. There are a number of trails, all starting from the lodge, whether you just want a gentle walk around the lake or a longer hike. The route to Consolation Lake (3.2km/2 miles) passes a stand of rock called the Tower of Babel; a steeper climb leads through Larch Valley (3.6km/2.2 miles) and, for an even more demanding hike, continues to Sentinel Pass; while the trail to Eiffel Lake (5.6km/3.5 miles), involving an ascent of almost 1,200m/3,936ft, is the least walked trail in spite of the grandiose scenery that awaits at its end.

Lovely at any time of the year, the area around the lake becomes unspeakably beautiful during the fall foliage season.

✚ 401 F16 ⓘ Banff and Lake Louise Tourism Bureau, P.O. box 1298, Banff, Alberta, T1L 1B3 ☎ 403/762-8421 ⓘ National Park Visitor Centre and Park Office, 224 Banff Avenue, Banff, Alberta, T1L 1K2 ☎ 403/762-1550 ⓘ Late Jun–end Aug daily 8–8; mid-May to late Jun and 1st 2 weeks in Sep daily 9–7; rest of year daily 9–5. Closed Dec 25 National Park fees: adult $8.80, child (6–16) $4.40, family $17.60

MT. REVELSTOKE NATIONAL PARK

www.parkscanada.gc.ca/revelstoke

Mt. Revelstoke National Park was

Above *Fast-flowing stream feeding into Moraine Lake*

established in 1914 after Revelstoke townspeople lobbied for action to preserve the beauty of the alpine meadows below the mountain summit, where wildflowers create a swathe of color in high summer.

Covering only 260sq km (101sq miles), Mt. Revelstoke is one of Canada's smallest parks. It offers walking on trails such as the Giant Cedars Trail, through a stand of ancient Western Red Cedars, and the Skunk Cabbage Trail, through jungle-like wetland, excellent for birdwatching. The park protects a small herd of the threatened mountain caribou, and provides habitats for grizzly bear and mountain goat.

The 26km (16-mile) Meadows in the Sky Parkway (closed when snow arrives—usually mid-Oct to early Jul), winds uphill through the dense old-growth rain forest of giant cedar and pine, then subalpine forest, and finally crosses alpine meadows and tundra to the Balsam Lake parking area. From here, the mountain summit can be reached either on foot or, in summer, by shuttle bus, a distance of 2km (1.25 miles). A gentle hike on the Meadows in the

Left The yacht club congregates in Oak Bay
Above First Nations war canoe on show at Georgia Park in Nanaimo

Sky Trail takes in the best of the woodland landscape.

Revelstoke itself is a quiet town of pretty clapboard houses nestling in the valley below the mountain. The view from the lookout near the start of the parkway is awe-inspiring. ✚ 400 E16 ✉ 300 3rd Street West, Box 350, Revelstoke, British Columbia, V0E 2S0 ☎ 250/837-7500 ◐ Park open when snow-free; welcome station kiosk: mid-Jun to end Aug daily 7am–10pm; park office: Mon–Fri 8.30–12, 1–4.30 during the snow-free season ⛺ Adult $6.80, child (6–16) $3.40, family $17.10

NANAIMO
www.tourismnanaimo.com
The town of Nanaimo revolves around its harbor. A working fishing fleet operates here, and there seem to be more pleasure boats, kayaks and sailboards on the water than there are cars in garages. On the last weekend in July the town holds the Nanaimo Marine Festival and Bathtub Race, when tubbers race around offshore islands before returning to Nanaimo. There's a lovely waterfront walk that takes you around the harbor from the apartment village in the south, around Georgia Park with its First Nations kayak and totems, and onto the Millstone River inlet where salmon come in the fall to spawn.

The local Snuneymuxw people fished here, and later the Hudson's Bay Company opened a trading post. The Bastion, built in 1853 and overlooking the harbor, was the company's attempt at fortification. The Nanaimo Museum relates the lives of the early settlers, local First Nations, geology and coal mining in the Port of Nanaimo Centre.
✚ 413 C16 ℹ Tourism Nanaimo, Beban House, 2290 Bowen Road, Nanaimo, British Columbia, V9T 3K7 ☎ 250/756-0106, 1-800/663-7337 🚌 Greyhound bus from Victoria 🚂 ViaRail's *Malahat* route runs along east coast of Vancouver Island from Victoria to Courtenay ⛴ BC Ferries from Horseshoe Bay northwest of Vancouver and from Tsawwassen south of Vancouver ✈ Regular scheduled flights from Vancouver

OAK BAY
www.tourismvictoria.com
This leafy suburb on the coast around 5km (3 miles) east of downtown Victoria is the nearest thing to a piece of Great Britain in Canada. Large family homes are surrounded by gardens planted with roses and hollyhocks. Most date from the early to mid-20th century, when wealthier residents of Victoria moved out of town. Many hotels and cafés here serve afternoon tea, often in locations that overlook the sea.

You can drive through Oak Bay on the scenic Marine Drive out of Victoria. Along the road there are good views of the architecture of the place, and glimpses of the rocky coves and sandy bays along the shoreline, and of the spectacular Cascade Mountains of Washington state (US), across the Strait of Georgia, dominated by Mt. Baker.
✚ 413 C17 ℹ Tourism Victoria, Greater Victoria Visitor and Convention Bureau, 4th Floor, 31 Bastion Square, Victoria, British Columbia, V8W 2B3 ☎ 250/414-6999 🚌 2, 2A from downtown Victoria

OKANAGAN
www.thompsonokanagan.com
The Okanagan River valley, with its lakes and rolling hills, is an area of fruit growing and wine production, and is a popular recreation spot, especially in summer. Many of the wineries welcome visitors to taste and buy their products, and products from around 70 wineries are showcased in the British Columbia Wine Information Centre (daily), which shares a distinctive building in Penticton with the Wine Country Visitor Centre. The Okanagan Wine Route takes in 25 wineries. Four wine festivals take place annually, one for each season.

From south to north, the main towns are Penticton, Kelowna and Vernon, all good bases from which to explore the region. The Historic O'Keefe Ranch (late Apr to mid-Oct daily 9–6), 11km (7 miles) north of Vernon, dates from the 1860s and was a family ranch for 100 years before opening its fascinating collection of old buildings There are plenty of opportunities for outdoor pursuits.
✚ 413 D17 ℹ Thompson Okanagan Tourism Association, 1332 Water Street, Kelowna, British Columbia, V1Y 9P4, ☎ 250/860-5999, 800/567-2275 ℹ Wine Country Visitor Centre, 553 Railway Street, Penticton, British Columbia, V2A 8S3 ☎ 250/493-4055, 800/663-5052 🚂 ViaRail services to Kamloops, 2 hours' drive to the north

PACIFIC RIM NATIONAL PARK
▷ 302–303.

PRINCE RUPERT/SKEENA VALLEY

www.tourismprincerupert.com

If you take the ferry north from Port Hardy on Vancouver Island along the Inside Passage, Prince Rupert is the last ferry stop before Alaska. A former Hudson's Bay Company post and natural deepwater port, it was chosen as the western terminus for the Grand Trunk Pacific Railway, begun in 1906 and completed in 1914. But two years earlier the railroad's chairman, Charles Hayes, died on the *Titanic*, and the town never achieved his dream of rivaling Vancouver in importance.

Cow Bay, a renovated area of stores, galleries and restaurants along the waterfront, has original 1905 clapboard buildings painted black and white like a Holstein cow. Totem poles carved by the Tsimshian and Haida peoples are dotted throughout the town, and the crafts and everyday items of these First Nations are on display in the Museum of Northern British Columbia (Jun–end Aug daily; rest of year Mon–Sat). Along the Skeena Valley you'll see waterfalls, tiny islands and densely forested slopes backed by snowcapped peaks. Look for the totem poles, too.

Near the small settlement of New Hazelton, where the road and the river part company, a traditional Gitksan village, Ksan Historical Vallage and Museum, has been reconstructed. An open-air museum (Apr–Sep daily, rest of year Mon–Fri for museum and giftshop only) preserving a vanishing culture, it features tribal longhouses, a carving school, and arts and crafts.

🚩 400 B14/C14 ℹ️ Prince Rupert Visitor Centre, Atlin Terminal, Suite 100, 215 Cow Bay Road, Prince Rupert, British Columbia, V8J 1A2 ☎ 250/624-5637 🚌 Geyhound, connecting at Prince George 🚢 BC Ferries from Port Hardy on Vancouver Island ✈ Scheduled flights from Vancouver

QUEEN CHARLOTTE ISLANDS/HAIDA GWAII

www.qcinfo.com

The remoteness of this archipelago of two larger and 150 smaller islands, lying around 130km (80 miles) from Prince Rupert across the Hecate Strait, is perhaps part of its attraction. Visitors come here for the spectacular, often mist-shrouded landscape, wildlife, hiking, boating and fishing, and to experience the culture of the Haida.

This First Nations tribe is believed to have been here for thousands of years before the islands were claimed for the British Crown in 1787 and named after the wife of King George III. Haida Gwaii means "islands of the Haida people," and the Haida are still thriving here, managing the islands and its tourism industry. Sat) is a multimillion dollar complex of large, modern cedar buildings incorporating the enlarged Haida Gwaii Museum, a performance venue, a carving house where demonstrations take place and various educational facilities for Haida artists and artisans. Examples of Haida carving on display here are unparalleled in their artistry and guided tours (summer only) interpret the significance of the totem poles around the site. The Haida Heritage Centre provides an excellent introduction to the culture of the Haida Nation.

The Gwaii Haanas National Park Reserve (May–end Oct) covers the southern tip of the archipelago, and protects the dense rainforest and accompanying wildlife, which would otherwise be threatened by logging interests. Occupying most of Moresby Island, it is home to several ancient Haida villages.

There is no vehicular access to the park, and independent visitors should have experience of wilderness travel. It's obligatory to make a reservation and attend an orientation session before being allowed to visit. Taking a trip with a local charter company approved by Parks Canada is your best option.

🚩 400 B14 ℹ️ Queen Charlotte Visitor Centre, 3220 Wharf Street, Queen Charlotte, British Columbia, V0T 1T0, ☎ 250/559-8316 🚢 BC Ferries from Prince Rupert to Skidegate ✈ Daily flights from Vancouver and Prince Rupert

Below left *A selection of wines from the vineyards of the Okanagan*
Below right *The Skeena River cuts through some spectacular scenery*

PACIFIC RIM NATIONAL PARK

INFORMATION

www.pacificrimtourism.ca
www.tourismtofino.com

✚ 413 C17 ℹ Pacific Rim National
Park Office, 2185 Ocean Terrace Road,
Ucluelet, British Columbia, V0R 3A0,
☎ 250/726-7721 or 250/726-7289
ℹ Pacific Rim Tourism, 3100 Kingsway,
"The Station," Port Alberni, British
Columbia, V9Y 3B1 ☎ 250/723-7529
☛ 2-hour guided walks on Long Beach
in summer

INTRODUCTION

Strung out along the wild Pacific coast, this huge park has three very different
ecosystems. As its name suggests, this national park, covering 49,962ha
(123,406 acres), sits on the very western edge of Canada on the Pacific side of
Vancouver Island. Many visitors come to see the whales that migrate through
the coastal waters, but the land and marinescapes demand equal attention,
with virgin temperate rainforest, fantastic beaches and remote offshore
islands. Summer sunsets are magnificent, and in winter pounding waves and
seaspray encourage storm-watching.

The park, running along the coastal strip, is divided into three main sections:
Long Beach, the Broken Islands and the West Coast Trail. There are regular boat
trips to the islands. To walk the West Coast Trail you must obtain a permit and
attend an orientation session. Port Alberni, though inland from the park, offers
access along Barkley Sound by boat and day trips on ferries.

Two small settlements—Ucluelet and Tofino—sit like bookends at either side
of Long Beach, and both offer a range of day trips, boat charters and seaplane
charters. Ucluelet, to the south, is the perfect departure point for trips to the
Broken Group Islands.

REMOTE FORESTS

The first European to explore this coast was Captain Cook in 1778, followed by
Captain Charles William Barkley, after whom Barkley Sound is named. The area
was populated by the Nuu-chah-nulth people, but settlers were not drawn to
the remote location, with an annual rainfall of 300cm (117in) and treacherous
waters known as "the Graveyard of the Pacific." As first-growth forest along
the coast began to fall to the lumberman's ax, it was its remoteness that saved
the forest. The national park now has some of the finest examples of first-
growth temperate rainforest in the world.

Though the First Nations population declined steeply in the 19th century,
they still have a presence here, and the national park protects 290 native
archeological sites.

WHAT TO SEE

LONG BEACH

This is the most accessible area of the park—a broad coastal plain between Barkley Sound and Clayoquot Sound protecting 13,715ha (33,876 acres), of which 7,690ha (18,994 acres) are on land. A walk along the beach here (▷ 326–327) is a wonderful experience, whatever the weather. Long sandy stretches of beach are broken by rocky outcrops and backed by temperate forest. The rolling swells of the mighty Pacific break on to the beach, making it a great place for surfing.

The Wickaninnish Interpretive Centre (mid-Mar to mid-Oct), nearing the end of a three-year renovation and improvement project, offers tours along the beach, information and a theater program.

THE BROKEN ISLANDS

Scattered across Barkley Sound in the coastal waters south of Long Beach are the Broken Group Islands, an archipelago of over 100 islets and rocks that protects populations of bald eagles, sea lions and seals. The islands are accessible only by boat, but you can take a daily charter from Ucluelet, or a full day trip (three times a week, year round) from Port Alberni on the MV *Lady Rose* or MV *Frances Barkley*.

THE WEST COAST TRAIL

Even more remote than the Broken Group Islands is the totally unspoiled strip of land south of Barkley Sound between the tiny settlements of Bamfield and Port Renfrew.

The West Coast Trail, originally designed as an escape route for sailors stranded by shipwreck in the 1880s and running for 75km (47 miles) along this strip, is not for novices; it takes around five days to complete.

MEARES ISLAND AND HOT SPRINGS COVE

These two attractions are both reached via Tofino. Meares Island consists of 8,800ha (21,736 acres) of pristine temperate forest said to be 1,500 years old. At Hot Springs Cove, reached along a half-hour boardwalk through forest, pungent sulfurous water at a temperature of 50°C (122°F) flows from natural fissures.

TIP

» Sightings are not guaranteed on whale-watching trips, but chances are very good during the migration season.

Opposite top *Passengers taking a boat trip on Clayoquot Sound*
Opposite bottom *A magnificent bald eagle at rest*
Below left *Sealions cling often bask on the rocks at Clayoquot Sound*
Below right *It's easy to explore the park on one of these boardwalks*

VANCOUVER

INFORMATION

www.tourismvancouver.com

🛈 Tourist InfoCentre, Plaza Level, 200 Burrard Street ☎ 604/683-2000 or 800/663-6000 🕓 Victoria Day weekend (mid-May) to mid-Sep daily 8.30–6; rest of the year Mon–Sat 8.30–5

HOW TO GET THERE

✈ **Vancouver International Airport**
13km (8 miles) south of the city center

🚆 🚌 **Pacific Central Station**
Southeast of downtown, houses the railroad and long-distance bus stations: take taxi or SkyTrain light transit to the center

Above *View of downtown Vancouver from Davie Street*
Opposite *Street entertainer on Granville Island, a lively area of the city*

INTRODUCTION

Downtown Vancouver occupies a peninsula, which juts into the Burrard Inlet, with the suburbs of North and West Vancouver across the inlet on the North Shore. Most sights are within walking distance of or close to downtown. Other highlights, such as Granville Island and the Vancouver Museum, are best reached by bus or ferry. Farther afield is the Museum of Anthropology, which requires a 20-minute bus or taxi ride. You'll also need public transportation to access the sights of the North Shore.

First Nations peoples inhabited the Vancouver area at least 10,000 years, but by European standards this is a new city, brought into being by the British Columbian gold rushes of 1858, when a small settlement on the Fraser River became a springboard for prospectors. In 1867, a sawmill, then a shanty town (Gassy's Town, now Gastown), were the focus of the city, which was named Vancouver in 1886. In the same year the transcontinental Canadian Pacific Railway reached the city, a lifeline that transformed Vancouver's fortunes.

WHAT TO SEE

CANADA PLACE

www.canadaplace.ca

Stroll the boardwalks at this stunning waterfront building for an impression of Vancouver's beautiful setting. The majestic white building, with five vast Teflon sails, the focal point, was designed by Eberhard Zeidler and constructed as the Canada Pavilion for World's Fair, Expo '86. In the following year it became home to the Vancouver Trade and Convention Center. Today, Canada Place houses an IMAX movie theater and chic hotels, restaurants and stores. Vancouver's cruise ship terminal is here—a huge cruise liner alongside Canada Place is one of the signature images of the city. Vancouver Port Authority now has an Interpretive Centre (Mon–Fri 8–5) at the north end, where you can load a container ship (virtually), experience the dockside world in front of giant video screens, and learn fun facts about shipping, trade and the cruise industry. Outside, there are 44 information boards of the Promenade into History.

✛ 304 B1 ✉ 504–999 Canada Place Way, Vancouver, British Columbia, V6C 3E1 ☎ 604/775-7200 ⊕ Daily ♨ Free 🚌 44 on Burrard; 5, 10, 16 on Granville 🚇 Skytrain: Waterfront 🍴 🛍

CHINATOWN

From Vancouver public library, a pedestrian walkway called the Silk Route (signed by banners on streetlights) leads through the impressive Millennium Chinese Gate into Vancouver's Chinatown, with its lively milieu of authentic restaurants, supermarkets, apothecaries, and stores. East Pender Street and the parallel Keefer house the bulk of the eateries, where you can find delicious dim sum, and on summer weekend evenings, (Jun–end Sep Fri–Sun 6–11) there's a night market, with everything from CDs and clothing to food specialties.

Dr. Sun Yat-Sen Classical Chinese Garden (daily) on Carrall Street is a beautiful and tranquil haven from the busy streets outside.

✛ 304 C2 ✉ Between East Pender, Abbot, Gore and Keefer streets, Vancouver, British Columbia 🚌 19, 22 east on Pender Street 🍴 🛍 🏛

GRANVILLE ISLAND

www.granvilleisland.com

Art schools, studios and workshop theaters make Granville Island one of the city's most vibrant cultural areas. Add the wonderful food market (daily), one of the best in North America, the inviting eateries, stores and the weekend street entertainers, and you have an unbeatable mix.

In the same building on Duranleau Street, the Model Trains Museum (Tue–Sun 10–5.30) has the largest collection of little locomotives in the world, while the Model Ships Museum (same hours) showcases diminutive seagoing vessels of all kinds. Don't miss the Net Loft (daily 10–7) and its surrounding galleries, with a comprehensive range of arts and crafts. The area was reclaimed from swampland after World War I for shipbuilding and ironworks. After the industry declined, the site became derelict, but regeneration in the 1970s transformed the area into the attractive waterside area it is today.

✛ Off map 304 A2 ✉ Across False Creek 🏠 1398 Cartwright Street, Vancouver, British Columbia, V6H 3R8 ☎ 604/666-5784 ⊕ Information Center: daily 9–6 ♨ Granville Island: free. One admission for all museums: adult $7.50, child $4, family $20 🚢 Aquabus, False Creek Ferry 🚌 4, 7, 10, 16, 70, (50 links to the Aquabus station) 🍴 🛍 🏛

MARITIME MUSEUM

www.vancouvermaritimemuseum.com

The prize exhibit of Vancouver's Maritime Museum is the Royal Canadian Mounted Police ship St. Roch, restored to her 1944 appearance. The first ship to navigate the Northwest Passage between Baffin Island and the Beaufort Sea, the St. Roch plied the route as a supply ship for the RCMP depots in the Arctic between 1928 and 1948. The museum tells stories of pirates, shipwrecks, cruising and the shipping trade, and illustrates Vancouver's strong ties with the sea with models, photographs and other interesting memorabilia. Marine enthusiasts can browse in the museum's library of research material and books relating to maritime history and technology.

✛ Off map 304 A2 ✉ 1905 Ogden Avenue, Vancouver, British Columbia, V6J 1A3 ☎ 604/257-8300 ⊕ Mid-May to early Sep daily 10–5; rest of year Tue–Sat 10–5, Sun 12–5 ♨ Adult $10, child (6–19) $7.50, family $25 (tax not included) 🚌 2, 22 🚢 False Creek Ferry

TIPS

» Granville Island is very busy at weekends. Aim to visit during the week, and don't take a car: parking is difficult.
» Day passes for the transit system are worthwhile only if you intend to make several trips outside the downtown area.
» Do make time to visit the North Shore sights: the SeaBus crossing is quick and efficient.
» If you're walking to Stanley Park from downtown, follow the waterfront: the approach on Robson and other streets is dull.
» Avoid rush hour if you're taking a bus, car or taxi to the North Shore—there are often long delays on the Lions Gate Bridge.
» If you make the journey to the Museum of Anthropology, be sure to see Wreck Beach and the Nitobe and Botanical gardens while you are there.

INFORMATION

www.moa.ubc.ca

✚ 304 off A5 ✉ 6393 North West Marine Drive, Vancouver, British Columbia, V6T 1Z2 ☎ 604/822-5087 🕐 Mid-May to early Oct daily 10–5 (Also Tue 5–9); rest of year Tue 11–9, Wed–Sun 11–5 ✋ Adult $9, child (6–17) $7, family $25, $5 flat rate Tue 5–9 🚌 4, 9, 17, 25, 41, 43, 44, 4999 to UBC ☛ Free self-guiding tours available in English, French, Italian, German, Spanish, Korean, Chinese and Japanese; free gallery walks (twice daily) 📖 Multilingual mini-guides: free 🍴 Café with a range of snacks 🛍 Gifts, books and Northwest Coast crafts

Below *The museum contains a remarkable collection of totems and carvings, such as this depiction of a bird*

MUSEUM OF ANTHROPOLOGY

This museum and vast store of ethnographic and archaeological artifacts displays objects and art of the local Haida, Salish, Tsimshian and Kwaiuti First Nations people, and is custodian of a vast archive relating to Haida traditional practices and social history. It was created at a time when the voices of First Nations were being heard, perhaps for the first time, in government circles—their demands for rights over tribal lands was a major political issue toward the end of the 20th century, with many tribes receiving land and millions of dollars in settlement of claims. The intense focus on First Nations' rights prompted an interest in their traditions, in contrast to efforts throughout the 19th and early 20th centuries to crush native ways.

THE COLLECTION

Although the collection covers all the tribes in British Columbia, precedence is given to the Haida, the most artistically creative of all North America's native peoples. It was they who fashioned totems as historical records (the forest of poles in the totem gallery is one of the highlights), carved exquisite jewelry and decorated household items.

Haida artist Bill Reid (1920–98) attracted world renown. A sculptor, carver, canoe-builder, poet and illustrator, Reid was at the forefront of the rebirth of First Nations' artistic endeavor, working tirelessly to keep the culture alive. The collection of his work here includes the powerful *The Raven and the First Men*, depicting the legend of the first Haida men, and the gallery also has fine examples of his jewelry, masks and sculpture, all in traditional materials.

THE BUILDING

The museum building was designed by Arthur Erickson in 1976. The huge Great Hall, created to reflect traditional longhouses, is a perfect setting for the totem collection, and is linked to the outside by more totems set in the gardens.

Two traditional Haida longhouses sit at Point Grey, overlooking the ocean. The Masterpiece Gallery houses jewelry and ceremonial masks, along with much of Bill Reid's work. A multimillion dollar "Renewal Project" is underway to expand the museum space by 50 percent and provide improved research facilities and a digital networking system. The work, anticipated to be complete in 2009, includes redesigned public spaces and a large new gallery for special exhibitions.

MORE TO SEE

NORTH SHORE

www.nvchamber.bc.ca

The North Shore has a different flavor from the rest of the city, and its own special attractions. There is a lively arts scene here, and the North Vancouver Museum and Archives (Tue–Sun pm) is the best of a clutch of museums. Shoppers will enjoy Park Royal mall and the market at Lonsdale Quay.

Hills rise steeply here, offering expansive views. Just 3km (2 miles) north of Lion's Gate Bridge, the Capilano River Regional Park protects rain forest and huge Douglas firs, and a fish ladder takes salmon around the Cleveland Dam to their spawning beds. Grouse Mountain cable car whisks visitors to a base station for panoramic views over the city, mountain-top trails, grizzly bears and falconry displays. Lighthouse Park, at the head of Burrard Inlet consists of 75ha (185 acres) of coastal virgin forest, with trails leading through the forest and down to the lighthouse.

✚ Off map, 304 C1 ℹ North Shore Tourism, 102–124 West 1st Street, North Vancouver, British Columbia, V7M 3N3, ☎ 604/987-4488 ⛴ Seabus

SCIENCE WORLD

www.scienceworld.bc.ca

The large geodesic dome of Science World is home to a hands-on science exhibits. Daily scientific demonstrations are given on the stage at the heart of the ground level. On the middle level, the main galleries explore the natural environment, and special areas are given over to children. The upper floor houses Omnimax, a curved screen showing the latest blockbuster movies.

✚ 304 C3 ✉ 1455 Quebec Street, Vancouver, British Columbia, V6A 3Z7 ☎ 604/443-7440, 604/443-7443 (recorded information) 🕐 Mon–Fri 10–5, Sat–Sun and public holidays 10–6; closed Christmas ✋ Adult $16, child 4–12) $11, (13–18) $13, family $54. Omnimax theater: combination ticket, adult $21, child (4–12) $16, (13–18) $18 🚌 22 🚇 Skytrain: Science World ⛴ Aquabus, False Creek Ferry 🖥 🎫

Above *The geodesci dome of Science World is a distinctive landmark*

STANLEY PARK

INFORMATION

www.city.vancouver.bc.ca

✚ Off map, 304 A1 ✉ Western tip of downtown Vancouver ℹ Vancouver Board of Parks and Recreation, 2099 Beach Avenue, Vancouver, British Columbia, V6G 1Z4 ☎ 604/257-8400 🕐 Daily 🎟 Free (fee for some attractions and facilities) 🚌 19. A free shuttle bus operates within the park from mid-Jun to late Sep 🍴 Restaurants at Prospect Point, Ferguson Point and Stanley Pavilion 🍽 Cafés at the Totem Poles, Lumberman's Arch, Third Beach, Lost Lagoon and swimming pool 🏛 Shop at the Brockton Park Visitor Centre (Totem Poles) sells a small range of First Nations crafts and Stanley Park souvenirs

INTRODUCTION

Often described as the "lungs" of Vancouver, Stanley Park is one of the largest urban parks in North America, providing a place where city-dwellers can have fun and keep fit in environments ranging from temperate forest to formal gardens and beaches. It is one of the largest urban parks in North America—a fantastic mix of forest, beaches, open parkland and formal gardens. Around 8 million people visit the park each year, which makes it all the more remarkable that it is still possible to feel alone here. The wilder forest side (over two-thirds of the total area) has trails for running, bicycling and hiking, while the eastern side—where most visitors tend to stay—has been transformed into a combination of open parkland and formal gardens. The park protects towering cedars, hemlock and fir trees, and the freshwater Lost Lagoon is a haven for birds and waterfowl. In December 2006 a violent storm devastated the park, flattening swathes of trees, downing power lines and damaging the Seawall. Restoration is still ongoing, but extensive tree-planting has taken place and work on the Seawall is expected to be complete by mid-2008. See also the walk, ▷ 322–323.

PARKS AND RECREATION

This area of first-growth forest was partly logged in the 1860s to accommodate the growing city, and was also used as an army camp. However, in an early act of environmental protection the newly formed city council designated the area as permanent public parkland in 1886, naming it for Lord Stanley, Canada's Governor General. An elected committee—the Vancouver Board of Parks and Recreation, unique in Canada—was appointed to oversee the management and running of this new resource. The board still exists, and now manages over 190 parks in the Greater Vancouver area.

In December 2006 a violent storm hit Stanley Park leaving such a trail of devastation that the park had to be closed to the public. Two further wind storms that winter resulted in the loss of an estimated 10,000 fine old trees, totalling an area of more than 45ha (111 acres). Parts of the sea wall were also damaged or overwhelmed with debris, and many park roads and trails were

Above *Strolling along the Seawall*

made impassable. Such was the damage that clearance and restoration work is expected to take until the end of 2008. Out of the destruction came the idea for the Stanley Park Environmental Art Project for the creation of temporary and semi-permanent works of art. This project commences in 2008 and promises to be a superb exhibition area.

WHAT TO SEE

THE SEAWALL
Surrounding the outer edge of the park is an 11km (7-mile) seawall, which was originally conceived in the early 1920s to prevent erosion, and took nearly 60 years to complete. Today, it is Vancouver's most popular recreational facility, with a walkway and a bicycle/Rollerblade track (counterclockwise direction only). There are wonderful views across to the North Shore and out into the Pacific Ocean beyond English Bay—the sandy beaches on this side come as a real surprise, being so close to the heart of this huge metropolis.

ACTIVITIES AND ENTERTAINMENT
There are plenty of activities in the park to amuse visitors of all ages. The best-known is Vancouver Aquarium (▷ 310), but there is also the Children's Farmyard and Miniature Railway, the Totem Pole garden at Hallelujah Point, the attractive Brockton Point Visitor Centre, the Nature Park, the Kid's Waterpark, the Theatre Under the Stars, a heated ocean-side swimming pool, tennis courts, a pitch and putt golf course, and wonderful flower gardens, including the spring-blooming Rhododendron Garden and Rose Garden, with 5,000 roses. In summer, take a trip on the free Stanley Park Shuttle, the route ensures that you take in all the most popular manmade attractions as well as the natural highlights.

LOST LAGOON
Once part of Coal Harbour, this 16ha (39-acre) body of water was cut off from the tide by the construction of the causeway in the 1920s and is now a fresh-water pond and bird sanctuary populated by swans, ducks, geese and heron. At the center of the pond, the Jubilee Fountain dates from 1936 and was installed to celebrate Vancouver's 50th anniversary. At the southeastern corner of the lagoon, the Lost Lagoon Nature House (daily) is run by the Stanley Park Ecology Society. Recently renovated, it offers displays offering insights into the ecology of the park, and guided walks depart from here every Sunday (1pm). There are also birding walks on the last Sunday of the month (9am).

Left *Figurehead of SS* Empress of Japan
Below The Girl in a Wetsuit *is a lifesize bronze statue in the park*

INFORMATION

www.vanaqua.org

🔶 Off map, 304 A1 ✉ 845 Avison Way, Stanley Park, Vancouver, British Columbia, V6B 3X8 ☎ 604/659-7443 🕐 Jul–Aug daily 9.30–7; rest of year daily 9.30–5 ✋ Adult $20, child (4–12) $12 or (13 and over) $15 🚌 35, 135 ☞ Various behind-the-scenes tours must be reserved in advance; e.g. Sea Otter Trainer Tour: adult $25, child $15; Beluga Encounters adult $150 ($210 1 adult plus 1 child) 🍴 Upstream Café 🛍 The Clamshell, with everything from educational to fun items to pure kitsch

VANCOUVER AQUARIUM

Located on the eastern edge of Stanley Park, this superb facility is one of the city's main draws with more than a million visitors annually, and is Canada's second most popular attraction—only Toronto's CN Tower (▷ 182–183) gets more visitors. It's the third-largest aquarium in North America, and contains more than 8,000 creatures representing 600 different species.

Stop first at the information board in the Upper Pacific Canada Pavilion to check out the shows and activities that are happening each day. A range of behind-the-scenes tours allows you to get closer to the animals with the Trainer Team, and learn about the research, conservation and animal care projects. Children (with a parent) can join a sleepover alongside the giant tanks (▷ 334).

Outdoor attractions include the BC Forest Headwaters exhibit, where you can see a salmon hatchery, and the Wild Coast pools, with above- and below-water viewing of sea lions, dolphins and seals. There's a separate pool for viewing the entertaining and enchanting sea otters, and the impressive Arctic Canada habitat contains graceful beluga whales, seals and walruses. An approved code of conduct is adhered to, and research carried out here has enabled many lives to be saved among creatures in the wild. Indoor exhibits include the Pacific Canada Pavilion, displaying marine life of the Strait of Georgia, just offshore from the city, and beavers that inhabit the freshwaters inland. Treasures of the BC Coast introduces creatures from deeper waters along the coast, including a huge octopus.

The Tropical Gallery features life on a reproduced coral reef, including sharks, stingrays and turtles, and there's a steamy Amazon Jungle area, which takes you away from the sea and into the rainforest—an ecosystem of bright tropical birds and fish, crocodiles, eels, snakes and somnolent giant sloths.

An expansion of the aquarium, providing larger and deeper pools, expanded dry habitats, better underwater landscapes and improved behind-the-scenes facilities is due to be completed in 2009.

Below *Sea otters were once hunted extensively for their fur*

STANLEY PARK

▷ 308–309.

VANCOUVER ART GALLERY

www.vanartgallery.bc.ca

Housed in the 1910 former Vancouver courthouse, this gallery concentrates mainly on historical and contemporary art and artists that represent the development of art in British Columbia.

A highlight is the permanent collection of the works of Emily Carr, perhaps the best-known British Columbian artist. A tour de force during the 1930s, her paintings of the deep British Columbia forests display a unique energy and intensity, and her influence is still strong today. The gallery also hosts prestigious international temporary exhibitions.

Vancouver's first law courts occupied this building, and murder victim William Hopkinson reputedly walks the corridors and haunts the catacombs below it with his ghost friend "Charlie." The gallery shop has an excellent range of

unique handcrafted items by both established and up-and-coming artists for sale.
✚ 304 A2 ✉ 750 Hornby Street, Vancouver, British Columbia, V6Z 2H7 ☎ 604/662-4700/4719 (24-hour information line) 🕓 Daily 10–5.30 (also Tue, Thu 5.30–9) 💷 Adult $15, child (5–12) $6, family $40 🚌 5, 15, and tourist trolley FSkytrain: Granville or Burrard 🖥 📷

VANCOUVER MUSEUM

www.vanmuseum.bc.ca

Set in a futuristic building designed by local architect Gerald Hamilton, the museum traces the history of Vancouver from its roots as a First Nations settlement to the development of the modern city. The fine First Nations Gallery depicts the area before Europeans arrived. The Pacific Rim Collection, with displays from China, Japan and Oceania, promotes cross-cultural pan-Pacific relations, while the World Heritage Collection contains objects from around the world.

Re-creations of the Vancouver of colonial times include an outpost

of the Hudson's Bay Company.
✚ 304 A2 ✉ 1100 Chestnut Street, Vanier Park, Vancouver, British Columbia, V6J 3J9 ☎ 604/736-4431 🕓 Jul–early Sep daily 10–5 (also Thu 5–9); rest of year Tue–Sun 10–5 (also Thu 5–9) 💷 Adult $17, child (5–17) $6, family $32 🚌 2, 22 and tourist trolley 📷

Above *Exhibit in the Vancouver Museum*
Top *The Vancouver Art Gallery*

VICTORIA

INFORMATION

www.tourismvictoria.com

✚ 413 C17 ℹ️ Victoria Visitor
Information Centre, 812 Wharf Street,
Victoria, British Columbia, V8W 1T3
☎ 250/953-2033; daily

Above *The Parliament Buildings are illuminated at night*

Below *A replica of a wooly mammoth in the Royal BC Museum*

INTRODUCTION

Victoria is often thought of as the prettiest city in western Canada and is regularly voted among the top ten cities in the world by *Traveler* magazine. Victoria sits on the southern tip of Vancouver Island on a fine natural harbor, with magnificent views of the U.S. state of Washington's Olympic Mountains to the south and Cascade Mountains to the east. It was among the leading settlements in colonial Canada and still has a very traditional English feel, with its historic buildings and red buses, and its post boxes, window boxes and hanging gardens.

The city is eminently walkable, with old-fashioned shopping streets devoted to craft and souvenir stores, and the main attractions located conveniently close together. The historic Inner Harbour is still at the heart of the city and, with its waterside promenade, is a wonderful place to stroll around. The yachts moored here during the summer add to the atmosphere, and the 1908 Empress Hotel and 1898 Legislature (known as the Parliament Buildings) are architectural treasures.

VANCOUVER ISLAND

In 1790 Vancouver Island was claimed for Spain by a shipwrecked Spanish sailor. However, it was the Hudson's Bay Company who brought European settlement in the form of a depot. A fort was built in the Inner Harbour in 1843 on a site now occupied by Bastion Square. In 1846 the new US border was created along the 49th parallel, dipping south at the Strait of Georgia leaving Victoria and southern Vancouver Island as non-US territory.

The British government granted the island to the Hudson's Bay Company in 1849, with the proviso that settlements be created and a new crown colony of Vancouver Island be declared, with Victoria as capital. In 1852 Fort Victoria became the city of Victoria and the town site was developed. Later in the decade, the Cariboo gold rush saw a great influx of people to Victoria, and the economic boom was further extended when the Royal Navy chose Esquimalt (just west of today's downtown) as a base. British Columbia became a crown colony in 1858, and Victoria was declared its capital when the mainland and island were amalgamated in 1868.

WHAT TO SEE

THE INNER HARBOUR

Heart of the city, the Inner Harbour is surrounded by many of the most interesting places in Victoria, including the superb Royal British Columbia Museum (▷ 314). The Parliament Buildings (mid-May to early Sep daily 9–5; rest of year Mon–Fri 9–4) are worth inspecting for their flamboyant architecture, a meld of Victorian Gothic, Italianate and American Romanesque styles.

The buildings were designed in 1893 by the eminent architect Francis Rattenbury and opened in 1898, replacing the original small and rather insignificant Legislature Building. Hundreds of lights over the exterior come on at dusk every evening, making a very pretty sight at sunset.

A VARIETY OF ATTRACTIONS

There is a huge choice of things to do nearby including the Pacific Undersea Gardens (Apr–end Jun daily 10–6; Jul–end Sep 9–8; Oct–end Mar 10–5), featuring more than 5,000 creatures native to the British Columbian coast. Miniature World (core opening hours daily 9–5) has 80 dioramas, including a fully operational miniature sawmill and a scale model of the Canadian Pacific Railway. Helmcken House (May–end Sep daily), the 1852 residence of doctor and politician John Helmcken and the oldest house in British Columbia, has a wonderful medical collection. The Royal London Wax Museum (daily 9.30–5), housed in a neoclassical building, exhibits wax figures of royalty, politicians, celebrities and historical figures.

The Crystal Garden (daily) occupies a huge glass-roofed conservatory originally designed as a swimming pool for the Empress Hotel in the style of London's Crystal Palace. Today, it houses over 50 endangered species of birds, small mammals, reptiles and butterflies in a tropical environment.

Slightly farther afield, the Victoria Bug Zoo (daily, check website for hours, www.bugzoo.bc.ca; ▷ 335) features a variety of creepy-crawlies from around the world, while Beacon Hill Park, a five-minute walk south of the Inner Harbour, covers 75ha (185 acres) and is a great place to stroll in the gardens or grassland, visit the children's farm or admire the world's largest freestanding totem pole, a dramatic sight.

Below *Beacon Hill Park totem pole*
Below left *A double decker bus passes the Empress Hotel*

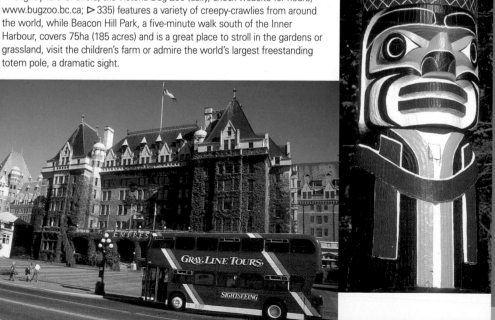

CRAIGDARROCH CASTLE
www.thecastle.ca
Built in the 1890s for coal magnate Robert Dunsmuir, this imposing 39-room Gothic mansion is a riot of Victorian ostentation, with some of the finest stained glass leaded windows in western Canada, exceptional wood paneling and fine period furniture.

Visitors take a self-guiding tour around the four floors of the castle, but there are docents stationed around the house to answer any questions. Finally, you climb up to the tower, from where there are spectacular views over the city and the Strait of Juan de Fuca to the distant Olympic Mountains. The house, now run by the Craigdarroch Castle Historical Museum Society, who are restoring everything—house and garden—to its original state, giving an accurate impression of the lifestyle enjoyed by the Dunsmuirs.
✉ 1050 Joan Crescent, Victoria, British Columbia V8S 3L5 ☎ 250/592-5323 🕓 Mid-Jun to early Sep daily 9–7.30 (last admission 7), early Sep to mid-Jun daily 10–5 (last admission 4.30) ✋ Adult $11.75, child (6–18) $3.75, under 6 free 🏛 🚉 Downtown, off Fort Street 🚌 11, 14

ROYAL BC MUSEUM
www.royalbcmuseum.bc.ca
Covering the natural, social and cultural history of British Columbia, this fine museum is regarded as one of the best in North America for its excellent displays—there are some superb dioramas. The Natural History Gallery illustrates how the planet has changed over the millennia, the evolution of its creatures, and how the climate relates to everything we do. The Ocean Station exhibit replicates a submarine view of marine life of the west coast. The First Peoples Gallery covers the periods before and after the arrival of European settlers in a groundbreaking approach to First Nations history. The Modern History Gallery concentrates on European influence in British Columbia: industry, agriculture, transportation and the development of cities. Street scenes and dioramas surround you with the sights, sounds and smells of the past, and there's a replica of Captain George Vancouver's HMS *Discovery*.
✉ 675 Belleville Street, Victoria, British Columbia, V8W 9W2 ☎ 250/356-7226, 888/447-7977 🕓 Daily 9–5 ✋ Adult $14, child (6–18) $9.50, family $37.50; combined tickets with IMAX also available

DOWNTOWN VICTORIA
Situated north of the Inner Harbour, downtown Victoria is a mixture of historic buildings and one-of-a-kind stores in a neat collection of narrow streets, and is

Above left *Ceramics and glassware on display in one of Victoria's craft shops*
Above right *Turn-of-the-20th-century street in the Royal BC Museum*

a great place for browsing. Bastion Square, close to the site of Fort Camosack's north bastion, contains the Maritime Museum (▷ below), while Market Square, built in 1858, is flanked by some fine period houses, now excellent stores, and has plenty of atmosphere.

MARITIME MUSEUM

www.mmbc.bc.ca

Housed in the former 1889 provincial courthouse in Bastion Square, the Maritime Museum reflects the importance of the sea to the development of Vancouver Island, British Columbia and, indeed, the whole of Canada.

On the first floor, exhibits cover centuries of exploration and BC's early maritime history, including the fur trade, whaling and fishing, shipbuilding and pirates. You can also see the vessel, *Tilikum*, which sailed around the world between 1901 and 1904. Up on the second floor there are some incredible ship models, plus exhibits on the Royal Canadian Navy, coastal steam ships, luxury ocean liners, racing yachts, ferries and the coast guard service. The third floor comes as something of a surprise, containing the beautifully restored courthouse that in the late 19th century meted out justice on provincial and maritime matters.

✉ 28 Bastion Square, Victoria, British Columbia, V8W 1H9 ☎ 250/385-4222, ext 101 ⏰ Daily 9.30–4.30 (mid-Jun to mid-Sep open to 5pm) 💲 Adult $10, child (6–11) $5, family $25

TIPS

❯❯ There's no better way to soak up the "English" atmosphere of Victoria than to take afternoon tea here, either in the Empress Hotel, or at The Blethering Place (▷ 339).

❯❯ The ferry companies down at the Inner Harbour also do some good sightseeing tours. The shorter trips provide superb views of the city and mountains, or you can take full days of whale-watching or exploring the Gulf of Juan de Fuca and the San Juan Islands.

❯❯ See also the drive on pages 324–325.

Below *The Empress is the most distinguished hotel in this stately city*

WATERTON LAKES NATIONAL PARK

www.pc.gc.ca
www.watertonchamber.com
Waterton Lakes is a tiny national park (525sq km/203sq miles), yet the four ecosystems that meet here—mountains, lakes, prairie and alpine meadows—support a fantastic variety of wildlife. The rugged peaks rise steeply out of the surrounding flat lands with very little in the way of foothills, and the views as you approach are dramatic. The mountains were formed by the Lewis Thrust, their sedimentary rocks pushed up over the younger rocks of the prairies. Erosion has carved deep valleys, often filled by lakes, and sharply sculpted peaks. Check out the view across the steep-walled Cameron Lake cirque, a glacial hollow. Grizzly and black bears—best viewed through binoculars—are attracted to the scree slope vegetation. Upper Waterton Lake is the deepest in the Canadian Rockies, and the unusually cold water in the park's chain of lakes supports rare fish species. Waterton town site is the social heart of the park, and it's a good place from which to take boat trips and road excursions.

In 1932, Waterton Lakes was linked with Montana's Glacier National Park (US$25 per vehicle; US$12 on foot) south of the U.S. border to form the Waterton-Glacier International Peace Park—the first peace park in the world. There are good long-distance hikes between the parks (non-Canadian visitors must enter Glacier at an official crossing with passport and visa).
✚ 400 F17 ✉ Box 200, Waterton Park, Alberta, T0K 2M0 ☎ 403/859-2224 ◷ Daily. Information centre: mid-May to early Oct 🎟 Adult $6.80, child (6–16) $3.50, family $17.50

WELLS GRAY PROVINCIAL PARK

www.wellsgray.ca
The best of British Columbia's provincial parks, Wells Gray has scenery to rival many national parks. It's a little off the tourist track, but you can take the scenic mountain route along Highway 5 from Jasper and Mt. Robson in the northeast, or make faster progress along the gentler road from Kamloops and the Okanagan in the south.

The access road from Clearwater leads to most of the attractions, including hiking trails. Spahats Falls, around 8km (5 miles) from Clearwater are a taster of what's to come. From the observation platform above the falls you get a good view of the Clearwater River below, framed by the pinky-gray volcanic rock that is found throughout the park. Green Mountain Lookout, just inside Wells Gray, gives a better view, revealing a superb panorama of the whole park. Dawson Falls are another cataract to look out for, while Helmcken Falls are definitely on the "must see" list. More than twice the height of Niagara, the waters here plunge 137m (450ft) into a deep bowl surrounded by dense forest, sending up plumes of spray. The road ends at Clearwater Lake, where there's a campsite and plenty of walking trails.
✚ 400 E15 ℹ Clearwater Visitor Centre, 425 East Yellowhead Highway, Clearwater, British Columbia, V0E 1N0 ☎ 250/674-2646

WHISTLER

www.mywhistler.com
www.tourismwhistler.com
Set to host the winter Olympic Games in 2010, Whistler is a year-round playground for Vancouverites, who live just two hours down the valley to the south. Most drive here via the scenic Sea to Sky Highway, taking in panoramas of Howe Sound (▷ 293), although the center of the resort is traffic-free. Nestling between the twin peaks of Whistler and Blackcomb, the village was developed only in 1977 and now has around 2 million visitors every year. The skiing is first class: plenty of snow, a long season, excellent visitor facilities, high-speed lifts, and a good range of slopes for all abilities, including one that runs for almost a vertical mile (1.6km).

In summer, Whistler is still a magnet for visitors, close to Garibaldi Provincial Park for hikers and mountain bikers, and with outdoor activities of all kinds. All of this is backed up by accommodations from campgrounds to luxury hotels, plus restaurants and great shopping.

Inevitably, the Winter Olympics have prompted masses of new facilities in Whistler. One of the most exciting innovations is the Peak to Peak Gondola, due to open in December 2008, which will cover the 4.4km (2.7-mile) distance between Whistler Mountain and Blackcomb Mountain. The world's longest and highest (415m/1,361ft) gondola will offer a breathtaking 11-minute trip for winter and summer visitors. Another new attraction is the Squamish Lil'wat Cultural Centre, opening in the summer of 2008, a complex that showcases the history, art, legends and lives of these two Nations.
✚ 413 C16 ℹ Tourism Whistler, 4010 Whistler Way, British Columbia, V0N 1B4 ☎ 604/938-2769. Whistler Visitor Centre, 4230 Gateway Drive, Whistler, British Columbia V0N 1B4 ☎ 604/935 3357 🚌 Several departures daily from Vancouver and Vancouver Airport

Left A snowboarder enjoys the slopes on Blackcomb Mountain

YOHO NATIONAL PARK

Yoho National Park, a stunning park that does justice to its name—a Cree First Nations word meaning "awesome,"—is 1,310sq km (511sq miles) in size, and was established in 1886. The park's history is inextricably linked with the Canadian Pacific Railway and the huge climb required to reach Kicking Horse Pass. The natural features, pretty lakes and spectacular waterfalls are surrounded by towering peaks, many over 3,000m (9,840ft) in height, and sit alongside spiral tunnels built deep into the mountainside.

KICKING HORSE PASS

When this stretch of the railway was being built, the route—which climbs rapidly from the valley floor—posed problems for the engineers. Runaway trains that headed down the pass and boilers that exploded under the strain of the uphill climb were not unknown. The solution was to create spiral tunnels under the hillsides, allowing the trains to climb and descend at a more sedate pace along a series of overlapping switchbacks. Kicking Horse Pass was named when Sir James Hector came to explore the site for the best rail and road route—he was kicked by a horse and taken for dead.

LAKES, FALLS AND FOSSILS

The park offers 400km (248 miles) of hiking, though many of the trails are long-distance ones. The most spectacular of these is to Lake O'Hara, a 22km (13,6-mile) return trip to a jewel of a lake surrounded by alpine meadows, while a guided hike is the only way you can get to see the Burgess Shale, an important geological feature containing some of the oldest fossils ever found, dating from more than 500 million years.

However, most of Yoho's highlights are accessible by car. Takakkaw Falls (from the Cree word meaning "magnificent") are reached via the twisting Yoho Valley Road. The falls, with a drop of 385m (1,263ft), are one of the highest in Canada, and the surrounding ice-capped peaks add to the splendor. Emerald Lake is another major attraction, and one of the prettiest vistas in the Rockies. The natural setting is enhanced by a couple of diminutive log cabins, the hand of man on this wild land.

INFORMATION

www.pc.gc.ca

⊞ 401 E16 🛈 Yoho Visitor Centre, Box 99, Field, British Columbia, V0A 1G0 ☎ 250/343-6783 🕘 Daily, including Visitor Centre 💰 Adult $8.80, child (6–16) $4.50, family $17.60

TIPS

» A bus shuttle (charge) runs to Lake O'Hara from mid-June to early October; numbers are limited, but you can reserve a seat up to three months in advance (☎ 250/343-6433).

» Contact the Yoho Burgess Shale Foundation (Box 148, Field, British Columbia, V0A 1G0 ☎ 1-800/343-3006, www.burgess-shale.bc.ca) to arrange a guided hike to the fossil site, which is otherwise off-limits.

Above *Emerald Lake Lodge sits right on the lakeshore*

ICEFIELDS PARKWAY DRIVE

This drive from Lake Louise to Jasper leads through some of the most majestic scenery in the Canadian Rockies, from Crowfoot Glacier in the south to the Athabasca Glacier in the north. It also puts you within easy walking distance of some of the area's most glorious natural sites, including Peyto Lake view, Mistaya Canyon, Sunwapta Falls and Athabasca Falls, and leads to the Columbia Icefields Centre, from where you can take an excursion onto a glacier.

THE DRIVE

Distance: 227km (143 miles)
Allow: One day; two if take longer walks and the Athabasca Glacier trip
Start: Lake Louise village ✚ 401 F16
End: Jasper ✚ 400 E15
How to get there: Lake Louise is a 2-hour drive north of Calgary on Highway 1

★ Stock up on snacks and water at the small shopping mall in Lake Louise village, then take Highway 1 north. Take the right exit for highway 93 (Icefields Parkway). About 2km (1.2 miles) along, you'll enter the park.

If you don't have a valid park pass, buy one here (adult $8.80

per day, child 6–16 $4.40 per day, family $17.60 per day). You'll pass Hector Lake some 16km (10 miles) beyond the ticket office, but the first important landmark comes when you've driven 34km (21 miles) from Lake Louise.

❶ Crowfoot Glacier, off to the left, is so named because the several fingers of ice hanging over the rock face resemble a bird's foot, though gradual melting is altering its shape.

After 6km (4 miles) look for the left turn to Peyto Lake view.

❷ From the parking area it is an

easy 750m (820-yard) walk to one of the most impressive panoramas in the Rockies, with turquoise Peyto Lake nestling at the base of the surrounding peaks.

Drive 26km (16 miles) to the parking area for Mistaya Canyon.

❸ Leave your car to take the 10-minute walk down a well-worn path to explore the water-eroded landscape.

Some 5km (3 miles) farther north you'll cross the wide boulder-strewn path of the North Saskatchewan River.

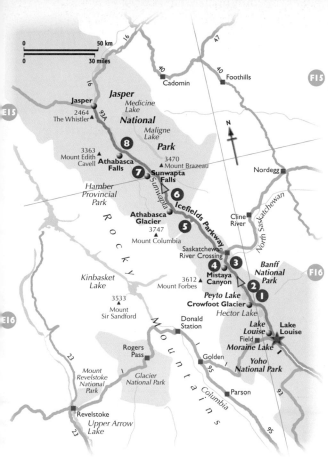

❽ Continue northward for another 16km (10 miles) to reach the Athabasca Falls. (At this waterfall, the drop is deeper and the gorge even narrower, allowing for more dramatic photos.)

From here it is 30km (19 miles) to Jasper (▷ 296–297).

WHEN TO GO
The road is open all year, weather permitting, but many of the accommodations and restaurants are open only April through October. Most footpaths are closed in winter.

WHERE TO EAT
✉ Baker Creek Bistro, Highway 1A, Bow Valley Parkway, Lake Louise ☎ 403/522-2182.
✉ The Crossing, Saskatchewan River Crossing ☎ 403/761-7000

WHERE TO STAY
✉ Fairmont Château Lake Louise Hotel, 111 Lake Louise Drive, Lake Louise ☎ 403/522-3511. ✉ Sunwapta Falls Resort Jasper ☎ 780/852-4852 or 888/828-5777

❹ Here you'll find refreshments, lodging and fuel—the last till Jasper, 130km (81 miles) north.

Beyond the crossing, the highway follows the route of the North Saskatchewan River.

❺ You'll see a series of jagged peaks on either side. Look for Cirrus Mountain on the right (parking area on the left side of the road) before you reach a huge curve, called Big Bend, that leads on up to a still higher plain. A parking area at the top of the bend is a great photo spot for the view back down the valley. Once on the plain, the 2.5km (1.5-mile) steep walk along Parker Ridge—120km (74 miles) from Lake Louise—on the left leads to views of the Saskatchewan Glacier.

Past Parker Ridge you'll cross the boundary of Banff National Park and enter Jasper National Park. Only 10km (6 miles) farther on are the Columbia Icefields.

❻ Here you can travel out onto Athabasca Glacier on a Snocoach from the Columbia Icefields Centre (▷ 294).

At North Columbia Icefield the mountains recede a little as the highway follows the wider flood plain of the Sunwapta River.

❼ The two main attractions on this section of the drive are both waterfalls. At the first, Sunwapta Falls, the river plunges 60m (197ft) through a narrow gorge.

Above *Athabasca Falls contain the greatest volume of water of any river in the Rockies* **Opposite** *Cirrus Mountain viewpoint in Banff National Park*

LAKE AGNES WALK

Follow in the footsteps of the genteel Victorian and Edwardian visitors to the Tea House at Lake Agnes, high above Lake Louise, along a route that offers excellent mountain panoramas. There are only two teahouses still operating in the Rockies, and the route to this one is the most popular walk in Banff National Park.

THE WALK

Distance: 7km (4.5 miles)

Allow: 4 hours

Start/end: Lake Louise parking area

How to get there: Lake Louise is a 2-hour drive north of Calgary on Highway 1

Warning: The path has some steep sections. The upper part of the walk follows the same route as the horse trek route from Lake Louise to the Tea House, so be careful around the horses and watch where you tread—horse droppings are not only unpleasant, but are also slippery underfoot.

From the Lake Louise parking area, make your way to the lakeshore promenade for exceptional water-level views of the landscape and the Fairmont Château Lake Louise Hotel. Keep the water on your left and walk along the lakefront until the path splits. Take the right-hand fork, which climbs immediately from the water's edge. The climb is quite steep, with few places to rest, so take your time. After 1.2km (0.75 miles) a magnificent lake view presents itself on the left.

From above the waterline, the unreal-looking blue tone of the lake is even more apparent. The coloration is caused by the minerals in the water absorbing some parts of the spectrum of light shining on them, and reflecting others. The viewpoint is a perfect place to take a photograph, especially when there are kayakers on the water.

The route takes a tight dogleg here, but the ascent continues to be just as steep. The path eventually reaches a plateau after 2km (1 mile).

Here you can pause for a while and admire Mirror Lake, a small body of water backed by a wall of rock and surrounded by mature shady trees. From here there are two possible routes onward to Lake Agnes.

Left and right *Views of Lake Agnes*

Take the path to the right from the lake where it sweeps to the east.

You have views across acres of woodland carpeting Bow Valley and stretching to the mountains on the lake's far flank. Notice the green strips on the mountain sides—in winter, these become the Lake Louise ski runs.

The path then swings left, west of the Little Beehive rock formation, before the final ascent to Lake Agnes. Climb the steps to the right of the rock wall.

This steep flight of steps often turns into a waterfall with overflow from the lake. At the top of the steps, the pretty setting of Lake Agnes presents itself immediately, with a curtain of peaks on all sides and the Big Beehive rock formation to your left. The lake is generally thought to have been named after Lady Agnes Macdonald, wife of the first prime minister of Canada, who hiked up here in 1886. The redoubtable lady is also known for taking a trip on a Canadian Pacific steam locomotive—riding on the cowcatcher.

Take time for some refreshment at the historic Tea House before the return journey. It was constructed in 1901 by the Canadian Pacific Railway and was one of several in the park—this is the highest at 2,134m (6,999ft)—to provide refreshment for parties of upper-class hikers. King Edward VIII, then the Prince of Wales, made his way up from the hotel to the Tea House during an official visit to Canada.

At this point you can return to the parking area by retracing your steps.

Optional Extended Walk

If you prefer, you can extend the walk into a circular route of 12km (8 miles) in total.

Leave the Lake Agnes Tea House, keeping the lake on your left (walk away from the path you took on your arrival at this point). After 1km (0.6 miles) you will see the left turning to the top of the Big Beehive. The route is a short but hard climb of 125m (135 yards) to the summit for extensive views across Mirror Lake, but the footpath is not maintained and is unclear in parts.

Return to the main path and continue walking away from Lake Agnes (turn left at the junction of the two footpaths). This is a steep descent into the valley bottom. After 900m (0.4 miles) this path intersects the Highline Trail. Turn right here, then after 1km (0.6 miles), fork left and after 700m (760 yards) you'll meet the Plain of Six Glaciers Trail.

As you approach the intersection, you have panoramic views up to the left to the Victoria Glacier above the Plain of Six Glaciers (the Plain of Six Glaciers is where the second teahouse is located, on the right 2km/1.2 miles along the trail).

Turn left where the Highland Trail meets the Plain of Six Glaciers Trail and walk just over 1km (0.6 miles) to the head of Lake Louise.

Your final 2km (1.2 miles) is a flat walk by the lakeshore toward Fairmont Château Lake Louise Hotel, with views of the reflections of the surrounding peaks on the surface of the azure water.

WHEN TO GO

You might want to take a lead from the Tea House, which opens when the snow melts and closes after the first snow falls (generally open May–end Oct). This is one of the most popular hikes in the country, so you might want to avoid the height of the summer and weekends. Set out as early as you can. Wildflowers up in the mountains will be in bloom around late July/early August; the larch trees are beautiful in the fall.

PUBLIC RESTROOMS

Fairmont Château Lake Louise Hotel and Lake Agnes Tea House.

WHERE TO EAT

Lake Agnes Tea House, Lake Agnes (there are also picnic tables up at the Tea House, if you want to carry your own supplies—these can be bought from the Château Deli, Fairmont Château Lake Louise Hotel). ✉ Mount Fairview Dining Room, Deer Lodge ☎ 403/522-3747

WHERE TO STAY

✉ Paradise Lodge and Bungalows, Lake Louise ☎ 403/522-3595. ✉ Fairmont Château Lake Louise Hotel, 111 Lake Louise Drive, Lake Louise ☎ 403/522-3511. ✉ Post Hotel, 200 Pipestone Road, Lake Louise ☎ 403/522-3938 or 800/661-1586

THINGS TO DO

As an alternative to the walk, you can go up to Lake Agnes on horseback. Treks are organized by the Fairmont Château Lake Louise Hotel daily (weather permitting), with a duration of about three hours ($40–$150).

WALK

AROUND STANLEY PARK'S SEAWALL

This walk around Vancouver's famous Stanley Park starts off with plenty of views of the city and park attractions, with the western section providing wonderful panoramas out to sea, invigorating fresh air, and peace and quiet.

THE WALK

Distance: 10.5km (6.5 miles)
Allow: 5 hours
Start/end: Parking area at the intersection of Denman Street and West Georgia
How to get there: Bus 5 stops at the intersection one block west of the start point, while highways 35 and 135 will take you to the information center in the park; or it's a 1.25km (0.75-mile) walk west of Canada Place
Warning: There are clearly marked lanes for walkers and joggers, and for bicyclists and in-line skaters. For safety reasons, stay in the appropriate lane.

Following a severe wind storm in 2006, during which many trees were blown down and damage sustained to the seawall, restoration work is expected to be ongoing until the end of 2008 but could last longer. Most trails are open, but heavy machinery is likely to be present and detours may be necessary

From the parking area, walk in the direction of the waterfront. Go left at the walkway, skirting between the ornamental gardens. This is the path you'll stay on all the way around the seawall.

The path sweeps around to the right and the first way point along your walk is the boathouse of the Vancouver Rowing Club, 200m (220 yards) from the park entrance. The tourist information kiosk is 500m (550 yards) from the park entrance, where you can pick up a map. Go past the yacht club boathouse on the left and continue for 1.2km (0.75 miles).

You pass the entrance of Deadman's Island, now a naval shore base named HMCS *Discovery*.

After another 300m (330 yards), you'll see the totem garden on

the left and pass the Nine O'Clock Gun, fired every evening across the harbor.

Here you can get some excellent photographs of the Vancouver skyline with Canada Place (▷ 304–305) directly across the water.

From Hallelujah Point, just beyond the gun, the path heads north around Brockton Point before turning to the west.

There are views at this point of the North Shore with its dramatic curtain of mountains behind.

Continue 400m (440 yards) to the small bronze statue, *Girl in a Wetsuit*. This life-size statue (1970), just offshore, is a homage to Copenhagen's *Little Mermaid*, and is the work of Budapest-born sculptor Elek Imredy.

Left *The city skyline is a splendid backdrop to the Royal Vancouver Yacht Club*
Above *The totem poles at Brockton Point attract alot of attention*
Right *The Nine O'Clock Gun stands along Stanley Park's Seawall*

Another 100m (110 yards) brings you to the bright oriental prow of the SS *Empress of China*, which sits in an ornamental shrub looking out over the narrowing waters. Continue past the children's play area before heading northwest.

You'll see the high Lion's Gate Bridge that spans the outlet as the open sea looms ever closer.

After you pass under the bridge, it's another 50m (55 yards) to Prospect Point.

This is the northernmost point in the park, and from here your views will be to the west across the Pacific Ocean.

From Prospect Point it's 1km (0.6 miles) to Siwash Rock, with views across English Bay, and then almost another 1km (0.6 miles) to Third Beach.

Whatever the time of year, you'll find bathers or beachcombers here.

Just beyond Third Beach is Ferguson Point, the most westerly place in Stanley Park. Some 8km (5 miles)

from the start of the walk, you come to Second Beach.

Here you'll find the large artificial Stanley Park Swimming Pool.

The path leaves the waterfront here and continues through some ornamental lawns. You come to an intersection, where you go left (follow signs for Lost Lagoon) under Stanley Park Road. You'll see a golf course on your right. Turn right at the far side of the golf course and walk past the Ted and Mary Greig Rhododendron Gardens on the right. Lost Lagoon will come into view on the left.

Lost Lagoon was given its name when the building of the Stanley Park Causeway cut it off from Coal Harbour.

Follow the path around the lake to reach the pass under the main road. At the intersection, go right, and after 200m (220 yards) you'll be back at the starting point.

WHEN TO GO
Year-round, any fine day will be a great time to join health-conscious

Vancouverites in their perambulations around the park.

PUBLIC RESTROOMS
Behind the information office.

WHERE TO EAT
✉ Sequoia Grill, Ferguson Point, Stanley Park ☎ 604/669-3281.
✉ Fish House, 8901 Stanley Park Drive (near 2nd Beach and Lost Lagoon), Stanley Park ☎ 604/681-7275
In addition, there are cafés at the totem poles, Lumbermen's Arch and Third Beach, and restaurants at Prospect Point and Stanley Park Pavilion.

WHERE TO STAY
✉ Lord Stanley Suites on the Park, 1889 Alberni Street ☎ 604/688-9299

ACROSS VANCOUVER ISLAND

This long day trip links such highlights of south Vancouver Island as the First Nations totems at Duncan, the beautiful murals at Chemainus and the natural splendor of Cathedral Grove. You'll leave the relative bustle of Victoria in the morning and by late afternoon arrive at the solitude of the Pacific Rim National Park to watch the sun set over the Pacific Ocean.

THE DRIVE

Distance: 316km (196 miles)
Allow: 6 hours (not including visits)
Start: Victoria ✚ 413 C17
End: Tofino (Pacific Rim National Park)

★ From the Empress Hotel on Victoria's waterfront at Inner Harbour, travel via Highway 1, or Island Highway. Take Douglas Street, which becomes Highway 1 and head through the northern suburbs. The road leads up and over Malahat Pass, at 352m (1,155ft) one of the highest points in southern Vancouver Island. Visibility may be limited by low cloud and fog. Some 60km (37 miles) from Victoria is Duncan (▷ 292).

❶ Known as the City of Totems (there are more than 80 of them in town and along the highway), Duncan is home to the Cowichan people, who are renowned for their carving skills. You can see carving in

Left *The Empress Hotel, Victoria*
Below left *The harbour at Port Alberni*
Below right *Trees in Cathedral Grove*

progress at the Quw'utsun Cultural and Conference Centre, and explore other aspects of their cultural background.

Some 11km (7 miles) north of the Lake Cowichan intersection, turn right on Westholme to Chemainus. This approach is much more picturesque than carrying on along the main road and taking the shorter link road farther north. When you reach the next intersection (a T-junction), turn left into Chemainus (▷ 292). You'll see an old steam engine opposite you at the intersection.

❷ Chemainus is famed for its murals and attractive shops. It is also known as "The Little Town That Did" because of its dramatic recovery from what seemed to be a terminal decline back in the early 1980s. The depression followed the closure of the town's traditional industries, but the idea of it becoming an artists' enclave—to breathe new life into the community—was championed. Many people said it couldn't be done, but after they were proved wrong, the plucky little town earned its cheery sobriquet.

Head back to Highway 1 and continue your drive north. When you've reached 110km (68 miles) from Victoria, you can visit Nanaimo (▷ 300). Highway 1 runs through the town and ends at the ferry port on Departure Bay, but if you'd rather

carry on, take Highway 19, a 4-lane bypass.

❸ Nanaimo is a lively town with an active fishing fleet and an interesting First Nations heritage. There's a pleasant seafront walk around the harbor and to the estuary of the Millstone River, where salmon come to spawn.

Travel north of Nanaimo on Highway 19 for 38km (24 miles) to reach a sign at the intersection of Highway 4 pointing the way to Port Alberni and the Pacific Rim National Park (also signposted to Tofino and Ucluelet). Turn left here and begin the westward drive. About 15km (9 miles) from the turning, Cameron Lake comes into view, followed after another 6km (4 miles) by Cathedral Grove and Port Alberni.

❹ The road skirts Cameron Lake, traveling through thick pine forest, then the majestic old growth forest of Cathedral Grove (▷ 292). Port Alberni is the leading town of the region. You can take boat trips down the Alberni Inlet to Barkley Sound in the Pacific Rim.

To reach Tofino and Ucluelet, make a right at the waterfront, following Highway 4 the whole way.

❺ This final section of the trip really takes you into untamed landscape. After Sproat Lake there is no fuel for 85km (53 miles), so check your tank.

Around 46km (29 miles) from Port Alberni, the road rises 175m (574ft)

at Sutton Pass through a series of dramatic switchbacks along the boulder-strewn Taylor River valley up onto the Clayoquot Plateau. You'll climb again at the other side of the plateau, before passing Lake Kennedy, on your right, on your final descent to the coast, eventually reaching an intersection (T-junction) that signposts Ucluelet south and Tofino north. Take the right turn to Tofino. You travel through the mainland section of Pacific Rim National Park (▷ 302–303) before reaching Tofino.

WHEN TO GO
Some of the attractions, including guided tours of the Duncan totems, operate only between May and end September. However, storm-watching is a popular winter pastime on the coastline near Tofino.

WHERE TO EAT
✉ Wharfside Eatery and Decks, 1208 Wharf Street, Victoria ☎ 250/360-1808.
✉ Dockside Pub/Blue Heron Restaurant, 634 Campbell Street, Tofino ☎ 250/725-3277

WHERE TO STAY
✉ Abigail's Hotel, 906 McClure Street, Victoria ☎ 250/388-5363 or 866/347-5054.
✉ Best Western Tin Wis Resort, 1119 Pacific Rim Highway, Tofino ☎ 250/725-4445 or 800/661-9995

WALK

A STROLL ON THE EDGE OF THE CONTINENT

Long Beach in Pacific Rim National Park is noted for its big waves, famed throughout the surfing world. Long, smooth strands backed by temperate rainforest make this the perfect place for strolling, while just offshore you may spot migrating whales or frolicking sea lions. Rather than taking in all 21km (13 miles) of Long Beach, this walk introduces you to the delights of its northernmost section nearest to the region's main town, Tofino.

THE WALK

Distance: 7.2km (4 miles) round trip
Allow: 4 hours
Start/end: Long Beach north parking area
How to get there: From Victoria, take Highway 1 north and after 38km (23.7 miles)—north of Nanaimo—turn left on Highway 4, a total distance of 316km (196 miles)

You'll need to display a Park Use Permit in your car, available from the Park Information Centre on Highway 4 at Long Beach (adult $6.80, chid (6–16) $3.40, family $17.10). From the Long Beach north parking area, head straight out onto the sand.

This part of Long Beach is the most popular with surfers, and you'll normally find a small group out on the water here in almost all weather conditions.

When you reach the waterline, turn left, walking along the shore with the ocean on your right.

Whatever the state of the tide, Long Beach presents a wonderful vista—high tide leaves only the soft golden grains visible, but low tide widens the strand considerably and provides lots of firm sand underfoot. As you stroll you'll see a small islet just offshore. Keep an eye out for

the occasional sea lion basking in the sea spray.

Continue walking along the waterline. You'll see a rocky headland ahead (if the tide is coming in and is close to the rocks, don't walk on the water-side of the headland as the waves can be powerful, take the footpath that runs along the landward side).

The north flank of the rocky outcrop has a bronze plaque commemorating the visit of Her Royal Highness Princess Anne when she officially opened the park

Left *Wild and windswept Long Beach, scattered with driftwood*
Below left *Boardwalks make the going easy and protect the delicate vegetation from trampling feet*
Below right *A gentle walk on the shore*

in 1971. The top of the outcrop is a great vantage point out to the open ocean, and to the left and right along Long Beach.

If you take the shore-side route you'll pass the path to Green Point Campground on your left, leading inland through thick shoreline vegetation. Beyond the outcrop is another long sandy bay. Walk along until you reach a stream of water cutting across your path (look also for a parking area at the top of the beach). Make your way to the vegetation line to reach the start of the 1.6km (1-mile) loop known as Combers Beach interpretive walk.

This boardwalk route leads through various levels of coastal vegetation, starting with the intercoastal tideland spruce forest at sea-level, before moving inland and climbing as the land level rises. Here you'll find mixed woodland and cedar-hemlock forest, containing some rare Sitka spruces, which are one of the world's tallest tree species.

This is old-growth forest with some gargantuan examples, along with a forest floor of ferns and fallen trees.

When you've completed the boardwalk, retrace your steps to the Long Beach parking area.

WHEN TO GO
Any time of year is good here, with whales offshore from March to October, beautiful sunsets in summer, and mild weather interspersed with spectacular storms in winter. The most important thing you should do is consult tide tables—you will get most out of the walk if you come at low tide, when there's more beach, more firm sand to walk on and more tidepools to explore. Tides change every six hours, so there are two low tides a day. High tide is best for kayaking or storm-watching, but for the latter stay off the beach—for safety and for better views, find a high vantage point away from the crashing waves. Park facilities are fully open mid-March through mid-October, and limited through the rest of the year.

PUBLIC RESTROOMS
North beach parking area.

WHERE TO EAT
✉ Pointe Restaurant, Wickaninnish Inn, 500 Osprey Lane, Tofino ☎ 250/725-3100 or 800/333-4604

WHERE TO STAY
✉ A Snug Harbour Inn, 460 Marine Drive, Ucluelet ☎ 250/726-2686 or 888/936-5222.
✉ Wickaninnish Inn, 500 Osprey Lane, Tofino ☎ 250/725-3100 or 800/333-4604

SOME ADVICE
To protect the environment and ensure your safety, heed the following advice:
» It is illegal to remove shells, stones, driftwood or any creatures—alive or dead.
» Explore rockpools gently, and respect the life in them.
» Watch where you tread on the rocks—they are covered with life, which is simply dormant until the sea returns.
» Beware of rogue waves and fast incoming tides.

WILDLIFE
Marine mammals abound in this protected environment, including whales offshore from March to October, and curious seals and sea lions that peer at you from the surfline or bask on the rocks. There's a bird sanctuary close by, and you'll see bald eagles, herons, oystercatchers and other species, including migrating shore birds. Inland, there are bears—some local outfitters run tours to view them safely.

WHAT TO DO

ALDERGROVE
GREATER VANCOUVER ZOO
www.gvzoo.com
Albus, a rare albino black bear, is just one of more than 700 animals at this 48ha (120-acre) park. There's a zoo train, and a tour bus that goes inside the North American Wilds exhibit.
✉ 5048 264th Street, Aldergrove, British Columbia, V4W 1N7 ☎ 604/856-6825 ⏰ Apr–end Sep daily 9–7; rest of year 9–4 💰 Adult $18, child (4–15) $14, family $60 🚗 Off Trans-Canada Highway between Vancouver and Abbotsford, south of exit 73 🍴 Fast food

ARMSTRONG
ARMSTRONG FARMERS' MARKET
www.bcfarmersmarket.org
This market offers a great variety and a great experience. It's the oldest of its kind in the region.
✉ IPE Fairgrounds, Pleasant Valley Road, PO Box 682, Armstrong, British Columbia, V0E 1B0 ☎ 250/546-1986 ⏰ Apr–end Oct Sat 8–12

BANFF
THE BANFF CENTRE
www.banffcentre.ca
An arts, culture and conference venue in a spectacular mountain lo-

cation. It has an interesting calendar of music, dance and comedy.
✉ 107 Tunnel Mountain Drive, Banff, Alberta, T1L 1H5 ☎ 403/762-6301, 800/413-8368 ⏰ Year-round 💰 Varies 🚗 On slope of Tunnell Mountain, four blocks east from Banff Avenue

BRIDAL FALLS
DINOTOWN
www.dinotown.com
This theme park in the Fraser Valley is one for young children. The 5ha (12-acre) park has cute dinosaur characters, gentle rides and a wet play area. There's a parade through a prehistoric town and a live stage show in the clubhouse.
✉ 53480 Bridal Falls Road, Rosedale, British Columbia, V0X 1X0 ☎ 604/794-3733 ⏰ Mid-Jun to end Aug daily 10–5 (to 7 Jul–Aug weekends); May to mid-Jun and Sep Sat–Sun 10–5 💰 $13 (children under 2 free) 🍴 Dinersaurus serves burgers, chicken strips and hotdogs

BRITANNIA BEACH
BC MUSEUM OF MINING
www.bcmuseumofmining.org
A filming location for dozens of movies and TV shows, this national historic site preserves the copper mining heritage of BC. The highlight

is climbing aboard the train in hard hats for a trip 364m (1,200ft) underground. You can also pan for gold, and keep any that you find.
✉ Highway 99, Britannia Beach, British Columbia ☎ 604/896-2233, 800/896-4044 ⏰ Early May to mid-Oct daily 9–4.30; rest of year Mon–Fri 9–4.30 💰 Adult $16.95, child (13–18) $13.95; winter rate $7.50 all ages 🚗 52km (32 miles) north of Vancouver on Sea-to-Sky Highway

BURNABY
METROPOLIS AT METROTOWN
http://metropolis.shopping.ca
An enormous shopping mall at the heart of downtown with nearly 500 stores of all kinds, including Sears, The Bay, Toys 'R' Us, Zellers, Winners HomeSense and Chapters. There are 16 movie theaters, restaurants and a calendar of special events such as a Lion Dance through the mall on Chinese New Year.
✉ Kingsway, Burnaby, British Columbia, V5H 4N2 ☎ 604/438-4715 ⏰ Mon–Fri 10–9, Sat 9.30–9, Sun 11–6 (some store hours may vary) 🚈 Skytrain Expo line, direction: King George or Millennium Line, direction: VCC-Clark 🚌 19, 49, 106, 110, 112, 116, 129, 130, 140 🚗 About 8km (5 miles) east of Vancouver 🍴 Several restaurants, plus a huge food court

CANMORE

ALPINE HELICOPTERS

http://alpinehelicopter.com

This company offers exhilarating sightseeing trips or half-day hikes for which you are dropped off by helicopter in remote mountain areas with an experienced guide.

✉ 91 Bow Valley Trail, Canmore, Alberta, T1W 1N8 ☎ 403/678-4802 🕐 Year-round by appointment (at least three days in advance) 🖐 Sightseeing $99–$259; Heli-hiking $349–499, plus tax 🚗 22km (13.5 miles east of Banff)

SILVER TIP GOLF RESORT

www.silvertipresort.com

A spectacular, world-class 6,675m (7,300-yard) golf course on the mountainside, with a 182m (600ft) elevation change and a 360-degree panoramic view.

✉ 2000 Silver Tip Trail, Canmore, Alberta, T1W 3J4 ☎ 403/678-1600, 877/877-5444 🕐 late May–early Oct daily 🖐 $105–$175 ($79 for 9 holes in evening). Club rental $48 per set (includes sleeve of balls) ❓ Power cart rule 🚗 Off Trans-Canada Highway (Canmore exit), 23km (14 miles) east of Banff

CHEMAINUS

CHEMAINUS THEATRE

This is a beautiful theater building, offering a good variety of new and classic drama and musicals, such as *Hay Fever*, *South Pacific* and *The Miracle Worker*. There's also an annual series of plays for children.

✉ 9737 Chemainus Road, Chemainus, Vancouver Island, British Columbia, V0R 1K0 ☎ 250/246-9820, 800/565-7738 🕐 Year-round 🖐 $30–$40. Dinner and theater: $49–$63 🍴 Playbill Dining Room (licensed) with hot and cold buffet

CLINTON

ECHO VALLEY RANCH AND SPA

www.evranch.com

A little bit of Thailand has been set down amid beautiful BC landscape, with a traditional Thai Baan building and Thai spa treatments, including massage, Ruesri-dat-ton stretching exercises and rejuvenation.

✉ Po Box 16, Clinton, Jesmond, British Columbia, V0K 1K0 ☎ 250/459-2386, 800/253-8831 🕐 Apr–end Oct and Dec

20–Jan 5 (primarily for overnight guests, but open to day visitors subject to availability) 🖐 Three nights all-inclusive from $720 🚗 About 30km (81 miles) northwest of Kamloops, off Highway 97 at Clinton

GRAND CACHE

U BAR TRAIL RIDES

www.ubartrailrides.com

Take overnight pack trips or spend just a few hours in the saddle. Beginners get instruction, then set off with a guide through meadows and mountains for wonderful views. Reservation required.

✉ Box 929, Grande Cache, Alberta, T0E 0Y0 ☎ 780/827-4884, 866/479-8227 🕐 Day rides begin 10am, one-hour ride at 4pm 🖐 1 hour $30, 2 hours $50, 5 hours $125–$150; overnight pack trip $195 🚗 Northern edge of Willmore Wilderness Park on the Big Horn Highway (40), 2.5 hours drive north of Jasper via Trans-Canada 16

INVERMERE

RIVERGEMS

www.rivergems.com

Here you will find some gorgeous jewelry made from richly colored Alberta ammolite and some shark-tooth necklaces. They also have stunning display of minerals that glitter or glow in the light, and fossils including ammonites.

✉ 613 12th Street, Invermere, British Columbia, V0A 1K0 ☎ 250/342-0177 🕐 Mar–Dec Mon–Sat 10–6, Sun 11–5; Jan–Feb Mon–Sat 11–5 🚗 Invermere is off Highway 93, south of Kootenay National Park and Radium Hot Springs

JASPER

ATHA-B CLUB

www.athabascahotel.com

A buzzing nightclub in a landmark hotel dating from 1929. It's a fun, noisy place with dancing every night, and live music most nights, including some international touring bands.

✉ Athabasca Hotel, 510 Patricia Street, Jasper, Alberta, T0E 1E0 ☎ 780/852-3386 🕐 Daily 4pm–2am 🚗 Near ViaRail station and bus depots

CHABA THEATRE

Two-screen movie theater showing latest releases and classic films.

✉ 604 Connaught Drive, Jasper, Alberta ☎ 780/852-4749 🕐 Daily

JASPER RAFT TOURS

www.jasperrafttours.com

A great trip for families, following the fur traders' route down the Athabasca River in big inflatables. The two- to three-hour round trip has some small rapids and calm stretches.

✉ Box 398, Jasper National Park, Jasper, Alberta, T0E 1E0 ☎ 780/852-2665, 1-888-553-5628 🕐 Jul, Aug tours depart Jasper railroad station 9am, 12.30pm and 7pm; mid-May to end Jun and Sep 12.30pm 🖐 Adult $49, child (6–16) £15, under 6 free ❓ Transportation from Jasper provided. Meet at the totem pole beside the train station, at 607 Connaught Drive

TOTEM SKI SHOP

www.totemskishop.com

It grew from a log-cabin general store of nearly a century ago, and now stocks a great range of outdoor clothing, footwear and equipment. They also offer rentals of summer and winter equipment, including climbing crampons and much more.

✉ 408 Connaught Drive, Jasper, Alberta, T0E 1E0 ☎ 780/852-3078, 800/363-3078 🕐 May–Oct daily 9.30am–10pm; Dec–Apr Sun–Thu 8am–6pm, Fri–Sat 8am–9pm 🚗 Ski Bus (winter only) 🚗 On main street, by Astoria Hotel

KELOWNA

SUMMERHILL PYRAMID WINERY

www.summerhill.bc.ca

There are a number of wineries in the Thompson Okanagan area. Wine here is aged in a four-story pyramid to enhance the flavor. You can tour the facility, sample the wine, and watch the sunset over dinner.

✉ 4870 Chute Lake Road, Kelowna, British Columbia, V1W 4M3 ☎ 250/764-8000, 800/667-3538 🕐 Daily 9–6. Tours at 12 and 2 🚗 20-min drive from Kelowna 🍴 Sunset Verandah (▷ 337)

108 MILE RANCH

THE HILLS HEALTH RANCH

www.spabc.com

A world-class spa on a vast western ranch. The Canadian Wellness Centre here has the largest staff of any spa in the country, and offers the full treatment.

✉ 108 Mile Ranch, British Columbia ☎ 250/791-5225, 800/668-2233 ⊕ Fully inclusive packages range from 2-night weekend to 30-night Weight Loss Special ✋ From $500 to more than $5,000 (based on two sharing a double room) ✗ Shuttle from Williams Lake airport ($60 round-trip) ➡ Greyhound Bus to 100 Mile House, then free chuttle ➡ Off Route 9, 12km (7.7 miles) north of 100 Mile House

NANAIMO
OCEAN EXPLORERS DIVING
www.oceanexplorersdiving.com
Diver and broadcaster Jacques Cousteau rated the waters off British Columbia as second only to the Red Sea for world-class diving. This outfitter offers diving charters that take you to explore artificial reefs and wrecks, and the package can include tuition and supplies. Wetsuit and equipment rental are available.

✉ 1690 Stewart Avenue, Nanaimo, British Columbia, V9S 4E1 ☎ 250/753-2055, 800/233-4145 ⊕ Year-round ✋ $60–$180, includes air and weights ➡ BC Ferries: Horseshoe Bay, Vancouver, to Nanaimo ❓ Free pick-up/drop-off to ferry terminal and airport ➡ Near Departure Bay ferry terminal

SIDNEY
TANNERS—A BOOKSTORE AND MORE
Sidney is known for its bookstores, most specializing in rare and second-hand books. This one has more mainstream interest, plus a selection of international newspapers and more than 2,000 magazines.

✉ 2436 Beacon Avenue, Sidney, British Columbia, V8L 1X6 ☎ 250/656-2345, 866/656-2345 ⊕ Daily 8–10 (till 9 in winter) ➡ Rapid bus (north) from Victoria ➡ Downtown, corner of Beacon and 4th

SURREY
FRASER DOWNS RACE TRACK
www.fraserdowns.com
This venue offers a good long season of harness-racing events, plus simulcast from Hong Kong.

✉ 17755 60th Avenue, Surrey, British

Columbia, V3S 1V3 ☎ 604/576-9141 ⊕ Live racing most weekends (Fri–Sun) and occasional weekdays, either 7pm or 1.15pm start. Simulcast: year-round ✋ Free P$2 for live racing, otherwise free ➡ 320 from Surrey Central station ⬛ Skytrain: Surrey Central, then bus ➡ Cloverdale, east of Pacific Highway

TELEGRAPH COVE
STUBBS ISLAND WHALE-WATCHING
www.stubbs-island.com
This was the first whale-watching company in British Columbia, and its experienced captains man vessels with cabin heating, restrooms, and hydro-phones to hear the whales. Extended tours also available.

✉ Box 2-2, Telegraph Cove, British Columbia, V0N 3J0 ☎ 250/928-3185, 800/665-3066 ⊕ Mid-Jul to mid-Aug daily 9am, 1pm, 5.30pm; May to mid-Jul and mid-Aug to early Oct daily 9am, 1pm. Cruises last around 3½ hours. Reservations recommended ✋ 9am and 5.30pm departures: $79 all ages; 1pm departures: adult $89, child (under 13) $79 ➡ Island Coach Lines: Victoria–Port Hardy ➡ At the north end of Vancouver Island, 11km (7 miles) from Highway 19 via Beaver Cove Road

VANCOUVER
ALCAN CHILDREN'S MARITIME DISCOVERY CENTRE
www.vancouvermaritimemuseum.com
There's plenty of opportunity for make-believe as well as educational fun here, taking the controls in a replica tugboat wheelhouse, working a remote-controlled deep-sea robot or visiting Pirates' Cove. There are also real boats to visit in the harbor.

✉ Vancouver Maritime Museum, 1905 Ogden Avenue, Vancouver, British Columbia, V6J 1A3 ☎ 604/257-8300 ⊕ Mid-May to early Sep daily 10–5, rest of year Tue–Sat 10–5, Sun 12–5 ✋ Adult $10, child (6–19) $7.50, family $25 ➡ 2, 22 ⛴ Aquabus, False Creek Ferry

BACKSTAGE LOUNGE
www.artsclub.com
Run by the Arts Club Theatre Company, behind the Granville Island Stage (▷ 331), this is one of the

city's foremost live music venues.

✉ 1585 Johnston Street, Vancouver, British Columbia, V6H 3R9 ☎ 604/687-1354 ⊕ Daily ✋ Cover charge varies 🍴 Pub food; 11 brews on tap

BARD ON THE BEACH
www.bardonthebeach.org
An annual professional Shakespeare festival presenting four classical productions and various special events.

✉ Theatre Tent, Vanier Park, Vancouver, British Columbia ☎ 604/739-0559, 877/739-0559 ⊕ Late May to late Sep Tue–Sun ✋ From $15 ⊗ ⛴ False Creek Ferry ➡ 2, 22

BLACKBERRY BOOKS
www.bbooks.ca
There is a welcoming atmosphere in this bookstore, run by the Stewart family for nearly 30 years.

✉ 1 Net Loft Building, 1666 Johnston Street, Granville Island, Vancouver, British Columbia, V6H 3S2 ☎ 604/685-6188, 604/685-4113 ⊕ Daily 9–6 ➡ 50 ⛴ False Creek Ferry or Aquabus

BC LIONS
www.bclions.com
Five-time Grey Cup winners, the BC Lions Canadian football team plays at the superb BC Place Stadium, which has a capacity for more than 60,000 and the biggest air-supported dome in the world.

✉ BC Place Stadium, 777 Pacific Boulevard, Vancouver, British Columbia, V6B 4Y8 ☎ 604/669-2300 (information), 604/280-4444 (tickets) ⊕ Season: late Jun–early Nov ✋ From $25 ➡ 15, 17 ⬛ Skytrain: Stadium

THE CELLAR
www.cellarjazz.com
Opened in 2000, the Cellar became the place to see the best local and touring jazz performers. Snug room; cabaret-style seating.

✉ 3611 West Broadway Street, Vancouver, British Columbia, V6R 2B8 ☎ 604/738-1959 ⊕ Mon and Wed 8pm–midnight, Thu–Sat 7pm–midnight, Sun 6–11, Tue 6.30–11.30 ✋ Minimum food and beverage charge: Sun–Thu $10, Fri–Sat $15; cover charges: Mon $5, Tue $15, Wed–Sun varies ➡ 99, 99B, 17

CN IMAX

www.imax.com/vancouver

Next to Canada Place, jutting out into the bay, this theater offers the usual IMAX huge-screen experience.

 Canada Place, 201–999 Canada Place, Vancouver, British Columbia, V6C 3C1 ☎ 604/682-4629 ⏰ Daily ✋ Adult $14, child (3–12) $13 🚉 Skytrain: Waterfront

CRAFTHOUSE

www.cabc.net

Run by the Crafts Association of British Columbia, this gallery is a nonprofit organization showcasing the work of more than 150 of its members. The imaginative layout and careful spotlighting highlight ceramics, glass, metal, wood, fabrics and furniture (shipping arranged), at prices from $5 to $2,500.

✉ 1386 Cartwright Street, Granville Island, Vancouver, British Columbia, V6H 3R8 ☎ 604/687-7270 ⏰ Daily 10.30–5.30 (extended seasonal hours) or by appointment 🚌 50 ⛴ False Creek Ferry, Aquabus 🚉 Near ferry terminal

FIREHALL ARTS CENTRE

www.firehallartscentre.ca

Housed in the old fire station, this is one of the busiest venues in the city, staging around 300 events a year: dance, theater and music.

✉ 280 East Cordova Street, Vancouver, British Columbia, V6A 1L3 ☎ 604/689-0926

⏰ Year-round ✋ $20–$28. Some pay-what-you-can matinées Wed 1pm following opening night (call to check) 🚌 3, 4, 7, 8 🚉 Skytrain: Waterfront 🚌 Eastside, corner of Gore Avenue 🍸 Gallery lounge serves snacks

GENERAL MOTORS PLACE

When it's not staging hockey or basketball, this 20,000-seat state-of-the-art arena hosts nearly 200 events a year, including big-name concerts.

✉ 800 Griffiths Way, Vancouver, British Columbia, V6B 6G1 ☎ 604/899-7676 ⏰ Year-round ✋ Varies 🚌 15 🚉 Skytrain: Stadium 🍴 More than 20 fast-food concessions and three formal restaurants; Brew House Grill has dinner-and-view tables

GRANVILLE ISLAND STAGE

www.artsclub.com

The Arts Club Theatre Company stages plays and musicals—here and at the Stanley Theatre.

✉ 1585 Johnston Street, Granville Island, Vancouver, British Columbia, V6H 3H9 ☎ 604/687-1644 ⏰ Year-round ✋ $17.50–$57 🚌 50 ⛴ Granville Island Ferry or Aquabus

H. R. MACMILLAN SPACE CENTRE

www.hrmacmillanspacecentre.com

This spectacular attraction offers exciting space-related activities. Best is the realistic virtual voyage, with a

pre-mission briefing then a ride in a spacecraft simulator. You can touch a moon rock, and visit the multimedia show and planetarium.

✉ 1100 Chestnut Street, Vancouver, British Columbia, V6J 3J9 ☎ 604/738-7827 ⏰ Daily 10–5 (closed Mon in winter) ✋ $15, child (5–18) $10.75, family $45; simulator rides $7; evening laser show $10.75. Combined tickets with Vancouver Museum and Vancouver Maritime Museum: adult $30, child (5–18) $24 🚌 2, 22 ⛴ Aquabus, False Creek Ferry

INUIT GALLERY OF VANCOUVER

www.inuit.com

A spacious gallery where individual works by Inuits of the eastern Canadian Arctic and Northwest Coast First Nations artists are displayed.

✉ 206 Cambie Street, Gastown, Vancouver, British Columbia, V6B 2M9 ☎ 604/688-7323, 888/615-8399 ⏰ Mon–Sat 10–6, Sun 11–5 (10–5 in summer) 🚌 50 🚉 Skytrain: Waterfront 🚌 Corner of Cambie and Water streets

LA RAFFINAGE SPIRIT SPA

www.laraffinage.com

Body, mind and spirit are soothed and nurtured in this relaxing haven in the heart of the city.

✉ 521 West Georgia Street, Vancouver, British Columbia, V6B 1Z5 ☎ 604/681-9933 ⏰ Mon–Wed 10–7, Thu–Fri 10–8, Sat 9–6 ✋ Treatments priced individually or as packages; massage/facials from about $80 5, 6, 8, 20 Skytrain: Granville Downtown, corner of West Georgia and Richards

LEONE

www.leone.ca

It's like stepping into the world of celebrity shopping at this fashion store. It has been constructed to look like an Italian street lined with designer boutiques—Versace, Prada, John Galliano, Armani and Jean-Paul Gaultier are just some of the labels. There's valet parking.

757 West Hastings Street, Vancouver, British Columbia, V6C 1A1 604/683-1133 Mon–Sat 10–6, Sun 12–5 44, 50 Skytrain: Waterfront Downtown, near Cruise Ship and Seabus Terminal Leone Café

LONSDALE QUAY

www.lonsdalequay.com

In a spectacular location overlooking the harbor, this mall has more than 90 stores and services, plus a traditional market with more than 60 vendors selling local produce and fish. Upstairs there are specialty boutiques and a playroom, and there's daily entertainment.

Lonsdale Avenue, North Vancouver, British Columbia, V7M 3K7 604/985-6261 Market level: daily 9.30–6.30, retail level: daily 10–6 (restaurants stay open later) 228, 242, 246 and others within North Vancouver Sea Bus from downtown (15 min) Several restaurants and cafés, plus International Food Court with 13 outlets

LYNN CANYON ECOLOGY CENTRE

www.dnv.org/ecology/

The center interprets the park's temperate rain forest, and children enjoy the Exploratorium. Outside, they can clamber across the suspension bridge over the creek and explore forests and waterfalls.

Lynn Canyon Park, 3663 Park Road, North Vancouver, British Columbia, V7J 3G3 604/990-3755 Ecology Centre: Jun–Sep daily 10–5, rest of year Mon–Fri 10–5, Sat–Sun and holidays 12–4. Park: daily from 7am; closes 7pm spring and fall, 9pm Jun–Sep, dusk in winter Park: free; Ecology Centre: donation 228, 229 Sea Bus to Lonsdale Quay, then bus North Vancouver off Trans-Canada Highway, via Lynn Valley Road and Peters Road Lynn Canyon Café

MAJESTIC

www.majesticvancouver.com

A cool, eclectic gay venue with a mixed crowd, good food, cocktails and varied entertainment. Wednesdays is "Bingo for Life" charity night; Thursdays hosts the Bob Loblaw Queer Comedy Troupe's improv show; there are drag dinner shows on Fridays and Saturdays; and on Sundays you can Brunch with the Queens at noon.

1138 Davie Street, Vancouver, British Columbia, V6E 1N1 604/669-2013 Mon–Fri from 4pm–3am, Sat 11am–3am, Sun 11am–6pm; entertainment starts between 7.30 and 8.30pm Wed–Sat Cover charge $5–$20; some events free 6, N6, C23 Downtown west of Burrard, between Thurlow and Bute streets

ODYSSEY

www.theodysseynightclub.com

In the heart of the city's gay village, this gay nightclub attracts a straight clientele too. Each night is different: the latest tracks, drag shows and naked male dancers. Minimum age: 19 years. Bring two pieces of ID if you look under 25.

1251 Howe Street, Vancouver, British Columbia, V6Z 1R3 604/689-5256 Mon–Thu 9pm–2am, Fri–Sat 9pm–3/4am, Sun 9pm–2.30am Varies Skytrain: Bay Between Drake and Davie, parallel with Granville Street

ORPHEUM

www.city.vancouver.bc.ca/theatres/orpheum/orpheum.html

Lavish 1927 building, now a national historic site, home to the Vancouver Symphony and BC Entertainment Hall of Fame. It has a full schedule of concerts.

884 Granville Street at Smithe Street, Vancouver, British Columbia 604/665-3050 Year-round $20–$100 4, 6, 7, 10 Granville Downtown, at Seymour

PACIFIC CENTRE

www.pacificcentre.com

This sparkling three-story mall stretches three blocks and has upward of 200 stores, including Sears, Harry Rosen, Gap and Holt Renfrew's new, enarged flagship store. It also links with The Bay, Sears and the Vancouver Centre. A major redevelopment of the center, including a new facade and some new stores inside, is due to be complete by mid-2008, and in 2009 the center will be linked to the

new Canada Line transit system at Vancouver City Centre station.

✉ 910–609 Granville Street, Vancouver, British Columbia, V7Y 1G5 ☎ 604/688-7235 🕐 Mon–Tue and Sat 10–7, Wed–Fri 10–9, Sun 11–6 🚊 5, 6, 8, 10, 11, 15 🚈 Skytrain: Granville 🚇 Downtown, between Robson, Pender, Howe and Seymour 🍴 Fast food ☕ Specialty coffee shops; Sierra Café and Grill

PLAZA

www.plazaclub.net

Classy club with huge dance floor, booth seats, mezzanine overlook and the best nightclub washrooms in town. Dance to Top 40, R&B, Latin, alternative, hip-hop and latest club hits. Live bands some nights. Dress code Friday and Saturday.

✉ 881 Granville Street, Vancouver, British Columbia, V6V 1K7 ☎ 604/646-0064 🕐 Nightly from 9pm 🎟 From $10 🚈 Skytrain: Granville 🚇 Between Robson and Smithe

PUBLIC MARKET

www.granvilleisland.com

At the heart of Granville Island, this market is a sensory delight, with colorful displays of fresh produce, the aroma of ethnic foods, roasting coffee, fragrant flowers and candy; and the sound of shoppers and street entertainers. There are 50 permanent vendors, visiting farmers, craftworkers and food producers.

✉ Johnston Street, Granville Island, Vancouver, British Columbia, V6H 3R8 ☎ 604/666-6655 🕐 Daily 9–7 (seasonal variations) 🚊 50 ⛴ False Creek Ferry, Aquabus 🚇 Near Ferry terminal at Duranleau 🍴 Food options include seafood and Mexican ☕ Coffee house

QUEEN ELIZABETH THEATRE COMPLEX

www.city.vancouver.bc.ca/theatres

This complex hosts a full and varied calendar of world-class dance, opera, musicals and rock concerts.

✉ 600 Hamilton Street, Vancouver, British Columbia, V6B 2R3 ☎ 604/665-3050 🕐 Year-round, but closed for construction work during 2008 and 2009 🎟 $20–$150 🚊 17 🚈 Stadium 🚇 Downtown, between Georgia and Dunsmuir

RENDEZVOUS ART GALLERY

www.rendezvousartgallery.com

This is a commercial gallery specializing in the work of Canadian artists, including traditional and contemporary paintings and sculptures.

✉ 323 Howe Street, Vancouver, British Columbia, V6C 3N ☎ 604/687-7466; 877/787-7466 🕐 Mon–Sat 10–5.30, Sun 11–5 🚈 Skytrain: Waterfront ⛴ Seabus G50 🚇 Downtown, one block back from waterfront near Sinclair Centre

RICHARDS ON RICHARDS

www.richardsonrichards.com

This is a cool venue for international touring bands, including progressive country, indie rock, world music, singer-songwriters and hip-hop.

✉ 1036 Richards Street, Vancouver, British Columbia ☎ 604/687-6794 🕐 Daily 🎟 $15–$35 🚈 Skytrain: Granville 🚇 Downtown, between Nelson and Helmcken

SALMAGUNDI

In an area that is bursting with antiques shops and other funky little stores, you should seek out this one. It specializes in "interesting things," and this encompasses a wide range of antiques, collectibles and quirky novelty items.

✉ 321 West Cordova Street, Gastown, Vancouver, British Columbia, V6B 1E5 ☎ 604/681-4648 🕐 Daily 10.30–5.30 🚊 6 🚈 Skytrain: Waterfront

SALVATORE FERRAGAMO

www.salvatoreferragamo.it

The place to come to pick up Italian-designed accessories, from a silk scarf or tie to a pair of sunglasses to a stylish purse. Also footwear, fashions and fragrances.

✉ 918 Robson Street, Vancouver, British Columbia V6Z ☎ 604/669-4495 🕐 Mon–Sat 10–6, Sun 12–6 (also Thu–Fri 6–9pm in summer) 🚈 Skytrain: Granville or Burrard 🚊 5, 50 🚇 Downtown, between Hornby and Burrard streets

SCIENCE WORLD AND OMNIMAX THEATRE

www.scienceworld.bc.ca

There are masses of interactive exhibits in this huge geodesic dome.

Centre Stage offers entertaining demonstrations and kids are sometimes called on to participate. The Science Theatre has electronic and live shows. KidSpace Gallery has bright exhibits that teach through pla. There's an Omnimax theater.

✉ 1455 Québec Street, Vancouver, British Columbia, V6A 3Z7 ☎ 604/443-7440; 604/443-7443 🕐 Mon–Fri 10–5, Sat, Sun and holidays 10–6 🎟 Adult $16, child (4–12) $11, (13–18) $13, family $54. Omnimax combination ticket: adult $21, child (4–12) $16, (13–18) $18 🚈 Skytrain: Main Street/Science World ⛴ Aquabus or False Creek Ferry

SCOTIABANK THEATRE VANCOUVER

www.cineplex.com

Formerly the Paramount Vancouver, this nine-screen movie theater shows new releases.

✉ 900 Burrard Street, Vancouver, British Columbia, V6Z 3G5 ☎ 604/630-1407 🕐 Year-round 🎟 Adult $12.50, child (under 14) $9.95 🚊 2, 5, 22, 44 🚈 Skytrain: Burrard 🚇 Downtown, at Smithe Street

SINCLAIR CENTRE

www.sinclaircentre.com

It's not a big mall, but it is certainly one of the classiest you'll find. In a restored heritage building, it has an elegant interior and upscale stores including Leone (▷ 332), Escada (designer clothing), the Perfume Shoppe and Charals ("executive lifestyle").

✉ 757 West Hastings Street, Vancouver, British Columbia, V6C 1A1 ☎ 604/682-1720 🕐 Mon–Sat 10–5.30 🚊 50 🚈 Skytrain: Waterfront ⛴ Seabus 🚇 Downtown, opposite Waterfront

STANLEY INDUSTRIAL ALLIANCE STAGE

www.artsclub.com

The Arts Club Theatre Company stages popular plays, new works and musicals—here and at the Granville Island Stage (▷ 331).

✉ 2750 Granville Street, Vancouver, British Columbia, V6H 3J3 ☎ 604/687-1644 🕐 Tue–Sat 🎟 $17.50–$57 🚊 8, 98B 🚈 Granville at 12th

VANCOUVER AQUARIUM
▷ 310.

VANCOUVER AQUARIUM SLEEPOVER
www.vanaqua.org/visit_us/sleepovers
After the aquarium closes, you can stay on to enjoy various activities, then sleep here. After breakfast there's a tour of the Marine Mammal Deck and Amazon Free Flight Gallery. Under-16s must be accompanied by an adult. Minimum age is 6.
✉ 845 Avison Way, Stanley Park, Vancouver, British Columbia, V6B 3X8 ☎ 604/659-3504 🕐 Specific dates; call for information 🖐 $100 🚌 35, 135 🍴 Light evening meal and breakfast included in the price

VANCOUVER CANUCKS
http://canucks.nhl.com
The Canucks hockey team play home games at the superb GM Place, one of the most active entertainment venues in North America.
✉ General Motors Place, 800 Griffiths Way, Vancouver, British Columbia, V6B 6G1 ☎ 604/899-7550. Tickets: 604/280-4400 🕐 Sep–end Mar 🖐 $49.25–$104.50 🚉 Skytrain: Stadium

VANCOUVER EAST CULTURAL CENTRE
www.vecc.bc.ca
This converted 1909 church hosts an exciting schedule of theater, music and dance, including premieres.
✉ 1895 Venables Street, Vancouver, British Columbia, V5L 2H6 ☎ 604/251-1363 🕐 Year-round 🖐 Varies, average $28 🚌 20 🚉 Skytrain: Broadway, then bus 20 🚌 Downtown Eastside, corner of Venables and Victoria

VANCOUVER THEATRE SPORTS LEAGUE
www.vtsl.com
Highly entertaining improv comedy company that uses various themes to showcase its considerable talent, including competitive improv.
✉ New Revue Stage, 1601 Johnston Street, Granville Island, Vancouver, British Columbia ☎ 604/738-7013 🕐 Wed–Sat 🖐 $10.50–$16.50 🚌 50 ⛴ Aquabus or False Creek Ferry

THE YALE
http://theyale.ca
The best rhythm and blues in Vancouver. Jam sessions on weekends.
✉ The Yale Hotel, 1300 Granville Street, Vancouver, British Columbia, V6Z 1M7 ☎ 604/681-9253 🕐 Sun–Thu 11.30am–

2am, Fri–Sat 11.30am–3.30am; music nightly, usually from 9 or 9.45pm (8pm Tue) 🖐 Varies $10–$20 🚌 50 🚌 Downtown at Granville and Drake

VERNON
OKANAGAN OPAL
www.opalscanada.com
The only opal mine in Canada has its own jewelry design studio and store. Stones in many different shades are set into gold-, silver- and rhodium-plated earrings, pendants and rings, or you can buy loose stones. You can also visit the mine site (Fri–Sun in summer) to dig for your own opals.
✉ 7879 Highway 97, Vernon, British Columbia, V1T 6M2 ☎ 250/542-1103 🕐 Mon–Fri 9–5, Sat–Sun 11–3 (call for winter hours) 🚌 6.4km (4 miles) north of Vernon; Pleasant Valley exit and follow signs

VICTORIA
BELFRY
www.belfry.bc.ca
An old church has been converted into this beautiful theater. It hosts nine shows a year, as well as jazz and pop concerts.
✉ 1291 Gladstone Avenue, Victoria, British Columbia, V8T 1G5 ☎ 250/385-6815 🕐 Aug to mid-May 🖐 $21–$36 🚌 22 🚌 Corner of Fernwood Road

LANGHAM COURT
www.langhamcourttheatre.bc.ca
Old carriage house and barn (c1880), converted in 1940 into this intimate theater. It stages classic and new drama, and comedies.
✉ 805 Langham Court, Victoria, British Columbia, V8V 4J3 ☎ 250/384-2142 🕐 Year-round 🖐 From $17 🚌 1 🚌 South of Rockland Avenue, between Linden Avenue and Moss Street

MCPHERSON
www.rmts.bc.ca
This theater is central to the city's entertainment scene, and hosts a variety of local and touring shows.
✉ 3 Centennial Square, Victoria, British Columbia, V8W 1E5 ☎ 250/386-6121, 888/717-6121 🕐 Year-round 🖐 $15–$60 🚌 Corner of Pandora and Government, behind City Hall 🍴 Snack concessions and bar

ROYAL
www.rmts.bc.ca

Home to Pacific Opera Victoria and the Victoria Symphony, this splendid 1913 building, with a 1,445 audience capacity, hosts varied events.
✉ 805 Broughton Street, Victoria, British Columbia, V8W 1E5 ☎ 250/386-6121, 888/717-6121 🕐 Year-round 🖐 $15–$60 🚌 16, 76 🚏 At Blanchard intersection

ROYAL BC MUSEUM SHOP
www.royalbcmuseumshop.bc.ca

This superb store stocks First Nations artwork sourced from Northwest Coast tribes.
✉ 675 Belleville Street, Victoria, British Columbia, V8W 9W2 ☎ 250/356-0505 🕐 Daily 9–5 🚌 5, 27, 28, 30, 31 🚏 Downtown, corner of Belleville and Douglas

VICTORIA BUG ZOO
www.bugzoo.bc.ca

See some of the most incredible live insects and creepy-crawlies—you can hold some, and there are even bugs for sale.
✉ 631 Courtney street, Victoria, British Columbia, V8W 1B8 ☎ 250/384-2847 🕐 Jun–Labor Day weekend daily 9.30–7; rest of year Mon–Sat 10–5, Sun 11–5.30 🖐 Adult $9, child (3–16) $5 🚌 5, 27, 28, 30, 31 🚏 Between Government and Douglas, a block north of Empress hotel

WHISTLER
CROSS COUNTRY CONNECTION
www.crosscountryconnection.ca

All you need for cross-country activities, including equipment rental, guided tours and tuition.
✉ Box 1235, Whistler, British Columbia, V0N 1B0 ☎ 604/905-0071 🕐 Mon–Sat 9–8, Sun 9–6 🖐 Varies, call for information 🚏 Edge of village at entrance to Lost Lake Park, off Lorimer Road

MILLENIUM
www.myplacewhistler.org

This center offers top-quality concerts, drama and art exhibitions.
✉ 4335 Blackcomb Way, Whistler, British Columbia V0N 1B4 ☎ 604/935-8410 🖐 Year-round 🖐 Varies, usually around $30 🚏 Between Village Gate Boulevard and Lorimer Road

FESTIVALS AND EVENTS

JANUARY/FEBRUARY
CHINESE NEW YEAR CELEBRATIONS
www.vancouverchinesegarden.com

The third-largest Chinese community in North America celebrates Chinese New Year at numerous city locations, centered on the Dr. Sun Yat-Sen Classical Chinese Garden.
✉ Vancouver, British Columbia ☎ 604/662-3207

MARCH
VANCOUVER INTERNATIONAL DANCE FESTIVAL
www.vidf.ca

Local, national and international dancers gather for nearly three weeks, with shows, films and workshops.
✉ Vancouver, British Columbia ☎ 604/662-7441

BRANT WILDLIFE FESTIVAL
www.brantfestival.bc.ca

Celebrates the return of over 20,000 Brent geese en route from Mexico to Alaska, with birdwatching, wildlife art, carving competition, lectures and guided walks. March to mid-April.
✉ Parksvill/Qualicum Beach, British Columbia ☎ 604/924-9771

APRIL
WORLD SKI AND SNOWBOARD FESTIVAL
http://whistler.mtv.ca

Action-packed 10 days of events featuring Olympic champions and extreme sports legends, plus live music and other entertainment.
✉ Whistler, British Columbia ☎ 604/938-3399, ext 28

MAY/JUNE
VANCOUVER INTERNATIONAL CHILDREN'S FESTIVAL
www.childrensfestival.com

Entertainment, the arts and lots of hands-on activities designed specifically for children, in candy-striped tents beside English Bay.

✉ Vancouver, British Columbia ☎ 604/708-5655

VANCOUVER INTERNATIONAL MARATHON
www.bmovanmarathon.ca

The whole city seems to be on the move, with the marathon, the team relay, the half-marathon, wheelchair half-marathon, a kids' MaraFun; lots of accompanying events, including 26 musical stations.
✉ Vancouver, British Columbia ☎ 604/872-2928

INTERNATIONAL JAZZ FESTIVAL
www.coastaljazz.ca

A great line-up of world-class performers delight jazz fans for 10 days. This is one of the best events of its kind in the world, with 400 concerts in 40 venues.
✉ Vancouver, British Columbia ☎ 604/872-5200

VANCOUVER ISLANDS AFRO-CARIBBEAN CARNIVAL
www.ahavi.ca

The waterfront at Selkirk goes tropical, with music, food, crafts and fashions from various Caribbean and African countries.
✉ Selkirk, British Columbia ☎ 250/727-6454

SEPTEMBER
VANCOUVER FRINGE FESTIVAL
www.vancouverfringe.com

Theater for everyone is the purpose of this popular festival.
✉ Vancouver, British Columbia ☎ 604/257-0366 (box office), 604/257-0350 (information)

NOVEMBER
SANTA LIGHT PARADE
Christmas comes early with this seasonal parade illuminated by glittering colored lights along the downtown route. There are usually around 50 floats.
✉ Victoria, British Columbia ☎ 250/382-3111

EATING

PRICES AND SYMBOLS

The restaurants are listed alphabetically within each town. The prices are for a two-course lunch (L) and a three-course à la carte dinner (D). Prices in pubs are for a two-course lunchtime bar meal and a two-course dinner in the restaurant, unless specified otherwise. The wine price is for the least expensive bottle.

For a key to the symbols, ▷ 2.

BANFF

BALKAN

www.banffbalkan.ca

A taste of the Mediterranean is not confined to the excellent Greek cuisine here—on Tuesdays and Thursdays you'll get the complete experience with plate smashing and belly dancing too. The signature dish, Arni Psito (roast lamb) is superb and everything, from the delicious range of mezes to various grills, moussaka and pastas are all homemade with fresh ingredients and authentic Greek expertise. The lunch menu has a great range of filled pittas, burgers and sandwiches

✉ 120 Banff Avenue, Banff, Alberta T1L 1A4 ☎ 403/762-3454 🄯 Daily 11am–11pm 🖐 L $15, D $45, Wine $25 🚌 Downtown, between Buffalo and Caribou streets

EVELYN'S COFFEE BAR

http://evelynscoffeebar.com

So successful was Evelyn's first coffee bar that two more had to be opened to cope with demand. Fresh baked goods, including cinnamon rolls, bagels, carrot cake, and croissants, entice from breakfast time on, while at lunchtime there are soups, salads, sandwiches that are bursting with fillings, or perhaps a hot dish like lasagne or chicken pot pie. Also at 119 Banff Avenue and 229 Bear Street.

✉ 201 Banff Avenue, Banff, Alberta T1L 1A4 ☎ 403/762-0352 🄯 Daily 6.30am–11pm 🖐 L $10 🚌 Downtown, at Caribou Street

FUZE

www.fuzedining.com

This chic restaurant has a terrific ambience, with its cozy plush

booths, subdued lighting and modern décor, and offers fine dining with international influences. Signature dishes include pan-roasted BC sablefish, herb-crusted rack of lamb, Thai-style risotto of shellfish and Indian spiced New York steak. There's also an interesting vegetarian menu, with four choices of main course and five appetizers, and a tapas/small plate menu.

✉ 2nd Floor, Clock Tower Village Mall, 110 Banff Avenue, Banff, Alberta T1L 1C9 ☎ 403/760-0853 🄯 Daily 6–9 🖐 D $60, Wine $40 🚌 Downtown, between Buffalo and Caribou streets

GIORGIO'S

www.giorgiosbanff.com

Glowing warm decor and candlelit tables offer a promise of something special, and the experience doesn't disappoint. A menu of classic Italian dishes prepared from the finest Canadian produce ranges from crisp wood-oven pizzas and home-made pastas to a melt-in-the-mouth *osso bucco*, tender Veal Marsala or the fabulous combination of Alberta

AAA beef tenderloin with truffle mash, lobster and mascarpone ravioli and grilled asparagus.
✉ 219 Banff Avenue, Banff, Alberta, T1L 1C4 ☎ 403/762-5114 ⊕ Daily from 5pm ✋ D $45, Wine $35 🚌 Downtown, between Caribou and Wolf streets

MAGPIE & STUMP / CANTINA
Lively and cheerful, this is a good family restaurant during the day and an evening hotspot with a four-hour "happy hour" in the Cantina after 10pm. The food is Mexican and Tex-Mex, with lunchtime listings including soups, salads, nachos, enchiladas, tostadas, tacos and burgers. The dinner menu has more of the same, plus burritos, chimi changas, fajitas, chili con carne, steaks, ribs, salmon and barbecued chicken.
✉ 203 Caribou Street, Banff, Alberta, T1L 1A8 ☎ 403/762-4067 ⊕ Daily noon–2am ✋ L $16, D $35, Wine $28 🚌 Downtown, off Banff Avenue at Bear Street

MAPLE LEAF GRILLE AND SPIRITS
www.banffmapleleaf.com
The two floors of this restaurant and bar-lounge are separated by a grand staircase, and natural wood creates a rustic elegance. Real Canadian cuisine is the focus of the menu.
✉ 137 Banff Avenue, Banff, Alberta, T1L 1C8 ☎ 403/760-7680 ⊕ Daily 11am–midnight ✋ L $12, D $40, Wine $36 🚭 Section 🚌 Banff Shuttle 🚌 Near Caribou Street intersection

CHEMAINUS
DANCING BEAN CAFE
www.dancingbean.ca
With the work of local artists on the walls, local crafts for sale, a monthly open-mic songwriters' night and regular live music (jazz, blues, roots, classical), this is an artsy little place with a good range of daytime food made from locally sourced ingredients wherever possible. This includes home-made soups, grilled panini sandwiches, salads and wraps, great traditional desserts, breakfasts until 11am, and evenings meals such as chicken stir-fry, pasta and steaks on show nights.

✉ 9752 Willow Street, Chemainus, British Columbia, V0R 1K0 ☎ 250/246-5050 ⊕ Daily (until 11pm on show nights) ✋ L $10, D $20 🚌 South of town off Highway 1A, via Mill Street

JASPER
PAPA GEORGE'S
www.astoriahotel.com
On the main floor of a family-run heritage hotel, this is a snug, casual restaurant with a pub-style interior featuring a big stone fireplace.
✉ Astoria Hotel, 404 Connaught Drive, Jasper, Alberta, T0E 1E0 ☎ 780/852-3351, 800/661-7343 ⊕ Daily 7–3, 5–10 ✋ L $13, D $25, Wine $18 🚭

KELOWNA
BOUCHONS BISTRO
www.bouchonsbistro.com
This is a French bistro with stylish casual decor and a spacious patio open in summer. The French chef/partner has impressive credentials and has created a classic bistro menu, including specialties of *bouillabaise* and cassoulet alongside perennial favorites such as duck confit glazed with honey and spices with sherry sauce, braised rabbit casserole in Meaux mustard and tarragon, beef tartare, and grilled beef tenderloin on a cognac and pepper sauce. The three-course table d'hôte menu is good value at $38.50.
✉ 105 – 1180 Sunset Drive, Kelowna, British Columbia, V1Y 9W6 ☎ 250/763-6595 ⊕ Daily from 5.30pm, but closed mid-Feb to mid-Mar ✋ D $50, Wine $26.50 🚌 Downtown, near lakeshore

DOC WILLOUGHBY'S
www.docspub.ca
This is a traditional pub, with a dark interior of polished wood, sturdy beams, exposed brickwork and interesting bits and pieces on the walls. The menu is traditional too, with a range of all-day breakfasts, pizzas, burgers, soups, sandwiches and fish and chips, plus a few more interesting dishes like coconut curry prawns (shrimp), tortilla-crusted tilapia with chipotle and lime, and Cajun-style Basa (a white fish) with

pineapple salsa. The pub is named after the owner's grandfather—a renowned doctor turned politician who lived to be 101. It is also a venue for regular live music.
✉ 353 Bernard Avenue, Kelowna, British Columbia, V1Y 6N6 ☎ 250/868-8288 ⊕ Daily from 10am ✋ L $20, D $35, Wine $22 🚌 Downtown, off Water Street

SUNSET VERANDAH
www.summerhill.bc.ca
This winery restaurant overlooks Okanagan Lake. The wide selection of creative dishes incorporate seafood and organic meats with interesting accompaniments.
✉ Summerhill Pyramid Winery, 4870 Chute Lake Road, Kelowna, British Columbia, V1W 4M3 ☎ 250/764-8000, 800/667-3538 ⊕ Daily 11–9 ✋ L $17 D $50, Wine $27 🚭 🚌 1 🚌 12km (7 miles) from Kelowna on Lakeshore Road

NANAIMO
BOLD KNIGHT
www.boldknight.ca
This restaurant has been popular for more than 30 years for its seafood and steaks, and if you find it difficult to make a choice there are a number of "surf and turf" combinations on the menu. There's a Greek influence here too, so *souvlaki* features among the specialties. The seafood chowder is renowned. House wines come from the Peller Estates.
✉ 1140 Island Highway South, Nanaimo, British Columbia ☎ 250/754-6411 ⊕ Tue–Thu 11am–2pm, 4.30–10pm, Fri 11am–2pm, 4.30–11pm, Sat 4–11pm, Sun 4–10pm ✋ L $20, D $45, Wine $28 🚌 Southern edge of city, on TransCanada Highway

LONGWOOD BREWPUB
www.longwoodbrewpub.com
Sure to draw the eye on your way into this pub is the sight of gleaming fermentation tanks of the on-site brewery. Come on a Saturday and you can get a proper tour and a tasting. There's a good range of food available, with expert culinary touches raising the bar on such pub standards as halibut and chips (with Longwood beer in the batter) and

burgers (local prime aged beef, wild sockeye with Cajun spices, Italian chicken) and an accomplished range of entrees, which might include Moroccan spiced lamb, wild salmon stuffed with rock crab and spinach with a lemon pepper cream sauce.
✉ 5775 Turner Road, Nanaimo, British Columbia, V9T 6L8 ☎ 250/729-8225 🕒 Mon–Sat 11am–11pm, Sun 10am–10pm 🖐 L $15, D $40, Wine $27 🚌 North part of town, off Island Highway North (Highway 19A) between Rutherford Road and Hammond Bay Road

PRINCE RUPERT
WATERFRONT RESTAURANT
www.cresthotel.bc.ca
Reserve a window seat here so that you can enjoy the stunning view across Tuck Inlet to the islands. But even without the view, it's worth coming here for the fresh local seafood, skilfully prepared by chef Willy Beaudry and his team. Gigantic Alaskan king crabs, local sable fish poached in milk, Pacific salmon, lemon-roasted halibut with a shrimp dill sauce and flying fish roe share the menu with prime Alberta steaks, and such dishes as slow-roasted lamb with mint-rosemary jus. There are vegetarian choices too, and if you want a lighter meal, the "casual plates" include home-made gourmet burgers, fish and chips, sandwiches and salads.
✉ Crest Hotel, 222 West 1st Avenue, Prince Rupert, British Columbia, V8J 1A8 ☎ 250/624-6771, 800/663-8150 🕒 Daily 6.30am–9.30pm 🖐 L $25, D $50, Wine $25 🚌 Downtown, on the waterfront just off McBride Street (Highway 16), between 1st and 2nd streets

PORT ALBERNI
LITTLE BAVARIA
www.littlebavariarestaurant.com
Established by a German immigrant in 1966, this perennially popular restaurant is now run by Croatian Kathy Krznaric, so the cuisine still focuses mainly on European comfort food, such as liver and onions, Hungarian goulash and ten types of schnitzel. There are also seafood and steak dishes, but the Bavarian Plate (for two or more people) is a great way to sample schnitzels and bratwurst, served with fried potatoes, *spätzle* and vegetables. The lunch menu also has sandwiches and salads.
✉ 3035 4th Avenue, Port Alberni, British Columbia ☎ 250/724-4242 🕒 Mon–Fri 11am–2pm and from 5pm, Sat–Sun from 5pm 🖐 L $17, D $35, Wine $18 🚌 Upper Port Alberni, between Argyle and Angus streets

TOFINO
BREAKERS
www.breakersdeli.com
If you are heading out for a hike on Long Beach, this is a great place to pick up a boxed lunch for your picnic—even if you are making an early start. Organic, free-range, sustainable and wholesome ingredients go into the food, which includes all-day breakfasts, sandwiches, wraps and burritos, salads, deli foods and pizzas.
✉ 430 Campbell Street, Tofino, British Columbia, V0R 2Z0 ☎ 250/725-2558 🕒 Daily 7am–10pm 🖐 L $12 🚌 Downtown in the Campbell House building

SOBO
www.sobo.ca
The name is a contraction of "sophisticated bohemian," which describes both the food and the owner/chef Chef Lisa Ahier, whose career included once being placed in Canada's top ten new restaurants… for a catering truck parked in the wilderness! The menu is refreshingly unpretentious, featuring the finest local ingredients in dishes that are interesting without being over-fussy. Fish and shellfish feature prominently. Starters might include hemp-seed crusted oyster with avocado ice, or tortillas filled with local fish and topped with fresh fruit salsa; recent main course choices have included traditional cedar-planked salmon with brown rice, red peppers and greens, sautéed in port wine vinaigrette. The children's menu offers similar dishes, simplified to suit young palates.

✉ 311 Neill Street, Tofino, British Columbia, V0R 2Z0 ☎ 250/725-2341 🕒 Mon–Tue 11–5.30, Wed–Sun 11–9 🖐 L $12, D $30, Wine $30 🚌 Downtown, in Conradi building

VANCOUVER
AURORA BISTRO
www.aurorabistro.ca
This is a chic, modern restaurant serving modern Canadian cuisine, with ingredients sourced from local organic farmers and ocean-friendly fish merchants. The wine list is exclusively BC wines.
✉ 2420 Main Street, Vancouver, British Columbia, V5T 3E2 ☎ 604/873-9944 🕒 Daily from 5.30pm 🖐 JL $25, D $45, Wine $40 🚌 South of False Creek, between West Broadway and 8th Avenue

BLUE WATER CAFÉ AND RAW BAR
www.bluewatercafe.net
This hip seafood and sushi restaurant still gets rave reviews. Two- or three-tier seafood towers (expensive), piled high with succulent shellfish, are great for sharing. Delectable desserts feature either chocolate or fruit.
✉ 1095 Hamilton Street, Vancouver, British Columbia, V6B 5T4 ☎ 604/688-8078 🕒 Daily 11.30–3, 5–midnight 🖐 L $25, D $60, Wine $27.50 🚫 Except patio 🚌 1 🚌 Yaletown, at Hamilton and Helmcken

CINCIN
www.cincin.net
The food here is first-rate modern Italian, including pizzas made in a wood-fired oven and a wide range of pastas and meat dishes.
✉ 1154 Robson Street, Vancouver, British Columbia, V6E 1B5 ☎ 604/688-7338 🕒 Mon–Fri 11.30–2.30, 5–10.30, Sat–Sun 5–midnight 🖐 L $15, D $20, Wine £25 🚫 🚌 All services to Robson 🚌 Car Downtown, between Bute and Thurlow streets

MOONSTRUCK TEA HOUSE
http://moonstruckteahouse.com
This specialist tea shop, offering an outstanding range of loose-leaf varieties, also has a café where you can sample the infusions (hot or cold) and get a snack,

including a range of dim sum, soup, sandwiches, cakes, and exotic nibbles like sweet-and-sour crispy plums or soy sauce tofu. You can also take part in a traditional tea ceremony.

 1590 Coal Harbour Quay, Vancouver, British Columbia V6G 3G1 ☎ 604/602-6669 ⏰ Late May to mid-Oct Thu–Tue 11–8.30, mid-Oct to late May Thu–Tue 11–7 ✋ L $10, D $10 🚌 Off West Georgia Street (Stanley Park end) near Westin Bayshore Resort

STEAMWORKS BREWPUB
www.steamworks.com
Both the beer and the food attract diners here. The menu includes seafood, burgers and wood-oven pizzas.
✉ 375 Water Street, Vancouver, British Columbia, V6B 5C6 ☎ 604/609-2739 ⏰ Mon–Wed 11.30–11.30, Thu 11.30am–midnight, Fri–Sat 11.30am–1am, Sun 11.30–11 ✋ L $15, D $35, Wine $23 🅂 🚇 Skytrain and West Coast Express to Waterfront 🚌 50 🚌 Edge of Gastown, intersection with Cordova Street

SUN SUI WAH SEAFOOD
www.sunsuiwah.com
For more than 30 years this has been one of the favorite restaurants of Vancouver's large and discerning Chinese community. It offers superb Cantonese cuisine.

✉ 3888 Main Street, Vancouver, British Columbia, V5V 3N9 ☎ 604/872-8822 ⏰ Daily 10–3, 5–10.30 ✋ L $40, D $60, Wine $29 🅂 🚇 Skytrain to Main Street 🚌 3 🚌 Downtown, at 23rd Avenue

VICTORIA
THE BLETHERING PLACE
www.thebletheringplace.com
This oak-paneled tearoom is the setting for a wonderful menu of teatime treats. Breakfasts and traditional lunches are also served, and there's entertainment on Saturday nights.
✉ 2250 Oak Bay Avenue, Victoria, British Columbia, V8R 1G5 ☎ 250/598-1413 ⏰ Daily 8am–9pm ✋ L $13, D $18, Wine $20 🅂 🚌 2, 8 🚌 Oak Bay Village, corner of Monterey

GLO EUROPUB AND GRILL
www.gloeuropub.com
In a fabulous waterfront location, this is a lively pub with a patio and cozy indoor booths. The menu offers sandwiches, soups, pasta and pizzas plus interesting appetizers (lobster and shrimp cakes, ginger chicken lettuce wrap), some of which feature on the late-night menu. Entrees range from fish and chips or barbecued ribs to pan-seared blackened red snapper with stone fruit compote. Value four-course menus are offered Sunday to Wednesday.

There's regular entertainment here, including live music and DJs.
✉ 104-2940 Jutland Road, Victoria, British Columbia V8T 5K6 ☎ 250/385-5643 ⏰ Daily 11am until late; brunch Sat, Sun and holidays 11–3 JL $20, D $35, Wine $26 🅿 🚌 8, 11 ⛴ Harbour Ferry Water Taxi 🚌 On Gorge Waterway north of downtown, via Government Street and Gorge Road East

MARINA
www.marinarestaurant.com
On the water's edge, a Pacific Northwest slant is given here to dishes that focus on fresh seafood. There's also a sushi bar, bar meals and a Sunday brunch buffet with cocktails.
✉ 1327 Beach Drive, Victoria, BC, V8S 2N4 ☎ 250/598-8555 ⏰ Mon–Thu 11.30–2.30, 5–10, Fri–Sat 11.30–2.30, 5–11, Sun 10–2.30, 5–10 ✋ L $15, D $25, Wine $21 🅂 🚌 2, 8 🚌 6km (4 miles) east of Victoria via Oak Bay Avenue

WHISTLER
VAL D'ISERE
www.valdisere-restaurant.com
This restaurant marries regional French cuisine with fresh local ingredients in creative dishes.
✉ 8-4314 Main Street, Bear Lodge, Town Plaza, Whistler, British Columbia, V0N 1B0 ☎ 604/932-4666 ⏰ Daily 5.30–10 ✋ L $35, D $50, Wine $25 🅂 🚌 Next to Sheraton Hotel

STAYING

PRICES AND SYMBOLS

Prices are the starting price for a double room for one night, unless otherwise stated. Breakfast is included unless noted otherwise. All the hotels listed accept credit cards unless otherwise stated. Note that rates vary widely throughout the year.

For a key to the symbols, ▷ 2.

BANFF
BREWSTER'S MOUNTAIN LODGE

www.brewstermountainlodge.com
Generations of the enterprising Brewster family have run this hotel in the Rockies. It has various rooms and suites with log furniture, rich decor, satellite TV, and full granite and tile bathrooms, some with jetted bathtubs. Some rooms have a private balcony.

✉ 208 Caribou Street, Banff, Alberta, T1L 1C1 ☎ 403/762-2900, 888/762-2900
✋ $109 ① 77 ⬆ 🚇 Downtown

CASTLE MOUNTAIN CHALETS

www.castlemountain.com
This isolated spot offers a true taste of the wilderness without the inconvenience. One- and two-bedroom log cabins have cathedral ceilings, Jacuzzis, fully equipped

kitchens with dishwasher and microwave, open stone fireplaces and satellite TV/VCR. There is excellent skiing, hiking and fishing, an old-fashioned style grocery store, laundry, steam room and library.

✉ Box 1655, Banff, Alberta, T1L 1B5 ☎ 403/762-3868, 1-877/762-2281
✋ $149 ① 21 chalets (non-smoking) 🍴
🚇 Castle Junction, on Bow Valley Parkway (Highway 1A), just off the Trans-Canada Highway.

CHASE
QUAAOUT RESORT AND CONFERENCE CENTRE

www.quaaout.com
Owned and run by the Little Shuswap, this lakeside resort combines modern accommodations with native culture. The modern rooms have private bathrooms, some with whirlpool, plus TV and refrigerator. There are also tepee accommodations. Guests can swim, waterski and boat on the lake, or follow trails through the surrounding woodland.

✉ Little Shuswap Lake Road, Chase, British Columbia, V0E 1M0 ☎ 250/679-3090 ✋ $89 ① 72 ⬆ 🍴 🚇 2.5km (1.5 miles) from Trans-Canada Highway, east

of Kamloops, exit Squilax Bridge

JASPER
FAIRMONT JASPER PARK LODGE

www.fairmont.com
Cabins with between one and eight bedrooms are available, all with cable TV, telephone, hairdryer, and iron and board. Loads of summer outdoor activites and a resident guide for scenic hikes. In winter, there's skating, sleigh rides and winter sports. On site parking with winter plug-ins and valet (fee).

✉ Old Lodge Road, Jasper, Alberta, T0E 1E0 ☎ 780/852-3301, 800/257-7544
✋ $169 ① 446 (non-smoking) ⬆ 🍴
🏊 Heated outdoor 🚇 4.8km (3 miles) northeast of Jasper via Highway 16

VANCOUVER
BARCLAY HOUSE IN THE WEST END

www.barclayhouse.com
A peaceful oasis amid the sky-scrapers of trendy West End, this B&B is in a restored Victorian home, complete with porch and garden. Each room has a private bathroom, some with clawfoot bathtubs, and TV/VCR and CD players are provided (with an extensive video and CD

library). The first-floor Garden Suite enjoys even greater privacy, with its own entrance and sitting room. No children under 12 years or pets allowed.

✉ 1351 Barclay Street, Vancouver, British Columbia, V6E 1H6 ☎ 604/605-1351, 800/971-1351 ✋ $155 ⓘ 6 (non-smoking) 🚇 Skytrain to Burrard 🚌 Downtown between Broughton and Jervis

BEAUTIFUL BED AND BREAKFAST
www.beautifulbandb.bc.ca
In a quiet residential area with convenient bus links to all the downtown attractions, this B&B is in a fine colonial home with antique furniture. The Honeymoon Suite has double sinks and an extra-large bathtub in its private bathroom. No children under 14 years.

✉ 428 West 40th Avenue, Vancouver, British Columbia, V5Y 2R4 ☎ 604/327-1102 ✋ $131 ⓘ 3 (all non-smoking) 🚌 15, airport shuttle 🚇 First block east of Cambie, in residential area

GRANVILLE ISLAND HOTEL
www.granvilleislandhotel.com
On the waterfront on vibrant Granville Island, this hotel has wonderful views across the water to the city and mountains— particularly if your budget runs to the Penthouse Suite on the top floor.

✉ 1253 Johnston Street, Vancouver, British Columbia, V6H 3R9 ☎ 604/683-7373 ✋ $125 ⓘ 85 (78 non-smoking) 🚇 🚌 🚌 4, 7, 10, 16, 17, 50 ⛴ Aquabus, False Creek Ferry 🚇 Northeast tip of Granville Island

GROUSE INN
www.grouseinn.com
Outside the city and handy for North Shore and the mountains. Accommodations (standard up to two-bedroom suites with full kitchen) are arranged around a landscaped courtyard; rooms have amenities such as TV/VCR, coffeemaker, hairdryer, iron and board, and mini-refrigerator.

✉ 1633 Capilano Road, North Vancouver, British Columbia, V7P 3B3 ☎ 604/988-7101, 800/779-7888 ✋ $69, continental breakfast included ⓘ 80 🚇 ⛴ Heated

outdoor 🏊 240, 250 from West Georgia Street 🚢 Seabus to Lonsdale Quay, then bus 239 to Marine Drive 🚇 North Vancouver, off Trans-Canada Highway (Highway 1), exit 14

HOSTELLING INTERNATIONAL
www.hihostels.ca
This is an above-average hostel, having some private rooms with TV and en-suite bathroom as well as four-bed dormitories.

✉ 1025 Granville Street, Vancouver, British Columbia, V6Z 1L4 ☎ 604/685-5335, 888/203-8333 ✋ $24.75 (per person, member in shared room) to $94 (non-member in private room) ⓘ 214 beds 🚇 🚇 Skytrain to Granville 🚌 4, 6, 7, 8, 10, 16, 50

"O CANADA" HOUSE
www.ocanadahouse.com
One of several version of the words to the national anthem were written here in 1909 by Ewing Buchan, who built this charming Victorian home in 1897. Spacious bedrooms and suites all include a sitting area, TV, VCR, refrigerator, telephone and en-suite bathroom. No children under 12.

✉ 1114 Barclay Street, Vancouver, British Columbia, V6E 1H1 ☎ 604/688-0555, 877/688-1114 ✋ $135 ⓘ 7 (all non-smoking) 🚇 Skytrain to Burrard 🚌 Downtown, west of Thurlow

SUTTON PLACE
www.suttonplace.com
The luxurious rooms and suites in this 21-story downtown hotel have a sleek, modern design and such amenities as in-room entertainment, flat-screen TV, dual-line telephone, high-speed internet and individual climate control.

✉ 845 Burrard Street, Vancouver, British Columbia, V6Z 2K6 ☎ 604/682-5511, 866/378-8866 ✋ $179 ⓘ 397 🚇 🚇 ⛴ Indoor 🚇 Skytrain to Burrard 🚌 98, 98b

WEDGEWOOD
www.wedgewoodhotel.com
A doorman ushers you into the city's foremost luxury hotel. Bedrooms are individually designed with antiques, fresh flowers and houseplants, and

original works of art.

✉ 845 Hornby Street, Vancouver, British Columbia, V6Z 1V1 ☎ 604/689-7777, 800/663-0666 ✋ $300 ⓘ 83 (75 non-smoking) 🚇 🚇 Skytrain to Burrard 🚌 5, 50, 98 🚇 Downtown, between Smithe and Robson

VICTORIA
ABIGAIL'S HOTEL
www.abigailshotel.com
Stylish boutique B&B with English gardens. The bedrooms have antiques, some four-poster beds, and coordinated interior designs. All have private bathrooms.

✉ 06 McClure Street, Victoria, British Columbia, V8V 3E7 ☎ 250/388-5363, 866/347-5054 ✋ $179 ⓘ 23 (all non-smoking) 🚌 Bus from ferry port 🚇 East of downtown, between Quadra and Vancouver

WHISTLER
DURLACHER HOF ALPINE INN
www.durlacherhof.com
This lovely little hideaway, an alpine chalet complete with a flower-decked wooden balcony, is run by an Austrian family. Rooms and suites have hand-carved pine furniture and all have bathrooms, some with whirlpool. No TVs or telephones.

✉ 7055 Nesters Road, Whistler, British Columbia, V0N 1B7 ☎ 604/932-1924, 877/932-1924 ✋ $130 ⓘ 8 (all non-smoking) ⛷ Outdoor 🚇 North on Highway 99

WESTIN RESORT AND SPA
www.westinwhistler.com
This splendid hotel offers the ultimate Whistler experience, with luxury accommodations, mountain views, superb gourmet cuisine, and a fantastic range of leisure and spa amenities. The suites have chic modern furnishings combined with the occasional rustic touch.

✉ 4090 Whistler Way, Whistler, British Columbia, V0N 1B4 ☎ 604/905-5000, 888/634-5577 ✋ $149 plus "resort fee" ⓘ 419 🚇 🚇 🚇 ⛴ Heated indoor/outdoor 🚇 Off Highway 99 on edge of Whistler village

THE NORTH

Northern Canada conjures up an image of frozen wastes, vast and inhospitable tundra and remote towns. While this could perhaps be regarded as a downside, it is in fact the main attraction. Here you will discover an untamed, unspoiled wilderness where wildlife outnumbers human population on a massive scale, where the experience of complete solitude amid awe-inspiring landscapes is something that will endure long after your return to "civilization."

Three territories comprise the north—the Yukon, the Northwest Territories and Nunavut—each evocative in its own way: there are reminders of the Klondike Gold Rush in Dawson City; Yellowknife, in the NWT, still has the strong First Nations associations that gave it its name (local tribes made knives from copper); Nunavut is clearly an Inuit territory, preserving a unique and artistic heritage though certainly not living in the past. The territorial capitals—Whitehorse, Yellowknife and Iqaluit, respectively—are not large, but are vibrant centers full of people who wouldn't live anywhere else but in the north.

Perhaps, surprisingly, it is not necessarily cooler up here. In fact, winter temperatures are sometimes higher here than in the Prairies. This paves the way for enjoying winter activities that range from dog-sledding to ice climbing to just watching the breathtaking natural spectacle of the northern lights. Summer days are not only warm but also long, and with at least 20 hours of daylight each day this a perfect time to enjoy the north to the full. There are plenty of opportunities for hiking, wildlife watching, fishing and kayaking, and plenty of local guides ready to take you to the best spots. New experiences are indeed plentiful, and even in the knowledge that you have a comfortable hotel awaiting, exploring this area offers a rare spirit of adventure.

ALASKA HIGHWAY

▷ 346–347.

BAFFIN ISLAND

www.nunavuttourism.com
www.baffinisland.ca

Baffin Island forms the major part of Canada's newest territory, Nunavut, created on April 1, 1999, from the eastern part of the Northwest Territories. Nunavut means "our land" in the language of the Inuit, who have lived here for 5,000 years. No longer nomads, they live mostly in conventional Western-style homes, and many work in offices, but they preserve elements of their former lifestyle—in spring, groups may go off on hunting and fishing expeditions.

Three-quarters of the land mass of Baffin Island lies north of the Arctic Circle, and the landscape is primeval and glaciated, with rugged peaks and vast areas of tundra. Ecotourism offers the chance to enjoy hiking, kayaking and canoeing, dogsledding, and snowmobiling. You can spot wildlife (polar bears, whales, narwhals, seals and walruses) on a boat trip or a floe-edge expedition, which could include staying in an igloo. Birdwatching is best in spring and summer, when migrant species return to nest.

✚ 409 Q7 🛈 Nunavut Tourism, Box 1450, Iqaluit, Nunavut, X0A 0H0 ☎ 867/979-6551 ✈ Flights to Iqaluit from Edmonton, Québec City and Montréal

DAWSON CITY

▷ 348.

DEMPSTER HIGHWAY

www.nwttravel.nt.ca www.dawsoncity.org

Completed in 1979, this 736km (457-mile) highway runs from 40km (25 miles) east of Dawson City in the Yukon to Inuvik in the Northwest Territories, and is the only Canadian highway to cross the Arctic Circle, which it does 450km (251 miles) from Dawson. It links remote settlements and crosses vast expanses of wilderness. Dawson City's Arctic Circle Gateway Interpretive Display has information.

There are two river crossings, the first over the Peel at 539km (334 miles) and the second over the Mackenzie at 608km (377 miles). In summer, ferries carry vehicles across, and in winter there are ice bridges. In the intermediate seasons, the road is impassable. The surface is mostly gravel, and there are few facilities, so an RV (motor-home) is a popular choice.

✚ 398 C8 🛈 Dempster/Delta Visitor Information Centre, Front Street at King Street; mid-May to mid-Sep daily 🛈 Klondike Visitors' Association, 1102 Front Street, Dawson City, Yukon ☎ 867/993-5575 or NWT Arctic Tourism, Inuvik, Northwest Territories ☎ 867/873-7200 ✈ Flights to Dawson City from Whitehorse. Flights from Inuvik serve the northern end of the highway

INUVIK

www.inuvik.ca

Inuvik is the largest Canadian settlement north of the Arctic Circle and makes a good base for exploring the western Arctic. First Nations Inuvailut and Gwich'in make up most of the population here, and live by hunting, sport hunting and ecotourism activities. Multicolored housing units are raised above the ground, clear of the permafrost, and water, sewage and heating run in conduits above the ground to prevent freezing. The Igloo Church of Our Lady of Victory on Mackenzie Road, built in 1958, is the town's major landmark—circular and white-walled, with lines to simulate blocks of ice. Inside, the Stations of the Cross were painted by a local Inuit artist, Mona Thresher.

The town lies in the delta of the Mackenzie River, surrounded by hundreds of tributaries that are separated by islands blanketed in baby pine forest. The mass of islets and channels of the delta, one of the world's most important wildlife corridors, is a haven for migratory wildfowl and large fish populations. Herds of caribou migrate here to calve, and the vast tundra is the ideal environment for polar bears.

Several national parks can be reached by small charter plane, and activities include whitewater rafting, kayaking and hiking. Guided wildlife viewing is popular. The aurora borealis is a big draw in winter, when you can explore by snowmobile, dogsled or snowshoe. Just east of Tuktoyaktuk, 164km (102 miles) north of Inuvik, is the world's largest area of pingos—odd, cone-shaped mounds formed when pockets of water freeze and are forced upward by pressure from the permafrost below.

✚ 398 D7 🛈 Western Arctic Visitor Centre, 284 Mackenzie Road, Inuvik, Northwest Territories ☎ 867/777-4727 or 867/777-4321 🚌 Twice-weekly connection between Dawson City and Inuvik (12- to 14-hour trip with lunch stop) ✈ Regular flights from Yellowknife

Opposite *A snow-covered mountain, seen beyond a stream running through the tundra*
Below *A Hudson's Bay Company Building, Pangnitung, Baffin Island*

REGIONS THE NORTH • SIGHTS

INFORMATION

www.cityfsj.com

www.touryukon.com

✛ 398 C11 ℹ Northern Rockies Alaska Highway Tourism Association, Box 6850, Suite 300, 9923 100th Street, Fort St. John, British Columbia, V1J 4J3 ☎ 250/785-2544, 1-888/785-2544

ℹ Tourism & Culture, Government of Yukon, Box 2703, Whitehorse, Yukon, Y1A 2C6 ☎ 867/667-5340, 1-800/661-0494

INTRODUCTION

The Alaska Highway stretches for 2,288km (1,422 miles) between Dawson Creek, BC, and Delta Junction, Alaska (US), and is an adventurous trip across the northern frontier of old. You'll need at least two days to drive the Canadian section of the highway, three if you want to continue to the end at Delta Junction, Alaska, and longer if you're going to do real justice to the experience. If you're planning to drive the entire route, remember that this involves crossing into the US, so make sure you have the necessary documentation and currency or credit cards. The Canadian customs point is at km1,937 (mile 1,201) and the official border with the US is at km1,967 (mile 1,220), from where it's another 321km (199 miles) to the end of the highway.

When northwestern Canada was first settled, its rivers provided the major routes—thousands traveled up the Yukon River in the 1890s during the Klondike gold rush, most taking the Inside Passage to Skagway before the struggle over the White Pass to reach the river. When the gold ran out, the population dropped and the Yukon almost returned to its untamed state.

DEFENCE MEASURES

Then, during World War II, Japan attacked Pearl Harbor and invaded the Aleutian Islands, threatening Alaska, and the US needed to strengthen its protection of the state. An overland route was planned, linking mainland US with Alaska across the Canadian north. The joint venture between the two countries began on March 9, 1942, and was completed on October 25 of the same year, built by 27,000 men at a rate of more than 13km (8 miles) a day. The work was hard, through mosquito-infested muskeg marshland turned into mud by the machinery. The original route was 2,452km (1,520 miles) long, but as many of the curves have since been taken out it is now 2,288km (1,422 miles).

WHAT TO SEE

DAWSON CREEK

The symbolic start to the trip is the Mile Zero marker in Dawson Creek. Other attractions of this small town are the Walter Wright Pioneer Village (daily), with original buildings and nine flower gardens, and Dawson Creek Station Museum (early May–early Sep daily; early Oct–early Apr Tue–Sat; rest of year Mon–Sat), housed in the old National Railroad Station, where you can watch an hour-long video about the building of the highway. It also houses the town's visitor center. Dawson Creek is on the verge of a major revitalization project, which will include the construction of an ambitious new interpretive center for the Alaska Highway.

FORT ST. JOHN

After 76km (47 miles), the route runs through Fort St. John, the oldest European settlement in mainland BC; it was founded in 1794 and served as field headquarters for the US Army during construction of the highway. The Fort St. John-North Peace Museum (summer daily; winter Mon–Sat) features thousands of exhibits from the surrounding area, including the re-creation of a trapper's cabin. Some 11km (7 miles) north of town, you can make a left off the highway to visit W. A. C. Bennett Dam, a huge earth-filled structure, now holding back the largest body of fresh water in British Columbia.

LAIRD RIVER HOT SPRINGS

The sulfur-laden pools here, at km799 (mile 496) west of Fort Nelson, have an average temperature of 42°C (107°F), and the resulting semitropical ecosystem around them even supports orchids.

WATSON LAKE

Styling itself the "Gateway to the Yukon," this town has an interpretive center (early May–late Sep daily), and also the Northern Lights Centre (Jun–end Aug daily), relating to the aurora borealis, but it is most famed for the "signpost forest." This was started by a homesick US soldier in 1942, who erected a makeshift signpost pointing the way to his home. Later, travelers added more signs, and today there are over 42,000.

TESLIN

This place, 179km (111 miles) south of Whitehorse, was home to the Tinglit people. George Johnston (1884–1972) photographed many of them early in the 20th century, and the town museum (mid-May to end Sep daily) displays these photographs, plus a collection of Tinglit objects.

TIP

» Although the highway is accessible year-round (weather permitting), the road conditions are very variable, with loose gravel, frost heave and potholes a constant problem—drive with care.

REGIONS THE NORTH • SIGHTS

Opposite top *The Alaskan Highway, built during World War II*
Opposite bottom *A magestic bald eagle*
Left *Sunset over the Yukon*
Below *Kluane National Park is home to a large bear population*

INFORMATION

www.dawsoncity.org
www.pc.gc.ca

⊞ 398 C9 ℹ Klondike Visitors Association, P.O. Box 389C, Dawson City, Yukon, Y0B 1G0 ☎ 867/993-5575, 1-877/GOLD-006 (465-3006) ℹ Tourism Yukon Visitor Reception, corner of Front and King streets, Dawson City, Yukon ☎ 867/993-5566; mid-May to late Sep daily 8–8 (closes at 6pm first and last weeks of season)
Parks Canada ✉ P.O. Box 390, Dawson City, Yukon, Y0B 1G0 C867/993-7200

TIPS

» Visitors who really want to re-create the gold-rush era can pan for gold at Claim No. 6 on Bonanza Creek.
» For a great view of Dawson City and the surrounding mountains, take the steep, winding Dome Road for 8km (5 miles) to the top of Midnight Dome (884m/2,900ft). Go on June 21 to see how it got its name—the sun is visible at midnight on that day.

Opposite *The natural grandeur of the glaciers of Kluane National Park*
Below *Learn more about Canada's heritage with a visit to Dawson City*

DAWSON CITY

When gold was discovered in the Yukon in 1896, word soon got around, and Dawson City was briefly the most happening place in the world, the epicenter of this amazing phenomenon. More than 100,000 people traveled here, yet within three years the rush came to a grinding halt and Dawson City went into decline, clinging to its role as capital of Yukon Territory while its clapboard houses slowly rotted away. Whitehorse took over as capital in 1950, but Dawson never quite died, and during the following decade a movement began to preserve it as a part of Canadian heritage. Today, over 30 buildings have been saved or renovated and are operated as historic sites, mainly by Parks Canada and by the Klondike Visitors' Association, which plows the admission money back into the community.

DIAMOND TOOTH GERTIE'S

Diamond Tooth Gertie's (mid-May to late Sep daily) is a turn-of-the-20th-century-style saloon and gambling casino. It is named after one of Dawson's most illustrious dancing girls, Gertie Lovejoy, who is said to have had a decorative diamond set into one of her front teeth. Here the atmosphere of the high-rolling gold-rush days is re-created, with costumed can-can dancers, blackjack, poker and roulette.

MUSEUMS

Dawson City's Museum (daily) is housed in the neoclassical Old Territorial Administration Building on 5th Avenue and covers both the gold-rush era and Dawson in the early 20th century. The local First Nations Han Hwech'in tribe, almost forgotten in the excitement of gold-rush history, still has a thriving population and their Danajo Zho Cultural Centre (mid-May to mid-Sep daily) depicts their hunter-gatherer lifestyle. Two of Dawson City's literary figures, Jack London and Robert Service, are remembered through re-creations of the cabins (late May to mid-Sep daily) in which they lived (on 8th Avenue). Readings of their works sometimes take place within these cabins. The former home of author Pierre Berton, also on 8th Avenue, has been restored for use as a private retreat for Canadian writers.

KLONDIKE HIGHWAY

www.touryukon.com

This highway follows the trail of the thousands of prospectors who stampeded north in search of gold in the 1890s. Starting at Skagway (in Alaska, US), where the hopefuls disembarked, the Klondike Highway, also called the Gold Rush Route, extends north to Dawson City in the Yukon. The prospectors traveled as far as Whitehorse (▷ 350–351) on foot or on horseback, then continued their journey by boat on the Yukon River. Today, this 540km (335-mile) northern section is about a six-hour drive, not counting detours, and much of it passes through barren wilderness. Around 6km (4 miles) from the start of the northern Klondike Highway you can take a 10km (6-mile) detour left to Takhini Hot Springs (daily) and relax in an outdoor pool fed by odorless mineral water at 40°C (104°F)—a great place to watch the aurora borealis in the fall and in winter.

Carmacks, 190km (118 miles) from Whitehorse, is a Tutchone village named for George Carmacks, co-discoverer of gold in the Klondike. Farther north, at Stewart Crossing, the Silver Trail heads east for 112km (69 miles) through the former mining communities of Mayo and Elsa to Keno City. At Glenboyle, 40km (25 miles) from Dawson City, the Klondike Highway joins the Dempster Highway (▷ 345) running northeast across the Northwest Territories to Inuvik.

✚ 398 C10 ℹ️ Tourist Reception centers at Whitehorse, Dawson City and Carmacks ☎ 867/993-5566 🚌 Bus services between Whitehorse and Dawson City (May–end Sep Mon–Fri) ✈️ Flights from Whitehorse

KLUANE NATIONAL PARK

www.pc.gc.ca

Kluane National Park is the ancestral home of the Southern Tutchone people and is one of Canada's most environmentally diverse parks. Within it, a series of mountain ranges runs parallel with the northern Canadian/Alaskan coast, and it is these majestic mountainscapes that draw visitors. Several giants rise to over 5,000m (16,400ft), including Mt. Logan, Canada's highest peak, at 5,959m (19,545ft). Kluane also encompasses the world's largest non-polar icefields. The moist Pacific air coming directly off the water creates ideal snow-producing conditions, and there is a vast network of more than 4,000 interior glaciers. Nearly 120 species of birds nest within Kluane, and the park supports large populations of Dall sheep and bears.

There is no road access into the park's interior, and the highway that skirts the park was not easy to construct. Destruction Bay on Kluane Lake recalls the storm that almost wiped out the road-builders' camp. The road offers tantalizing views west, but to explore this area you need to set out on foot, by kayak or on horseback—or take a tour in a small plane. There are three reasonably short hiking trails (▷ 356–357 walk), but the rest involve one or more nights of wilderness camping and require good navigational skills.

✚ 398 B10 ✉️ P.O. Box 5495, Haines Junction, Yukon, Y0B 1L0 ☎ 867/634-7250 🕐 Park daily; Kluane and Tachal Dhal Visitor Reception Centers mid-May to mid-Sep daily ✋ Free ℹ️ Haines Junction Visitor Centre, Haines Junction: ☎ 867/634-7208, mid-May to mid-Sep daily

NAHANNI NATIONAL PARK

www.pc.gc.ca

Located in the southwest corner of the Northwest Territories, Nahanni protects sections of the Mackenzie Mountains, an unspoiled wilderness of high peaks, deep canyons, rivers, forest, hot springs and tundra. Nahanni is one of the most remote of Canada's national parks, and in 1978 became the first place in the world to be designated a UNESCO World Heritage Site. The park is wonderful for those wanting to escape civilization, but getting there is not straightforward. There is no easy vehicular access (most visitors arrive by charter seaplane), and campers must take all supplies and equipment.

Attractions include canyons up to 1,200m (3,936ft) deep, created by river erosion; the Ribbitkettle Hot Springs, at a constant 20°C (68°F); and Virginia Falls at 92m (302ft), which is twice the height of Niagara.

The spectacularly wild South Nahanni River is renowned as the world's premier whitewater-rafting location. Only very experienced rafters are allowed to take to the rapids unescorted, and most rafters undertake the trip with a licensed outfitter. For intrepid mountaineers, there is the challenge of the sheer rocky peaks of the Cirque of the Unclimbables.

✚ 398 D11 ✉️ Box 348, Fort Simpson, Northwest Territories, X0E 0N0 ☎ 867/695-3151 🕐 Mid-Jun to mid-Sep daily; Park office: mid-Jun to mid-Sep daily 8–12, 1–5; rest of year Mon–Fri 8.30–12, 1–5 ✋ Free

TOP OF THE WORLD HIGHWAY
▷ 352.

WHITEHORSE AND THE WHITE PASS

INFORMATION

www.visitwhitehorse.com
www.touryukon.com
www.city.whitehorse.yk.ca
www.skagway.com

✚ 398 C10 ℹ Whitehorse Visitor
Reception Centre, 100 Hanson
Street, Whitehorse, Yukon, Y1A 3S9
☎ 867/667-3084 ℹ Skagway
Convention and Visitors Bureau, 2nd
Avenue and 245 Broadway, P.O. Box
1029, Skagway, Alaska 99840, USA
☎ 907/983-2854, 1-888/762-1898

INTRODUCTION

Although it's not particularly attractive, especially when compared with Dawson
City or Skagway, Whitehorse is the perfect starting point for exploration of the
Yukon and White Pass area. It has the only major airport in the territory, along
with plenty of adventure outfitters. Whitehorse may be visited mainly as the
jumping-off point for trips into the wilderness, but it has a few attractions of its
own. See also the drive on pages 354–355.

CAPITAL CITY

The town of Whitehorse was established during the gold rush, when, to ease
their journey to the Klondike, most prospectors navigated the Yukon River,
which flows north through the territory. Two of the many obstacles in their
path were Miles Canyon, an impenetrable narrow funnel with sheer walls
that forced them to carry their equipment for 5km (3 miles), and the fierce
Whitehorse Rapids, so named because the flurry of white water resembles a
horse's mane. Rudimentary towns sprang up at Canyon City and Whitehorse as
prospectors rested and planned how to negotiate the obstacles.

In 1897, a tramway was built on either side of the canyon, making the
journey easier, but it was superseded by the White Pass and Yukon Route
Railway, which bypassed Miles Canyon. Canyon City faded away (the
ramshackle remains of its timber buildings can still be seen today), while
Whitehorse flourished, taking over from Dawson City as the capital of Yukon
Territory in 1950.

WHAT TO SEE

WHITEHORSE MUSEUMS

You can find out more about the gold rush at the Macbride Museum (mid-May to early Sep daily; winter hours vary) which has a really good explanatory display about the frenzy that followed the discovery of gold in the Klondike, including a gold-rush tent housing the typical equipment used by the prospectors, and some genuine gold nuggets found in the area. There's also a series of dioramas showing stuffed animals in their native surroundings.

The Old Log Church Museum (late May–early Sep daily), housed in a church built in 1900, tells the tale of the Yukon's early explorers, from whalers to missionaries. There is also an interpretive display relating to the lives of the First Nations peoples since the arrival of Europeans. The Yukon Transportation Museum (mid-May to early Sep daily) looks at Yukon's favorite methods of transportation, from dogsleds to floatplanes and riverboats, and provides information on the historic routes.

The fascinating Yukon Beringia Interpretive Centre (late May to mid-Sep daily) explores the geology of the land bridge called Beringia, that joined Russia and Alaska before the last Ice Age, together with the flora and fauna that crossed it.

THE WHITE PASS

The White Pass is a narrow and very steep ravine that runs southwest of Whitehorse to Skagway, Alaska. It is an impressively dramatic route whether traversed by car or—much more fun—by the narrow-gauge railway (early May–late Sep daily) from Skagway to Lake Bennet (with a bus connection to Whitehorse), whose tracks hug the south side of the ravine, carried over seemingly rickety wooden bridges. One of the most memorable sections is Dead Horse Gulch, where the bones of over 3,000 pack animals lie. Horses, it turned out, were not tough enough to survive the harsh environment; instead, both men and dogs acted as pack animals during the gold rush.

SKAGWAY

The beautifully preserved town of Skagway, in Alaska (US), looks very much as it did 100 years ago, when it was the port for prospectors arriving by sea for the Klondike gold fields. Several blocks of downtown are subject to a preservation order and have been designated the Klondike Goldrush National Historic Park (daily), a living museum with saloons, hotels and stores—look for the costumed actors throughout the town. Skagway has a wonderful position, crowded by high peaks at the head of the fiord-like Lyn Canyon waterway. It is still a busy port, and on certain days of the week it can be very full. The Chilkoot Gold Rush Footpath is a popular hiking route heading north from Skagway. The climb out of town takes a full day, but in summer you can return to the town by train.

TIPS

» The Whitehorse to Skagway route involves crossing the US border. Visitors will need to show passports, and certain nationalities will require a visa to enter Alaska. Visitors from countries belonging to the Visa Waiver Program must have an e-passport, if it was issued after October 26, 2006. For full details see www.dhs.gov/xtrvisec/crossingborders/#2

» The City of Whitehorse issues free three-day parking permits, should you need one: ask at City Hall, Second Avenue at Steele Street (Mon–Fri 8.30–4.30).

» Take a look at the unique log scraper (actually four stories high) on Lambert Street.

Opposite *The skeleton of an abandoned silver mine at White Pass*
Left *The wooden clapboarded Caribou Hotel on the White Pass route between Skagway and Whitehorse*
Below *SS* Klondike *moored at Whitehorse*

INFORMATION

www.touryukon.com

✚ 398 B8 🕐 Highway open mid-May to mid-Oct, weather permitting

ℹ️ Tourism Yukon Visitor Reception Centre, Front and King streets, Dawson City, Yukon ☎ 867/993-5566; mid-May to late Sep daily 8–8 (closes at 6pm first and last weeks of season)

TOP OF THE WORLD HIGHWAY

The 105km (66-mile) Top of the World Highway—more prosaically known as Highway 9—leads from Dawson City to the Alaska border and is one of the most picturesque routes in northern Canada. Its wonderful name was inspired by its high northerly latitude, and because much of it lies above the treeline, it has breathtaking, seemingly never-ending panoramic views across mountain peaks and valleys blanketed in Yukon forest.

The route begins at the northern end of Dawson City's Front Street, with a free ferry ride (May–end Sep daily 24 hours) across the wide Yukon River. From here the highway climbs steadily until, just under 4.5km (3 miles) along, there's a viewpoint with a stunning vista back over Dawson City, the Yukon River and its tributaries that really highlights the settlement's remote location.

After 15km (9 miles), the highway breaks through the treeline and follows the top of the ridges, so that you really feel that you are on top of the world. After 56km (35 miles) there is a collection of strange rock formations known as Castle Rock.

Though plenty of people travel this route without incident, it is not necessarily an easy drive. It is narrow and winding, with some vertiginous drop-offs in places and few guard rails. Potholes in the road surface are another hazard. The best policy is to drive slowly and carefully, make plenty of stops so that the driver can also safely enjoy the views, and don't even think of making the journey in an RV (motorhome). The highway is surfaced with asphalt, but is not cleared of snow in winter and closes with the first major snowfall, or when the river freezes. In addition, the border crossing into the US is open only in summer (8am–8pm Alaska time).

If you want to continue driving across the border into Alaska, make sure you bring all the proper documentation for the vehicle and all passengers.

Below *A wild expanse viewed from the Top of the World Highway, near Dawson*

YELLOWKNIFE

Yellowknife, located on the northeast shore of the Great Slave Lake, is the capital of the Northwest Territories and the jumping-off point for exploring the area's natural attractions. The intrepid traveler Samual Hearne named the settlement in 1770 after seeing the yellow- (copper-) bladed knives used by the native Dogrib Dene peoples. Prospectors discovered gold in the region in 1934, and by 1937 Yellowknife was a boom town. Although gold-mining is still active, in the 1990s Yellowknife pioneered diamond-mining in Canada—the Diavik Diamond Mines Visitor Centre has displays about mining, cutting and polishing. The actual Diavik diamond mines are located some 300km (200m miles) northwest of Yellowknife. The town is now known as the 'Diamond Capital of North America'.

The Prince of Wales Northern Heritage Centre (daily), on Highway 4, is the main museum for the whole of the Northwest Territories. It includes galleries with dioramas relating to the traditions and lifestyles of the First Nations from the area, European settlement, and the modern industrial and social infrastructure, plus temporary exhibitions and family activities.

The other principal reason to come here is for the area's natural attractions, not least the midnight sun in summer and the magnificent spectacle of the aurora borealis in winter. There are also lots of opportunities for wildlife watching in the surrounding wilderness and along the Mackenzie River. Outdoor pursuits include kayaking, canoeing, rafting and hunting, or taking a summer cruise.

INFORMATION

www.northernfrontier.com

✚ 399 G11 ℹ Yellowknife Visitor Centre, 4 4807–49th Street, Yellowknife, Northwest Territories, X1A 3T5

☎ 867/873-4262, 1-877/881-4262; Jun–end Aug daily 8.30–6; rest of year Mon–Fri 9–5, Sat–Sun and holidays 12–4

Above *The spectacular sight of the aurora borealis attracts many visitors to Yellowknife*

THE GOLDEN CIRCLE DRIVE

This spectacular drive, following in the footsteps of the gold rush prospectors, traverses some of the most pristine landscapes in North America, and takes you to two countries as you cross the Canadian border into Alaska. Majestic peaks in Kluane National Park, the Bald Eagle preserve near Haines City, the fierce incline of the White Pass, and the world's smallest desert are just some of the natural highlights.

THE DRIVE
Distance: 483km (299 miles)
Allow: 2 days (not including time for hiking on park trails)
Start/end: Whitehorse
How to get there: The best way to reach Whitehorse is by air—regular flights from Vancouver (4 hours) and Edmonton (about 3 hours). Overland, from Vancouver take Highways 97, 16, then 37, or 97 then the Alaska Highway; from Edmonton take Highway 43 then the Alaska Highway
Warning: Distances between settlements are large. Keep an eye on your fuel gauge at all times and plan ahead for overnight stops. You'll be crossing into the US, so have necessary documentation for the vehicle and all passengers, plus US$6 per person for the visa waiver green card. If you need a visa to enter the US, obtain it from the US embassy in your home country before leaving

From Whitehorse, travel via 4th Avenue and Two Mile Hill to Highway 1, the famed Alaska Highway (▷ 346–347), which takes you in a northwest direction toward Haines Junction.

❶ This is pretty unremarkable countryside by Yukon standards, but as you get within 1.5km (1 mile) or so of Haines Junction, the mighty peaks of Kluane National Park (▷ 349) come into view directly ahead.

At Haines Junction, 161km (100 miles) along the route, take the Haines Highway south toward Haines City; in 27km (17 miles) you'll see a turning right to Kathleen Lake, a popular place for hiking and camping, but continue to the 44km (27-mile) point.

❷ You can stop here to take the short 800m-long (875-yard) Rock Glacier Trail, leading through a glacial landscape.

Sweep on past Dezadeash Lake at 51km (31.5 miles), to Klukshu.

❸ At this traditional First Nations fall camp, 500m (550 yards) left off the highway, you can see fish being caught and smoked during the salmon run, which takes place between late October and early November), and shop at the craft store (Jun–Sep). The camp is deserted early November through May.

Some 90km (56 miles) from Haines Junction you'll cross from the Yukon into British Columbia. The views here are dominated by the St. Elias Mountains to the right, and the road leads gradually up to the Chilkat Pass.

4 The Chilkat Pass is the highest point on this highway, at 1,065m (3,493ft), and was one of the main conduits for prospectors in the 1898 gold rush. Beyond, there are sweeping views south into Alaska.

You'll cross into Alaska, US, after traveling 179km (111 miles).

5 The customs post is open 7am–11pm, Alaska Time (one hour ahead of the time on the Canadian side).

Once the formalities are over, head on to the Chilkat Bald Eagle Preserve, 33km (20 miles) farther.

6 Thousands of bald eagles gather on the Chilkat Valley flats, especially in late fall when salmon spawn. Don't park at the roadside—only use designated parking spaces.

From the preserve it's only 35km (22 miles) to diminutive Haines City, a good place for an overnight stop. Take the one-hour ferry ride to Skagway, an old gold rush town, and follow the Klondike Highway north, climbing the steep ascent to White Pass, completed in 1978.

7 Over 90,000 prospectors traveled on foot through this and the parallel Chilkoot Pass in the late 1890s. There are dramatic views of the footpath, White Pass and Yukon narrow-gauge rail tracks climbing through the narrow ravine.

White Pass summit is 23km (14 miles) from Skagway, just before the Canadian border. It's another 12km (7 miles) to the customs post (daily 24 hours in summer). At 50km (31 miles), Tushti Lake comes into view and the road follows its banks for a few miles until you cross from BC back into the Yukon. North of Carcross, at 106km (66 miles), is a surprising landscape.

8 The Carcross Desert is the world's smallest, at just over 2km (1 mile) long.

Some 117km (73 miles) from Skagway is Emerald Lake, known for its brilliant blue-green hues. Klondike Highway meets the Alaska Highway 40km (25 miles) on, from where it's only 15km (9 miles) back to Whitehorse, although you should take the turn to the right 11km (7 miles) from the intersection to view Miles Canyon before heading back into town.

WHEN TO GO
Extra-long summer days make this an ideal time to travel in the north. The best time to see bald eagles is during the salmon spawn (mid-Oct to mid-Nov), but most hotels and restaurants will close October through April.

WHERE TO EAT
✉ Sam 'n' Andy's, 506 Main Street, Whitehorse ☎ 867/668-6994 ✉ Raven Hotel, Haines Junction ☎ 867/634-2500.

WHERE TO STAY
www.highcountryinn.yk.ca
✉ High Country Inn, 4051 4th Avenue, Whitehorse ☎ 867/667-4471.

Above *The traditonal clapboard architecture of the Carcross Church at White Pass*
Opposite *The restored White Pass and Yukon railroad runs through beautiful scenery between Skagway and Whitehorse*

KING'S THRONE TRAIL IN KLUANE NATIONAL PARK

One of the most spectacular of the shorter trails in Kluane National Park, the King's Throne Trail climbs steeply from the shores of Kathleen Lake to a wonderful mountain cirque, offering panoramic views north across the Dezadeash Valley and the Kluane mountain range. Then, if you feel fit enough, climb above the cirque onto the King's Throne, with majestic vistas to the west across the glacial mountainscapes that make Kluane famous.

THE WALK

Distance: 10km (6 miles)

Allow: 6 hours

Start and end at: Kathleen Lake parking area

How to get there: From Whitehorse (▷ 350–351 Golden Circle drive), take the Alaska Highway. Total distance is 165km (101 miles) and the journey takes about 2 hours

Make your way to the trailhead to the left side of the parking area as you look at the lake. The route is wide here and well worn, but watch out for the huge tree roots crisscrossing it. After 750m (820 yards) the footpath skirts the lake on your right. Continue 350m (380 yards) along the trail to where the route splits, and follow the King's Throne Trail signs that lead left.

The Cottonwood Trail, which leads on beside the lakeshore, is one of the longest trails in the park at 83km (52 miles).

The King's Throne route begins to climb through the mature woodland away from the lake. When you reach a second split in the trail, take the left route and continue climbing.

The path soon becomes a series of tight switchbacks and narrows to a single file. Then it breaks through the treeline, offering the first panoramic view north—a breathtaking vista, with Kathleen Lake in the foreground, a carpet of forest along the valley and the high peaks of the park to the left. It's also worth looking up at the route ahead, which is almost vertical at this point with a tightly twisting trail.

Keep on climbing until you arrive at the lip of the cirque, a rock bowl gouged out of the mountain peak by glacial action.

After the climb, you will want to take time to sit and admire the full spectacle of the Yukon countryside spread out far below. Then explore the rock-strewn surface of the cirque, with its relatively smooth sides.

Above *The Kings Throne Trail offers some of the most breathtaking views of the park*
Opposite *The vastness of the Dezadeash Valley, Kluane National Park*

From the cirque it's possible to hike along the ridge to the King's Throne summit.

There are stunning views to the west over some of the most typical Kluane landscape, the remote Kennedey-Hubbard-Alverstone peaks seemingly set in the icefields.

This part of the trail is not marked as clearly as on the lower section, so extra care is needed. Return to your car by retracing the route.

WHEN TO GO

With its very steep sections and poorer markings in the higher reaches, this walk definitely calls for a bright, clear day when the ground is dry and free of ice to make the most of it.

PUBLIC RESTROOMS

Kathleen Lake parking area.

WHERE TO EAT

✉ Kluane Park Inn, Haines Junction ☎ 867/634-2261.

WHERE TO STAY

✉ The Cabin Bed-and-Breakfast, Haines Junction ☎ 867-634-2626. ✉ Alcan Motor Inn, Junction of Alaska and Haines Highways ☎ 867/634-2371 or 888/265-1018.

WHAT TO DO

CARCROSS

CARIBOU CROSSING TRADING POST

www.cariboucrossing.ca

Within a museum of Yukon natural history, this store specializes in Yukon-made gifts and products, including handcarved antler and horn, and fur products. Some of the items on sale are made for this outlet by local artisans, and there's an artist-in-residence.

✉ Carcross, Yukon, Y0B 1B0 ☎ 867/821-4055 🕐 Mid-May to mid-Sep, call for hours 🚌 3km (2 miles) north of Carcross off the Klondike Highway 🍴 Restaurant (reservation required) ☕ Coffee house and ice cream parlor

DAWSON CITY

BONANZA MARKET

More of a food store than a traditional-style market, but it's a good place to meet the locals, and if you're looking for provisions for a picnic, it's worth a visit. It's the only place in town that has fresh fruit and vegetables, and there's a good European/ Canadian deli counter that's strong on German delicacies.

✉ 2nd Avenue and Princess Street, Bag 5020, Dawson City, Yukon, Y0B 1G0 ☎ 867/993-6567 🕐 Mon–Sat 9–8, Sun 9–7. Call for winter hours

DIAMOND TOOTH GERTIE'S GAMBLING HALL

Canada's oldest casino, in a 1901 building named after a famous dance-hall queen. Blackjack, roulette, sic bo, slots and cancan shows raise money for the community and local conservation projects. Age limit applies.

✉ Queen Street, Dawson City, Yukon, Y0B 1G0 ☎ 867/993-5575 🕐 Mid-May to late Sep Mon–Fri 7pm–2am, Sat–Sun 2–2; some year-round events 💵 $6

GOLDBOTTOM MINE TOURS

www.goldbottom.com

Finding a glittering fragment of gold among the gravel evokes the excitement of the gold rush. You get a tour with guides who tell lots of fascinating stories before they let you loose on the creek. You keep what you pan, and you might even see bear or moose. Wear sturdy footwear. After the GoldBottom Mine tour you'll be driven out to tour the goldfields area, including the spot where gold was first discovered in the area and a restored dredge.

✉ Hunker Creek Road, Box 912, Dawson City, Yukon, Y0B 1G0 ☎ 867/993-5023 🕐 Jun until freeze-up daily 11–7 💵 Full tour: adult $20, child (12–15) $10, under 12 free; gold-panning only: downtown site $6, creek site $10–£25, includes transportation from Dawson City 🚌 Shuttle from Dawson City 🚗 East of Dawson City, 15km (9 miles) south of intersection of Klondike Highway North and Hunker Creek Road

KODIAK WILDERNESS TOURS

www.kodiaktours.ca

You can build your own trip with this company, run by local guides who'll take you out on quads, by riverboat or canoe, and in winter by snowmobile, to explore the wild north.

✉ Box 248, Dawson City, Yukon, Y0B 1G0 ☎ 867/993-6333 🕐 Year-round 💵 Varies

PALACE GRAND THEATRE

Lavish theater dating to 1899, now superbly restored. It's home to the Gaslight Follies, a professional musical comedy with a gold-rush theme.

✉ King Street, Dawson City, Yukon, Y0B 1G0 ☎ 867/993-6217 🕐 Mid-May to end Sep 💵 Adult $15–$17, child $7.50

TOP OF THE WORLD GOLF COURSE

www.topoftheworldgolf.com

Canada's most northerly course with grass greens has nine challenging holes amid rugged scenery. Hazards may include old mining equipment and moose. Driving range, pro shop, cart and club rentals.

✉ Bag 189, Dawson City, Yukon, Y0B 1G0 ☎ 867/993-5888 (mid-May to mid-Sep only) 🕐 Depends on weather; no tee-time reservations required; 24-hour daylight in high summer 🎫 9 holes $25, 18 holes $39, club rental $20

IQALUIT
RANNVA DESIGN
www.rannva.com
You might find Rannva's sealskin garments elsewhere in Canada (they're even exported to Italy), but there's a real thrill in buying direct from the designer in such a far-flung corner of the world—and in the old Hudson's Bay Company trading post at that. Fur has long been a traditional trade up here, and Rannva uses it to create beautiful, exclusive and original designs.

✉ Apex Beach, Old Hudson Bay Building 3606, Iqaluit, Nunavut, X0A 0H0 ☎ 867/979-0333 🕐 Sat 2–6, Sun 2–4, or by appointment during the week

WHITEHORSE
BERINGIA
www.beringia.com
This unique interpretive center about animals that roamed Beringia 40,000 years ago is full of models, skeletons and dioramas of strange-looking creatures—the 4m-high (13ft) woolly mammoth, the 3m-long (10ft) giant sloth, scimitar cat, yesterday's camel, American lion and giant beaver.

✉ Mile 914 Alaska Highway, Whitehorse, Yukon, Y1A 2C6 ☎ 867/667-8855 🕐 Mid-May to late Sep 9–6; rest of year Sun 1–5 or by appointment 🎫 Adult $6, child (6 and over) $4 🚌 Next to Whitehorse International Airport 🍴 Light refreshments and drinks

BLUE KENNELS
www.bluekennels.de
A dogsled trip is one of the ultimate Canadian experiences, and not just a winter activity. In summer, to keep the dogs fit and in training, they pull buggies instead. You can help put the huskies into their harnesses, and

after the trip there's a barbecue.

✉ Box 31523, Whitehorse, Yukon, Y1A 6K8 ☎ 867/633-2219 🕐 Call for details 🎫 1 hour $97, 3 hours $190, 6 hours $300. Five- to 15-day tours from $1,225–$3,500 🚌 50km (31 miles) west of Whitehorse at Mile 956 on Alaska Highway

ED-VENTURES FOR KIDS
www.yukonconservation.org
Two-hour and 2.5-hour hikes are specially designed for families, so that parents and children can share the natural wonders of the north in the expert company of YCS trail guides. Tuesday hikes are for four- to six-year-olds, while Thursdays are aimed at seven- to ten-year-olds.

✉ Yukon Conservation Society, 302 Hawkins Street, Whitehorse, Yukon, Y1A 1X6 ☎ 867/668-5678 🕐 Schedules change yearly. Generally hikes run July to mid-Aug twice daily 🎫 Free

FOLKNITS/KNIT NOW
www.folknits.com
This store specializes in qiviuq (the down of the musk ox), one of the rarest natural fibers in the world, plus garments made from regular yarns. Also knitting supplies.

✉ 2123 3rd Avenue, Whitehorse, Yukon, Y1A 1E6 ☎ 867/456-4192 🕐 Mon–Fri 10–5.30, Sat 10–5

FRANTIC FOLLIES
www.franticfollies.com
The vaudeville tradition of the gold-rush era brought to life. Don't expect cerebral entertainment—just old-fashioned singing, dancing and skits.

✉ Westmark Whitehorse Hotel, 201 Wood Street, Whitehorse, Yukon, Y1A 2E4 ☎ 867/668-2042 🕐 Mid-May to mid-Sep 🎫 Adult $24, child (under 13) $10

GOLDSMITHS
www.yukoninfo.com/goldsmith
David Ashley and Cheryl Rivest create and sell beautiful original pieces of jewelry and metal art, which are all designed and made on the premises. You can also get gold nuggets (with a certificate of authenticity) and Canadian Polar Bear Diamonds that originate in the Arctic. Commissions accepted.

✉ 106 Main Street, Whitehorse, Yukon, Y1A 2A7 ☎ 867/667-7340 🕐 Mon–Fri 10.30–5.30

KANOE PEOPLE
www.kanoepeople.com
Experts here make sure you get just what you need for a canoe trip: suitable craft, dry bags, coolers, cooking equipment and bear repellent spray. Then they get it, and you, to your starting point. Tuition is offered, and guided adventure tours are also available.

✉ P.O. Box 5152, Whitehorse, Yukon, Y1A 4S3 ☎ 867/668-4899 🕐 Year-round from 2.5-hour trips to inclusive 8-day tours 🎫 From $60 for 2.5–4 hour excursion, plus optional insurance ❓ Transportation can be provided to put-in or pick-up point 🚌 First Avenue and Strickland Street, on the Yukon River

MAC'S FIREWEED BOOKS
www.yukonbooks.com
This is one of the best-known bookstores in the Yukon, and you can't miss the big blue storefront on Main Street. Inside, you will find a modern layout with a great selection of books about the Yukon, including evocative tales of pioneer days, sumptuous picture books to remind you of your visit, travel planners and maps, plus all the usual bestsellers, magazines and international newspapers.

✉ 203 Main Street, Whitehorse, Yukon, Y1A 2B2 ☎ 867/668-6104, 800/661-0508 🕐 Jun–end Aug 9am–midnight; rest of year Mon–Fri 8am–9pm, Sat 9–9, Sun 9–9

MEADOW LAKES GOLF COURSE
www.meadowlakesgc.com
Public nine-hole, par 36 course of 1,756–2,548m (1,930–2,800 yards), designed for target golfers, with lots of hazards, but suitable for beginners too. Wonderful views, practice areas, pro shop and rentals.

✉ 90849 Alaska Highway, Whitehorse, Yukon, Y1A 5S8 ☎ 867/668-4653 🕐 Year-round, weather and light permitting 🎫 Green fees $30, cart and club rental from $20 🚌 South of Whitehorse on Alaska Highway

UNIQUE TAILORS

www.uniquetailors-yukon.com

There's a crucial need to keep warm up here, and this store has a good selection of very distinctive parkas and anoraks, fur hats and gloves that will keep the winter chill at bay. It also has some First Nations clothing, such as beaded leather dresses and shirts, moccasins and mukluks, as well as beaded necklaces, earrings and dreamcatchers.

✉ 4101 4th Avenue, Whitehorse, Yukon, Y1A 1H6 ☎ 867/668-2042

YUKON ARTS CENTRE

www.yukonartscentre.com

The Yukon Arts Centre is the foremost arts facility in the north, with a 424-seat theater featuring innovative drama, modern dance, classical recitals, country, roots, singer-songwriters and cabaret.

✉ 300 College Drive, Yukon College Campus, Box 16, Whitehorse, Yukon, Y1A 5X9 ☎ 867/667-8574 ◷ Year-round. Box office Mon–Fri 10–3 and 1 hour before performances ♿ Most shows and exhibitions: adult $25; child $15

YUKON CINEMA CENTRE

wwwlandmarkcinemas.ca

Modern movie house with two theaters, each seating just over 200, showing selected latest releases and kids' movies.

✉ 304 Wood Street, Whitehorse, Yukon, Y1A 2E6 ☎ 867/668-6644 (infoline), 867/667-6105 ◷ Daily ♿ Adult $9 (matinees and Tue $6), child (13–17) $7.50, under 13 $5.50, Tue $5.50 all ages

YUKON CONSERVATION SOCIETY

www.yukonconservation.org

A variety of hikes with YCS trail guides, including easy two-hour walks to the Yukon Fish Ladder or Canyon City, day-long hikes up Grey Mountain or through forests to visit remote lakes.

✉ 302 Hawkins Street, Whitehorse, Yukon, Y1A 1X6 ☎ 867/668-5678 ◷ Jul to mid-Aug hikes run twice daily; call for details. Office: Mon–Fri 10–2 ♿ Free 🚗 Most hikes meet at YCS office in Whitehorse; Canyon City Hike meets at Miles Canyon suspension bridge

FESTIVALS AND EVENTS

FEBRUARY
YUKON QUEST INTERNATIONAL SLED DOG RACE

www.yukonquest.com

A 1,637km (1,023-mile) race between Whitehorse and Fairbanks (Alaska), alternating in direction each year. Between 20 and 40 teams complete, and Whitehorse, Braeburn, Carmacks, Pelly Crossing and Dawson City are good viewing places.

✉ Whitehorse, Yukon ☎ 867/668-4711

MAY/JUNE
YUKON INTERNATIONAL STORYTELLING FESTIVAL

www.storytelling.yk.net

One of the largest festivals of

YUKON ESCAPES

www.yukonescapes.com

Ice-fishing is just one of many tours organized by this company. You get a snowmobile driving lesson, then head out with your guide on a scenic route before cutting a hole in a frozen lake and fishing through the ice. Summer trips include ATV (quad-bike) tours, hikes, fishing and boating, as well as an exciting jet-boat tour to Lake Labarge.

✉ 4158 4th Avenue, Whitehorse, Yukon ☎ 867/668-6005 ◷ Year-round for various tours ♿ Guided tours: from $150 per day; rentals (boats, ATVs, snowmobiles): from $100 per day plus fuel and £1,000 damage deposit per machine. Insurance cover not provided ❓ Door-to-door service offered from your accommodations

YUKON WILDLIFE PRESERVE

www.yukonwildlife.ca

Caribou, moose, Dall sheep, musk oxen and other wild animals roam relatively freely in their beautiful natural habitat, which is as close as you'll get to a real wildlife experience.

✉ Box 20191, Whitehorse, Yukon, Y1A 7A2 ☎ 867/633-2922 ◷ Jun–end Sep daily. Tours depart at 8, 10, 12, 2 and 4. Oct–end

its kind in the world, gathering together storytellers from many countries.

✉ Whitehorse, Yukon ☎ 867/633-7550

AUGUST
KITIKMEOT NORTHERN GAMES

www.nunavuttourism.com

You can witness the intense competition as entrants from across the region compete in traditional and modern games over three days. The event also includes a northern feast. Locations change each year.

✉ Kitikmeot Region, Nunavut ☎ 867/979-6551 (Nunavut Tourism)

May tours by arrangement ♿ Guided tours: adult $22, student/child (6–17) $12, under 6 free 🚗 At km8 (mile 5) on Takhini Hot Springs Road, 25 min north of Whitehorse

YELLOWKNIFE
AURORA VILLAGE

www.auroravillage.com

A winter experience, based at an authentic tepee village, offering a taste of First Nations life. Various packages include dogsledding, snowmobiling, ice-fishing, snowshoeing, wildlife flight tours, and aurora borealis viewing. Winter clothing for rent.

✉ Box 1827, Aurora Village, Yellowknife, Northern Territories, X1A 2P4 ☎ 867/669-0006 ◷ Late Nov to mid-Apr ♿ Packages start at $385 for 2 viewings ❓ Pick-up from Yellowknife included

CAPITOL THEATRE

www.movies.yk.com

Three comfortable, modern theaters with superb acoustics and views.

✉ 4920 52 Street, Yellowknife, Northern Territories, X1A 3S9 ☎ 867/873-2302 (infoline), 867/873-2861 ◷ Daily 7pm, 9.30pm plus Sat–Sun 2pm ♿ Adult $11 (matinees $7), students $10, child (under 14) $7

PRICES AND SYMBOLS

The restaurants are listed alphabetically within each town. The prices are for a two-course lunch (L) and a three-course à la carte dinner (D). Prices in pubs are for a two-course lunchtime bar meal and a two-course dinner in the restaurant, unless specified otherwise. The wine price is for the least expensive bottle.

For a key to the symbols, ▷ 2.

DAWSON CITY
JACK LONDON DINING ROOM

www.downtownhotel.ca

Named after the famous author of *Call of the Wild*, this is a good restaurant with formal dining inside and a patio for summer barbecues. Fresh Yukon salmon is always on the menu. Food is also available in the hotel's Sourdough Saloon, famous for its Sour Toe Cocktails (ask what's in it before you order one).

✉ Downtown Hotel, Box 780, Dawson City, Yukon. Y0B 1G0 ☎ 867/993-5346 ◐ Sun–Thu 6am–10pm, Fri–Sat 6am–11pm ✋ L $16, D $40, W $20 🚌 Downtown, corner of 2nd Avenue and Queen

KLONDIKE KATE'S

www.klondikekates.ca

Canadian and ethnic food is on the menu here.

✉ Box 417, Dawson City, Yukon, Y0B 1G0 ☎ 867/993-6527 ◐ Mid-May to mid-Sep daily 6.30am–11pm ✋ L $13, D $18, Wine $27 🚭 🅿 Street (free) 🚌 At Third and King streets

IQALUIT
GRANITE ROOM

One of the best places in the territory for a special meal, the Granite Room offers both table d'Hôte and à la carte menus with such dishes as caribou steak with peppercorn sauce, ovenbaked Pangnirtung halibut with hazelnut and crab, and smoked Arctic char. The Sunday brunch is popular too.

✉ Discovery Lodge Hotel, PO Box 387, Iqaluit, Nunavut, X0A 0H0 ☎ 867/979-4433 ◐ Daily 6.30–9, 11–2, 6–9 ✋ L $30,

D $70, W $29 🚌 Southern edge of town, off Niaqunngusiariaq

WHITEHORSE
KLONDIKE RIB AND SALMON

If you are looking for a real flavor of the north, you'll find it in this historic building, with a menu featuring bison, caribou, musk-ox and fish from the local rivers and the closest oceans. If it's on the menu order the bumbleberry pie, whether you are still hungry or not. If the weather's right, opt to dine on one of the decks (heated on cooler evenings).

✉ 2116 2nd Avenue, Whitehorse, Y1A 1B9 ☎ 867/667-7554 ◐ Daily 11–3.30, 4–9 ✋ L $18, D $40, W $23 🚌 Downtown, corner of Steele Street

SAM 'N'ANDY'S

Lively, fun and colorful describes the place and the food. There are vegetarian options on the menu alongside the Tex-Mex, seafood, burgers and other dishes.

✉ 506 Main Street, Whitehorse, Yukon Y1A 2B9 ☎ 867/668-6994 ◐ Daily 11–9 ✋ L $10, D $26, W $5.25 (glass) 🚌 Downtown.

STEELE STREET RESTAURANT AND LOUNGE

www.westmarkhotels.com/whitehorse.php

This is a nice, laid-back kind of place with a good bar menu and beers brewed locally by the Yukon Brewing Company. In summer you can eat on the patio.

✉ Westmark Hotel, 201 Wood Street, Whitehorse, Yukon Y1A 2E4 ☎ 867/393-9700 ◐ Daily 11am–midnight (hours may vary) ✋ L $12, D $35, W $13 🚌 Downtown

TALISMAN

www.yuk-biz.com/talismancafe

This great little café is geared toward families and vegetarians, and offers international dishes.

✉ 2112 2nd Avenue, Whitehorse, Yukon, Y1A 1B9 ☎ 867/667-2736 ◐ Mon–Wed 8–7, Thu–Sat 9–9, Sun 10–2 ✋ L $13,

D $19 🚌 Downtown, next to Toronto Dominion Bank

YUKON MINING COMPANY

www.highcountryinn.yk.ca

Fresh home-made fare, with an all-day menu of soups, appetizers, sandwiches, salads, burgers, pastas, fish and chips. The barbecue on the deck is fired up at 5pm to grill a variety of beef and bison steaks and ribs, burgers, chicken, salmon and game sausages.

✉ 4051 4th Avenue, Whitehorse, Yukon Y1A 1H1 ☎ 867/667-4471 ◐ Daily 6am–11pm ✋ L $20, D $45, W $32 🚌 Downtown, between Main Street and the waterfront

YELLOWKNIFE
BLACK KNIGHT PUB

www.blackknightpub.com

Billing itself as a 'Scottish' pub, the Black Knight is renowned for its lively atmosphere and very good food. The lunchtime line-up includes typical bar meals—swoops, sandwiches, burgers, salads, and British-style comfort food such as shepherd's pie, bangers and mash and fish and chips. The even longer dinner menu has more of the same plus pasta, steaks, and Cajun and Mexican specialties. The pub also has live music most Saturday nights.

✉ 4910 49th Street, Yellowknife, Northwest Territories X1A 1P3 ☎ 867/920-4041 ◐ Mon–Sat until 2am ✋ L $20, D $30 🚌 Downtown, at junction of 49th Street and 49th Avenue

L'ATITUDES

www.yellowknifeinn.com

This modern eatery serves a good range of food throughout the day.

✉ Yellowknife Inn, Central Square Mall, 5010 49th Street, Yellowknife, Northwest Territories, X1A 2N4 ☎ 867/873-2601 ◐ Mon–Sat 7–5, Sun 8–3 ✋ L $13, D $23, W $30 🚌 1, 2 (also 3 on Sat and during summer school vacation) 🚌 Downtown, off Main Street beside shopping mall

PRICES AND SYMBOLS

Prices are the starting price for a double room for one night, unless otherwise stated. Breakfast is included unless noted otherwise. All the hotels listed accept credit cards unless otherwise stated. Note that rates vary widely throughout the year.

For a key to the symbols, ▷ 2.

CARCROSS
DUNROAMIN' RETREAT

www.dunroaminretreat.com
This remote, TV-free haven is a log-built home beside Crag Lake, run by accomplished and well-traveled hosts with a mission to provide both interest and stress-reduction for their guests. By day you can enjoy several hiking trails or take part in one of the craft workshops on offer, and in the evening there's a cozy lounge where you can read by the log fire, or perhaps take a steam sauna and a dip in the lake.
✉ PO Box 169, Carcross, Yukon, Y0B 1B0
☎ 867/821-3492 ⊕ Year-round 🖐 $125
🛈 1 cabin (non-smoking) 🚌 13.7km (8.5 miles) northeast of Carcross on Highway 8; shuttle service from Carcross or Whitehorse, subject to availability

DAWSON CITY
BOMBAY PEGGY'S

www.bombaypeggys.com
Built in 1900, this hotel (pictured above) has a mixed history, but it's the era when it was a brothel that lives on, albeit only in the name. Luxuriously restored, it retains a touch of decadence. The Lipstick Room has red walls and black velvet bedding; the exotic Purple Room has a 2m-high (7ft) carved headboard.
✉ Box 411, 2nd Avenue, Dawson City, Yukon, Y0B 1G0 ☎ 867/993-6969
⊕ Year-round 🖐 $89 🛈 9 (all non-smoking) 🔁 🚌 One street back from the river front at 2nd and Princess Street

WESTMARK INN

www.westmarkhotels.com
Cheerful complex built around a central lawned courtyard, where locally renowned Klondike barbecues are held. The rooms and suites have private bathroom, TV, honor bar, hairdryer and iron; some have a kitchen.
✉ P.O. Box 420, Dawson City, Yukon, Y0B 1G0 ☎ 867/993-5542, 800/283-6622
⊕ Mid-May to end Sep 🖐 $129 🛈 177
🚌 Downtown at 5th and Harper streets

FORT SIMPSON
NORTH NAHANNI NATURALIST LODGE

www.nnnlodge.ca
Amid spectacular scenery beside Cli Lake, this traditional log building is run by members of the local Liidli Kue First Nation. The wilderness experience begins even before you arrive if you choose the jet boat (or snowmobile in winter) means of transportation rather than the fly-in option. Rooms include standard doubles, small dormitory-style shared rooms and individual housekeeping cabins, and there's a spacious lounge. Much of the furniture is hand-crafted from local lumber. Various activity packages are available.
✉ PO Box 807, Fort Simpson, Northwest Territories, X0E 0N0 ☎ 867/695-2116. 888/880-6665 ⊕ Year-round; minimum 2-night stay 🖐 $400 per person, per day all inclusive (meals, guide service, facilities and equipment); housekeeping cabins (4–6 people) $300 per cabin per day 🛈 ??? Info to follow 🚌 Transportation provided from Fort Simpson by plane, jet-boat or snowmobile; cost depends on number of guests sharing the trip

HAINES JUNCTION

THE RAVEN
www.yukonweb.com/tourism/raven
This is a delightful little hotel in a picturesque Alaska Highway village, below the St. Elias Mountains. Rooms all have private bathroom, TV and telephone. There's also a large sundeck and a small RV (motor caravan) park.

✉ 181 Alaska Highway, Box 5470, Haines Junction, Yukon, Y0B 1L0 ☎ 867/634-2500 🕐 May–end Sep 🖐 $130, continental breakfast included 🛏 12 🚗 Short drive out of town

INUVIK

ARCTIC CHALET
www.arcticchalet.com
In a beautiful location between two lakes and the Mackenzie River, this B&B offers a wonderful northern experience. Rooms and cabins all have satellite TV and phone; most have private bathroom and private entrance. In winter you can take a dogsledding trip. In summer there's fishing and canoeing on site. Guests who fly into the resort can get a "room plus car" rate and use one of their 4x4 vehicles.

✉ 25 Carn Street, PO Box 1099, Inuvik, Northwest Territories, X0E 0T0 ☎ 867/777-3535, 1-800/685-9417 🕐 Year-round 🖐 $110 🛏 11 (all non-smoking) 🚗 3km (2miles) from centre of Inuvik, off Airport Road

IQALUIT

CAPITAL SUITES
www.capitalsuites.ca
In a good central location, this all-suites hotel offers one- and two-bedroom apartments with fully equipped kitchens and pleasant décor and furnishings, including original local artworks. High-speed Internet is available in all the rooms. Discounts offered for longer stays.

✉ PO Box 2510, Iqaluit, Nunavut, X0A 0H0 ☎ 867/975-4000 🕐 Year-round 🖐 $169 🛏 42 (all non-smoking)

FROBISHER INN
www.frobisherinn.com
This modern hotel, with spectacular views over Koojesse Inlet, is where visiting dignitaries from around the world choose to stay, most likely in the corner suites which have fireplaces and Jacuzzis. The standard rooms feature quality furnishings, full bathroom, coffee, hairdryer and TV; deluxe rooms feature Inuit artworks, larger-screen TV and VCR.

✉ P.O. Box 4209, Iqaluit, Nunavut, X0A 0H0 ☎ 867/979-2222, 877/422-9422 🕐 Year-round 🖐 $220 🛏 95; no smoking floors 🅿 Indoor 🚗 Downtown

WATSON LAKE

WATSON LAKE HOTEL
www.watsonlakehotels.com
This hotel was built to service the personnel involved in the Alaska Highway project, and occupies a rustic log building dating from 1942. Kept up to date, the rooms are spacious and modern, with cable TV and private bathroom; family suites have a full kitchen.

✉ Alaska Highway, Box 370, Watson Lake, Yukon, Y0A 1C0 ☎ 867/536-7712 🕐 Year-round 🖐 $100 🛏 48

WHITEHORSE

HIGH COUNTRY INN
www.highcountryinn.yk.ca
You can't miss this inn—it has a 15m-high (50ft) Mountie guarding its door. Inside you'll find four floors of rooms ranging from standard doubles to sumptuous suites with two-person Jacuzzis. Rooms with kitchenette are also available. All have private bathroom, cable TV, two telephone lines and modem, and tea/coffee. The inn has a continental-style bistro and a gold-mining themed pub with Canadian specialties.

✉ 4051 4th Avenue, Whitehorse, Yukon, Y1A 1H1 ☎ 867/667-4471, 800/554-4471 🕐 Year-round 🖐 $149 🛏 85 📺 🚗 Six blocks east of Main Street, three blocks from waterfront

TOWN AND MOUNTAIN HOTEL
www.townmountain.com
In a good central location, within walking distance of all the main attractions, this is a bright and spacious boutique hotel with pleasant, unfussy décor, modern furnishings and coordinated fabrics. There are two styles of rooms: those on the second floor have two double beds, while those on the third have one king-size bed and a kitchenette. All have an ensuite bathroom, cable TV and telephone, and Internet access may be available. There are two eating options here—the traditional Sourdough Dining Room and the pub-style Lizard's Bar and Grill with a menu of wood-oven pizzas, ribs and steaks.

✉ 401 Main Street, Whitehorse, Yukon, Y1A 2B6 ☎]867/668-7644, 800/661-0522 (toll-free in Yukon and northern BC only) 🕐 Year-round 🖐 $7 🛏 29

WESTMARK WHITEHORSE HOTEL AND CONFERENCE CENTRE
www.westmarkhotels.com
The Yukon's biggest hotel has been renovated, and offers international style rooms and suites (some with a Jacuzzi), a full range of conference and meeting facilities, and a nice restaurant with seasonal heated patio. There's also a guest laundry, Northern Wonders gift shop and a barber shop on the premises.

✉ 201 Wood Street, Whitehorse, Yukon Y1A 2E4 ☎ 867/393-9700, 800/544-0970 (central reservations) 🕐 Year-round 🖐 $129–$169 🛏 180 [all non-smoking in summer; 6–7 rooms for smokers in winter)

YELLOWKNIFE

CHATEAU NOVA
www.chateaunova.com
One of Yellowknife's newer hotels, opened late 2000, provides big-city standards, with large, elegant rooms and suites. All have private bathroom, bathrobes, tea- and coffee-making facilities and hairdryer, plus high-speed internet connection, TV, and telephone with voice mail.

✉ 4401 50th Avenue, Yellowknife, Northwest Territories, X1A 2N2 ☎ 867/873-9700, 877/839-1236 🕐 Year-round 🖐 $199 🛏 80 📶 📺 🚗 Downtown 🚌 Free bus shuttle from airport

PRACTICALITIES

This section gives you all the important practical information you will need during your visit from money matters to emergency phone numbers.

CLIMATE AND WHEN TO GO

Canada is an enormous country, encompassing many different climatic zones with tremendous variations from summer to winter. The country's cold winters and heavy snowfall produce some spectacular skiing, and the warmth of summer gives rise to myriad outdoor festivals and activities. Although any time of year has its attractions depending on your interests, the vast majority of visitors seek the pleasures of Canada between mid-May and mid-October. Outside these months, facilities may be much reduced, unless you are going to a ski area or a major city. It is thus advisable to check in advance that hotels and sights will be open if you plan to travel outside the peak season.

REGIONAL VARIATIONS
East Coast

The east coast has lovely warm summers, but rain and fog are always a possibility, especially on or near the coast. The Atlantic shores can also be very windy, particularly in Newfoundland. The fall colors in this area are lovely. Winters are relatively mild, but there is snow too—in New Brunswick it often figures among the highest in the country—and ice floes (or massive icebergs in the case of Newfoundland and Labrador) can be seen drifting not far offshore.

Canadian Shield—Ontario and Québec

Because of their size, there is considerable variation within these two huge central provinces. Québec, covering an area greater than Texas, stretches from the temperate south to the Arctic and the weather varies accordingly.

The southern parts of both Ontario and Québec are extremely hot and humid in mid-summer. From the end of June through August the temperature can easily remain in the 30s°C (90s°F) for days on end. This can be extremely uncomfortable in the big cities as there is high humidity. As a result, central Canadians use air conditioning in summer and humidification in winter—in some homes, the same machine does both jobs.

In the winter you can expect the other extreme, with cold temperatures and lots of snow. Central Canadians continue life as normal whatever the season and adjust to the extremes. Visitors should try to do the same.

The Niagara Peninsula, the country's top fruit-growing and wine-producing region, has relatively milder winters. Snow sometimes falls, and in the coldest winters Niagara Falls looks spectacular when it freezes.

Between winter and summer, there is a short, crisp spring. Later, the mild fall produces brilliant foliage, and unsurprisingly this is a popular time to visit.

Prairies

The landlocked Prairies have bitterly cold and drawn-out winters, but beautiful warm summers. They don't suffer from the humidity of the Canadian Shield country (Ontario and Québec) and they don't suffer from bugs either. Thunderstorms occur in summer: They can be seen coming from a long way off, so you can usually avoid getting soaked. Night skies in mid-summer are unbelievable, with more stars than can possibly be counted.

Rocky Mountains

Famous for their rocky profiles and snow-capped peaks, the Canadian Rockies experience heavy snowfall in the winter. Roads are icy and dangerous at this time. The season draws skiers, snowboarders and enthusiasts for dangerous sports such as climbing frozen waterfalls.

Like all mountain areas, the weather can change dramatically in a few hours in any month of the year. Rainstorms can appear from nowhere and turn to snow at high altitudes, even in July. In May the lakes are often still frozen over, so most visitors prefer to enjoy the great mountain parks (such as Banff and Jasper) from June through August.

West Coast

The weather of the west coast, especially Vancouver Island, is tempered by the Pacific Ocean. It's not too hot in summer and the winters are mild with little or no snow, but both seasons can be wet.

Away from the coast the climate is much hotter and drier. Inland, the Okanagan is a major fruit-growing and wine-making region, though rainfall is so low that irrigation is required to grow the crops.

The North

In the north of the country summers are short and warm with 24 hours

QUEBEC
TEMPERATURE

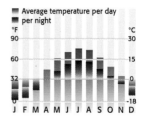

RAINFALL

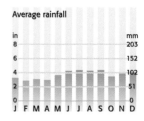

of daylight. Winters are long, dark and Siberia-like, with incredibly low temperatures. Plan any trip here carefully, getting as much information as possible from the tourist offices or local outfitters.

TIME ZONES
Canada is the second-largest country in the world, and spans six of the world's 24 time zones. However, there's only a 4 1/2-hour difference between the east and west coasts because Newfoundland and a part of Labrador have their own special zone—half an hour ahead of Atlantic Standard Time, which, itself, is 4 hours behind GMT (sometimes known as UTC). AST is observed in the rest of Labrador and the other Maritime provinces.

Most of Québec (except a section of the North Shore) and Ontario (except the extreme west) observe Eastern Standard Time (GMT -5). Manitoba and Saskatchewan observe Central Standard Time (GMT -6). Alberta and a section of south eastern British Columbia observe Mountain Standard Time (GMT -7). The rest of British Columbia and the Yukon observe Pacific Standard Time (GMT -8). The Northwest Territories

WEATHER WEBSITE
The federal government agency, Environment Canada, has an excellent website (www.weatheroffice.gc.ca), which gives a good idea of what to expect in any given part of the country in any particular month.

observes the two time zones to the south—Central and Mountain—while Nunavut observes Eastern Standard Time.

Daylight Saving Time is effective in all provinces and territories except Saskatchewan, but the dates it starts (March/April) and ends (October/November) vary depending on where you are. Saskatchewan keeps the same time all year (▷ 9, Time Zones map).

WHAT TO PACK
With the possibility of long hot summer days, fierce rainstorms, beautiful evenings and bright, cold winters, making sure that you pack the right things can be a problem.

East Coast
Rainwear and sweaters for evenings are a good idea on the east coast, even in mid-summer. The wind can

be fierce on the Atlantic coast, so pack a light wind-breaker if you'll be spending time outside.

TIME ZONES

CITY	TIME DIFFERENCE	TIME AT 12 NOON EST (MONTRÉAL AND TORONTO)
Amsterdam	+6	6pm
Berlin	+6	6pm
Brussels	+6	6pm
Buenos Aires	+2	2pm
Calgary	-2	10am
Chicago	-1	11am
Dublin	+5	5pm
Halifax	+1	1pm
Johannesburg	+6	6pm
London	+5	5pm
Los Angeles	-3	9am
Madrid	+6	6pm
Miami	0	12 noon
New York	0	12 noon
Paris	+6	6pm
Perth, Australia	+13	1am
Rome	+6	6pm
San Francisco	-3	9am
Sydney	+15	3am
Tokyo	+14	2am
Vancouver	-3	9am

TORONTO
TEMPERATURE

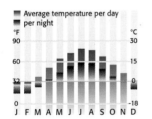

RAINFALL

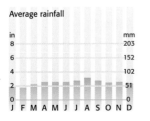

VANCOUVER
TEMPERATURE

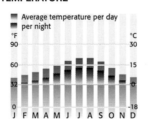

RAINFALL

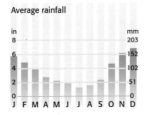

WINNIPEG
TEMPERATURE

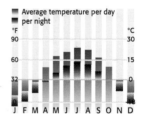

RAINFALL

West Coast

Make sure you are equipped with rainwear if you plan to hike or do other outdoor activities. An umbrella is handy in Vancouver. In the winter months you will need warm clothing only if you go to a ski resort.

The North

Sunglasses are important as the light in the north is surprisingly bright and daylight lasts for 24 hours in summer.

On northern trips sunscreen is important in summer; dress relatively lightly but cover yourself against lengthy exposure to the sun. Insects are a problem in the early part of the season (April and May). Long-sleeve shirts, slacks and a hat with mosquito netting are recommended for any prolonged periods of outdoor activity, such as camping or canoeing.

Winter Wear

For winter visits to Canada, except for the west coast (▷ above), pack warm clothing: a parka or coat, a woolen hat (preferably with ear-flaps), gloves, long underwear, and also waterproof boots. All the above can be purchased once you've arrived if necessary, though you could freeze between the airport and the nearest clothing store. In the north in January especially, cover yourself up in thermal Arctic gear from head to foot.

DOCUMENTS
ENTRY REQUIREMENTS

Like those of any country, Canadian entry requirements vary depending on your nationality, and are also subject to change without notice. Check requirements prior to a visit and follow news events that may affect your situation.

US VISITORS

American citizens must show proof of citizenship when entering Canada. At the present time a passport is not essential, though it is the best and easiest means to prove your citizenship. Otherwise any documentation with photo ID can be used, such as your certificate of naturalization, if you were not born in the US; a birth or baptismal certificate with photo ID; a social security card; or a voter's card. No visa is necessary. If you are a permanent US resident but not a citizen, you must carry your Alien Registration Card (green card).

The rules for re-entering the US from Canada are changing, and citizens will need specific documentation when returning home, whether by air, land or sea. Check the latest situation with the Department of Homeland Security (www.dhs.gov).

VISITORS FROM THE EUROPEAN UNION AND AUSTRALIA

Citizens of Australia and of European countries that are part of the European Union do not require a visa to enter Canada, but they must carry a valid passport.

VISITORS FROM OTHER PARTS OF THE WORLD

Entry visas are required for citizens of more than 130 countries. As political and economic changes take place around the world, the list of countries changes frequently, depending on what's going on at the time. You can check the situation for any particular country by contacting with the local Canadian embassy, or by visiting the website of the Canadian government's Citizenship and Immigration (www.cic.gc.ca).

If you do require a visa, you will need to apply for it at the Canadian embassy in your home country. The visa must be issued before you leave home—and you'll need to plan this well in advance because the process is not always speedy.

YOUNG PEOPLE AND SENIORS

Any person under 19, alone or in a group, is required to show a letter from a parent or guardian giving them permission to visit Canada; the letter must state the individual's name and the duration of the trip. In addition they must carry proof of identity. If you are traveling with any children under 16 and you are not their parent or guardian, you must have a letter from their parent or guardian authorizing their entry into Canada. If only one parent or guardian is accompanying a child, they should carry permission from the other parent or guardian, or documentation to prove there is no other guardian. Students should also have their ID handy for claiming reductions on travel fares and admission charges.

Throughout Canada, seniors need to prove their age to receive reduced fares or admission charges.

CUSTOMS
Firearms—strict regulations

If you are going on a hunting trip, make sure you check restrictions and have the necessary documentation before you arrive at the border. If you are flying in, consult airport security for advice.

CANADIAN EMBASSIES AND CONSULATES ABROAD

COUNTRY	ADDRESS	WEBSITE
Australia	Commonwealth Avenue, Canberra, ACT 2600; tel (02) 6270 4000	http://geo.international.gc.ca/asia/australia
France	35 avenue Montaigne, Paris, 75008; tel 01 44 43 29 00	www.dfait.maeci.gc.ca/canada-europa/france
Germany	Leipziger Platz 17, 10117 Berlin; tel (030) 20 31 20	international.gc.ca/canada%Deuropa/germany
Ireland	3rd Floor, 7–8 Wilton Terrace, Dublin 2; tel (01) 234 4000	http://geo.international.c.ca/canada-europa/ireland
Italy	Via Zara 30, 00198 Roma; tel (06) 85 44 41	www.international.gc.ca/canada-europa/italy
New Zealand	PO Box 8047, Level 11, 125 The Terrace	http://geo.international.gc.ca/asia/newzealand/
Spain	Calle Nuñez de Balboa 35, 28001 Madrid; tel (034) 91 423 3250	www.dfait-maeci.gc.ca/canada-europa/spain
South Africa	1103 Arcadia Street, Hatfield, Pretoria 0028; tel (012) 422 3000	www.dfait.maeci.gc.ca/southafrica
UK	Canada House, Trafalgar Square, London SW1Y 5BJ; tel (020) 7258 6600	www.dfait-maeci.gc.ca/canadaeuropa/united_kingdom
US	501 Pennsylvania Avenue NW, Washington D.C. 20001-2114; tel (202) 682-1740	http://geo.international.gc.ca/can-am/washington

Organic Imports

There are many regulations concerning the importation of plants, flowers and other vegetation and this matter is taken very sriously. It is not advisable to bring anything of this sort into Canada. For more information and details of the regulations are available from the Canada Border Services Agency; tel 800/461-9999 (within Canada), 204/983-3500 or 506/636-5064 (from outside Canada), or consult its website: www.cbsa-asfc.gc.ca/.

Pets

Pets can accompany you to Canada, but they must have been vaccinated against rabies within the preceding 12 months, and you must carry the vaccination certificate with you.

VEHICLE DOCUMENTATION

If you drive a vehicle into Canada, you must carry its registration papers and proof of insurance coverage, in addition to a valid driver's license. Be aware that your vehicle is likely to be searched for illegal substances at the border, and be prepared to show your documentation to police officers if you are pulled over while driving within Canada.

INSURANCE

To enter Canada you are not obliged to have any personal form of insurance other than for your vehicle. It is advisable, however, to arrange health coverage. Canada's health system is available free to Canadians, but is not similarly available to foreigners. Bills for quite simple procedures can be more than you would pay at home, and some Canadians may have an out-of-province premium to pay.

Your own insurance company is probably the best source of advice on what is best for you. Insurance on your personal property, especially if you will be carrying valuables with you, is also important.

Most residential insurance policies provide some coverage, even when you are journeying in a foreign country—check with your insurer before leaving home. If anything does get lost or stolen, it is usually necessary to have a police report in order to make a claim.

MONEY

CURRENCY

Canada's currency is the Canadian dollar, which consists of 100 cents. Canadian currency has almost the same denominations as US money, with the exception of the $1 and $2 bills, which no longer exist. Single Canadian dollars are in the form of a gold-colored coin bearing an image of a loon (a bird found in Canada) and, as a result, the coin has been nicknamed the "loonie". Two-dollar coins have gold centers and silver rims (and are called "twonies").

EXCHANGING MONEY

Exchange facilities are found in large hotels, airports and train stations, but rates are often poor and commission fees high. Most banks offer exchange facilities, but may charge a fee. Outside major cities and resort areas, there are few places devoted solely to currency exchange. American dollars are widely accepted in Canada, but be aware of the official exchange rate.

TRAVELER'S CHECKS

The best way to carry money is in the form of traveler's checks (cheques). You can purchase American Express or Visa checks from your own bank before you leave home. Have the traveler's checks made out in Canadian dollars and they can then be used as cash in most stores, restaurants and filling stations across the country. There is no limit to the amount of Canadian or foreign currency that can be exchanged in or brought into or out of the country.

AUTOMATED BANKING MACHINES

The simplest means of obtaining money is by using your bank card at an automated banking or telling machine (ABM or ATM). Bank cards are generally connected to either the MasterCard (Cirrus) or Visa (Plus) system. You may have to check a couple of machines before you find one that accepts your card.

CREDIT AND DEBIT CARDS

A credit card is a convenient means to pay for things when visiting Canada. It is also safer than carrying a lot of cash. Most hotels, restaurants and stores accept the major cards. However, you will probably need cash in local grocery stores, newsstands and small establishments.

Before leaving home, you should check with your bank as to whether your debit card will be accepted out of your home country. Some stores, hotels and restaurants may not accept a UK microchip debit card, although this may change now that Canadian Visa issuers are introducing a similar system.

TIPPING

Tipping is widespread across Canada and remains an acknowledgment of good service. Service charges are not automatically added to restaurant checks (bills), except in a few rare cases. It is customary to tip as follows:

» About 15 percent of the check (bill), before taxes, for waiters and waitresses.

» About 15 percent for taxi drivers and hairdressers.

» At your hotel, you should give the bellman (porter) $1 per bag, the valet $2, and room service staff 10 percent of the check (bill) before taxes have been calculated.

» If you take a guided city tour, it is customary to offer the tour guide a small token of your appreciation. In general, $1 per person is adequate.

TAXES
▷ 372, 283.

LOST/STOLEN CREDIT CARDS

American Express	905/474-9280; www.americanexpress.com
Diners Club	800/363-3333; www.dinersclub.com
MasterCard	800-307-7309; www.mastercard.com/canada
Visa	800/847-2911; www.visa.com

10 EVERYDAY ITEMS AND HOW MUCH THEY COST

Takeaway sandwich	$5–$7
Bottle of water	$1.50–$2
Cup of tea or coffee	$1.80
Bottle of beer	$2–$3
Glass of wine	$5–$7
Daily newspaper	$1
Roll of camera film	$5–$9
20 cigarettes	$10
An ice cream	$2–$3
A liter of fuel (petrol)	$1.05

ABM/ATM TIPS

» To be able to use your bank card at an ABM/ATM in Canada, it must be programmed with a personal identification number, or PIN. Without this you will not be able to access either your bank or credit card account.

» Before leaving home, you should check the restrictions on the amount of money you can withdraw at any one time or on any one day.

BANKS

NAME	TELEPHONE	WEBSITE
Bank of Montréal	800/363-9992	www.bmo.com
Royal Bank of Canada	800/769-2511	www.royalbank.com
Scotiabank	800/472-6842	www.scotiabank.com
Toronto Dominion	866/222-3456	www.td.com

HEALTH

BEFORE YOU GO
Vaccinations
No vaccinations are required before entering Canada for visitors from Europe, the US, Australia or New Zealand. You should check current requirements if you are arriving from the Far or Middle East, Africa, or South or Central America, and especially if you are coming from a known infected area. For details contact the Canadian embassy in your country or visit the Canadian government's Citizenship and Immigration website, www.cic.gc.ca.

Prescription Drugs
You should carry a full supply of any prescription drug that you have to take. Over-the-counter drugs are readily available in pharmacies (nright), but no Canadian pharmacy will accept or refill an out-of-province prescription. If you run out of or lose your supply, you will have to visit a Canadian doctor and get a new prescription recognized locally. There will be a cost for this service.

HEALTH HAZARDS
For most visitors there are no significant health hazards involved in a trip to Canada. The few problems that could occur are associated with the outdoors. For example, "beaver fever" comes from a parasite (Giardi lamblia) that thrives in small streams or shallow lakes in summer. You are well advised to boil all drinking water when camping. Beaver fever normally lasts only a day or so, but seek medical aid if it persists.

In southern Ontario and Québec poison ivy can be prevalent in woodland. It causes inflammation and rashes, and can be very uncomfortable, but will normally disappear after about 10 days. Rag-weed can cause similar irritations. Creams are available in pharmacies to help alleviate any discomfort.

Less serious but still irritating are the hordes of biting insects that are common in central Canada and the north any time after April, but especially in May and June. Insect repellents work with only limited effectiveness on some people. You should wear long-sleeve, light-toned clothing when outdoors — especially after 5pm on a hot day.

PHARMACIES
There is no shortage of pharmacies (chemists) in Canadian cities, some staying open 24 hours. Ask at your hotel reception or call the police in an emergency for addresses.

City pharmacies are generally large stores selling a variety of cosmetics and other beauty products in addition to prescription and over-the-counter drugs. The pharmacist is a good source of advice if you are not sure what to buy for a particular condition, such as the effects of poison ivy (▷ Health Hazards), or if you are suffering from an unknown malady.

In case of emergency, it is wise to make a note of the generic name of any prescription medications that you take before you leave home — they may be sold under a different trade name in Canada. See also the section on prescription drugs (▷ this page).

DOCTORS AND DENTISTS
If you require medical or dental help in Canada, ask at your hotel reception. Most hotels keep a list of doctors, dentists and medical centers handy, which can save you considerable time. Otherwise, try the local visitor center or the Yellow Pages telephone book; emergency services, such as an ambulance, are usually listed inside the front cover. When you pay for any medical services, keep the receipts and other paperwork for future insurance claims.

HEALTHY FLYING

Visitors coming to Canada via long-haul flights may be concerned about the effect on their health. The most widely publicized fear is deep vein thrombosis, or DVT. Misleadingly labeled "economy-class syndrome," DVT is the clotting of the blood in a vein deep below the skin, particularly in the legs. The clot can move around the bloodstream and may be fatal. Flying increases the likelihood of DVT because passengers are often seated in a cramped position for long periods of time and may become dehydrated. Those most at risk include the elderly, pregnant women and those using the contraceptive pill, smokers, and the overweight. If you are at increased risk of DVT, see your doctor before departing.

To minimize the risk of DVT:
» Drink water (not alcohol)
» Don't stay immobile for hours at a time — stretch and exercise your legs periodically
» Wear elastic flight socks, which support veins and reduce the chances of a clot forming

Exercises

Ankle rotations	Calf stretches	Knee lifts
Lift feet off the floor. Draw a circle with the toes, moving one foot clockwise and the other counterclockwise	Start with heel on the floor and point foot upward as high as you can. Then lift heels high, keeping balls of feet on the floor	Lift leg with knee bent while contracting your thigh muscle. Then straighten leg, pressing foot flat to the floor

Other health hazards are airborne diseases and bugs spread by the plane's air-conditioning system. If you have a serious medical condition, seek advice from a doctor before leaving home.

BASICS

ELECTRICAL ADAPTERS

Throughout Canada, the voltage is 110 volts AC, the same as in the US. European appliances require a transformer and a plug adaptor with two flat prongs (occasionally three prongs).

Modern electric razors and hairdryers are often designed to work on both 220 volts and 110 volts, but you still need the appropriate adapter. You can buy these at most airports and travel stores in Canada, though it is advisable to purchase one before you leave home.

LAUNDRY SERVICES

Dry cleaning and laundry services are widely available in Canadian cities. Your hotel can make arrangements for you or provide some addresses; tourist offices can also supply this information.

Be warned that laundry services are not necessarily cheap. If you wish to do your own laundry and find a hotel washbasin inadequate, don't expect to find laundromats on every downtown corner—instead seek out a student area, where they are more plentiful.

MEASUREMENTS

Canada uses the metric system of weights and measures, with fuel sold in liters, and food in grams and kilograms. However, clothing sizes and food amounts may still be given in the imperial (American) system.

PUBLIC WASHROOMS

Canadian cities are not usually equipped with public washrooms (toilets) accessed from the outdoors, as is often the case in Europe. The main reason for this is the problem of servicing them in winter and making sure they don't freeze up.

One of the best places to find washrooms is the local tourist office, where they will be clean. Train and bus stations also provide washrooms though they are not always spotlessly clean. Other good places include the lobbies of major hotels, department stores, museums and other tourist attractions, restaurants (but only if you are eating there) and gas (petrol) stations. Public washrooms are usually free of charge and of a high standard.

SMOKING AND ALCOHOL

Smoking is increasingly frowned upon in Canada, and is forbidden in office buildings, most indoor public places, and on buses and subway systems. Smoking is banned in restaurants in all provinces, although rules on smoking in bars, restaurants and cafés, and other entertainment venues vary from province to province.

Cigarettes are sold in supermarkets and other grocery stores, newspaper and magazine stores, and bars.

The legal age to purchase and drink alcoholic beverages is 19 in all provinces except Alberta, Manitoba and Québec, where the age is 18. Laws regarding the sale of beer, wine and other alcoholic beverages vary from province to province.

In most provinces hard liquor can be purchased only at government stores, or at special stores in Ontario. An exception is Québec, where wine and beer are sold in food stores.

TAXES

A 5 percent Goods and Services Tax (GST) is added to everything you buy in Canada except food from a supermarket or grocery store. It is also applicable on all hotel and restaurant checks (bills), on tickets for all types of transportation and on admission charges to tourist sights.

In addition, most provinces add their own Provincial Sales Tax (PST), so you may find yourself paying a surcharge of anything between 5 percent in Alberta (GST only—there is no PST) to 17 percent in Newfoundland, where the rate of PST is 12 percent. The Atlantic provinces operate a Harmonized Sales Tax (HST), which combines GST and PST into one system. These are not hidden taxes: They are added to the check (bill) and itemized on the sales slip.

VISITING WITH CHILDREN

If you take children to Canada, they must have their own documentation, such as a birth certificate and passport. If you are a parent traveling without the child's other parent, or if you are not the legal guardian, you must carry a letter of permission from the other parent, parents or legal guardian. Divorced parents are required to carry legal documents establishing their status. These restrictions have recently been imposed because of the number of divorced parents absconding to Canada with their children, against the wishes of the other parent.

CONVERSION CHART

From	To	Multiply by
Inches	Centimeters	2.54
Centimeters	Inches	0.3937
Feet	Meters	0.3048
Meters	Feet	3.2810
Yards	Meters	0.9144
Meters	Yards	1.0940
Miles	Kilometers	1.6090
Kilometers	Miles	0.6214
Acres	Hectares	0.4047
Hectares	Acres	2.4710
Gallons	Liters	4.5460
Liters	Gallons	0.2200
Ounces	Grams	28.35
Grams	Ounces	0.0353
Pounds	Grams	453.6
Grams	Pounds	0.0022
Pounds	Kilograms	0.4536
Kilograms	Pounds	2.205
Tons	Tonnes	1.0160
Tonnes	Tons	0.9842

When renting a car, request a child's car seat at the time of making the reservation. When flying, check the carry-on allowance, especially in the case of buggies; some airlines require that they are checked as baggage. You should ask for children's meals in advance too.

Most hotels in Canada allow children under a certain age to stay free in their parents' room. The age limit for this varies from establishment to establishment, and some places treat children as extra adults and charge accordingly. Check carefully when reserving.

Most restaurants, especially those in popular tourist areas, will offer a children's menu and have high chairs or booster seats, but this is worth checking in advance. Certain museums (for example, the National Gallery of Canada, ▷ 224–225) offer children's activity rooms in addition to their child-related exhibits.

CULTURE AND ETIQUETTE

Although Canadians may appear just like Americans to some Europeans, many of them do not appreciate being told so. It's probably a topic to avoid. If you push the cultural similarities too far expect to receive a lecture on how Canada developed and just how different it is. Having said that, Canadians are increasingly informal and there is very little that shocks them.

Dress Code

Visitors can dress casually in jeans, T-shirts and sneakers and feel at home in most parts of the country, especially during the daytime.

Outside the major cities, in some of the popular resorts for example, you may find that Canadians tend to dress a little more formally in the evening.

Toronto, Ottawa, Montréal and Vancouver are important business places, with well-dressed office workers, and you may therefore prefer to dress up a little, especially for shopping trips and when visiting museums. All four cities have world-class restaurants, and while they may not impose a dress code they are unlikely to get the best service or a good table if you are dressed too casually.

Visiting Churches

As everywhere else in the world, you should be appropriately dressed when visiting a church or other place of religious worship. The Basilique Notre-Dame de Montréal will not admit people in very short shorts or in tank tops with "spaghetti" straps, and visitors must wear shoes.

First Nations

It is important to respect the traditional lifestyle of Canada's native peoples. It is an insult, for example, to call the northern peoples Eskimos—a derogatory word meaning "eaters of raw meat." Likewise, the word Indians should be used only in the context of the people of the Indian subcontinent. Canada's native peoples, or First Nations, are generally referred to by their tribal affiliation, such as the Cree of northern Québec, the Ojibwa of northern Ontario, and the Assiniboine of the Prairies.

French Canada

In Québec and parts of New Brunswick be prepared to acknowledge that French is the first and sometimes the only language of the resident population. Learning a few words can only enhance your visit (▷ 381). If you do have a problem expressing yourself, a friendly smile and a polite apology for not knowing the language will go a long way to assuring help and good service.

Tipping

For etiquette regarding tipping, ▷ 370.

Places of Religious Worship

Major hotels in the cities usually have a list of places of worship close to them. If not, the local tourist office can provide a list (▷ 378–379). There will normally be a Roman Catholic church, an Anglican church (Episcopal), a United church (Methodists and Presbyterians), and sometimes a Baptist church. In addition, all the major cities have synagogues and most have a mosque, and a Buddhist and a Hindu temple.

COMMUNICATIONS

TELEPHONES

Public phones are widely available. They accept coins, telephone credit cards and pre-paid phone cards. US telephone credit cards are also readily accepted.

Pre-paid phone cards are sold in a variety of places including most convenience stores, visitor centers and some hotels, and are available in various amounts starting at $10. They are probably the most convenient means to make a long-distance call from a public phone.

TIP

» Hotels charge a premium rate for making calls from your room, which can be substantial. However, local calls are sometimes free.

MAKING CALLS

To call within Canada, press 1 followed by the provincial or city code (▷ panel) . If you are making a local call, you will mostly just dial the seven-digit number, but after September 2008, for all calls within BC and Alberta, you will need to include the provincial code. In the major cities you must use the provincial or city code even for local calls.

It is easy to make calls directly to the US. Again, press 1 followed by the state or city code and telephone number.

To make calls to Europe or elsewhere outside North America, you must know the country code. Most phone books list country codes along with instructions for making an overseas call. If you have any problems placing a call or you don't know or cannot find the country code, press 0 and ask for the overseas operator.

To call Canada from overseas, use the country code 1, the same as for the US.

TIPS

» Local calls are free in Canada; hotels normally add a nominal charge while public phones require 25 cents.
» Rates for long-distance calls are greater

during business hours—the cheapest time is generally after midnight and before 6am.

CELL PHONES

Check with your server to find out whether your cell phone will work in Canada—some do, some don't and you may need to organize a "roaming agreement" prior to your trip. Making calls this way can be expensive.

POSTAL SERVICES

Canada is not noted for speedy mail delivery. In addition, the cost of postage stamps tends to rise frequently.

There is one mail delivery per day, Monday to Friday. For more information on the mail service, contact Canada Post: www.canadapost.ca

Alternatively, Priority Post is a fast and somewhat expensive service that promises "next day delivery" within Canada. It is available 24 hours a day, seven days a week.

STAMPS

Post offices are generally open Monday to Friday 8.30 to 5.30. Certain small convenience stores are licensed to sell stamps, and postal outlets are often found inside larger stores and train stations—look for the "Canada Post" sign. Such outlets may open on Saturday mornings and keep longer hours on weekdays than regular post offices. Stamps may also be available at hotel reception desks.

EMAIL AND INTERNET ACCESS

Almost every Canadian is online, so emails are an efficient form of communication. Many hotels offer internet access, sometimes included in the room rate, but often at a price, in which case you are probably better off seeking out the nearest internet café or WiFi hotspot. Visitor centers have the addresses of local internet cafés, or there may be internet access at the nearest large bookstore or a university campus. Internet cafés are also listed in the Yellow Pages telephone book.

COUNTRY CODES FROM CANADA

Australia	011 61
Belgium	011 32
France	011 33
Germany	011 49
Greece	011 30
Ireland	011 353
Italy	011 39
Netherlands	011 31
New Zealand	011 64
Spain	011 34
Sweden	011 46
UK	011 44
US	1

PROVINCIAL TELEPHONE CODES

Alberta	South	403
	North	780
British	Vancouver	604 and 778
Columbia	rest of BC	250
Manitoba		204
New Brunswick		506
Newfoundland and Labrador		709
Northwest Territories		867
Nunavut		867
Nova Scotia		902
Ontario	Toronto	416 and 647
	Toronto region	905 and 289
	Central and North	705
	Southwest	519 and 226
	Ottawa region	613
	Northwest	807
Prince Edward Island		902
Québec	Montréal	514 and 438
	Montréal region	450
	West and North	819
	East	418
Saskatchewan		306
Yukon		867

USEFUL TELEPHONE NUMBERS

» For directory assistance within a city, press 411.
» To call collect within North America or have your call charged to your home number, press 0 before making your call and listen to the options. Again, speak to an operator if you have a problem.

ESSENTIAL INFORMATION

PRACTICALITIES

FINDING HELP

PERSONAL SAFETY

Canada is a relatively crime-free country and you should not be overly concerned about personal safety. However, some city areas are best avoided and reasonable caution should be exercised elsewhere. These few simple precautions will help prevent unfortunate incidents.

» Don't leave bags or other valuables visible in your car—put everything in the trunk (boot).

» Consider carrying your passport and credit cards in a pouch or belt, and walk along only well-lit streets at night. If you do have anything stolen, report it immediately to the police and/or your hotel.

EMERGENCIES

To contact the police, the fire department, or ambulance service in most parts of Canada, dial 911. Where the 911 service is not in effect (Vancouver Island, Prince Edward Island, Nova Scotia, Yukon, Northwest Territories and Nunavut), press 0 for the operator and say that it is an emergency. This is much the best way to report a crime or other emergency and saves you searching for a police station or hospital.

POLICE

The Royal Canadian Mounted Police is Canada's federal police force. The "Mounties" also act as the regular police in all provinces except Ontario and Québec, which have their own provincial forces. On duty, RCMP officers look just like those of any other police force and drive cars. (Horses are no longer used, and the red jackets, stetson hats and boots with spurs are worn only on ceremo- nial occasions.) All major cities have their own police forces in addition to the RCMP and/or provincial force.

LOST PROPERTY

The police are the best people to contact if you mislay something valu- able. Don't use the emergency 911 number in such cases, but instead check the phone book or ask your hotel reception for the local number. If you make an insurance claim for any losses, you must obtain a police report (▷ 369 Insurance).

Lost Passport

In the case of a lost or stolen passport, you will have to contact your local embassy or consulate. Generally, these are in Ottawa, Montréal, Toronto and Vancouver, and occasionally elsewhere (▷ below).

EMBASSIES AND CONSULATES

Australian High Commission
7th Floor, Suite 710, 50 O'Connor Street, Ottawa, Ontario, K1P 6L2
Tel 613/236-0841
www.ahc-ottawa.org
In addition to its embassy, Australia maintains
consulates in the following cities:

Australian Consulate General Toronto
Suite 1100, 175 Bloor Street East, Toronto,
Ontario, M4W 3R8
Tel 416/323-1155

Australian Consulate Vancouver
Suite 1225, 888 Dunsmuir Street, Vancouver,
British Columbia, V6C 3K4
Tel 604/684-1177

British High Commission
80 Elgin Street, Ottawa, Ontario, K1P 5K7
Tel 613/237-1530
www.britainincanada.org
In addition to its embassy, the United Kingdom
maintains consulates in the following cities:

British Consulate General Montréal
Suite 4200, 1000 rue de la Gauchetière Ouest,
Montréal, Québec, H3B 4W5
Tel 514/866-5863

British Consulate General Toronto
777 Bay Street, Suite 2800, Toronto,
Ontario, M5G 2G2
Tel 416/593-1290

British Consulate General Vancouver
1111 Melville Street, Suite 800, Vancouver,

British Columbia, V6E 3V6
Tel 604/683-4421

French Embassy Canada
42 Sussex Drive, Ottawa, Ontario, K1M 2C9
Tel 613/789-1795 www.ambafrance-ca.org
There are French consulates in Moncton,
Québec, Montréal, Toronto and Vancouver.

German Embassy, Canada
1 Waverley Street, Ottawa, Ontario, K2P 0T8
Tel 613/232-1101
www.ottawa.diplo.de
There are German consulates in Montréal,
Toronto and Vancouver.

Italian Embassy Canada
275 Slater Street, 21st Floor, Ottawa, Ontario,
K1P 5H9
Tel 613/232-2401
www.ambottawa.esteri.it
There are Italian consulates in Montréal,
Toronto, Edmonton and Vancouver.

Spanish Embassy Canada
74 Stanley Avenue, Ottawa, Ontario, K1M 1P4
Tel 613/747-2252, 613/747-7293
www.maec.es
There are Spanish consulates in Toronto and
Montréal.

US Embassy Ottawa
490 Sussex Drive, Ottawa, Ontario, K1N 1G8
Tel 613/688-5335
http://canada.usembassy.gov

In addition to its embassy, the US maintains
consulates in the following cities:

US Consulate Halifax
Suite 904, Purdy's Wharf Tower II, 1969 Upper
Water Street, Halifax, Nova Scotia, B3J 3R7
Tel 902/429-2480

US Consulate Montréal
1155 rue St.-Alexandre, Montréal, Québec,
H2Z 1Z2
P.O. Box 65, Postal Station Desjardins, Montréal,
Québec, H5B 1G1
Tel 514/398-9695

US Consulate Québec City
2 place Terrasse-Dufferin, C.P. 939, Québec City,
Québec, G1R 4T9
Tel 418/692-2095

US Consulate Toronto
360 University Avenue, Toronto, Ontario,
M5G 1S4
Tel 416/595-1700

US Consulate Winnipeg
860-201 Portage Avenue, Winnipeg, Manitoba,
R3B 3K6
Tel 204/940-1800

US Consulate Calgary
615 Macleod Trail S.E., Calgary, Alberta,
T2G 4T8, Tel 403/266-8962

US Consulate Vancouver
1095 West Pender Street, Vancouver, British
Columbia, V6E 2M6
Tel 604/685-4311

MEDIA

NEWSPAPERS AND MAGAZINES

Nationals

There are two so-called "national" newspapers in Canada, *The Globe and Mail* and *The National Post*. Both are sold at newsstands and convenience stores across the country, though because they are published in Toronto some Canadians do not consider them truly "national."

Macleans Magazine is a monthly news magazine published in Toronto, and contains good listings of what is happening throughout Canada; you can usually find it at newsstands across the country.

For lifestyle issues in the major cities, try either *Toronto Life* magazine, famous for its restaurant listings, or *Vancouver* magazine, which is a similar publication. Montréal does not have a comparable magazine.

Local Newspapers

The major Canadian cities have their own newspapers, with circulations that can be greater than that of the nationals. Toronto newspapers include the *Toronto Star* and the *Toronto Sun*.

In Montréal the major daily in English is the *Montréal Gazette*. There are several newspapers in French, the most popular being *La Presse* and the tabloid *Le Journal de Montréal*.

The two major newspapers in Vancouver are the *Vancouver Province* and the *Vancouver Sun*. Ottawa has two major dailies, the *Ottawa Citizen* and the *Ottawa Sun*. In Québec City, the major newspaper is *Le Soleil*. All the above have internet versions.

Other important publications include the *Calgary Herald*, the *Edmonton Journal* and the *Winnipeg Free Press*. There is also a variety of ethnic publications in major cities.

The following website provides access to a wide range of Canadian newspapers as soon as they are published: www.broadcast-live.com/newspapers/canadian.html.

Foreign Press

American newspapers are sold at newsstands in the major cities, notably the *New York Times*, the *Financial Post*, the *Wall Street Journal* and *USA Today*. They are less common elsewhere.

Certain other foreign newspapers are available in specialized stores in the major cities (tourist offices can supply the names of these outlets), including *The Times* of the UK, the French paper, *Le Monde*, and *Der Spiegel* from Germany.

TELEVISION AND RADIO

Television reaches most Canadian homes, even in the extreme north, which benefits from satellite service. The major broadcaster of English and French television and radio across Canada is the publicly funded Canadian Broadcasting Corporation, or CBC (www.cbc.ca). CBC television has commercials, though there are none on the radio stations.

On the cable network, the CBC has a 24-hour news channel, "CBC Newsworld," which broadcasts in both official languages. Other national broadcasters include CTV and Global in English and TVA in French.

CABLE CHANNELS

Where cable service is available, there is a wide choice of channels. Popular Canadian cable channels include the Weather Network; Bravo!, an arts channel; TSN, the Sports Network; MuchMusic, Canada's rock music channel; the Discovery Channel, Canadian science; the Canadian History Channel; and the Life Network, a Canadian lifestyles channel.

Many American cable networks are also accessible, including the major television networks CBS, ABC, NBC and PBS.

***Opposite** Chapters Bookshop and Paramount IMAX cinema on Peter Street, downtown Toronto*

BOOKS AND MOVIES

BOOKS

Canada has a number of writers of international acclaim. In recent years three have won the Booker prize—Yan Martel (*The Life of Pi*; 2002), Margaret Atwood (*The Blind Assassin*; 2000) and Michael Ondaatje (*The English Patient*; 1992), though none of these books is set in Canada.

Considered the grand old man of Canadian literature, Robertson Davies set many of his books in his native Ontario. The Deptford Trilogy is among his best-known works: *Fifth Business* (1970), *The Manticore* (1972) and *World of Wonders* (1975). Among others, he also wrote the Cornish Trilogy: *The Rebel Angels* (1981), *What's Bred in the Bone* (1985) and *The Lyre of Orpheus* (1988).

Two other Ontario classics are Stephen Leacock's *Sunshine Sketches of a Little Town* (1912) and Ralph Connor's *The Man from Glengarry* (1901).

Farley Mowat's adventure stories are mainly set in northern Canada: *People of the Deer* (1952), *Lost*

in the Barrens (1956), *Never Cry Wolf* (1963) and The Snow Walker (1975). He wrote a fascinating but somewhat controversial book on Newfoundland, *A Whale for the Killing* (1972).

Two splendid historical novels are set in Québec City during the French Regime: *William Kirby's The Golden Dog* (1877), and Willa Cathar's *Shadows on the Rock* (1931).

To understand linguistic tensions, read Hugh Maclennan's *Two Solitudes* (1945), or Gabrielle Roy's *The Tin Flute*—a translation of *Bonheur d'Occasion* (1945).

Two very different views of Montréal life include the works of playwright Michel Tremblay, *Albertine in Five Times* (1986) and *Les Belles Soeurs* (1992); and Mordecai Richler's stories of Jewish Montréal, *The Apprenticeship of Duddy Cravitz* (1959) and *St. Urbain's Horseman* (1971).

A Prairie classic is W. O. Mitchell's *Who has Seen the Wind* (1947), while a unique take on the First Peoples of British Columbia is artist Emily Carr's *Klee Wyck* (1941). The nature books of Archie Belaney (a.k.a. Grey Owl) include *Pilgrims of the Wild* (1934), *The Adventures of Sajo and her Beaver People* (1935) and *Tales of an Empty Cabin* (1936).

Pierre Berton has written many popular, readable history books. His volumes on the construction of the Canadian Pacific Railway, *The National Dream* (1970) and *The Last Spike* (1971), are required reading before taking the train across Canada. He also wrote two books on the War of 1812: *The Invasion of Canada* (1980) and *Flames across the Border* (1982).

Before visiting Prince Edward Island, read Lucy Maud Montgomery's wonderful *Anne of Green Gables* (1908). Of the several film versions, the best was a series produced by the CBC in the 1980s.

The books of Thomas Raddall bring Nova Scotia to life, notably *The Governor's Lady* (1960). American writer E. Annie Proulx's *The Shipping News* (1993) won a Pulitzer prize; this tale of outpost life in Newfoundland was made into a movie starring Kevin Spacey in 2001.

MOVIES

I Confess (Alfred Hitchcock, 1953)

Montgomery Clift plays a priest framed for murder in Québec.

Kamouraska (Claude Jutra, 1973)

French writer Anne Hébert set this classic love story in the village of Kamouraska in the Lower St. Lawrence.

The Apprenticeship of Duddy Kravitz (Ted Kotcheff, 1974)

Mordecai Richler's best-selling novel, set in Montréal, features a young schemer (played by Richard Dreyfuss) growing up in a poor Jewish neighborhood.

Maria Chapdelaine (TGilles Carle, 1985)

Louis Hémon's haunting story of a young girl and the three men who loved her stars Carole Laure.

Jesus of Montréal (Denys Arcand, 1989)

Lothaire Bluteau stars in this dramatic story set in Montréal.

Black Robe (Bruce Beresford, 1991)

Beresford's splendid historical movie traces the life of a young Jesuit priest in the 17th century in the area that is now Ontario. It stars Lothaire Bluteau.

Grey Owl (Richard Attenborough, 1999)

This dramatic movie relates the life of Englishman, Archie Belaney, who took an Amerindian name, Grey Owl, and ethnic identity. Pierce Brosnan stars.

TOURIST OFFICES

PROVINCIAL TOURIST OFFICES

The best place to start collecting information on Canada or on a particular region is at the provincial tourist departments. Each Canadian province or territory operates a tourist office, which you can contact for free information (npanel below). They will send you a map of the province or territory, a list of accommodations, a list of things to do, and a host of other information. Contact them by mail, phone or email. Normally you cannot visit in person but they all operate websites. Some are really helpful and user-friendly, but others are more commercial and have less to interest vsitors.

LOCAL AND CITY TOURIST OFFICES

It's worthwhile stopping at the local tourist office in the towns and cities you visit. They can help you find accommodations, supply you with free maps, and direct you to sights, tourist attractions and restaurants.

Gas (petrol) stations sell useful maps. However, they will not be as good as the maps that you can get free at the tourist office.

Montréal

www.tourism-montreal.org

Montréal's tourist office, Centre Infotouriste, is at 1001 Dorchester Square in the heart of downtown. It's open daily 9 to 6, with extended hours in the summer months. Maps, a visitor guide and a variety of free information are available for the whole of Québec, as well as the city. Bus tours start from here (☎ 514/873-2015). There's also a tourist information center in Vieux Montréal, at 174 rue Notre-Dame Est.

Vancouver

www.tourismvancouver.com

Vancouver's TouristInfo Centre is at 200 Burrard Street in the Waterfront Centre. Free maps, a visitor guide and information on local attractions are available, and city bus tours start here. Open daily 8.30–6 with extended hours in the summer months (☎ 604/683-2000).

Toronto

www.torontotourism.com

Toronto does not have a good central tourist office, but you can visit Tourism Toronto at 207 Queens Quay West on the waterfront. This is not a proper tourist office, though the staff will give you a free visitor guide and map if you ask, and there are a few brochures you can pick up here. The office is open only business hours (☎ 416/203-2600).

Ottawa

www.canadascapital.igc.ca

The National Capital Commission runs an information center opposite the Parliament Buildings (90 Wellington Street, ☎ 613/239-5000 or 800/465-1867; www. canadascapital.gc.ca). Free maps, a visitor guide and other information are available. The center is open daily and there is a selection of videos. Ottawa Tourism has its office at 130 Albert Street, Suite 1800 (☎ 613/237-5150 or 800/363-4465; www.ottawatourism.ca), and visitors are welcome to call in for information.

PROVINCIAL TOURIST OFFICES

Alberta
Travel Alberta
P.O. Box 2500, Edmonton, Alberta, T5J 2Z4
Tel 780/427-4321, 800/252-3782
www.travelalberta.com

British Columbia
Tourism British Columbia
Box 9830, 1803 Douglas Street, Suite 300, Victoria, British Columbia, V8W 9W5
http://uk.britishcolumbia.travel

Manitoba
Travel Manitoba
7th Floor, 155 Carlton Street, Winnipeg, Manitoba, R3C 3H8
Tel 204/927-7800, 800/665-0040
www.travelmanitoba.com

New Brunswick
Tourism and Parks, P.O. Box 12345, Campbellton, New Brunswick, E3N 3T6

Tel 800/561-0123
www.tourismnewbrunswick-canada.com

Newfoundland and Labrador
Newfoundland and Labrador Department of Tourism, Culture and Recreation
P.O. Box 8700, St. John's, Newfoundland, A1B 4J6
Tel 800/563-6353
www.newfoundlandandlabrador.com

Northwest Territories
Northwest Territories Tourism
P.O. Box 610, Yellowknife, Northwest Territories, X1A 2N5
Tel 867/873-7200, 800/661-0788
www.explorenwt.com

Nova Scotia
Nova Scotia Tourism
P.O. Box 456, Halifax, Nova Scotia, B3J 2R5

Tel 800/565-0000, 902/425-5781
http://.novascotia.com

Nunavut
Nunavut Tourism
P.O. Box 1450, Iqaluit, Nunavut, X0A 0H0
Tel 867/979-6551, 866/686-2888
www.nunavuttourism.com

Ontario
Ontario Tourism
Queen's Park, Toronto, Ontario, M7A 2E1
Tel 905/282-1721, 800/668-2746
www.ontariotravel.net

Prince Edward Island
Tourism PEI
P.O. Box 940 Charlottetown, Prince Edward Island, C1A 7M5
Tel 902/368-4444, 800/463-4734
www.gov.pe.ca/visitorsguide/

Québec
Tourisme Québec
P.O. Box 979, Montréal, Québec, H3C 2W3
Tel 877/266-5687, 514/873-2015, (toll-free from UK: 0800/051/7055)
www.bonjourquebec.com

Saskatchewan
Tourism Saskatchewan
1922 Park Street, Regina, Saskatchewan, S4N 7M4
Tel 877/237-2273
www.sasktourism.com

Yukon
Department of Tourism and Culture
P.O. Box 2703, Whitehorse, Yukon, Y1A 2C6
Tel 800/661-0494
http://traveltouryukon.com

Québec City

www.quebecregion.com

Québec's tourist office is at 835 avenue Wilfrid-Laurier, near the eastern end of the Parc des Champs-de-Bataille. Free maps, a visitor guide and information on all attractions in the province are available. The office is open daily 10 to 4 with extended hours in the summer (☎ 418/522-0830).

Halifax

www.halifaxinfo.com

The International Visitor Centres in Halifax are at situated on Scotia Square Mall on Duke Street, near the Barrington Street intersection, and at Sackville Landing on the Waterfront. At these offices you can pick up a free map of the city and the province, a visitor guide to the city and to each region of Nova Scotia, and a whole range of other tourist information. The center is open daily (☎ 902/490-4000).

OPENING TIMES

BANKS

Banking hours are usually Monday through Friday 9.30 to 4, though this can vary with the branch (some open at 9am, others close at 3pm). In addition, some branches have extended hours (until 5pm or 6pm) on certain days, usually Thursday or Friday. All banks are closed on public holidays. As far as changing money is concerned, currency exchange offices have longer operating hours than banks and often lower service charges. Hours tend to be Monday to Friday 9am to 5pm, and Saturday 9am to 12 noon.

DOCTORS AND PHARMACIES

Every Canadian town or city has a pharmacy that is open 24 hours, and in major urban areas pharmacies are often open until 11pm. Tourist offices or police stations can supply their addresses and also the locations of medical clinics and their hours. Major urban areas have clinics operating seven days a week, but not necessarily all night.

MUSEUMS AND GALLERIES

Opening hours of museums and the principal art galleries can vary widely. Museums usually open Tuesday to Sunday 10am to 5pm; art galleries often open at 11am. Many museums are closed on Mondays, especially off-season. Most major museums have one evening a week when they are open late (until about 9pm) and they are usually free after 5.30pm on that evening. Small museums in out-of-the-way places may close for lunch.

OFFICES

Canadian offices have increasingly gone over to flexible working hours, with employees arriving and leaving over a staggered period. In general, though, someone should always be available Monday to Friday between 9am and 5pm (or 4pm in government offices).

STORES

In general, stores open Monday to Friday 9am to 6pm, with later hours (usually 9pm) on Thursday and Friday evenings. In some cities, the downtown stores open Monday to Friday at 10am. Normal Saturday hours are 9am to 5pm, and, where open, Sunday hours are usually 12 noon to 5pm.

Shopping malls tend to have longer hours than the downtown stores; they often close between 7.30pm and 9pm. In certain tourist areas (for example Old Montréal and

PUBLIC HOLIDAYS

National holidays are celebrated across the country:
(Government offices and banks are closed, some stores are open)

New Year's Day	January 1	
Good Friday	Easter	
Easter Monday	Easter	
Victoria Day	3rd Monday of May	
National Aboriginal Day	June 21	
Canada Day	July 1	
Labor Day	1st Monday of September	
Thanksgiving	2nd Monday of October	
Remembrance Day	November 11	
Christmas Day	December 25	
Boxing Day	December 26	
Holidays in particular provinces or regions:		
Family Day	3rd Monday of February	Alberta, Ontario and Saskatchewan
St. Patrick's Day	March 17	Newfoundland and Labrador
St. George's Day	April 23	Newfoundland and Labrador
National Day	June 24	Québec
Discovery Day	June 24	Newfoundland and Labrador
Nunavut Day	July 9	Nunavut
Orangeman's Day	July 12	Newfoundland and Labrador
Heritage Day	1st Monday of August	Alberta
British Columbia Day	1st Monday of August	British Columbia
New Brunswick Day	1st Monday of August	New Brunswick
Civic holiday	1st Monday of August	Ontario, Manitoba, Saskatchewan, Northwest Territories, Nunavut
Natal Day	1st Monday of August	Nova Scotia
	(varies in Halifax — usually July or August)	
Natal Day	Usually 1st Monday of August (by proclamation)	Prince Edward Island
Regatta Day/ civic holiday	August (fixed by council orders)	Newfoundland and Labrador
Discovery Day	3rd Monday of August	Yukon

www.canadianvintners.com
The website of the Canadian Vintners Association gives details of wines and wine producing areas.

Parks Canada
www.pc.gc.ca
The website gives comprehensive information about more than 40 national parks in Canada and more than 160 national historic sites.

Post
www.canadapost.ca
Information on postal services and postage rates within Canada.

Rail
www.viarail.ca
For details on passenger train travel including online booking.

Sport
www.pch.gc.ca/progs/sc
Information on Canadian sports at the government's Sport Canada website.

Visas
http://cic.gc.ca
The Canadian Government Citizenship and Immigration Service website gives details of the requirements for entry into Canada.

Visitors with Disabilities
www.ccdonline.ca
Council of Canadians with Disabilities
926–294 Portage Avenue, Winnipeg, Manitoba, R3C 0B9
Tel 204/947-0303
www.canparaplegic.org
Canadian Paraplegic Association
1101 Prince of Wales Drive, Suite 230, Ottawa, Ontario, K2C 3W7
Tel 613/723-1033
The above organizations offer advice to mobility-challenged visitors.

Weather
www.weatheroffice.gc.ca
Environment Canada's website is a good stop for planning for the weather.

Québec), stores selling souvenirs and other tourist-related items will remain open late into the night if there's any chance of customers dropping by.

SUPERMARKETS
Supermarkets in the suburban areas of the large towns and cities often have longer hours than regular stores, though they can suffer from a shortage of check-out personnel at certain times of the day. These supermarkets tend to stay open until 10 or 11pm every night.

RESTAURANTS
Restaurants that offer breakfast will naturally be open early—6am or even before that. Otherwise they generally open for lunch from around 12 noon to 3pm, close for the afternoon, and then open again at around 6pm or 7pm for the evening. All of the big cities will have late-night establishments, catering to the after-theater and nightclub crowd.

USEFUL WEBSITES
GENERAL INFORMATION ABOUT CANADA
http://canada.gc.ca
http://canadainternational.gc.ca
These government of Canada websites provide information and services about culture, immigration, tourism and more.
www.travelcanada.ca
This is the dedicated travel website of the Canadian Tourism Commission.

Customs
www.cbsa-asfc.gc.ca
Find out what you can and cannot import into or take out of Canada.

Culture and History
www.culturecanada.gc.ca
Canadian government websites for visitors seeking Canadian culture and heritage.
www.culture.ca
A useful one-stop national lifestyle guide.
www.histori.ca
The bilingual educational website of the magazine Historica promotes the teaching of Canadian history and heritage.

Currency
www.bank-banque-canada.ca/ en/ exchform.htm
To see how many Canadian dollars you can buy, check the Bank of Canada's website.

Festivals
www.tourismexchange.com/ exchange/festivalseeker/en/ searchform.jsp
A one-stop search engine for details on the multitude of festivals and other events that are held across Canada, especially during the summer months.

Food and Wine
www.agr.gc.ca
The Agriculture Canada website provides a great deal of useful information.

LANGUAGES OF CANADA

Canada has two official languages — English and French. The reasons for this are historical. French settlement in the St. Lawrence Valley started in the early 17th century. No English-speaking settlers arrived until after the British conquest of 1760. At the time of Canadian Confederation in 1867, the English- and French-speaking populations were more or less equal in size. Today, less than a quarter of Canadians speak French as their mother tongue (6.7 million out of 31 million).

The country has large communities of peoples of other nationalities and languages, but none has official recognition.

FRENCH-SPEAKING COMMUNITIES

French Canadians are in every province, but their greatest concentration is in the province of Québec, where they comprise more than 85 percent of the population. These are the people known as the Québécois.

French-speaking people form more than a third of the population of New Brunswick, and are also prominent in Nova Scotia and Prince Edward Island—these are the Acadiens. Ontario has a sizable French-speaking population in Toronto and in the eastern part of the province, who are known as Franco-Ontariens.

Manitoba's distinct French-speaking community is in St.-Boniface and are known as Franco-Manitobins. There are also small French-speaking communities in Saskatchewan, Alberta and British Columbia.

THE FRENCH LANGUAGE

If you speak the French of France, you will find the language in Québec has a strong and highly recognizable accent—as close to the language of the mother country as the Texas accent is to the English of the UK.

The French spoken by the Acadians is different again. For instance, oui sounds like "why," and non is pronounced "nah." If you

have a good ear, you can detect the difference and a somewhat softer accent. It resembles the French of old France more than the dynamic language of French Montréal.

Differences of vocabulary that can cause unfortunate misunderstandings include words used for meals. In Québec, you eat *déjeuner* first thing in the morning, *dîner* at lunchtime, and *souper* in the evening. In France, breakfast is *petit-déjeuner*, the lunchtime meal is *déjeuner*, and *dîner* is the evening meal. If you are invited for *dîner* check what time to go or you may arrive for the wrong meal.

OTHER LANGUAGES

The official Canadian census of 2006 recorded a population of just over 32.6 million, of whom more than 17.8 million spoke English as their mother tongue and 6.8 million spoke French. The third-largest language group was Chinese, with more than a million people, followed by Italian and German, with just under half a million each.

Polish, Spanish and Tagalog (Filipino) speakers accounted for around 350,00 people each, and, Portuguese, Punjabi and Arabic were the mother tongue of more than 200,000 people each. Dutch, Greek and Vietnamese are each spoken by more than 100,000 individuals. Of First Nations languages, Cree has the most speakers, with 77,000. Inuktitut is spoken by about 32,000 people.

USEFUL FRENCH WORDS AND PHRASES

French	English
bonjour / bonsoir / bon nuit	good day / good evening / good night
au revoir	goodbye
oui / non	yes / no
merci / bienvenue	thank you / you're welcome
s'il vous plaît	please
Comment ça va?	How are you?
Très bien, merci	Very well, thank you
Ça va?	How's it going? (more colloquial)
douanes / frontière	customs / international border
autoroute / chemins / rue	highway / road / street
arrêt	stop (road sign)
aéroport	airport
métro / autobus / taxi	subway / bus / taxi
gare / train / billets	station / train / tickets
entrée / sortie	entrance / exit
droit / gauche	right / left
tout droit	straight ahead
nord / sud / est / ouest	north / south / east / west
matin / après-midi	morning / afternoon
soir / nuit	evening / night
Où est le restaurant / hôtel?	Where's the restaurant / hotel?
le menu / table d'hôte	the menu / table d'hote (fixed-price meal)
L'addition / la facture, s'il vous plaît	The check (bill), please
Combien?	How much?
déjeuner / dîner / souper / le thé	breakfast / lunch / dinner / tea
banque / toilettes	bank / washrooms (toilets)
cinéma / théâtre / concert	cinema / theater / concert
librarie / bibliothèque	bookstore / library
cathédrale / église	cathedral / church
musée / galerie d'art	museum / art gallery
centre d'achat / boutique de souvenirs	shopping mall / souvenir store
édifice / place	building / city square

SHOPPING

Canada has some wonderful shopping, with the opportunity to buy all kinds of goods in all kinds of retail outlets: cutting-edge technology in smart downtown locations; distinctive designer fashions in chic neighborhood boutiques; superb art and crafts from First Nations galleries; old-fashioned preserves and candies in re-created pioneer settlements; and the whole gamut of high-street stores selling just about everything you can think of.

Stores are generally well laid out, spotless and well stocked, and places to eat or grab a coffee and doughnut are never far away. In addition to the range of goods, there is a real pleasure in the retail experience that is due entirely to the exceptionally friendly and helpful service you receive from the staff. It seems that they really do want you to have a nice day.

SHOPPING MALLS

The malls in Canada are huge and modern—indeed, Canada has both the largest and second-largest malls in the world at Edmonton in Alberta and Burnaby in British Columbia. Many incorporate a multiplex movie theater, some have nightclubs, and all have food courts and restaurants. There might be a play area for kids, special discount offers for tourists (check at the information booth on arrival) and special events.

Some of the city malls occupy conversions of older buildings, like the splendidly upscale Queen's Quay Terminal in Toronto, or Vancouver's characterful Lonsdale Quay, complete with a bustling market area.

Though they can vary considerably in size, most of the malls have pretty much the same national and international chain stores, and the same fast-food chains in their food courts, which means you can set out with some confidence about finding what you are looking for. This doesn't necessarily detract from the

pleasure of browsing, particularly for visitors from outside North America who are not familiar with the stores, and it certainly doesn't mean that when you've seen one, you've seen them all.

DISCOUNT MALLS

Shoppers with an eye for a bargain will want to head for one of the discount malls—and there is no

Above *Eaton Centre*
Opposite *Seal skin garments at Rannva Designs, Nunavut*

shortage of these: there's even one over on Prince Edward Island. Here you'll find brand-name and designer outlets with up to 70 percent off the normal retail price, mostly for discontinued lines. One of the biggest and best known is the Dixie Mall, just outside Toronto, which has a range of low-price goods of variable quality.

DOWNTOWN SHOPPING

Main Street shopping can be tiring, but if you enjoy pounding the city streets you'll find a huge variety of stores and services, with fashion, electronics, sports goods and other specialty stores mingling with downtown malls, banks and restaurants.

Much more interesting, though, are the little enclaves that have developed their own specialties. Most obvious are the Chinatowns, Little Italys and other nationality-based areas. Some towns are entirely influenced by a particular nationality, such as Kitchener, Ontario, with a large German population (and consequently a really good Oktoberfest, ▷ 241). You will also find that in the bigger cities independent fashion designers' boutiques tend to cluster together in trendy neighborhoods; antiques dealers and fine art galleries do the same, or share one large building to create a market atmosphere; and there will always be street markets with lots of noise and character. Tourist offices can point you in the right direction.

SMALL TOWN SHOPPING

Just about every province has small towns or villages that are known for their concentration of craftspeople, artists, book-sellers and individual boutiques, and these are wonderful places to visit, invariably peaceful, low-key and friendly. you can amble in and out of stores crammed with interesting unusual items. Mennonite towns, where the lifestyle has remained unchanged for a century, are fascinating, with residents in old-style clothing getting around by pony and trap. First Nations craft stores are also worth a visit, but not every reservation is geared toward tourists, so make inquiries locally about where you should go.

SOUVENIRS

There are many distinctively Canadian goods that will recall your visit for many years to come, including Inuit soapstone carvings and other First Nations art and crafts. There are plenty of galleries that guarantee authenticity, in addition to those run by the artists and artisans themselves. Up in the Yukon there are a number of jewelry designers producing pieces from local gold and gemstones—or you can just buy a raw nugget.

Much of the clothing available is unmistakably Canadian—not just the T-shirts and sweatshirts with destinations or maple leaves emblazoned on the front, but also real lumberjack shirts, moccasins, cowboy boots and traditional First Nations beaded suede shirts and dresses. Sport fans will enjoy the range of team shirts and hats from the leading hockey and baseball teams.

Maple syrup is an obvious choice, available everywhere from supermarkets to the sugar shacks where it is produced. Canadian confectionery includes the Ganong brand from New Brunswick and Laura Secord chocolates.

There is nothing like the written word to bring back fond memories, and good choices here include *The Spell of the Yukon*, a collection of Robert Service's frontier ballads; *The Shipping News* by Annie Proulx, set in Newfoundland; *The Apprenticeship of Duddy Kravitz* reflecting author Mordecai Richler's Montréal roots; or the Prince Edward Island classic, *Anne of Green Gables* by Lucy Maud Montgomery.

FURS

Some visitors may be surprised, even shocked, to see so many

stores selling furs and clothing made from sealskin. Remember, however, that trade in these items is vital to the survival of many First Nations and Inuit communities, and that where demand has declined, these people have had to find alternatives to provide a livelihood, such as giving over their land to oil exploration or forestry, which has a devastating effect on the local ecology

TAXES

One thing that can catch visitors out is the fact that price tags do not include tax. When you pay for goods, 5 percent will be added for GST (Goods and Service Tax; TPS in Québec) plus PST (Provincial Sales Tax; TVQ in Québec). PST varies between the provinces (zero in oil-rich Alberta).

New Brunswick, Nova Scotia, and Labrador/Newfoundland now have HST (Harmonized Sales Tax), which is a combination of GST and PST.

OPENING HOURS

Stores are generally open from 9 or 10am to 5.30 or 6pm, with late opening on Thursday and Friday, and many are open on Sundays from noon. Times vary though, and big cities will have stores open well into the evening most days. Shopping malls also stay open late, generally closing between 7.30 and 9pm.

Canada has produced many world-class performers in all branches of the arts, and the range of entertainments available is enormous. Toronto is the entertainment hub of the country, the third-largest film and TV production center in North America (after LA and New York), and is alive with theater, orchestral concerts, comedy and live music performances year-round. Montréal and Vancouver are close behind, with their own slant on things, and every major city has plenty going on, from classical performances to pub music. Throughout the country, arts festivals provide concentrated culture at regular intervals, and some First Nations gatherings are open to all.

Canadians might be known as outdoors people—and they certainly do enjoy communing with nature—but they know how to party too, and the opportunities for living it up into the early hours (or even till dawn) are plentiful, at least in the cities. As everywhere, things are quieter out in the country, and in the north might be confined to gathering for a drink beneath the midnight sun or the aurora borealis, depending on the time of year.

THEATER

There's a thriving theater scene in Canada, including musicals and long-running plays in big city theaters, and the classics, such as the renowned Shakespeare Theatre in Stratford, Ontario, and Shaw Festival at Niagara-on-the-Lake. Modern plays and experimental works by local writers are often staged. There are also open-air theater performances in some spectacular locations.

CLASSICAL MUSIC AND DANCE

Canada's cultural institutions include a National Ballet and National Opera Company, in addition to world-class provincial orchestras and soloists.

There are superb concert halls in all the major cities, which attract top musicians, orchestras and opera companies from around the world. Every major city will have a schedule of classical music concerts.

FILM

Canada's National Film Board was awarded an Oscar to mark its 50th anniversary, recognizing the fine contribution it has made to the world of cinema.

Canada has a reputation for producing quality art films and animations, and its cities and landscapes have become popular among US movie and TV companies for location work: Vancouver hosted many series of *The X-Files*, and Toronto will have between 20 and 40 film crews on location on any day of the year (it's often used as a stand-in for New York).

COMEDY

Canada has produced a long, long list of comedians who have earned international fame, including Jim Carrey, Mike Myers, Dan Aykroyd, John Candy and Martin Short.

The international Just For Laughs Festival in Montréal (▷ 85) is televised worldwide, and all the

Below *The storm scene in* Pericles, Prince of Tyre, *performed during the 2003 season at Bard on the Beach, Vancouver*

major cities have comedy clubs, notably Toronto's Second City, and the Yuk Yuks chain.

POPULAR MUSIC
Bryan Adams, Avril Lavigne, Alanis Morissette, Shania Twain, Neil Young and Céline Dion are just a few of Canada's many musicians who are known internationally. All kinds of music can be found throughout Canada, and Toronto, Vancouver, Calgary and Montréal feature on most world-tour schedules of the big-name singers and bands.

World-class jazz clubs are easy to find and blues clubs are equally widespread.

FOLK AND COUNTRY MUSIC
Singers such as Gordon Lightfood and Anne Murray introduced the world to Canadian folk music, and folk clubs are thriving throughout the country, with lots of summer festivals. The Maritimes have a strong tradition of fiddle music and Celtic song.

Country music is popular everywhere, but especially in the Prairies, where the cowboy culture is alive and well.

SMOKING
There's a general no-smoking rule in all places of public entertainment, including most open-air venues.

NIGHTCLUBS
All the big cities have a choice of nightclubs. There are plenty of high-tech dance clubs, with DJs spinning the latest rhythms, big-screen music videos and perhaps more than one dance floor; some of these clubs include chill-out areas and food service. Most of them won't really get going before 11pm or midnight and will continue till between 2am and dawn.

There are also cabaret clubs, cocktail lounges and piano bars, attracting a more mature crowd.

CASINOS
Gambling has been legal in Canada only since 1969, but you will find plenty of chances to indulge, with superb casinos in or near the major cities—and Niagara Falls has three. In addition to all the favorite table games—roulette, blackjack, craps, and so on—they usually have thousands of slot machines, restaurants and spectacular shows. Some casinos, such as Diamond Tooth Gerties, have been set up to raise funds for local causes.

There will always be an age limit—usually over 18 or 19—and admission is free (though there may be a charge for stage shows).

LIVE MUSIC VENUES
Canada's vibrant music scene gives rise to a huge number of venues featuring national or international bands, or showcasing local acts. You might see a soon-to-be-famous band in a fairly modest club, but even if it's just the local favorites, standards are pretty high everywhere.

Many venues specialize in a particular type of music, so it's easy to find a place to suit your taste. Others feature different styles on different nights of the week.

Some clubs levy a cover charge while others don't; sometimes it depends what is on, or which night of the week you go. The music usually kicks off at about 9 or 10pm, and bars that are open all day will start charging admission only after a certain time.

PUBS AND BARS
Sometimes all you need is good company, and that's the time to head for one of the many pubs and neighborhood bars. Canadians are generally outgoing and interested in their visitors, so conversation comes easy. In summer you can usually find a place with tables outside.

Pubs vary in character, sometimes replicating an English pub, sometimes with an Irish theme and sometimes more Americanized.

Unlike British pubs, you will get table service for drinks as well as food. tips are expected, even if you stand at the bar.

GAY CLUBS
Canada is very positive toward gay people: Toronto has huge Gay Pride and Aids Awareness events every year, and Montréal is a renowned gay destination.

Every major city has at least one or two gay clubs (Montréal has more than 100), with dancing and stage shows. Many are popular with—and welcoming to—a straight crowd too.

SMOKING
Canada is still struggling with legislation over smoking in bars. After imposing a blanket ban, many provinces had to backtrack following vociferous opposition from bar owners, who claimed they were losing custom. Rules vary from place to place, so check in advance if it's important to you.

Below *Yuk Yuk's Comedy Theatre, Toronto*

SPORTS AND ACTIVITIES

An entire book could easily be devoted to sports and activities in Canada—especially activities. There are seemingly endless possibilities, summer and winter, in every part of the country. There is also avid support for certain spectator sports. Hockey is a national obsession, and baseball and Canadian football games attract big crowds—the atmosphere at any of these can be electric. Violence (at least off the playing surface) is not an issue, and even if you are not a sports fan, the experience of being among all the hotdog-munching, enthusiastically vocal supporters is great fun.

BASEBALL

http://mlb.mlb.com

Baseball has a strong following, particularly in Toronto—its Blue Jays have played in the American League since 1976 and won the World Series in 1992 and 1993. Toronto was also the city in which the legendary Babe Ruth scored his first home run.

The season runs from April through September/October, so games are often played in bright sunshine—wear a hat, sunglasses and sunscreen, and bring binoculars if you can: some of the seats are a long way from the field. For the full experience, buy plenty of hotdogs and sodas, and join in the waves and interval keep-fit session.

BASKETBALL

www.nba.com

Although the game was invented by a Canadian, it is not particularly prominent here at a professional level, but the Toronto Raptors, established only in the mid-1990s, have made something of a mark in the NBA. The season runs from October through June.

CANADIAN FOOTBALL

www.cfl.ca

This is similar to American football, and therefore quite incomprehensible to most visitors from Europe, but if you're an enthusiast you can see CFL (Canadian Football League) games in Montréal, Toronto, Hamilton, Calgary, Edmonton, Ottawa, Regina, Winnipeg and Vancouver. The season is from late June to early November.

Important differences from American football—bigger ball, longer pitch, deeper end zone, field goalpost positioning, 12 players instead of 11, three downs instead of four—make for a faster game with more passing and less rushing at the opponents.

CLIMBING

Climbers automatically think of the Rocky Mountains and Laurentians,

Above *Snowboarding at Gray Rocks, Quebec*
Opposite *Slmon Arm, British Columbia*
Far right *The Manitoba Moose ice hockey team*

and those ranges certainly do have some great climbs (though they are not the only options by any means), with outfitters offering tuition, equipment and guided climbing trips. If you come in winter you can have a go at climbing a frozen waterfall too. It's sometimes hard to imagine the severity of the Canadian winter, so even experienced climbers should think very carefully about when to go.

FISHING
There are superb fishing opportunities, summer and winter, in the rivers and lakes, but you will need a license and regulations are strictly enforced, with regular warden patrols in even the remotest areas. Contact the tourist information office or make inquiries at an equipment store or outfitter.

Offshore fishing trips can be arranged at various points along the Atlantic and Pacific coasts. If you accidentally catch a lobster down east, throw it back immediately. Lobster fishing is a huge industry here and is strictly licensed.

In winter, ice-fishing is a popular pastime, in which you venture out onto a frozen lake, saw a hole through the thick ice, drop your line through it... and wait. In some places the hole is already cut for you, and you might get a little wooden hut on the ice where you can warm yourself.

GOLF
www.golfcanada.com
Golf is hugely popular in Canada, and there are more than 2,000 courses throughout the country in all kinds of territory, from spectacular mountains to seaside links and parklands. A number were designed by famous golfers. Glen Abbey, at Oakville, Ontario, is one of the best; the Top of the World course in Dawson City, Yukon (▷ 250), is the most northerly, with 24-hour daylight in mid-summer. The Canadian Open is held at a different venue each year.

For players, there's a great choice, including resort hotels that have superb golf courses on the grounds—Jasper is notable among these. Many ordinary hotels offer golf packages using nearby courses. Visitors are generally welcome, but it's advisable to make reservations for tee times, particularly in summer. Most courses have clubs and carts for rent. As everywhere, green fees vary.

The playing season very much depends on weather conditions, but summers are pretty reliable, and spring and autumn can be glorious.

HIKING AND WALKING
Canadians are keen hikers, and there is a huge number of good trails of varying length all over Canada, particularly in the national and provincial parks. They are well mapped, sometimes signposted,

and guided hikes with a naturalist are often available.

If you plan to set off into the wilderness, check weather conditions, make sure you are fully equipped and wearing the proper gear, and let someone know where you are going. Good maps are available from park information offices and specialist bookstores.

HOCKEY
www.canadianhockey.ca
www.nhl.com
Don't call it ice hockey. To Canadians it's just hockey, and the other kind is called field hockey. The season runs from October to early April, when excitement reaches fever pitch as Canada's top teams vie with their US counterparts for the NHL (National Hockey League) championship. The national team is one of the best in the world, and in the 2006 Winter Olympics in Turin, Canada took the gold medal in the women's event.

Hockey is fast and furious (often literally), with a reputation for violence on the ice—a favorite joke goes: "I went to a boxing match last night, and a hockey game broke out"—but when the teams behave, it's tremendously exciting. Wear warm clothing, including a hat and gloves—it gets very cold sitting by the ice.

HORSE RACING

www.woodbineentertainment.com
Racetracks are located within proximity of all the major population centers, but the top one is the Woodbine track near Toronto, which hosts Canada's premier races with the richest prizes. Two-thirds of Canada's horse racing takes place in Ontario. Racetracks usually also have casino-style slot machines, feature thoroughbred, standard-bred or harness racing (sometimes all three), and when there's no live racing, events are beamed in from the US, Hong Kong and Australia.

HORSEBACK RIDING

The Prairies are Canada's cowboy country, with great opportunities for taking to the saddle. And there are places all over the country where you can go out on horseback, either on a guided ride or on your own (as long as you can demonstrate your competence). Stables offer trail-riding by the hour, the day or multiday trip, or you can stay at a guest ranch and work on the farm, round up cattle and ride for pleasure.

If you just want to watch expert riders, try to get to one of the many rodeos that are regularly held on the Prairies during summer.

HUNTING

Hunting is strictly regulated in Canada. Whatever you do, do not shoot a moose—even the locals have to enter a lottery to win a license to do so, and penalties for flouting the rules are severe, including imprisonment. First Nations and Inuits are exempt from these rules.

If you want to bring your own gun into Canada, you will need to contact the Canadian embassy in your country of residence to check on the regulations and consult customs and excise officials about airport security.

WATER SPORTS

The popular image of Canada usually includes a canoe on a stretch of calm water, with spectacular moun-tain scenery in the background. Wherever there is water, there's likely to be an outfitter providing canoes and kayaks. Sea-kayaking is also popular, and is a wonderful way to explore remote areas of the Atlantic and Pacific coastlines. Best of all, you can kayak among whales off both the Atlantic and BC coasts during the season.

Inland, on the majestic rivers, you can go whitewater rafting through boiling rapids—particularly exhilarating in spring and early summer when the meltwater adds extra power to the torrent. There are plenty of specialist companies here that have excellent safety records.

Divers can explore some of the clearest waters in the world off both the Atlantic and Pacific coasts, where, in addition to the marine life, there are wrecks to explore.

WILDLIFE WATCHING

The opportunity of seeing a bear or herd of caribou in the wild, or a pod of whales surfacing close to your boat, is a huge attraction in Canada, and there are plenty of companies offering organized trips. It's probably best to use these experts, since they know where to find what you are looking for and how best to maintain safety and not alarm the wildlife. Nevertheless, even a short hike in one of the national or provincial parks may offer sightings, and park offices can give advice about what is around.

You'll often see moose along the roadsides in certain areas—drive carefully. Aside from not wanting to harm the animal, it is akin to driving into a wall in terms of damage and injury.

For birdwatchers there are count-less reserves and observation points on migratory flight lines.

WINTER SPORTS

www.ski-guide.com/
Naturally, there are exceptionally good opportunities for winter sports in Canada. All over the country, winter snows bring the chance to do cross-country (or Nordic) and

Above Walking in the shade of Vancouver's Stanley Park
Right World Waterpark's wave pool is popular with all of the family

downhill skiing, snowboarding, snow-tubing, snowmobiling, snowshoeing, dogsled trips and skating.

The west and the Laurentians have the best resorts, notably Whistler, where the premier downhill and extreme sports competitions take place; it is set to co-host the 2010 Winter Olympics with Vancouver. Other premier locations include Blackcomb, Banff and Lake Louise, Kicking Horse near Calgary, and Tremblant in Québec. In Ontario, head for Collingwood and the Blue Mountain Resort. Even in top resorts, ski passes tend to cost less than in Europe, and elsewhere it's even cheaper.

There are thousands of skating rinks throughout Canada, but it's much more fun out in the open on lakes, ponds, rivers and canals (always check the ice is strong enough). Popular areas often have floodlighting for night-time skating, piped music and booths selling hot drinks and snacks. Rinks and some outdoor sites offer skate rental.

HEALTH AND BEAUTY

After lots of activities there's nothing like a bit of pampering, and Canada offers a wide range of ways to indulge.

There are lots of spas with a range of soothing options, from single treatments to visits tailored to your requirements. If you're in the Rockies, you can just go for a soak in one of the natural hot springs.

FOR CHILDREN

Canada is a fun country for kids, with lots of attractions, including theme parks, waterparks, zoos and wildlife parks, open farms, and science centers full of hands-on exhibits. Even the big cities have a larger number of things specifically for children than you would find in their European counterparts, and this is equally true of more modestly sized towns. In addition to the specific attractions, children will enjoy many of the same outdoor activities as their parents—enhanced, for them, by the sight of so many adults acting just like kids.

ACTIVITIES
There's a long list of activities that children will enjoy in Canada, including panning for gold in the Yukon, horseback riding on the Prairies, whale-watching off the British Columbian or the Atlantic coast, learning to ski, or simply Rollerblading around one of Canada's excellent city parks.

BEACHES
You might not think of Canada for a beach vacation, but there are some wonderful unspoiled stretches of sand on both the east and west coasts. Many of the lakes have sandy beacheswith safe swimming.

CONCESSIONS
There are invariably reduced admission charges for children and students (which sometimes can extend to age 30 in some places, with proof of student status), except in theme parks and waterparks, where only the tiniest toddlers and grandparents get a lower price. Many attractions offer a discounted charge for families.Children are not allowed in any bars, pubs, nightclubs or casinos.

MUSEUMS
Canada's museums are particularly child-friendly, and often have lively areas designed specially for kids, with interactive exhibits, interpreters to engage their interest, and fun demonstrations. Winnipeg, Ottawa and London (Ontario) have children's museums devoted entirely to the younger generation. Science museums also have a particular appeal, and just about every provincial capital has one.

Open-air museums are good for kids, too, where they can see real people role-playing in historic costumes. They can explore old homes, take a wagon ride and taste traditional candy.

NATIONAL AND PROVINCIAL PARKS
Canada has 39 national parks and hundreds of provincial parks. These are great places to let off steam and perhaps spot some wildlife you'd only see in a zoo back home—and many have special events for children. The relevant national park offices have details. Most offer canoeing or kayaking and other activities too.

SUMMER CAMPS
If your children have an independent nature, you can sign them up for a spell at summer camp (www.camppage.com/canada) where they can make new friends and have an exciting Canadian experience. There are camps for every kind of interest, from wilderness adventures to circus skills, and you can choose between residential or day camps.

THEME PARKS AND WATERPARKS
Canada has plenty of amusement parks, but Canada's Wonderland (▷ 240) in Ontario is the best; allow a full day or more to sample all the thrill rides and shows. Waterparks are abundant, and incorporate giant water slides and splash pools. These are usually open from about May to late August or September, when the weather is at its best and some may be heated. In winter, there are some indoor amusement complexes.

ZOOS, WILDLIFE PARKS AND AQUARIUMS
A sure bet for entertaining the little ones are the superb Toronto Zoo (▷ 193) and Vancouver Aquarium (▷ 310).

EATING

Canadian cuisine is a somewhat nebulous concept, given that it's such a young country with so many outside influences. Some say it doesn't exist at all, and in some restaurants it simply means they are using the best Canadian products. Nevertheless, there are certainly a few traditional dishes that you won't find anywhere else in the world, and top chefs in all the major cities are producing inventive and exciting dishes that can truly be regarded as Canadian.

Fusion remains a buzz word on the restaurant scene, notably in the Pacific Rim cuisine of the west coast, incorporating Canadian and Oriental influences. Elsewhere, the longer established French and British cuisines are mixed with Native Canadian, and further embellished with the ethnic culinary skills of more recent arrivals. This has created such exotic dishes as seared sea scallops on a potato pancake with lemongrass lobster sauce, or venison wellington stuffed with enoki mushrooms. The original Canadian cuisine is, of course, that of the First Nations, and there are opportunities to sample this, for instance at one of the many tribal pow-wows that take place during the year. Tourist offices will have details (▷ 378).

The choice of restaurants in Canada has increased enormously in recent years as the immigrant population has brought about a gastronomic revolution. Cities such as Toronto, Montréal and Vancouver are now compared with New York for quality and diversity. The abundance of fresh produce, wild game, locally reared beef, and freshly caught fish and shellfish, along with award-winning Canadian beers and wines, make dining throughout Canada a delectably memorable experience. In the major cities you'll find Greek, Italian, Polish, Ukrainian, Chinese, Vietnamese, Korean and Thai restaurants, to name just a few.

Not surprisingly, American chain restaurants have a strong presence. While meat and fish play a central role in many regional dishes, vegetarians and vegans can today find enough choice in most of the country, especially in the larger cities. Away from the cities choice of cuisine is more limited, but home-style cooking is often excellent and the service is friendly.

REGIONAL SPECIALTIES
The Atlantic provinces have their Acadian French, English and Scottish traditions, and proudly serve a tantalizing variety of seafood,

Above *Enjoy a picturesque meal at Cadero's Restaurant on the waterfront, Vancouver*

from robust chowders to dainty deep-sea scallops. Freshly caught Atlantic cod, lobster, shrimp and mussels are equally traditional fare. Steakhouses are popular, serving top-quality beef cooked to order, and many restaurants offer bison and caribou, adding their uniquely Canadian tastes and textures to many dishes. The rich ethnic flavors are reflected in dessert choices such as shoofly pie, chocolate mousse and strawberry cheesecake. Newfoundland's unusual cuisine includes brewis, a hard bread soaked and boiled with salt cod, which is eaten with fried salt-pork squares called scrunchions. Cod tongues and cheeks, and seal-flipper pie are other traditional dishes.

In Québec, restaurants offer a gastronomic pageant of fine French-style cooking. Laurentian pea soup, made of yellow split peas, is a Québecois specialty, as are fiddleheads (also a favorite in the Maritimes), the young shoots of the ostrich fern. The musical name refers to the similarity of the tightly curled fronds to the scroll of a violin head; they taste like a blend of broccoli, asparagus and globe artichoke. *Tarte au sucre* (sugar pie) is the favorite dessert choice here. Visitors to Montréal should sample the smoked meats, served in high-rise piles between two slices of rye bread. Most restaurants have an English-language menu, but you may have to ask for it. In restaurants with no liquor license, it's common practice to bring your own bottle of wine; they will happily open your bottle and provide glasses.

Ontario, especially Toronto, is where fusion cooking excels. Here, chefs create masterpieces using a palette of fine ingredients mixed with the inspiration of the world's cuisines in dishes such as maple-glazed duck or tea-smoked sea bass. Toronto's multiethnic population is reflected in the abundance of restaurants, from Japanese robata bars to Mexican cantinas. Locally produced Canadian cheddar originated in Ingersoll, Ontario, where raw milk

is used to make this tasty cheese. Corn, pumpkin, beans and peaches are locally grown and provide inspiration for such delights as pumpkin mousse. Traditional shoofly pie is a molasses dessert that satisfies anyone with a sweet tooth. Ottawa, like Toronto, offers a wide variety of choices.

In the Prairies the abundance of grain and game features on menus in the form of sourdough bread, bannocks (a griddle-baked flatbread made of oats or barley), Manitoba wild rice, barbecued ribs, Prairie-grazed beef, caribou, wild boar and bison. Traditional Native American fare, including turkey, cornbread, and Saskatoon pie, made of berries similar to blueberries, is popular. In the Rockies and British Columbia, Pacific and Arctic fish, Alaskan king crab and Fanny Bay oysters, plus wild game, appear on menus. Vancouver is recognized as having some of the best restaurant chefs in the country, who import the latest trends from Seattle, across the border. This city also has one of North America's largest Chinatowns, with some exceptionally good, authentic Chinese restaurants. However, it is the Ukrainian *pierogi* (filled dumpling) that is practically a national dish here.

The sparsely populated north is rather limited compared to other regions, but the quality, quantity and freshness of such wonderful home-made fare as home-smoked salmon, moose sausages, breads and jams guarantee wholesome, tasty meals.

MEALS

Breakfast and brunch: A typical Canadian breakfast includes fresh fruit, yogurt, cereal, bacon and eggs, sausages, home-smoked kippers, pancakes or waffles with maple syrup, hash browns, bannocks, forach (oatmeal, cream and sugar), toast, bagels, homemade preserves, and muffins. Continental breakfasts of croissant, bread, butter and jam are a lighter option, while brunch is a feast of breakfast and lunch dishes. Usually available weekends only, and generally a buffet, brunch may come with complimentary cocktails or wine, and can cost as little as $15 in some places, but not if wine is included!

Lunch: Set menus are excellent value in the larger cities, where you can eat for between $10 and $20.

Dinner: Dinner for two in a restaurant (excluding drinks) averages out to between $30 and $150. At top restaurants, the decor is often exquisite, but equally enjoyable are the little family-run restaurants that show off local heritage. The views from your table can offer such exotic sights as the aurora borealis in the north or Niagara Falls in Ontario.

WHERE TO EAT

Cafés and bistros: Cafés in all the cities offer an informal atmosphere with simple but good food at reasonable prices. Bistros are less formal than restaurants and the food is often of a very high standard.

Bars, brewpubs and pubs: Many bars in the cities have a happy hour, where you can enjoy free snacks along with your half-price drinks. Brewpubs offer a great selection of beers and standard pub food such as fish and chips, nachos and burgers. Pubs are informal, offering inexpensive burgers and pasta.

Restaurants: Some restaurants offer table d'hôte—a set menu with a set price, which is less expensive than choosing from the à la carte menu, although choices are limited.

WHAT TO DRINK

Coffee: In most diners and restaurants you pay for your first cup of coffee and the waiter or waitress refills it as many times as you like. Coffee is either regular (caffeinated) or decaf, black or with half-and-half (half milk, half cream) or cream—Canadians don't understand the term "white coffee." Sidewalk cafés like the Toronto-based Second Cup offer a large selection of excellent Italian coffees, and the US chain Starbucks has also moved in, although Tim Horton's is the one you'll see most.

Tea: Tea shops offer a selection of teas, including herbal, served with milk or lemon. If you want your tea brewed in the correct way—boiling water poured directly onto the tea or tea bag—you will have to spell it out carefully, otherwise you are likely to get a cup of hot water and a tea bag in the saucer.

Beer: Canadian beers, like American brews, are light and fizzy, and are always served ice cold. Canadians are fond of their native Molson and Labatts beers, and Moosehead, brewed in New Brunswick, and Great Western Beer from Saskatchewan are also popular. Foreign beers, including Heineken made under license in Canada, are widely available. Real-ale devotees should not despair. Canada has an increasing number of microbreweries producing a variety of British-style real ales, along with lagers, pilsners and bock. Brewpubs offer beers brewed on the premises (tours are sometimes available). If you are in a group, it's cheaper to purchase a pitcher of beer to share.

Wine: Wine drinking has gained popularity in the past decade and most restaurants offer a fine selection of imported wines, but do try Canada's own. Since the 1980s, Canadian wines, both red and white, under a VQA (Vintner's Quality Assurance) have gained international acclaim. Ontario's Niagara Peninsula produces wines similar to those of Burgundy and the Loire Valley. British Columbia's Okanagan region and Vancouver's coastal islands produce some very good Chardonnay, Merlot and Pinot Noir, as well as German varieties such as Riesling and Gewürztraminer. In addition, Ontario has become the largest producer of ice wine, a pricey dessert wine made from grapes picked and crushed while still frozen. There are also some vineyards in Québec and the Maritimes.

Spirits: A wide selection of spirits is available. Canadian Club is known all over the world, and has been based in Walkerville, Ontario, for about 150 years. VO rye whiskey is another domestic favorite. Cocktails using gin, rum, vodka kahlua and other spirits usually run from $6–$12, depending on the establishment.

Non-alcoholic drinks: Milkshakes, sodas, floats (soda and ice cream), and smoothies are all alternatives. In Canada, cider is a non-alcoholic apple drink, except in Québec.

MENU READER

apple butter: thick, dark brown apple preserve
Arctic char: a fish from the salmon family
assiette anglaise: cold meats
bangbelly: pork rice bun
biscuit: savory scone
brewis: hard bread boiled with salt cod
butter tarts: tarts made with butter, brown sugar, corn syrup and raisins
capelin: tiny fish similar to smelts
chokeberry: small deep-purple berry also called aronia
chowder: thick seafood soup usually made with milk or cream
cipate chicken: meat and vegetable casserole with biscuit topping
cookie: biscuit
cranberry: a red North American berry rich in vitamin C
crème brûlée: creamy baked custard with caramelized sugar
cretons: spicy pork pâté
decaf: decaffeinated coffee
dim sum: Chinese breakfast and lunch buffet of hors d'oeuvres
dulse edible: dried deep-purple seaweed from the Bay of Fundy
escargot: snails in garlic butter
fat archie: Cape Breton molasses cookie
fiddleheads: young green shoots of the ostrich fern
finnan haddie: smoked haddock
foie gras: liver of specially fattened goose or duck
fricot: a hearty chicken soup
grunt: stewed fruit and dumplings
hash browns/home fries: pan-fried diced potatoes
ice wine: white wine made from pressed frozen grapes
Lunenburg sausage: Nova Scotia's hot spicy sausage
maple taffy: hot maple syrup chilled on snow and wrapped onto a stick
molasses thick: dark syrup produced from refining sugar or sorghum

Nanaimo bars: chocolate bars, originating in Nanaimo, Vancouver Island
partridgeberry: red berries used in preserves and pies
pemmican: dried meat preserved in cranberries and fat; a staple for mountaineers
pierogi: Ukrainian dumplings filled with cheese, potato, meat or vegetables
Posole stew: hominy and meat stew
poutine: french fries, curd cheese and gravy
poutine rappé: potato dumpling with salt-pork filling
rapie pie: meat pie topped with potato
Saskatoon pie: berry pie popular in Saskatchewan
scone: small, round, sweet cake
scrapple: fried pork
scrunchions: fried salt-pork squares
shoofly pie: molasses or brown-sugar pie
snow crab: crab of polar waters with enormously long legs
Solomon Grundy: marinated herring
sourdough: bread made from fermented dough
sugar pie/tarte au sucre: open tart with a caramel-flavor or molasses filling
tourtière: meat and potato pie
toutons: pork bread
trempette: bread, cream and maple syrup

STAYING

Canadians in general have a reputation for being polite and friendly, and this is nowhere more apparent than in the hospitality industry. You may occasionally meet an indifferent motel receptionist or a tetchy waiter, but it's extremely unusual, and for the most part you are made to feel very welcome wherever you go—and this is true across the board, from swanky downtown hotels to budget motels.

Canada has every type of accommodation: luxury hotels and vacation resorts equal to any in the world; chic boutique-style "designer" hotels in the cities; and beautiful historic properties serving as intimate bed-and-breakfasts. There are international-style, mid-range chain hotels in all the main towns and cities, and roadside motels are dotted along all the principal highways. To all of these, you can add the places that offer something particular, like the ranches where you can experience the cowboy's life, the fishing lodges that give access to Canada's premier fishing lakes and rivers, hotels with a championship golf course on the grounds, and winter resorts that have snowmobile parking and a handy ski-lift. Every kind of location is there, whether you want to be in the hub of the downtown action, or get so far away from it all that you have to fly in on a floatplane.

RESERVATIONS AND LATE ARRIVALS

Usually you can travel at will in Canada and find somewhere to stay without too much difficulty. In most cases, the supply fits the demand, and all towns, cities and vacation hotspots are well served with hotels, motels and restaurants. However, popular locations do fill up quickly in high season, so it is advisable to make a reservation well in advance. This is also true if your requirements are specific, or if there's a festival or convention coinciding with your visit. If you are heading north to the more remote areas, take a look at a map, make sure you understand the scale and get to grips with the enormous distances that can exist between settlements. These trips will need careful planning and you should make sure you have a room waiting for you at the end of each day. Should you be running late on your journey, it's a wise precaution to call

the hotel and let them know your expected arrival time so that you don't lose the room. If you do show up in town without a reservation, the tourist office may be able to help.

CATEGORIES OF ACCOMMODATIONS

Hotels in large cities range from high-price luxury establishments to dingy downtown joints, with fewer hotels available in the mid-price range. Luxury hotels charge from around $250 for a double room, with $350 getting you a deluxe room with amenities such as refrigerator, microwave, high-speed internet access, CD-player and VCR. In some boutique hotels rates can soar to more then $1,000 per night. For a mid-price hotel, around $130 for a double, head for one of the chains such as Best Western or Holiday

Above *Experience the wilderness in comfort with a log cabin set amongst the forests of Wells Grey Provincial Park*

Inn, where you'll get a room that's comfortable and clean, but without the fine linen and extras. The lower end of the scale, at about $45 to $70 for a double, gets you a room that is central, often above a bar, and clean but run down.

Motels are usually on the highways outside of towns and may be called motor hotels, lodges or inns. Prices mostly range from $45 to $120 for a double, with many offering free beds for children sharing a room with parents. Weekly rates can reduce the overall price, so don't forget to ask if you're interested. Motels vary in what they have to offer, but all will provide a comfortable bed, private bathroom, TV and phone. Food is not usually available on the premises other than from a vending machine, so ask where the nearest restaurant is before you settle in. Some motels have a few rooms equipped with small kitchenettes, which add little if anything to the price. Parking is free.

Cottages and cabins with one or more bedrooms, a bathroom and kitchen are available in many areas, and can be rented for a single night or longer. They are often in scenic areas, and may have a veranda and barbecue, with onsite facilities such as laundry rooms and playgrounds. Prices can start at little more than you'd pay for a motel room. Holiday home rentals, in regular houses and apartments, are usually available only by the week, and are considerably more expensive.

Bed-and-breakfasts, or gîtes du passant, offer pleasantly furnished, comfortable rooms with a double bed and breakfast for around $80 more. In some cities and towns hosts provide transportation to and from the airport, which can be very useful. Ask ahead if they offer a full hot breakfast or only a continental breakfast so that you are sure what you will be getting for your money. Tourist offices are very helpful in finding available bed-and-breakfasts for you and can often show you pictures to help you decide (▷ 378). Location is important, as some are well outside of the town or city.

Hostels affiliated with Hostelling International (HI) are graded as basic, simple, standard and superior. These normally have single-sex dormitories and from around $10 to $25 for members, many offering membership on the spot or a surcharge for non-members that can double the price. Most hostels will accept credit card bookings, some for up to six months in advance. There are HI offices around the world where you can obtain the Hostelling North America handbook. In Canada, contact Hostelling International, Room 400, 205 Catherine Street, Ottawa, Ontario, K2P 1C3 (tel 613/237-7884, www.hihostels.ca). City university residences are also available during the summer vacation period.

Campgrounds, usually open from May to the end of October, are run on a first-come, first-served basis, but some are beginning to offer advance reservations. July and August is the high season, when campgrounds in or near resorts fill up early in the day. Municipal campgrounds are inexpensive, normally about $5 per tent and $10 per RV (motor caravan), but are very basic. Private grounds often have more facilities, including stores, laundries, restaurants, swimming pools, tennis courts and other amenities. Some have fully winterized tepees for rent, and provide winter sports such as dogsledding and showshoeing. Prices vary. National and provincial parks offer camping between May and the end of September, but if you wish to camp outside of this period, it is often permitted and an "honesty box" is provided for collecting your fees. Backcountry camping is not for most people, but if you want to rough it in the wild, check that fires are permitted before starting one and use fire pits if provided. If you are in bear country, make sure you know all the necessary safety precautions, especially regarding the storage of food (racoons will also raid tents for food at night).

Resorts are usually open year-round and range from luxurious hotel accommodations to cozy log cabins in the mountains and tepees alongside lakes, with prices between $100 and $500 depending on the location and facilities. Mountain resorts have spectacular views and offer winter sports. Lakeside resorts are pleasant and relaxing, with boating, waterskiing and swimming in summer, skating and cross-country skiing in winter. Many resorts have superb restaurants, some have pools, health and fitness suites, weekly entertainment and kids clubs, and some have their own golf courses.

Farms, ranches and fishing lodges offer a real Canadian experience. On farms and ranches you can often give a hand with the chores and will certainly have the opportunity to explore (or perhaps help round up the cattle) on horseback. You can expect great home-cooked food, lots of fresh air and as much exercise as you like. Fishing lodges cater to the real angling enthusiast, and are often located right on the edge of a scenic lake or riverbank.

RATINGS

Standards in Canada are generally high, and there are a couple of organizations that back this up with a ratings system. The AAA (commonly called Triple A), the US motoring organization, inspects and rates many hotels and restaurants across Canada using its one- to five-diamond categories. Information is published, in conjunction with the CAA (Canadian Automobile Association), in three regional guidebooks. Not all Canadian accommodations are covered, and they tend to major on the big guys—chain hotels and more luxurious places—though not to the total exclusion of more individual establishments. The other outfit is called Canada Select (www.canadaselect.com), which inspects and rates participating hotels and bed-and-breakfasts with a one- to five-star system. Properties within this scheme show a distinctive "maple leaf with a roof" symbol. Canada Select also has a scheme for campgrounds, called Camping Select (www.campingselect.ca).

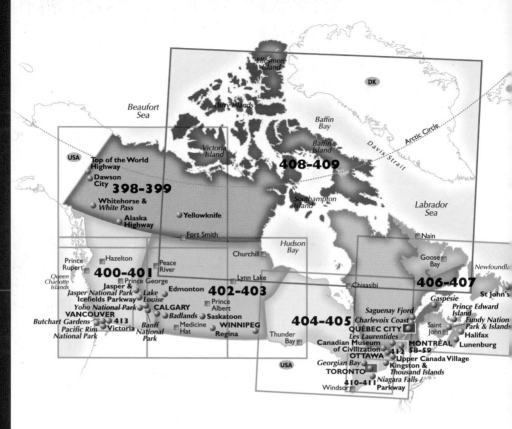

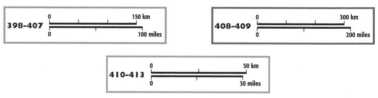

398-399
400-401
402-403
404-405
406-407
408-409
410-411
412-413

Scale bars:

398-407 — 0 – 150 km / 0 – 100 miles

408-409 — 0 – 300 km / 0 – 200 miles

410-413 — 0 – 50 km / 0 – 30 miles

Legend:

- Toll motorway (Turnpike)
- Motorway (Expressway)
- National road
- Other road
- International boundary
- Administrative region boundary
- City / Town
- National / Provincial park
- Featured place of interest
- Airport
- 1531 ▲ Height in metres
- Ferry route
- Mountain pass

MAPS

Map references for the sights refer to the atlas pages within this section or to the individual town plans within the regions. For example, Halifax has the reference ✚ 407 X16, indicating the page on which the map is found (407) and the grid square in which Halifax sits (X16).

12 B C D E

ALASKA

USA

Skagway

Cassiar Highway

Spatsizi
Plateau
Wilderness
Park

13

Graham
Island

Masset

Naikoon
Provincial
Park

Skeena Mountains

Williston
Lake

Wonowon

Fort
Nelson

Summit
Lake

97

Queen
Charlotte
City

Prince Rupert

Skidegate

Skeena

Terrace

16

Skeena Valley

37

Babine
Lake

Smithers

New
Hazelton

16

MacKenzie

Fort
St John

29

Chetwynd

97

Dawson
Creek

Fort
McLeod

39

Fort
St James

27

Vanderhoof

Dawson
Creek

Tumbler
Ridge

Beaverlode

29

14
Queen
Charlotte
Islands

Gwaii Haanas
National Park
Reserve

Banks
Island

Pitt
Island

Kitimat

Burns Lake

16

Fraser
Lake

Moresby Island

Butedale

Princess
Royal
Island

Eutsuk
Lake

Tweedsmuir
Provincial
Park

Prince
George

Prince George

97

Fraser

16

Grande
Cache

Bella
Bella

Bella
Coola

Anahim
Lake

BRITISH
COLUMBIA

Bowron Lake
Provincial
Park

Mount Robso
Provincial
Park

Columbia Mountains

Inside Passage

20

Quesnel

3954

Mount Robson

Jasper

15

Queen
Charlotte
Sound

Cape Scott

Queen Charlotte Str.

Fraser

Williams
Lake

Plateau

Wells Gray
Provincial
Park

3863

Mount Edith
Cavell

Port Hardy

4017

Mount
Waddington

One Hundred Mile House

24

Clearwater
Lake

Clearwater

Monashee Mountains

Kinabask
Lake

Glacier
Nationa
Park

Port
McNeill

Ts'yl-os
Provincial
Park

16

Vancouver
Island

Gold
River

19

28

Strathcona
Provincial
Park

Campbell River

Powell River

Pemberton

Clinton

Lillooet

99

Cache Creek

Kamloops

Chase

Mount Revelstoke
National Park

Revelstoke

Purce

413

Courtenay

Tofino

Cathedral
Grove

Port Alberni

Nanaimo

Bamfield

Pacific Rim
National Park

Port Renfrew

Squamish

Gibsons

Whistler

Garibaldi
Provincial
Park

Golden Ears
Provincial Park

Howe
Sound

Fraser
Canyon

Hell's
Gate

5

Okanagan
Lake

Vernon

Lumby

Nakusp

23

Selki

VANCOUVER

Vancouver
International

Fort Langley

ABBOTSFORD

97C

KELOWNA

Duncan

Chemainus

Butchart
Gardens

Victoria
International

Chilliwack

Bellingham

3

Penticton

Keremeos

3A

33

Kootenay
Lake

VICTORIA

Oak
Bay

WASHINGTON

Okanagan

Rossland

3

17

Everett

SEATTLE

Columbia

Spokane

Bellevue

TACOMA

Seattle Tacoma International

18

USA

Wenatchee

SPOKANE

Spokane
International

IDAHO

B C D E

Longview

Yakima

408

Gillam

Winisk River
Provincial Park

Polar
Bear
Provincial
Park

James
Bay

15

Severn

Big Trout
Lake

Winisk

Winisk
Lake

Attawapiskat

Opasquia
Provincial Park

Sandy
Lake

North
Caribou
Lake

Albany

16

403

Lake
St Joseph

Albany

Attawapiskat
Lake

ONTARIO

Abitibi

Woodland
Caribou
Provincial
Park

Red Lake

Lac
Seul

Armstrong

Lake
Nipigon

Geraldton

Longlac

Hearst

Kapuskasing

Hornepayne

17

44

17

71

Sioux Lookout

Vermillion
Bay

72

Dryden

502

599

Ignace

642

17

Manitouwadge

Long
Lake

Terrace
Bay

614

Marathon

163

Chapleau

101

Wawa

12

Rainy
Lake

622

Atikokan

11

THUNDER BAY

527

Ouimet
Canyon

17

Pukaskwa
National
Park

17

Agawa
Canyon

556

Fort
Frances

Quetico
Provincial
Park

101

Lake Superior
Provincial Park

18

2

Virginia

Lake Superior

**Sault
Ste Marie**

Thessalo

59

Duluth

Marquette

Cheboyga

Iron Wood

MINNESOTA

Escanaba

10

10

71

USA

MICHIGAN

19

71

WISCONSIN

Marinette

Traverse
City

Cadillac

12

Wausau

Coon
Rapids

Green Bay

59

212

MINNEAPOLIS

Austin Straubel International

Eau Claire

Appleton

Stevens Point

Ludington

212

Minneapolis-St Paul
International

ST PAUL

Lake
Michigan

59

**GRAND
RAPIDS**

20

14

71

Rochester

La Crosse

MILWAUKEE

Wyoming

59

90

M

N

P

MADISON

Waukesha

Q

Kalamazoo

404

IOWA

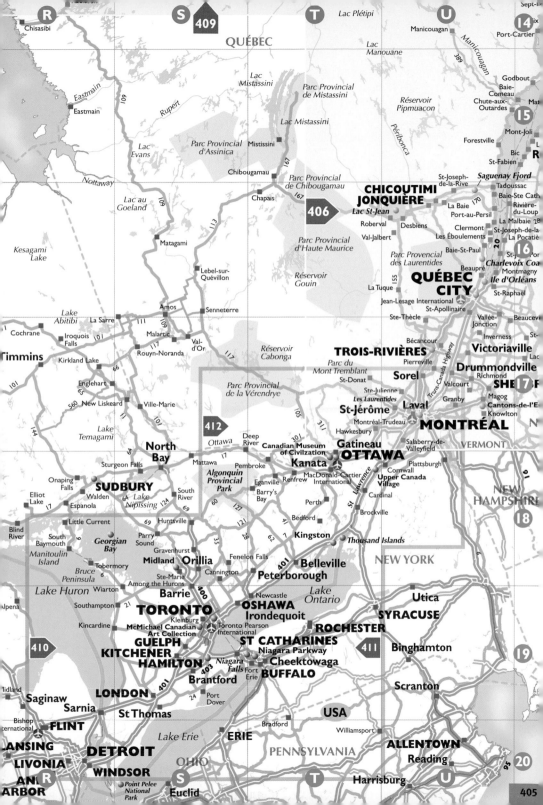

Axel
Heiberg
Island

Queen Elizabeth
Islands

Melville
Island

Parry
Islands

Devon
Island

Qausuittuq
(Resolute)

Lancaster Sound

Banks
Island

Victoria
Melville
Sound

Ikpiarjuk
(Arctic Bay)

Pond
Inlet

Amundsen
Gulf

Somerset
Island

Prince
of
Wales
Island

Gulf of Boothia

Victoria
Island

Boothia
Peninsula

Igloolik

Taloyoak

NUNAVUT

Kugluktuk
(Coppermine)

Coronation Gulf

Ikaluktutiak
(Cambridge Bay)

King
William
Island

Ursuqtuq
(Gjoa Haven)

Melville
Peninsula

399

Great Bear
Lake

Naujat
(Repulse Bay)

Southampton
Island

Garry
Lake

Back

Salliq
(Coral Harbour)

Aylmer
Lake

Qamanittuaq
(Baker Lake)

Fisher Str

Coats
Island

Rae-Edzo
Yellowknife

NORTHWEST
TERRITORIES

Thelon

Dubawnt
Lake

Yellowknife

Great Slave
Lake

Hay River

Fort Resolution

Enterprise

Arviat
(Eskimo Point)

Hudson
Bay

Fort Smith

Nueltin
Lake

35

High Level

Wood
Buffalo
National
Park

Uranium City

Stony
Rapids

Wollaston
Lake

Churchill

Cape Churchill

697

Lake
Athabasca

402

Reindeer
Lake

MANITOBA

Churchill

403

Manning

88

ALBERTA

SASKATCHEWAN

Southern
Indian
Lake

Nelson

Fort
Severn

Slave Lake

63

Fort McMurray

La Loche

Lynn
Lake

Leaf Rapids

280

Ilford

Gillam

ONTARIO

GREENLAND

DK

Baffin
Bay

Kangiqlugaapik
(Clyde River)

Davis Strait

**Baffin
Island**

Auyuittuq
National Park

Nettilling
Lake

Pangnirtung

Prince
Charles
Island

Cumberland Sound

Foxe
Basin

Amadjuak
Lake

Iqaluit

Labrador
Sea

Frobisher Bay

Kingait
(Cape Dorset)

Kimmirut

Hudson Strait

Cape Chidley

1729
▲ Mount
Caubvick

Quaqtaq

Ivujivik

Ungava
Bay

Mansel
Island

**Péninsule
d'Ungava**

Kuujjuaq

Labrador

Cartwright

Lake
Melville

L'Anse Aux
Meadows

Caniapiscau

North West River

Smallwood
Reservoir

Happy Valley-
Goose Bay

Blanc
Sablon

Inukjuak

QUÉBEC

Schefferville

500

Churchill

**NEWFOUNDLAND
AND LABRADOR**

Lac
Caniapiscau

Lac
Bienville

▼**406**

Labrador City

▼**407**

Kuujjuarapik

Gulf of Saint
Lawrence

P Polar Bear
Provincial
Park

Q

R

Chisasibi

S

T Réservoir
Manicouagan

U

Rivière-au-
Tonnerre

Sept-
Îles

Gallix

Mingan

138

V

Île
d'Anticosti

W

409

P Q R S T U V W

3
4
5
6
7
8
9
10
11
12
13

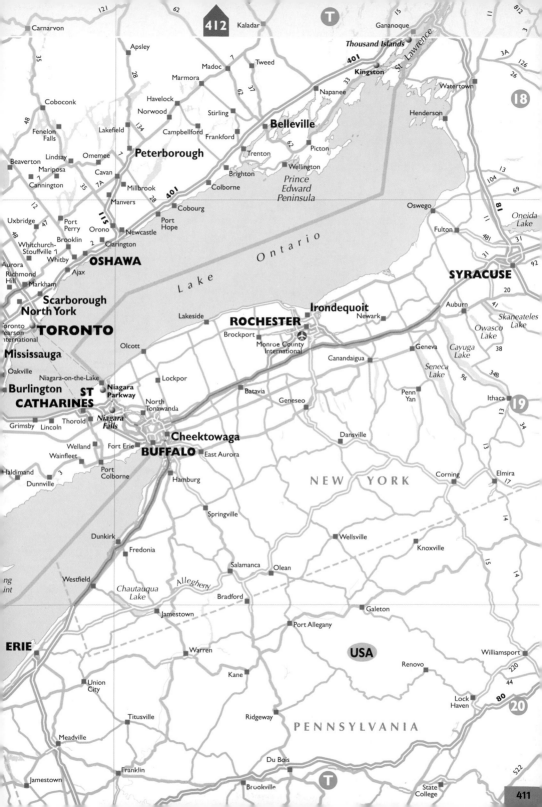

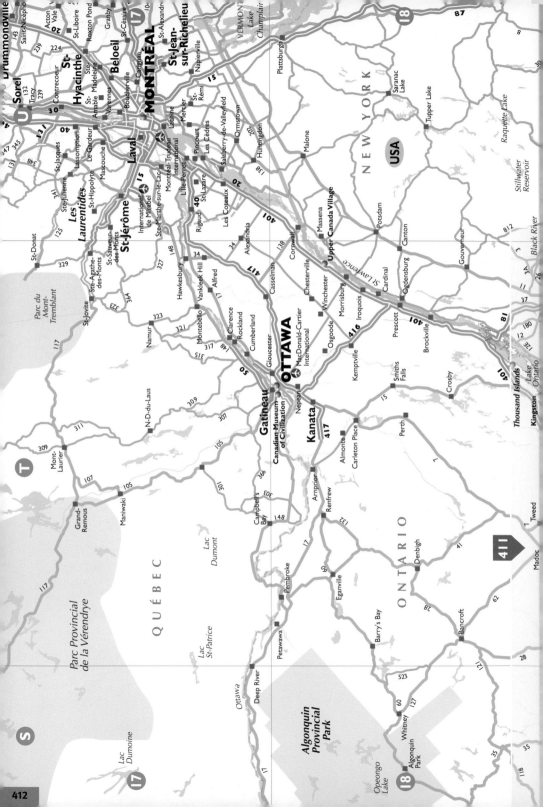

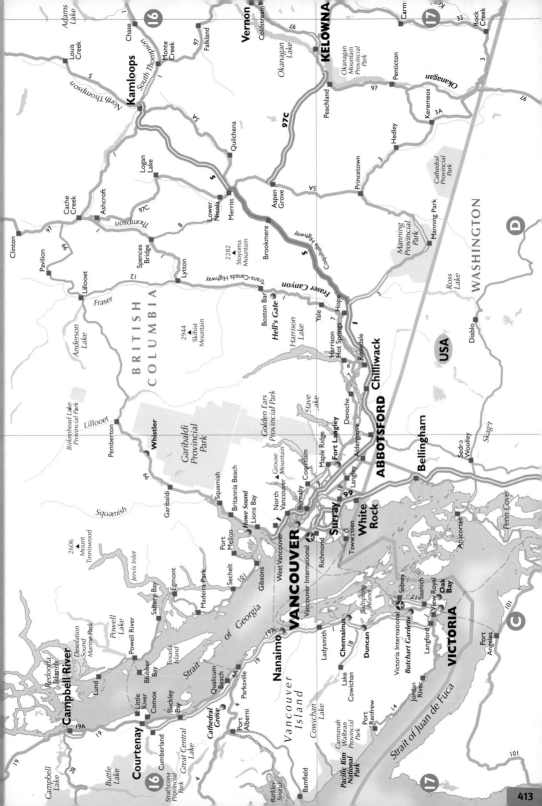

MAPS | INDEX

Place	Page	Grid	Place	Page	Grid	Place	Page	Grid
Souris	407	X15	Tracy	412	U17	Whistler	413	C16
Southampton	410	S19	Traverse City	404	Q19	Whitby	411	S19
South Baymouth	410	R18	Trenton	411	T18	Whitchurch-Stouffville	411	S19
Southend	402	J14	Trois-Rivières	406	U17	Whitecourt	401	F15
Southfield	410	R20	Truro	407	X16	Whitehorse	398	C10
South Indian Lake	403	K14	Tsawwassen	413	C17	White Rock	413	C17
South River	405	S18	Tuktoyaktuk	398	E7	Whitney	412	S18
South River	407	Z13	Tumbler Ridge	400	E14	Wiarton	410	S19
Spences Bridge	413	D16	Tungsten	398	D10	Wilkie	402	H16
Spirit River	401	E14	Tupper Lake	412	U18	Williams Lake	400	D15
Spokane	400	E18	Tweed	411	T18	Williamsport	411	T20
Springdale	407	X13				Winchester	412	T18
Springfield	407	W16	Uluqsaqtuuq	399	G7	Windsor	407	X16
Springhill	407	X16	Union City	411	S20	Windsor	410	R20
Springville	411	T19	Unity	402	H16	Wingham	410	S19
Squamish	413	C16	Uranium City	402	H13	Winnipeg	403	L17
State College	411	T20	Ursuqtuq	408	L9	Wonowon	400	E13
Stayner	410	S19	Utica	405	U19	Woodstock	407	V16
Steinbach	403	L17	Uxbridge	411	S19	Woodstock	410	S19
Stephenville Crossing	407	X13				Wrigley	399	E10
Sterling Heights	410	R20	Valcourt	406	U17	Wynyard	402	J16
Stettler	401	G16	Val-d'Or	405	S17	Wyoming	404	Q20
Stevens Point	404	P19	Val-Jalbert	406	U16	Wyoming	410	S19
Stewart Crossing	398	C9	Vallée-Jonction	406	U16			
Stirling	401	F17	Valleyview	401	F14	Yakima	400	D18
Stirling	411	T18	Vancouver	413	C16	Yale	413	D17
Stonewall	403	L17	Vanderhoof	400	D14	Yarmouth	407	W17
Stony Plain	401	F15	Vankleek Hill	412	T17	Yellowknife	399	G11
Stony Rapids	402	J13	Varennes	412	U17	Yorkton	402	J17
Stratford	410	S19	Vegreville	401	G15			
Strathmore	401	F16	Vermilion	401	G15			
StrathroyIngersoll	410	S19	Vermillion Bay	403	M17			
Sturgeon Falls	405	S18	Vernon	413	E16			
Sudbury	405	R18	Victoria	413	C17			
Summerside	407	W15	Victoriaville	406	U17			
Summit Lake	400	D12	Viow Royal	413	C17			
Sundre	401	F16	Viking	401	G16			
Surray	413	C17	Ville-Marie	405	S17			
Sussex	407	W16	Virden	403	K17			
Sutton	410	S19	Virginia	404	N18			
Swan Hills	401	F15	Vulcan	401	F17			
Swan River	403	K16						
Swift Current	402	H17	Wabana	407	Z13			
Sydney	407	X15	Wainfleet	411	S19			
Sylvan Lake	401	F16	Wainwright	401	G16			
Syracuse	411	T19	Walden	405	R18			
			Walkerton	410	S19			
Tacoma	400	C17	Wallaceburg	410	R20			
Tadoussac	406	U16	Warman	402	H16			
Taloyoak	408	L8	Warren	411	T20			
Teeswater	410	S19	Warwick	410	S19			
Terrace	400	C14	Waterloo	410	S19			
Terrace Bay	404	P17	Watertown	411	T18			
Teslin	398	C11	Watford	410	S19			
Tetlin Junction	398	B8	Watrous	402	J16			
The Pas	403	K15	Watson Lake	398	D11			
Thessalon	404	R18	Waukesha	404	P20			
Thompson	403	L14	Wausau	404	P19			
Thornbury	410	S19	Wawa	404	Q17			
Thorold	411	S19	Welland	411	S19			
Three Hills	401	F16	Wellington	407	W15			
Thunder Bay	404	P18	Wellington	411	T18			
Tilbury	410	R20	Wellsville	411	T19			
Tillsonburg	410	S19	Wenatchee	400	D18			
Timmins	405	R17	Westfield	411	S19			
Tisdale	402	J16	Westlock	401	F15			
Titusville	411	T20	West Lorne	410	S20			
Tobermory	410	R18	West Vancouver	413	C16			
Tofino	400	B16	Wetaskiwin	401	F15			
Torbay	407	Z13	Weyburn	402	J17			
Toronto	411	S19	Wheatley	410	S20			

INDEX CANADA

PICTURES

The Automobile Association wishes to thank the following photographers and organisations for their assistance in the preparation of this book.

Abbreviations for the picture credits are as follows –
(t) top;
(b) bottom;
(l) left;
(r) right;
(c) centre;
(dps) double page spread;
(AA) AA World Travel Library

2 AA/P Bennett;
3t AA/P Bennett;
3ct AA/P Bennett;
3cb AA/N Sumners;
3b AA/N Sumner;
4 AA/P Bennett;
5 AA/C Sawyer;
6 AA/C Sawyer;
8l Courtesy of Newfoundland and Labrador Tourism/Michael Hockney;
8r AA/N Sumner;
9 AA/P Bennett;
10 AA/N Sumner;
11l Courtesy of Newfoundland and Labrador Tourism/Barrett and MacKay;
11r AA/P Bennett;
12 AA/N Sumner;
13 Tourisme Montréal/Festival International de Jazz de Montréal 2001, Jean-François LeBlanc;
14 Tourisme Montréal/Festival International de Jazz de Montréal 2001, Caroline Hayeur;
15t AA/P Bennett;
15b Ulf Andersen/Getty Images;
16 AA/J F Pin;
17l AA/J Davison;
17r Raymond Boyd/Michael Ochs Archives/Getty Images;
18 Gary M. Prior/Getty Images;
19t Calgary Stampede;
19b Tourism Saskatoon;
20 AA/N Sumner;
21l AA/N Sumner;
21r AA/N Sumner;
22 Jeff Vinnick/Getty Images;
23 AA/P Bennett;
24 AA/N Sumner;
25t AA/M Dent;
25b AA/J F Pin;

26 AA/J F Pin;
27l AA/P Bennett;
27r AA/N Sumner;
28 Hulton Archive/Getty Images;
29t AA/C Coe;
29b AA/N Sumner;
30 Kirby/Topical Press Agency/Getty Images;
31 AA/P Aithie;
31r Mary Evans Picture Library;
32 Paul Schutzer/Time Life Pictures/Getty Images;
33t AA/N Sumner;
33b Daniel Wiener/Time Life Pictures/Getty Images;
34 Ponopresse/Rex Features;
35l Timothy A Clary/AFP/Getty Images;
35r Tourisme Montréal/ Festival International de Jazz de Montréal 2001, Jean-François LeBlanc;
36 Kevin Frayer/AFP/Getty Images;
37 VIA Rail;
38 Aéroports de Montréal;
40 AA/P Bennett;
41 Digital Vision;
42t AA/N Sumner;
42b AA/N Sumner;
45 STM;
46t AA/P Bennett;
46b AA/P Bennett;
47 AA/P Bennett;
48t AA/P Bennett;
48b AA/P Bennett;
50 VIA Rail;
51t AA/J F Pin;
51b AA/P Bennett;
52t AA/C Coe;
52b AA/N Sumner;
53 AA/C Sawyer;
55 Alan Marsh/First Light/Getty Images;
56 Tourisme Montréal/© Canadian Tourism Commission, Pierre St-Jacques;
62 AA/J F Pin;
63 AA/J F Pin;
64 AA/J F Pin;
65 Tourisme Montréal/© Tourisme Montréal, Stéphan Poulin;
67 Tourisme Montréal/© Tourisme Montréal, Shutterstock;
68 Tourisme Montréal/© Tourisme Montréal, Stéphan Poulin;
70t Tourisme Montréal/© Tourisme Montréal, Rosalie Pépin;
70b AA/J F Pin;

71 Roderick Chen, Pointe-a-Callière, Montréal Museum of Archaeology and History;
72 Le 1000 de La Gauchetière;
73l Tourisme Montréal/© Tourisme Montréal, Pierre Luc Dufour;
73r AA/J F Pin;
74 Tourisme Montréal/© Quays of the Old Port of Montréal, Paul labelle Photographes;
75l Tourisme Montréal/© www.old.montreal.qc.ca, le photographe masqué;
75r Tourisme Montréal/© Tourisme Québec;
76 Tourisme Montréal/Donald Courchesne;
77 Tourisme Montréal/Marie-Reine Mattera;
78 Tourisme Montréal/Old Port of Montréal Corporation 5 – Benoit Chalifour;
80 Tourisme Montréal/Stéphan Poulin;
82 Tourisme Montréal/Anton Fercher;
84 AA/J F Pin;
86 Ingram;
88 Stockbyte Royalty Free;
89 Weinstein and Gavino's Pasta Bar Factory;
90 Auberge de la Fontaine;
92 AA/N Sumner;
96 AA/J F Pin;
97 AA/N Sumner;
98 AA/N Sumner;
99 AA/J F Pin;
100 © Hemis/Corbis;
101 © Hemis/Corbis;
102 AA/N Sumner;
103 AA/N Sumner;
104 AA/J F Pin;
105 AA/N Sumner;
106 AA/N Sumner;
108 Aux Anciens Canadiens;
110 Stockbyte Royalty Free;
112 AA/N Sumner;
114 Yves Marcoux/Getty Images;
115 AA/N Sumner;
116 Canadian Museum of Civilization, Harry Foster, MCC;
117 Canadian Museum of Civilization, photographer Stephen Alsford;
118 AA/N Sumner;
119l AA/J F Pin;
119r AA/N Sumner;
120 © Atlantide Phototravel/Corbis;
121 AA/J F Pin;

122 AA/J F Pin;
123 AA/N Sumner;
124 AA/N Sumner;
125 AA/N Sumner;
126 AA/N Sumner;
127t AA/N Sumner;
127b Courtesy of Newfoundland and Labrador Tourism/Barrett and Mackay;
128 AA/J F Pin;
129 AA/J F Pin;
130 Cosmo Condina/The Image Bank/Getty Images;
131t Marie LeBlanc;
131b Marie LeBlanc;
132 Corbis Royalty Free;
134 Photodisc;
136 AA/J F Pin;
137 Photodisc;
138 AA/S McBride;
139 Wakefield Mill;
140 AA/N Sumner;
142 AA/N Sumner;
143 AA/N Sumner;
144l AA/N Sumner;
144r AA/N Sumner;
145 AA/N Sumner;
146 AA/N Sumner;
147 AA/N Sumner;
148 AA/N Sumner;
149t AA/N Sumner;
149b AA/N Sumner;
150 AA/N Sumner;
151 AA/N Sumner;
152 Tourism Prince Edward Island/John Sylvester;
153 AA/N Sumner;
154 AA/J F Pin;
155 AA/N Sumner;
156 AA/N Sumner;
158 AA/J F Pin;
159 AA/N Sumner;
160 AA/N Sumner;
161 AA;
162 © Wolfgang Kaehler/Corbis;
163l Kim Thomas;
163r AA/N Sumner;
164 AA/P Bennett;
167 AA/T Souter;
168 Magic Valley Family Fun Park;
170 AA/N Sumner;
172 AA/N Sumner;
173 Lincoln House Bed and Breakfast;
174 AA/N Sumner;
179 AA/N Sumner;
180 AA/N Sumner;

181 Art Gallery of Ontario;
182 AA/N Sumner;
183 AA/N Sumner;
184l AA/N Sumner;
184r AA/J Davison;
185 AA/J Davison;
186t AA/N Sumner;
186b AA/N Sumner;
187l AA/N Sumner;
187r AA/N Sumner;
189 AA/J Davison;
190 Copyright Royal Ontario Museum, 2008. All rights reserved;
191 AA/J Davison;
192 AA/J Beazley;
193 AA/N Sumner;
194 AA/N Sumner;
196 AA/N Sumner;
199 AA/N Sumner;
200 The Helicopter Inc.;
201 AA/N Sumner;
202 360 The Restaurant at the CN Tower;
204 AA/J Davison;
206 Renaissance Toronto Hotel at Skydome;
2088 AA/N Sumner;
210 AA/N Sumner;
211 McMichael Canadian Art Collection;
212t AA/J F Pin;
212b AA/N Sumner;
213 AA/N Sumner;
214 AA/N Sumner;
215l AA/N Sumner;
215r AA/N Sumner;
216l AA/N Sumner;
216r AA/N Sumner;
217t AA/N Sumner;
217b AA/N Sumner;
218t AA/N Sumner;
218b AA/N Sumner;
2119l AA/N Sumner;
219r AA/N Sumner;
220 AA/N Sumner;
221 AA/N Sumner;
223 AA/N Sumner;
224 National Library of Canada;
225t AA/J F Pin;
225b Photolibrary Group;
226 AA/N Sumner;
227 Copyright Upper Canada Village;
228 AA/J F Pin;
230 AA/N Sumner;
231t AA/N Sumner;
231b AA/N Sumner;
232 African Lion Safari;

233 Thousand Island Playhouse;
235 Centrepoint Theatre;
236 AA/N Sumner;
239 AA/P Bennett;
241 AA/N Sumner;
242 Terrior la Cachette;
245 Imagestate Royalty Free;
246 AA/A Mockford and N Bonetti;
248 AA/P Bennett;
250 AA/P Bennett;
251 AA;
252 Tourism Calgary/www.tourism-calgary.com;
253t AA/C Sawyer;
235bl AA/P Bennett;
235br AA/P Bennett;
254l AA/P Bennett;
254r AA/P Bennett;
255t AA/C Sawyer;
255c AA/P Bennett;
256 © Richard Cummins/Corbis;
257l AA/P Bennett;
257r Tourism Calgary/www.tourism-calgary.com;
258l AA/P Bennett;258r AA/C Sawyer;
259l AA/P Bennett;
259r Calgary Stampede;
260 AA/P Bennett;
261 AA/P Bennett;
262t AA/P Bennett;
262b AA/P Bennett;
263 John Perret/Stone/Getty Images;
264 AA/P Bennett;
265l AA/P Bennett;
265r AA/P Bennett;
265r AA/P Bennett;
266l AA/P Bennett;
266r AA/P Bennett;
267l AA/P Bennett;
267r AA/P Bennett;
268t © Mike Grandmaison/Corbis;
268b Prince Albert National Park;
269 Prince Albert National Park;
270 AA/P Bennett;
271t AA/P Bennett;
271b AA/P Bennett;
272 Calgary Stampede;
275 Epcor Centre for the Performing Arts;
277 AA/P Bennett;
278 West End Cultural Centre/Brock Hamilton;
279 The Forks North Portage Partnership CentreCourt;
280 Buchwakker Brewpub;
282 The Inns & Spa at Heartwood;

284 AA/C Sawyer;
286 AA/P Bennett;
287 AA/C Sawyer;
288 AA/P Bennett;
289l AA/C Coe;
289r AA/P Bennett;
290l AA/P Bennett;
290r AA/P Bennett;
291t AA/C Sawyer;
291b AA/P Bennett;
292l AA/P Bennett;
292r AA/P Bennett;
293 AA/M Dent;
294 AA/P Bennett;
295t AA/P Bennett;
295bl AA/P Bennett;
295br AA/P Bennett;
296 AA/C Sawyer;
297bl AA/C Sawyer;
297br AA/C Sawyer;
298 AA/C Sawyer;
299 AA/P Bennett;
300l AA/P Bennett;
300r AA/P Bennett;
301l AA/C Coe;
301r AA/C Coe;
302t AA/P Bennett;
302b AA/P Bennett;
303l AA/P Bennett;
303r AA/P Bennett;
304 AA/J A Tims;
305 AA/C Sawyer;
306 AA/C Sawyer;
307 AA/P Bennett;
308 AA/P Bennett;
309l AA/P Bennett;
309r AA/P Bennett;
310 Vancouver Aquarium;
311t AA/J A Tims;
311b AA/J A Tims;
312t AA/P Bennett;
312b AA/C Sawyer;
313l AA/P Bennett;
313r AA/P Bennett;
314l AA/C Sawyer;
314r AA/C Sawyer;
315 AA/C Sawyer;
316 AA/P Bennett;
317 AA/P Bennett;
318 AA/P Bennett;
319 AA/P Bennett;
320 © Adam Burton/Alamy;
321 © Stephen Finn/Alamy;
322 AA/P Bennett;
323l AA/P Bennett;
323r AA/P Bennett;
324 AA/P Bennett;

325l AA/C Sawyer;
325r AA/P Timmermans;
326 AA/C Coe;
327l Parks Canada/Hikers Log Bridge rainforest & trail by A. Corneluer;
327r Parks Canada/Walks on Long Beach by W. McIntyre, 1975;
328 AA/P Timmermans;
331 Lonsdale Quay;
332 Banff Centre/Donald Lee;
334 AA/P Bennett;
336 AA/C Sawyer;
339 Sunset Verandah;
340 AA/P Bennett;
342 Paul Nicklen/National Geographic/Getty Images;
334 AA/C Coe;
345 Robert Harding Picture World Imagery;
346b AA/P Bennett;
347r AA/P Bennett;
348 Photolibrary Group;
349 AA/C Coe;
350 AA/C Coe;
351l AA/C Coe;
351r AA/P Bennett;
352 Photolibrary Group;
353 Robert Postma/First Light/Getty Images;
354 AA/C Coe;
355 AA/C Coe;
356 Parks Canada;
357 Parks Canada;
358 Blue Kennels & Dog Sled Trips;
362 Hawkins House Bed and Breakfast;
364 AA/J A Tims;
365 AA/J A Tims;
368 AA/P Bennett;
369 AA/C Coe;
370 AA/N Sumner;
372 AA/J Davison;
373 AA/N Sumner;
376 AA/N Sumner;
377 AA/N Sumner;
380 AA/N Sumner;
382 AA/N Sumner;
383 Rannva Designs;
384 Bard on the Beach/David Blue;
385 Yuk Yuk's Club, Toronto;
386 Grays Rocks;
387l AA/P Bennett;
387r Manitoba Mouse Hockey Club;
388 AA/P Timmermans;
389 AA/P Bennett;
390 AA/C Sawyer;
391 Photodisc;

392 Imagestate;
394 AA/C Sawyer;
397 AA/P Bennett

Every effort has been made to trace the copyright holders, and we apologise in advance for any unintentional omissions or errors. We would be pleased to apply any corrections in any following edition of this publication.

Managing editor
Sheila Hawkins

Design
Drew Jones, pentacorbig, Nick Otway

Picture research
Vivien Little

Image retouching and repro
Sarah Montgomery

Mapping
Maps produced by the Mapping Services
Department of AA Publishing

Main contributors
Terry Arsenault, Susi Bailey, Lindsay Bennett,
Jenni Davis, Fiona Malins, Penny Phenix,
Paul Waters

Updater
Penny Phenix

Indexer
Marie Lorimer

Production
Lyn Kirby, Karen Gibson

Published by AA Publishing, a trading name of Automobile Association Developments Limited, whose registered office is
Fanum House, Basing View, Basingstoke, RG21 4EA. Registered number 1878835.
A CIP catalogue record for this book is available from the British Library.

ISBN 978-07495-5958-8

KeyGuide is a registered trademark in Australia and is used under license.
Colour separation by Keenes, Andover, UK
Printed and bound by Leo Paper Products, China

We believe the contents of this book are correct at the time of printing. However, some details, particularly prices, opening times and
telephone numbers do change. We do not accept responsibility for any consequences arising from the use of this book.
This does not affect your statutory rights. We would be grateful if readers would advise us of any inaccuracies they may encounter, or any
suggestions they might like to make to improve the book. There is a form provided at the back of the book for this purpose, or you can email us
at Keyguides@theaa.com

A03307
Maps in this title produced from map data © Tele Atlas N.V. 2007   Tele Atlas
Transport maps © Communicarta Ltd, UK
Weather chart statistics © Copyright 2004 Canty and Associates, LLC.

Find out more about AA Publishing and the wide range of travel publications and services the AA provides by visiting our website at
www.theAA.com/bookshop

READER RESPONSE

Thank you for buying this KeyGuide. Your comments and opinions are very important to us, so please help us to improve our travel guides by taking a few minutes to complete this questionnaire.

You do not need a stamp (unless posted outside the UK). If you do not want to cut this page from your guide, then photocopy it or write your answers on a plain sheet of paper.

Send to: **KeyGuide Editor, AA World Travel Guides**
FREEPOST SCE 4598, Basingstoke RG21 4GY

Find out more about AA Publishing and the wide range of travel publications the AA provides by visiting our website at www.theAA.com/bookshop

ABOUT THIS GUIDE

Which KeyGuide did you buy?
....

Where did you buy it?
....

When? .... month .... year

Why did you choose this AA KeyGuide?
☐ Price ☐ AA Publication
☐ Used this series before;
title
☐ Cover ☐ Other (please state)

Please let us know how helpful the following features of the guide were to you by circling the appropriate category:
very helpful (VH), helpful (H) or little help (LH)

Size	VH	H	LH
Layout	VH	H	LH
Photos	VH	H	LH
Excursions	VH	H	LH
Entertainment	VH	H	LH
Hotels	VH	H	LH
Maps	VH	H	LH
Practical info	VH	H	LH
Restaurants	VH	H	LH
Shopping	VH	H	LH
Walks	VH	H	LH
Sights	VH	H	LH
Transport info	VH	H	LH

What was your favourite sight, attraction or feature listed in the guide?

Page .... Please give your reason ....
....
....

Which features in the guide could be changed or improved? Or are there any other comments you would like to make?

ABOUT YOU

Name (Mr/Mrs/Ms)..

Address ....

....

....

Postcode.. Daytime tel nos..

Email..
Please only give us your mobile phone number/email if you wish to hear from us about other products and services from the AA and partners by text or mms.

Which age group are you in?
Under 25 ☐   25–34 ☐   35–44 ☐   45–54 ☐   55+ ☐

How many trips do you make a year?
Less than1 ☐   1 ☐   2 ☐   3 or more ☐

ABOUT YOUR TRIP

Are you an AA member?   Yes ☐ No ☐

When did you book?.............. month................. year

When did you travel?.............. month................. year

Reason for your trip?   Business ☐   Leisure ☐

How many nights did you stay? ....

How did you travel?   Individual ☐   Couple ☐   Family ☐   Group ☐

Did you buy any other travel guides for your trip? ....

If yes, which ones?..

Thank you for taking the time to complete this questionnaire. Please send it to us as soon as possible, and remember, you do not need a stamp (unless posted outside the UK).
AA Travel Insurance call 0800 072 4168 or visit www.theaa.com

Titles in the KeyGuide series:

Australia, Barcelona, Britain, Brittany, Canada, China, Costa Rica, Croatia, Florence and Tuscany, France, Germany, Ireland, Italy, London, Mallorca, Mexico, New York, New Zealand, Normandy, Paris, Portugal, Prague, Provence and the Côte d'Azur, Rome, Scotland, South Africa, Spain, Thailand, Venice, Vietnam, Western European Cities.
Published in July 2009: Berlin

AA Travel Insurance call 0800 072 4168 or visit www.theaa.com

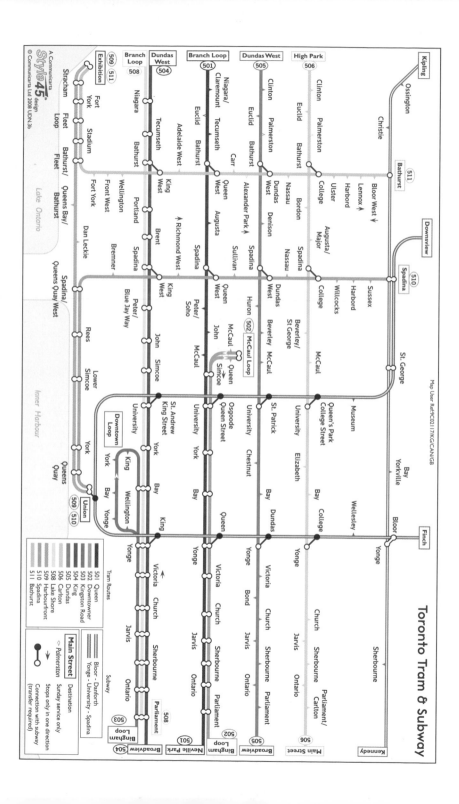

Toronto Tram & Subway

A Communicarta
Style45® design
© Communicarta Ltd 2008 UDN.3b

Map User Ref:9C021I7/KG/CAN/GB

Lake Ontario

Inner Harbour